O9-ABG-843
300 YEARS OF GERMANS IN AMERICA
CONCORD
1683
1983
300 JAHRE DEUTSCHE IN AMERIKA

CARE
U.S.A.

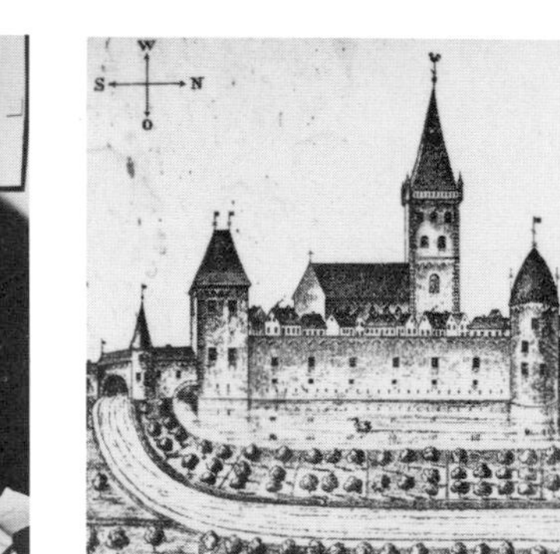

PROLES FLOREBIT ★ RELIGIONE INDUSTRIA ET FORTITUDINE GERMANA

Three Hundred Years of German Immigrants in North America
Dreihundert Jahre Deutsche Einwanderer in Nordamerika

1683-1983

Their Contributions to the Evolution of the New World

Ihre Beiträge zum Werden der Neuen Welt

A pictorial history with 510 illustrations Edited by Klaus Wust and Heinz Moos

Eine Bilddokumentation mit 510 Abbildungen Herausgegeben von Klaus Wust und Heinz Moos

„300 Jahre Deutsche in Amerika“ Verlags-GmbH

Managing Editor / Redaktion: Thomas Piltz

Contributors / Mitarbeiter:

Karl J. R. Arndt, Worcester, Mass. Donald Arthur, München Joseph Ballerstaller, München Louis Bloom, München Lutz A. Bormann, München Paula Domzalski, Los Angeles Anita Eichholz, München Vincent Fitzpatrick, Baltimore Brigitte Fleischmann, München Wolfgang J. Fuchs, München Hanns-Theodor Fuß, München Hermann Glessgen, Landau Anneliese E. Harding, Boston Armin Hermann, Stuttgart Alexander Graf von Keyserlingk, München Sigbert Kluwe, München Sabine Lahusen, München Detlev Moos, Baltimore Anneliese Nowak, München Thomas Piltz, München Patricia Reber, München Renate Reifferscheid, München Bob Rice, München Brad Robinson, München Conny Schröder-Lipp, Baltimore Horst Ueberhorst, Bochum Burt Weinshanker, Boston Rüdiger B. Wersich, Frankfurt

The chapters on "The Old Homeland," "The New World" and "Individuals and Groups" were written by Klaus Wust.

Den Text der Kapitel „Die alte Heimat", „Die Neue Welt" und „Einzelgänger und Gruppen" verfaßte Klaus Wust.

English Translations / Übersetzungen ins Englische:

Louis Bloom (Editor); Donald Arthur, Patricia Reber, Brad Robinson

German Translations / Übersetzungen ins Deutsche:

Lutz Bormann, Anita Eichholz, Thomas Piltz

Typesetting / Satzarbeiten:
Lichtsatz Ebach, München Fotosatz Weihrauch, Würzburg
Fotosatz-Atelier Scheiderer, Martinsried bei München

Reproductions / Reproduktionen:
Oestreicher und Wagner, München

Distribution in the United States:

Heinz Moos Publishing Co., Inc.,
Rotunda Office Center, 711 West 40th Street,
Baltimore, Maryland 21211

ISBN 3-7879-0206-6

Printed in the Federal Republic of Germany

Cover: The founding of Germantown, the first German settlement in North America, by Francis Daniel Pastorius and the Krefeld Mennonites in October, 1683. The idealized portrayal in the illustration is from a model for a Pastorius monument by the American sculptor of Swiss-German descent, J. Otto Schweizer (1890–1965).

Umschlagbild: Die Gründung Germantowns, der ersten deutschen Ansiedlung in Nordamerika, durch Franz Daniel Pastorius und die Krefelder Mennoniten im Oktober 1683; die idealisierte Darstellung stammt vom Modell eines Pastorius-Denkmals des amerikanischen Bildhauers deutsch-schweizerischer Abstammung J. Otto Schweizer (1890–1965).

Back cover: an "immigrant work of art", the "Spherical Caryatid N.Y." by the German sculptor Fritz Koenig, in front of the quarter-of-a-mile-high towers of the World Trade Center in New York (see also p. 105).

Hinteres Umschlagbild: Ein »Kunstwerk, das auswanderte« – die »Kugelkaryatide N.Y.« des deutschen Bildhauers Fritz Koenig vor den 410 Meter hohen Türmen des World Trade Center in New York (siehe auch Seite 105)

Preface Vorwort

On 6 October 1683, thirteen Mennonite families from Krefeld arrived at Philadelphia harbor on board the vessel Concord, and proceeded to found the settlement of Germantown. Their migration marks the start of the history of over seven million immigrants who, in the course of three centuries, left the German-speaking regions of Europe to head for the shores of North America. As the numerically largest single ethnic group, whose descendants currently comprise 28 percent of the total U.S. population according to a survey published in 1982, they played no small part in shaping the development of their new homeland in all phases of social and cultural life.

The intention of this book is to relate that saga of transatlantic migration by means of an illustrated historical survey and a selection of concise biographies exemplifying the diverse social, religious, political and personal motives for pulling up stakes, and the reasons why North America was chosen as a particularly favored destination. Both heartaches and spectacular successes are part of the story of making a fresh start in the New World. Without invoking the past to gratify our current political climate, the editors and the publisher are convinced that the material presented here in a bilingual edition can provide an impulse to dispel stereotypes widespread on both sides of the Atlantic, and moreover be a stimulating source of information especially for young readers – and not only for those in America of German extraction.

Am 6. Oktober 1683 trafen dreizehn aus Krefeld ausgewanderte Mennonitenfamilien an Bord der Concord in Philadelphia ein, wo sie die Siedlung Germantown gründeten. Mit ihnen beginnt die Geschichte von über sieben Millionen, die im Lauf von drei Jahrhunderten aus den deutschsprachigen Ländern Europas nach Nordamerika zogen. Als zahlenmäßig größte Einwanderergruppe, von der, laut einem 1982 veröffentlichten Umfrageergebnis, über 28 Prozent der Bürger der heutigen USA abstammen, haben sie die Entwicklung ihrer neuen Heimat auf allen Gebieten des sozialen und kulturellen Lebens mitgeprägt.

Das vorliegende Buch will in einem geschichtlichen Überblick und einer Reihe von exemplarischen Kurzbiographien von dieser transatlantischen Wanderung berichten: von den historischen Ursachen und den persönlichen Motiven für die Emigration; von den Gründen, die die Auswanderer gerade Nordamerika als Ziel wählen ließen; von den Enttäuschungen und Erfolgen beim Neubeginn in der Neuen Welt. Ohne die Vergangenheit in den Dienst des politischen Alltags stellen zu wollen, sind Herausgeber und Verlag überzeugt, mit diesem zweisprachigen Band gerade jungen Lesern – in den Vereinigten Staaten keineswegs nur solchen deutscher Abstammung – ein Informationsangebot machen zu können, das geeignet ist, einige der beiderseits verbreiteten Stereotypen abzubauen.

Contents Inhalt

When the United States became independent in 1776, between 70,000 and 100,000 German immigrants had already taken up residence in the colonies. Among the many German-Americans who participated in the struggle for independence were (clockwise from top): Johann Peter Gabriel Muhlenberg (1746–1807), Lutheran clergyman who led a regiment of German volunteers and later became lieutenant governor of Pennsylvania; Johann de Kalb (1721–1780) from Hüttendorf in Bavaria, who came to America with Lafayette and was killed in the battle of Camden; Nicholas Herkimer (1728–1777), who fell at the battle at Oriskany Creek, becoming one of the first heroes of the Revolutionary War; David Rittenhouse (1732–1796), astronomer and inventor, constructor of the first planetarium in America, and the first director of the young nation's Federal Mint; Maria Ludwig-Hayes (1754–1832), who became a legendary figure in American folklore under the nickname "Molly Pitcher"; and Friedrich Wilhelm von Steuben (1730–1794), inspector general and reorganizer of the Continental Army.

Als die Vereinigten Staaten 1776 unabhängig wurden, waren bereits siebzig- bis hunderttausend deutsche Einwanderer in den Kolonien an Land gegangen. Für die deutschamerikanischen Teilnehmer am Kampf um die Unabhängigkeit stehen (im Uhrzeigersinn, beginnend oben): Johann Peter Gabriel Muhlenberg (1746–1807), lutherischer Geistlicher, Führer eines deutschen Freiwilligenregiments und später Vizegouverneur von Pennsylvanien; Johann de Kalb (1721–1780) aus Hüttendorf in Bayern, der mit Lafayette nach Amerika kam und in der Schlacht von Camden den Tod fand; Nicholas Herkimer (1728–1777), einer der ersten Helden des Revolutionskriegs, gefallen in der Schlacht am Oriskany Creek; David Rittenhouse (1732–1796), Astronom und Erfinder, Erbauer des ersten Planetariums in Amerika und später Direktor der Staatlichen Münze der jungen USA; Maria Ludwig-Hayes (1754–1832), die als „Molly Pitcher" zu einer Figur der amerikanischen Folklore wurde; Friedrich Wilhelm von Steuben (1730–1794), Generalinspekteur und weitblickender Reformator der Kontinentalarmee.

In the nineteenth century, over five million Germans found a new home in the United States. Among them were (clockwise from top): Carl Schurz (1829–1906), German revolutionary in 1848 who fled to the United States, where he later became senator from Missouri and then secretary of the interior under President Hayes; John Peter Altgeld (1847–1902), Democratic governor of Illinois; Ottmar Mergenthaler (1854–1899), inventor of the Linotype machine; John Augustus Roebling (1806–1869), who, together with his son Washington Augustus, constructed the Brooklyn Bridge; Leopold Damrosch (1832–1885), concert and opera conductor; Friedrich Hecker (1811–1881), also a „Forty-Eighter" who fled Germany and later was a general of the Union troops during the Civil War.

Im neunzehnten Jahrhundert fanden über fünf Millionen Deutsche eine neue Heimat in den Vereinigten Staaten. Unter ihnen waren (im Uhrzeigersinn, beginnend oben): Carl Schurz (1829–1906), als deutscher Revolutionär von 1848 in die USA geflohen, dort Senator von Missouri und schließlich Innenminister unter Präsident Hayes; John Peter Altgeld (1847–1902), demokratischer Gouverneur von Illinois; Ottmar Mergenthaler (1854–1899), der Erfinder der Linotype-Setzmaschine; John Augustus Roebling (1806–1869), zusammen mit seinem Sohn Washington Augustus Erbauer der Brooklyn-Bridge; Leopold Damrosch (1832–1885), Konzert- und Operndirigent; Friedrich Hecker (1811–1881), ebenfalls geflohener „Achtundvierziger" und General der Unionsarmee im Bürgerkrieg.

Among the Americans whose emigration from Germany in the twentieth century was the consequence of Nazi persecution were (clockwise from top): the "pope of physics" Albert Einstein (1879–1955); the conductor Bruno Walter (1876–1962); the social philosopher Hannah Arendt (1906–1975); and the political scientist and politician Henry Kissinger (b. 1923). Space travel pioneer Wernher von Braun (1912–1977) (top left) was one of the German scientists who entered the United States and became naturalized citizens in the aftermath of World War II.

Deutschstämmige Amerikaner, die im zwanzigsten Jahrhundert auf der Flucht vor nationalsozialistischer Verfolgung in die USA kamen (im Uhrzeigersinn, beginnend oben): der „Papst der Physik", Albert Einstein (1879–1955); der Dirigent Bruno Walter (1876–1962); die Sozialphilosophin Hannah Arendt (1906–1975); der politische Wissenschaftler und Politiker Henry Kissinger (geboren 1923). – Wernher von Braun (1912–1977) (links oben), der Pionier der Weltraumfahrt, war unter jenen deutschen Wissenschaftlern, die nach Beendigung des Zweiten Weltkriegs in die Vereinigten Staaten kamen und später amerikanische Bürger wurden.

The old homeland in the century when emigration commenced: general map of the German-speaking realm of central Europe, drawn by Matthäus Merian the Elder (Frankfurt, 1643). Fifty-two million Americans today have ancestors who originally came from the cities and rural areas of these Germanic domains.

Die alte Heimat im Jahrhundert der ersten Auswanderung: Übersichtskarte der deutschsprachigen Länder Mitteleuropas von Matthäus Merian d. Ä., Frankfurt, 1643. Aus den Städten, Dörfern und Landschaften dieses »Teutschland« stammen die Vorfahren von 52 Millionen der heute lebenden Amerikaner.

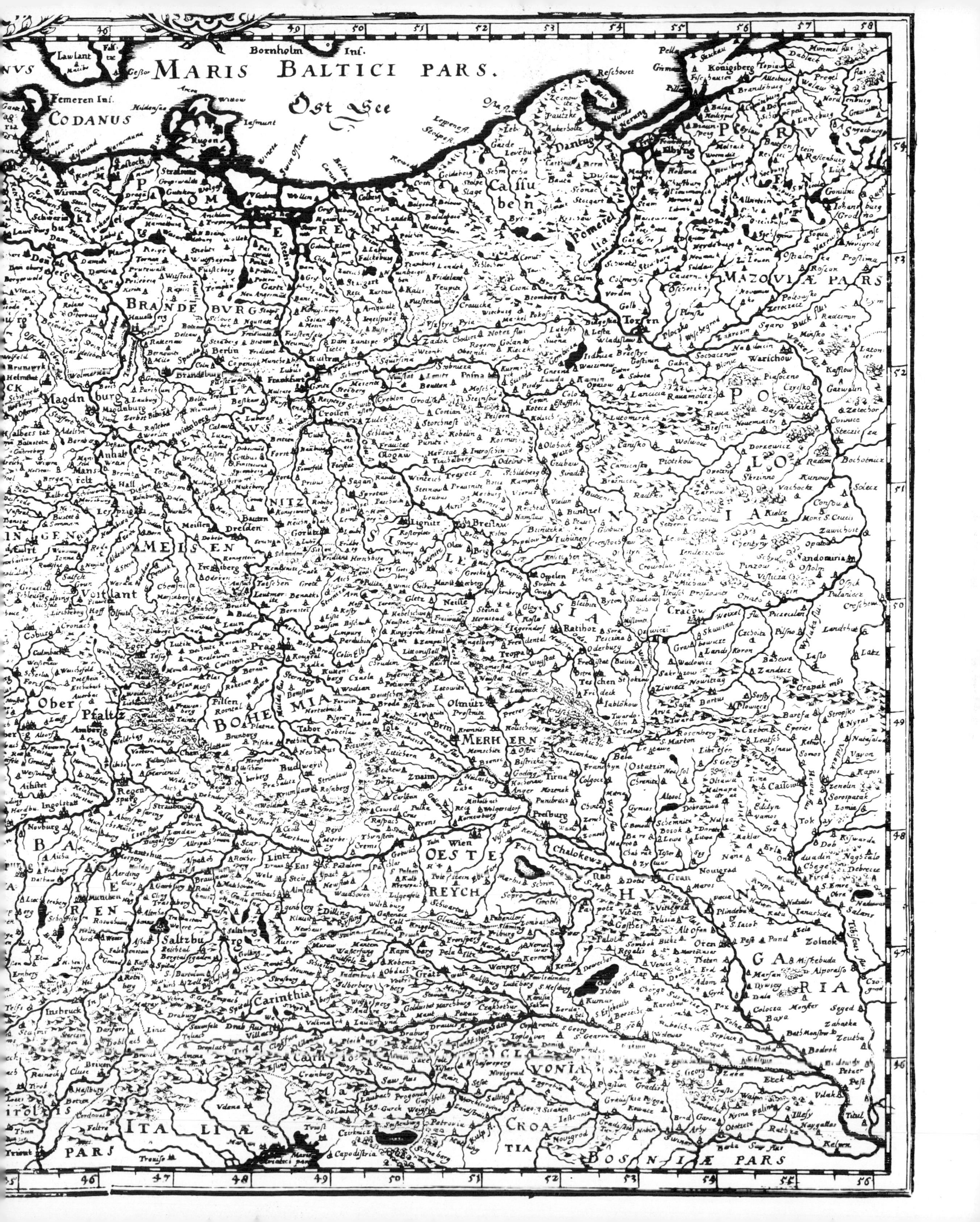

MARIS BALTICI PARS.
Ost See
CODANUS
Bornholm Inf.
BRANDEBURG
MAZOVIÆ PARS
POLONIA
SILESIA
BOHEMIA
MERHERN
MEISEN
Voitlant
Ober Pfaltz
OESTEREYCH
HVNGARIA
Carinthia
Saltzburg
SCLAVONIA
CROATIA
ITALIÆ PARS
BOSNIÆ PARS
Cassuben
Pomerelia
Magdenburg
Danzig
Konigsberg
Prag
Wien
Cracow
Breslaw
Torn

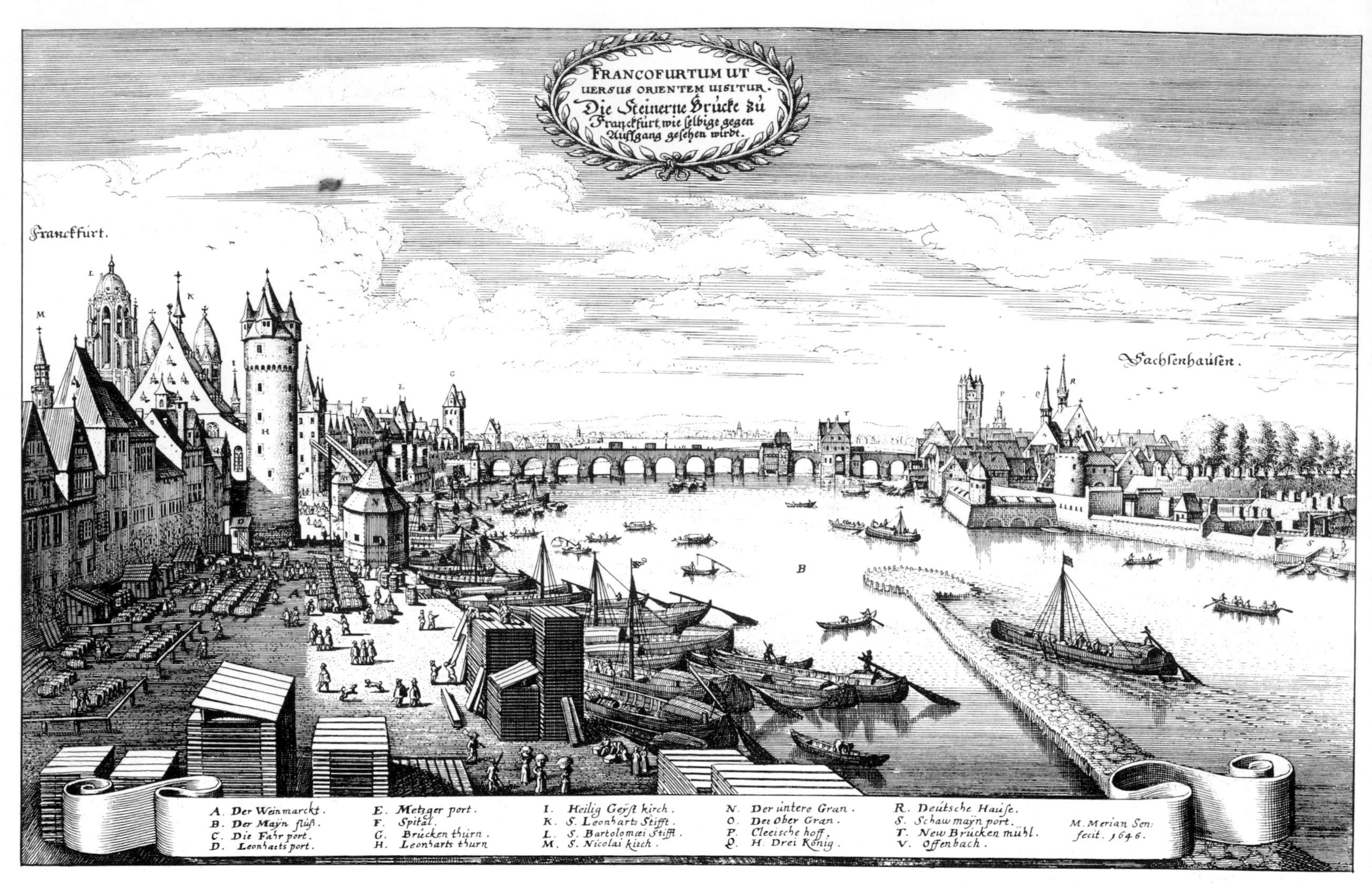

Copperplate by Matthäus Merian the elder, 1646

Kupferstich von Matthäus Merian d. Ä., 1646

Frankfurt on the Main, free imperial city, center of trade, and site of the Holy Roman Emperor's coronation between 1562 and 1792, was also where the first effort was made to organize group emigration from Germany to North America. Stimulated by William Penn's promotion visit in August 1677, a congregation of Frankfurt Pietists founded a company which purchased fifteen thousand acres of land in Pennsylvania, with the intention of leasing plots to fellow believers wishing to emigrate. In 1683, the thirty-two-year-old doctor of law Francis Daniel Pastorius travelled to Philadelphia as authorized agent of the "Frankfurt Company" to make preparations for the first group of settlers, the Krefeld Mennonites.

Frankfurt am Main, freie Reichsstadt, Handelszentrum und Krönungsort der deutschen Kaiser von 1562 bis 1792, war auch der Ausgangspunkt der ersten organisierten deutschen Auswanderung nach Nordamerika: Angeregt durch einen Besuch William Penns im August 1677 gründeten Frankfurter Pietisten eine Handelsgesellschaft, die 15 000 Morgen Land in Pennsylvanien erwarb, um sie an auswanderungswillige Glaubensgenossen zu verpachten. Als bevollmächtigter Agent dieser »Frankfurter Compagnie« reiste 1683 der damals zweiunddreißigjährige Doktor beider Rechte Franz Daniel Pastorius nach Philadelphia, um die Ansiedlung der Krefelder Mennoniten vorzubereiten.

The Old Homeland

The motivations of German emigrants against the background of European history

Die alte Heimat

Motive deutscher Auswanderer vor dem Hintergrund der europäischen Geschichte

Johanna Eleonore Petersen (1644 – 1724), member of the "Saalhof Pietists" and one of the initiators of the "Frankfurt Company". Pastorius was the only member of the society who actually turned the planned emigration into reality. None of the others, including Johanna, could conquer their fear of a voyage into the unknown.

Johanna Eleonore Petersen (1644–1724), Mitglied der »Saalhof-Pietisten« und eine der Initiatorinnen der »Frankfurter Compagnie«. Pastorius blieb der einzige Angehörige der Gesellschaft, der den Auswanderungsplan in die Tat umsetzte; alle anderen, auch Johanna, schreckten vor der Reise ins Unbekannte zurück.

The history of German emigration to North America does not necessarily mirror the ups and downs of German history. The three centuries of emigration since 1683 rather were dominated by seemingly contradictory "push-and-pull" effects. Often the transatlantic pull was stronger than the prospects, or even the reality, of an economic boom at home. The push, in turn, was frequently a local one not affecting other, even neighboring localities. The decision to emigrate has always been a highly individual one. Even in times of an emigration craze, the individual must be receptive to the pull. In the competition of countries seeking emigrants from Germany, America remained the most constantly preferred destination throughout the three centuries. The foundation for this trend was firmly laid in the 18th century. Therefore, the factors leading to the American orientation of the Europe-weary will be dealt with in more detail than the course of the migration itself, which attained massive proportions in the 19th century.

In 300 years Germany experienced the final decline of the Holy Roman Empire of German Nation, the emergence of Prussia, the Napoleonic wars, the loose German Confederation with repressions and frustrated revolts, Bismarck's *Reich*, the Weimar Republic, twelve years of Nazi rule and finally the present division of the residual heartland. It is a story of expanding and contracting frontiers with a frequently vague concept of what, and who, was and is German. Yet in the following 18th century testimonies, the term "German" is used by contemporaries who always seemed to know what it meant.

"I behold the woeful judgments of wrath and severe chastisement which, in the irrevocable course of divine justice, will be poured out over Europe till this abhorrent Babylon is completely perished. Now, dearly beloved parents, if you want to escape the plagues destined for Germany, do not partake of her sins but go and leave her," wrote Francis Daniel Pastorius to his parents in March, 1684, less than a year after his arrival in Pennsylvania. This apocalyptic view of the leader of the first organized German settlement in the New World was not unique. Pastorius had traveled extensively throughout Germany before he was received into the circle of Lutheran pietists at the Saalhof in Frankfurt, where lay people gathered for devotions and pious conversations according to the doctrine of the spiritual priesthood of believers. It was from this circle that the *"Frankfurt Company"* emerged. The company acquired land in Pennsylvania in order to lay the foundations for a projected retreat which would offer them refuge from the tribulations of life in Germany.

In der Geschichte der deutschen Auswanderung nach Nordamerika spiegelt sich nur sehr bedingt das Auf und Ab der deutschen Geschichte wider. Die drei Jahrhunderte der Emigration seit 1683 waren eher von scheinbar widersprüchlichen Schub- und Sogwirkungen bestimmt. Oft überwog der transatlantische Sog die Hoffnung auf eine mögliche oder sogar schon einsetzende Verbesserung der wirtschaftlichen Lage zu Hause. Der Schub wiederum ging häufig von einem eng umgrenzten Gebiet aus, ohne selbst unmittelbar benachbarte Regionen zu beeinflussen. Von jeher war der Entschluß zur Auswanderung eine äußerst individuelle Entscheidung. Selbst in Epochen allgemeiner Auswanderungsbegeisterung mußte der Einzelne für die Sogwirkung empfänglich sein. Unter den Ländern, die sich um deutsche Einwanderer bewarben, blieb Amerika drei Jahrhunderte lang unverändert das bevorzugte Ziel. Die Grundlagen für diese Vorliebe wurden bereits im 18. Jahrhundert gelegt. Daher sollen hier die Gründe, die zur Amerikaorientierung der Europamüden führten, ausführlicher behandelt werden als der spätere Verlauf der Emigration, die im 19. Jahrhundert die Ausmaße einer Völkerwanderung annahm.

In dreihundert Jahren erlebte Deutschland den endgültigen Zerfall des Heiligen Römischen Reiches Deutscher Nation, den Aufstieg Preußens, die Napoleonischen Kriege, den losen Zusammenschluß deutscher Einzelstaaten zum Deutschen Bund mit seinen inneren Repressionen und gescheiterten Revolten, die Bismarcksche Reichsgründung, die Weimarer Republik und zwölf Jahre der Naziherrschaft bis hin zur heutigen Teilung des Landes in zwei deutsche Staaten. Es ist eine Geschichte sich ausdehnender und wieder zusammenziehender Grenzen, die es häufig im unklaren lassen, wer oder was man noch als „deutsch" bezeichnen kann. In den folgenden Zeugnissen aus dem 18. Jahrhundert wird dieser Begriff von Zeitgenossen gebraucht, die immer genau zu wissen schienen, was sie damit meinten.

„Ich sehe die trübselige Zorn- und schwere Straff-Gerichte / welche nach dem unhintertreiblichen Lauff göttlicher Gerechtigkeit über Europa biß zur gäntzlichen Verderbung dieses abscheulichen Babylons / außgegossen werden. Wolt Ihr nun / liebwerthste Eltern / diesen über Teutschland bestimmten Plagen entfliehen / so macht Euch nicht theilhafftig ihrer Sünden / sondern gehet davon aus!" Dies schrieb Franz Daniel Pastorius im März 1684 an seine Eltern, weniger als ein Jahr nach seiner Ankunft in Pennsylvanien. Und der Führer der ersten organisierten deutschen Auswanderung in die Neue Welt stand mit solchen apokalyptischen Anschauungen keineswegs

Only one generation had grown up since the end of the Thirty Years' War which had reduced the population of Germany to nearly half its prewar size. The war had left farms and homes in ruins in many parts of Central Europe. While the Atlantic nations embarked on exploration and exploitation of other continents, the center of Europe was only slowly recovering from the ravages of wars and epidemics. Millions of people were uprooted and roamed the countryside in search of land that could be cultivated. Southwestern Germany, the Palatinate in particular, experienced significant population shifts. The lands on both sides of the upper Rhine had been the scene of much unrest before the Great War, when peasants had risen against their oppressors in the first revolutionary movement in German history. Despite setbacks and renewed misery, a spark of the erstwhile rebellion remained alive among the frightened, bewildered peasantry.

The Lutheran, Reformed and Catholic Churches which had been established and sanctioned by the peace treaties of 1648, provided but little solace in their rigidity and orthodoxy. Moreover, the preference of the local ruler could determine which faith his subjects were allowed to practice. The multitudes of men and women who were shuffled from one ruler to another due to territorial changes, and who were alienated from the churches by the clergy's ever-increasing disinterest in everyday life, took refuge in a personalized, simple piety. While most gathered for prayer and Bible-reading in small groups without abandoning their ties to organized religion, many joined one of the virtually hundreds of factions of Christian dissenters that sprang up during the second half of the 17th century. Adherents to the old Anabaptist faith, relentlessly persecuted in their Swiss homes, settled in deserted parts of the Palatinate. Intolerance in many principalities and imperial cities forced groups of radical pietists into the underground. Some emerged in areas or towns where they were tolerated, notably Krefeld, Kriegsheim and Wittgenstein.

It was during the pietist assemblies, both within and without the organized Protestant churches, that the first impulse came for migration to a new world. The Krefeld and Kriegsheim Mennonites and Quakers, whose settlement Pastorius prepared and guided through its initial years, were no impractical dreamers. But as Pastorius stated, they were "tired of seeing and sampling European vanities". For them a new country, even though it was a wilderness, held the promise of "a quiet and Christian life." Sectarians all over the Rhinelands and beyond eagerly awaited news from those who had taken this immense step, irrevocable as it then seemed.

allein. Pastorius war geraume Zeit durch Deutschland gereist, bevor er in den Kreis lutherischer Pietisten im Frankfurter Saalhof aufgenommen wurde, wo sich Laien zu Gebet und frommer Unterhaltung getreu ihrer Überzeugung von der geistlichen Priesterwürde der Gläubigen zusammenfanden. Aus diesem Kreis ging die *„Frankfurter Compagnie"* hervor, die in Pennsylvanien Land erwarb, um sich dort ein Refugium zum Rückzug aus der Drangsal des Lebens in Deutschland zu schaffen.

Seit dem Ende des Dreißigjährigen Krieges, der Deutschlands Bevölkerung um nahezu die Hälfte reduziert hatte, war erst eine Generation herangewachsen. In weiten Gebieten Mitteleuropas lagen Bauernhöfe und Häuser in Schutt und Asche. Während die seefahrenden Nationen am Atlantik mit der Erforschung und Ausbeutung fremder Kontinente begannen, erholte sich das europäische Binnenland nur langsam von den Verwüstungen durch Krieg und Seuchen. Millionen von Menschen waren heimatlos geworden und durchstreiften die deutschen Staaten auf der Suche nach kultivierbarem Land. Das südwestliche Deutschland und vor allem die Pfalz erlebten bedeutende Bevölkerungsverschiebungen. Die Landstriche zu beiden Seiten des Oberrheins waren schon vor dem großen Krieg Schauplatz zahlreicher Unruhen gewesen, als sich die Bauern in der ersten revolutionären Bewegung der deutschen Geschichte gegen ihre Unterdrücker erhoben. Trotz aller Rückschläge und des neuerlichen Elends war ein Funke dieser ersten Rebellion bei der verwirrten und geängstigten Bauernschaft lebendig geblieben.

Die drei Kirchen – die lutherische, die reformierte und die katholische –, die durch die Friedensverträge von 1648 etabliert und bestätigt worden waren, konnten in ihrer orthodoxen Strenge nur wenig Trost bieten. Hinzu kam, daß das Recht der Landesfürsten, die Religion ihrer Untertanen zu bestimmen, auch nach 1648 im Prinzip unangetastet blieb. Ein Großteil der Menschen, die sich durch territoriale Veränderungen von einem Herrscher zum anderen geschoben sahen und sich angesichts der wachsenden Gleichgültigkeit des Klerus vor den Problemen des täglichen Lebens von ihren Kirchen entfremdeten, suchte bei individuellen, einfachen Formen der Frömmigkeit Zuflucht. Während sich die meisten in kleinen Gruppen zu Gebet und Bibellesung zusammenfanden, ohne dabei ihre Bindungen an die institutionalisierte Religion aufzugeben, schlossen sich viele andere den buchstäblich Hunderten von Sekten christlicher Dissidenten an, die in der zweiten Hälfte des 17. Jahrhunderts aufblühten. Anhänger des alten Wiedertäuferglaubens, die in ihrer schweizerischen Heimat erbarmungslos

Martin Luther (1483 – 1546): the schism he involuntarily brought about with his 95 theses on the misuse of indulgences determined the course of European history well past the conclusion of the Thirty Years' War. (Woodcut based on a painting by Lucas Cranach the elder.)

Martin Luther (1483–1546): die Glaubensspaltung, die er mit seinen 95 Thesen gegen den Ablaßmißbrauch 1517 ungewollt auslöste, bestimmte die europäische Geschichte bis über den 30jährigen Krieg hinaus. (Holzschnitt nach einem Gemälde von Lucas Cranach d. Ä.)

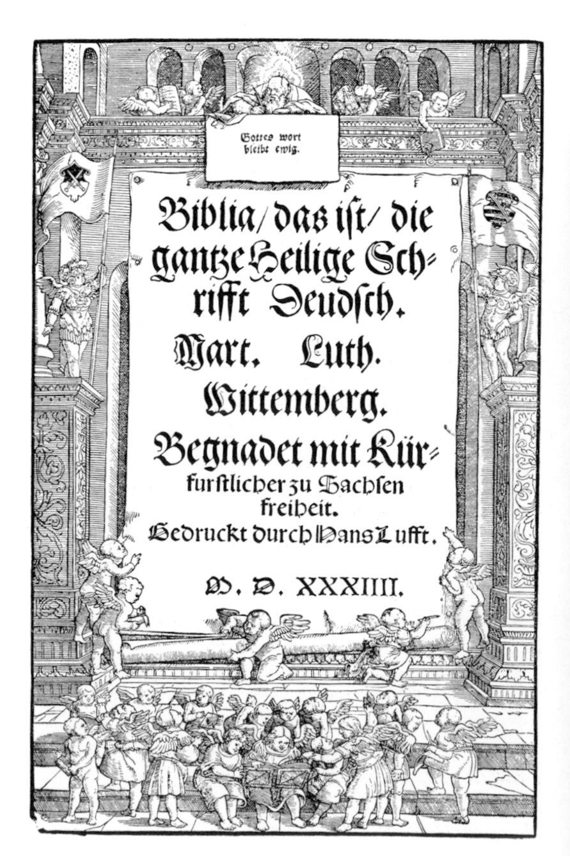

Gottes wort bleibt ewig.

Biblia/das ist/die gantze Heilige Schrifft Deudsch.
Mart. Luth.
Wittemberg.
Begnadet mit Kürfurstlicher zu Sachsen freiheit.
Gedruckt durch Hans Lufft.
M. D. XXXIIII.

Title page of the first complete edition of Luther's translation of the Bible, published in 1534 in Wittenberg, with woodcuts from the atelier of Lucas Cranach the elder. The wide distribution of this Bible – made possible by Johannes Gutenberg's invention of printing with movable type in 1445 – made it the foundation of modern literary High German. Two centuries later, Luther's translation also provided the text for the first Bible printed in a European language in North America – published in 1743 by the Pennsylvania Dutch printer, Christopher Saur in Germantown.

Titelblatt der ersten vollständigen Ausgabe der Lutherschen Bibelübersetzung, 1534 in Wittenberg erschienen, mit Holzschnitten aus der Werkstatt Lucas Cranachs d. Ä. Seine weite Verbreitung – ermöglicht durch den 1445 von Johannes Gutenberg erfundenen Buchdruck mit beweglichen Lettern – ließ dieses Werk zum Fundament der neuhochdeutschen Schriftsprache werden. Zwei Jahrhunderte später lieferte Luthers Übersetzung auch den Text für die erste Bibel, die in Nordamerika in einer europäischen Sprache gedruckt wurde – 1743 von dem pennsylvaniendeutschen Drucker Christopher Saur in Germantown.

Titelholzschnitt der »Bundschuh-Flugschrift«, 1513: links versammeln sich Bauern unter ihrem Feldzeichen, das einen auf dem traditionellen Symbol des Bauernstandes (dem Bundschuh als Gegensatz zum bespornten Rittersiefel) stehenden gekreuzigten Heiland zeigt; rechts schwören Bauern auf die Harke als das Sinnbild ihrer Arbeit. Die Bauernaufstände, die unter dem Zeichen des Bundschuhs von 1493 bis 1517 in eben jenen Gebieten Südwestdeutschlands aufflackerten, deren Bevölkerung sich später auch als die auswanderungsfreudigste erweisen sollte, waren das Vorspiel zum großen Bauernkrieg von 1524/25. Hier wie dort begehrten die Bauern unter Berufung auf das »göttliche Recht« gegen die feudalistische Gesellschaftsordnung mit ihren Lehns- und Tributspflichten auf, die endgültig erst zu Beginn des 19. Jahrhunderts abgeschafft wurden.

Title woodcut from the "Bundschuh Pamphlet," 1513: on the right the farmers are gathered beneath their standard, which depicted a crucified Saviour above the traditional symbol of the peasant class (the thonged shoe – "Bundschuh" – in contrast to the spurred riding boot of the nobility); on the right, farmers are seen swearing an oath on the rake, the symbol of their work. The peasant revolts, which flared up beneath the sign of the thonged shoe from 1493 to 1517 in those very parts of southwestern Germany where the population would subsequently provide the most enthusiastic emigrants, were the prelude to the great peasants' revolt of 1524/25. In both cases, the peasants appealed to their "divine right" to take arms against feudal society with its system of vassalage and tributes, abuses which were not completely done away with until the beginning of the 19th century.

"Diversions enjoyed by persons of rank and others in Virginia": an early report on the first English colony in North America, published by Johann-Theodor de Bry in Oppenheim in 1618, the year the Thirty Years' War began.

Zehender Theil Americæ.
XI.
Was die Adelspersonen vnd andere
in Virginia für Kurtzweil haben können.

Frühe Nachricht über die erste englische Kolonie in Nordamerika, erschienen 1618, im ersten Jahr des Dreißigjährigen Krieges, bei Johann-Theodor de Bry in Oppenheim.

Die Boten, die 1648 die Nachricht von den Vertragsschlüssen des »Westfälischen Friedens« (mit Schweden in Osnabrück, mit Frankreich in Münster) durch die deutschen Staaten trugen, ritten durch ein verwüstetes Land: Kampfhandlungen, Seuchen, Plünderungen und Hungersnöte hatten die Bevölkerung Deutschlands gegenüber dem Vorkriegsstand – 1618 etwa 20 Millionen Menschen – um 40 Prozent schrumpfen lassen. Besonders umkämpfte Gebiete wie die Pfalz waren regelrecht entvölkert: dort lebten von 500 000 Bewohnern noch ganze 43 000. In seiner wirtschaftlichen Entwicklung war Deutschland um zwei Jahrhunderte zurückgeworfen. Die psychologischen Kriegsfolgen bei den Überlebenden – ein tiefverwurzeltes Gefühl der Unsicherheit und des Ausgeliefertseins – blieben noch jahrzehntelang unterschwellig wirksam und manifestierten sich nicht zuletzt in der Blüte des pietistischen Sektenwesens mit seiner Sehnsucht nach Erweckung und Verinnerlichung. Politisch brachten die Friedensverträge, neben der Regelung der Konfessionsfrage, eine Stärkung der fürstlichen »Libertät« gegenüber der kaiserlichen Zentralgewalt. Das Reich, bestehend aus 355 Einzelstaaten, löste sich in einen lockeren Staatenbund auf, der die politische und militärische Ohnmacht Deutschlands besiegelte.

Holzschnitt aus einem Friedensflugblatt, Oktober 1648

The messengers who bore the news of the "Westphalian Peace" treaties of 1648 (with the Swedes in Osnabrück and in Münster with the French) through the German states rode through a devastated country; military engagements, epidemics, pillage and famine had reduced Germany's population by 40 percent from its prewar level of some twenty million people in 1618. Scenes of particularly bitter hostility, such as the Palatinate, were virtually depopulated: the population of 500,000 there was reduced to 43,000. Germany had been thrown back two centuries in its economic development. The psychological consequences of the war for the survivors – a deeply rooted sense of insecurity and abandonment – remained subliminal factors for decades and manifested themselves noticeably in the flowering of the pietistic sects with their longing for awakening and spiritualization. Politically, in addition to a regulation of the religious issue, the peace treaties brought about a strengthening of the "liberties" of the individual princes vis-à-vis the central powers vested in the emperor. The Empire, which consisted of 355 individual states soon dissolved into a loose confederation which inevitably led to Germany's political and military impotence.

Woodcut from a peace handbill, October 1648.

A remarkable group of some forty mystics set out for Pennsylvania in 1694. They were led by Johann Jacob Zimmermann, a noted mathematician and astronomer. Zimmermann had calculated that the world would end in the autumn of that year and he planned to await the Millennium in the New World. When he died before embarkation, his disciple, John Kelpius, led the group across the sea. Most left their mark on the early intellectual history of the American colonies. One of their group, Daniel Falckner, an ordained Lutheran minister, wrote the first practical guide for would-be emigrants on request of the founder of pietist schools and orphanages in Halle, August Hermann Francke. Published in 1702, Falckner's book, together with tracts and letters written by Pastorius, familiarized people all over Germany with the potential and promise that Pennsylvania represented. In the preface to his manuscript Falckner expressed feelings of doom shared by many other pietists in Germany: "Ought not a time of dearth and famine come unto you, ought not pestilence, epidemics, the French and other plagues overtake you? Ought not deluded men, wild dissolute tyrants rule over us? Ought not war or strife arise, should not an evil government come about in the German States? Sodom and Gomorrah were not one tenth as wicked as Germany is at present; they had neither God's Holy Word nor the ministry which we have gratuitously. But we act like those who would that both the Lord and his word, all discipline and honor perish. If this is to be the rule in Germany, I shall regret that I am born a German, or ever spoke or wrote German."

Thus the first real impulse for German transatlantic migration came from religious groups whose uneasiness about the present and the future in their "European Egypt" made them long for a far-off "Canaan." Eventually entire sects followed the example of the Krefeld Mennonites. News about their emigration travelled by word of mouth and through letters and publications. Much curiosity was aroused by the new continent across an ocean that had hitherto seemed so remote to people living hundreds of miles inland.

The generally precarious economic situation of the peasant population and the brutal and destructive French incursions into the Palatinate and adjacent provinces in 1688/89 and again in 1692/93 seemed reason enough to assume that news from Pennsylvania fell upon fertile ground. But the question remained of how to pay for the journey and for land. From 1699 onwards another English colony, Carolina, was mentioned repeatedly in German publications. French Protestant refugees were welcomed and helped in Carolina and Virginia. So far only religiously motivated, organized groups had left for the New World. Such

verfolgt wurden, ließen sich in entlegenen Teilen der Pfalz nieder. Religiöse Intoleranz in vielen Fürstentümern und freien Reichsstädten trieb Gruppen radikaler Pietisten in den Untergrund. Einige von ihnen tauchten in Gegenden und Städten wieder auf, wo sie und ihr Glaube geduldet wurden, darunter vor allem Krefeld, Kriegsheim und Wittgenstein.

Von solchen pietistischen Versammlungen, sowohl innerhalb wie außerhalb der organisierten protestantischen Kirchen, ging der erste Anstoß zur Auswanderung in eine Neue Welt aus. Die Mennoniten und Quäker aus Krefeld und Kriegsheim (bei Worms), deren Ansiedlung in Amerika Pastorius vorbereitete und durch die ersten Jahre führte, waren keineswegs unrealistische Träumer. Aber sie waren es, in Pastorius' Worten, „müde, Europens Eitelkeiten zu sehen und (zu) probiren". Für sie versprach ein neues Land, selbst eine Wildnis, die Aussicht auf „ein stilles und christliches Leben". Sektierer in allen rheinischen Ländern und weit darüber hinaus warteten nun begierig auf Nachrichten von jenen, die diesen ungeheueren und, wie es damals scheinen mußte, unwiderruflichen Schritt getan hatten.

Eine bemerkenswerte Gruppe von etwa vierzig Mystikern brach 1694 nach Pennsylvanien auf. Ihr Anführer war Johann Jakob Zimmermann, ein angesehener Mathematiker und Astronom. Zimmermann hatte errechnet, daß die Welt im Herbst desselben Jahres untergehen würde, und er wollte das Millennium in der Neuen Welt erwarten. Als Zimmermann noch vor der Einschiffung starb, übernahm sein Schüler Johann Kelpius die Führung der Gruppe über den Ozean. Die meisten ihrer Mitglieder haben in der frühen Geistesgeschichte der amerikanischen Kolonien ihre Spuren hinterlassen. Einer von ihnen, Daniel Falckner, ein lutherischer Pfarrer, schrieb auf Veranlassung von August Hermann Francke, dem Gründer pietistischer Schulen und Waisenhäuser in Halle, das erste Handbuch mit praktischen Anweisungen für Auswanderungswillige. Zusammen mit einer Reihe von Traktaten und Briefen aus der Feder von Pastorius machte Falckners 1702 veröffentlichtes Buch die Menschen in ganz Deutschland mit den vielversprechenden Möglichkeiten vertraut, die sich in Pennsylvanien boten. In seiner Vorrede kam jene Untergangsstimmung zum Ausdruck, die damals bei vielen Pietisten in Deutschland herrschte: „Solte nicht theure Zeit kommen, solt nicht Pestilentz, Schweiß, Frantzosen und andere Plagen uns finden, solten nicht verblendete Leute, wilde, wüste Tyrannen regiren, solt nicht Krieg und Hader entstehen, solt nicht ein böses Regiment in teutschen Landen werden. Sodoma und Gomorra sind das zehende Theil nicht so böse gewesen als jetzo Teutschland ist,

Johann Kelpius (1673 – 1708), mystic, astrologer and founder of a theosophical community on Wissahickon Creek in Pennsylvania, painted by Christopher Witt around 1705.

Johann Kelpius (1673–1708), Mystiker, Astrologe und Gründer einer theosophischen Gemeinschaft am Wissahickon Creek in Pennsylvanien, um 1705 gemalt von Christopher Witt

Moses looks down at the Promised Land; the return of the scouts from Canaan; the destruction of Sodom: copperplate engravings from the workshop of Matthäus Merian the elder. The biblical motives were the 17th and 18th centuries' way of illustrating the contrast between Europe and America.

Mose schaut in das gelobte Land; Rückkehr der Kundschafter aus Kanaan; die Vertilgung Sodoms: Kupferstiche aus der Werkstatt Matthäus Merians d. Ä. mit biblischen Motiven, die in der Gedankenwelt des 17. Jahrhunderts den Gegensatz Amerika/Europa illustrierten.

denn sie haben Gottes Wort und Predigt-Ambt nicht gehabt, so haben wir es umbsonst und stellen uns, als die da wollten, daß beyde Gott sein Wort, alle Zucht und Ehre unterginge. Wann es so soll in Teutschland gehen, so ist mirs Leyd, daß ich ein Teutscher gebohren bin, oder je teutsch geredet oder geschrieben habe."

Der erste konkrete Anstoß zur Auswanderung über den Ozean kam also von religiösen Gruppen, deren Unbehagen angesichts der gegenwärtigen Zustände und der Zukunftsaussichten ihres „europäischen Ägypten" die Sehnsucht nach einem fernen „Kanaan" geweckt hatte. Bald folgten ganze Sekten dem Beispiel der Krefelder Mennoniten. Die Nachrichten von ihrer Auswanderung gingen von Mund zu Mund, verbreiteten sich durch Briefe und Schriften. Neugier erwachte auf diesen neuen Kontinent jenseits eines Meeres, das den Menschen tief im Binnenland bis dahin selbst schon weit entfernt erschienen war.

Die allgemeine wirtschaftliche Not der Bauern und die brutalen Überfälle der Franzosen auf die Pfalz und die benachbarten Provinzen in den Jahren 1688/89 und 1692/93 lassen es nur plausibel erscheinen, daß die Neuigkeiten aus Pennsylvanien auf fruchtbaren Boden fielen. Es blieb nur die Frage, wie man das Geld für Überfahrt und Landerwerb aufbringen sollte. Seit 1699 finden sich in deutschen Druckschriften wiederholt Hinweise auf eine weitere englische Kolonie, Carolina, in der protestantische Flüchtlinge aus Frankreich willkommen waren und, ebenso wie in Virginia, Unterstützung fanden. Die Auswanderung in die Neue Welt war bis dahin generell die Domäne religiös motivierter, organisierter Gruppen gewesen. Sie konnten sich bei ihrer Reise auf die tatkräftige Hilfe Gleichgesinnter verlassen, häufig der Quäker, deren Interesse an der Gewinnung neuer Siedler keineswegs völlig uneigennützig war.

A view of Krefeld around 1730. Located in the Dutch-German borderland region, it became a place of refuge for victims of religious persecution from all of Germany in the 17th century.

Krefeld, im deutsch-holländischen Grenzgebiet gelegen und im 17. Jahrhundert Zufluchtsort für Glaubensflüchtlinge aus ganz Deutschland, auf einer Ansicht um 1730

The Dutch religious reformer Menno Simons (1496–1561), founder of the Anabaptist "Mennonite" sect, persecuted because of its pacifistic aloofness from the state; the likeness was painted in 1683, the year the first German settlers emigrated to America.

Der holländische Theologe Menno Simons (1496–1561), Begründer der wegen ihres konsequenten Pazifismus verfolgten Wiedertäufersekte der »Mennoniten«; das Gemälde stammt aus dem Jahr der ersten Auswanderung, 1683.

Von wegen der Evangelischen Religion bin ich gefangen gesetzt worden / da hat man mich auf dem Rath-Hauß zu Red gesetzt / wegen meines Glaubens / so gabe ich zur Antwort: Wann euer Glaub gerecht ist / so führt mich nach Maria-Plan / kan ich alsdann vor dem wunderthätigen Marien-Bild aufrecht und gerad stehen / so glaub ich / daß euer Glaube gerecht / auf diese Red wurde ich mit Ketten und Banden geschlossen / und in ein Loch gesteckt welches 7. Klafftern tieff war / und das 7. Tag und Nacht / auch kümmerlich mit Wasser und Brod gespeißt wurde / und das bey grosser Kält / in dieser Trangsal ruffte ich zu GOtt: HERR! vergib ihnen / dann sie wissen nicht was sie thun.

Geschehen / den 24. Januarij Anno 1732.

Frantz Antoni Baumgarten / Bergknapp / aus dem Rastatter Gericht gebürtig / seines Alters 32. Jahr.

Religious persecution in the 18th century: the lament of miner Franz Antoni Baumgarten from the province of the prince-bishops of Salzburg, whose entire Protestant population of over 20,000 was banished from the region in the winter of 1732/33. The great portion of these exiles found homes in Prussia; about 80 families resettled in the newly established American colony of Georgia.

Religiöse Verfolgung im 18. Jahrhundert: Klage des Bergknappen Franz Antoni Baumgarten aus dem Fürstbistum Salzburg, dessen gesamte evangelische Bevölkerung von mehr als 20 000 Menschen im Winter 1732/33 außer Landes gejagt wurde. Der größte Teil der Vertriebenen fand in Preußen Aufnahme, etwa 80 Familien ließen sich in der neugegründeten amerikanischen Kolonie Georgia nieder.

The "Franckesche Stiftungen" building in Glaucha near Halle on a copperplate engraving made in 1799. Founded by the theologist, pedagogue and orientalist, August Hermann Francke (1663 – 1727), the Francke Foundations, which exist to this day, became a center of the Pietist Protestant reform movement in the early 18th century. Many of their members numbered among the first German emigrants to America.

Die Gebäude der »Franckeschen Stiftungen« in Glaucha bei Halle auf einem Kupferstich aus dem Jahr 1799. Von dem Theologen, Pädagogen und Orientalisten August Hermann Francke (1663–1727) begründet, wurden die noch heute bestehenden Franckeschen Stiftungen im frühen 18. Jahrhundert zu einem europäischen Zentrum der protestantischen Reformbewegung des Pietismus, dessen Anhänger einen großen Teil der frühen deutschen Amerika-Emigranten stellten.

The year in which German emigration to America commenced, 1683, was also the year in which Turkish armies laid siege to Vienna for the final time. Their defeat in the battle on the Kahlenberg (12 September) marked the end of the centuries-long Muslim Turkish threat to Christian central Europe. (Contemporary etching by Romeijn de Hooghe)

Im selben Jahr 1683, in dem die deutsche Amerikaauswanderung einsetzte, standen die Türken zum letztenmal vor Wien. Ihre Niederlage in der Schlacht am Kahlenberg am 12. September markiert das Ende der jahrhundertelangen türkischen Bedrohung Mitteleuropas. (Zeitgenössische Radierung von Romeijn de Hooghe).

bands were assisted along the way by kindred spirits, often by Quakers whose interest in attracting settlers was not altogether altruistic.

In 1704 a number of Thuringians in Langensalza formed the *"High German Society"* to effectuate the emigration of several hundred, partly well-to-do, families. They sent an emissary to Pennsylvania and a delegation to London where they negotiated with the Quaker John Archdale, the Governor of Carolina. No religious reasons are given for their action but their leader, Polycarpus Rechtenbach, cited "the great impost and grievances laid upon their property" which were "day by day growing higher". The Saxon government employed a spy to report on the movements of the delegation and their talks with Quakers at the Carolina Coffee House. Acting on reports of the Saxon envoy in London, King Augustus the Strong of Poland and Elector of Saxony ordered Rechtenbach's arrest and the prevention of the entire project in August, 1706.

Josua Harrsch, a Lutheran pastor from Eschelbronn in the Palatinate, had also gone to London in 1704 under the assumed name of Kocherthal to find out how poor Palatines could be shipped to America. He was given detailed information by eager proprietors of lands in Carolina and Pennsylvania, and was urged to compile a book which was published in Germany in 1706. In his preface Kocherthal vividly described the situation from the time of the French invasions of the 1690s which had prompted his inquiries: "Not long afterwards, namely after the ill-fated end of the Campaign in 1703, a great many places of our Germany had fallen into a very precarious state. While, on one hand, the French forces had taken possession of the fortress of Landau and thus exposed again the entire region to severe troubles and pressures, on the other hand, considerable Bavarian advances brought terror to all neighboring lands, many people were prompted thereby to think of the said province of Carolina and to consider

Im Jahre 1704 schlossen sich einige Thüringer in Langensalza zur *„Hoch-Teutschen Sozietät"* zusammen, um die Auswanderung einiger hundert, teils wohlhabender, Familien in die Wege zu leiten. Sie entsandten einen Boten nach Pennsylvanien und eine Abordnung nach London, die mit dem Quäker John Archdale, dem Gouverneur von Carolina, Verhandlungen aufnahm. Für ihre Auswanderungsabsicht werden keinerlei religiöse Gründe genannt: statt dessen erwähnt ihr Anführer, Polycarpus Rechtenbach, die „hohen Steuern und Abgaben auf ihr Eigentum", die „von Tag zu Tag größer" würden. Die sächsische Regierung bediente sich eines Spions, um über die Absichten der Delegation und den Fortgang der Verhandlungen mit den Quäkern im Carolina Kaffeehaus auf dem laufenden zu bleiben. Auf Grund der Berichte des sächsischen Gesandten in London ordnete August der Starke, Kurfürst von Sachsen und König von Polen, schließlich im August 1706 die Verhaftung Rechtenbachs und die Blockierung des Projekts an.

Ebenfalls 1704 war Josua Harrsch, ein lutherischer Pfarrer aus Eschelbronn in der Pfalz, unter dem angenommenen Namen Kocherthal nach London gekommen, um die Möglichkeiten zu erkunden, die es für arme Pfälzer gab, sich nach Amerika einzuschiffen. Interessierte Grundbesitzer aus Carolina und Pennsylvanien versahen ihn mit detaillierten Informationen und drängten ihn, darüber ein Buch zu schreiben, das 1706 in Deutschland erschien. In seinem Vorwort schildert Kocherthal anschaulich die Lage, in der sich Südwestdeutschland seit der Zeit der französischen Einfälle in den 90er Jahren befand und die ihn zu seinen Erkundungen veranlaßt hatte:

„Da nun nicht lange hernach, nemlich nach der 1703 unglücklich geendigten Campagne sehr viele Oerter unseres Teutschlands in einen sehr gefährlichen zustand verfallen, indem einerseits die Frantzösischen Waffen der Vestung Landau sich bemächtiget, und

Ezéchiel, Comte de Mélac, French general, whose troops laid waste huge stretches of the Palatinate and burned down the cities of Mannheim and Heidelberg during the War of Palatine Succession (1688 - 97).

Ezéchiel Graf von Mélac, französischer General, dessen Truppen im Pfälzischen Erbfolgekrieg (1688–97) weite Landstriche der Pfalz verwüsteten und die Städte Mannheim und Heidelberg niederbrannten.

Heavy ice drift on the Rhine near Cologne; copy of an 18th century etching

Schwerer Eisgang auf dem Rhein bei Köln; nach einem Stich aus dem 18. Jahrhundert

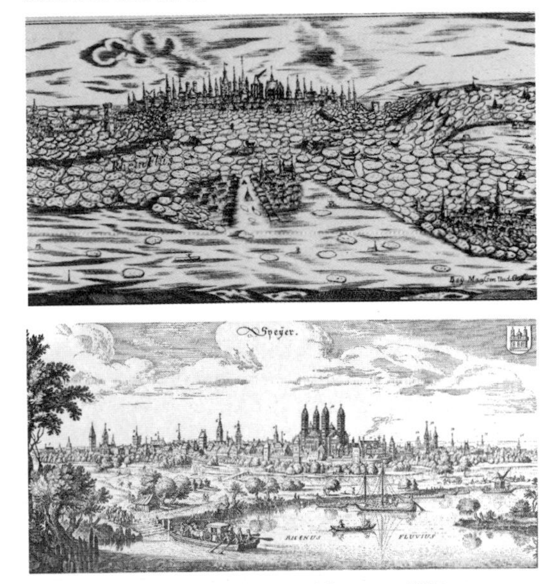

The episcopal cities of Speyer, Mainz and Trier on contemporary etchings

Die Bischofsstädte Speyer, Mainz und Trier auf zeitgenössischen Stichen

whether it were not advisable to leave hard-pressed Germany and go over there."

Toward the end of 1707 Kocherthal went to London with 61 young adult Palatines. They were helped liberally by people along the way. Kocherthal appealed directly to Queen Anne who ordered spontaneously that these fellow-Protestants from the German province most exposed to encroachments by hostile Catholic powers be transported to New York. Kocherthal was prevailed upon by English promoters to describe the help received from the Queen and others in a postscript to his book, which was re-issued early in 1709 and quickly went through three further editions. Little did he or his English sponsors dream that the report of the Queen's largesse would trigger off a stampede and influence the migration from Central Europe for decades to come.

The reasons cited by Kocherthal against the background of the military situation in the Palatinate seemed plausible enough, but a decided hesitation to leave even an embattled, impoverished homeland was still discernable. During the Winter of 1708/09 however, the ultimate push was provided by nature. It was as if a new ice age had suddenly broken out. Hans Stauffer of Alsheim recorded in his notebook which he brought to America: "In 1708, in the autumn, apples and apple blossoms were together on the same branches", and "in the year 1709 the Rhine was closed with ice for five weeks. On January 10, the Rhine closed". The severe weather destroyed many of the vineyards, one of the mainstays of the Palatine and Franconian economy. Stored wine froze into solid blocks of ice and birds on the wing fell dead from the air, so the story goes. Many saw these events as a sign of doom and the coming of the end of the world.

When Spring finally came and the rivers were free of ice, families packed their bundles and headed for the Dutch ports. First a few hundred from the Palatinate, then thousands from the entire Southwest of the Empire: the bishoprics of Worms, Speyer, Mainz and Trier, from Hanau and Darmstadt, Nassau, Alsace, Baden and Franconia. 6,000 emigrants had reached London in June, and at the end of the year this number had swelled to 14,000. Many others were stranded along the Rhine and in Holland. Somehow word had spread from village to village that Queen Anne had invited all to come. Mysterious agents and books, notably Kocherthal's, which passed from hand to hand only strengthened these rumors.

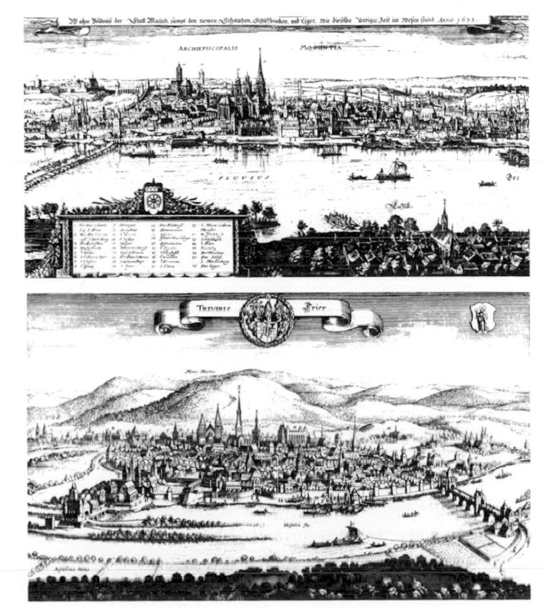

mithin die gesamte Landschaften jenseits Rheins wieder in viele harte Troublen und Pressuren gesetzet; andererseits aber die sehr große Bayerische Progressen allen benachbarten Landen zum Schrekken gerathen: seynd viele dadurch veranlasset worden, an besagte Landschaft Carolina zu gedencken und in Deliberation zu ziehen, ob nicht rathsam sey auß dem so viel- und hart-bedrängten Teutschland außzugehen und sich dahin zu begeben."

Ende 1707 führte Kocherthal eine Gruppe von 61 jungen Pfälzern nach London. Bereits während der Reise erfuhren sie überall bereitwillige Unterstützung. Kocherthal wandte sich direkt an Königin Anne, die spontan anordnete, daß die protestantischen Glaubensgenossen aus der den Übergriffen feindlicher katholischer Mächte am meisten ausgesetzten deutschen Provinz nach New York gebracht werden sollten. Kocherthal wurde von seinen Gönnern dazu überredet, die von der Königin und anderen gewährte Hilfe in seiner Nachschrift zu seinem Buch zu würdigen, das 1709 neu erschien und bald drei weitere Auflagen erlebte. Weder Kocherthal noch seine englischen Förderer ahnten, daß diese Schilderung der königlichen Großzügigkeit einen wahren Exodus auslösen und die Auswanderung aus Mitteleuropa für Jahrzehnte beeinflussen würde.

Mußten Kocherthals Argumente für die Auswanderung vor dem Hintergrund der militärischen Lage in der Pfalz auch einleuchtend genug erscheinen, so war doch immer noch eine deutliche Zurückhaltung zu spüren, selbst ein umkämpftes und verarmtes Heimatland zu verlassen. Den endgültigen Anstoß dazu gab die Natur selbst. Es war, als wäre plötzlich eine neue Eiszeit hereingebrochen. Im Notizbuch eines Hans Stauffer aus Alsheim, der seine Aufzeichnungen nach Amerika mitnahm, lesen wir, daß die Bäume im Herbst 1708 Äpfel und Apfelblüten zugleich trugen und daß der Rhein am 10. Januar 1709 für volle fünf Wochen zufror. In den Weingärten, dem Haupterwerbszweig der pfälzischen und fränkischen Wirtschaft, ließ der strenge Frost die Rebstöcke eingehen; in den Fässern gefror der Wein zu Eisblöcken, und die Vögel, so die Überlieferung, fielen mitten im Flug tot vom Himmel. Viele sahen in dieser Wetterkatastrophe ein böses Omen – ein Vorzeichen des nahenden Endes der Welt.

Als endlich der Frühling einzog und die Eisdecken tauten, packten ganze Familien ihre Habseligkeiten zusammen und machten sich auf den Weg nach den holländischen Häfen. Erst waren es ein paar hundert Pfälzer, dann folgten Tausende aus ganz Südwestdeutschland: den Bistümern Worms, Speyer, Mainz und Trier, aus Hanau und Darmstadt, aus Nassau, dem Elsaß, Baden und Franken. Im Juni waren 6 000 Auswanderer in London eingetroffen, bis zum Ende des Jahres insgesamt 14 000. Viele weitere waren entlang des Rheins und in Holland hängengeblieben. Von Dorf zu Dorf ging das Gerücht um, Königin Anne habe sie alle zum Kommen aufgefordert. Geheimnisvolle Agenten und Bücher, vor allem Kocherthals, die allgegenwärtig waren, gossen nur neues Öl in die Flammen.

Eine Flut von Auswanderungsanträgen überschwemmte die Behörden in den betroffenen deutschen Staaten – und viele Emigranten machten sich gar nicht erst die Mühe, den amtlichen Segen einzuholen. In mehreren Fällen wurden spezielle Anhörungsverfahren durchgeführt. In der Grafschaft Nassau-Weilburg gaben die Antragsteller einhellig zu Protokoll, daß sie aus Armut und wegen mangelnder Verdienstmöglichkeiten in ihren erlernten Berufen auswandern wollten. Die meisten erwähnten auch die

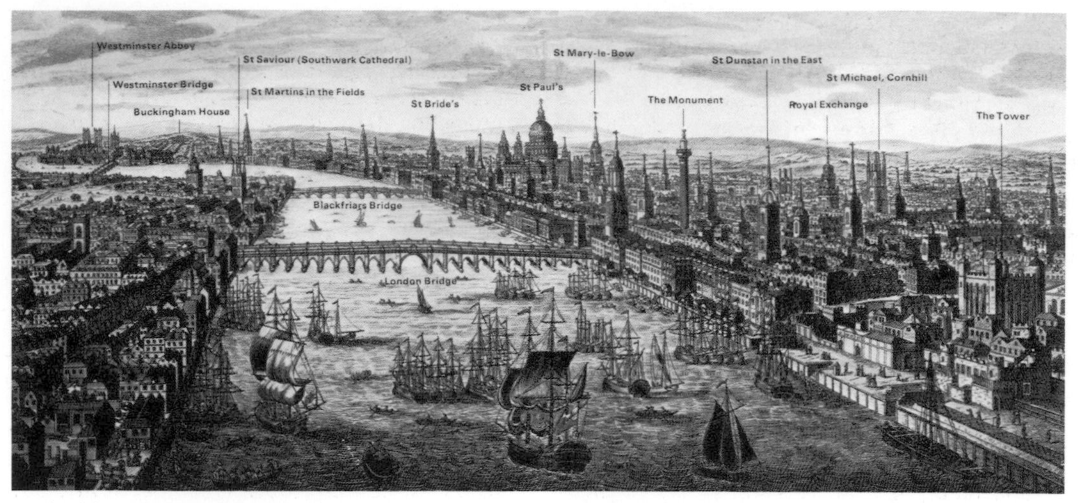

View of 18th-century London

Ansicht Londons im 18. Jahrhundert

Authorities in the affected German states were flooded with applications for emigration by those who bothered to obtain permission. In several cases special hearings were conducted. Applicants interrogated in Nassau-Weilburg all pleaded poverty or the inability to earn a decent livelihood in their trades as reasons for their leaving. Most of them also spoke of the books that had been passed around, copied by teachers, read to illiterates and propounded from the pulpits. Master-baker Jost Schneider wrote to the prince of Nassau-Dillenburg that he had to go "because I do not know how to make ends meet here anymore. Also the heavy taxation and debts take everything, and my craft is so badly paid that I don't know how to make a single penny. Therefore I won't be able to subsist here much longer."

The complaints and the reasons given by numerous individuals were common to most of the peasantry and lower middle class. Without persuasion most might never have thought of leaving home. Apart from a few scores of Mennonites from the Palatinate and Switzerland, none had compelling reasons to flee intolerance. Catholics and Protestants alike were among the multitudes streaming down the Rhine. In June 1709 the Reformed Consistory of the Palatinate condemned the move as "groundless Pretences of such People to go out of the Country on Account of the said Religious persecution."

The emigrants were helped by the impotence and disorganization of the Empire. There was no central power, as in France, that could have put a halt to the crazed masses. The authorities had been so taken by surprise that they could not coordinate their policies. However, they were also not prepared to prohibit emigration altogether. The most severe measures threatened by some were confiscation of all property. The government of Sayn-Wittgenstein stated with resignation that "those who have fallen for the *principium emigrandi* are so bent upon it, that like desperate people they rather leave everything behind, than change their mind." Eberhard Ludwig, Duke of Wurttemberg decreed in June that no emigrant could sell his property, but this only served as a deterrent for a few people. Prince Wilhelm of Nassau-Dillenburg resorted to a different course of action. He announced that taxes were to be lowered, fired a number of civil servants, reprimanded others and appealed to the clergy to stop preaching rebellious sermons. Pastor Dietz of Emmerichhayn was singled out for a particular investigation because he had admonished his flock that "the time had come that God the Lord had revealed a promised land in order to save His people from Egyptian servitude."

Bücher, die von Hand zu Hand gegangen, von Schulmeistern abgeschrieben, den Analphabeten vorgelesen und sogar von den Kanzeln herab verkündet worden waren. In einem erhalten gebliebenen Brief eines Bäckermeisters, Jost Schneider, an den Fürsten von Nassau-Dillenburg werden als Auswanderungsgründe ebenfalls finanzielle Schwierigkeiten, zumal die hohe Steuer- und Zinsenlast und die schlechten Preise, die auf dem Markt zu erzielen seien, angeführt.

Solche Argumente und Klagen, die von vielen Emigranten überliefert sind, trafen für die große Mehrheit des Bauernstandes und der unteren Mittelschicht zu. Ohne äußeren Anstoß hätten die meisten von ihnen nie daran gedacht, ihre Heimat zu verlassen. Abgesehen von ein paar pfälzischen und schweizerischen Mennonitengruppen hatte niemand zwingende Gründe, wegen religiöser Intoleranz außer Landes zu gehen. Unter den Auswandererströmen, die den Rhein hinunterzogen, befanden sich Katholiken ebenso wie Protestanten, und der Rat der reformierten Kirche in der Pfalz bezeichnete die Berufung mancher Auswanderer auf religiöse Verfolgungen im Juni 1709 als „unbegründeten Vorwand".

Die Machtlosigkeit und Desorganisation des Reiches kam den Auswanderern zu Hilfe. Es existierte keine Zentralgewalt – wie etwa in Frankreich –, die der Auswanderungswut der Massen hätte Einhalt gebieten können. Die Behörden waren von den Ereignissen so überrascht worden, daß sie ihre Gegenmaßnahmen nicht koordinieren konnten. Auch zu einem gänzlichen Auswanderungsverbot vermochten sie sich jedoch nicht zu entschließen. Als drakonischster Schritt wurde den Emigranten in einigen Staaten die Beschlagnahme ihres gesamten Besitzes angedroht. Die Regierung von Sayn-Wittgenstein stellte resignierend fest, daß „diejenigen, welche auf das *principium emigrandi* einmahl fallen, darinnen so verbicht sind, dass sie gleichsam wie desperate Leute lieber alles zurücklaßen, als ihr Vorhaben ändern wollen". Herzog Eberhard Ludwig von Württemberg verfügte im Juni 1709, daß kein Auswanderungswilliger seinen Besitz verkaufen dürfe, doch auch davon ließen sich nur wenige abschrecken. Fürst Wilhelm von Nassau-Dillenburg suchte bei Präventivmaßnahmen Zuflucht: Er kündigte eine Steuersenkung an, feuerte einige seiner Beamten, ergriff Disziplinarmaßnahmen gegen andere und appellierte an den Klerus, seine rebellischen Predigten einzustellen. Ein Pfarrer Dietz aus Emmerichhayn wurde besonderer Untersuchung unterzogen, weil er seiner Gemeinde verkündigt hatte, „daß es nun ahn deme seye, daß Gott Der Herr sein Volck aus der Egyptischen Dinstbarkeit zu erretten ein gelobtes Landt gezeiget hatte".

"Good Queen Anne" Stuart (1665 – 1714) at the time of her accession (1702)

Die »gute Königin«, Anne Stuart (1665–1714), zur Zeit ihrer Thronbesteigung (1702)

Duke Eberhard Ludwig (1676 – 1733), regent of Wurttemberg from 1693, a notorious spendthrift

Herzog Eberhard Ludwig (1676–1733), Regent Württembergs seit 1693, für seine Verschwendungssucht berüchtigt

Elisabeth Charlotte ("Liselotte") von der Pfalz (1652–1722) became duchess of Orléans upon her marriage to Duke Philippe I. (Portrait by Hyacinthe Rigaud, 1713)

Elisabeth Charlotte (»Liselotte«) von der Pfalz (1652 bis 1722), seit 1671 als Gattin Philipps I. Herzogin von Orléans. (Gemälde von Hyacinthe Rigaud, 1713)

The Elector of the Palatinate, Johann Wilhelm, known and praised for his tolerant policies, faced the most critical situation of all. More than 8,500 of his subjects had left. His advisers started using the term "depopulation" and reported that there was a scarcity of grain and bread largely due to the departure of so many farmers. For the very first time, governments in Germany were confronted with a problem that had hitherto been almost beneficial. Beneficial because previously only religious dissenters and a few disgruntled or adventurous individuals had wanted to emigrate, but now everybody seemed to want to leave. It was a problem that was to remain with various governments for the rest of the century and well beyond.

Despite the tragic turn which the 1709 emigration took, as will be dealt with elsewhere, departures for America continued. British shipping companies in Rotterdam were beginning to carry Germans on credit arrangements to Pennsylvania. It enabled those who could not pay for the passage to enter into work contracts upon arrival and thus "redeem" their passage. When this system was initiated, the French followed suit and offered free transporation to their colonies. Under the auspices of John Law's *Compagnie de l'Occident*, emissaries swarmed out across the Rhine and signed up about 4,000 people, mostly young families from the Palatinate, Baden and surrounding areas. When the Palatine princess Elisabeth Charlotte, wife of Duke Philip of Orleans, Regent of France, received news in May 1720 of the trek of 75 Palatine families on their way through France, she wrote: "Tears came to my eyes on account of them. I fear that our Lord will severely punish the Elector. If the punishment could only strike the damned clergy, it would be fair: but I fear the Elector himself will have to pay for it." She expressed her own disillusionment strongly: "One hears and sees nothing but falsehood and deception which renders life terribly tiresome and sour. It almost makes me consider that the Palatines who go to Mississippi and get away from Europe are most fortunate."

Der für seine Toleranz bekannte und gepriesene pfälzische Kurfürst Johann Wilhelm sah sich in der schwierigsten Lage. Mehr als 8 500 seiner Untertanen hatten das Land verlassen. Seine Ratgeber begannen, den Begriff „Depopulation" zu gebrauchen und berichteten, daß es großen Mangel an Brot und Getreide gäbe, da so viele Bauern ausgewandert seien. Zum ersten Mal wurde für die Regierungen in Deutschland zum Problem, was sich bis dahin eher positiv ausgewirkt hatte – positiv, weil die Auswanderung von religiös Andersdenkenden, Abenteuerern und Unzufriedenen durchaus nicht unerwünscht war. Jetzt jedoch wollten plötzlich alle gehen. Es war ein neues Problem entstanden, das die Regierungen bis zum Ende des Jahrhunderts und darüber hinaus beschäftigen sollte.

Obwohl die Hoffnungen der Auswanderer von 1709 zum großen Teil unerfüllt blieben – davon später –, hielt der Emigrantenstrom nach Amerika an. Britische Reedereien in Rotterdam gingen dazu über, deutsche Auswanderer auf Kreditbasis nach Pennsylvanien mitzunehmen. Wer die Überfahrt nicht bezahlen konnte, ging nach seiner Ankunft einen mehrjährigen Arbeitsvertrag ein, mit dem er sich gegenüber dem Schiffseigner auslösen konnte. Als dieses Verfahren eingeführt wurde, zogen die Franzosen nach und offerierten freie Beförderung in ihre Kolonien. Im Auftrag von John Laws *Compagnie de l'Occident* schwärmten Emissäre über den Rhein hinüber und warben etwa 4 000 Menschen an, größtenteils junge Familien aus der Pfalz, aus Baden und den umliegenden Gebieten. Als die pfälzische Prinzessin Elisabeth Charlotte, Gemahlin des französischen Regenten, Herzog Philipp von Orleans, im Mai 1720 von einem Treck von 75 pfälzischen Familien hörte, der sich auf dem Weg durch Frankreich befand, brachte sie folgendes zu Papier: „Die threnen seindt mir darüber in den Augen kommen. Ich fürchte, daß unser herrgott den churfürsten hart straffen wirdt. Wen die straffe nur auff die verflüchte pfaffen konte fallen, were es gutt; aber ich fürchte, der churfürst es selber wirdt bezahlen." Für ihre Enttäuschung und Resignation fand sie klare Worte: „Man hort und sieht nichts, alß falschheit und betrug; daß macht daß leben greulich müde undt sawer. Daß macht mich schir die Pfaltzer glücklich finden, so in Missisipi gehen undt auß Europa weg kommen."

Emigrants to America from Switzerland go aboard the river barges that will take them down the Rhine to their embarkation point in Rotterdam; woodcut by Johan Heinrich Heitz from "Letters from America by a Farmer from Basel", 1806

Schweizerische Amerikaauswanderer besteigen in Basel die Flußkähne, die sie rheinabwärts zu ihrem Auswanderungshafen Rotterdam bringen sollen; Holzschnitt von Johan Heinrich Heitz aus »Briefe aus Amerika von einem Basler Landmann«, 1806

If a Palatine princess could express such thoughts, it is not surprising that thousands of ordinary people reacted to the prospect of a better life. Religious motivation became blurred as time went on. True, sporadic flare-ups of persecution, or merely official disapproval, continued to send entire groups of dissenters across the sea. Political instability and intermittent warfare contributed to the resolve to emigrate but, even at times of heightened emigration fever, the decision was a highly individual one. Once a basis for comparison existed, by which an individual – within the context of his class – could measure his present situation against opportunities elsewhere, the temptation to emigrate took hold. Poverty only became a factor in pushing an individual or a family to leave home for an unknown destination when comparison with something better made their situation more apparent. The fearful, the really downtrodden hardly ever yielded to it.

Wenn selbst eine pfälzische Prinzessin solchen Gedanken anhängen konnte, ist es kaum überraschend, daß auch Tausende von gewöhnlichen Bürgern auf die Aussicht auf ein besseres Leben reagierten. Die religiösen Auswanderungsmotive verwischten sich im Lauf der Jahre, auch wenn es immer wieder zu einem sporadischen Aufflackern der Glaubensverfolgungen oder zu behördlichen Schikanen kam, die ganze Gruppen von Dissidenten über den Atlantik segeln ließen. Politische Instabilität und immer neue kriegerische Auseinandersetzungen trugen zum Entschluß zur Auswanderung bei, doch blieb diese Entscheidung, selbst in Zeiten allgemeinen Auswanderungsfiebers, stets eine höchst individuelle und persönliche. Natürlich mußte die Versuchung zur Emigration wachsen, sobald erst einmal eine Vergleichsbasis existierte, die es den Menschen erlaubte, ihre derzeitige Lage – im Rahmen ihrer sozialen Klasse – gegen die anderswo sich bietenden Chancen abzuwägen. Armut konnte für den einzelnen oder eine Familie erst dann zum auslösenden Faktor für den Aufbruch in eine ungewisse Zukunft werden, wenn der Vergleich mit etwas Besserem die eigene Situation deutlich gemacht hatte. Die Ängstlichen, wirklich Getretenen gaben solcher Versuchung kaum jemals nach.

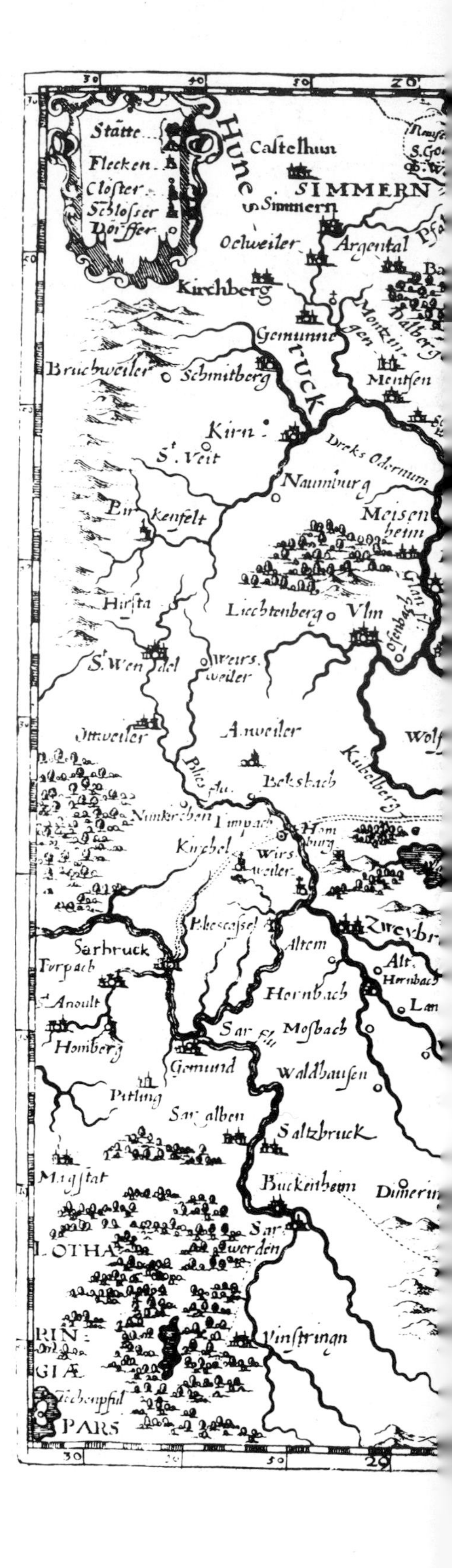

The War of the Palatinate (also known as the War of the League of Augsburg, 1688–97) was set off by claims of inheritance made by King Louis XIV of France after the death of the Palatine Elector Karl, who died without issue in 1685, on behalf of the Palatine's sister Elisabeth Charlotte ("Liselotte") von der Pfalz, who had married a member of the French royal family. In the course of the war, the city of Heidelberg was plundered by the French both in 1689 and 1693. One of the illustrations shows Heidelberg in flames; the other is a Merian etching of the city of Worms from the middle of the 17th century, on which the flames were painted in later to give the viewer an idea of the horrors of war.

Der Pfälzische Erbfolgekrieg (1688–97) entzündete sich an den Erbansprüchen, die der französische König Ludwig XIV nach dem Tod des kinderlos verstorbenen pfälzischen Kurfürsten Karl (1685) für dessen Schwester, die an den französischen Hof verheiratete Elisabeth Charlotte (»Liselotte«) von der Pfalz, erhob. Die Abbildungen zeigen das brennende Heidelberg, das 1689 und 1693 von den Franzosen geplündert wurde, und einen Merian-Stich der Stadt Worms aus der Mitte des 17. Jahrhunderts, der nachträglich mit Flammen übermalt wurde, um einen Eindruck von den Kriegsgreueln zu geben.

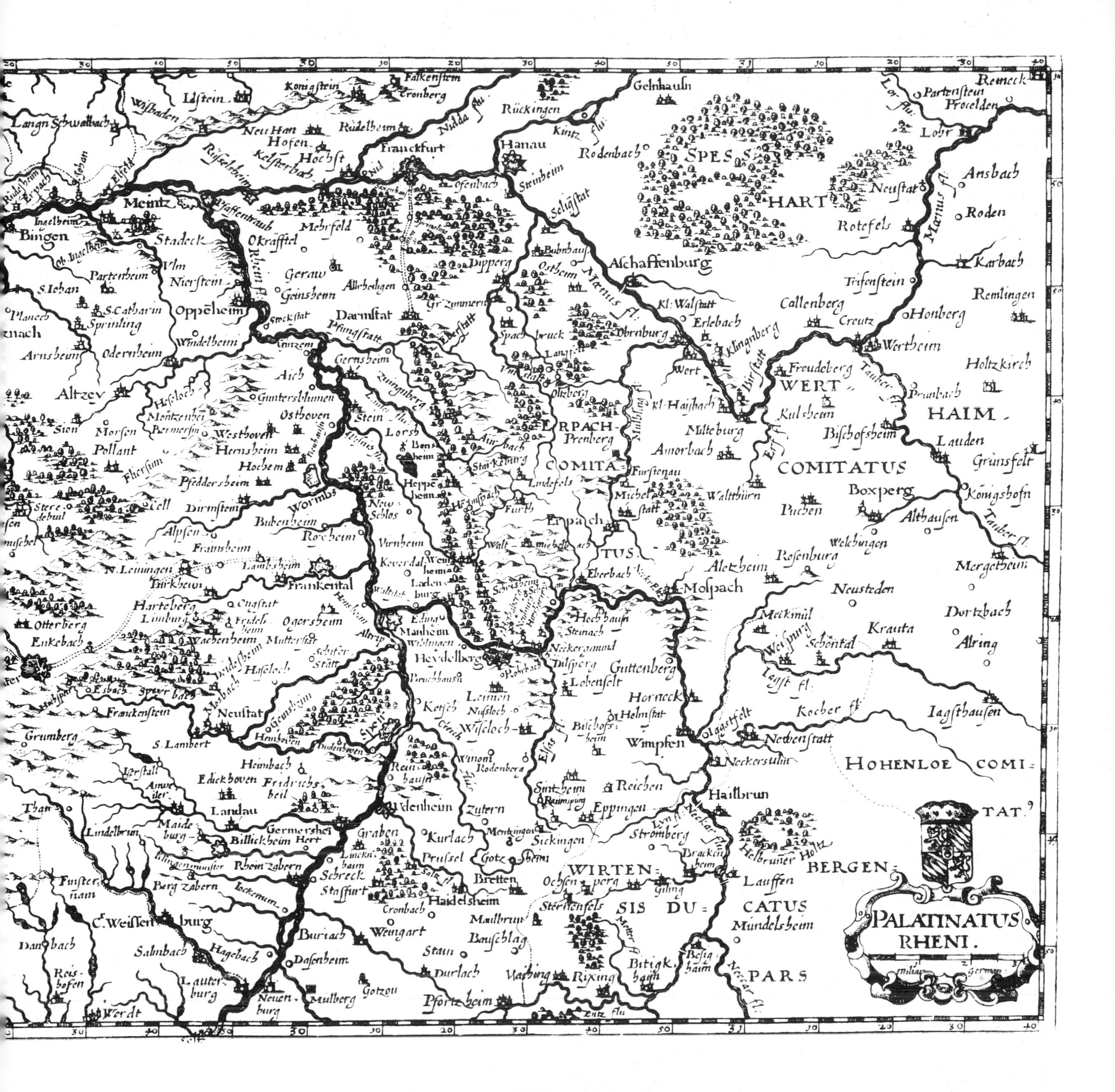

The Rhenish sections of the Electoral Palatinate, situated on both sides of the upper Rhine to the south of its tributory the Main, as shown on a map by Matthäus Merian the Younger, Frankfurt, 1672. With France on its western border, the district was repeatedly overrun by foreign troops for almost a century, from the start of the Thirty Years' War (1618) until the end of the War of the Spanish Succession (1714). Such a high percentage of early German emigrants to America had originated from that area that for a time the expression "Palatines" became synonymous with "Germans".

Die rheinischen Gebiete der Kurpfalz, zu beiden Seiten des Oberrheins südlich der Einmündung des Mains gelegen, auf einer Karte von Matthäus Merian d. J., Frankfurt, 1672. Das im Westen an Frankreich grenzende und vom Beginn des Dreißigjährigen Krieges (1618) bis zum Ende des Spanischen Erbfolgekrieges (1714) fast ein Jahrhundert lang immer wieder von fremden Truppen heimgesuchte Land stellte einen so großen Anteil der frühen deutschen Amerikaauswanderer, daß der Begriff »Palatines« (Pfälzer) in Nordamerika vorübergehend zu einem Synonym für »Deutsche« wurde.

Overpopulation, so frequently cited as a cause for migration, is also a relative concept. For a century after the Thirty Years'. War many parts of southwest Germany did not reach the pre-war population density. The Palatinate and Wurttemberg were areas that actually received immigrants from other regions.
Social restraints for the small peasantry and the lower middle-class in town and village during the last phase of feudalism were numerous and often overwhelming. Vassalage was still in effect but in most cases in the German Southwest, personal bondage no longer existed beyond the obligation to provide services. Such obligations of course, could be quite burdensome, as there were also heavy taxes to pay. Even nominal vassals had to obtain their legal freedom through manumission if they wanted to leave their ruler's territory, an act frequently requiring the payment of a stiff fee. The farming population consisted largely of people with very small holdings due to the custom of dividing the inheritance among all surviving children. Viticulture, which had provided a livelihood for many, was reduced by diseases and harsh winters. Though the culture of American crops, potato, corn and tobacco, replaced many a vineyard in the Palatinate, most farmers lived close to the subsistence level. Prospects of more land in far-away places never failed to appeal to the more enterprising elements of the rural population. Artisans of all types of craft labored under a closely regulated guild system which excluded gifted people if they had not served the prescribed course as apprentice and journeyman. Lastly, though morals had been affected by wars, occupations and frequent population shifts, clergy and officials watched over strict moral standards in communities. Undesirables were driven to emigrate. Sexual promiscuity, drunkenness and chronic laziness were the main targets of social pressure by peers.

Auch die Überbevölkerung, die häufig als Auswanderungsgrund genannt wird, ist ein relativer Begriff. Noch ein Jahrhundert nach dem Dreißigjährigen Krieg hatte die Bevölkerung in vielen Teilen Südwestdeutschlands den Vorkriegsstand nicht wieder erreicht. Die Pfalz und Württemberg waren sogar Regionen, die ihrerseits Einwanderer aus anderen Gebieten aufnahmen.
Die sozialen Einschränkungen für Kleinbauern und untere Mittelschicht in den Städten und Dörfern des ausklingenden Feudalismus waren vielfältig und oft niederdrückend. Die Lehnspflicht war noch geltendes Recht, wenn auch in den meisten südwestdeutschen Staaten außer der Möglichkeit zur Dienstverpflichtung keine persönliche Leibeigenschaft mehr existierte. Zusammen mit der erheblichen Steuerlast konnten solche Dienstpflichten natürlich eine schwere Bürde darstellen. Selbst Lehnsmänner, die es nur noch dem Namen nach waren, mußten sich um die formelle Freilassung durch ihren Herrscher bemühen, wenn sie dessen Territorium verlassen wollten - ein Rechtsakt, den sich der Fürst nicht selten teuer bezahlen ließ. Unter der bäuerlichen Bevölkerung verfügten die meisten nur über sehr wenig Grundbesitz, da es alter Brauch war, die Erbschaften unter allen überlebenden Kindern aufzuteilen. Der Weinbau, einst Existenzgrundlage für viele, war durch Schädlinge und strenge Winter zurückgegangen. Obwohl der Anbau von Getreide und den aus Amerika importierten neuen Pflanzen Kartoffel, Mais und Tabak an die Stelle so manches pfälzischen Weingartens getreten war, lebten die meisten Bauern am Rande des Existenzminimums. Die Aussicht auf mehr Grund und Boden in einem fernen Land konnte ihre Wirkung auf den unternehmungslustigeren Teil der Landbevölkerung nicht verfehlen. Im Handwerkerstand sorgte das erstarrte Zunftsystem für Unzufriedenheit, das auch begabte

Palatine farmer and his wife, based on a contemporary illustration

Pfälzisches Bauernpaar, nach einer zeitgenössischen Darstellung

Everyday town-and-country life under the signs of Mercury, the god of commerce, and Saturn, the patron god of the peasantry; wood carving by Hans Sebald Beham.

Alltagsleben in der Stadt und auf dem Land, unter den Zeichen Merkurs, des Gottes der Kaufleute, und Saturns, des Gottes der Landbauern, in Holzgeschnitten von Hans Sebald Beham.

Inn sign with the mark of the Aschaffenburg builders' guild, 1715

Herbergsschild mit dem Zunftzeichen der Bauhandwerker von Aschaffenburg, 1715

8. Personen, so verkauffet werden sollen, in Königsberg.

Es hat jemand folgende Unterthanen zu verkauffen: 1) Einen Koch, etliche 40. Jahr seines Alters, welcher wol kochen kan, auch nicht nur mit der Küche, sondern auch mit Garten guten Bescheid weiß, und zur Aufwartung und auf Reisen sehr wol zu gebrauchen. 2) Sein Weib eben von etliche 40. Jahren, welche gut Linnen wircken kan. 3) Eine Tochter von 13. Jahren. 4) Eine Dito von 12. Jahren, und 5) Eine Dito von 9. Jahren, welche alle zu Diensten gebräuchlich. 6) Noch ein Mensch von 20. Jahren, welcher das, was zur Jagd gehöret, bey einem Königl. Förster lernet. Wer nun die vorspecificirte 6. Personen an sich zu kauffen Willens ist, derselbe wolle sich bey dem Cantzelley-Boten bey der hiesigen geheimten Cantzelley Abraham Ernst Müller, so Vor- und Nachmittage daselbst zu treffen ist, beliebig melden, und wegen des Preises der Leute zu einigen.

Contemporary testimony of the feudalistic social structure around the middle of the 18th century: above, an advertisement from the "Königsberger Intelligenzwerk" (1744), offering serfs for sale; on the right, a lord of the manor exercising his corporal punishment privileges.

Zeitgenössische Zeugnisse der feudalistischen Gesellschaftsstruktur um die Mitte des 18. Jahrhunderts: Oben eine Anzeige aus dem »Königsberger Intelligenzwerk« von 1744, in der leibeigene Untertanen zum Verkauf angeboten werden; rechts ein Gutsherr bei der Ausübung des ihm zustehenden Züchtigungsrechts.

Ready conclusions as to the causes of emigration to America may be drawn from the economic and social factors enumerated here, and indeed, most were evoked by the emigrants themselves in applications for manumission, in letters and diaries, or in hearings conducted by the authorities. Except for vassalage, which disappeared from Germany after the French Revolution and the Napoleonic Wars, reasons given by those who emigrated during the 19th century differed little from the earlier testimonies.

But there is another dimension to the America migration. It was more than misery, constraint and unease that made people in certain areas more responsive than others. People longed for a life as individuals, beyond the niche of the hierarchical society into which they had been born. It was the refutation of an existing economic, social and moral order and of a limited horizon. Among the young, it was also a yearning for adventure and for action which could not be satisfied within the constraints of dwarfish principalities. For many it was neither mere wanderlust nor only hunger for land. There were other open spaces beckoning the landless peasant, far less distant than America. However, a Wurttemberger expressed his preference in 1754 with the following explanation: "We were told that whoever wanted to move to Prussia would be given money for travel and as much land as in America. But, oh, what is a free inhabitant compared to a slave or serf? What pleasure would a man have in a country in which he has to work himself to death for an overlord, and where his sons are at no hour safe from the miserable soldier's life?"

It is true that Germany lost many of her rebellious sons and daughters to America. Amidst the often abjectly servile wording of petitions for emigration, criticism of local officials and complaints about unjust taxation are discernible. Wagonmaker Lorenz Albert of the county of Wertheim in 1754 refuted accusations of having merely caught the "emigration fever" from others: "It is neither impudence nor pleasure which drives me from the country but poverty and concern for wife and child." In 1752 Rhenish emigrants to South Carolina were asked to state the reasons for their departure. A single girl, Barbara Ratgeb, simply replied that she was "desirous to see more of the world". Several others wanted to go to a land where they could make their fortune and a score or so had decided to go in order to join friends and relatives who had left before them.

Handwerker von der Berufsausübung ausschloß, wenn sie nicht den traditionellen Ausbildungsgang mit Lehr- und Wanderjahren durchlaufen hatten. Und schließlich gab es noch die engen Moralbegriffe, die, obwohl bereits von Kriegen, Besatzungszeiten und häufigen Bevölkerungsverschiebungen aufgeweicht, doch von Klerus und Beamtenschaft streng überwacht wurden. Wer gegen sie verstieß, sah sich zur Auswanderung genötigt. Sexuelle Promiskuität, Trunksucht und chronische Faulheit waren die Hauptangriffspunkte des sozialen Drucks der Gemeinschaft.

Die Bedeutung der geschilderten wirtschaftlichen und gesellschaftlichen Faktoren für die Auswanderung liegt auf der Hand, und in der Tat finden sich eben diese Gründe in den Anträgen der Emigranten auf Entlassung aus der Lehnspflicht, in Briefen und Tagebüchern und in den Protokollen offizieller Anhörungen aufgeführt. Mit Ausnahme der Lehnspflicht, die nach der französischen Revolution und den Napoleonischen Kriegen aus Deutschland verschwand, unterscheiden sich die Auswanderungsgründe, die die Emigranten des 19. Jahrhunderts angaben, nur wenig von den älteren Zeugnissen.

Doch die Auswanderung nach Amerika hat eine weitere Dimension. Neben Verelendung, sozialen Zwängen und Unzufriedenheit gab es noch etwas anderes, das die Menschen in bestimmten Regionen stärker reagieren ließ als andere. Man sehnte sich nach einem Leben als freies Individuum, jenseits der Nische innerhalb einer hierarchischen Gesellschaft, in die man hineingeboren war. Der Auswanderungswunsch war zugleich eine Ablehnung der bestehenden wirtschaftlichen, sozialen und moralischen Ordnung mit ihren beschränkten Horizonten. Er war, bei den Jüngeren, auch ein Ausdruck der Sehnsucht nach Abenteuer und Handlungsfreiheit, die in der Enge der oft winzigen Fürstentümer nicht befriedigt werden konnte. Bei vielen aber ging es um mehr als bloße Wanderlust und Landhunger. Schließlich gab es andere dünnbesiedelte Gegenden, weit näher als Amerika, die sich dem landlosen Bauern anboten. Ein Württemberger begründete seine Bevorzugung Amerikas im Jahr 1754 mit den folgenden Worten: „Man hat uns gesagt, daß, wer nach Preussen ziehen wolle, der bekome Reiß-Geld und Land, wie in America; Aber Ach! Was ist ein *freyer* Einwohner gegen einen Sclaven oder Leib-eigenen? Was für ein Vergnügen kan ein Mensch haben in einem Land, darin er sich vor die Herrschaft zu tod arbeiten muß, und wo die Söhne keine Stunde vor dem elenden Soldaten-Leben sicher sind?"

Tatsächlich hat Deutschland viele seiner rebellischen Söhne und Töchter an Amerika verloren. In den oft bis zur Servilität unterwürfigen Formulierungen vieler Bittgesuche um Auswanderung lassen sich versteckte Kritik an örtlichen Beamten und Klagen über ungerechte Besteuerung entdecken. Der Stellmacher Lorenz Albert aus der Grafschaft Wertheim entgegnete 1754 auf den Vorwurf, er sei nur vom Auswanderungsfieber angesteckt worden: „Es ist kein Vorwitz oder Lust, der mich aus dem Land treibt, sondern die Armut und die Sorge für Weib und Kind." Im Jahr 1752 wurden rheinländische Auswanderer nach Süd-Carolina nach ihren Gründen befragt. Ein lediges Mädchen, Barbara Ratgeb, antwortete einfach, sie wolle „mehr von der Welt sehen". Einige andere gaben an, sie wollten in ein Land gehen, in dem sie ihr Glück machen konnten, und etwa zwanzig emigrierten, um Freunden und Verwandten zu folgen, die ihnen vorausgegangen waren.

In 1727 the minutes of the police court of Schwaigern in Wurttemberg simply noted that Johann Georg Teter, son of the village mayor, decided "to render himself to Pennsylvania in pursuit of his expected success". Four citizens of Oberingelheim got in trouble in 1747 because they had "sent their sons, whose names were on the new military conscription list, to the New Land, and with the knowledge of the entire town, had given each of them 100 florins and some food for the voyage."
Toward the end of the 18th century some emigrants were no longer mincing their words. Hammersmith Franz Spiess of Siegen countered the authorities and the guild (who were both trying to prevent the loss of skilled workmen), with an indictment of the masters of his trade. Referring to frequent shutdowns of the mills, Spiess claimed it was done "without any regard to the dayman who may languish meanwhile. The dayman is thus expected to live on his own fat until it pleases the owner to use him again like his pack animal. Should we not have just cause, if we are made to stay, to demand that the hammersmiths' guild first compensate us for what we have lost in 3 or 4 years?"
Half a century earlier, in 1742, when the inhabitants of Ziegelhausen petitioned the Elector of the Palatinate to turn forests into arable land, they included the veiled threat that in the case of rejection "Ziegelhauseners ... would then take refuge in the New Land, or Pennsylvania." The forest land was converted. Many of the rulers lived extravagantly and spent the revenues from the taxes and tributes which had been exacted from their people, rather freely. The attitude seems to have been the following: try to keep useful, tax-yielding citizens at home and ship useless ones off to America! Much effort was spent to dissuade would-be migrants from leaving. The cooper Franz Kuhn in 1764 requested an audience with Duke Karl Eugen of Wurttemberg when minor authorities refused to let him go. The duke himself was unable to dissuade him. Authorities were wary of returning emigrants. Some rulers received letters from former subjects in America giving them advice and admonishments. Georg Käsebier, a Schwarzenau Baptist, felt compelled to remind Count Casimir of Berleburg "to act like a father in your land so that God may also act like a father unto you." And he admonished the count: "If someone comes and asks you for a mite for the journey in order to migrate to this country, open your generous hand and share as much as you can." Brewer Zacharias Endress in Philadelphia suggested in 1771 to his former sovereign, Carl Ludwig, Count of Löwenstein-Wertheim that he should finance the building of a town in Pennsylvania which could accomodate 100 mechanics and farmers from Wertheim. Somehow the decision to emigrate made people lose meekness and submissiveness.

In den Protokollen des Polizeigerichts von Schwaigern in Württemberg heißt es im Jahre 1727, der Sohn des Dorfbürgermeisters, Johann Georg Teter, habe sich zum Aufbruch nach Pennsylvanien entschlossen, weil ihm sein dortiger Erfolg gewiß sei. Vier Bürger aus Oberingelheim gerieten 1747 in Schwierigkeiten, weil sie ihre Söhne mit 100 Gulden und einer Wegzehrung versehen und, mit Wissen der ganzen Stadt, in das „Neue Land“ geschickt hatten, um einer Zwangsaushebung zum Militärdienst zuvorzukommen.
Gegen Ende des 18. Jahrhunderts wagten einige der Emigranten eine deutlichere Sprache. Der Hammerschmied Franz Spiess aus Siegen gab den Behörden und der Zunft (die beide versuchten, die Abwanderung ausgebildeter Arbeitskräfte zu verhindern) mit schweren Vorwürfen an die Adresse seiner Meister Kontra. Bezugnehmend auf die häufige Schließung der Mühlen, behauptete Spiess, dies geschehe „ohne auf den Taglöhner – der interdessen schmachten möchte – einige Rücksicht zu nehmen. Da soll also der Taglöhner mittlerweile von seinem eigenen Schmalz zehren, und wenn es dem Eigenthümer gefällig ist, will er jenen erst wieder wie sein Lasttier gebrauchen. Wir hätten doch wohl gerechte Ursache zu verlangen, dass, wenn wir bleiben sollten, uns die Hammerschmidtszunft zuerst das vergüten müste, was wir seit 3–4 Jahren zugesetzt haben.“
Bereits 1742, ein halbes Jahrhundert zuvor, hatten die Einwohner von Ziegelhausen ihrer Eingabe an den pfälzischen Kurfürsten, Wälder zur Gewinnung von Ackerland roden zu lassen, die verhüllte Drohung beigefügt, sie würden im Fall einer Ablehnung „in das neue Land, oder Pinsilvanien, flüchtig werden.“ Der Wald wurde gerodet. Die Herrscher, die oft einen extravaganten Lebensstil pflegten und ihre Einnahmen aus Steuern und Tributzahlungen bedenkenlos verpraßten, schienen bei der Behandlung der Auswanderer nach einer Art Faustregel zu verfahren: nützliche, steuerzahlende Bürger hielt man nach Möglichkeit im Lande; die anderen, nutzlosen, schiffte man nach Amerika ein. Oft wurden große Anstrengungen unternommen, Auswanderungswillige zum Bleiben zu überreden. Der Küfer Franz Kuhn forderte und erhielt 1764 eine Audienz bei Herzog Karl Eugen von Württemberg, nachdem ihm untergeordnete Behörden die Ausreise verweigert hatten. Auch dem Herzog gelang es nicht, ihn von seiner Überzeugung abzubringen. Vor wieder zurückkehrenden Auswanderern waren die Behörden auf der Hut. Einige Herrscher erhielten Briefe von ehemaligen Untertanen, die nun aus Amerika gute Ratschläge und Ermahnungen erteilten. Georg Käsebier, Baptist aus Schwarzenau, fühlte sich veranlaßt, den Grafen Casimir von Berleburg daran zu erinnern, „doch väterl. in dero Lande zu verfahren auf daß auch Gott möge väterl. mit sie verfahren“. Seine dringliche Mahnung: „Wenn iemand kommen möchte und sie ansprechen, um einen Reise Pfennig, um hier in dieses Land zu ziehen, daß sie ihro Milde Hand auf Thun wolten und nach vermögen mittheilten.“ Der Brauer Zacharias Endress aus Philadelphia schlug 1771 seinem ehemaligen Herrscher, dem Grafen Carl Ludwig von Löwenstein-Wertheim vor, er möge doch die Errichtung einer Stadt in Pennsylvanien finanzieren, die hundert Handwerker und Bauern aus Wertheim aufnehmen könnte. Augenscheinlich hatte der Entschluß zur Auswanderung die Menschen ihre Demut und Unterwürfigkeit verlieren lassen.

The life-style of the "Amish people", members of a conservative Mennonite sect founded in 1693 by Jacob Ammann, their customs, manner of dressing, and type of community settlements originated in Alsace and the German-speaking part of Switzerland, whence most of them emigrated to Pennsylvania in the 18th century. The c. 50,000 present-day members of the American "Old Order Mennonite Church" still dwell in the areas to which they originally immigrated and still lead an uncompromising and unchanging 18th-century way of life.

Aus der deutschsprachigen Schweiz und dem Elsaß stammen Trachten, Siedlungsformen und Gebräuche der »Amische«, einer 1693 von Jakob Ammann begründeten und im 18. Jahrhundert größtenteils nach Pennsylvanien ausgewanderten konservativen Mennonitengruppe. Die heute 50 000 Angehörigen der amerikanischen »Amisch-Mennoniten Kirche Alter Verfassung« leben nach wie vor in den ursprünglichen Einwanderungsgebieten und haben den Lebensstil des 18. Jahrhunderts unverändert beibehalten.

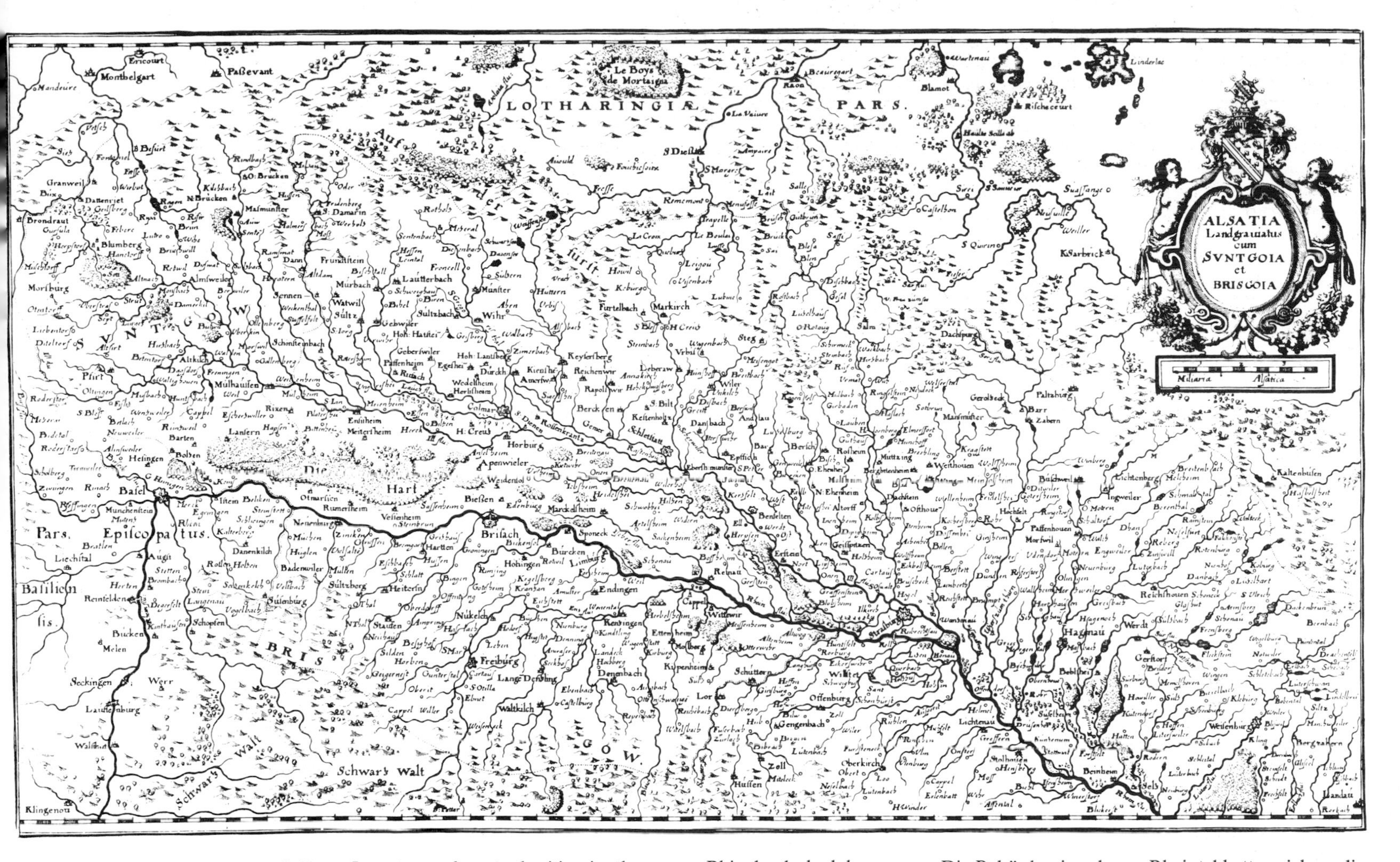

The Rhenish frontier regions of Alsace-Lorraine and Baden on a map drawn along a vertical west-east axis (with north toward the right) by Matthäus Merian the Younger in 1663. Seen at the bottom are the Breisgau and Black Forest districts, which adjoin the southern Palatinate and were part of the southwest German area where early emigration chiefly originated. Those fleeing Alsace, a primarily German-speaking province which had come under French rule in the second half of the 17th century, made their way mainly to the purlieus of German settlement in Pennsylvania, however there were some smaller groups which opted for the French territory of Louisiane (named after Louis XIV), which did not become a part of the U.S. until 1803, anglicized as "Louisiana".

Elsaß und Baden mit Breisgau und Schwarzwald, die südlich an die Pfalz anschließenden Teile des südwestdeutschen Hauptauswanderungsgebietes, auf einer nach Westen ausgerichteten (Norden = rechts) Karte von Matthäus Merian d. J. aus dem Jahr 1663. Die Auswanderer aus dem überwiegend deutschsprachigen Elsaß, das in der zweiten Hälfte des 17. Jahrhunderts unter französische Herrschaft gekommen war, ließen sich zum größten Teil in den deutschen Siedlungsgebieten in Pennsylvanien nieder; kleinere Gruppen entschieden sich für die französische (nach Ludwig XIV. benannte) Kolonie Louisiane, die 1803 zu den USA kam.

Authorities in the upper Rhinelands had become accustomed to emigration. In the first four decades of the 18th century the centers of this population unrest were largely limited to the Protestant areas near the upper and middle Rhine, basically the Swabian-Alemanic region and the Franconian areas on the Rhine and Moselle. It included some German-speaking cantons of Switzerland, lower Alsace and Mosellan Lorraine, all of which no longer belonged to the Empire. The percentage of migrants from the Palatinate was so high at times that after a while all German-speaking persons, regardless of their origin, were referred to in England and her colonies as "Palatines". Wurttemberg and the Nassau principalities experienced heavy emigration at intervals but particularly from 1749 to 1754 when agents (the so-called newlanders) canvassed these areas with remarkable success. During the same period, which coincided with the peak years of 18th-century German emigration to North America, recruiters for shipping companies and land schemes widened their range of activity to the Protestant imperial cities in upper Swabia and into central Germany. The Rhine had hitherto been the major route for Rotterdam-bound wanderers, now English emigrant ships loaded in Hamburg for the first time. American emissaries spread into the hinterland of the Elbe as far as Thuringia and Saxony. But here they ran into formidable obstacles from Prussian and Saxon authorities.

Die Behörden im oberen Rheintal hatten sich an die Auswanderung gewöhnt. In den ersten vier Jahrzehnten des 18. Jahrhunderts beschränkten sich die Unruheherde, von denen die Wanderungsbewegung ausging, im wesentlichen auf die protestantischen Bezirke am oberen und mittleren Rhein, also den schwäbisch-alemannischen Raum und die fränkischen Gebiete an Rhein und Mosel. Am Rande wurden auch einige nicht mehr zum Reich gehörende Regionen erfaßt, so etliche deutschsprachige Kantone der Schweiz, das untere Elsaß und die an die Mosel grenzenden Teile Lothringens. Der Prozentsatz der Auswanderer aus der Pfalz war zu manchen Zeiten so hoch, daß in England und den englischen Kolonien bald alle deutschsprachigen Emigranten, ohne Rücksicht auf ihre Herkunft, als „Pfälzer" bezeichnet wurden. Die württembergischen und nassauischen Fürstentümer erlebten mehrere Auswanderungswellen mit Höhepunkten zwischen 1749 und 1754, als werbende Agenten, sogenannte „Neuländer", diese Gegenden mit bemerkenswertem Erfolg durchkämmten. Im selben Zeitraum, in den auch die absoluten Spitzenjahre der deutschen Auswanderung im 18. Jahrhundert fallen, erweiterten die Werber der Schiffahrts- und Landerwerbsgesellschaften ihren Aktionsradius auf die protestantischen Kaiserstädte Oberschwabens und bis nach Mitteldeutschland hinein. War der Rhein bis dahin die Hauptroute für Reisende via Rotterdam gewesen, so begannen englische Auswandererschiffe nun auch in Hamburg anzulegen. Amerikanische Werber drangen ins Hinterland der Elbe vor und gelangten bis nach Thüringen und Sachsen, wo sie jedoch auf beträchtliche Schwierigkeiten mit den preußischen und sächsischen Behörden stießen.

The larger territories of the Empire, Prussia and Austria, had generally endeavored to keep their subjects from emigrating. Both were eager to attract settlers from other German territories in order to secure their eastern provinces. While Austria had no emigration problem during the 18th century, Prussia was in the unique position of possessing river ports on the Rhine, Weser and Elbe, which emigrant transports to America had to pass. In 1753 Frederick II ordered that all transit be halted at Cleve, Minden and Magdeburg. When Chamber President von Massow in Minden asked for clarification of the order as to whether it also applied to transports from non-Prussian territories, the king jotted down in his own hand: "Transit shall be prohibited them under the pretext that they want to lead people away from us." The hardest hit was the Rhine transport to Rotterdam. The Elector Palatine also had emigrant boats intercepted at Oppenheim; the Elector of Mainz, at Mainz and Stockstadt. Hannover dispatched agents to Altona near Hamburg who removed their subjects from emigrant ships. Surprisingly, more than 11,000 Germans made it to Philadelphia, several thousand more to other American ports in 1753 and 1754. Many of them had moved overland in slow, cumbersome treks to circumvent control stations along the rivers. The outbreak of the Indian War in America and the concurrent Seven Years' War in Europe suspended all transatlantic movement of emigrants. Twelve years later the Revolutionary War caused an interruption from 1775 until 1784.

In the period between these two wars Prussia renewed the river closings in 1764 and intensified her own solicitations for settlers. By the 1780s one third of Prussia's population were immigrants, or children of immigrants from other German states, Switzerland and France. Austria was trying to entice landless people from the Swabian and Franconian areas of the Empire to its Danube frontier. These projects of the two large German powers were not only threatened by the attraction America represented, but also by an invitation to Russia's new eastern provinces that Catherine the Great extended in 1763 to German peasants, and by a massive recruiting effort of the French to attract emigrants to Guyana in 1764. Several governments issued a ban on emigration but local measures had little effect. Finally, in 1768, Emperor Joseph II made an unprecedented move. On July 7th he issued an imperial edict against all emigration into "lands which are not in any way connected with the Empire." This careful wording left the doors open to emigration for those parts of Austria and Prussia which, though not within the borders of the Empire (notably East Prussia, Hungary and Transylvania), were "connected" with it. Unlike many other imperial edicts, this one found unanimous approval. Even Prussia, archenemy of the Habsburg dynasty, enforced it and so did the imperial cities which had been traditional collecting points for emigrant transports. The movement to America was temporarily halted. Only 300 Germans landed in Philadelphia in 1769, none in other ports. As time went on, the restrictions were relaxed and from 1771 through 1773 transports to Philadelphia and Balitmore annually reached the 1,000 mark.

Die beiden großen Territorialstaaten im Verband des Reiches, Preußen und Österreich, hatten ihre Untertanen im allgemeinen von der Auswanderung abzuhalten versucht. Beide Länder waren daran interessiert, Siedler aus anderen deutschen Gebieten zu gewinnen, um mit ihnen ihre östlichen Provinzen zu sichern. Während Österreich im 18. Jahrhundert kein Auswanderungsproblem kannte, befand sich Preußen in der besonderen Lage, an Rhein, Weser und Elbe Binnenhäfen zu besitzen, die von Auswanderertransporten nach Amerika passiert werden mußten. Im Jahr 1753 ordnete Friedrich II. von Preußen an, daß jeglicher Transitverkehr in Cleve, Minden und Magdeburg aufgehalten werden sollte. Als Kammerpräsident von Massow aus Minden rückfragte, ob diese Order auch für Transporte aus nicht-preußischen Gebieten gelten solle, notierte Friedrich der Große eigenhändig folgenden Randbescheid auf den Brief: „Sol ihnen der Durchgang verbohten werden unter Pretecst Sie heten uns Leute Debauchiren wollen." Am schwersten wurde der Auswanderertransport auf dem Rhein nach Rotterdam beeinträchtigt. Der pfälzische Kurfürst ließ Auswandererschiffe in Oppenheim abfangen, der Kurfürst von Mainz in Mainz und Stockstadt. Hannover entstandte Agenten nach Altona bei Hamburg, um seine Untertanen wieder von den Schiffen holen zu lassen. Trotz aller dieser Behinderungen gelangten in den Jahren 1753/54 über 11 000 Deutsche nach Philadelphia, einige weitere Tausend nach anderen amerikanischen Häfen. Viele von ihnen hatten die Kontrollstationen an den Flüssen auf langwierigen und mühseligen Landwegen umgangen. Erst der Ausbruch des Siebenjährigen Kriegs in Amerika und Europa brachte den transatlantischen Auswandererstrom zu einem vorübergehenden Stillstand. Zwölf Jahre später sorgte der amerikanische Unabhängigkeitskrieg von 1775 bis 1784 für eine neue Unterbrechung.

In der Zeit zwischen den Kriegen wiederholte Preußen seine Flußsperrungen (1764) und verstärkte seine Bemühungen, selbst Siedler ins Land zu locken. Um 1780 bestand ein Drittel der preußischen Bevölkerung aus Einwanderern der ersten und zweiten Generation, die aus anderen deutschen Staaten, der Schweiz und Frankreich gekommen waren. Österreich versuchte, landlose Bauern aus den schwäbischen und fränkischen Reichsteilen an seine Donaugrenze zu locken. Die Siedlungsprojekte der beiden deutschen Großmächte mußten zu dieser Zeit nicht nur mit der Anziehungskraft Amerikas konkurrieren, sondern auch mit der von Katharina der Großen 1763 ausgesprochenen Einladung an die deutschen Bauern, sich in den neuen Ostprovinzen Rußlands niederzulassen. Hinzu kamen massive Anwerbungskampagnen der Franzosen im Jahr 1764 für eine Einwanderung nach Guayana. Verschiedene Regierungen erließen Auswanderungsverbote, doch solche lokalen Maßnahmen blieben ohne durchschlagende Wirkung. Da entschloß sich Kaiser Joseph II. im Jahre 1768 zu einer noch nicht dagewesenen Maßnahme: Am 7. Juli erließ er ein kaiserliches Edikt, das jede Auswanderung „in andere, mit dem Reich in keiner Verbindung stehende Länder" verbot. Diese vorsichtige Formulierung ließ die Möglichkeit offen, in jene Gebiete Österreichs und Preußens zu über-

Frederick II, "the Great" (1712 – 86), King of Prussia from 1740 (statue by Christian Daniel Rauch)

Friedrich II., der Große (1712–86), König von Preußen seit 1740 (Statue von Christian Daniel Rauch)

Maria Theresia (1717 – 80), Archduchess of Austria, Queen of Hungary and Bohemia; from 1745, as wife of Franz I, Empress of the Holy Roman Empire (painting by Martin Meytens the younger, ca. 1745)

Maria Theresia (1717–80), Erzherzogin von Österreich, Königin von Ungarn und Böhmen, seit 1745 als Gattin Franz I. Kaiserin des Heiligen Römischen Reiches (Gemälde von Martin Meytens d. J., um 1745)

"...and most graciously do make known herewith, that We, by these presents, in the first years of Our reign over Our entire rightfully inherited dominions, do most specifically prohibit that any one of Our vassals or subjects shall presume to travel to foreign countries without having previously applied to Us and received Our most gracious permission so to do": Maria Theresia's decree banning emigration, enacted on June 30, 1752.

»... und geben hiemit gnädigst zu vernehmen, welcher gestalten Wir allschon in denen ersteren Jahren Unserer Regierung in gesamten Erbkönigreichen und Landen scharf verbothen, daß niemand von Unseren Vasallen, und Unterthanen, ohne vorherig bey Uns angesucht- und erhaltenen gnädigsten Erlaubnuß in auswärtige Länder zu reisen sich unterfangen solle«: Dekret Maria Theresias gegen die Auswanderung, erlassen am 30. Juni 1752.

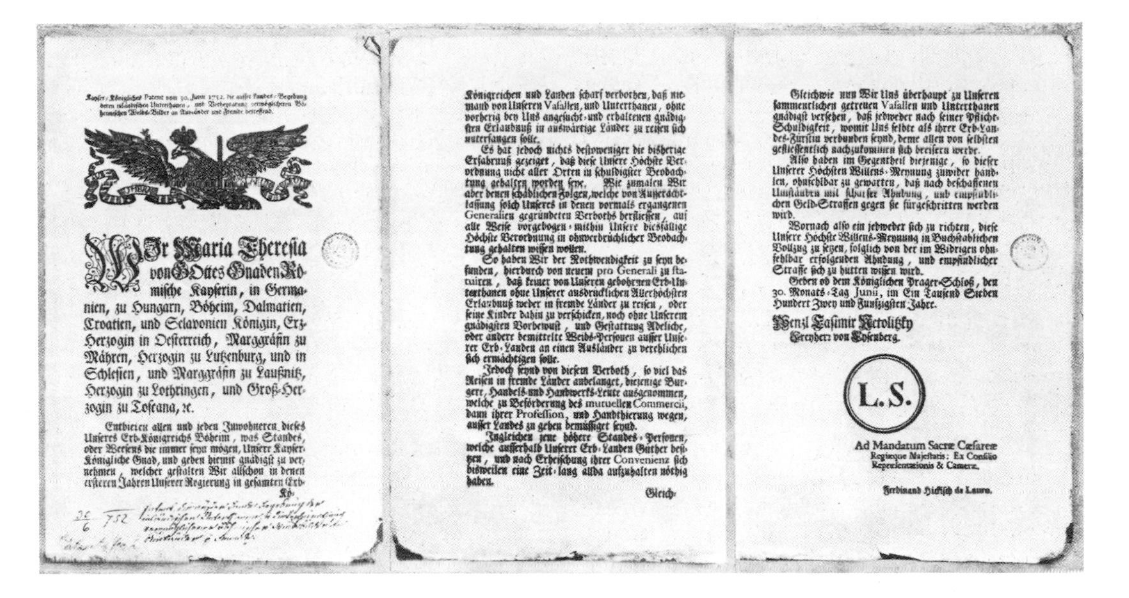

Kayser-Königliches Patent vom 30. Junii 1752. die ausser Landes-Begebung deren inländischen Unterthanen, und Verheyratung vermöglicheren Böheimischen Weibs-Bilder an Ausländer und Fremde betreffend.

Wir Maria Theresia von GOttes Gnaden Römische Kayserin, in Germanien, zu Hungarn, Böheim, Dalmatien, Croatien, und Sclavonien Königin, Erz-Herzogin in Oesterreich, Marggräfin zu Mähren, Herzogin zu Lutzenburg, und in Schlesien, und Marggräfin zu Laußnitz, Herzogin zu Lothringen, und Groß-Herzogin zu Toscana, rc.

Entbieten allen und jeden Inwohneren dieses Unseres Erb-Königreichs Böheim, was Standes, oder Weesens die immer seyn mögen, Unsere Kayser-Königliche Gnad, und geben hiemit gnädigst zu vernehmen, welcher gestalten Wir allschon in denen ersteren Jahren Unserer Regierung in gesamten Erb-Königreichen und Landen scharf verbothen, daß niemand von Unseren Vasallen, und Unterthanen, ohne vorherig bey Uns angesucht- und erhaltenen gnädigsten Erlaubnuß in auswärtige Länder zu reisen sich unterfangen solle.

Es hat jedoch nichts destoweniger die bisherige Erfahrnuß gezeiget, daß diese Unsere Höchste Verordnung nicht aller Orten in schuldigster Beobachtung gehalten worden seye. Wie zumalen Wir aber denen schädlichen Folgen, welche von Ausseracht-lassung solch Unseres in denen vormals ergangenen Generalien gegründeten Verboths herfliessen, auf alle Weise vorgebogen, mithin Unsere diesfällige Höchste Verordnung in ohnverbrüchlicher Beobachtung gehalten wissen wollen.

So haben Wir der Nothwendigkeit zu seyn befunden, hierdurch von neuem pro Generali zu statuiren, daß keiner von Unseren gebohrnen Erb-Unterthanen ohne Unserer ausdrücklichen Allerhöchsten Erlaubnuß weder in fremde Länder zu reisen, oder seine Kinder dahin zu verschicken, noch ohne Unserem gnädigsten Vorbewust, und Gestattung Adeliche, oder andere bemittelte Weibs-Personen ausser Unserer Erb-Landen an einen Ausländer zu verehlichen sich ermächtigen solle.

Jedoch seynd von diesem Verboth, so viel das Reisen in fremde Länder anbelanget, diejenige Burgere, Handels- und Handwerks-Leute ausgenommen, welche zu Beförderung des mutuellen Commercii, dann ihrer Profession, und Handthierung wegen, ausser Landes zu gehen bemüssiget seynd.

Ingleichen jene höhere Standes-Personen, welche ausserhalb Unserer Erb-Landen Güther besitzen, und nach Erheischung ihrer Convenienz sich bisweilen eine Zeit-lang allda aufzuhalten nöthig haben.

Gleichwie nun Wir Uns überhaupt zu Unseren sammentlichen getreuen Vasallen und Unterthanen gnädigst versehen, daß jedweder nach seiner Pflicht-Schuldigkeit, womit Uns selbte als ihrer Erb-Landes-Fürstin verbunden seynd, deme allen von selbsten geflissentlich nachzukommen sich beeifern werde.

Also haben im Gegentheil diejenige, so dieser Unserer Höchsten Willens-Meynung zuwider handlen, ohnfehlbar zu gewarten, daß nach beschaffenen Umständen mit scharfer Ahndung, und empfindlichen Geld-Straffen gegen sie fürgeschritten werden wird.

Wornach also ein jedweder sich zu richten, diese Unsere Höchste Willens-Meynung in Buchstablichen Vollzug zu setzen, folglich von der im Widrigen ohnfehlbar erfolgenden Ahndung, und empfindlicher Straffe sich zu hütten wissen wird.

Geben ob dem Königlichen Prager-Schloß, den 30. Monats-Tag Junii, im Ein Tausend Sieben Hundert Zwey und Funfzigsten Jahre.

Wenzl Casimir Netolitzky
Freyherr von Eysenberg.

L.S.

Ad Mandatum Sacræ Cæsareæ Regiæque Majestatis: Ex Consilio Repræsentationis & Cameræ.

Ferdinand Hickisch de Lauro.

Von GOttes Gnaden LUDWIG,

Landgraf zu Hessen, Fürst zu Hersfeld, Graf zu Catzenelenbogen, Diez, Ziegenhain, Nidda, Hanau, Schaumburg, Isenburg und Büdingen, rc. rc. Ihro Russisch-Kayserlichen Majestät bestellter General-Feld-Marschall, des St. Andreas- wie auch Königlich-Preussischen schwarzen Adler-Ordens Ritter rc. rc.

"Any of our subjects or vassals, male or female, bondsman or freeman, who secretly or openly migrate to territories outside my jurisdiction without having applied for and received dispensation, shall be penalized by confiscation of effects and property. The same penalty shall be applied to those who demonstrate intention to flee by selling off their cattle and other goods": Decree restricting emigration issued in 1787 by Landgrave Ludwig of Hessia, detailing sanctions to be taken against offenders. Not until the establishment of the German Reich in 1871 did unrestricted freedom of emigration become an inalienable human right.

Liebe Getreue !

Wir haben mißfälligst wahrgenommen, daß, ohnerachtet derer von Unsern Vorfahren am Regiment Christmildesten Gedächtnüsses in den Jahren 1630. 1643. 1658. und 1692., und von Uns annoch neuerdings in den Jahren 1770. und 1772. erlassenen allgemeinen Verboten, daß kein Unterthan ohne vorher erhaltene Erlaubnuß weder in fremde Colonien auswandern, oder sich in solchen ansäßig machen, noch auch sich außer Landes häuslich niederlassen oder ansäßig machen solle, und wo auf die Uebertrettung des ersten Falles besonders und ausdrücklich der Verlust des Vermögens gesetzt worden ist, dennoch seither mehrere Unserer Unterthanen diesen höchsten Verordnungen schnurstracks zuwider entweder gar nicht, oder erst nach ihrer Auswanderung aus Unsern Fürstl. Landen, oder Niederlassung und Ansäßigkeit in auswärtigen Landen bey Uns um den Abschieds-Brief und Verabfolgung ihres Vermögens nachgesucht: Und Wir dann diesem Ordnungswidrigen Benehmen nicht länger nachzusehen gewilliget sind: Als ist hiermit Unser wiederholter ernster Wille, daß

1) alle Auswanderungen und häusliche Ansäßigkeit in fremden Colonien, heimliche und öffentliche, welche ohne Unsere zuvor ausgebrachte Landesherrliche Dispensation geschehen, Unsern Unterthanen und Angehörigen, männlichen- und weiblichen Geschlechtes, Leibeigenen und Freyen, sie mögen auch schon gehuldiget haben, oder nicht, fürderhin durchaus, und ohne daß einer der Verwandten einiger Gnade sich hierunter zu getrösten habe, bey Strafe der Vermögens-Confiscation verboten seyn sollen, wie dann auch diejenige Unterthanen, welche aus Gewinnsucht, oder ohne sattsame Ueberlegung, von solchen pflichtsvergessenen Personen, welche sich heimlich auf- und außer Land machen, ihre Effecten, Vieh und andere Sachen zu kaufen, und solche theils heimlich, theils nächtlicher Weile in deren Häusern, abzuholen in Sinn kommen lassen mögten, nicht besser als die Flüchtlinge selbst betrachtet- nach befindenden Umständen mit scharfer Leibesstrafe beleget- zugleich auch niemalen als rechtmäßige Besitzere von dem an sich nichtig erkauften Guth angesehen- sondern dasselbe oder dessen Werth ihnen deßfalls confiscirt werden solle; woben ausserdem, absonderlich Unsern Fürstlichen Beamten, geschärftest aufgegeben wird, auf alle hin und wieder versteckte Emissarien, welche, wie Uns hinlänglich bekannt ist, oftmals unter Vorspiegelung beglückterer Umstände Unsere getreue Unterthanen zur Wandersucht zu verleiten suchen, genau zu invigiliren, und solche sowohlen als die Auswanderer im Betrettungsfall sogleich gefänglich niederzuwerfen, welche sonach mit harter Leibes- und die Emissarien nach Umständen mit Lebensstrafe belegt werden sollen. Sodann verordnen Wir

2) daß alle diejenigen Unserer Fürstl. Unterthanen und Angehörigen, sie seyen männlichen- oder weiblichen Geschlechts, sie seyen Leibeigene oder nicht, sie mögen auch bereits gehuldiget haben, oder nicht, welche zwar nicht in fremde Colonien förmlich auswandern, oder doch ohne Unsere vorher ausgebrachte Landesherrliche Erlaubnis und Dispensation in auswärtigen Landen sich ansäßig machen, oder häuslich niederlassen, außer denen sonst gewöhnlichen Prästationen und Abzugs-Geldern annoch Fünf vom Hundert von ihrem zu exportirenden Vermögen zur Strafe entrichten, und dieses Quantum sofort jederzeit und ohne alle Rücksicht davon einbehalten werden solle. Wornach sich also unterthänigst zu achten, und zu dem Ende diese Unsere Verordnung zu jedermanns Nachricht und Nachachtung nicht allein öffentlich gewöhnlicherweise, sondern auch von denen Canzeln zu publiciren. Insbesondere aber wird Unsern Beamten, Adelichen- und andern Gerichts-Vorgesetzten zur eigenen Pflicht gemacht, bey eigner Verantwort- und Haftung darauf genau zu wachen und zu halten, auch die Schultheißen und Ortsvorsteher gemessenst anzuweisen, dergleichen Fälle sobalden als sie solche in Erfahrung bringen, ohne den mindesten Verzug bey Vermeidung scharfer Ahndung jedesmal bey Amt anzuzeigen. Versehens Uns und seynd Euch mit Gnaden wohlgewogen.

Darmstadt, den 10. Februar 1787.

Ex speciali Commissione SERENISSIMI.

Fürstl. Hessische Präsident, Canzlar, und Geheime Räthe daselbsten.

A. P. Hesse. D. Bayert.

Erlaß des hessischen Landgrafen zur Eindämmung der Auswanderung aus dem Jahr 1787 mit detaillierten Angaben über die Sanktionen, die gegen Emigrationswillige verhängt werden konnten. Zu einem unbeschränkten Grundrecht wurde die Auswanderung in Deutschland erst nach der Reichsgründung von 1871.

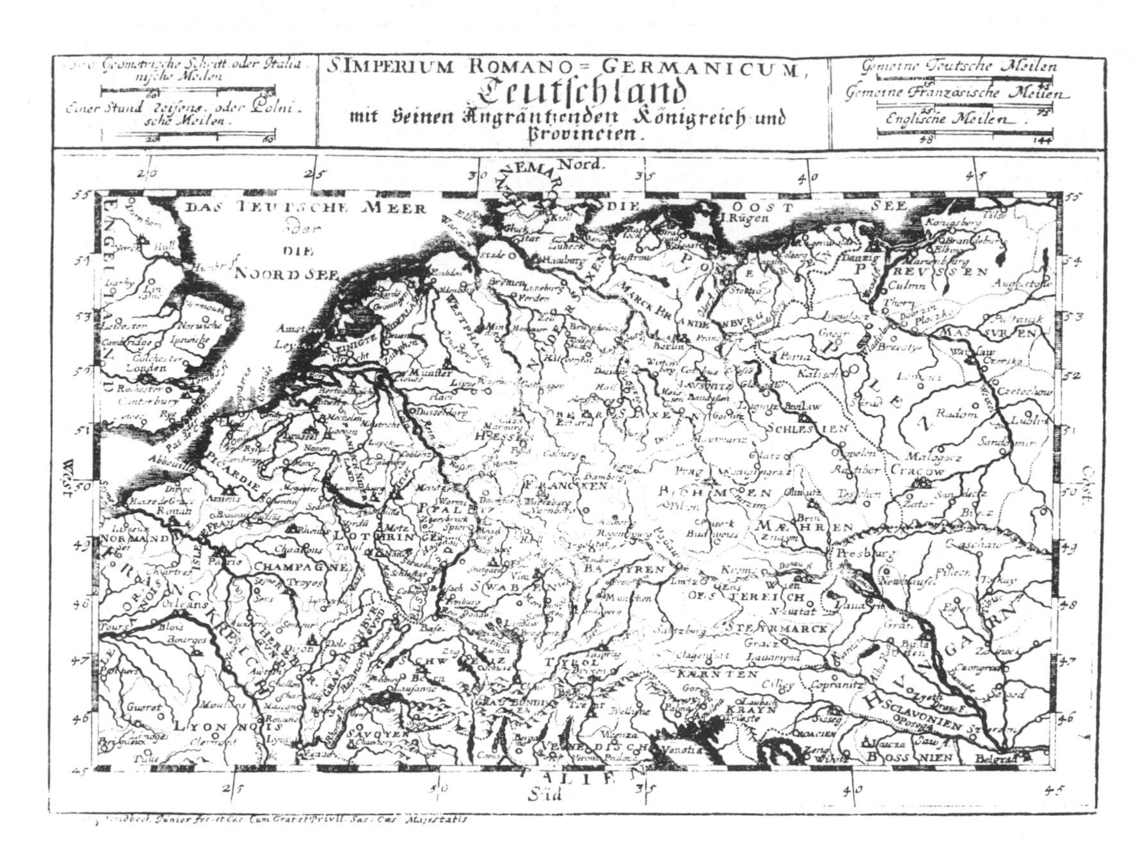

Map of the Holy Roman Empire ("Sacrum Imperium Romano-Germanicum") and neighboring kingdoms, made in Augsburg around 1700 by Johann Stridbeck the Younger. The appellation (in German, "Heiliges Römisches Reich Deutscher Nation") was coined in the late Middle Ages and designated the old German realm which nominally existed from the coronation as emperor of the "Roman Empire" of Otto the Great (962) until the abdication of Emperor Francis II (1806). The terms "holy" and "Roman" apply to the original alliance with the Church (imperial coronation by the pope) and the claim to being the secular heir to the Roman Empire (west). Founded as an aggregation of medieval feudal fiefdoms, the Empire was unable to develop into a modern type of national state, and disintegrated into a loose association of increasingly independent individual countries, among which Prussia and Austria (repeatedly at war with each other) gained preeminence. This dissolution of the Empire was one of the historical factors why Germany did not pursue any policy of colonization on its own in the 17th and 18th centuries, but instead became a source of emigration.

Karte des Heiligen Römischen Reiches Deutscher Nation (»Sacrum Imperium Romano-Germanicum«) von Johann Stridbeck d. J., Augsburg, um 1700. Die Formel »Heiliges Römisches Reich Deutscher Nation« ist eine spätmittelalterliche Bezeichnung für das alte Deutsche Reich, das man von der Kaiserkrönung Ottos des Großen (962) bis zur Abdankung Kaiser Franz' II. (1806) rechnet. Die Begriffe »Heilig« und »Römisch« beziehen sich auf die ursprüngliche Verbindung mit der Kirche (Kaiserkrönung durch den Papst) und die beanspruchte Fortsetzung des weströmischen Reiches. Als mittelalterlicher Lehnsverband entstanden, konnte sich das Reich nicht zu einem Nationalstaat moderner Prägung entwickeln und zerfiel zu einem immer loseren Verband immer unabhängigerer Einzelstaaten, unter denen Preußen und Österreich, mehrfach in Kriege miteinander verwickelt, die Vorherrschaft gewannen. Diese Zersplitterung des Reiches ist einer der historischen Gründe, warum Deutschland im 17. und 18. Jahrhundert keine eigene Kolonialpolitik betrieb und statt dessen zum Auswanderungsland wurde.

The Austrian Habsburg dominions and the Danubian countries on a map drawn around 1650 by S. Sanson of Nürnberg. Austrian emigration to America was negligible during the 18th century, as after the wars of 1683–99 and 1714–18 against the Turks of the Ottoman Empire, the migration of Germans from the core of the archduchy of Austria was mainly eastward to the lands of the lower Danube. Not until the turn of the 20th century did the decline of the heterogeneous Austrian monarchy and its collapse in 1918 lead to waves of mass emigration with the U.S. as the primary destination.

Karte Österreichs und der Donauländer von S. Sanson, Nürnberg, um 1650. Die Besiedlung des östlichen Donauraums, der in den beiden letzten Türkenkriegen von 1683–99 und von 1714–18 unter habsburgische Herrschaft kam, ließ die österreichische Amerikaauswanderung im 18. Jahrhundert gering bleiben. Erst der Niedergang der Vielvölkermonarchie um die Wende zum 20. Jahrhundert und ihr Zusammenbruch 1918 führten zu Massenauswanderungswellen, deren Ziel vorwiegend die USA waren.

Arrival of Hessian troops in New York harbor; based on a contemporary etching

Ankunft hessischer Truppen im Hafen von New York; nach einem zeitgenössischen Stich

A mercenary recruit taking his physical: sketch drawn by Johann Wolfgang Goethe in 1779.

Musterung eines rekrutierten Söldners: gezeichnet wurde diese Skizze 1779 von Johann Wolfgang Goethe.

Recruitment of mercenaries in the 18th century – the number of German soldiers sold to fight on the side of the British in the American War of Independence was given as 29,875 men by Friedrich Kapp, the New York City Commissioner of Immigration, in his standard work, "German Princes' Sale of Soldiers for America", which the descendant of German immigrants published in 1874. The soldiers had been recruited in six German principalities, but as the majority of them were the almost 17,000 Hessian subjects, they all came to be known as "Hessians". According to Kapp, 17,313 mercenaries returned to Germany after the war. He calculates that half of the remaining number died in battle, leaving the generally accepted estimate of 6,000 former mercenaries who preferred to remain in the United States after the war.

Söldneranwerbung im 18. Jahrhundert. – Die deutschen Subsidientruppen, die im amerikanischen Unabhängigkeitskrieg auf der Seite Englands kämpften, umfaßten nach den Berechnungen, die Friedrich Kapp, der deutschstämmige Einwanderungskommissar der Stadt New York, 1874 in seinem Standardwerk »Der Soldatenhandel deutscher Fürsten nach Amerika« veröffentlichte, insgesamt 29 875 Mann. Sie waren in sechs deutschen Fürstentümern angeworben worden, werden jedoch nach der Mehrheit von fast 17 000 hessischen Untertanen traditionsgemäß als »Hessen« bezeichnet. Laut Kapp kehrten 17 313 Söldner nach dem Krieg nach Deutschland zurück. Vom Differenzbetrag setzt er die Hälfte als gefallen an, woraus sich die allgemein akzeptierte Schätzung von 6 000 ehemaligen Söldnern ergibt, die es nach dem Krieg vorzogen, in den USA zu bleiben.

Hessian commander von Lossberg's general amnesty for repentant deserters

Generalamnestie des hessischen Kommandanten von Lossberg für reuige Deserteure

GENERAL PARDON.

Sr. Excellenz FRIEDRICH WILHELM von LOSSBERG, *General Lieutenants, und Commandeurs en Chef des in Koeniglich* Groſs Britannischen *Diensten ſtehenden Auxiliair Corps Fuerſtlich Heſſiſcher Truppen, Ritters des Ordens Pour la Vertu Militaire, &c. &c. &c.*

ALLEN und jeden von den Fuerſtlich Heſſiſchen Truppen, in Nord-America, Deſſertirten, unter Officiers und Gemeinen, wird hierduch bekannt gemacht, daſs ſie einen freyen und volligen Pardon erhalten ſollen, wenn ſie ſich vor dem 1ſten Tage des naechſt kuenftigen Monats Auguſt, 1783, bey denen Koeniglichen Truppen einfinden, und by ihren Regementern darauf ſtellen werden.

Gegeben unter meiner Hand, New-York, den 9ten May, 1783.

Auf Sr. Excellentz Befehl, LOSSBERG
JUSTIN HENRICH MOTZ.

BY HIS EXCELLENCY

FRIEDRICH WILHELM de LOSSBERG, *Lieutenant-General, Commander in Chief of the Auxiliary troops of Heſſe, in the ſervice of Great Britain, Knight of the Order,* Pour la Vertu Militaire, *&c. &c. &c.*

A FREE and GENERAL PARDON

IS hereby offered to all Non-commiſſioned Officers, and Privates Deſerters from the Heſſian Troops in North-America, who ſhall repair to any of his Majeſty's Troops before the 1ſt day of Auguſt next, in order to re-join their reſpective Regiments or Corps.

Given under my Hand at NEW-YORK, *this 9th Day of May,* 1783.

By his Excellency's Command, LOSSBERG.
JUSTIN HENRY MOTZ.

Georgia. To John Gorham esquire County Surveyor for the County of Franklin

YOU are hereby authorized and required to admeaſure and lay out, or cauſe to be admeaſured and laid out, unto Jacob Russell – – – a Tract of Land, which ſhall contain Two hundred and thirty —— Acres, in the ſaid County of Franklin
a Bounty agreeable to Gov.r Martins proclamation for Hessian Deserters. –
Taking eſpecial Care that the ſame has not heretofore been laid out to any Perſon or Perſons: And you are hereby alſo directed and required to record the Plat of the ſame in your Office, and tranſmit a Copy thereof, together with this Warrant, to the Surveyor General, within three Months from this Date. Given under my Hand, this 11th Day of February 1785

A Hessian defector was rewarded with 250 acres of land in Georgia.

Belohnung eines hessischen Überläufers mit 250 Morgen Land in Georgia

Recruitment advertisement of the Prince of Anhalt-Zerbst, who sent the smallest contingent of 1,160 mercenaries to America. The amount he received for this was considerable: Anhalt-Zerbst was paid 110,000 pounds sterling. Kapp estimates the aggregate figure paid by England for German mercenaries to have been seven million pounds, which would be equivalent to several hundred million dollars in modern buying power.

Werbungsanzeige des Fürsten von Anhalt-Zerbst, der das kleinste Kontingent von 1160 Söldnern nach Amerika sandte. Die dafür erlösten Summen waren beträchtlich: Anhalt-Zerbst nahm ca. 110 000 Pfund Sterling ein. Die Gesamtsumme, die England für die deutschen Söldner bezahlte, schätzt Kapp auf sieben Millionen Pfund, was nach heutiger Kaufkraft einem Betrag von mehreren hundert Millionen Dollar entsprechen dürfte.

During the Revolutionary War, knowledge about the new country was kept alive and even furthered by frequent reports in the German press. Letters from German soldiers of the subsidiary troops hired by Britain from the Electorate of Hesse, Brunswick, Ansbach-Bayreuth, Hanau, Waldeck and Anhalt-Zerbst depicted a vast country full of bewildering contradictions. The Palatine regiment Deux-Ponts and other German auxiliaries in the French army came to the aid of the Americans. This hiring out of mercenaries by German princes was bitterly resented throughout the Empire. However, a report from Hessian headquarters in America indicated that some recruits had plans other than fighting for the glory of England and the coffers of the Elector: "Many of them may have been prompted to take the chance of a free passage to this country, and thus in this manner finally get away from Europe, instead of having to work about four years to redeem the cost of their crossing." At least 6000 of these men remained in America.

After the war the desire to emigrate to America seemed even greater than before. With the British Navigation Laws no longer in effect, many transports now left from Bremen and Hamburg. Until 1806, when the Continental Blockade virtually closed off the European mainland, some 30,000 Germans, mostly young people, headed for various American ports in order to escape the uncertain future of a Europe where the old feudal system was crumbling, and the new order ushered in by the French Revolution seemed a rather frightening alternative.

As the 18th century came to its close, the pros and cons of emigration became a favorite subject of public and academic discussion. The Palatine statistician, Th. Traiteur, caused an uproar when he stated in 1788 that "the body politic can do without a few ounces of blood and, if healthy inside, may rid itself of untimely and useless matter in order to be cleansed from time to time." The prevailing view of mercantilists and cameralists of the day was that a dense population was an element of national strength. Friedrich Nicolai, publicist and critic, wrote of an encounter with a Wurttemberger who described the surprising result of the steps taken to release emigrants from comburghery. By making it hard for a poor man who had always considered himself of little import, by trying to dissuade him and having him cited before the duke for a final, personal audience, such a man could not help but feeling that he was of importance to the dukedom. Such methods contributed to a growing feeling of individual merit and personal freedom. Authorities in the main emigration centers also tried to explain away an otherwise inexplicable subject. As an apologist for the Wurttemberg government, Georg Christoph Heinrich Bunz found in 1796 that game damage, firewood shortages and other constant vexations, together with the complexity of the legal and bureaucratic system made many people all the more receptive to pictures of the New World that were full of promise and hope. Johann Wolfgang Goethe, himself a high government official in Weimar, had seen many treks of German emigrants during his youth in Frankfurt. In *Wilhelm Meisters Wanderjahre* he characterized German emigration to America as follows: "The impulsive urge for America at the beginning of the 18th century was so great because everyone who felt uncomfortable over here, hoped to settle over there in freedom. This urge was nourished by desirable possessions which one could still acquire before the population spread further to the West."

siedeln, die bereits außerhalb der Grenzen des Heiligen Römischen Reichs lagen, aber natürlich mit ihm „in Verbindung standen" (vor allem Ostpreußen, Ungarn und Siebenbürgen). Im Gegensatz zu vielen anderen kaiserlichen Erlässen fand dieser einmütige Zustimmung. Selbst Preußen, der Erzfeind der Habsburger Dynastie, ließ ihn bei sich in Kraft treten, und auch die freien Reichsstädte, die traditionellen Sammelpunkte der Auswanderertransporte, schlossen sich an. Die Emigration nach Amerika wurde fast völlig zum Erliegen gebracht. Ganze 300 Deutsche gingen 1769 in Philadelphia an Land, kein einziger in den anderen Häfen. Im Lauf der Zeit wurden die Verbotsbestimmungen jedoch allmählich gelockert, und zwischen 1771 und 1773 erreichten die Transporte nach Philadelphia und Baltimore wieder Umfänge von über tausend Menschen jährlich.

Während des Unabhängigkeitskrieges wurde das Wissen über das neue Land durch zahlreiche Artikel in der deutschen Presse lebendig gehalten und noch erweitert. Briefe deutscher Soldaten der Subsidientruppen, die die Briten bei den Fürsten von Hessen-Kassel, Braunschweig, Ansbach-Bayreuth, Hessen-Hanau, Waldeck und Anhalt-Zerbst gedungen hatten, berichteten von einem riesigen Land voller verwirrender Widersprüche. Das pfälzische Regiment Deux-Ponts und andere deutsche Hilfstruppen innerhalb der französischen Armee zogen nach Amerika, um die Aufständischen zu unterstützen. Überall im Reich wurde die Verschacherung deutscher Söldner durch ihre Landesherren mit Verbitterung registriert. Aus einem Bericht aus dem Hauptquartier der Hessen in Amerika läßt sich jedoch schließen, daß einige der Rekrutierten anderes im Sinn hatten, als für den Ruhm Englands oder die Privatschatulle ihres Kurfürsten zu kämpfen. Viele der Söldner, so heißt es dort, dürften vor allem die Gelegenheit zu einer freien Überfahrt gesucht haben, um so endlich aus Europa wegzukommen, ohne sich nach der Ankunft zur Begleichung der Passage auf etwa vier Jahre verdingen zu müssen. Mindestens 6 000 der deutschen Söldner blieben in Amerika.

Nach dem Krieg schien die Sehnsucht, nach Amerika auszuwandern, sogar noch größer geworden zu sein. Da die englischen Schiffahrtsgesetze nun keine Gültigkeit mehr hatten, legten viele Auswandererschiffe auch in Hamburg oder Bremen ab. Bis 1806, als die Kontinentalsperre das europäische Festland praktisch vom Ozean abriegelte, übersiedelten etwa 30 000 meist junge Deutsche nach Nordamerika, um so der unsicheren Zukunft ihres Heimatkontinents zu entfliehen, in dem das alte Feudalsystem zerbröckelte, während die neue, mit der französischen Revolution eingeläutete Ordnung eine eher furchteinflößende Alternative darzustellen schien.

Gegen Ende des 18. Jahrhunderts wurde das Für und Wider der Emigration zum beliebten Gegenstand öffentlicher und akademischer Debatten. Der pfälzische Statistiker Th. Traiteur verursachte einen Aufschrei der Empörung, als er 1788 feststellte, der Staatskörper könne „ein paar Unzen Blut entbehren, und wenn er im Innern gesund ist, um sich von Zeit zu Zeit zu reinigen, auch unzeitige und unnütze Materie von sich stossen". Die vorherrschende Ansicht unter den merkantilistischen und kameralistischen Staatsdenkern der Zeit war, daß eine hohe Bevölkerungsdichte ein Garant für nationale Stärke sei. Friedrich Nicolai, Publizist und Kritiker, berichtete von einem Gespräch mit einem Württemberger, der ihm die überraschenden Wirkungen schilderte, die die ver-

Letzter Ruf

der

frey gewordenen Franken

an

die unterdrückten Deutschen.

Im Monat Augst 1791. des dritten Jahrs
der Freyheit.

Fühlet eure Sclaverey, edle Deutsche! sehet es endlich ein, daß euch Fürsten zu unglücklichen Werkzeugen des Mordes gegen uns Franken brauchen wollen, — Franken, die euch Freundschaft angelobten; eure Verfassungen nie stören wollen, die euch nachbarlich lieben, und die dem ohngeachtet von euren Despoten nur um deswillen bekriegt werden sollen, weil sie die eisernen Ketten abschüttelten, die ihr noch traget.

Wir Franken wollen für diese unsre Freyheit

Kämpfen, siegen, — oder sterben.

Und ihr, verblendete Deutsche, wollt für eure Fürsten, die euer Mark aussaugen, eurer Söhne, Gatten und Freunde Blut aufopfern, um nach zweydeutigem Siege euch in vestere Ketten schmieden zu lassen?

Ha! welch Unternehmen!

Wir steckten euch die Fackel der Freyheit auf; wir gaben euren Fürsten einen Wink, was Tyranney vermag, und wie eine Nation endlich müde der Unterdrückung würde. Und doch frohnet ihr noch ihrem Stolz, wollt Leben und Eigenthum wagen, um bey uns wieder Verschwender, Barbaren und nach Herrschsucht geizende Ungeheuer in ihre entrissenen Ungerechtigkeiten einsetzen zu helfen? — weil dies eure Fürsten wollen!

Thun dies Deutsche?

Hört unsre Meynung!

Zerreißt die Sclaven-Ketten eurer verschwenderischen Fürsten, und ihrer raubbegierigen Minister; wir bieten euch die Hand, fechten und sterben mit, und für euch; schützen eure Freyheit, euer Eigenthum, und sichern euern Herd ....

Ihr seyd mit uns frey, und unsre Brüder!!

Wollt ihr aber doch Sclaven bleiben, nicht hören die Stimme eines freyen Volkes, euren Fürsten, und unsern entwichenen Schaaren stolzer Bösewichter die Hand zu mörderischen Unternehmungen bieten — Ha! so seyd ihr unsrer Schonung nicht werth; und wir machen euch, wie einst unser Despot vor hundert Jahren, zu Bettlern, schonen eures Blutes und Eigenthums nicht, und siegen, oder sterben für unsre Freyheit allein ....

Denn wir sind Franken!

The murder of the dramatist August von Kotzebue (1761–1819), who had published poetry ridiculing the liberal movement, by the radical Karl Ludwig Sand, member of a student "Burschenschaft", provided an ostensible cause for the so-called "suppression of demagogues" (the Carlsbad decrees against liberalism), which deprived the unification movement of any legal basis and occasioned the emigration of many of its adherents. Kotzebue's plays, today all but forgotten, once enjoyed immense popularity in post-revolutionary America.

Europe churning in upheaval: A "final appeal" in a 1791 leaflet from revolutionary France on the part of "liberated Frenchmen" urging their "oppressed German neighbors" to heed their example and "break the bonds of slavery to wastrel princes and rapacious ministers."

Europa im Umbruch: Flugblatt der französischen Revolution aus dem Jahr 1791, in dem die »verblendeten Deutschen« aufgefordert werden, ebenfalls ihre »Sclaven-Ketten« zu zerreißen.

"Patriotic Observations regarding the Great Student Festival on the Wartburg of 18/19 October 1817": contemporary report on the first political demonstration against Metternich's restoration policies by liberal students agitating for a united Germany.

Das »Wartburgfest« liberaler Burschenschaftler im Oktober 1817 war die erste große Demonstration der nationalen Bewegung gegen die Metternichsche Restaurationspolitik.

Die Ermordung des Dramatikers August von Kotzebue (1761–1819), der Spottgedichte auf die liberale Bewegung veröffentlicht hatte, durch den radikalen Burschenschaftler Karl Ludwig Sand war der äußere Anlaß für die sogenannte »Demagogenverfolgung«, die der Einigungsbewegung die legale Basis entzog und viele ihrer Anhänger zur Auswanderung veranlaßte. Kotzebue, der heute fast Vergessene, war übrigens einer der meistgespielten Autoren auf den deutschamerikanischen Bühnen des 19. Jahrhunderts.

Napoleon I Bonaparte (1769 – 1821), conqueror of Prussia in the double battle of Jena and Auerstedt (1806), on his retreat from Berlin removed the Victory Goddess's four-horse team from the Brandenburg Gate to Paris. (Contemporary copperplate engraving)

Napoleon I. Bonaparte (1769–1821), Besieger Preußens in der Doppelschlacht von Jena und Auerstedt (1806), entführt bei seinem Abzug aus Berlin das Viergespann der Siegesgöttin vom Brandenburger Tor nach Paris. (Zeitgenössischer Kupferstich)

The struggle for German unity, which began with the War of Liberation against Napoleon, culminated in the abortive revolution of 1848. The illustration portrays the "Consecration of the Lützow Free Corps", a troop of volunteer soldiers organized in 1813; along with patriotic students, the poets Joseph von Eichendorff and Theodor Körner and the "father of German gymnastics" Friedrich Jahn served in the corps.

Mit den Befreiungskriegen gegen Napoleon begann der Kampf um die deutsche Einheit, der 1848 in einer gescheiterten Revolution kulminierte. Die Abbildung zeigt die »Einsegnung des Lützowschen Freikorps«, einer 1813 aufgestellten Freiwilligentruppe, der neben patriotischen Studenten auch die Dichter Joseph von Eichendorff und Theodor Körner sowie der »Turnvater« Friedrich Jahn angehörten.

Patriotische Betrachtungen

über

das große Burschenfest

auf

der Wartburg

am 18/19ten des Siegesmonds 1817

von

Fr. Fr. v. Bw.

Wähntest du etwa,
Ich sollte das Leben hassen,
In Wüsten fliehen,
Weil nicht alle
Blüthenträume reiften? —
Prometheus von Göthe.

Hamburg 1818.

Bey Hoffmann und Campe.

"The General World Peace": allegory on the peace treaty of Paris, signed on May 30, 1814, which put an end to the era of the Napoleonic wars. The victorious powers waived all rights to reparations – with the exception of the quadriga from the Brandenburg Gate, which Prussia took back to Berlin.

»Der allgemeine Weltfriede«: Allegorie auf den Friedensschluß von Paris vom 30. Mai 1814, der die Ära der Napoleonischen Kriege beendete. Die Siegermächte verzichteten auf alle Kriegsentschädigungen – nur die Quadriga vom Brandenburger Tor holte Preußen wieder nach Berlin zurück.

The Congress of Vienna, 1814/15: With the reactionary-minded Austrian chancellor Prince Metternich presiding, the five major European powers (Austria, Prussia, France, Great Britain and Russia) restored the balance of power which the French Revolution and Napoleon had put out of joint. (Contemporary political cartoon)

Der Wiener Kongreß, 1814/15: Unter Vorsitz des um Restauration bemühten österreichischen Kanzlers Fürst Metternich stellen die fünf europäischen Großmächte Österreich, Großbritannien, Frankreich, Rußland und Preußen ihr durch die französische Revolution und Napoleon verwirrtes Kräftegleichgewicht wieder her. (Zeitgenössische Karikatur)

By 1815, the year that peace finally came to Europe, neither a unified German Empire nor the liberties which many of the young people had hoped and fought for, were realized. Territories were shuffled around again so that the old powers could reassert themselves. The first post-war emigration to America began where it had been the most prevalent during the 18th century: in southwest Germany. Political and territorial changes were more radical there than in northern and central Germany. The Palatinate and the Rhineland north of it were now ruled from distant Munich and Berlin. The once proud and free imperial cities became mere provincial towns with the exception of Frankfurt. Economic adjustments to peace and multitudes of discharged veterans would alone have created an auspicious atmosphere for emigration, not to speak of a revival of pietism in Wurttemberg. But, as in 1708/09, nature provided the necessary push. The year 1816 was a year without a summer. Cold, steady rain prevailed from May through September and a harsh winter set in by October. Again many saw the hand of God behind the catastrophic weather.

schiedenen Schritte bis zur Bewilligung der Auswanderungserlaubnis zeitigten: Einem Armen, der sich selbst stets nur als unbedeutender Untertan empfunden habe, zusätzliche Schwierigkeiten in den Weg zu legen, indem man ihm die Auswanderung auszureden versuche und ihn endlich gar zu einer letzten, persönlichen Audienz beim Herzog vorlade, könne bei diesem Mann nur das Gefühl stärken, daß seine Existenz für das Herzogtum von Bedeutung sei. Solche Methoden trügen zu einem wachsenden Selbstwertgefühl bei und stärkten das Bewußtsein persönlicher Freiheit. Auch die Behörden in den Hauptauswanderungsgebieten gaben sich alle Mühe, das ihnen Unerklärliche hinwegzuargumentieren. Georg Christoph Heinrich Bunz versuchte 1796 die Regierung von Württemberg aus der Verantwortung zu retten, indem er die Anfälligkeit der Bevölkerung für die Versprechungen der Neuen Welt mit Wildschäden in Wald und Flur, mit Brennholzknappheit, daneben freilich auch mit der Undurchschaubarkeit des heimischen Rechts- und Verwaltungswesens, erklären zu können glaubte. Johann Wolfgang Goethe, selbst hoher Regierungsbeamter in Weimar, hatte in seiner Jugend in Frankfurt viele Auswanderertrecks durch die Stadt ziehen sehen. In *Wilhelm Meisters Wanderjahren* charakterisierte er die deutsche Amerikaauswanderung wie folgt: „Der lebhafte Trieb nach Amerika im Anfange des achtzehnten Jahrhunderts war gross, indem ein jeder, der sich diesseits einigermassen unbequem ſand, sich drüben in Freiheit zu setzen hoffte; dieser Trieb ward genährt durch wünschenswerte Besitzungen, die man erlangen konnte, ehe sich noch die Bevölkerung weiter nach Westen verbreitete."

Als die Befreiungskriege gegen Napoleon beendet waren und 1815 Frieden in Europa einzog, waren weder der ersehnte Nationalstaat noch die politischen Freiheiten Wirklichkeit geworden, für die so viele junge Patrioten gekämpft hatten. Wieder wurden Grenzen hin und her geschoben, bis die alten Mächte ihre Positionen neu gefestigt hatten. Die erste Auswanderungswelle der Nachkriegszeit nahm in den gleichen Gebieten ihren Ausgang wie schon im 18. Jahrhundert: in Südwestdeutschland. Hier waren die politischen und territorialen Veränderungen sehr viel einschneidender gewesen als in Nord- und Mitteldeutschland. Die Pfalz und das angrenzende Rheinland wurden nun von dem entfernten München und dem noch ferneren Berlin aus regiert. Die einst freien und stolzen Reichsstädte waren, mit Ausnahme Frankfurts, zu unbedeutenden Provinzstädten geworden. Die Umstellung auf die Friedenswirtschaft und die Heerscharen entlassener Kriegsteilnehmer hätten allein schon genügt, ein günstiges Klima für die Auswanderung zu schaffen, ganz abgesehen von dem Wiederaufleben des Pietismus in Württemberg. Doch gerade wie im Winter 1708/09 war es die Natur, die den letzten Anstoß gab. Das Jahr 1816 war ein Jahr ohne Sommer. Kalter, fast ununterbrochener Regen fiel von Mai bis September, und im Oktober setzte ein strenger Winter ein. Wieder glaubten viele, die Naturkatastrophe sei ein Fingerzeig Gottes.

Late in 1816 the stampede began, down the Rhine to America, and eastward to Russia. The magnitude of this migration caught shipping companies unprepared. By June 1817, despite overloading and unseasonable departures, 30,000 people were crowding the Dutch ports. In 1817 and 1818 altogether 50,000 reached America. The miseries and hardships accompanying this exodus were so great that protests arose everywhere. Confronted with accusations, the Wurttemberg government commissioned a young economist, Friedrich List, to investigate the causes. List's assessment of the situation made it clear that profound uneasiness provoked by the lack of freedom, plus economic hardships coupled with pietist fervor, all contributed to the outbreak of the "emigration epidemic".

A conservative, albeit nationalistic, view of the crisis was expressed by Hans von Gagern who represented the Netherlands (for Limburg and Luxemburg) in the *Bundestag* of the German Confederation, the loose association of states which had replaced the defunct Empire since 1815. Gagern, former chief minister of Nassau-Weilburg, had witnessed emigration from his area for many years. He found emigration "within limits" an excellent means to rid a country of rebellious, Jacobinic and revolutionary elements. The misery in the Dutch ports and the burden such stranded wayfarers represented to the host country were the main reason for Gagern's step to make the conditions known to the *Bundestag*. For a brief span, emigration became a political topic. The subsequent decline in emigration to America until 1830 did not, however, remove the New World from public awareness.

The first political refugees heading for America came from German universities which were bristling with student unrest. The students protested against the repressive measures that had been carried out against the democrats. Initiated by the Austrian chancellor Metternich, they were seconded by most German states. In 1829 Gottfried Duden, a graduate in law and medicine, who had settled in the newly-opened Missouri territory five years earlier, published his *Journey to the Western States of North America*. It was the right book at the right time. In a skillful manner Duden depicted the vast spaces and the democratic life of America and compared both with the social and political pressures that the individual had to bear in Germany. Several editions found avid readers all over the country. Soon a flood of other books followed. Letters from successful settlers in the United States were even more effective in enticing relatives and friends to think of emigrating. The expansion of trade between Bremen and American ports also had a singular effect. The ships bringing bulky American staples from Baltimore and New Orleans, especially tobacco and cotton, lacked freight on their outward voyage. Emigrants therefore became the favorite America-bound freight. Shipping companies became ardent solicitors in the German hinterland.

Gegen Ende des Jahres 1816 begann eine panische Flucht, rheinabwärts nach Amerika und ostwärts nach Rußland. Die Schiffahrtsgesellschaften waren auf einen solchen Ansturm nicht vorbereitet. Im Juni 1817 bevölkerten rund 30 000 Menschen die holländischen Häfen – obwohl die Schiffe überladen wurden und auch bei ungünstiger Witterung in See stachen. Insgesamt 50 000 deutsche Einwanderer kamen in den Jahren 1817/18 in Amerika an. Die menschlichen Tragödien und Härten, die diesen Massenexodus begleiteten, riefen überall heftige Proteste hervor. Die württembergische Regierung, ebenfalls in die Schußlinie geraten, beauftragte einen jungen Ökonomen, Friedrich List, mit der Untersuchung der Ursachen. In seinen Ergebnissen kam List zu dem Schluß, daß ein „tiefes Unbehagen" angesichts der politischen Unfreiheit, verbunden mit wirtschaftlichen Nöten und pietistischem Glaubenseifer, zum Ausbruch dieser „Auswanderungsepidemie" geführt habe.

Eine konservativ-nationalistische Beurteilung erfuhr die Krise durch Hans von Gagern, den Vertreter der Niederlande (für Limburg und Luxemburg) im Frankfurter Bundestag des losen deutschen Staatenbundes, der 1815 das Heilige Römische Reich Deutscher Nation abgelöst hatte. Von Gagern, ehemals leitender Minister von Nassau-Weilburg, hatte die Auswanderung in seiner Heimatregion jahrelang beobachten können. Er fand, daß eine Auswanderung „in Grenzen" ein ausgezeichnetes Mittel sei, das Land von rebellischen, jakobinischen und revolutionären Elementen zu befreien. Das Elend in den holländischen Häfen und die Belastung, die die gestrandeten Reisenden für das Gastland darstellten, waren von Gagerns eigentliche Gründe, die Angelegenheit vor den Bundestag zu bringen. Für kurze Zeit wurde die Auswanderung zum politischen Thema. Der bald darauf einsetzende Rückgang der Amerikaauswanderung bis 1830 ließ die Neue Welt jedoch nicht aus dem Bewußtsein der Öffentlichkeit verschwinden.

Die ersten politischen Flüchtlinge, die nach Amerika aufbrachen, kamen von den deutschen Universitäten, wo unter der Studentenschaft die Unzufriedenheit gärte. Man protestierte gegen die antidemokratische Restaurationspolitik und die „Demagogenverfolgung", die der österreichische Kanzler Metternich initiiert hatte und die in fast allen Staaten des Deutschen Bundes beflissene Vollstrecker fand. 1829 publizierte der Jurist und Mediziner Gottfried Duden, der sich fünf Jahre zuvor in dem damals gerade in die Union aufgenommenen Bundesstaat Missouri niedergelassen hatte, seinen *Bericht über eine Reise nach den westlichen Staaten Nordamerika's*. Es war das richtige Buch zur richtigen Zeit. Geschickt schilderte Duden die geographische Weite und das demokratische Leben Amerikas und stellte beides den gesellschaftlichen und politischen Zwängen gegenüber, denen der Bürger in Deutschland ausgesetzt war. Mehrere Auflagen erschienen kurz hintereinander und fanden im ganzen Land begierige Leser. Rasch folgte eine wahre Flut ähnlicher Reiseberichte. Mehr noch als Bücher trugen Briefe erfolgreicher Siedler aus Übersee dazu bei, die zurückgebliebenen Freunde und Verwandten zur Auswanderung zu motivieren. Der wachsende Seehandel zwischen Bremen und den amerikanischen Häfen half auf eigene Weise mit, die Emigration zu verstärken: Die Schiffe, die mit amerikanischer Stapelware, vor allem Tabak und Baumwolle aus Baltimore und New Orleans, nach Europa kamen, brauchten eine Rückfracht – und als solche boten sich die Emigranten an. So wurden bald die Reedereien zu eifrigen Auswanderungswerbern im deutschen Hinterland.

To the right: The July Revolution of 1830 in Paris, which deposed Charles X and led to the accession of the "citizen king" Louis Philippe, sparked a resurgence of nationalistic and liberal movements on the entire continent. There was rioting in several German cities, and a formidable popular insurrection in Warsaw. Many European countries proclaimed sympathy with the Polish cause but none came to its aid, enabling Russia to crush the uprising in the following year. The 1830 revolution at Brussels, however, succeeded in winning independence for Belgium from the Netherlands and the pig-headed Dutch king, William I.

Rechts: Die Pariser Juli-Revolution des Jahres 1830, durch die Karl X. vertrieben wurde und der »Bürgerkönig« Louis Philippe an die Macht kam, führte in ganz Europa zu einer Neubelebung der nationalen und liberalen Ideen. In mehreren deutschen Städten kam es zu Unruhen, in Warschau zu einer Volkserhebung. Die übrigen europäischen Länder ergriffen für die polnische Sache Partei, leisteten jedoch keine Hilfe, so daß der Aufstand im folgenden Jahr von Rußland niedergeschlagen werden konnte. Erfolgreich verlief die Revolution in Belgien, das seine Unabhängigkeit von den Niederlanden errang.

Bericht

über eine Reise

nach den

westlichen Staaten Nordamerika's

und einen mehrjährigen Aufenthalt am Missouri (in den Jahren 1824, 25, 26 und 1827), in Bezug auf Auswanderung und Uebervölkerung,

oder:

Das Leben

im

Innern der Vereinigten Staaten

und dessen Bedeutung für die häusliche und politische Lage der Europäer, dargestellt

a) in einer Sammlung von Briefen,

b) in einer besonderen Abhandlung über den politischen Zustand der nordamerikanischen Freistaaten, und

c) in einem rathgebenden Nachtrage für auswandernde deutsche Ackerwirthe und Diejenigen, welche auf Handelsunternehmungen denken,

von

Gottfried Duden.

Gedruckt zu Elberfeld im Jahre 1829 bei Sam. Lucas, auf Kosten des Verfassers.

Title page of Gottfried Duden's widely circulated report on his four years' sojourn along the Missouri River.

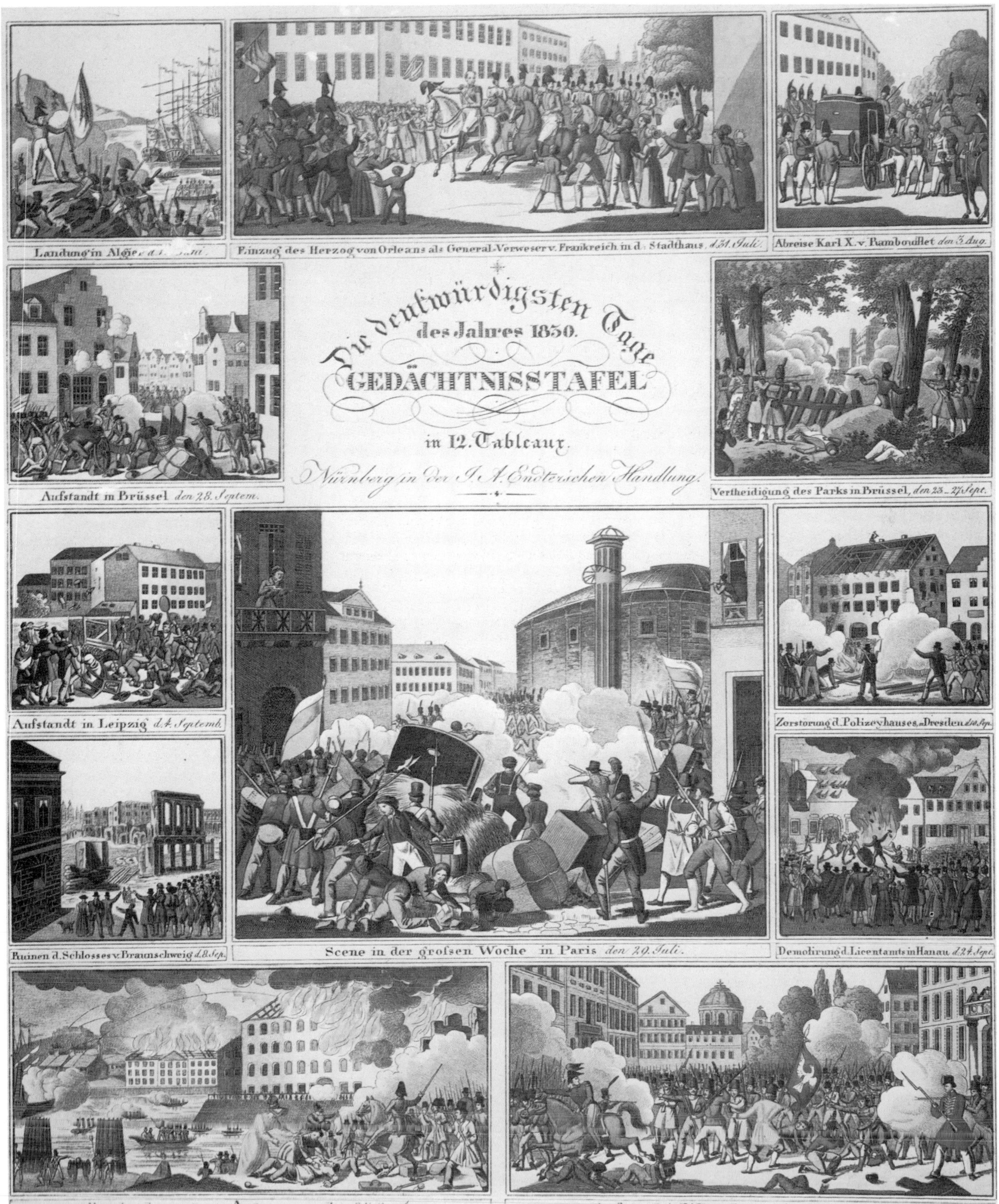
Die denkwürdigsten Tage
des Jahres 1830.
GEDÄCHTNISSTAFEL
in 12. Tableaux.
Nürnberg in der J. A. Endterischen Handlung.
Landung in Algie
Einzug des Herzog von Orleans als General-Verweser v. Frankreich in d. Stadthaus, d. 31. Juli.
Abreise Karl X. v. Rambouillet den 3. Aug.
Aufstandt in Brüssel den 28. Septem.
Vertheidigung des Parks in Brüssel, den 23 – 27. Sept.
Aufstandt in Leipzig d. 4. Septemb.
Zerstörung d. Polizeyhauses, Dresden d. 10. Sep.
Ruinen d. Schlosses v. Braunschweig d. 8. Sep.
Scene in der grofsen Woche in Paris den 29. Juli.
Demolirung d. Licentamts in Hanau d. 24. Sept.
Bombardement von Antwerpen, den 27. October.
Aufstand in Warschau, den 29. November.

After 1836 the majority of emigrants no longer came from the traditional southwestern states. Hesse, Franconia, Westphalia, Hanover and Oldenburg experienced heavy migration. In the 1840s almost 450,000 people left for America. Governments and public opinion in Germany accepted this as more or less inevitable. Rising nationalistic feeling found its expression in occasional remarks that this bloodletting deprived Germany of substance and talent. Next to nothing was done to protect emigrants against the exploitation that they inevitably encountered along their way. They had chosen to shut the door behind them and were on their own. Humanitarian concern was voiced occasionally, often only when hordes of emigrants in transit created local problems. Only Prussia, still interested in attracting settlers in the East, tried to stem the tide. But a royal decree to unite Lutheran and Reformed churches into one state church suddenly brought the emigration problem home to Prussian authorities. In 1838, conservative Lutherans decided to escape the enforced church union and began to leave for America. News of their move spread into the lands east of the Elbe from whence emigrants began to join other Germans in ever-increasing numbers. Densely populated Saxony and sparsely peopled Mecklenburg were both losing their share of people to America, a further indication that population pressure was not a decisive factor.

Despite the long periods of apparent calm and economic stability, people in the German states felt that the smoldering liberal movement on the one hand, and the repressive government measures on the other hand, would lead to a revolution. There was a strong feeling of discontent which, as the saying went, made the pessimists leave for America and the optimists get ready for battle. Many relatively prosperous families went on their way to America to avoid becoming involved in an uprising. The revolution finally came to Germany in 1848. Initial successes in Berlin, Vienna and southwest Germany encouraged liberals in their hope for unification and democracy. It was argued in the German National Assembly in Frankfurt, that the achievement of these goals would put an end to mass emigration. But the revolt ended with the triumph of the old powers. Active participants were relentlessly persecuted and some 4000 of them eventually went to America. They went as emigrés, exiled men and women looking for a temporary asylum until the fight for liberty in Germany could be resumed.

Was ist des Deutschen Vaterland?

To the left: "What country is a fatherland to the Germans?" is the question in this caricature from the days of the unsuccessful 1848 revolution, which drove thousands of political refugees to the U.S.

Links: zeitgenössische Karikatur der deutschen Amerika-Flüchtlinge in den Jahren nach 1848

Nach 1836 kam die Mehrzahl der Emigranten nicht mehr aus den traditionellen Ursprungsländern im Südwesten Deutschlands. Hessen, Franken, Westfalen, Hannover und Oldenburg erlebten starke Auswanderungswellen. In den 1840er Jahren brachen nahezu 450 000 Menschen nach Amerika auf. Die Regierungen und die öffentliche Meinung in Deutschland nahmen dies als mehr oder weniger unvermeidlich hin. Wachsendes Nationalgefühl äußerte sich gelegentlich in der Bemerkung, solcher Aderlaß beraube Deutschland an Substanz und Talent. So gut wie nichts wurde zum Schutz der Emigranten vor Übervorteilung unternommen, wie sie ihnen auf ihrem langen Weg zwangsläufig widerfahren mußte. Sie hatten die Tür hinter sich zugeschlagen und blieben nun sich selbst überlassen. Zu humanitären Bedenken, die gelegentlich laut wurden, kam es in der Regel nur, wenn durchziehende Auswandererhaufen lokale Probleme verursachten. Allein Preußen, das immer noch an Siedlern für seine Ostgebiete interessiert war, versuchte, sich der Flut entgegenzustemmen. Da konfrontierte ein königlicher Erlaß zur Vereinigung der lutherischen und reformierten Kirchen zu einer Staatskirche plötzlich auch die preußischen Behörden mit dem Auswanderungsproblem. 1838 begannen orthodoxe Lutheraner, sich der erzwungenen Einheitskirche zu entziehen, indem sie sich nach Amerika absetzten. Die Nachricht von ihrem Fortzug verbreitete sich rasch in den Ländern östlich der Elbe, von wo nun ebenfalls ständig steigende Auswandererzahlen gemeldet wurden. Das dicht besiedelte Sachsen und das nur spärlich besiedelte Mecklenburg verloren beide einen Teil ihrer Bevölkerung an Amerika – ein weiteres Indiz dafür, daß die Bevölkerungsdichte kein ausschlaggebender Faktor für die Auswanderung war.

Trotz der scheinbaren äußeren Ruhe und wirtschaftlichen Stabilität der Biedermeierzeit spürten nicht wenige Menschen, daß es zwischen dem untergründig schwelenden Liberalismus und der repressiven Politik der Regierungen zu einer revolutionären Auseinandersetzung kommen mußte. Ein Gefühl der Unzufriedenheit war weit verbreitet, und eine Redensart der Zeit behauptete, es ließe die Pessimisten nach Amerika ziehen und die Optimisten ihre Waffen schärfen. Viele relativ wohlhabende Familien machten sich auf den Weg nach Amerika, um nicht in eventuelle Aufstände verwickelt zu werden. 1848 war es schließlich soweit: die Revolution kam nach Deutschland. Anfangserfolge in Berlin, Wien und Südwestdeutschland schienen den liberalen Hoffnungen auf nationale Einigung und Demokratie recht zu geben. In der Nationalversammlung zu Frankfurt wurde argumentiert, daß die Verwirklichung dieser Ziele auch der Massenauswanderung ein Ende setzen würde. Doch die Revolte endete mit dem Sieg der etablierten Mächte. Die Revolutionäre wurden erbarmungslos verfolgt, etwa 4 000 von ihnen nach Amerika getrieben. Sie gingen als politische Flüchtlinge, als Exilierte, die nur nach einem vorübergehenden Asyl suchten, bis der Kampf um die Freiheit in Deutschland wieder aufgenommen werden konnte.

Trotz ihrer relativ geringen Zahl erweckten die emigrierten „Achtundvierziger" eine große öffentliche Anteilnahme, die ihrerseits wieder dazu beitrug, das Bewußtsein von Amerika als einem sicheren Zufluchtsort vor Not und Drangsal jeder Art zu vertiefen. Es muß der Spekulation überlassen bleiben, ob und inwieweit die nun einsetzende Auswanderungswelle von der Revolution, ihrem Scheitern und ihrem Nach-

A session of the Frankfurt National Assembly, which convened in the Paulskirche from 18 May 1848 until the end of May, 1849.

Sitzung der Frankfurter Nationalversammlung, die vom 18. Mai 1848 bis Ende 1849 in der Paulskirche tagte.

"Panorama of Europe in August, 1849": after the failure of the revolutions and reform attempts the previous year, the counterrevolution now dominates the picture. German freedom-fighters are shown being swept by the Prussian/clerical reactionaries into Switzerland and France, from where Louis Napoleon ships them off to America. The peoples of Austria and Hungary try in vain to restrain the Habsburg feudal regime, while, in the rest of Europe – see Warsaw – the light has already gone out. Trade flourishes in Queen Victoria's England; in Denmark, the king triumphs. But in Frankfurt a parliamentary scarecrow grows stunted, while Reverend Beer-Mug snoozes away in Munich. (Lithograph by F. Schroeder)

»Rundgemaelde von Europa im August 1849«: Nach dem Scheitern der Revolutionen und Reformversuche des Vorjahrs beherrscht die Konterrevolution das Bild. Deutsche Freiheitskämpfer werden von der preußisch-klerikalen Reaktion in die Schweiz und nach Frankreich gekehrt, von wo sie Louis Bonaparte nach Amerika verschifft. Die Völker Österreichs und Ungarns versuchen vergebens, dem habsburgischen Feudalregime in den Arm zu fallen, während im übrigen Europa – siehe Warschau – das Licht schon ausgegangen ist. In England floriert unter Königin Victoria der Handel, in Dänemark triumphiert der König. In Frankfurt aber verkümmert eine parlamentarische Vogelscheuche, und in München döst ein pfäffischer Bierseidel. (Lithographie von F. Schroeder)

Nro. 28 der Agentur Coblenz

Schiffs-Accord.

Nro.

Joseph Stöck in Kreuznach,

im Königreich **Preußen** concessionirter **Unternehmer**, verpflichtet sich urkundlich dieses Vertrages, gemäß Vollmacht und durch Vermittlung von

Karl Joh. Klingenberg,

Schiffsmackler in **Bremen**,

1. Franz Kolb 48 Jahre Kaufmann in Coblenz
2. Christine Kolb 40 " "
3. Therese Kolb 18 " "
4. Clara Kolb 16 " "
5. Mathias Kolb 15 " "
6. Christine Kolb 10 " "
7. Franz Jos. Kolb 7 " "
8. Wilhelm Kolb 6 "

2 [illegible] II Cajüte

5 Erwachsene und Kinder über 10 Jahre 3 Kinder von 1 bis 10 Jahre und — Säugling unter 1 Jahr, zusammen 8 Personen, laut Uebereinkunft von Coblenz nach Bremen und von da auf dem in der Quittung zu benamenden Schiffe an dem in derselben zu bestimmenden Abfahrttage, unter nachstehenden Bedingungen, nach New York — zu befördern.

§. 1. Die Passagiere erhalten zur Fahrt von oben genanntem Orte die nöthigen Fahr-Billets bis Bremen.

Auf dieser Fahrt hat jeder Erwachsene freien Transport von zwei Centner und jedes Kind von 1 bis 12 Jahren von einem Centner Reisegepäcke. Für Uebergewicht wird der tarifmäßige Preis von Rthl. 2. per Centner erhoben.

§. 2. Die Kosten der Visitation an den Gränzen und des Durchzugs des wirklichen Reisegepäcks haben die Schiffbefrachter zu tragen. Die Nachtheile unrichtiger Angabe, oder einer Verheimlichung ihrer Effekten und Waaren fallen lediglich den Eigenthümern zur Last.

§. 3. In den Städten, in welchen übernachtet wird, müssen die Passagiere auf ihre eignen Kosten logieren; dagegen werden ihre Effekten, für sie kostenfrei, von einem Dampfschiffe auf das andere sowie auf die Eisenbahn und von Bremen nach Bremerhafen in das Seeschiff gebracht.

§. 4. Die Inhaber dieses Vertrages müssen spätestens 2 Tage vor der bestimmten Abfahrt in Bremen eintreffen. Verspätungen, sowie unrichtige Angaben des Alters der Kinder machen der Ansprüche im §. 9. verlustig; letztere verpflichten noch insbesondere zur Nachzahlung des ganzen Tarifpreises.

§. 5. Mit ansteckenden Krankheiten behaftete Personen können nicht eingeschifft werden; sie erhalten jedoch nach ihrer Genesung auf dem zuerst abfahrenden Schiff ihre Beförderung, selbstredend bis dahin ohne Entschädigung für ihren Aufenthalt.

§. 6. Folgenden Personen ist die Landung in New-York gesetzlich verboten:

1) Geisteskranke, Einäugige, Blinde, Taube, Stumme;
2) Gebrechliche, d. h. in krüppelhaftem Zustande sich Befindende;
3) Frauen mit kleinen Kindern und Schwangere ohne Männer;
4) Leute über 60 Jahre ohne arbeitfähige Familien-Angehörige;

und müssen daher von den Agenten und Conducteurs zurückgewiesen werden.

§ 7. Die Schiffskost, welche die Passagiere vom Tage der bedungenen Abfahrt an bis zur Landung im Ausschiffungshafen kostenfrei zubereitet täglich erhalten, besteht in gesalzenem Ochsen- und Schweinefleisch, Erbsen, Bohnen, Grütze, Reis, Mehlspeise, Sauerkraut, Kartoffeln, Pflaumen u. s. w., sowie Schiffsbrod (Zwieback); ferner Morgens und Abends Caffee oder Thee, Brod und Butter, Trink-Wasser; — Alles hinreichend und gut.

Bei Bereitung der Speisen für die Passagiere haben stets Einige von denselben dem Schiffskoche hülfreiche Hand zu leisten.

In Krankheitfällen werden dienliche Speisen und die erforderliche Medizin gereicht.

Diese Beköstigung ist in dem in §. 8. bedungenen Ueberfahrtbetrage inbegriffen.

Die Eß-, Trink- und Wasch-Geschirre, sowie das erforderliche Bettzeug müssen die Auswanderer jedenfalls selbst stellen, ohne welche sie nicht eingeschifft werden können.

§. 8. Die Eingangs genannte Person , welche alle Bedingungen dieses Vertrages kenn und ann , verpflichte sich, baar und jedenfalls vor der Einschiffung zu bezahlen:

für 5 Personen über 10 Jahre . . . à Thlr. Thlr.
" 3 Kinder von 1 bis 10 Jahren . à Thlr. Thlr. } 247 Thlr.

sage: Thaler Zweihundert sieben und vierzig —

worauf bei Abschluß dieses Accordes der sub I. unten quittirte Betrag entrichtet werde. — Restzahlungen in Bremen können in preußischem oder Vereins-Gelde, fl. 7 zu Rthl. 4 gerechnet, geleistet werden.

§. 9. Gegen Bezahlung des Aufgeldes werden die Einschreibungen auf einen festen Abfahrttag ertheilt, und hiernach Diejenigen, welche die ganze Ueberfahrtsumme entrichtet haben, während des, ohne ihre eigene Schuld verursachten Aufenthaltes, von der festgesetzten Abfahrt an, selbst höhere Gewalt, wie Sturm und Wetter, nicht ausgenommen, für Rechnung der Schiffbefrachter verköstiget und beherbergt, oder täglich mit 12 Sgr. für die erwachsene Person und mit 8 Sgr. für jedes Kind entschädigt.

§. 10. Auf dem angewiesenen Schiffe hat jeder eingeschriebene Passagier sich der gesetzlichen Schiff-Ordnung zu fügen und erhält:

a) einen Platz im Zwischendeck,
b) freien Transport des Reisegepäcks und der zum eigenen Gebrauche bestimmten Geräthschaften,
c) Bettstelle und nöthigenfalls Apotheke,
d) Täglich zubereitete reichliche Kost,
e) süßes Wasser und Licht; und ist bei der Ankunft im Ausschiffungshafen New York
f) berechtigt, 48 Stunden Aufenthalt auf dem Schiffe mit gutem Trinkwasser und Seekost anzusprechen;
g) frei von Entrichtung des Spital- oder Armen-Geldes, da solches im obigen Betrage begriffen ist.

§. 11. Die Schiffbefrachter sind verpflichtet, die Auswanderer und deren Effekten auch in dem Falle um den bedungenen Preis an den bestimmten Ort zu bringen, wenn das betreffende Schiff unterwegs durch irgend einen Unfall an der Fortsetzung der Reise verhindert wird.

§. 12. Jedem Passagier, welcher unter Begleitung eines Conducteurs reiset, wird für die richtige Ablieferung seines Reisegepäckes in Bremen garantirt, wofür ein Procent vom angegebenen Werthe bezahlt wird.

Sowie einerseits die Unternehmer, resp. die Schiffbefrachter hoher Verordnung gemäß verpflichtet sind, den Betrag der Ueberfahrt nebst 20 Thlr. per Kopf Bewendungsgelder ~~zu versichern, —~~ so müssen anderseits die Passagiere für gleiche Versicherung ihrer Effekten und Lebensmittel gegen See-Gefahr zwei Procent des erklärten Werthes im Seehafen entrichten.

§. 13. Der Unternehmer verpflichtet sich in Beziehung auf alle wegen des gegenwärtigen Vertrags zwischen ihm und den Auswanderern entstehenden Streitigkeiten, vor den Königlichen Gerichten Recht zu geben und auf Einreden, welche auf etwaige, im Ausland geschlossene, den Bestimmungen der einschlägigen Verordnug zuwiederlaufende Verträge gegründet werden möchten, Verzicht zu leisten. Während der Reise, namentlich in Seestädten, etwa entstehende Streitigkeiten werden durch die Vermittlung des Preußischen Gesandten oder Konsuls beigelegt, dessen Schiedsspruch die Befrachter sich unbedingt unterwerfen, wenn dieser auch ganz allein als Schiedsrichter von dem Auswanderer angerufen werden sollte.

§. 14. Dieser Vertrag kann einseitig weder gekündet oder gebrochen, noch, da er nur für die oben eingeschriebenen Personen und, bei bereits ertheilter spezieller Einschreibung, nur auf das betreffende Seeschiff gültig ist, auf Andere, übertragen und für eine spätere Abfahrt geltend gemacht werden. Der zuwiderhandelnde Theil verliert alle darin bedungenen Rechte und Ansprüche. Wird mit Umgehung desselben, ein neuer Schiffs-Accord mit einem Dritten abgeschlossen, so ist der Verletzende verpflichtet, dem Verletzten die gerichtlich zu bestimmende Entschädigung zu entrichten.

Dieser Vertrag ist aufgelöset, wenn der Passagier vor der Abreise die verordnete Reiselegitimation nicht vorweist.

So geschehen, doppelt ausgefertigt, von den Contrahenten unterzeichnet und jedem Theil ein Original-Exemplar eingehändigt: Coblenz am 1ten August 1855

E. W. von Zülow
Haupt Agent.

Unterschrift der Auswanderer:

F. Kolb

Quittung I.

Auf nebenstehenden Accord das Aufgeld als erste Anzahlung empfangen mit Thlr. 247.
sage Thaler Zweihundert sieben und vierzig —
und wird hiermit de Accordanten gleichzeitig die Ankunft und Anmeldung auf der Agentur in Coblenz spätestens auf den 28 August die Fahrt von da nach Bremen auf den darauffolgenden Tag und die Fahrt von Bremen nach New York auf den 1 September mit dem Seeschiff [illegible] geführt von dem Capitän oder einen andern gleichguten, am nämlichen Tage abseegelnden Schiffe, festgesetzt.

Coblenz den 28ten August 1855.

E. W. von Zülow
Haupt Agent.

Quittung II.

Den Restbetrag auf nebenstehenden Accord mit Thlr
sage Thaler.
empfangen zu haben, bescheinigt
den ten 185

Schiffs-Accord Nro. Nro. der Agentur

hat am mit
für Person über 10 Jahre, von 1 bis 10 Jahre Säugling Platz auf dem am von Bremen abfahrenden Schiffe
abgeschlossen für die Summa von . . . . Thlr.
und außerdem bezahlt:
1) für Uebergewicht . . . . Thlr.
2) „ Effekten-Assecouranz bis Bremen . . Thlr.
3) „ See-Versicherung . . . . Thlr.
Total . . . Thlr.

Bezahlt wurde:
I. An den Agenten . . . Thlr.
II. In . Thlr.
III. In Bremen . . . . Thlr.
IV. Außerdem:
1) an
für Uebergewicht . . Thlr.
2) an
für Effekt-Assec. . . . Thlr.
3) an
für See-Verf. . . . . . Thlr.
Total . Thlr.

Contract to transport all eight members of the emigrant Kolb family from Coblenz to New York: from the year 1855

Vollständiger Beförderungsvertrag der achtköpfigen Auswandererfamilie Kolb von Koblenz nach New York aus dem Jahr 1855

Facilitation of emigration as an easy solution to social problems: the Frankfurt agent H. Bernard's letter to the mayor of the town of Gross-Gerau concerning the transportation of two impoverished persons to America at community expense.

Die Auswanderung als bequeme Lösung sozialer Probleme: Schreiben des Frankfurter Agenten H. Bernhard an den Bürgermeister der Kleinstadt Groß-Gerau, betreffend den Transport zweier Bedürftiger nach Amerika auf Gemeindekosten.

"There is lively competition among shipowners and managers to make the voyage as pleasant as possible for the emigrants. The assigned cabins are bright, airy and comfortable, so that nothing will give rise to the slightest complaint": excerpt from an emigration-agency's advertisement, given the lie by a caricature illustrating the actual conditions.

»Unter den Schiffsrhedern und Expeditenten herrscht ein reger Wettstreit, den Auswanderern die Reise auf das angenehmste zu machen. Die ihnen überwiesenen Schiffsräume sind hell, luftig und bequem, so daß keine Gelegenheit gegeben ist zur geringsten Klage« – Reklametext eines Auswanderungsagenten, illustriert mit einer Karikatur der tatsächlichen Zustände.

At right: "While I am still young and strong enough to earn my living by the labor of my own hands, I request you to make it seem plausible to the community council that it would be advantageous for the town if they approved financing my emigration with community funds. If perhaps the rest of my prison sentence could be suspended, I would immediately depart for America and the township would be rid of me forever which would furthermore be cheaper than if they had to pay for my welfare in my old age…": a prisoner's petition (1857) to be deported to America. His request must have remained unfulfilled, as the 18th-century practice on the part of certain German principalities (occasionally revived in the 1830s and 40s) of emptying local jails and houses of correction by shipping the inmates to North or South America had gradually been abandoned by the middle of the 19th century; protests issued by the American authorities led to the prohibition of any further "convict transports" at Bremen and Hamburg, the ports of embarkation for emigrants. As the deportations took place clandestinely, it is difficult to estimate the number of criminals (-and incidentally, deportation had always been restricted to those involved in minor offenses only-) who emigrated with official support; they could only have accounted for less than 1% of total emigration.

Rechts: »… Da ich nun jetzt noch jung und stark bin daß ich mich mit meiner Hände Arbeit ernähren kann; so bitte ich Sie es dem Gemeinde Vorstand vorzustellen daß es am besten für die Stadt ist wenn sie mir die Mittel zur Auswanderung aus der Gemeindekassa verwilligen. Ich kann dann vielleicht einen Theil von meiner Strafe geschenkt kriegen und sogleich von hier aus nach Amerika auswandern, und die Stadt ist mich auf immer los, und kommt billiger dazu als wenn ich ihr im Alter zur Last falle«: Gesuch eines Zuchthäuslers um Abschiebung nach Amerika aus dem Jahr 1857. Der Wunsch wird unerfüllt geblieben sein, da die im 18. Jahrhundert übliche und auch in den 30er und 40er Jahren des 19. Jahrhunderts in verschiedenen deutschen Fürstentümern wieder aufgegriffene Praxis, die heimischen Gefängnisse und Korrektionsanstalten durch Verschiffung der Insassen nach Nord- und Südamerika zu leeren, um die Jahrhundertmitte zum Erliegen gekommen war: Proteste der amerikanischen Behörden hatten die Auswanderungshäfen Bremen und Hamburg veranlaßt, keine solchen »Häftlingstransportationen« mehr zuzulassen. Da die Abschiebungen heimlich stattfanden, läßt sich die Zahl der mit Amtshilfe ausgewanderten Kriminellen (unter denen sich übrigens niemals Schwerverbrecher befanden) nur schätzen: sie dürfte unter einem Prozent der Gesamtauswanderung gelegen haben.

Naturalization certificate of the former Prussian subject Johann (John) Menz, issued on 3 May 1859, after Menz had resided the required five years in the United States.

Einbürgerungsurkunde des ehemaligen preußischen Untertanen Johann (John) Menz, nach vorgeschriebenem fünfjährigem Mindestaufenthalt in den Vereinigten Staaten ausgestellt am 3. Mai 1859.

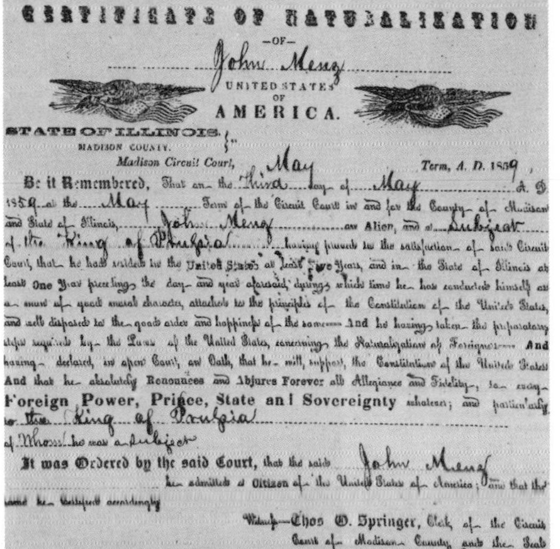

CERTIFICATE OF NATURALIZATION
—OF—
John Menz
UNITED STATES
OF
AMERICA.

STATE OF ILLINOIS, }
MADISON COUNTY. } ss.

Madison Circuit Court, May Term, A. D. 1859,

Be it Remembered, That on the Third day of May A. D. 1859 at the May Term of the Circuit Court in and for the County of Madison and State of Illinois, John Menz an Alien, and a Subject of the King of Prussia having proved to the satisfaction of said Circuit Court, that he has resided in the United States at least Five Years, and in the State of Illinois at least One Year preceding the day and year aforesaid, during which time he has conducted himself as a man of good moral character, attached to the principles of the Constitution of the United States, and well disposed to the good order and happiness of the same — And he having taken the preparatory steps required by the Laws of the United States, concerning the Naturalization of Foreigners — And having declared, in open Court, an Oath, that he will support the Constitution of the United States And that he absolutely Renounces and Abjures Forever all Allegiance and Fidelity, to every Foreign Power, Prince, State and Sovereignty whatever; and particularly to the King of Prussia of Whom he was a Subject

It was Ordered by the said Court, that the said John Menz be admitted a Citizen of the United States of America; and that the same be certified accordingly

Witness — Thos O. Springer, Clerk of the Circuit Court of Madison County and the Seal thereof, at Edwardsville, this Third day of May A. D. 1859

Thos. O. Springer Clerk

This relatively small number of exiles received a great deal of public attention, which in turn contributed to the steadily widening awareness of America as a safe refuge from all sorts of tribulations. It must be left to speculation as to what extent the subsequent emigration tide was influenced by the revolution, its failure and its aftermath. Of the 976,000 Germans who arrived in the United States from 1850 to 1859, 215,000 came in 1854 alone, as many in a single year as had arrived during the entire 18th century.

At the 1853 agricultural county fair at Landau, Palatinate, an emigrant chest shared the exhibit with farm implements. It bore the inscription from the 37th Psalm: "Remain in the country, and support yourself honestly". The chronicler wrote that it was not a prank but the chest stood there as a true symbol of Palatine conditions. It represented "a cure for the social vagabondism in many an infected and rotten Palatine community." He went on to tell of the corrupted Rhenish village whose people went on their journey singing amidst festive illuminations: they had set fire to their old abodes! In Saxony, where numerous Emigration Societies were active during this period, Carl Andreas Geyer, a horticulturist, tried to make his emigration activities palatable to the authorities by extolling them as a means to prevent "the breaking of dams under the floodwaters of the proletariat." Yet, in most cases, it was not the proletariat that left but what society then considered the sturdy middle-class families and young, enterprising farmers.

During the years of the American Civil War, 1861–65, and of the German wars in 1864 and 1866, emigration slowed down somewhat, but Prussia's triumph over Austria and her allies provided a push in those areas annexed by the Prussians. The creation of the German Empire, the *Reich,* during the Franco-German War in 1871, and the economic surge known as the "founders' years", were believed by many to have dealt the death blow to America fever. The *Reich* government tried to gain control of emigration through special commissioners, but to no avail. 1872 and 1873 were peak years for the movement to America. Altogether 1½ million Germans left for overseas countries between 1871 and 1885, 95 per cent of them for the United States. Much of this emigration originated in the rural areas of the northern and eastern parts of the country. Families and young men who preferred the prospect of farming in America to life in the industrial cities on the Ruhr

spiel beeinflußt war. Jedenfalls übersiedelten im Jahrzehnt von 1850 bis 1859 insgesamt 976 000 Deutsche in die USA – davon 215 000, mehr als im gesamten 18. Jahrhundert, allein im Jahr 1854.

Auf einem Kreislandwirtschaftsfest in Landau in der Pfalz war 1853 neben landwirtschaftlichen Geräten auch eine Auswanderertruhe zu sehen. Sie trug eine Inschrift aus dem 37. Psalm: „Bleibe im Lande und nähre dich redlich." Ein Chronist bemerkte, dies sei mehr als „bloß ein guter Witz". Die Truhe stünde hier als ein „bedeutsames Wahrzeichen pfälzischer Zustände, ein Heilmittel des sozialen Vagabundentums in mancher angesteckten und verdorbenen pfälzischen Gemeinde". Sein weiterer Bericht erzählte von einem gottlosen Dorf im Pfälzischen, dessen Bewohner singend und unter festlicher Beleuchtung zu ihrer großen Reise angetreten waren: sie hatten Feuer an ihre eigenen Häuser gelegt! In Sachsen, wo zu dieser Zeit zahlreiche Auswanderungsgesellschaften tätig waren, versuchte der Gärtner Carl Andreas Geyer den Behörden seine Anwerbungskampagnen schmackhaft zu machen, indem er sie als ein Mittel anpries, das „Brechen der Dämme unter den Fluten des Proletariats" zu verhindern. In den meisten Fällen war es jedoch keineswegs das Proletariat, welches das Land verließ: es waren die tatkräftigen Familien der Mittelschicht und junge, unternehmungslustige Bauern.

Der amerikanische Bürgerkrieg von 1861 bis 1865 und die beiden deutschen Kriege 1864 und 1866 ließen die Auswanderung zunächst zurückgehen, bis der Sieg Preußens über Österreich und dessen Verbündete einen neuen Anstieg in den von Preußen annektierten Gebieten bewirkte. Nach der Entstehung des zweiten deutschen Kaiserreichs im deutsch-französischen Krieg von 1870/71 und dem sich anschließenden Wirtschaftsaufschwung der sogenannten Gründerjahre erwarteten viele, daß das Amerikafieber der Deutschen nun endgültig geheilt sein müsse. Die Regierung setzte Auswanderungskommissare ein, um die Emigration unter Kontrolle zu bringen, doch ohne durchschlagenden Erfolg. Die Jahre 1872 und 1873 waren neue Spitzenjahre für die Wanderungsbewegung nach Amerika. Zwischen dem Reichsgründungsjahr 1871 und 1885 gingen insgesamt anderthalb Millionen Deutsche in überseeische Länder, davon 95 Prozent in die USA. Ein Großteil der Auswanderer kam nun aus den ländlichen Gebieten im Norden und

Echoes of the Franco-German War of 1870/71 in New York and Washington: left, "Victory celebration of the German-Americans in New York", illustration from the German magazine "Over Land and Sea"; right, "The Curtain is Raised," exposing the illegal sale of American weapons to France in the fall of 1870: caricature representing U.S. senators Carl Schurz and Charles Sumner, who brought the affair before Congress.

Der deutsch-französische Krieg von 1871 in New York und Washington: links »Die Friedensfeier der Deutsch-Amerikaner in New York«, Illustration aus der Zeitschrift »Über Land und Meer«; rechts »Der Vorhang wird gelüftet«, Karikatur der U.S.-Senatoren Carl Schurz und Charles Sumner, die den illegalen Verkauf amerikanischer Waffen an Frankreich im Herbst 1870 vor den Kongreß brachten.

The founding of the second German Empire: Prussia's Hohenzollern King, Wilhelm I (1797 – 1888), is proclaimed Emperor of Germany on 18 January 1871 in the hall of mirrors of the Versailles palace; at the right in front of the dais, Chief Minister Bismarck and General von Moltke. (Painting by Anton von Werner, 1877)

Die Gründung des zweiten deutschen Kaiserreichs: der preußische König Wilhelm I. (1797 – 1888) wird am 18. Januar 1871 im Spiegelsaal des Schlosses von Versailles zum deutschen Kaiser ausgerufen; rechts vor dem Podium Bismarck und Moltke. (Gemälde von Anton von Werner, 1877)

GERHART HAUPTMANN.

De Waber.

(Die Weber.)

Schauspiel aus den vierziger Jahren.

Dialekt-Ausgabe.

Berlin.
S. Fischer, Verlag
1892.

First edition of the original dialect version of the social drama "The Weavers" by Gerhart Hauptmann (1862–1946), in which the author incorporated observations he made on a trip through the weaving region of Silesia in the spring of 1891.

Erstausgabe der ursprünglichen Dialektfassung von Gerhart Hauptmanns (1862 – 1946) sozialem Drama »Die Weber«, in dem Hauptmann die Eindrücke einer Reise durch das schlesische Webergebiet im Frühjahr 1891 verarbeitete.

A leaf by Käthe Kollwitz (1867 – 1945) from her series "The Weavers' Revolt" (1897). Rapid industrialization not only led to the economic upsurge of the "Gründerjahre" (the period after 1871), but also produced a new abject proletariat, and therewith new potential emigrants. In the 1880s und 90s, for the first time in the history of German emigration, the proportion of unskilled laborers among the emigrants outweighed that of the craftsmen and farmers.

Blatt aus dem Zyklus »Der Weberaufstand« (1897) von Käthe Kollwitz (1867 – 1945): der wirtschaftliche Aufschwung der Gründerjahre mit seiner raschen Industrialisierung ließ ein neues Elendsproletariat und damit ein neues Auswandererpotential entstehen. Erstmals in der Geschichte der deutschen Emigration begann in den 80er und 90er Jahren der Anteil der ungelernten Arbeiter unter den Emigranten über die Handwerker und Bauern zu dominieren.

and Rhine, turned their backs on a jubilant, triumphant homeland. Avoiding three years of service in the Emperor's army was no doubt an added incentive for some young fellows. This was quite obviously true in the annexed provinces of Lorraine and Alsace which, though still largely German-speaking, had become quite French in sentiment over two centuries of sharing triumphs and defeats with France.

In the eastern provinces of Prussia and in Mecklenburg, agricultural labor was still so dependent on the large landowners that it bordered in many cases on the vassalage of old. Those among the young generation who did not want to exchange that dependency for one in a factory, chose America. Despite an occasional boom and labor shortage, such emigration continued. From 1890 until the outbreak of World War I in Europe in 1914, there was a steady, though somewhat smaller, stream of America-bound migrants. Official statistics become unreliable because they included considerable numbers of Poles from Poznan, the Vistula area and upper Silesia as "Germans".

During the last decades before the Great War, when the *Reich,* as a latecomer on the scene of European imperialism, was rushing to catch up with the established colonial empires, nationalistic circles in Germany remembered the millions of "lost brothers and sisters" overseas. Attempts were made, almost exclusively by private organziations, to assist the emigrants in America in preserving a distinct "Germanness". While Bismarck had still looked on them as "mere deserters", writers in Germany now began to extoll their achievements in the United States. Nationalists in the *Reich* fostered the illusion that in view of the sheer numbers of Germans in America, there would be enough sympathy for German causes to prevent an armed conflict between the two countries. The rude awakening came with the entry of the United States into the war in 1917.

New York celebrating the armistice of 11 November 1918. One and a half years of participation in the war cost America 130,000 lives.

New York feiert den Waffenstillstand vom 11. November 1918. Die anderthalb Kriegsjahre hatten Amerika 130 000 Menschenleben gekostet.

Osten des Reichs. Familien und junge Männer, die die Aussicht auf ein Dasein als unabhängige Farmer dem Leben in den Industriestädten an Rhein und Ruhr vorzogen, kehrten ihrem siegestrunkenen Vaterland jährlich zu Zigtausenden den Rücken. Die Möglichkeit, auf diese Weise dem dreijährigen Militärdienst in der kaiserlichen Armee zu entgehen, war für viele junge Burschen sicher ein zusätzlicher Anreiz – vor allem im 1871 zu Deutschland gekommenen Elsaß-Lothringen, dessen Bewohner, obwohl überwiegend deutschsprachig, in den zwei Jahrhunderten ihrer Zugehörigkeit zu Frankreich auch im Denken und Fühlen französisch geworden waren.

In den Ostprovinzen Preußens und in Mecklenburg lebten die Landarbeiter immer noch in einer Abhängigkeit von den Großgrundbesitzern, die dem alten Lehnswesen kaum nachstand. Diejenigen unter ihnen, die ihre Abhängigkeit nicht mit der Abhängigkeit des Industriearbeiters vertauschen wollten, wählten Amerika. Trotz Phasen der Wirtschaftsblüte und des Arbeitskräftemangels hielt diese Auswanderung an. Auch in den fünfundzwanzig Jahren von 1890 bis zum Ausbruch des Ersten Weltkriegs floß ein stetiger, wenn auch langsam zurückgehender Strom von Emigranten in die Neue Welt. Die offiziellen Statistiken sind für diesen Zeitraum irreführend, da sie eine beträchtliche Anzahl von Polen aus Posen, dem Weichselgebiet und Oberschlesien als „Deutsche" aufführen.

In den letzten Jahrzehnten vor dem großen Krieg, als das Deutsche Reich – der Spätankömmling auf der Szene des europäischen Imperialismus – gegenüber den etablierten Kolonialmächten aufzuholen versuchte, erinnerten sich nationalistische Kreise in Deutschland der Millionen von „verlorenen Brüdern und Schwestern" in Übersee. Man versuchte, fast ausschließlich durch private Organisationen, die Auswanderer in Amerika bei der Bewahrung ihres „Deutschtums" zu unterstützen. Während Bismarck in ihnen „eigentlich nur ... Überläufer" gesehen hatte, begannen deutsche Schriftsteller nun, ihre Leistungen in den Vereinigten Staaten zu rühmen. Deutsche Nationalisten gaben sich der Illusion hin, die schiere Anzahl deutscher Einwanderer in Amerika würde genügen, bei den USA Sympathie für die deutsche Sache zu erwecken und einem bewaffneten Konflikt zwischen den beiden Ländern vorzubeugen. Das jähe Erwachen kam mit dem Kriegseintritt der Vereinigten Staaten im Jahr 1917.

Enemy aliens are taken to an internment camp in Gloucester, New Jersey (1918)

Feindliche Ausländer werden in Gloucester, New Jersey, in ein Internierungslager gebracht (1918).

The era of mass immigration was nearing its end in 1906 when this ship docked at Ellis Island.

Das Zeitalter der Masseneinwanderung ging seinem Ende entgegen, als dieses Schiff 1906 in Ellis Island anlegte.

Mobilization in Germany on 1 August 1914: conscripted civilians being taken to receive uniforms.

Mobilmachung am 1. August 1914: einberufene Zivilisten werden zur Einkleidung geführt.

New York American

WAR WITH GERMANY

BAKER ASKS AN ARMY OF 1,200,000

Gibbons Prays God May Guide Nation in War

THREE BILLION AND A HALF IN WAR BUDGET

FOUR GERMAN SHIPS TOWED TO CITY PIER

Americans in Belgium May Be Interned

CARRANZA'S TROOPS MASS UPON BORDER

Austria and Turkey Hope to Stay Neutral

HOUSE BACKS UP WILSON, 373 TO 5L

The "New York American" of 7 April 1917: Germany's declaration of total submarine warfare was what led the U.S. to join the hostilities.

Der »New York American« vom 7. April 1917: die Erklärung des uneingeschränkten U-Boot-Kriegs durch Deutschland hatte zum amerikanischen Kriegseintritt geführt.

A spectral hand signing the peace treaty at Versailles: prophetic caricature by Boardman Robinson, 1919

Eine Todeshand unterzeichnet den Friedensvertrag von Versailles: prophetische Karikatur von Boardman Robinson, 1919

Out of Germany's defeat came the creation of the democratic Weimar Republic amidst political chaos. Harsh economic conditions imposed by the victors and continued international ostracism were not a very propitious stage for a democracy which could otherwise have been a realization of what earlier generations had striven for. Relations between Germany and the United States were normalized by a separate peace treaty in 1921. At the same time America closed her doors to unbridled immigration.
Under the quota laws, based on rather academic assessments of the national origins of the inhabitants, Germany did not fare badly compared to the quotas of other countries. Throughout the years of the Weimar Republic until the Great Depression in 1929 a steady trickle of emigrants continued to leave for America. Many went because they could not adjust to the conditions in post-war Germany. The majority consisted of mechanics, craftsmen and people looking for a small business of their own.

Aus der Niederlage Deutschlands entstand, inmitten des politischen Chaos, die demokratische Weimarer Republik. Die harten wirtschaftlichen Auflagen der Siegermächte und die anhaltende internationale Ächtung Deutschlands schufen kein günstiges Klima für eine junge Demokratie, die unter anderen Umständen vielleicht verwirklicht hätte, wofür frühere Generationen gekämpft hatten. Die Beziehungen zwischen Deutschland und den Vereinigten Staaten wurden 1921 durch einen separaten Friedensvertrag normalisiert. Gleichzeitig machte Amerika der ungehinderten Einwanderung durch Quotierungsgesetze ein Ende.
Bei der Zuteilung der Quoten, die nach ziemlich akademischen Begriffen von nationaler Zugehörigkeit vorgenommen wurde, kam Deutschland, verglichen mit anderen Ländern, nicht einmal schlecht weg. So floß der Emigrantenstrom von einst durch die Jahre der Weimarer Republik bis zur Weltwirtschaftskrise von 1929 wenigstens als stetiges Rinnsal weiter. Viele verließen Deutschland, weil sie mit den Lebensbedingungen der Nachkriegszeit nicht mehr zurechtkamen. Die Mehrheit dieser Auswanderer bestand aus Handwerkern, Mechanikern und Angehörigen ähnlicher Berufe, die sich drüben selbständig zu machen hofften.

"Germany's Children are Famished!", drawn by Käthe Kollwitz in 1924

»Deutschlands Kinder hungern!«, 1924 gezeichnet von Käthe Kollwitz.

"Quaker meals" being distributed in a Munich school. The American Relief Administration, organized by Herbert Hoover before he became president, as well as private organizations such as the Quakers offered aid to the needy German populace in the aftermath of World War I.

Quäkerspeisung in einer Münchner Schule. Das von dem späteren amerikanischen Präsidenten Hoover gegründete »Amerikanische Hilfswerk« und private Organisationen, vor allem der Quäker, halfen nach dem Ersten Weltkrieg, die Not der deutschen Bevölkerung zu lindern.

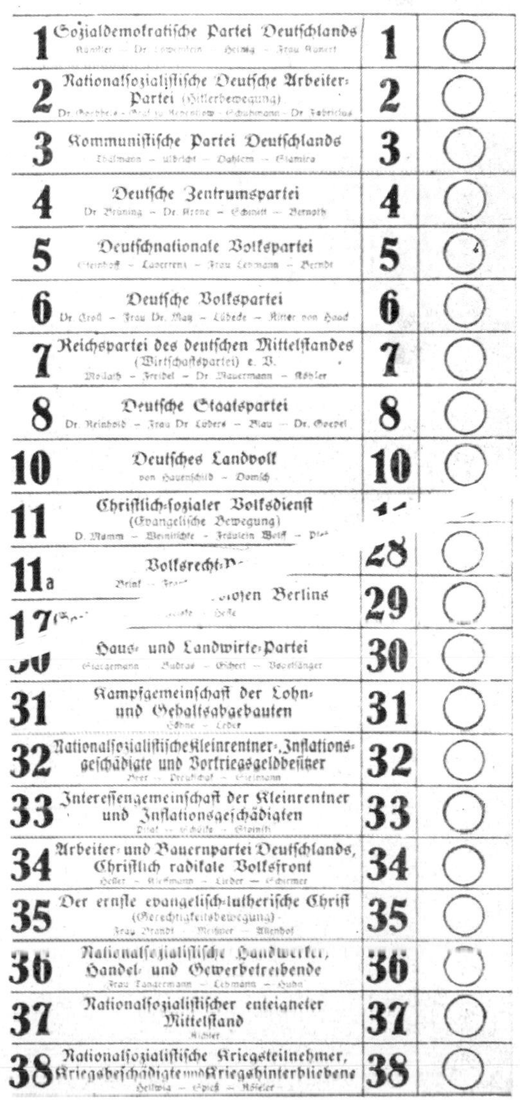

Reichstagswahl 1932

Wahlkreis Potsdam II.

1	Sozialdemokratische Partei Deutschlands	1	○
2	Nationalsozialistische Deutsche Arbeiter-Partei (Hitlerbewegung)	2	○
3	Kommunistische Partei Deutschlands	3	○
4	Deutsche Zentrumspartei	4	○
5	Deutschnationale Volkspartei	5	○
6	Deutsche Volkspartei	6	○
7	Reichspartei des deutschen Mittelstandes (Wirtschaftspartei) e. V.	7	○
8	Deutsche Staatspartei	8	○
10	Deutsches Landvolk	10	○
11	Christlich-sozialer Volksdienst (Evangelische Bewegung)	[illegible]	
11a	Volksrecht-[illegible]	28	○
[illegible]	[illegible] Berlins	29	○
30	Haus- und Landwirte-Partei	30	○
31	Kampfgemeinschaft der Lohn- und Gehaltsabgebauten	31	○
32	Nationalsozialistische Kleinrentner-, Inflationsgeschädigte und Vorkriegsgeldbesitzer	32	○
33	Interessengemeinschaft der Kleinrentner und Inflationsgeschädigten	33	○
34	Arbeiter- und Bauernpartei Deutschlands, Christlich radikale Volksfront	34	○
35	Der ernste evangelisch-lutherische Christ (Gerechtigkeitsbewegung)	35	○
36	Nationalsozialistische Handwerker, Handel- und Gewerbetreibende	36	○
37	Nationalsozialistischer enteigneter Mittelstand	37	○
38	Nationalsozialistische Kriegsteilnehmer, Kriegsbeschädigte und Kriegshinterbliebene	38	○

Ballot for the 1932 German national election: of the altogether 38 parties running in this last free election of the disintegrating Weimar Republic, Hitler's NSDAP received 33.1% of the votes; the Communist party, 19.9%.

Stimmzettel zur Reichstagswahl 1932: insgesamt 38 Parteien bewarben sich in den letzten freien Wahlen der zersplitterten Weimarer Republik um die Wählergunst. Hitlers NSDAP erhielt 33,1, die Kommunistische Partei 19,9 Prozent der Stimmen.

With the advent of Hitler's National Socialist regime in Germany in 1933, and later on in most other parts of Europe, past persecutions for conscience's or for religion's sake looked like mere inconveniences. The race theories underlying the Nazi program raised anti-Semitism from an ever-present but often latent prejudice to the status of official policy. The race laws affected all people of Jewish descent, most of whom had been so totally integrated over the centuries that they were nothing but German. Other policies of the Nazi government were directed against elements in the Christian churches and the labor movement who opposed the narrowly nationalistic theories because they believed in a brotherhood of all men. From 1933 onwards, tens of thousands of racially and politically persecuted Germans fled across the borders. The restrictive U.S. immigration policies made the obvious and traditional haven unattainable for many German refugees. In a decade only some 129,000 victims of Nazi measures in Germany and Austria managed to be admitted to the United States.

Emigration was virtually forbidden for all "Aryan" Germans. The ultimate aim of Nazi policy was to extend Germany's borders to all areas inhabited by people "of German descent and blood". Those scattered overseas were not excluded from the scheme. Repeated attempts were made to attract at least recent emigrants to the new *Reich* with minimal success: altogether some 6,800 persons heeded the siren call and returned from the United States which, as Nazi *Gauleiter* A.E. Frauenfeld expressed with dismay in 1940, had become "the common grave of the German emigrants."

Mit der Machtergreifung der Nationalsozialisten 1933 und den bald einsetzenden Übergriffen Hitlers auf die Nachbarländer und schließlich fast ganz Europa begann eine Schreckensherrschaft, die alle früheren Verfolgungen aus Glaubens- und Gewissensgründen in den Schatten stellte. Die der Nazi-Ideologie zugrundeliegende Rassentheorie machte den Antisemitismus, der als Vorurteil immer latent vorhanden gewesen war, zur offiziellen Staatspolitik. Die Rassengesetze betrafen alle Menschen jüdischer Herkunft – von denen die meisten aus Familien stammten, die sich im Lauf der Jahrhunderte so vollkommen integriert hatten, daß sie nichts anderes waren als Deutsche. Auch bestimmte Gruppierungen innerhalb der christlichen Kirchen und die Arbeiterbewegung, die an die Brüderlichkeit aller Menschen glaubten und in natürlicher Opposition zur völkisch-nationalistischen Weltanschauung der Nationalsozialisten standen, wurden zu Opfern des Regimes. Zehntausende von aus rassischen oder politischen Gründen Verfolgten flohen ab 1933 über Deutschlands Grenzen. Doch der traditionelle Zufluchtsort, der sich ihnen angeboten hätte, war durch die restriktive Einwanderungspolitik der US-Regierung für die Mehrzahl der Vertriebenen unerreichbar geworden. Innerhalb eines Jahrzehnts gelang es nur etwa 129 000 Verfolgten des Naziregimes aus Deutschland und Österreich, die begehrte Einreiseerlaubnis in die USA zu erhalten.

Den Deutschen „arischer" Abstammung war die Auswanderung praktisch verboten. Zu den erklärten Absichten nationalsozialistischer Politik gehörte die Ausweitung des deutschen Staatsgebietes auf alle Territorien, in denen Menschen „deutscher Abstammung und deutschen Blutes" lebten. In diesem Zusammenhang waren auch die Überseedeutschen für das Regime von Interesse. Wiederholt wurden Versuche unternommen, zumindest Auswanderer der ersten Generation „heim ins Reich" zu holen, doch nur mit minimalen Erfolg: Ganze 6 800 Personen folgten dem Sirenenruf und verließen die Vereinigten Staaten, die, wie Nazi-Gauleiter A.E. Frauenfeld 1940 erschreckt feststellte, zum „Massengrab der deutschen Auswanderer" geworden seien.

The book burnings of 10 May 1933 marked the start of the campaign which drove an entire intellectual elite out of Nazi Germany. Most of those who fled took refuge in the United States.

Die Bücherverbrennungen vom 10. Mai 1933 setzten das Fanal zur Vertreibung der intellektuellen Elite Deutschlands. Die meisten der Flüchtlinge fanden schließlich in den USA Zuflucht.

Boycott of Jewish-owned shops on 1 April 1933. Immediately after Hitler came into power, German Jews became the victims of terror and brutality. Gentiles who protested were derided as being "handmaids to the Jews."

Boykott jüdischer Geschäfte am 1. April 1933. Sofort nach Hitlers Machtübernahme setzte auch der Terror gegen die deutschen Juden mit aller Brutalität ein. Wer protestierte, war ein »Judenknecht«.

American antiaircraft gun in front of the bombed-out Frankfurt opera house, 1945

Ein amerikanisches Flakgeschütz vor der Ruine der Frankfurter Oper, 1945

U.S. Seventh Army tanks enter a devastated Nürnberg on 20 April 1945.

Panzer der 7. amerikanischen Armee dringen am 20. April 1945 in das zerstörte Nürnberg ein.

At the end of the war: an American field chaplain leading prayers of thanksgiving in the ruins of a German church at Übach.

Kriegsende: ein amerikanischer Feldgeistlicher hält seinen Dankgottesdienst in einer zerstörten deutschen Kirche in Übach.

General Jodl signing the unconditional surrender of the German armed forces at General Eisenhower's headquarters at Reims on 7 May 1945.

Im Hauptquartier General Eisenhowers in Reims unterzeichnet Generaloberst Jodl am 7. Mai 1945 die bedingungslose Kapitulation der deutschen Wehrmacht.

The historic and emotional moment when American GIs met soldiers of the Red Army at the Elbe River in April, 1945.

Ein GI und ein russischer Soldat umarmen sich nach der historischen Begegnung der amerikanischen und der sowjetischen Truppen an der Elbe im April 1945.

The leaders of the Allied forces of World War II at the Potsdam conference in July, 1945: Churchill, Truman and Stalin.

Die »großen Drei« der Anti-Hitler-Koalition des Zweiten Weltkriegs, Churchill, Truman und Stalin, auf der Konferenz von Potsdam im Juli 1945.

The total collapse of Nazi Germany in 1945 was in itself the deepest incision in German history. Reduced to the territory of pre-colonization days in the East, divided along the political concepts of the victors, there would have been mass emigration from Germany had America or other overseas countries opened their gates. Before limited emigration to the United States became possible again, a controversial group of a few hundred Germans was shipped to America by the military occupation authorities. Dubbed "Operation Paperclip", the scheme provided limited contracts to scientists and technicians in fields where Germans had made significant advances. As human war booty, these men accompanied tons of confiscated records, patents and blueprints and shiploads of prototype equipment and products. In due course most of this sophisticated contract labor force turned into bonafide immigrants. 550 men and their families, 85 per cent of the total number, elected to become American citizens.

From 1948 until the mid-sixties the German immigration quota of 28,000 persons annually was readily filled. A good portion of the emigrants consisted of young people looking for careers in industry and business. Others were expellees from the lost eastern territories or the Soviet-dominated land between the Oder and Elbe, now the German Democratic Republic. Though not eligible on the German quota, ethnic Germans deported from Eastern Europe, where their ancestors had moved in the 18th and 19th century, were among the new emigrants. Lastly, thousands of German women who had married American soldiers stationed in Germany went to the States with their returning husbands.

More recently, emigration from the Federal Republic of Germany has become insignificant, amounting rarely to 5,000 people a year. Jet travel, close political, business and military ties between the two countries have blurred the distinction between visitor and immigrant. Going to America is no longer the almost irreversible step it was in the past. There is hardly any doubt that the presence of millions of descendants of German emigrants in the United States contributes to the emergence of a "special relationship" which, given continued propitious circumstances, could eventually match that which has bound the United States and Britain despite their wars of the past.

Statistics on postwar immigration to America in accordance with special quota regulations applicable to "displaced persons" and to political refugees from the communist sphere.

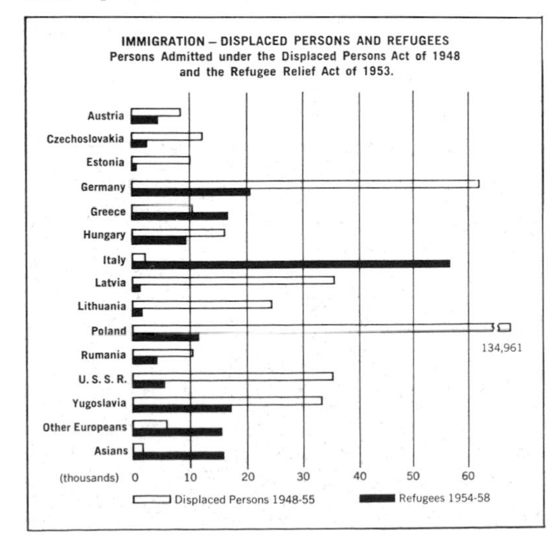

Der vollständige Zusammenbruch des „Dritten Reiches" im Jahr 1945 bedeutete den tiefsten Einschnitt in der ganzen deutschen Geschichte. Angesichts des Verlustes von Ostgebieten, die seit dem 18. Jahrhundert und länger zu Deutschland gehört hatten, und der Teilung des Landes nach den politischen Gesichtspunkten der Siegermächte, wäre es zweifellos zu einer Massenauswanderung gekommen, hätten Amerika oder andere überseeische Länder ihre Tore geöffnet. So blieb es bei Ausnahmen wie jener umstrittenen Gruppe von nur wenigen hundert Deutschen, die lange vor dem Beginn einer neuen, quotierten Amerikaauswanderung von den Besatzungsbehörden in die USA gebracht wurde. *Operation Paperclip* lautete das Codewort für dieses Unternehmen, bei dem hochqualifizierte Techniker und Wissenschaftler aus jenen Fachgebieten, auf denen Deutschland technologische Durchbrüche erzielt hatte, ihre Arbeit mit zeitlich begrenzten Verträgen fortsetzen konnten. Als „menschliche Kriegsbeute" begleiteten sie Tonnen von beschlagnahmten Aufzeichnungen, Patentschriften und Blaupausen und ganze Schiffsladungen von Prototypen und technischem Gerät. Es dauerte nicht lange, bis diese hochspezialisierten „Gastarbeiter" regulären Einwanderern gleichgestellt wurden. 85 Prozent von ihnen – insgesamt 550 Männer – entschlossen sich schließlich, mit ihren Familien in den USA zu bleiben und amerikanische Bürger zu werden.

Von 1948 bis zur Mitte der 60er Jahre wurde die deutsche Einwanderungsquote von 28 000 Personen jährlich beständig ausgeschöpft. Viele der Emigranten waren junge Leute, die in Industrie und Wirtschaft Karriere machen wollten. Andere kamen als Heimatvertriebene aus den verlorenen Ostgebieten oder der sowjetisch besetzten Zone zwischen Oder und Elbe, der heutigen Deutschen Demokratischen Republik. Nicht auf die deutsche Quote angerechnet wurden die Einwanderer aus deutschstämmigen Minderheiten Osteuropas, die nun aus jenen Ländern ausgesiedelt wurden, in die ihre Vorfahren im 18. und 19. Jahrhundert emigriert waren. Als letzte Sondergruppe bleiben jene Tausende von deutschen Frauen zu erwähnen, die in Deutschland stationierte amerikanische Soldaten heirateten und später mit ihren Männern in die USA übersiedelten.

In jüngster Zeit ist die Auswanderung aus der Bundesrepublik Deutschland in die Vereinigten Staaten praktisch bedeutungslos geworden: nur selten erreicht sie noch Größenordnungen von 5 000 Menschen pro Jahr. Der moderne Flugverkehr und die engen politischen, wirtschaftlichen und militärischen Bande zwischen den beiden Staaten haben den Unterschied zwischen vorübergehenden Besuchern und Emigranten verwischt. Nach Amerika zu gehen ist kein irreversibler Schritt mehr, wie er es in der Vergangenheit so oft war. Heute kann kaum noch ein Zweifel daran bestehen, daß die Gegenwart von Millionen Menschen deutscher Abstammung in den Vereinigten Staaten zur Entwicklung einer „besonderen Beziehung" beiträgt, die, wenn die Voraussetzungen weiterhin günstig bleiben, eines Tages jener gleichkommen könnte, die die Vereinigten Staaten und Großbritannien, trotz früherer Kriege, miteinander verbindet.

Statistik der amerikanischen Nachkriegseinwanderung unter den Sondergesetzen für »Displaced Persons« (im und nach dem Krieg Zwangsverschleppte bzw. Heimatvertriebene) und für politische Flüchtlinge aus dem kommunistischen Machtbereich.

Top right: The "European Recovery Program" (ERP), known for short as the "Marshall Plan" after its initiator, Secretary of State George C. Marshall, was a landmark in the establishment of postwar German-American relations, as was likewise the Berlin Airlift, organized by General Lucius D. Clay during the Berlin blockade of 1948/49. Two countries, formerly enemies, became political partners and enjoyed an era of halcyon amity lasting well into the 60s.

Rechts oben: Das »Europäische Wiederaufbauprogramm«, nach seinem Initiator George C. Marshall kurz »Marshallplan« genannt, und die von General Lucius D. Clay während der Blockade Berlins 1948/49 organisierte »Luftbrücke« waren zwei Marksteine in den deutsch-amerikanischen Beziehungen der Nachkriegszeit. Die ehemaligen Gegner, zu politischen Partnern geworden, wuchsen zu Freunden zusammen, deren Verhältnis bis weit in die 60er Jahre hinein so gut wie ungetrübt war.

The personal initiative of American citizens led to the founding of the relief organization CARE in 1946 (Cooperative for American Remittances to Europe) which up until 1963 distributed donations valued at over 300 million Marks to the needy in West Germany and Berlin. The illustration shows Dr. Ernst Reuter, the Governing Mayor of Berlin from 1948 to 1953, presenting the one-millionth CARE package.

Amerikanische Privatinitiative gründete 1946 die Hilfsorganisation CARE (»Cooperative for American Remittances to Europe«, etwa: Arbeitsgemeinschaft zur Weiterleitung amerikanischer Hilfsgelder nach Europa), die bis 1963 Spenden im Wert von über 300 Millionen Mark an Bedürftige in Deutschland und Berlin verteilte. Die Abbildung zeigt Dr. Ernst Reuter, Berlins Regierenden Bürgermeister von 1948 bis 1953, bei der Übergabe des millionsten CARE-Pakets.

"All free men, wherever they may live, are citizens of Berlin, and, therefore, as a free man, I take pride in the words: 'Ich bin ein Berliner'": President John F. Kennedy addressing the people of Berlin on June 26th, 1963.

»Alle freien Menschen, wo immer sie leben mögen, sind Bürger Berlins, und deshalb bin ich als freier Mann stolz darauf, sagen zu können: ›Ich bin ein Berliner!‹«. Präsident John F. Kennedy in seiner Rede vor dem Schöneberger Rathaus am 26. Juni 1963.

Bottom row of photos, from the left: Chancellor Willy Brandt, visiting the U.S. in September 1973 on the occasion of the Federal Republic's becoming a member of the United Nations, seen here together with the U.S. Secretary of State and immigrant from Germany, Henry Kissinger; 1975 in Washington: Walter Scheel, then president of the Federal Republic of Germany, presenting John J. McCloy, former American high commissioner for Germany, the charter of the German "McCloy Fund" establishing a German-American exchange program (at the right, President Gerald Ford; in the background, Secretary of State Henry Kissinger and Foreign Minister Hans Dietrich Genscher); June, 1982, in Bonn: President Ronald Reagan and First Lady Nancy on their state visit, receiving a present from Chancellor Helmut Schmidt (left, with his wife Loki): two American eagles which were raised in Germany.

Untere Bildreihe von links: Der deutsche Bundeskanzler Willy Brandt, im September 1973 anläßlich der Aufnahme der Bundesrepublik in die Vereinten Nationen zu Besuch in den USA, mit dem amerikanischen Außenminister und Deutschland-Emigranten Henry Kissinger; Bundespräsident Walter Scheel präsentiert dem früheren amerikanischen Hochkommissar für Deutschland, John J. McCloy, 1975 in Washington die Gründungsurkunde der deutschen »McCloy-Stiftung« für deutsch-amerikanischen Austausch (rechts Präsident Gerald Ford, im Hintergrund die Außenminister Henry Kissinger und Hans Dietrich Genscher); Präsident Ronald Reagan und seine Gattin Nancy erhalten während ihres Staatsbesuchs in Bonn 1982 von Bundeskanzler Helmut Schmidt (links, mit Loki Schmidt) zwei in Deutschland gezogene Weißkopf-Seeadler – das amerikanische Wappentier – zum Geschenk.

The first two chancellors of the Federal Republic of Germany on official visits to the U.S.: Konrad Adenauer with President Dwight D. Eisenhower (a descendent of 18th-century German immigrants), and Ludwig Erhard with President Lyndon B. Johnson.

Die beiden ersten Kanzler der Bundesrepublik Deutschland auf Staatsbesuch in den USA: Konrad Adenauer mit Präsident Dwight D. Eisenhower, einem Nachfahren deutscher Einwanderer des 18. Jahrhunderts, und Ludwig Erhard mit Präsident Lyndon B. Johnson.

Philadelphia in 1702, a year after receiving its charter as a city. The "City of Brotherly Love", which derived its name from an early Christian community in Asia Minor, was set up as the proving ground for William Penn's "holy experiment", a colony where – in accordance with Quaker beliefs and the philosophy of the Enlightenment – religious tolerance, pacifism and peaceful community living with the natives was to be achieved. Germantown, incorporated into Philadelphia in 1854, was then two hours away in the primeval forest.

Philadelphia 1702, ein Jahr nach seiner offiziellen Erhebung zur Stadt. Der Ortsname, der »Bruderliebe« bedeutet und auf eine frühchristliche Gemeinde in Kleinasien zurückgeht, war programmatisch für William Penns »Heiliges Experiment« einer Kolonie, in der – entsprechend dem Quäkerglauben und der Philosophie der Aufklärung – religiöse Toleranz, Pazifismus und ein friedliches Zusammenleben mit den Eingeborenen verwirklicht werden sollten. – Germantown, seit 1854 ein Stadtteil Philadelphias, lag damals noch zwei Wegstunden außerhalb im Urwald.

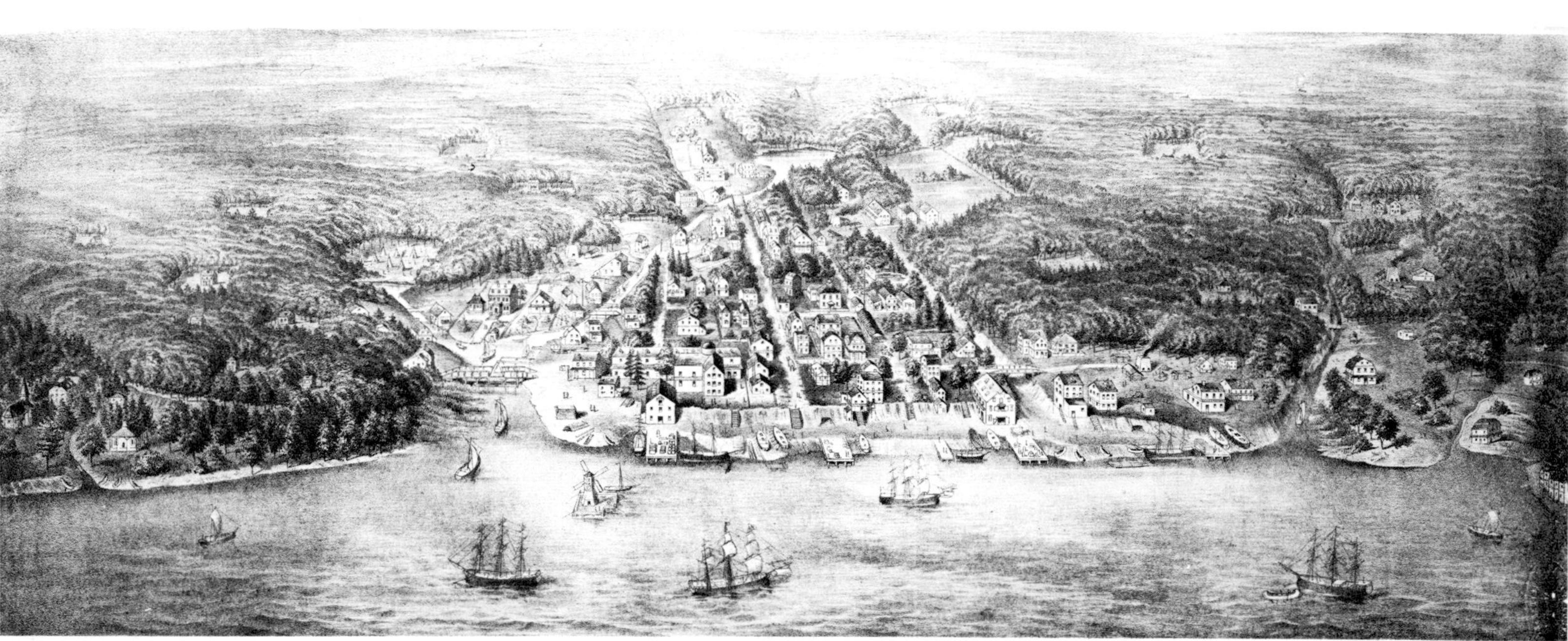

THE CENTENNIAL CITY, WHEN TWENTY YEARS OLD.

PHILADELPHIA IN 1702

The New World

The diverse expectations of German immigrants in the changing course of American history

Die Neue Welt

Wechselnde Erwartungshorizonte deutscher Einwanderer im Verlauf der amerikanischen Geschichte

Nachlaß. Zahme Xenien. IX. 137

Den Vereinigten Staaten.

Amerika, du hast es besser
Als unser Continent, das alte,
Hast keine verfallene Schlösser
745 Und keine Basalte.
Dich stört nicht im Innern,
Zu lebendiger Zeit,
Unnützes Erinnern
Und vergeblicher Streit.

750 Benutzt die Gegenwart mit Glück!
Und wenn nun eure Kinder dichten,
Bewahre sie ein gut Geschick
Vor Ritter-, Räuber- und Gespenstergeschichten.

Goethe's oft-quoted verse greeting to the United States, the pithiest of all the statements issuing from Europe over the course of centuries, in which the "New World" was apostrophized as a new beginning, a nation without a history. First published in "Wendts Musenalmanach für 1831" when the poet was 81 years old.

Goethes vielzitierte Verse an die Vereinigten Staaten, das prägnanteste Zeugnis für den Mythos des Neubeginns und der Geschichtslosigkeit, mit dem Europa die »Neue Welt« jahrhundertelang umgab. Erstmals veröffentlicht in »Wendts Musenalmanach für 1831«, im 82. Lebensjahr des Dichters.

The German emigrants' pattern of expectations in the New World, on the surface at least, seems to have remained unchanged over the last three centuries. On the idealistic, intangible side there was "freedom"; on the materialistic, tangible side there were "possessions" which the emigrant hoped to acquire. Goethe expressed contempt for the reactionary and stifling limitations of the Old World in his famous dictum, "America, your lot is fairer." In more recent times both aspects were blended into the much flaunted maxim: "America, the land of unlimited opportunities."

Since the great majority of Germans who swarmed to North America obviously came for economic reasons, the entire phenomenon of migration has readily been classified by its opponents, and by disenchanted emigrants themselves, as a crassly materialistic movement. In contrast there is the romantic view, exemplified by banished Anabaptists or the persecuted political activist, of haunted, chased men and women and children finding freedom at last on American soil. Such oversimplifications, tempting as they are, lose sight of the fact that the seven to eight million Germans came from every conceivable rung of the social ladder in Germany, from Nobel Prize laureates to deported convicts, to cite the extremes. They also came at entirely different periods of history. Not only did the conditions in their homeland differ drastically over the period but also the America of their expectations did not remain the same. Those who came during the formative years were part of the forces that shaped the new society, whereas the latecomers were shaped by a nation to which they were merely additions.

Until 1681, when William Penn was given the proprietorship of a large stretch of virgin land, absolving the British government of a debt owed his father, no appeal was made to solicit settlers from continental Europe. The other European powers, France, Spain, Holland and Sweden, who shared in the earliest stage of colonization in North America, were not too eager to let foreigners migrate to their settlements on the coast. The presence of a few Germans in various colonies during the 17th century does not alter the fact that New France, New Spain, New Netherland, and New Sweden were thought of as extensions of the power of the respective motherlands. Eventually, the English prevailed along the entire coastal area that was to become the territory of the original 13 American states. The French and the Spaniards remained at the northern, western and southern fringes.

Die von den deutschen Emigranten an ein Leben in der Neuen Welt geknüpften Erwartungen scheinen – zumindest an der Oberfläche – über die drei Jahrhunderte hinweg unverändert geblieben zu sein. Auf der idealistischen, immateriellen Seite war es die „Freiheit", auf der materiell greifbaren der Wohlstand, den man zu erlangen hoffte. Goethes berühmter Vers: „Amerika, du hast es besser" ließ Verachtung für die lähmenden, reaktionären Beschränkungen im alten Europa spüren, während eine spätere Epoche den materiellen und den idealistischen Aspekt zu dem vielzitierten Wort verschmolz: „Amerika, das Land der unbegrenzten Möglichkeiten."

Da die große Mehrzahl der Deutschen, die nach Amerika zogen, ganz unverkennbar wirtschaftliche Motive hatte, konnte die Auswanderung von ihren Gegnern (und von enttäuschten Emigranten selbst) als eine krass materialistische Bewegung dargestellt werden. Dem gegenüber steht die romantische Vorstellung – illustriert mit verbannten Wiedertäufern oder politischen Flüchtlingen – von den verfolgten und gehetzten Männern, Frauen und Kindern, die erst auf amerikanischem Boden ihre Freiheit fanden. Derartige Vereinfachungen, so verführerisch sie sein mögen, verlieren die Tatsache aus den Augen, daß die sieben bis acht Millionen deutschen Einwanderer aus allen nur vorstellbaren Schichten des sozialen Spektrums kamen – vom Nobelpreisträger bis zum deportierten Sträfling, um zwei Extreme zu nennen. Überdies kamen sie in gänzlich verschiedenen historischen Epochen: nicht nur die Verhältnisse in ihrer Heimat wandelten sich in den drei Jahrhunderten von Grund auf – auch das Amerika ihrer Hoffnungen und Sehnsüchte blieb nicht das gleiche. Diejenigen, die in einer frühen Entwicklungsphase kamen, wurden Teil jener Kräfte, die die neue Gesellschaft prägten und gestalteten; die Spätankömmlinge hingegen wurden von der Nation geprägt, zu der sie nur noch Hinzufügungen waren.

Bis 1681, als William Penn von der britischen Regierung in Abzahlung einer gegenüber seinem Vater bestehenden Schuld ein ausgedehntes Stück unberührten Landes als Eigentümerkolonie zugesprochen erhielt, hatte England keinerlei Anstrengungen unternommen, Siedler aus dem kontinentalen Europa nach Amerika zu locken. Auch die anderen europäischen Mächte – Frankreich, Spanien, Holland und Schweden –, die sich in die früheste Phase der Kolonisierung Nordamerikas teilten, waren nicht sonderlich daran

In the 1600s, until the creation of Pennsylvania, Germans were to be occasionally encountered as contract labor of colonization companies. The first handful came to Jamestown in 1608, just one year after the founding of the first English colony. Captain John Smith, president of the first council in Virginia, had trouble with these "High Germans" when they tried to cast their lot with the Native Americans. He bestowed upon them the famous epithet "those damned Dutchmen" which was to remain alive in American speech for three centuries. The beginnings of English colonization in America are still frequently overshadowed by the aura created by the migration of persecuted Puritans more than a decade later, but Captain Smith had a clearer view of the colonist's expectations: "Who is he, that hath judgement, courage, and any industry, or quality, with understanding will leave his country . . . were it not to advance his fortunes by enjoying his deserts!"

To advance their fortunes, men like Peter Minnewit and Jacob Leisler had signed up for service with the Dutch and Swedish companies, men like Augustin Herman and Peter Hack had entered the profitable tobacco trade, but they would have gone anywhere else if opportunity had beckoned.

When the Quaker, William Penn, obtained the American province that was to carry his family's name, the picture seemed to change. Penn, who had previously visited kindred spirits in the Palatinate, the Rhineland and the Netherlands, envisaged a colony where men could live a saintly life. Not cut off from the world, but in a climate in which even the successful businessman could be free from the temptations of greed and power. It was to be a New World in every respect where the newly arrived Europeans would live in harmony with the native inhabitants. It was to be the "Holy Experiment". In 1681, Penn proceeded to appeal directly to religious dissenters in England, Holland and Germany to join him in this experiment. The German edition of his promotional tract, *Some Account of the Province of Pennsylvania in America,* became the first book on America that had a common appeal. Pastorius and others tell how this account was eagerly read in sectarian circles along the Rhine.

interessiert, fremde Nationalitäten in ihren Kolonien Fuß fassen zu lassen. Die Anwesenheit einzelner Deutscher in verschiedenen Kolonien bereits im 17. Jahrhundert ändert nichts an der Tatsache, daß Neu-Frankreich, Neu-Spanien, Neu-Niederlande und Neu-Schweden vor allem als Erweiterungen des Machtbereichs des jeweiligen Mutterlandes gedacht waren. Auf dem Ostküstenstreifen, auf dem sich später die 13 Staaten der ursprünglichen USA konstituierten, errang schließlich England die alleinige Vorherrschaft. Franzosen und Spanier behaupteten sich in den nördlich, westlich und südlich anschließenden Gebieten.

Vor der Gründung Pennsylvaniens kamen im 18. Jahrhundert einzelne Deutsche im Dienst der Kolonialgesellschaften nach Amerika. Eine Handvoll Deutscher findet sich bereits 1608 in Jamestown, nur ein Jahr nach der Gründung der ersten englischen Kolonie. Captain John Smith, Vorsitzender des ersten Bürgerrates von Virginia, hatte mit diesen „Hochdeutschen" seine Schwierigkeiten, als sie begannen, sich mit den amerikanischen Ureinwohnern einzulassen. Smith entfuhr der berühmte Ausspruch von den *damned Dutchmen*, den „verdammten Deutschen", der in der amerikanischen Umgangssprache über drei Jahrhunderte lebendig bleiben sollte. Das Bild der ersten englischen Kolonisatoren wird bis heute von der Aura der Pilgerväter, der vor religiöser Verfolgung geflüchteten Puritaner bestimmt, doch diese trafen erst ein Jahrzehnt später in der Neuen Welt ein. Captain Smith beurteilte die Erwartungen der frühen Siedler wesentlich nüchterner: „Wer, der klaren Verstand, Mut, Fleiß oder eine besondere Fähigkeit sein eigen nennt, würde sein Vaterland verlassen . . . wäre es nicht, um sein Los zu verbessern und seinen wohlverdienten Lohn zu genießen!"

Um ihr „Los zu verbessern" hatten sich Männer wie Peter Minnewit und Jacob Leisler bei den holländischen und schwedischen Gesellschaften verpflichtet, waren Augustin Herman und Peter Hack in den gewinnträchtigen Tabakhandel eingestiegen – doch sie alle wären in ein anderes Land gegangen, hätten sich dort bessere Chancen geboten.

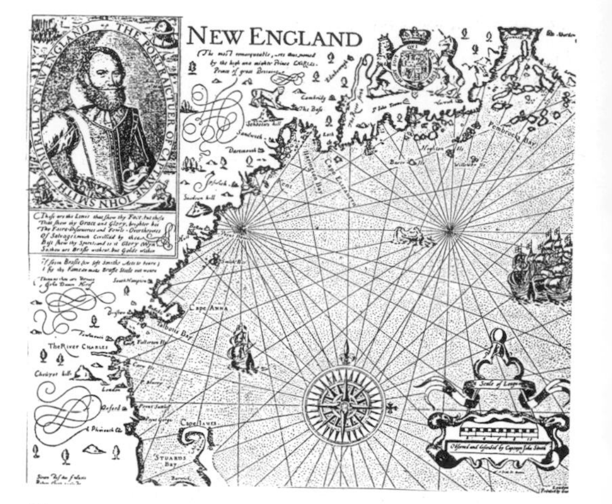

The coast of New England on a map drawn in 1614 by its explorer, John Smith. Even before the establishment of Pennsylvania, we can find German settlers in the early colonies; their total number, however, was of no great significance.

Die Küsten Neu-Englands auf der von ihrem Erforscher John Smith 1614 gezeichneten Karte. Bereits vor der Gründung Pennsylvaniens lassen sich in den frühen Kolonien vereinzelt deutsche Siedler nachweisen; ihre Gesamtzahl fällt jedoch kaum ins Gewicht.

Peter Minnewit (also known as Minuit) from Wesel on the Rhine making his legendary bargain with the Algonquin Indians, in which he purchased Manhattan Island on behalf of the Dutch West India Company for beads and fabrics worth a mere 60 guilders.

Peter Minnewit (auch Minuit) aus Wesel am Rhein bei seinem legendären Tauschhandel mit den Algonkin-Indianern, der die Insel Manhattan 1626 für Ketten und Tuche im Wert von 60 Gulden in den Besitz der niederländischen Westindischen Kompanie brachte.

Wiliam Penn receiving the charter of his new colony from the hand of King Charles II. This "Charter of Establishment", which calls the colony Pennsylvania in honor of Penn's father, was signed by the king on 14 March 1681.

William Penn erhält die am 14. März 1681 unterzeichnete Gründungscharter für die nach seinem Vater benannte Kolonie Pennsylvanien aus der Hand von König Charles II.

William Penn's missive to the Delaware Indians, written in England in the spring of 1682. Penn promises the natives of his colony that he will "order all things in such manner that we may all live in love and peace one with another." At the left, a note written by the deliverer of the message, in which he tells us that it was read to the Indians with the assistance of an interpreter. The famous treaty between Penn and the Delawares was probably not signed until November of 1683, after the arrival of the first German settlers.

Sendschreiben William Penns an die Delaware-Indianer, abgefaßt in England im Frühjahr 1682. Penn verspricht den Ureinwohnern seiner Kolonie, »alle Dinge so zu ordnen, daß wir in Liebe und Frieden zusammenleben können«. Links unten ein Vermerk des Überbringers, wonach die Botschaft den Indianern mit Hilfe eines Dolmetschers vorgelesen worden sei. Der berühmte Vertragsabschluß zwischen Penn und den Delawaren fand wahrscheinlich erst im November 1683, bereits nach Ankunft der ersten deutschen Siedler, statt

The Great God who is the power and wisdom that made you and me Incline your hearts to Righteousness Love and peace. This I send to Assure you of my Love, and to desire your Love to my friends, and when the Great God brings me among you I intend to order all things in such manner that we may all live in Love and peace one with another which I hope the Great God will Incline both me and you to do. I seek nothing but the honor of his name, and that we who are his workmanship, may do that which is well pleasing to him. The man which delivers this unto you, is my Special friend Sober wise and Loving, you may believe him. I have already taken Care that none of my people wrong you, by good Laws I have provided for that purpose, nor will I ever allow any of my people to sell Rumme to make your people Drunk. If any thing should be out of order, expect when I come, it shall be mended, and I will bring you some things of our Country that are useful and pleasing to you. So I rest In ye Love of our god yt made us I am

England 25: 2: 1682

Your Loving Freind

Wm Penn

I read this to the Indians by an Interpreter the 6 mo 1682 Tho Holme

Like the English Quakers, German and Swiss Mennonites were immensely practical people. No matter how burdensome life on earth might be, it had to be mastered in order to pave the way to heaven. All they were longing for was a form of society in which they and other Christian believers could work their looms or till their land unfettered by kings and popes. It was this search for a perfect society under God that prompted the first believers to embark on a new start in America. Enthusiasm for the novelty of the experiment was not dampened by the long, onerous voyage or by the hardships of the first years.

Not even impractical enthusiasts who followed later – men and women who went to the New World to be better prepared for the impending end of the world altogether – had illusions before embarking nor regrets after experiencing the wilderness. The humble baker, Conrad Beissel, who landed in Boston in 1720 with several companions in search of a saintly life, knew precisely why he had gone to an unknown world: "America sees a lily blooming," he wrote, whereas "for Europe the sun has set at bright midday." By the way, Beissel and friends experienced early what innumerable immigrants found out the hard way: the tremendous distances in America. They took several months to get from Boston to Pennsylvania, their original destination.

New York harbor at the time of Frankfurt-born Jacob Leisler, who took over the administration of the colony in 1689 when its English governor left New York in connection with the political turmoil caused by the Glorious Revolution in his homeland. In 1691 Leisler was executed for high treason, but exonerated posthumously four years later.

Der Hafen von New York zur Zeit Jacob Leislers, eines gebürtigen Frankfurters, der 1689 die Regierung der Kolonie übernahm, nachdem der englische Gouverneur die Stadt im Zusammenhang mit den politischen Umwälzungen im Mutterland verlassen hatte. 1691 als Verräter hingerichtet, wurde Leisler vier Jahre später posthum rehabilitiert.

Erst als der Quäker William Penn zum Eigentümer der amerikanischen Kolonie wurde, die den Namen seiner Familie tragen sollte, schien sich das Bild zu wandeln. Penn, der schon früher Gleichgesinnte und Glaubensgenossen in der Pfalz, dem Rheinland und den Niederlanden aufgesucht hatte, plante eine Kolonie, in der die Menschen ein frommes Leben führen konnten: nicht abgekapselt von der Welt, sondern in einem Klima, das selbst den erfolgreichen Geschäftsmann vor den Versuchungen der Macht und der Besitzgier bewahren würde. Es sollte in jeder Hinsicht eine „Neue Welt" sein, in der die Neuankömmlinge aus Europa auch mit den Eingeborenen in Eintracht zusammenlebten – ein „heiliges Experiment". 1681 wandte sich Penn an religiöse Dissidenten in England, Holland und Deutschland und forderte sie auf, bei seinem Experiment mitzutun. Die Übersetzung seines Werbetraktats, *Eine Nachricht wegen der Landschaft Pennsylvania in Amerika,* wurde zum ersten Werk der Amerikaliteratur, dem in Deutschland Breitenwirkung beschieden war. Pastorius und andere berichten von der Begierde, mit der Penns Schrift in den Sektiererkreisen entlang des Rheins gelesen wurde.

Wie die englischen Quäker, so waren auch die deutschen und schweizerischen Mennoniten ungemein lebenstüchtige Menschen. Wie beschwerlich das irdische Dasein auch immer sein mochte – sie wollten es meistern, um sich auf diese Weise den Weg ins Himmelreich zu ebnen. Sie sehnten sich nach nichts anderem als einer Gesellschaftsform, in der sie und andere Menschen christlichen Glaubens unbehelligt von Königen oder Päpsten ihr Land bestellen oder an ihrem Webstuhl arbeiten konnten. Es war diese Suche nach einer vollkommenen Gesellschaft unter Gott, die die ersten von ihnen zu einem neuen Anfang in die Neue Welt ziehen ließ. Auch die lange, beschwerliche Seereise und die Mühsal der ersten Jahre taten ihrer Begeisterung angesichts der Neuartigkeit des Experiments keinen Abbruch.

The success of Penn's Holy Experiment and the attending publicity led to the awakening of a desire to better oneself among many who were not religiously motivated. Those with means of their own could simply head for a Dutch port and wait for a vessel that would take them to England where, in turn, they could contract with a captain for the voyage to Philadelphia. Only ships under the English flag were allowed to carry passengers and goods to the English colonies. The English government was unconcerned, however, as to who was taking passage to Pennsylvania or other American colonies. It was not until the mass exodus from the Rhinelands in 1709 that the government found itself confronted with the emigration problem. Even then, only 2,841 men, women and children were provided with free passage in exchange for future work on the production of naval stores in the colony of New York.

Land speculators and promoters tried time and again to interest the English government in their projects, conveniently describing them as useful defense barriers against encroachments of the French along the western frontiers of Pennsylvania and Virginia. With the exception of the subsidized transport of Germans to Nova Scotia in the 1750s which was organized in order to people a colony depleted by the deportation of the Catholic French settlers, no project was ever aided by the government again. The entire Atlantic migration thus became a population transfer solely carried out by private enterprise with an occasional helping hand from religious bodies.

Initially, enterprising Quakers had a firm grip on the passenger trade. Some established themselves in Rotterdam where immigrants were loaded on English ships, some also Quaker-owned, and after the required stopover in an English port, they sailed on to Philadelphia. The early proprietors of Carolina followed this pattern. A Swiss-born Quaker in London, John Ochs, tried with less luck to include Virginia in this trade. For years Quakers deftly mixed their devotion to the meeting house with their keen interest in the counting house. Thousands of willing emigrants from German-speaking regions became a desirable return-freight for ships that were bringing colonial staples to England. When paying passengers were becoming scarce, a credit system was devised that was organized on the same lines as those of the transportation of indentured servants, which had worked well for many decades. These servants, mainly from the British Isles, had been signed up under service contracts for a certain

At right: In 1727 Pennsylvania became the first colony to require immigrants to swear an oath of allegiance. The illustration shows the signatures attested to that oath on 16 October 1727 by new arrivals from the Palatinate.

Rechts: Pennsylvanien begann 1727 als erste Kolonie, von den Einwanderern die Ablegung eines Treueids zu verlangen. Die Abbildung zeigt am 16. Oktober 1727 unter einen solchen Eid gesetzte Unterschriften pfälzischer Neuankömmlinge.

Selbst weniger lebenspraktische Begeisterte, die ihnen später folgten – Männer und Frauen, die in die Neue Welt gingen, um besser auf den bevorstehenden Untergang alles Irdischen vorbereitet zu sein – hatten weder Illusionen vor der Einschiffung, noch bedauerten sie ihren Schritt, nachdem sie die Wildnis kennengelernt hatten. Conrad Beissel, der bescheidene Bäcker, der 1720 auf der Suche nach einem „heiligen Leben" mit einigen Begleitern in Boston landete, wußte genau, warum er in eine unerforschte Welt gezogen war: „Amerika siehet eine Lilie blühen", so schrieb er, während ihm für „Europa die Sonne am hellen Mittag untergegangen" war. Übrigens blieb auch Beissel und seinen Freunden die Erfahrung nicht erspart, die nach ihnen noch unzählige Einwanderer späterer Generationen machen mußten: wie gewaltig die Entfernungen in Amerika waren. Sie brauchten mehrere Monate, um von Boston nach Pennsylvanien, ihrem eigentlichen Ziel, zu gelangen.

Der Erfolg von Penns Heiligem Experiment und das Aufsehen, das es erregte, ließ auch unter vielen nicht religiös Motivierten den Wunsch entstehen, ihr Leben zu bessern. Wer über die Mittel verfügte, brauchte nur in einen holländischen Hafen zu reisen und auf ein Schiff zu warten, das ihn nach England mitnahm, wo er dann mit einem englischen Kapitän seine Überfahrt nach Philadelphia aushandeln konnte. Nur Schiffe unter englischer Flagge durften Passagiere und Waren in die englischen Kolonien befördern. Wer diese Passagiere waren, die sich nach Pennsylvanien oder anderen Kolonien in Amerika einschifften, war der englischen Regierung zunächst relativ gleichgültig. Erst durch den Massenexodus aus den rheinischen Ländern im Jahre 1709 sah man sich in England unmittelbar mit dem Auswandererproblem konfrontiert. Selbst jetzt beschränkte sich das Engagement der Regierung jedoch auf die Finanzierung der Überfahrt für nur 2841 Männer, Frauen und Kinder, die sich dafür als Arbeitskräfte bei der Produktion von Schiffsausrüstung in der Kolonie New York verpflichten mußten.

Landspekulanten und Auswanderungswerber versuchten immer wieder, die englische Regierung für ihre Siedlungsprojekte zu interessieren, indem sie diese als nützliche Barrieren gegen französische Übergriffe an den Westgrenzen Virginias und Pennsylvaniens anpriesen. Mit Ausnahme eines Transports von Deutschen nach Nova Scotia im Jahre 1750, wo eine durch die Deportation französischer Katholiken entvölkerte Kolonie neu besiedelt werden sollte, hat die englische Regierung jedoch keines dieser Projekte aufgegriffen. So entwickelte sich die transatlantische Auswanderung auf rein privatwirtschaftlichen Bahnen, allenfalls mit gelegentlicher Unterstützung durch religiöse Körperschaften.

In den ersten Jahrzehnten wurde die Passagierbeförderung von unternehmerischen Quäkern dominiert. Einige ließen sich in Rotterdam nieder, wo die Auswanderer auf englische Schiffe – teils ebenfalls in Quäker-Besitz – verfrachtet wurden, die sie nach dem obligatorischen Zwischenstopp in einem englischen Hafen nach Philadelphia beförderten. Die ersten Eigentümer von Carolina verfuhren nach dem gleichen Schema. Ein schweizerischer Quäker in London namens John Ochs versuchte, auch Virginia in dieses Geschäft mit einzubeziehen, jedoch mit geringerem Erfolg. Dergleichen gerechte Teilung ihrer Hingabe an Kirche und Kontorkasse war lange Jahre ein Charakteristikum der Angehörigen der „Gesellschaft der Freunde". Tausende williger Emigranten aus deutschsprachigen Ländern wurden so zur beliebten Rück-

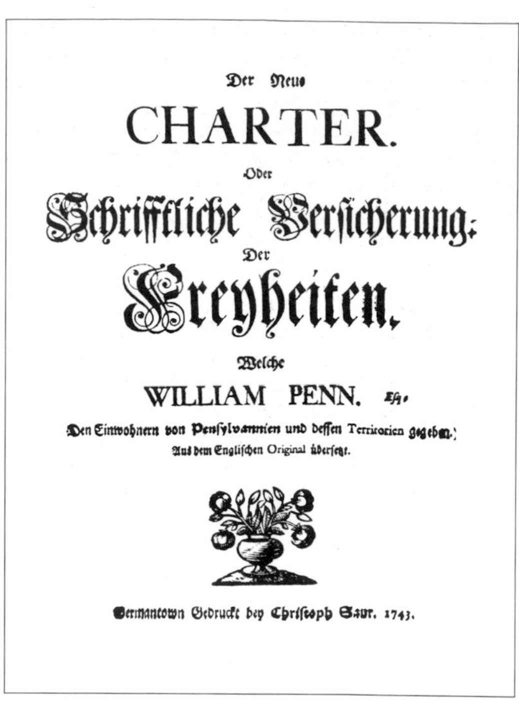

Der Neue
CHARTER.
Oder
Schrifftliche Versicherung:
Der
Freyheiten,
Welche
WILLIAM PENN. Esq.
Den Einwohnern von Pensylvanien und dessen Territorien gegeben;
Aus dem Englischen Original übersetzt.

Germantown Gedruckt bey Christoph Saur, 1743.

The title page of a German translation of the "Charter of Privileges", a revised fundamental law for the colony of Pennsylvania, which went into effect in 1701

Titelseite einer 1743 in Germantown gedruckten deutschen Übersetzung der »Charter of Privileges«, des 1701 in Kraft getretenen, revidierten Grundgesetzes der Kolonie Pennsylvanien.

Map of the English colonies in North America from the year 1754. The largest concentration of German settlers was located in Pennsylvania, with others to be found in Georgia, South and North Carolina, Virginia and Maryland. New York received the greater portion of the mass emigration from the Palatinate in 1708/09, but lost much of its attractiveness after the Palatine immigrants were recruited into forced labor. The immigration to the American interior started with the opening up of the West at the beginning of the 19th century.

Karte der englischen Kolonien in Nordamerika aus dem Jahr 1754. Neben dem statistisch dominierenden Pennsylvanien waren im 18. Jahrhundert auch Georgia, Süd- und Nord-Carolina, Virginia und Maryland wichtige Siedlungsgebiete deutscher Einwanderer. New York nahm einen großen Teil der pfälzischen Massenauswanderung von 1708/09 auf, verlor jedoch an Anziehungskraft, nachdem die Pfälzer dort zu Zwangsarbeiten herangezogen worden waren. Die Einwanderung ins amerikanische Binnenland begann erst mit der Erschließung des Westens zu Beginn des 19. Jahrhunderts.

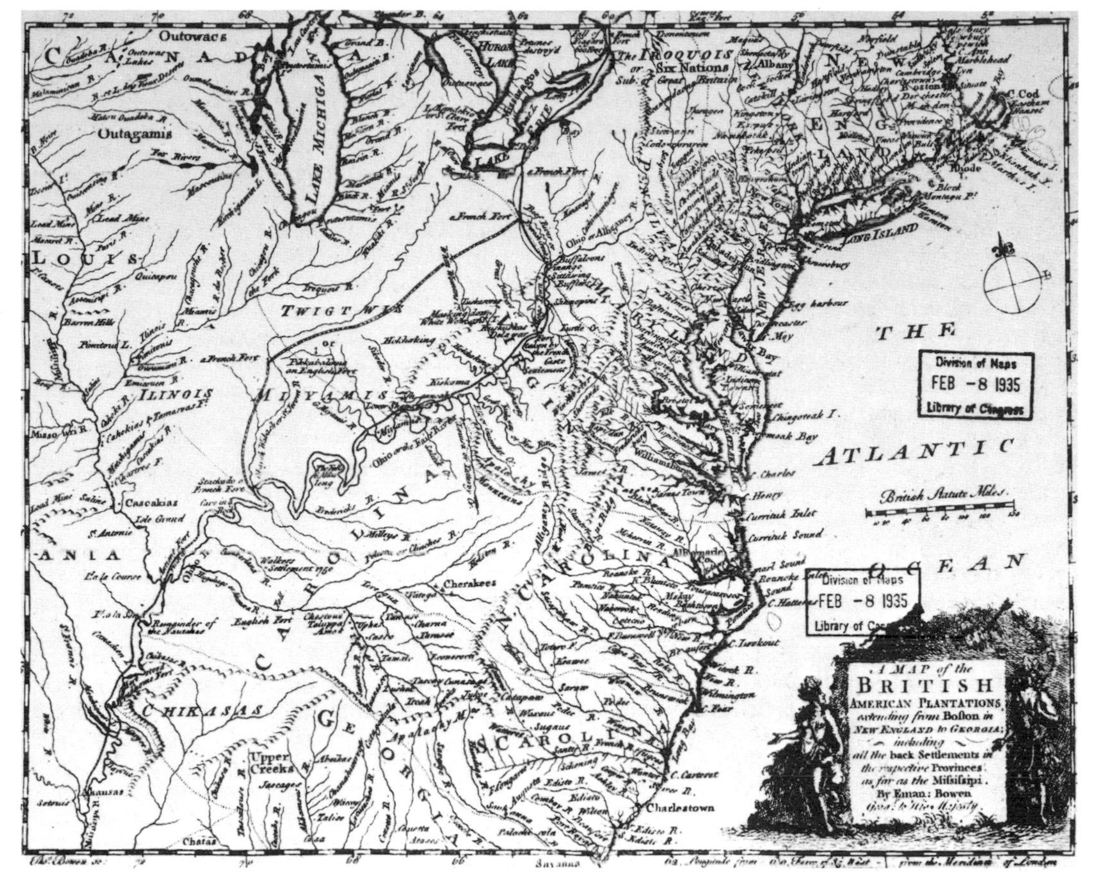

Printed and sold by Andrew Steuart, in Second-street.

This Indenture

Witnesseth, That Mary Elizabeth Bauer with the consent of her Father [illegible] Samuel Pleasants for her passage from Holland as also for other good Causes, she the said Mary hath bound and put her self, and by these Presents doth bind and put her self Servant to the said Samuel to serve him his Executors and Assigns, from the Day of the Date hereof, for and during the Term of five Years thence next ensuing. During all which Term, the said Servant her said Master his Executors, or Assigns, faithfully shall serve, and that honestly and obediently in all Things, as a good and dutiful Servant ought to do. AND the said Master his Executors and Assigns, during the Term, shall find and provide for the said Servant sufficient Meat, Drink, Apparel, Washing and Lodging,

freedom Dues

And for the true Performance hereof, both Parties bind themselves firmly unto each other by these Presents. In Witness whereof they have hereunto interchangably set their Hands and Seals, Dated the Twenty second Day of October in the Seventh Year of his Majesty's Reign; and in the Year of our Lord, one Thousand, seven Hundred and Sixty-Seven

Signed sealed and delivered in the Presence of

[illegible] Mayor

Maria Elisabetha Bauerin

German immigrant Maria Elisabeth Bauer's contract of redemption from the year 1767

Auslösungsvertrag der deutschen Einwanderin Maria Elisabeth Bauer aus dem Jahr 1767.

Herbert Hoover (1874–1964), president of the United States from 1929 to 1931; his ancestors bore the name Huber when they emigrated from Germany in the 18th century.

number of years in England and Ireland. Unless he had prior commitments from colonists, the captain would offer the services of his passengers "for sale" in the American port against payment of the passage money. For the increasing number of German and Swiss passengers who had no cash to pay upon embarkation, or who preferred to turn their cash into saleable goods, a modified system was devised. Upon entering the ship, the emigrant signed a regular passage contract payable upon or shortly after arrival. This did not make him technically a servant. In port, relatives, friends or persons willing to take him into service for 4 to 6 years, could pay the captain and the contract was fulfilled. Another method was used by those who brought merchandise with them. They would offer it to merchants in port and with the proceeds pay for their passage. Such were the ways of redeeming the passage under the "redemption system".

It can be stated that the great majority of German immigrants throughout the period from 1719 to the early part of the 19th century came as "redemptioners", including the Hoover, Eisenhower and Rockefeller families. For many thousands it was the only way to reach the desired destination. Most emigrants were fully aware of their obligations for a passage on credit. Some were duped, and as the system became extended to ever larger numbers of people, numerous abuses were committed. Illiterate, ignorant people could easily become victims of unscrupulous captains or merchants, but there are also the advertisements of captains looking for passengers who fled the ship after arrival.

Herbert Hoover (1874–1964), Präsident der USA von 1929–31, ein Nachfahre deutscher Einwanderer des 18. Jahrhunderts mit Namen Huber.

fracht für die Schiffe, die Kolonialwaren aus Amerika nach England gebracht hatten. Als zahlende Passagiere rar zu werden begannen, wurde ein Kreditsystem eingeführt, das jenem ähnelte, mit dem bereits seit Jahrzehnten Dienstpersonal von den britischen Inseln nach Amerika gebracht worden war. Diese Diener hatten sich bereits vor der Abreise schriftlich für eine bestimmte Anzahl von Jahren verpflichtet. Nach der Ankunft bot der Kapitän, soweit ihm nicht bereits Vormerkungen der Kolonisten vorlagen, die an Bord befindlichen *indentured servants* (vertraglich verpflichteten Diener) zum „Verkauf" an, womit er die ihm entstandenen Überfahrtskosten deckte. Für die wachsende Anzahl deutscher und schweizerischer Passagiere, die ohne Geld zur Einschiffung erschienen oder es vorzogen, ihr Bargeld in wiederverkäufliche Güter zu investieren, wurde dieses System modifiziert: Der Emigrant schloß, sobald er das Schiff betrat, einen normalen Beförderungsvertrag ab, der jedoch erst bei oder kurz nach der Ankunft zahlbar war. Auf diese Weise wurde er zum Schuldner, aber nicht zum vertraglich gebundenen, rechtlosen Diener. Nach der Ankunft konnten Verwandte, Freunde oder auch andere Personen, die ihn vier bis sechs Jahre bei sich arbeiten lassen wollten, die Überfahrt beim Kapitän bezahlen, und der Vertrag war erfüllt. Diejenigen Einwanderer, die Waren mitgebracht hatten, boten diese den Händlern im Hafen zum Kauf an und verschafften sich so das Geld zur Bezahlung der Passage. Dies waren die beiden Möglichkeiten, die Kosten der Überfahrt innerhalb des sogenannten „Redemptions-" oder Auslösungsverfahrens zu tilgen.

Ohne zu übertreiben kann man sagen, daß fast alle deutschen Einwanderer zwischen 1719 und dem Anfang des 19. Jahrhunderts als „Redemptionisten" nach Amerika kamen – einschließlich der Familien Hoover, Eisenhower und Rockefeller. Für viele Tausende war dies der einzige Weg, das Ziel ihrer Wünsche zu erreichen. Die meisten Auswanderer waren

The redemption system worked well on the whole. The most negative testimony on record was recorded precisely because it was not the norm. The worst abuses occurred after the Napoleonic wars. Increased publicity and the legislative activities of immigrant aid societies, such as the German societies in various ports, led to the abolition of the practice.
Prospective emigrants were in most cases better informed of what to expect than anti-emigration proclamations by governments would lead to believe. Numerous trans-atlantic letters warned and informed people. Christopher Saur, in a widely distributed letter, wrote from Germantown in 1725: "Nobody should sell himself to the Captain, but promise to pay on this side." Johannes Naas of Krefeld explained the redemption system in a letter from America in 1733: "For many young people it is very good that they cannot pay their own freight. These will sooner be provided for than those who have paid theirs, and they can have their bread with others and soon learn the ways of the country."
It is true that the expectations of emigrants differed according to their social status at home. Genuine farmers and trained craftsmen convinced of their own merit tended to be more realistic than destitute or unskilled people. The latter tended to expect an almost miraculous turn in their fortunes. Letters written after arrival in the new country often express to what extent expectations were met. Many waited with writing more than just greetings until they had sized up the country and had found a place for themselves. There were the negative letters too, which were carefully preserved by authorities to be used in anti-emigration campaigns. Many positive letters were intercepted and destroyed. But from among those that have survived we can gather one ever-recurrent theme – the freedom of the new country. Freedom, of course, meant many things to as many people. For Jochim Rieck, one of the convicts unloaded by the Hamburg authorities in 1752, it was most literal when he expressed his gratitude to the guardian of the workhouse. Christopher Saur wrote in 1740 to a prominent Frankfurt type-founder of the freedom to exercise any craft a person could reasonably master, and praised the absence of restrictive guilds. Johann Wilhelm Hoffmann confided to his diary in 1741: "On May 16th, 1741, I . . . left the village of Eysern in the Catholic part of Nassau-Siegen, and my fatherland in Europe. Glory to God alone, and may God be thanked many thousand times therefore." Then Hoffmann proceeds to refer to "the servitude in Siegen, in the form of manual labor and money." Jacob Gallmann wrote from Saxe-Gotha in South Carolina in 1738: "So you can see that I did well by my children to have left my fatherland and to have come here. We live under a very good, mild government."

sich der Verpflichtungen voll bewußt, die sie mit ihrer Überfahrt auf Kredit eingingen. Einige gingen Betrügern auf den Leim, und als das System auf immer zahlreichere Emigranten angewendet wurde, kam es auch zu zahlreichen Mißbräuchen. Ungebildete Analphabeten konnten nur allzu leicht skrupellosen Kapitänen oder Kaufleuten zum Opfer fallen – doch umgekehrt existieren auch Suchanzeigen von Schiffseignern, die ihrer vor Bezahlung der Passage durchgebrannten Passagiere wieder habhaft zu werden versuchten.
Im großen und ganzen funktionierte das Auslösungsverfahren nicht schlecht. Die negativsten Zeugnisse wurden eben deshalb aufgezeichnet, weil sie nicht die Norm waren. Zu den schlimmsten Auswüchsen kam es nach den Napoleonischen Kriegen. Erhöhte Publizität und juristische Gegenmaßnahmen der Einwandererhilfsorganisationen – etwa der „Deutschen Gesellschaften" in verschiedenen Hafenstädten – führten schließlich zur Abschaffung des Systems.
Die zukünftigen Emigranten waren in den meisten Fällen wesentlich besser über das informiert, was sie in Übersee erwartete, als es die Anti-Auswanderungs-Proklamationen der Regierungen vermuten lassen. Zahlreiche Briefe aus Amerika informierten die Menschen in der alten Heimat und machten sie auf mögliche Gefahren aufmerksam. Christopher Saur warnte 1725 in einem Brief aus Germantown, der weite Verbreitung fand: „Keiner verkauffe sich an der Capitain, jedoch verspreche diesseits zu bezahlen." Ein Johannes Naas aus Krefeld pries das Auslösungssystem in einem Brief aus dem Jahr 1733 mit der Begründung, daß es vielen jungen Leuten am ehesten zu Arbeit und Brot und dadurch auch zur Kenntnis der Lebensart des neuen Landes verhelfe.
Beträchtliche Unterschiede findet man in den Erwartungen, die Einwanderer mit unterschiedlichem sozialem Status nach Amerika mitbrachten. Hauptberufliche Bauern und ausgebildete Handwerker, die von ihrem Können überzeugt waren, sahen die Dinge realistischer als Habenichtse und ungelernte Arbeiter. Letztere neigten dazu, eine mirakulöse Wendung zum Besseren in ihrem Leben zu erhoffen. Viele der Briefe, die nach der Ankunft geschrieben wurden, lassen erkennen, inwieweit sich solche Erwartungen erfüllten. Andere Einwanderer zögerten, mehr als nur Grüße in die Heimat zu schicken, solange sie sich nicht in ihrem neuen Land umgesehen und einen Platz für sich gefunden hatten. Es kamen auch negative Briefe, die von den deutschen Behörden sorgfältig aufbewahrt wurden, um in Anti-Auswanderungs-Kampagnen Verwendung zu finden. Positive Berichte wurden nicht selten abgefangen und vernichtet. In den Briefen, die erhalten geblieben sind, findet sich ein ständig wiederkehrendes Hauptthema: die Freiheit, die man in der neuen Heimat genoß. Natürlich bedeutete „Freiheit" für jeden, der dieses Wort gebrauchte, etwas anderes. Für Jochim Rieck, einen der Sträflinge, die 1753 von den Hamburger Behörden nach Amerika abgeschoben wurden, war es Freiheit im wortwörtlichsten Sinn, wofür er sich in einem Brief an den Schließer seiner ehemaligen Besserungsanstalt bedankte. Christopher Saur schilderte einem bekannten Frankfurter Schriftgießer 1740 die Freiheit, jedes Handwerk auszuüben, das man einigermaßen beherrsche, ohne von den Zwängen des Zunftwesens gegängelt zu werden. Johann Wilhelm Hoffmann vertraute seinem Tagebuch 1741 folgende Herzensergießung an: „Am 16. Mai 1741 verließ ich das Dorf Eysern im katholischen Teil von Nassau-Siegen und mein Vaterland in Europa. Dem Herrn sei's gelobt und dem

The "redemptioner system", by which emigrants without means were coerced into selling themselves into slave-like service in return for passage, led to the foundation of the first German protective organizations. The building depicted is that of the German Society of Philadelphia.

Gebäude der 1764 zum Schutz deutscher Einwanderer gegründeten Deutschen Gesellschaft von Pennsylvanien in Philadelphia. Ähnliche Selbstschutzorganisationen entstanden in den folgenden Jahrzehnten auch in New York, Baltimore und Charleston.

"Tolerance" – an allegorical etching in the spirit of the Enlightenment by Daniel Chodowiecki (1726 – 1801).

Die Toleranz – allegorische Radierung aus dem Geist der Aufklärung von Daniel Chodowiecki (1726–1801)

New settlement in the wilderness: a log cabin is built in a clearing in the virgin forest, the way is cleared for fields to be planted, gardens and outbuildings are added, the forest recedes to the horizon line, and finally a new stone house replaces the old wooden one – illustrations of an immigrant's dream taken from O. Turner's "Pioneer History of the Holland Purchase", 1850.

Neuansiedlung in der Wildnis: auf einer Urwaldlichtung wird eine Blockhütte errichtet, Rodungen schaffen Raum für Felder, Gärten und Nebengebäude kommen hinzu, der Wald weicht an den Horizont zurück und schließlich ersetzt ein Steinhaus das alte hölzerne – Illustrationen eines Einwanderertraums, entnommen aus O. Turners »Pioneer History of the Holland Purchase«, 1850.

As unlikely as it may seem, the turbulent period of the American Revolution produced the largest number ever of German travel books on North America: the army doctor J.D. Schöpf (1752–1800) was only one of many officers of the German subsidiary troops who put pen to paper and published their observations on the land and its inhabitants, thereby creating a long-enduring incentive to immigration.

Reise
durch einige der mittlern und südlichen
vereinigten
nordamerikanischen Staaten
nach Ost-Florida und den Bahama-Inseln
unternommen in den Jahren 1783 und 1784
von
Johann David Schöpf
d. A. W. D. Hochfürstl. Brandenb. Onolzb. und Culmb. Hof- und Militär-Medikus, Landphysikus, des Mediz. Colleg. zu Bayreuth Rath und der Gesellschaft naturforschender Freunde zu Berlin Mitglied.

Erster Theil.

Mit einem Landchärtchen.

Erlangen
bey Johann Jacob Palm. 1788.

Einen quantitativen Höhepunkt erlebte die deutsche Reiseliteratur über Nordamerika paradoxerweise im Gefolge des Unabhängigkeitskrieges: der »Militär-Medikus« J.D. Schöpf (1752–1800) war nur einer von vielen Offizieren der deutschen Subsidientruppen, die ihre Erfahrungen mit Land und Leuten zu Papier brachten und damit langfristige Auswanderungsanreize schufen.

Johannes Müller, one of 1709 emigrants from Nassau-Dillingen, recalled the initial hardships in New York, but then continued in a letter to his relatives: "We wish no more to live in your forsaken Egypt. We have here a land, free of all German servitude. One pays taxes once a year which are so negligible that many spend more in one visit to the tavern." In 1752, John Hayn, formerly a cowherd in Nassau, explains the colonial election system to his friends back home, extolls "justice and law", and tries to convey an idea of the size of America: "People sell out and move on. Nobody knows yet how large the country is. On a map Europe would be like Dillenburg compared to Frankfurt. The best land is still lying waste. They travel some 700 miles and yet do not find the end." The most touching testimony came from Johannes Schlessmann near Germantown in 1753: "I and my children and my wife thank and praise God a thousand times, that we are in this healthful country. We expect to support ourselves much better here than in Germany, for this is a free country."

Throughout the 18th century, immigration, if dealt with officially at all, was a matter for the provincial governments. For a while the individual colonies even dealt with the naturalization of foreigners until Parliament passed an act in 1740 that would grant naturalized foreign-born inhabitants of the colonies in America full civil and political rights. Pennsylvania, the colony most effected by German immigration, required the registration of all newcomers from non-British countries as early as 1727. But an act for the protection of German passengers from abuse by captains or merchants was not passed until 1765, despite much urging from the German community over the years. Massachusetts, in a vain effort to divert some of the immigrants from the Mid-Atlantic colonies, had passed such an act as early as 1750.

Herrn sei tausendmal Dank dafür!" Weiter erwähnt Hoffmann „die Knechtschaft in Siegen, in Gestalt händischer Arbeit, und durch Geld". Ein Jacob Gallmann schrieb 1738 aus Sachsen-Gotha in Süd-Carolina: „So kann man sehen, das ich meine Kinder wohl getan, das ich mein Vaterland verlassen habe und hier bin. Wir läben gar unter gutter, gelinder Regierung." Johannes Müller, einer der Emigranten aus Nassau-Dillingen vom Jahr 1709, erinnert sich in einem Brief an die Verwandtschaft an die erste schwere Zeit in New York, fährt dann jedoch wie folgt fort: „Wir wünschen also nicht mehr, in euer verlassenes Egypten zu wohnen. So haben wir von allen teutschen Auflagen ein frey Land. Wir zahlen Steuern einmal das Jahr, welche so gering sind, das gar mancher bei einem Besuch in der Wirtschaft mehr ausgiebt." Im Jahr 1752 versucht Johannes Hayn, einst Kuhhirt in Nassau, seinen daheimgebliebenen Freunden das koloniale Wahlrecht zu erläutern, preist „Gerechtigkeit und Recht" und versucht, eine Vorstellung von der Größe Amerikas zu vermitteln: „Die Leute verkauffen und gehen weiter fort. Es weis noch kein Mensch, wie groß das Land ist. Euroba ist als Dillenburg gegen Franckfurt in der Landkarte. Das beste Land liegt immer noch brach. Manche haben schon 700 Meilen gereist und finden doch kein Ende." Einer der anrührendsten Briefe kam 1753 von Johannes Schlessmann aus der Nähe von Germantown: „Ich und meine Kinder und meine Frau danken und loben Gott tausend Mal, daß wir in dem gesunden Land sind, wir denken uns viel besser ernähren denn in Deutschland, denn dieses ist ein Fry land."

Im gesamten 18. Jahrhundert blieb die Einwanderung, soweit sie von den Behörden überhaupt beachtet wurde, eine Sache der jeweiligen Kolonial- oder Provinzregierung. Geraume Zeit waren die Kolonien sogar selbst mit der Naturalisierung der Neuankömmlinge befaßt, bis das englische Parlament 1740 ein Gesetz erließ, das naturalisierten, im Ausland geborenen Einwohnern der amerikanischen Kolonien uneingeschränkte politische und bürgerliche Rechte gewährte. Pennsylvanien, die am stärksten von der deutschen Einwanderung betroffene Kolonie, hatte bereits seit 1727 die Registrierung aller Neuankömmlinge aus

There were virtually no obstacles in the way of anybody who wanted to come. From time to time Catholics were specially noted in the arrival records, but no instance of returning any to Europe is known. Occasionally there were expressions of concern about the increasing number of Germans in certain areas. Pennsylvania again went periodically on record against being overrun by these foreigners. Often such nativistic voices were politically motivated. They did not reach the ears of the immigrants and did not influence the flow of migration at any time. Not even Benjamin Franklin's occasional outbreaks were noted in Europe. His least restrained remarks in *The Increase of Mankind,* in March 1751, came just before the largest German immigration period, on which it had no effect whatsoever: "Why should the Palatine Boors be suffered to swarm into our Settlements, and by herding together establish their Language and Manners to the Exclusion of ours?" Nor was Franklin very prophetic when he predicted that they "will shortly be so numerous as to Germanize us instead of our Anglifying them, and will never adopt our Language or Customs, any more than they can acquire our Complexion." Only thirty years later, J. Hector St. John Crèvecœur, in his *Letters from an American Farmer,* could write with much justification that a synthesis was emerging from the various European elements in the New World: "From this promiscuous breed, that race now called Americans have arisen."

The creation of an independent American republic and the return to peace after the Revolutionary War brought soaring expectations to emigration-minded Germans. Many felt that it was now really true that America "saw the lily bloom". The New World now also was outwardly the great experiment of humankind unburdened by European ties. A recent newcomer to Pennsylvania in 1794 sent a poem to the *Philadelphische Correspondenz* which expressed the admiration and the hope of many a young German emigrant with respect to the United States. The anonymous poet enthusiastically describes the "free air" which quickens the beat of his heart in a country where only "he who nourishes fairness in his bosom is great and highly honored", where "neither medals nor ribbons, not even the black cloth" (of the clergy) convey privileges to the wearer. One of his verses deserves inclusion in its original wording:

Hier wo die Freyheits-Fahne weht,
Wo die Vernunft gebeut,
Wo jeder, als ein freyer Mann,
Frey sprechen, glauben, würken kan:
Hier ist die güldene Zeit!

(Here where the flag of freedom flies / Where reason rules / Where each as a free man / Can freely speak, believe, and work: / Here is the golden age!). This voice of a gifted immigrant was more articulate than that of most of his fellow Germans, but even in the correspondence of simple folk, republican sentiment is frequently encountered. The economic possibilities of the new country, granted they were extolled in many European publications, were often overestimated by emigrants. For decades after the end of the War of

nicht-britischen Ländern verlangt. Ein Gesetz zum Schutz der deutschen Passagiere vor Ausbeutung durch Kapitäne oder Kaufleute wurde allerdings erst 1765 erlassen, obwohl die deutsche Gemeinde jahrelang darauf gedrängt hatte. Massachusetts, das den Strom der Einwanderer von den mittelatlantischen Kolonien zu sich umlenken wollte (was mißlang), hatte ein solches Gesetz bereits 1750 in Kraft treten lassen.

Hinderungsgründe, die die Einwanderung unmöglich gemacht hätten, gab es praktisch für niemanden. Von Zeit zu Zeit wurden Katholiken in den Einwanderungsregistern gesondert aufgeführt, doch ist kein Fall bekannt, in dem sie tatsächlich abgewiesen worden wären. Gelegentlich wurden Bedenken angesichts der wachsenden Zahl von Deutschen in bestimmten Gebieten laut. Wieder war es Pennsylvanien, das sich mehrfach zur Gefahr der Überfremdung durch ausländische Siedler zu Wort meldete. Häufig waren solche nativistischen Äußerungen innenpolitisch motiviert. Sie erreichten weder das Ohr der Einwanderer, noch vermochten sie die Wanderungsbewegung jemals im geringsten zu beeinflussen. Selbst Benjamin Franklins gelegentliche Ausbrüche blieben in Europa unbemerkt. Seine unbeherrschtesten Bemerkungen fielen in *The Increase of Mankind* im März 1751 – unmittelbar vor der größten deutschen Einwanderungswelle des Jahrhunderts, auf die sie keinerlei Einfluß hatten: „Warum sollten wir es hinnehmen, daß diese pfälzischen Bauern in unsere Siedlungen schwärmen und dort zusammenhecken, bis ihre Sitten und Sprache das Unsrige verdrängt haben?" Franklin war auch ein schlechter Prophet, als er voraussagte, es würden „ihrer bald so viele sein, daß sie uns germanisieren werden, anstatt daß wir sie anglisieren. Unsere Sprache und Gebräuche werden sie niemals annehmen, genausowenig, wie sie in unsere Haut schlüpfen können". Nur dreißig Jahre später konnte J. Hector St. John Crèvecœur in seinen *Briefen eines amerikanischen Landmanns* konstatieren, daß sich aus den verschiedenen europäischen Elementen in der neuen Welt eine Synthese entwickelte: „Aus dieser gemischten Nachkommenschaft ist nun ein neuer Menschenschlag, genannt der Amerikaner, entstanden."

Die Gründung einer unabhängigen amerikanischen Republik und die Rückkehr zum Frieden nach dem Revolutionskrieg ließ bei den auswanderungsbereiten Deutschen hochfliegende Erwartungen aufkeimen. Viele spürten, daß Amerika nun tatsächlich „eine Lilie blühen" sah: Die Neue Welt war nun auch äußerlich zum großen, von europäischen Fesseln befreiten Experiment der Menschheit geworden. Ein Neuankömmling in Pennsylvanien schickte 1794 ein Gedicht an die *Philadelphische Correspondenz*, in dem er der Bewunderung und den Hoffnungen Ausdruck verlieh, die viele junge deutsche Einwanderer mit den Vereinigten Staaten verbanden. Mit enthusiastischen Worten schilderte der unbekannte Dichter die „freye Luft", die sein Herz schneller schlagen lasse in diesem Land, in dem „nur der groß und hoch geehrt,/Der Redlichkeit im Busen nährt" und wo „kein Ordensstern, noch Band, ja selbst kein schwarz Gewand" (nämlich des Klerus) seinem Träger Privilegien verschaffe. Eine seiner Strophen verdient es, zur Gänze zitiert zu werden:

Hier wo die Freyheits-Fahne weht,
Wo die Vernunft gebeut,
Wo jeder, als ein freyer Mann,
Frey sprechen, glauben, würken kan:
hier ist die güldene Zeit!

George Washington, victor in the war against the British and first president of the U.S., was admired as the very personification of democratic ideals both in America and on the European continent. In Germany he was eulogized by Christian Friedrich Daniel Schubart (1739–91) as "Hercules-Washington, the Guardian of Liberty." On a more human plane – notwithstanding the idealistic treatment – is this 1842 portrait of the Founding Father by a Pennsylvania Dutch naive painter, with fractur lettering proclaiming "Freedom, Equality, Unity and Brotherly Love."

George Washington, der Besieger der englischen Kolonialmacht und erste Präsident der USA, wurde in Europa wie in Amerika zur Personifizierung der demokratischen Idee. In Deutschland besang ihn Christian Friedrich Daniel Schubart (1739–91) als »Herkules-Washington, der Freiheit Schutzgott«. Von menschlicherem Maß ist das abgebildete Idealporträt des Gründungsvaters, das ein pennsylvaniendeutscher Naiver 1842 schuf.

"America has now become an open refuge for all those who sigh under the yoke of the old forms of government in Europe." A clear-sighted appraisal of the American Revolution and its significance to politically motivated immigration to America, published by the German printers Steiner and Cist in the "Philadelphisches Staatsregister" on July 28, 1779.

Leitartikel aus dem von den deutschen Druckern Steiner und Cist herausgegeben »Philadelphischen Staatsregister« vom 28. Juli 1779: bereits vor Beendigung des Unabhängigkeitskrieges eine hellsichtige Einschätzung der amerikanischen Revolution und ihrer Bedeutung für die politisch motivierte Amerikaauswanderung.

The United States as a symbolic ark "with liberty and justice for all" to nourish the hungering immigrants of every species.

Die Vereinigten Staaten als Arche, in der, bei »freiem Eintritt«, »Gleichheitsbohnen«, »Freiheitsmais« und »Selbstbestimmungskorn« auf die hungrige Einwanderer-Tierwelt warten.

The signing of the Louisiana Purchase contract by Talleyrand and President Jefferson's secretary of state James Monroe on 30 April 1803, as depicted on a relief by the American sculptor of German descent Karl Bitter. The French territory of almost a million square miles, for which the United states paid 15 million dollars, included the city of St. Louis in what later became the state of Missouri, both of which were heavily settled by 19th-century German immigrants.

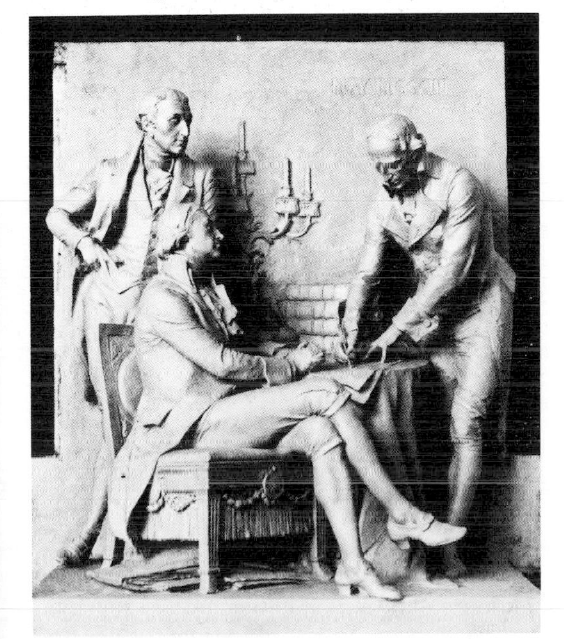

Die Unterzeichnung des Louisiana-Vertrags durch die Außenminister Monroe und Talleyrand am 30. April 1803 auf einem Relief des deutschstämmigen amerikanischen Bildhauers Karl Bitter. Zu dem 2,1 Millionen Quadratkilometer großen französischen Territorium, das die USA für 15 Millionen Dollar kauften, gehörte mit St. Louis und dem späteren Bundesstaat Missouri eines der wichtigsten Siedlungsgebiete deutscher Einwanderer im 19. Jahrhundert.

1779. Num. 2.

Philadelphisches Staatsregister:

Enthaltend

Die neuesten Nachrichten von den merkwürdigsten In- und Ausländischen

Kriegs- und Friedens-Begebenheiten;

nebst verschiedenen andern gemeinnützigen Anzeigen.

Mittwochs, den 28 July.

Der vortheil von der in America geschehenen revolution muß allen liebhabern und gönnern der freyheit in Europa von äusserster wichtigkeit seyn. Es scheint, daß der Himmel ihnen zugleich wohl gewollt, indem er diese Staaten mit einem solchen glück gesegnet---America ist nun ein offener zufluchtsort für alle diejenigen geworden, die unter dem druck der alten Regierungsformen in Europa seufzen. Die einwohner der dortigen Staaten werden die last der willkührlichen Regierungen jetzt empfindlicher fühlen, wenn sie wissen, daß es einen ort in der welt gibt, wo freyheit und billigkeit herrschen, und das verlangen dieses glücks theilhaftig zu werden, wird viele bewegen nach diesen gegenden herüber zu kommen. Und nicht allein diese, sondern auch diejenigen die zurück bleiben, werden einen grossen vortheil davon ziehen; indem die dortigen Regierungen, besonders England und Irland gezwungen seyn werden, die strenge ihrer macht nachzulassen, aus furcht die zurückgebliebenen zu verlieren. Wir fechten derohalben nicht allein für unsere sache, sondern für die sache des ganzen menschlichen geschlechts, und insbesondere unserer ehmaligen mitunterthanen von Groß-Brittannien und Irland. Millionen die nicht in America wohnen, werden die weisheit, tapferkeit und standhaftigkeit dankbarlich segnen, wodurch diese glückselige revolution bewirkt worden, und den unterthanen dieser Staaten müssen die annehmlichkeiten der freyheit doppelt süsse gemacht werden, durch den gedanken, daß die eroberung derselben entfernten nationen zum heil gereichet. Dis muß bey der unpartheyischen welt dem glück unserer waffen einen besondern glanz ertheilen, und die namen derjenigen, deren weisheit und tapferkeit eine so glückliche veränderung hervorgebracht, unter die berühmtesten helden und größten wohlthäter des menschlichen geschlechts versetzen.

Independence the United States underwent much adjustment, both with respect to external trade and internal improvement. The reckless confidence of new German immigrants contrasted with the rather cautious attitude of old-timers who were recovering from the losses sustained during the war years and the subsequent depression. Many plunged right into the new frontier-lands that were opening up along and beyond the Ohio.

From 1806 until 1815 German emigration to the United States was completely interrupted. America, although freer and less encumbered by traditions than any other country, was not as influenced by the ideas of European enlightenment as many young Germans had expected. The years of interruption of the transatlantic migration became a period of self-reliance. It was a time for consolidating what had been won. The Louisiana Purchase and the extension of effective control over vast territories in the Northwest opened up opportunities where now the native-born American would always be one step ahead of the newcomer from Europe. Though enlightened thought had helped to formulate the new freedom and had separated church and state, basically Americans had remained a people under God. Puritans, Quakers, Presbyterians, Lutherans and others of traditional faiths, the Baptists, the Methodists and Evangelical United Brethren of the great revivals, all felt the same horror of the godlessness that was spreading in Europe. This new man, the

So beredt wie dieser begabte Einwanderer waren nicht alle seiner Landsleute, doch selbst in den erhaltenen Briefen einfacher Menschen kommen häufig republikanische Gefühle zum Ausdruck. Die wirtschaftlichen Möglichkeiten im neuen Land – wie sie ja auch in zahlreichen europäischen Veröffentlichungen gepriesen wurden – wurden von vielen Einwanderern überschätzt: Noch Jahrzehnte nach dem Unabhängigkeitskrieg befanden sich die Vereinigten Staaten in einem schwierigen Anpassungsprozeß, sowohl auf dem Gebiet des Außenhandels wie auch im Inneren. Die kühne Zuversicht vieler Neuankömmlinge aus Deutschland stand in charakteristischem Gegensatz zur vorsichtig abwartenden Haltung der Alteingesessenen, die sich erst von den Verlusten erholen mußten, die sie in den Kriegsjahren und der anschließenden Wirtschaftsflaute erlitten hatten. Viele der neu Eingewanderten zogen nun erstmals direkt ins Landesinnere, an die neue Westgrenze am und jenseits des Ohio.

Zwischen 1806 und 1815 war die deutsche Auswanderung in die USA vollständig unterbrochen. Obwohl freier und weniger von Traditionen belastet als jedes andere Land, wurde Amerika von den Ideen der europäischen Aufklärung weniger beeinflußt, als es viele junge Deutsche erwartet hatten. Die Jahre, in denen die transatlantische Völkerwanderung unterbrochen war, wurden für die USA zu einer Periode der Selbstbesinnung. Es war nun Zeit, das Erreichte zu konsolidieren. Durch den Erwerb Louisianas und die Ausdehnung des Machtbereichs auf riesige Territorien im Nordwesten eröffneten sich Möglichkeiten, bei deren Ausschöpfung der in Amerika Geborene den Neueinwanderern immer eine Nasenlänge voraus sein würde. Obwohl die Ideen der Aufklärung in die Formulierung der neuen Freiheiten eingegangen waren und zur Trennung von Kirche und Staat geführt hatten, blieben die Amerikaner ein gottesfürchtiges Volk. Puritaner, Quäker, Presbyterianer, Lutheraner und andere traditionelle Glaubensgemeinschaften, Baptisten, Methodisten und Evangelische Vereinigte Brüder aus den großen Erweckungsbewegungen, sie alle empfan-

American, regardless of his origins, carried a Bible wherever he built a cabin in the new West. It was this new freedom under God which baffled generations of immigrants from Germany, who equated civil liberties with an absence of, or at least with less emphasis on, personal piety. It also attracted conservative religious groups during the 19th century. But basically the German immigrant of this century which saw the largest flood of newcomers, did not expect the religious overtones on daily life that he encountered almost everywhere. America had indeed become a different world, with established institutions which the newcomer could no longer remove but only influence subtly here and there. In due course, the new country was to shape the immigrant. It turned out not to be a process of mere assimilation. There was a give-and-take. Yet the institutions of the republic proved lasting and strong enough to provide the framework into which millions of newcomers eventually fitted.

Immigration from Germany during the 19th century was one of the greatest achievements of private enterprise in an emerging capitalistic society. Those who had expected that the American government would appeal to the disenchanted masses of Europe to come and people the vast new lands in the West, or who had hoped that the government would at least take a guiding role in this process, were to be disappointed. Unlike the Russian tsar who invited Germans and others to come to his new domains, no American government made any appeal. Right at the beginning of the resumption of emigration after 1815, abuses in redemptioner trade led to governmental concern on both sides of the Atlantic. The system of transporting emigrants on credit had worked relatively well for most of the preceding century as long as it had operated under the restraints of the British Navigation Act. Now it had become a free-for-all.

The first steps that were taken to interest the government in immigration were organized by the German Societies in the port cities. The Fürstenwärther mission of 1817 to Baltimore and Washington, and legislative efforts of the German Society of Maryland, acquainted Secretary of State John Quincy Adams, and Attorney General William Wirt, with the problems.

John Quincy Adams (1767–1848), President of the United States from 1825 to 1829 (Engraving by A. B. Durand after a painting by Thomas Sully, 1826)

John Quincy Adams (1767–1848), Präsident der USA von 1825 bis 1829 (Stich von A.B. Durand nach einem Gemälde von Thomas Sully, 1826)

den den gleichen Abscheu vor der in Europa sich ausbreitenden Gottlosigkeit. Der Amerikaner, dieser neue Mensch, der seine Herkunft abgestreift hatte, nahm eine Bibel mit in die Wildnis, wo immer er seine Blockhütte errichtete. Es war diese neue Freiheit vor Gott, die Generationen von deutschen Einwanderern verblüffte, hatten sie doch mit bürgerlicher Freiheit unwillkürlich ein Verschwinden oder wenigstens Zurücktreten der individuellen Frömmigkeit verbunden. Natürlich gab es im 19. Jahrhundert auch orthodoxe religiöse Gruppen, die sich gerade deshalb nach Amerika aufmachten. Die überwiegende Mehrheit der deutschen Umsiedler in diesem Jahrhundert der Massenauswanderung war jedoch nicht auf die religiösen Untertöne vorbereitet, die sie beinahe überall im täglichen Leben antrafen. Amerika war in der Tat zu einer anderen Welt geworden – mit festgefügten Institutionen, die der Neuankömmling nicht mehr umstoßen, sondern allenfalls hier und da ein wenig beeinflussen konnte. Umgekehrt wurde der Einwanderer von seiner neuen Heimat geprägt. Es war ein Prozeß des Gebens und Nehmens, bei dem sich die Institution der Republik als stark und dauerhaft genug erwiesen, den Millionen von Neubürgern einen Rahmen anzubieten, in den sie sich endlich einfügten.

Die Einwanderung aus deutschen Ländern während des 19. Jahrhunderts war, schon rein zahlenmäßig, eine der größten Leistungen des privaten Unternehmertums der sich heranbildenden kapitalistischen Gesellschaft. Wer erwartet hatte, daß die amerikanische Regierung die desillusionierten Massen aus Europa auffordern würde, zu kommen und die endlosen Weiten des Westens zu bevölkern, wurde genauso enttäuscht, wie die Hoffnung, die Regierung würde wenigstens eine lenkende Funktion übernehmen. Anders als der russische Zar, der Deutsche und andere Nationalitäten zur Besiedlung seiner neuen Provinzen aufgerufen hatte, forderte keine amerikanische Regierung jemals zur Einwanderung auf. Unmittelbar nach der Wiederaufnahme des Transatlantikverkehrs nach 1815 ließen Auswüchse im Redemptionistenhandel die Behörden auf beiden Seiten des Ozeans aktiv werden. Das Auslösungssystem hatte sich im vergangenen Jahrhundert relativ gut bewährt, solange es unter den Bedingungen der britischen Navigationsakte betrieben worden war. Jetzt stand es jedermann offen.

Die ersten Initiativen, die ergriffen wurden, um die Regierung für die Probleme der Einwanderer zu interessieren, gingen von den Deutschen Gesellschaften in den Hafenstädten aus. Die Untersuchungen Moritz von Fürstenwärthers, der 1817 Washington und Baltimore besuchte, und Gesetzesanträge, die von der Deutschen Gesellschaft von Maryland eingebracht wurden, machten den Außenminister John Quincy Adams und Justizminister William Wirt mit der einschlägigen Problematik vertraut. Beide Männer hatten dafür ein offenes Ohr: Adams war amerikanischer Gesandter in Berlin gewesen, während Wirt selbst von einem schweizerischen Redemptionisten und einer aus Württemberg eingewanderten Mutter abstammte. Dennoch zögerten beide, die Bundesbehörden direkt mit diesen Angelegenheiten zu befassen. Nach den Verhandlungen faßte John Quincy Adams den offiziellen Standpunkt der amerikanischen Regierung in bezug auf die Einwanderung erstmals zusammen: „Die Republik", so schrieb er, „fordert niemanden auf, zu kommen. Sie weist auch niemanden ab, der den Mut hat, den Atlantik zu überqueren. Neuankömmlinge werden nicht als Fremde benachteiligt werden. Genausowenig dürfen sie besondere Vorteile erwarten. Im Ausland Geborene und hier Geborene haben

The City of Eden on paper and in reality: contemporary illustrations for Charles Dickens' novel about emigrants, "The Life and Adventures of Martin Chuzzlewit" (1844). During Dickens' trip to America in 1842, the fact that great expectations often lead to great disillusionment was driven home to him when he fell for a fraudulent settlement project with the highfalutin name of "Cairo" (the "Eden" of the novel).

Die Stadt Eden auf dem Papier und in der Wirklichkeit: zeitgenössische Illustrationen zu Charles Dickens' Auswandererroman »Leben und Abenteuer Martin Chuzzlewits« (1844). Die Erfahrung, daß Versprechungen und Realitäten schmerzlich auseinanderklaffen konnten, hatte Dickens bei seiner Amerikareise von 1842 selbst gemacht, als er einem betrügerischen Siedlungsprojekt mit dem hochtrabenden Namen »Cairo« (das »Eden« des Romans) aufsaß.

Trained craftsmen represented a greater-than-average percentage – occasionally up to a third – of the German immigrants. The lithographs by G.M. Kirn, produced at the beginning of the 19th century, show, from left to right: weaver, blacksmith, gold and silversmith, carpenters, compass maker and toolsmith, mason.

Ausgebildete Handwerker stellten einen überdurchschnittlichen Prozentsatz – zeitweise bis zu einem Drittel – der deutschen Einwanderer. Die Lithographien von G. M. Kirn, zu Beginn des 19. Jahrhunderts entstanden, zeigen von links nach rechts: Tuchweber, Hufschmied, Gold- und Silberschmied, Zimmerleute, Zirkel- und Zeugschmied, Maurer.

Both men were particularly attentive. Adams had served as head of the Amercian legation in Berlin. Wirt's father had come as a redemptioner from Switzerland, his mother from Wurttemberg. But they were hesitant to get the federal authorities directly involved. After the negotiations, John Quincy Adams summarized for the first time the official American position as regards immigration. "The Republic", Adams wrote, "invites none to come, nor will it keep out those who have the courage to cross the Atlantic. Newcomers will suffer no disabilities as aliens, nor can they expect special advantages. Foreign-born and natives face the same opportunities and their success will depend upon their individual activity and good fortune." Never again was American immigration policy, which was to remain in force for over a century, expressed so succinctly.

In March 1819, Congress passed the first law making immigration a federal concern: regulating the number of passengers a vessel could carry, and organizing the registration of arriving aliens which had previously been carried out by the states. This statute set no restrictions on the number of immigrants who might be admitted. Thus the population transfer from one continent to the other was left to the forces of the marketplace. Solicitation and transportation of emigrants was up to those who expected to profit from it. Occasionally state government would try to direct the stream of emigrants their way but, by and large, it was private enterprise that handled all aspects.

German government official: "But kids, when you've got it so good here, with laws and authorities galore, why on earth do you want to go to a lawless land where they don't even have policemen?" – German caricature of 19th century emigrants.

Amtmann: »Aber Kinder, ihr habt es hier so gut, Gesetze und Beamte in Fülle, und da wollt ihr in ein gesetzloses Land gehen, wo es nicht einmal Polizei gibt?« – deutsche Auswanderer-Karikatur, um die Mitte des 19. Jahrhunderts.

die gleichen Chancen; ihr Erfolg wird von ihrer individuellen Unternehmungslust und ihrem Glück abhängen." Nie wieder wurde die amerikanische Einwanderungspolitik, wie sie noch ein Jahrhundert lang gültig sein sollte, ähnlich bündig formuliert.

Im März 1819 erließ der Kongreß das erste Gesetz, das sich auf Bundesebene mit der Einwanderung befaßte. Es setzte Belegungsobergrenzen für den Passagiertransport fest und vereinheitlichte die Registrierung der einreisenden Ausländer, die bis dahin den Einzelstaaten überlassen geblieben war. Eine zahlenmäßige Beschränkung der Einwanderung war nicht vorgesehen. Die Völkerwanderung von einem Kontinent zum anderen blieb ganz dem freien Spiel des Marktes überlassen. Anwerbung und Beförderung von Auswanderern blieben die Domäne derer, die sich davon einen Gewinn erwarteten. Gelegentlich versuchte die eine oder andere Regierung eines Bundesstaates, den Einwandererstrom in ihre Richtung umzulenken, aber im großen und ganzen blieben alle Aspekte der Einwanderung in privatwirtschaftlicher Hand.

Die öffentliche Meinung in den USA war generell positiv zur Einwanderung eingestellt. Aufgrund der in der Kolonialzeit gemachten Erfahrungen waren die Deutschen als Farmer hoch geschätzt, und auch als Handwerker genossen sie einen guten Ruf. In früheren Generationen hatten sie sich als loyale und hilfsbereite Mitbürger erwiesen. Es gab nichts zu fürchten für die Millionen, die mit dem Gedanken spielten, ihre Heimat, in der ihr Marktwert (mit Friedrich List gesprochen) so gering war, mit einem Land zu vertauschen, in dem sie als Personen ungleich wertvoller eingeschätzt wurden. Sie folgten Ratschlägen wie diesem, den Chrisostomus Weis 1818 seinem Bruder gab: „Libster Bruder was glaubst du willst du kommen ja ich rathe dir du sollst kommen wir haben schon 100 mal gewunschen wenn nur unser Bruder und Schwestern bei uns wären und ich rathe allen die Willens sind zu kommen sie sollen nur kommen sie machen ihr leben besser als in Teutschland." Obwohl sein eigener Start in der neuen Heimat unter keinem guten Stern gestanden hatte, ließ auch Weis die Worte früherer Immigranten anklingen, als er Amerika „ein Frey-

Public opinion in the United States was generally favorable toward immigration. As a result of the colonial experience, Germans were highly regarded as farmers and also enjoyed a good reputation as craftsmen. Earlier generations had proven loyal and willing fellow-citizens. There was nothing to fear for the millions who were thinking of leaving a country where, as Friedrich List had put it, their own person as a ware was "of little value, and they are going to a place where it has great value." They were following such advice as Chrisostomus Weis offered his brother in 1818: "Dearest Brother, do you think you will come, yes, I advise you to come. 100 times we have wished if only our brothers and sisters were with us, and I advise all who are willing to come they must simply come. They will make a better living here than in Germany." Then Weis, whose start in the new life had been all but fortunate, echoes the message of earlier immigrants when he calls America *ein Freyland*, a "free country": "it is subject to no potentate". Weis concluded with the admonition: "If you were in this country and you would work here as in Germany, you could make a good future for your children."

No promotion agency could have provided better and more convincing testimony to meet the expectations of those back home who were thinking of going to America. Even letters that were critical of the new country did not have a negative effect. Many willing to emigrate wanted to hear the whole truth and though all embarked with great hopes, most had tried to secure as much information about the new country as possible. Young Ludwig Stassfort of Frankfurt wrote to his parents in May 1840, a few months after "having reached the land of liberty," in a vein that showed mature judgment and a lack of illusion: "The folks aboard ship formed great plans for their future, all of which quickly vanished after landing . . . Those who in Germany perhaps have been lawyers, preachers, merchants, craftsmen and farmers, vie with each other in pushing a wheelbarrow. No one need imagine that the Americans are awaiting at the dock to welcome the Germans." Stassfort, who founded a successful family in Baltimore, also found the "puritan" life-style at first

land" nannte: „es steht unter keinen Bodenda" (Potentaten). Er schloß seinen Brief mit der Mahnung: „Wenn du in diesem Land wärst und dort arbeiten wie in Teutschland so thätest deinen Kindern gute Zeiten machen."

Kein Werber und Agent hätte den Sehnsüchten der Auswanderungswilligen in der Heimat bessere und überzeugendere Nahrung geben können. Doch selbst Briefe, in denen Kritisches über das neue Land geäußert wurde, blieben ohne abschreckende Wirkung. Die zukünftigen Auswanderer wollten die ganze Wahrheit erfahren, und wenn sie auch alle mit großen Hoffnungen in See stachen, hatten doch die meisten vorher so viele Informationen über ihre neue Heimat zusammenzutragen versucht, wie ihnen möglich war. Der junge Ludwig Stassfort schrieb seinen Eltern im Mai 1840, kurz nach seiner Ankunft „im Lande der Freiheit", einen Brief, der von klarem Urteil und nüchternen Erwartungen zeugt: „Wenn die Leute vom Schiffe kommen haben sie meist große Pläne im Kopf, diese verlieren sich aber so bald sie den Fuß an Land setzen . . . Jene, welche in Deutschland Advocaten, Pfarrer, Kaufleute, Handwerker und Bauern waren, fahren hier die Schiebkarre mit einander um die Wette . . . Es muß sich niemand einbilden, daß die Americaner am Ufer stehen und lauern auf die Deutschen." Stassfort, der in Baltimore eine Familie gründete, die es zu Wohlstand und Ansehen brachte, war anfangs auch über den ihm völlig unerwarteten „puritanischen" Lebensstil verblüfft: „Der Sonntag wird auf das Strengste gefeiert; alle Läden sind geschlossen; kein Wagen fährt auf der Strasse, und nur die Kirchen sind zum Gottesdienst geöffnet; daher weiss der Americaner auch nichts als arbeiten und beten."

Es war diese Kollision verschiedener Lebensstile – vor allem die deutsche Vorstellung vom Sonntag als einem Tag der Fröhlichkeit und der Erholung und die deutsche Vorliebe für Bier in einer Gesellschaft, in der die Temperenzbewegung noch immer gegen den Fluch des frühen Grenzerlebens, den hohen Alkoholkonsum, zu kämpfen hatte –, die zu Feindseligkeit zwischen Einwanderern und gebürtigen Amerikanern englischer Herkunft führte. Etwa um die Jahr-

Statuten

des Vereins zum Schutze deutscher Einwanderer in Texas.

I. Capitel.

Bildung des Vereins, dessen Zweck und Wirksamkeit.

§ 1.

Der Verein bildet sich durch die Inhaber der Aktien. Der Sitz desselben ist: **Mainz** oder **Mannheim.**

§ 2.

Die Dauer des Vereins ist vorläufig auf 25 Jahre festgesetzt, vom Tage dessen wirklicher Constituirung an gerechnet. Ein Beschluß der General-Versammlung kann diese Dauer prorogiren.

§ 3.

Hauptzweck des Vereins ist:

1) Verbesserung des Zustandes der arbeitenden Classe ohne Arbeit, hierdurch Verminderung des Pauperismus.
2) Eröffnung neuer Absatzwege für die Producte der National-Industrie.
3) Entwickelung des Seehandels.

Die Wirksamkeit des Vereins besteht darin:

1) In Deutschland's Interesse den Zug deutscher Auswanderer zu regeln und zu ordnen, die Auswanderer nach einem Punkt hinzuleiten und zwar nach Texas.

2) Ackerbau-Industrie- und Handels-Niederlassungen zu gründen, sich ohne oder gegen Vergütung Ländereien dort zu verschaffen, diese zu vergeben, zu verkaufen, urbar zu machen und anzubauen und die Producte von Texas auszubeuten.

3) Commerzielle Beziehungen zwischen diesem Lande und Deutschland anzuknüpfen.

4) Denjenigen Deutschen, welche sich auf dessen Colonial-Niederlassungen befinden, oder dort einwandern, seinen Schutz angedeihen zu lassen.

§ 5.

Es giebt der Verein den mittellosen Einwanderern Ländereien, ohne Vergütung dafür anzusprechen, deren Flächeninhalt das Colonial-Statut firirt. Er verschafft ihnen die Mittel zur Existenz und zur Arbeit, verhilft ihnen zu Schul- und Religions-Unterricht nach Maßgabe der Bevölkerung.

So geschehen: **Mainz**, den 25. März 1844.

Der Präsident
Fürst **Leiningen.**

The statutes of the "Society for the Protection of German Immigrants in Texas", a separatist settlement project established by German aristocrats, aimed at the establishment of a German-dominated immigrant colony in Texas, an area which, at the time, did not yet belong to the Union. After this "Society" – a corporation in the eyes of the law – had brought several thousand settlers to Texas, internal mismanagement and the effects of the Mexican-American War of 1846–48 led to the bankruptcy of the company.

Die Statuten des »Vereins zum Schutze deutscher Einwanderer in Texas«, eines separatistischen Siedlungsprojekts deutscher Adeliger, das auf die Schaffung einer deutsch dominierten Einwandererkolonie im damals noch nicht zur Union gehörenden Texas abzielte. Nachdem der »Verein« – juristisch eine Aktiengesellschaft – mehrere tausend Siedler nach Texas gebracht hatte, führten interne Mißwirtschaft und die Auswirkungen des mexikanisch-amerikanischen Krieges von 1846/48 zum Bankrott des Unternehmens.

Prince Carl von Solms-Braunfels, general commissioner of the "Texas Society" and founder of the city named for him, New Braunfels (1845). After his economic downfall, Solms-Braunfels returned to Europe; his successor was Hans Otfried von Meusebach.

Prinz Carl von Solms-Braunfels, Generalkommissar des »Texasvereins« und Gründer der nach ihm benannten Stadt New Braunfels (1845). Nach seinem wirtschaftlichen Scheitern kehrte Solms-Braunfels nach Europa zurück; sein Nachfolger wurde Hans Otfried von Meusebach.

A share of "Texas Society" stock

Eine Aktie des »Texasvereins«

Sunday evening in a German beer tavern: illustration from "Harper's Weekly", October 1859.

Sonntagabend in einem deutschen Bierlokal: Illustration aus »Harper's Weekly«, Oktober 1859.

Beer as a political issue: anti-German cartoon on a postcard from the early prohibition era.

Bier als Politikum: antideutsche Karikatur auf einer Postkarte aus der frühen Prohibitionszeit

Brawl between workers of Germanic origin and Know-Nothings at a May Day celebration in Hoboken, New Jersey, in 1851. "Know-Nothings" was the nickname for members of a secret political organization violently antipathetic toward immigrants; so called because they replied "I know nothing" when questioned about the party's activities.

Schlägerei zwischen deutschstämmigen Arbeitern und »Know-Nothings« auf einer Maifeier in Hoboken, New Jersey, 1851: »Know-Nothings« war der Spitzname der Mitglieder eines nativistischen politischen Geheimbundes, die ihre Beteiligung an einwandererfeindlichen Ausschreitungen mit einem stereotypen »Ich weiß von nichts« abzuleugnen pflegten.

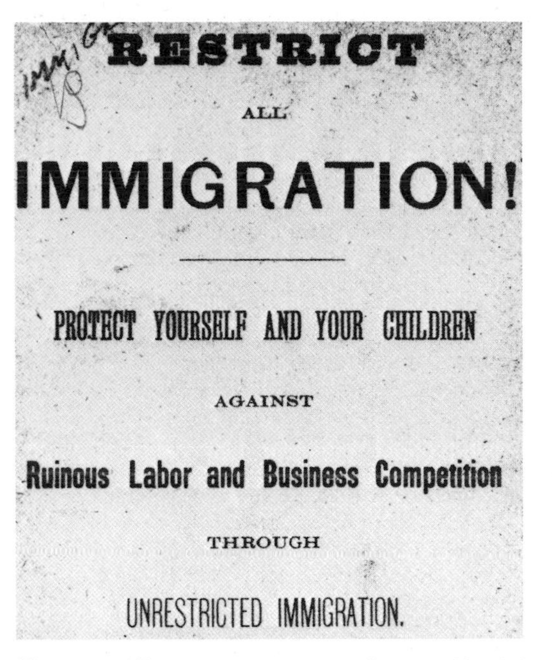

RESTRICT

ALL

IMMIGRATION!

PROTECT YOURSELF AND YOUR CHILDREN

AGAINST

Ruinous Labor and Business Competition

THROUGH

UNRESTRICTED IMMIGRATION.

The surge of European immigrants in the second half of the 19th century led to protests in the more heavily populated States of the Union, demanding restrictive laws: anti-immigration pamphlet from 1885.

Die Flut europäischer Einwanderer in der zweiten Hälfte des 19. Jahrhunderts ließ in den dichter besiedelten Staaten der Union die Forderung nach einer gesetzlichen Beschränkung laut werden: Anti-Einwanderungs pamphlet aus dem Jahr 1885.

bewildering and most unexpected: "Sunday is strictly observed here. All shops are closed; no wagons run and only the church doors are open for divine service. From which it follows that your American knows nothing but work and prayer."

It was this clash of different life-styles – especially the German concept of the Sunday as a day of relaxation and frolicking, and the Germans' love of beer in a society where the temperance movement was still struggling to free the people from one of the scourges of early frontier life: heavy drinking – that led to antagonism between immigrants and natives. About the middle of the century, when German and Irish immigration reached its first peak, the political movement of the Know Nothing tried to create an anti-immigrant climate. It ultimately only served to weld Germans together who, like their Irish counterparts, finally took to the streets to counter the policy of the Know Nothing. More effectively, they also helped to defeat them at the polls. News of the revival of the "damned Dutchmen" concept did not have a deterrent effect on emigration from Germany. Precisely at that time emigrants were singing with undaunted enthusiasm:

When we arrive in Baltimore,
Our hands are pointed to the shore,
We loudly shout Victoria,
We made it to America!

As new territories opened up in North America, there was repeated talk about creating an area that would be entirely German. Patriotic German liberals had such dreams as Paul Follenius expressed: "We may in at least one of the American territories create a state that is German from its foundations up." The reality of the United States made such wild expectations futile. A distinguished German-American, Gustav Körner,

"The Last Yankee" – viewed as a curiosity by immigrants: caricature from "Frank Leslie's Illustrated Newspaper", September 1888.

»Der letzte Yankee« – von Einwanderern als Kuriosität bestaunt: Karikatur aus »Frank Leslie's Illustrated Newspaper«, September 1888.

hundertmitte, als die deutsche und die irische Einwanderung ihre ersten Höhepunkte erreichten, versuchte die politische Bewegung der *Know Nothings,* ein einwandererfeindliches Klima zu schaffen. Doch der Druck schmiedete die Deutschen nur um so enger zusammen, bis sie schließlich, wie die Iren, ebenfalls auf die Straße gingen, um den *Know Nothings* entgegenzutreten. Noch wirkungsvoller war der Beitrag, den sie zur Niederschlagung der nativistischen Bewegung an den Wahlurnen leisteten. Auf die deutsche Amerikaauswanderung hatten die Nachrichten vom Wiederaufleben des Schlagworts von den *damned Dutchmen* keine Auswirkung. Genau zur selben Zeit sangen die Auswanderer mit ungebrochenem Enthusiasmus:

Sind wir dann in Baltimore,
Werfen wir die Händ' empor,
Und rufen laut Victoria,
Jetzt sind wir in Amerika!

Die Erschließung immer neuer Territorien in Nordamerika ließ wiederholt Pläne aufkeimen, ein rein deutsches Siedlungsgebiet zu schaffen. Patriotische deutsche Liberale wie Paul Follenius träumten davon, „wenigstens in einem der amerikanischen Territorien einen, seinem Grundwesen nach deutschen Staat (zu) gründen", doch die amerikanischen Realitäten ließen dieses wie andere verwegene Projekte hinfällig werden. Gustav Körner, wie Follenius ein liberaler Flüchtling der 30er Jahre und später Vizegouverneur von Illinois, fand solche „Versuche von seiten der deutschen Einwanderer nachteilig für Wohlergehen und Fortbestand dieses freien Landes".

Als die deutsche Einwanderung in den 40er und 50er Jahren die Ausmaße einer Flut annahm, entstanden in den größeren Städten des Ostens und des mittleren Westens so viele deutsche Stadtviertel (*little Ger-*

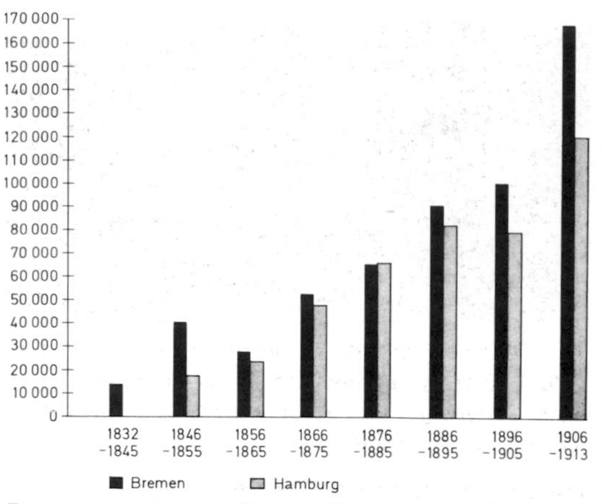

Passenger statistics of Germany's two major 19th-century emigration ports, Bremen (incl. Bremerhaven) and Hamburg

Statistik der Passagierzahlen in den beiden wichtigsten deutschen Auswanderungshäfen des 19. Jahrhunderts, Bremen (mit Bremerhaven) und Hamburg

Embarkation at Bremerhaven, after a woodcut by Johannes Gehrts

Abreise in Bremerhaven, nach einem Holzstich von Johannes Gehrts

The Hoboken docking piers of the Bremen "Norddeutscher Lloyd" (left) and the Hamburg HAPAG companies (right) in New Jersey.

Die Piers des bremischen Norddeutschen Lloyd (links) und der hamburgischen HAPAG (rechts) in Hoboken, New Jersey

The "Hamburg-Amerikanische Packetfahrt-Actien-Gesellschaft" (HAPAG), founded in 1847, was the first German shipping line to introduce regularly scheduled Atlantic crossings. Like HAPAG, the second oldest large-scale German shipping line, the ten-years-younger Norddeutscher Lloyd, owes its existence and success primarily to the increase in emigration to America in the second half of the nineteenth century.

Als erste deutsche Reederei führte die 1847 gegründete Hamburg-Amerikanische Packetfahrt-Actien-Gesellschaft (HAPAG) den regelmäßigen Transatlantikverkehr nach Fahrplan ein. Wie die HAPAG, verdankt auch die zweite deutsche Großreederei, der zehn Jahre jüngere Norddeutsche Lloyd, Entstehung und Aufschwung in erster Linie der Zunahme der Amerikaauswanderung in der zweiten Hälfte des 19. Jahrhunderts.

The F. Missler emigration agency in Bremen, around 1910. Left, the mezzanine entrance for saloon passengers; the ticket office for passengers in steerage is hidden away downstairs on the right.

Die Auswandereragentur F. Missler in Bremen, ca. 1910: links im Hochparterre der Eingang für die Passagiere der »ersten Kajüte«, rechts im Souterrain versteckt der Kartenschalter für das Zwischendeck.

The HAPAG shipping company's business report of February 1889, announcing that Carl Schurz had become their American representative, a position Schurz held until 1892.

Geschäftsbericht der HAPAG vom Februar 1889 mit Bekanntgabe der Verpflichtung von Carl Schurz als amerikanischer Repräsentant der Reederei. Schurz übte dieses Amt bis 1892 aus.

Hamburg-Amerikanische Packetfahrt-Actien-Gesellschaft.
Hamburg.

Hamburg, den 5. Februar 1889.

An unsere Herren Agenten.

Indem wir nicht versäumen, Ihnen für Ihre geschätzte, während des vergangenen Jahres geleistete Mitarbeit unsere volle Anerkennung und unseren besten Dank hiermit auszudrücken, gereicht es uns zum Vergnügen, zu sagen, daß unsere Arbeit keine vergebliche war. Das Jahr 1888 war von erfreulichen Erfolgen für die Gesellschaft begleitet, und unser Betrieb ist zu unserer großen Genugthuung von größeren Unfällen verschont geblieben.

Dies günstige Ergebniß und die lebhafte Zunahme des Verkehrs haben der Gesellschaft gestattet, eine Erweiterung ihres Unternehmens und eine namhafte Vermehrung ihres Betriebsmaterials vorzunehmen. Die vier großen und tüchtigen Dampfer „Australia", „Polynesia", „Polaria" und „California" sind von uns erworben und außerdem der Bau von sieben weiteren transoceanischen Dampfern angeordnet worden. Von den letzteren sind die „Flandria" und die „Helvetia" bereits geliefert worden, die „Croatia" soll noch in diesem Monate in Fahrt gesetzt werden, während die Fertigstellung der „Galizia" zu Anfang April, diejenige der „Dania", „Scandinavia" und „Russia" gegen die Mitte des Jahres erwartet wird. Die drei letztgenannten Schiffe werden Ihrer besonderen Aufmerksamkeit begegnen, da sie ausschließlich für die Beförderung von Passagieren dritter Klasse bestimmt und eingerichtet sein werden. Die großen Dimensionen von 373 Fuß Länge bei 43 Fuß Breite werden jedem dieser stattlichen Fahrzeuge die Aufnahme von 1600 Zwischendecks-Reisenden erlauben, während die innere Ausstattung und Raumvertheilung an Zweckmäßigkeit und Bequemlichkeit innerhalb der berechtigten Ansprüche dieser Klasse von Passagieren kaum noch übertroffen werden kann. Der ganze Raum ist mit Schlafkammern versehen und außerdem sind gesonderte große Abtheilungen vorhanden, welche für den Aufenthalt der Reisenden bei Tage und zum Einnehmen der Mahlzeiten eingerichtet sind. Alle Räumlichkeiten sind electrisch beleuchtet. Diese neuen Dampfer bieten mithin den Passagieren eine in jeder Weise angenehme und bequeme Unterkunft, welche selbst die weitgehendsten Erwartungen befriedigen wird, und die Gesellschaft darf erwarten, daß dieselben sehr bald zu den vom reisenden Publikum bevorzugtesten Schiffen ihrer Linie gehören werden.

Die beiden Doppelschrauben-Schnelldampfer, welche für uns im Bau begriffen sind und welche die beiden größten Schiffe sein werden, welche die Handelsmarine Deutschlands besitzt, sehen ihrer Vollendung entgegen. Wie Sie der Segelliste entnehmen werden, soll die „Augusta Victoria", welcher Ihre Majestät die deutsche Kaiserin die Führung ihres Namens huldreichst gestattet hat, bereits am 2. Mai, und die „Columbia" am 20. Juni ihre erste Reise antreten. Angesichts der eingehenden Schilderungen, welche die deutsche Presse über die glänzende Einrichtung und den bewundernswerthen Bau diesen, das Beste der Gegenwart in sich vereinigenden beiden Dampfern, bereits gebracht hat, können wir auf eine nähere Beschreibung derselben an dieser Stelle verzichten. Erwähnen wollen wir aber, obwohl auch dies Ihnen schon bekannt sein wird, daß Seine Majestät der Kaiser Wilhelm II. gelegentlich seiner letzten Anwesenheit in Stettin unseren fast vollendeten Schnell-Dampfer mit einem längeren Besuche beehrt, und mit großer Befriedigung von dem Bau und allen Einzelheiten der Einrichtungen des Schiffes Kenntniß genommen hat.

Die Gesellschaft hat ferner die Genugthuung gehabt, es am Tage des Stapellaufs der „Augusta Victoria" verkünden zu können, daß sie für den neu geschaffenen Posten eines amerikanischen Directors der Hamburg-Amerikanischen Packetfahrt-Actien-Gesellschaft mit dem Sitze in New-York die Person des ehemaligen Ministers und Senators der Vereinigten Staaten **Karl Schurz** zu gewinnen vermochte. Es kann uns Deutschen nur zur Freude gereichen, das Talent und die Arbeitskraft, sowie die staatsmännische und wirthschaftliche Potenz unseres berühmten Landsmannes für die Pflege der Beziehungen und des Verkehrs zwischen beiden Nationen durch unsere Gesellschaft in Wirksamkeit gebracht zu sehen.

Um den andrängenden Bedürfnissen des Verkehrs gerecht werden zu können, haben wir uns veranlaßt gesehen, von einer am 12. September 1888 einberufen gewesenen General-Versammlung unserer Actionäre eine Erhöhung des Grundkapitals der Gesellschaft von 20 auf 25 Millionen Mark zu erbitten. Durchdrungen von der vollen Berechtigung dieser Forderung hat sich aber die General-Versammlung bewogen gefunden, der Verwaltung nicht 5, sondern 10 Millionen zur Verfügung zu stellen und damit zugleich, wie wir mit großem Danke zu erwähnen nicht unterlassen wollen, derselben ein ehrenvolles Zeugniß des Vertrauens gegeben.

Die Gesellschaft sieht sich in Folge dieses Beschlusses in die erfreuliche Lage gebracht, jederzeit mit dem Bau weiterer Schnelldampfer vorgehen zu können, sobald die Erfahrung gezeigt haben wird, daß die Construction und Einrichtung der beiden zunächst in den Dienst einzustellenden sich bewähren. Wie Sie ferner aus den Abfahrtslisten ersehen haben werden, haben wir eine Linie Hamburg-Baltimore errichtet. Ueber die Passage-Preise 2c. kommen wir Ihnen in einem Special-Circulair demnächst näher.

Wir geben uns mit Vergnügen der Erwartung hin, daß die vorstehenden Mittheilungen dazu beitragen werden, uns Ihre Regsamkeit und Freudigkeit für den Dienst der Gesellschaft zu bewahren und begrüßen Sie

Hochachtungsvoll

Hamburg-Amerikanische Packetfahrt-Actien-Gesellschaft.

"The Growth of the Hamburg-America Line, 1847–1904". This descriptive painting, commissioned by the HAPAG company, illustrates its development from a freight-hauling fleet of sailing vessels on which – apart from the expensive deck cabin – passengers could only be carried in a degrading steerage area above the cargo holds, to passenger steamships similar to what we see today; also a side-effect of the mass emigration which made strictly passenger-carrying vessels profitable for the first time.

»Die Entwicklung der Hamburg-Amerika-Linie, 1847 bis 1904«. Das im Auftrag der HAPAG gemalte Schaubild illustriert die Entwicklung vom frachttragenden Segler, in dem zur Passagierbeförderung – neben der teuren Deckskajüte – nur das menschenunwürdige »Zwischendeck« über den Frachträumen zur Verfügung stand, zum Passagierdampfer heutiger Prägung: ebenfalls eine Folgeerscheinung der Massenauswanderung, durch die reine Passagierschiffe erstmals rentabel wurden.

himself a liberal refugee of the 1830s and later lieutenant-governor of Illinois, called such "attempts on the part of German immigrants injurious to the welfare and the permanence of this free country."
With German immigration reaching flood proportions for two decades, there were so many "Little Germanies" evolving in the larger cities of the East and Midwest, that a newcomer could find a small universe of his own familiar surroundings. German shops, theaters, churches, schools, newspapers and the ever-present clubs were natural shock absorbers during the initial period. They also could have a limiting effect on the immigrant if he remained in this narrow sphere without striking out for better opportunities outside German America. On the whole, it proved beneficial to most to find communities of people with the same background.
In the history of German immigration the first station for newcomers, Ellis Island, never held the importance it has had for millions of immigrants from other countries. Opened in 1892, it came into being at a time when German immigration was already declining. In the lore of German immigrants the wharves of Philadelphia, Castle Garden in New York, Locust Point in Baltimore and the New Orleans docksides play a similar role. During the height of the movement from Germany, an emigrant could purchase an entire travel package, which included departure from Germany, Holland or Belgium, the steerage class on the ship and a railroad ticket to his ultimate destination in America. Some even made a down payment on land which they hadn't even seen. Payments were made to the agents of American railroad and steamship companies who were stationed at strategic points in Europe.
By sheer numbers the Germans and other German-speaking immigrants were an important factor in America at the beginning of the 20th century. More were still coming in, though less than before. By and large they had earned the acceptance and respect of their fellow citizens. They had proved no disappointment to those who had steadfastly defended them against nativists. Indeed, they had fulfilled what a newspaper editor in 1855 in the hostile Know Nothing climate had predicted in the Richmond (Virginia) *Enquirer*: "Our American Germany will be a great blessing to us, enlarging our wealth, confirming our freedom, balancing the Celtic immigration by its

manies), daß der Neuankömmling ein kleines Universum mit der von daheim vertrauten Umgebung vorfinden konnte. Deutsche Läden, Theater, Kirchen, Schulen, Zeitungen und die allgegenwärtigen Vereine dienten in der Eingewöhnungszeit als natürliche Schockdämpfer. Natürlich konnten sie auch eine isolierende Wirkung haben, wenn der Einwanderer in diesem deutschen Milieu befangen blieb und nicht den Mut fand, nach besseren Chancen außerhalb zu greifen. Im allgemeinen war die Existenz dieses „Deutsch-Amerika" jedoch segensreich für die vielen, die sich nach der Gesellschaft von Menschen gleicher Herkunft sehnten.
In der Geschichte der deutschen Einwanderung hat Ellis Island, die berühmte Durchgangsstation für Einwanderer in New York, nie eine ähnliche Bedeutung besessen wie für Millionen von Neuankömmlingen aus anderen Ländern. 1892 eröffnet, nahm Ellis Island den Betrieb erst auf, als die deutsche Einwanderung bereits zurückzugehen begann. In der Saga der deutschen Einwanderer spielen die Kais von Philadelphia, Castle Garden auf Manhattan, Locust Point vor Baltimore und das Hafenviertel von New Orleans eine vergleichbare Rolle. Auf dem Höhepunkt der Völkerwanderung konnte der Emigrant seine Reise als komplettes Paket buchen, von der Anreise zum Einschiffungshafen in Deutschland, Holland oder Belgien über die Beförderung im Zwischendeck bis zur Eisenbahnfahrt an seinen endgültigen Zielort in Amerika. Manche Auswanderer leisteten sogar schon vor der Abreise eine Anzahlung auf ein Stück Land, das sie noch nie gesehen hatten. Die Zahlungen wurden von Agenten der amerikanischen Eisenbahn- und Dampfschiffahrtsgesellschaften entgegengenommen, die an strategischen Punkten über ganz Europa verstreut waren.
Allein durch ihre Anzahl waren die Einwanderer aus Deutschland und den anderen deutschsprachigen Ländern in den USA des beginnenden 20. Jahrhunderts zu einem wichtigen Bevölkerungsfaktor geworden. Und die Einwanderung dauerte immer noch an, wenn auch mit abnehmender Tendenz. Von wenigen Ausnahmen abgesehen hatten sich die Deutschamerikaner die Anerkennung und den Respekt ihrer Mitbürger erwerben können. Jene, die sie immer wieder vor einwandererfeindlichen Kampagnen in Schutz genommen hatten, waren nicht enttäuscht worden. Es war in Erfüllung gegangen, was ein Redakteur des *Enquirer* aus Richmond, Virginia, im feindseligen Know-Nothing-Klima des Jahres 1855 prophezeit hatte: „Unser amerikanisches Deutschland wird ein großer Segen für uns sein. Es wird unseren Wohlstand mehren, unsere Freiheit sichern, durch seine geistige Unabhängigkeit und seine Strebsamkeit ein Gegengewicht zur keltischen Einwanderung schaffen, und es verspricht zumindest, sich auch die Sparsamkeit der Angelsachsen zu erwerben und diesen dafür von seinem künstlerischen Geschmack und seinen mitmenschlichen Gefühlen mitzuteilen."
Dieser lange und langwierige Prozeß der freiwilligen Integration von vielen Millionen Deutschen in ihre neue Nation wurde durch die Ereignisse in der alten Welt brutal unterbrochen. Während der ersten beiden Jahre des Ersten Weltkrieges, als die Vereinigten Staaten noch neutral waren, hatten zahlreiche Deutschamerikaner keinen Hehl aus ihrer Sympathie für die Sache ihrer alten Heimat gemacht – genauso, wie viele andere Amerikaner offen Partei für die Alliierten ergriffen. John W. Wayland, ein Nachfahre deutscher Einwanderer aus der Kolonialzeit, notierte in seinen Kriegsaufzeichnungen: „Einige wenige schienen

Locust Point, Baltimore's immigration harbor with direct railroad connections, via the Baltimore and Ohio Railroad, to the areas of settlement in the Middle West.

Locust Point, Baltimores Einwandererhafen mit direktem Eisenbahnanschluß, über die Baltimore and Ohio Railroad, nach den Siedlungsgebieten des mittleren Westens

The southernmost point of Manhattan in a lithograph by A. Gocht, 1850. At the lower left, the round Castle Garden edifice, then still a concert hall, but between 1859 and 1892, reception center for millions of immigrants.

Die Südspitze Manhattans auf einer Lithographie von A. Gocht, 1850. Links unten der Rundbau von Castle Garden, damals noch Konzertsaal, von 1859 bis 1892 Durchgangsstation für Millionen von Einwanderern.

To the left: An unidentified girl at the reception center for immigrants on Ellis Island; picture taken in 1905 by the master photographer and trained sociologist Lewis H. Hine.

Links außen: Ein unbekanntes Mädchen, im Einwanderer-Empfangszentrum Ellis Island 1905 fotografiert von dem ausgebildeten Soziologen und Meisterfotografen Lewis W. Hine.

The Erie Railroad's immigration ferry at Castle Garden in 1874. The middle western states became the principal settlement region for 19th-century German immigrants: as of 1820, Ohio, and as of 1840, Illinois and Wisconsin.

Einwandererfähre der Erie-Eisenbahn vor Castle Garden, 1874. Der Mittlere Westen mit den Bundesstaaten Ohio (ab 1820 erschlossen) sowie Illinois und Wisconsin (ab 1840) wurde im 19. Jahrhundert zum deutschen Haupteinwanderungsgebiet.

Schutzwehr gegen Betrug.

Für Emigranten und Reisende.

Das Eisenbahn-Bureau,

No. 85, Greenwich-Straße,

nahe Rector-Straße.

Die billigste, schnellste, und sicherste Linie nach dem Westen.

Einwanderer und sonstige Leute, die ins Innere zu reisen gedenken, können sich versichert halten, daß sie billiger, bequemer und schneller als mit irgend einer andern Bahn reisen, wenn sie sich der

New-York- und Erie-Eisenbahn

bedienen.

Abgang der Züge jeden Abend (ausgenommen Sonntags) **6 Uhr.**

In a German-language advertisement, the Manhattan office of the New York & Erie Railroad offers the "cheapest, fastest and most comfortable fraud-proof transportation to destinations west for emigrants and other travellers."

In New-York werden bei der Landung in Castle-Garden alle diejenigen, welche diese Karte am Hute oder an der Brust tragen, von Pastor Berkemeier oder dessen Agenten in Empfang genommen.

Der Besitzer dieser Karte wird empfohlen an

Pastor Berkemeier

im deutschen Emigrantenhause

Nr. 26, State Street, New-York,

Castle-Garden gegenüber.

Man trage diese Karte bei der Ankunft in Castle-Garden am Hute oder an der Brust.

Man lasse sich diese Karte, welche von zuverlässiger Seite gegeben ist, durch keine Vorspiegelungen wegnehmen, weder auf der Reise zur Hafenstadt, sowie in dieser selbst, noch auf dem Schiffe, da in New-York die Auswanderer in vielen Gasthäusern den ärgsten Betrügereien ausgesetzt sind.

Buchdruckerei von J. H. Broom, Bremen.

A card printed in Bremen claims that the bearers who, upon arrival in Castle Garden, wear it visibly "on their hat or on their breast" will be met by Pastor Berkemeier or his agent, and shielded from exploitation by tricksters by receiving accommodations in New York's "House of German Emigrants".

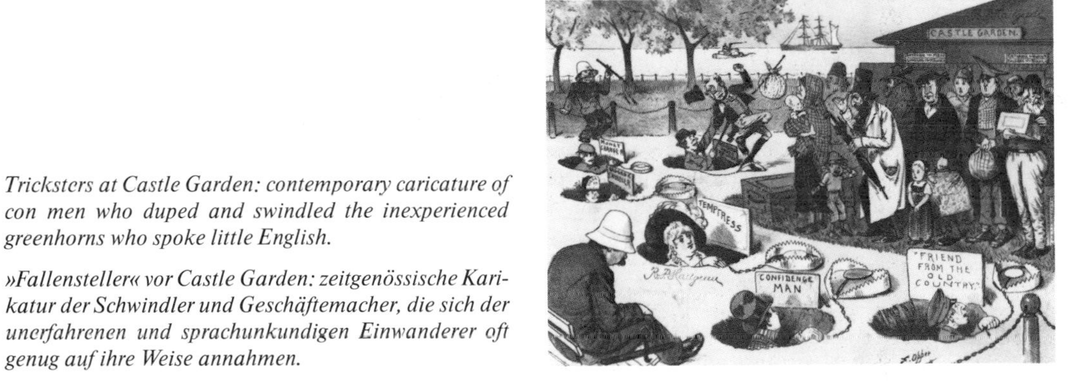

Tricksters at Castle Garden: contemporary caricature of con men who duped and swindled the inexperienced greenhorns who spoke little English.

»Fallensteller« vor Castle Garden: zeitgenössische Karikatur der Schwindler und Geschäftemacher, die sich der unerfahrenen und sprachunkundigen Einwanderer oft genug auf ihre Weise annahmen.

New Orleans, the major port of entry for immigrants in the U.S. South, as it looked in 1851, at a time when the city's population included around twelve thousand German immigrants.

New Orleans, der wichtigste Einwanderungshafen im Süden der USA, im Jahre 1851; etwa 12 000 deutsche Einwanderer lebten zu diesem Zeitpunkt in der Stadt.

intellectual independence and habitual pursuits, and promising at least to learn the thrift and quicken the artistic taste and social feelings of the Anglo-Saxon." This long, slow process of the voluntary integration of millions of Germans into a new nation was brutally interrupted by events in the Old World. During the first two years of World War I when the United States was neutral, many German-Americans made no attempt to hide their sympathies for the German homeland just as many other Americans openly championed the Allied cause. A descendant of colonial German immigrants, John W. Wayland, wrote in his wartime notes: "A few at first seemed to take a sort of sportsman's zest in watching the efficiency of the huge Prussian machine. The skill with which it operated was admired by some, almost applauded by a few . . . but as time passed, changes came . . ." These changes were so subtle at first that most supporters of the German cause did not notice them. When the United States entered the war on the Allied side, it was too late to begin to convince the other Americans of their loyalty for their adopted country. Suddenly everything German was engulfed in a sea of hatred and bigotry. While certain measures of the Federal government were dictated by understandable security considerations, the ugly drive aimed at German-born businessmen and wage-earners, often motivated by instincts of competition, is the darkest chapter of the hysteria that befell otherwise normal citizens.

The Germans were numbed during these weeks where neighbors turned enemies, and authorities, pledged to the protection of all citizens, haunted them like outcasts. While German-Americans answered the call to arms like any other Americans, hysterical "patriots" slaughtered dogs of German breeds in public parks and threw German books into huge bonfires. After two years the terror subsided. German America was gone but millions of Americans of German birth and ancestry remained. They had contributed more than their share to the war effort and yet many who lived through those trying years could

A donation campaign conducted by German-Americans in San Francisco for the benefit of the warring German Reich in the year 1915.

Spendenaktion der Deutschamerikaner von San Francisco für das kriegführende Deutsche Reich im Jahr 1915

The fate wished upon the German Kaiser in this cartoon actually happened to immigrant Robert Prager from Dresden on April 4, 1918, in Collinsville, Illinois: he was hanged by an angry mob. This lynch murder – the only one perpetrated against a German immigrant during the First World War – marks the tragic culmination of anti-German hysteria after the entry of America into the war in April 1917.

Was diese Karikatur dem deutschen Kaiser zudachte, geschah dem Einwanderer Robert Prager aus Dresden am 4. April 1918 in Collinsville, Illinois: er wurde von einer aufgebrachten Menschenmenge gehenkt. Dieser Lynchmord – der einzige, der während des Ersten Weltkriegs in den USA an einem deutschen Einwanderer verübt wurde – markiert den traurigen Höhepunkt der antideutschen Hysterie nach dem amerikanischen Kriegseintritt im April 1917.

The sinking of the British passenger steamer, "Lusitania", by a German submarine on May 7, 1915, which sent 128 American passengers among the 1, 198 casualties to their deaths, mobilized public opinion in the United States against Germany: advertisement by the Cunard Line and warning from the German Embassy in Washington concerning the use of British ships, published on May 1, 1915.

Die Versenkung des englischen Passagierdampfers »Lusitania« durch ein deutsches U-Boot am 7. Mai 1915, bei der unter 1198 Opfern auch 128 amerikanische Passagiere den Tod fanden, mobilisierte die öffentliche Meinung in den USA gegen Deutschland: Anzeige der Cunard Line und Warnung der deutschen Botschaft in Washington vor der Benutzung englischer Schiffe, veröffentlicht am 1. Mai 1915.

EUROPE VIA LIVERPOOL
LUSITANIA
Fastest and Largest Steamer
now in Atlantic Service Sails
SATURDAY, MAY 1, 10 A. M.
Transylvania, Fri., May 7, 5 P.M.
Orduna, - - Tues., May 18, 10 A.M.
Tuscania, - - Fri., May 21, 5 P.M.
LUSITANIA, Sat., May 29, 10 A.M.
Transylvania, Fri., June 4, 5 P.M.
Gibraltar–Genoa–Naples–Piraeus
S.S. Carpathia, Thur., May 13, Noon

NOTICE!
TRAVELLERS intending to embark on the Atlantic voyage are reminded that a state of war exists between Germany and her allies and Great Britain and her allies; that the zone of war includes the waters adjacent to the British Isles; that, in accordance with formal notice given by the Imperial German Government, vessels flying the flag of Great Britain, or of any of her allies, are liable to destruction in those waters and that travellers sailing in the war zone on ships of Great Britain or her allies do so at their own risk.
IMPERIAL GERMAN EMBASSY
WASHINGTON, D. C., APRIL 22, 1915.

Count von Bernstorff, German Ambassador in Washington from 1908 to 1917, leads Uncle Sam before the "hyphenated Americans" (of German origin) on the long leash of "solemn assurances": caricature by W.A. Rogers, illustrating Bernstorff's attempts to keep the United States from entering the war.

Graf von Bernstorff, deutscher Botschafter in Washington von 1908 bis 1917, läßt Uncle Sam am langen Zügel »feierlicher Versicherungen« vor den »Bindestrich-Amerikanern« (den deutschen Einwanderern) paradieren: Karikatur von W. A. Rogers auf die Bemühungen von Bernstorffs, den Kriegseintritt der USA zu verhindern.

Rally held by the "Friends of New Germany" in Los Angeles in 1934. The total number of organized Nazi sympathizers in the United States never exceeded 20,000.

Kundgebung der »Freunde des neuen Deutschlands« in Los Angeles, 1934. Die Gesamtzahl organisierter Anhänger des Nationalsozialismus in den USA erreichte nur wenig mehr als 20 000.

never rid themselves of the trauma of being branded enemies in their own, often self-chosen country. Only a loyal people could sustain such wounds and close ranks.

History did not repeat itself in Word War II. There were inconveniences and a few Nazi sympathizers were rounded up or isolated, but on the whole no public outrage was directed against German-Americans. After both wars some immigration from Germany continued. It is indicative of the profound nature of the relationship between America, the goal of so many Germans, and Germany, the home of so many Americans, that two world wars and the accompanying intense propaganda, have wrought little change in the expectations and their fulfillment on the part of German immigrants. When asked about his feeling upon acquiring American citizenship, one of the scientists of "Operation Paperclip" spoke of "how wonderful this experience was for me to have found a 'new way', from extreme disaster and misery." Photographer Ernst Haas in 1975 spoke from his heart:

An immigrant has to learn to digest.
No one becomes suddenly American . . .
I have great love for this country.
I am very grateful for the liberty it gives me to choose
Without pressure, and I feel for myself
That the time is right
To cherish this freedom and never to take it for granted.

That was also what Johannes Schlessmann meant in 1753 when he stated "This is a free country."

anfangs ein sportliches Interesse daran zu haben, die riesige preußische Kriegsmaschine in Funktion zu sehen. Ihre Präzision und Genauigkeit wurde von einigen bewundert, von wenigen sogar fast beklatscht . . . aber mit der Zeit änderte sich das . . ." Es änderte sich anfangs so unmerklich, daß viele Sympathisanten des Deutschen Reiches den Klimawechsel nicht bemerkten. Als die Vereinigten Staaten dann auf seiten der Alliierten in den Krieg eintraten, war es für die Deutschamerikaner zu spät, ihre Landsleute noch von ihrer Loyalität gegenüber ihrer Wahlheimat zu überzeugen. Plötzlich sah sich alles, was deutsch war, von einem Ozean aus Haß und Fanatismus umgeben. Während gewisse Maßnahmen der Bundesregierung von verständlichen Sicherheitserwägungen diktiert waren, bleiben die blindwütigen Ausschreitungen gegen deutschstämmige Geschäftsleute und Arbeiter, oft von Konkurrenzneid angeheizt, eines der dunkelsten Kapitel dieser Hysterie, die bislang normale Bürger befiel.

Die Deutschen waren wie gelähmt in diesen Wochen, als ihre Nachbarn sich in Feinde verwandelten und die Behörden, statt allen Bürgern gleichermaßen Schutz zu bieten, sie wie Aussätzige verfolgten. Während die Deutschamerikaner dem Ruf zu den Waffen Folge leisteten wie alle anderen Amerikaner auch, wurden deutsche Schäferhunde von hysterischen „Patrioten" in öffentlichen Parks geschlachtet und deutsche Bücher auf riesigen Scheiterhaufen verbrannt. Nach zwei Jahren war der Terror überstanden. Das deutsche Amerika gehörte der Vergangenheit an, doch Millionen von Amerikanern deutscher Abstammung blieben. Sie hatten mehr, als ihr Teil gewesen wäre, zur Kriegsanstrengung beigetragen und mußten doch nach diesen Jahren mit dem Trauma weiterleben, in ihrem eigenen, oft selbstgewählten Heimatland als „Feinde" abgestempelt worden zu sein. Es brauchte viel Loyalität, um solche Wunden zu ertragen und die Reihen wieder zu schließen.

Die Geschichte wiederholte sich im Zweiten Weltkrieg nicht. Es gab gelegentliche Unannehmlichkeiten, und einige Nazi-Sympathisanten wurden festgenommen oder interniert, aber es kam im allgemeinen nicht zu öffentlichen Ausschreitungen gegen die Deutschamerikaner. Nach beiden Kriegen dauerte die Einwanderung aus Deutschland – im Rahmen der Quotierung – an. Es ist bezeichnend für die tiefgreifende Beziehung zwischen Amerika (dem Ziel so vieler Deutscher) und Deutschland (der Heimat so vieler Amerikaner), daß selbst zwei Weltkriege mit der dazugehörigen intensiven Propaganda an den Erwartungen der Umsiedler und den Möglichkeiten zu ihrer Verwirklichung keine großen Veränderungen bewirkt haben. Als einer der Wissenschaftler der *Operation Paperclip* über seine Gefühle beim Empfang der amerikanischen Staatsbürgerschaft befragt wurde, antwortete er: „Für mich war es etwas Wunderbares, diesen neuen Anfang zu machen, nach so viel Leid und Elend." Und 1975 sprach der Fotograf Ernst Haas aus seinem Herzen:

Ein Einwanderer muß lernen, zu verdauen.
Niemand wird von einem Tag auf den anderen zum Amerikaner . . .
Ich liebe dieses Land sehr.
Ich bin sehr dankbar für die Freiheit zur Wahl,
Die es mir läßt ohne Druck, und ich spüre für mich,
Daß die Zeit reif ist,
Diese Freiheit zu schätzen
und niemals für selbstverständlich zu halten.

Nichts anderes meinte auch Johannes Schlessmann, als er 1753 feststellte: „dieses ist ein Fry land."

"Arrival of the Emigrants in the USA", mural by the Lithuanian-born American painter Ben Shahn (1898–1969) for the community center of a textile workers' settlement in Roosevelt, New Jersey, 1937/38.

»Ankunft der Emigranten in den USA«. Wandgemälde des aus Litauen gebürtigen amerikanischen Malers Ben Shahn (1898–1969) für das Gemeinschaftshaus einer Textilarbeitersiedlung in Roosevelt, New Jersey, 1937/38

Stained-glass window in the building of the German Society of Pennsylvania, located in Philadelphia

Glasfenster im Gebäude der Deutschen Gesellschaft von Pennsylvanien in Philadelphia

Individuals and Groups

Their influence in the fields of social life, the manual arts, technology, military affairs, science and culture

Einzelgänger und Gruppen

Ihr Wirken in Gesellschaft, Handwerk, Technik, Militärwesen, Wissenschaft und Kultur

Among the 21,028 German immigrants who came to the U.S. in 1839 were the shoemaker Ernst August Radue and his wife Henriette. They took up residence in the German settlement of Freistadt in Wisconsin, became well-to-do farmers, and were the common ancestors of the group which gathered together a century later for the photograph below.

Zwei von den 21 028 deutschen Einwanderern, die beispielsweise 1839 in die USA kamen: der Schuhmacher Ernst August Radue und seine Frau Henriette. Sie ließen sich in der deutschen Siedlung Freistadt in Wisconsin nieder und wurden wohlhabende Farmer – und die Stammeltern der ein Jahrhundert später für das Gruppenfoto unten versammelten Nachkommenschaft....

The millions of German immigrants who came to America during the last three centuries seem to many observers of historical events to be an amorphous mass largely submerged in a predominantly Anglo-Saxon culture. To be sure, a certain number of outstanding individuals has always been singled out for special treatment such as in the biographical sketches contained in this volume. But the seeming anonymity of millions of immigrants who came from all walks of life in Germany and that of their descendants, cannot alter the fact that entire areas and communities in the United States today are keenly aware of the imprint individuals and groups have left wherever they settled. Entire sections of towns and cities bear testimony to this immigration and in many rural areas Germans created a distinct cultural landscape that has left traces easily discernible today. This is true in the Schoharie and Mohawk valleys of New York, in western New Jersey, in much of eastern Pennsylvania, and in parts of Maryland, Virginia and the Carolinas. More than two centuries after the first colonization, the erstwhile German settlements can still be distinguished from those of the other colonial immigrants. The same is true of many rural settlements begun in the Midwest and in Texas by 19th century immigrants.

In May 1982 the U.S. Census Bureau published the results of a nationwide survey in which Americans were asked to report their known ethnic origins. Although 17 percent either had no recollection of their origins or simply put down "American", 28.8 percent of all Americans had reported that they were at least partly of German ancestry. That means about 52 million Americans are aware of their German forebears who are all but anonymous to them. Earlier census calculations had revealed that German-Americans were almost equally divided between urban and rural areas and, despite heavy concentration in the Middle Atlantic and North Central states, were present in sizeable numbers in almost all parts of the country. In consequence, their impact on both agriculture and industry has been considerable. In cities as well as in the countryside they were, and often still are, particularly well represented among craftsmen.

Die Millionen von deutschen Einwanderern, die in den vergangenen dreihundert Jahren nach Amerika kamen, mögen vielen Beobachtern der historischen Szene als amorphe Masse erscheinen, die von einer überwiegend angelsächsischen Kultur mehr oder minder aufgesogen wurde. Natürlich ist eine gewisse Anzahl herausragender Persönlichkeiten stets besonderer Betrachtung gewürdigt worden, wie es ja auch in den Kurzbiographien in diesem Buch geschieht. Doch auch die scheinbare Anonymität der Millionen, die aus allen Bereichen des Lebens in Deutschland kamen, ändert nichts an der Tatsache, daß sich die Bewohner ganzer Landstriche und Ortschaften der heutigen USA sehr wohl des prägenden Einflusses bewußt sind, den die Einwanderer, als Individuen und als Gruppe, in allen ihren Siedlungsgebieten ausgeübt haben. Ganze Stadtviertel legen Zeugnis von dieser Einwanderung ab, und in vielen ländlichen Gebieten haben die Deutschen eine Kulturlandschaft von unverwechselbaren Zügen hinterlassen, deren Merkmale noch heute zu erkennen sind. Dies trifft für das Schoharie- und das Mohawk-Tal im Staat New York zu, für das westliche New Jersey, große Teile des östlichen Pennsylvaniens und Teile von Maryland, Virginia und den beiden Carolinas. Mehr als zwei Jahrhunderte nach der ersten Kolonisation sind die ehemals deutschen Siedlungen immer noch von denen anderer Einwanderer zu unterscheiden. Das gleiche gilt für viele ländliche Niederlassungen, die von deutschen Einwanderern des 19. Jahrhunderts im mittleren Westen und in Texas gegründet wurden.

Im Mai 1982 veröffentlichte das statistische Bundesamt der USA die Ergebnisse einer landesweiten Befragung, in der die Amerikaner über ihre ethnische Herkunft, soweit bekannt, Auskunft geben sollten. Während 17 Prozent der Befragten nichts über ihre Abstammung aussagen konnten oder einfach „amerikanisch" angaben, bezeichneten sich 28,8 Prozent aller Amerikaner als ganz oder teilweise deutschstämmig. In absoluten Zahlen sind das etwa 52 Millionen Bürger der Vereinigten Staaten, die sich ihrer – nun gar nicht mehr so anonymen – deutschen Vorfahren bewußt sind. Frühere Volkszählungen hatten ergeben, daß die deutschstämmigen Amerikaner fast zu gleichen Teilen in städtischen und in ländlichen Siedlungsgebieten beheimatet waren und daß sie, trotz einer deutlichen Konzentration in den mittleren Ostküstenstaaten und den nördlichen Staaten des Mittelwestens, in so gut wie allen Teilen des Landes einen nennenswerten Bevölkerungsanteil stellten. Infolgedessen war ihr Einfluß auf Landwirtschaft und Industrie gleichermaßen beträchtlich. In Städten wie auch auf dem flachen Land waren sie – und sind es häufig heute noch – besonders unter den Handwerkern stark vertreten.

As a group, German-Americans earned consistent praise as farmers. From the days of frontier agriculture to today's agribusiness, the share of Germans has been large, often to such an extent that certain crops like alfalfa and winter wheat were dominated by them. According to one calculation, German immigrants started no less than 672,000 family farms during the 19th century. Theirs was also a prominent role in setting up the scientific foundations for improvements in farming. It suffices to mention here Eugene Hilgard, the father of soil research in the United States, who transferred his knowledge acquired in German universities to the fledgling experiment stations of America. Forestry was another field in which Germans brought contemporary European methods to both the conservation and exploitation of natural wealth. Bernhard Fernow, for many years chief of the Forestry Division of the Department of Agriculture, was instrumental in creating the national forest system in 1891.

Als Gruppe haben sich die Deutschamerikaner vor allem in der Landwirtschaft einen guten Ruf erworben. Von den Tagen der *frontier* bis zur heutigen Agrarindustrie war ihr Anteil an der Farmwirtschaft stets überdurchschnittlich, auf manchen Gebieten, wie dem Anbau von Luzernen und winterhartem Weizen, sogar dominierend. Einer statistischen Berechnung zufolge gründeten deutsche Einwanderer im 19. Jahrhundert nicht weniger als 672 000 Familienfarmen. Eine wichtige Rolle spielten sie auch bei der Erarbeitung der wissenschaftlichen Grundlagen für die Verbesserung von Ackerbau und Viehzucht. Hier sei nur Eugene Hilgard erwähnt, der Vater der Bodenforschung in den Vereinigten Staaten, der sein an deutschen Universitäten erworbenes Wissen an die jungen Experimentierstationen Amerikas weitergab. Auch in der Forstwirtschaft waren die Deutschen an der Einführung zeitgenössischer europäischer Methoden zur Erhaltung und Nutzung der natürlichen Reserven maßgeblich beteiligt. Bernhard Fernow, viele Jahre lang Leiter der forstwirtschaftlichen Abteilung des Landwirtschaftsministeriums, spielte eine führende Rolle bei der Neuorganisation der Bundesforsten im Jahre 1891.

Cutting out a clearing in the virgin forest. The beginning of one of the many farms which were established in the 19th century (Contemporary illustration).

Rodungsarbeiten im Urwald: der Anfang einer von vielen Farmneugründungen des 19. Jahrhunderts (zeitgenössische Illustration)

A century after German Mennonites had emigrated to Russia under the reign of Catherine the Great (1762–96), their descendents were compelled to leave the country and resettled in America. Bringing new hardy varieties of wheat with them to Kansas, they contributed to that state's fame in America's wheat belt. The illustrations, both from the March 20, 1875 issue of "Frank Leslie's Illustrated Newspaper," show the Russo-German village of Gnadenau, Kansas (above), and a group of Mennonite immigrants in temporary accommodations in Topeka (below).

Deutsche Mennoniten, die zur Zeit Katharinas der Großen nach Rußland ausgewandert und später von dort nach Amerika vertrieben worden waren, brachten neue winterharte Weizensorten nach Kansas und halfen mit, diesen Staat zur Kornkammer Amerikas zu machen. Die Abbildungen, beide aus »Frank Leslie's Illustrated Newspaper« vom 20. März 1875, zeigen das rußlanddeutsche Dorf Gnadenau in Kansas (oben) und eine mennonitische Einwanderergruppe in einem Zwischenquartier in Topeka (unten).

A land office in Sedgewick County, Kansas, in 1874 (illustration taken from "Harper's Weekly").

Ein Landverteilungsamt in Sedgewick County, Kansas, im Jahr 1874 (Illustration aus »Harper's Weekly«)

An American ten-Taler bill, adorned with portraits of Mozart and the theologian/physiognomist Lavater; issued by the German Lumbermen's Bank in Warren, Pennsylvania, probably around the middle of the 19th century.

Amerikanische Zehn-Taler-Note, geschmückt mit den Porträts von Mozart und Lavater, ausgegeben von der deutschen Holzfäller-Bank in Warren, Pennsylvanien, wahrscheinlich um die Mitte des 19. Jahrhunderts.

H. L. Mencken (German-American contribution to linguistic culture, left) in front of an ornate painted poster of the Pabst brewery (German-American contribution to drinking culture, right). Attorney Clarence Darrow (middle) appears not to hold either one in contempt.

Henry Louis Mencken (deutschamerikanischer Beitrag zur Sprachkultur, links) vor einem gemalten Prachtprospekt der Brauerei Pabst (deutschamerikanischer Beitrag zur Trinkkultur, rechts). Anwalt Clarence Darrow (Mitte) scheint beides nicht zu verschmähen.

As early as the colonial era, German immigrants were prominent in the milling of small grain. Later on, new immigrants became magnates in the processing and distribution of food. There were the "sugar kings" of the Havemeyer and Spreckels families; Henry J. Heinz, who founded one of the largest food canning firms in the world; and Ferdinand Schumacher, the first successful producer of packaged breakfast cereals. Despite present-day conglomerates and mergers, super-market shelves still hold products that once were sold in the innumerable corner groceries run by German families. Musselman's preserves, Mueller's noodles and Hecker's flour were and are familiar staples across the country. Speaking of food and agricultural products, we might just as well include an industry in which German-Americans were practically unchallenged: beer brewing. In the wake of every wave of German immigration, breweries were founded. German-style lager beer soon took the place of ale and porter in American esteem and by 1900 the United States was the second largest beer-producing country in the world after Germany. Despite the long years of Prohibition, and despite business consolidations, the names of the immigrant brewers still adorn the labels of America's favorite brands, Blatz, Miller, Pabst, Schlitz, Stroh and Anheuser-Busch. There were thousands of saloons and beer gardens run by Germans which competed with the Irish pubs. They were excelled in numbers only by the legions of German bakers, butchers, grocers and restaurateurs whose lasting influence is reflected in many words that have entered the American language like sauerkraut, liverwurst, delicatessen, stein, frankfurter or rathskeller.

It has often been said that German Gentiles catered to America's eating and drinking needs but German Jews provided the clothing for Americans. By the end of the 19th century, 90 percent of all ready-made wholesale clothing and 80 percent of the retail business was in the hands of German Jews. These clothiers created inexpensive garments which had a tremendous impact on the democratization of American society, by eliminating dress as an exterior sign of

Bereits in der Kolonialzeit waren deutsche Einwanderer überdurchschnittlich in der Getreidemüllerei vertreten. Einwanderer späterer Generationen brachten es in der Lebensmittelindustrie zu Macht und Reichtum – so die „Zuckerkönige" der Familien Havemeyer und Spreckels; Ferdinand Schumacher, der als erster abgepackte Frühstücksflocken in industriellem Maßstab produzierte; oder Henry J. Heinz, dessen Firma zu einem der größten Konservenhersteller der Welt wurde. Trotz heutiger Konzernverflechtungen und -fusionen stehen in den Regalen amerikanischer Supermärkte immer noch Produkte, die schon in den Gemischtwarenläden deutscher Einwanderer angeboten wurden. Musselmans Konserven, Muellers Nudeln und Heckers Mehl waren und sind vertraute Namen im ganzen Land. Im Zusammenhang mit Lebensmitteln und Landwirtschaftsprodukten soll auch ein Industriezweig erwähnt werden, in dem die Deutschamerikaner praktisch konkurrenzlos waren: die Bierbrauerei. Jede deutsche Einwanderungswelle hatte neue Brauereigründungen im Gefolge. Nach deutscher Art hergestelltes Lagerbier verdrängte in der Beliebtheitsskala der Amerikaner bald das englische Ale oder Porter, und schon um 1900 waren die Vereinigten Staaten zum nach Deutschland zweitgrößten Bierproduzenten der Welt geworden. Trotz der langen Jahre der Prohibition und späterer Firmenfusionen finden sich die Namen der eingewanderten deutschen Brauer noch heute auf den Etiketten der beliebtesten amerikanischen Biermarken: Blatz, Miller, Pabst, Schlitz, Stroh und Anheuser-Busch. Es gab Tausende von deutschen Kneipen und Biergärten, die mit den irischen Pubs konkurrierten. Sie wurden zahlenmäßig nur von den Legionen deutscher Bäcker, Fleischer, Lebensmittelhändler und Speisewirte übertroffen, deren bleibender Einfluß sich in vielen Wörtern widerspiegelt, die in die amerikanische Alltagssprache eingegangen sind: *sauerkraut, liverwurst* (Leberwurst), *delicatessen, stein* (Bierkrug), *frankfurter* oder *rathskeller.*

Man hat oft gesagt, daß die deutschstämmigen Christen für die leiblichen Bedürfnisse der Amerikaner sorgten, während die deutschen Juden für die Kleidung zuständig waren. Tatsächlich befanden sich gegen Ende des 19. Jahrhunderts 90 Prozent des Konfektionskleidungsgroßhandels und 80 Prozent des Einzelhandels in der Hand deutschstämmiger Juden. Die preiswerte Kleidung, die diese Konfektionäre schufen, hatte beträchtlichen Einfluß auf die Demokratisierung der amerikanischen Gesellschaft, indem sie die Garderobe von ihrer klassischen europäischen Funktion befreite, ein äußeres Zeichen der sozialen Schichtenzugehörigkeit zu sein. Deutschstämmige Juden gründeten auch die meisten der großen Kaufhäuser in den Vereinigten Staaten. Andere, wie Simon Guggenheim, August Belmont, Jacob Schiff und Solomon Loeb schafften den Aufstieg in die Welt der Hochfinanz zu einer Zeit, da Risiken und Profite gleichermaßen groß waren und das Bankwesen alten Zuschnitts von der Finanzierung der wirtschaftlichen Expansion überfordert gewesen wäre, die mit der rapiden Besiedlung eines ganzen Kontinents einherging.

The "Brauhaus" in Yorkville, a section of Manhattan extending on both sides of 86th Street, which today still bears the stamp of German immigrants.

Das »Brauhaus« in Yorkville, dem bis heute von deutschen Einwanderern geprägten Teil Manhattans beiderseits der 86. Straße

A Bavarian immigrant by the name of Levi Strauss invented that which was to become "the" American clothing article par excellence – Blue Jeans.

Ein bayerischer Einwanderer namens Levi Strauss erfand, was zum amerikanischen Kleidungsstück par excellence wurde: die Blue Jeans.

class distinction which was so prevalent in Europe at that time. German-Jewish families also founded most of the large department stores across the United States. Others like Simon Guggenheim, August Belmont, Jacob Schiff and Solomon Loeb worked their way up into the world of finance at a time when both risks and profits were high and the banking establishment of old could not have financed the economic surge that followed the sudden peopling of an entire continent.

German craftsmen during the colonial period helped lay the foundations for industries of a later era. Most notable among their achievements were the so-called Kentucky rifle, first developed from European prototypes in Pennsylvania, and the Conestoga wagon. Both of these creations played an essential role in the westward movement. Germans were also among the pioneers of the colonial iron industry. Early ironmasters like "Baron" Stiegel and John Huber of Pennsylvania, Peter Hasenclever in New York and Dirk Pennybaker in Virginia produced not only utensils and stoves but provided the foundation for the infant armament industry of the Revolutionary War. Descendants of colonial immigrants like Henry C. Frick and Charles M. Schwab later became the giants of America's steel industry. The inventiveness of German-Americans provided spectacular advances in American technology in the late 19th and early 20th century. George Westinghouse whose greatest invention was the air brake, John A. Roebling, the bridge builder, Ottmar Mergenthaler who invented the Linotype machine, and Charles P. Steinmetz whose work paved the way for mass production of generators and electrical motors, are just a few of the most renowned contributors.

The prevalence of German names in the pharmaceutical, chemical and optical industries such as Dohme, Pfizer, Erhart, Vogel, Merck, Bausch and Lomb is evidence of the transfer of theoretical knowledge acquired in German universities and laboratories to practical production in the New World. An entire generation of immigrant chemists and instrument builders successfully helped the United States to challenge Germany's lead in these fields.

Deutsche Handwerker halfen in der kolonialen Ära mit, die Grundlagen für ganze spätere Industriezweige zu schaffen. Zu ihren bemerkenswertesten Entwicklungen zählen die sogenannte Kentucky Rifle, die in Pennsylvanien auf der Basis europäischer Vorbilder entstand, und der Conestoga Wagon. Beide Produkte, Gewehr und Planwagen, spielten eine entscheidende Rolle bei der Erschließung des Westens. Deutsche befanden sich auch unter den Pionieren der kolonialen Eisenverarbeitung. Frühe Hüttenbesitzer wie der „Baron" Stiegel oder John Huber aus Pennsylvanien, Peter Hasenclever in New York und Dirk Pennybaker in Virginia fertigten nicht nur haus- und landwirtschaftliche Geräte und Öfen, sondern legten auch Grundlagen für die Anfänge des amerikanischen Zeugwesens im Unabhängigkeitskrieg. Nachfahren von Einwanderern der Kolonialzeit wie Henry C. Frick und Charles M. Schwab wurden später zu Magnaten der amerikanischen Stahlindustrie. Auch im 19. und 20. Jahrhundert sorgte der Erfindungsreichtum deutschamerikanischer Ingenieure für spektakuläre Fortschritte. George Westinghouse, dessen größte Erfindung die Luftdruckbremse war, John A. Roebling, der Brückenbauer, Ottmar Mergenthaler als Erfinder der Linotype-Setzmaschine und Charles P. Steinmetz, dessen Forschungen erst die Massenproduktion von Dynamomaschinen und Elektromotoren ermöglichten, seien stellvertretend für viele genannt.

Die Vorherrschaft deutscher Namen wie Dohme, Pfizer, Erhard, Vogel, Merck, Bausch und Lomb in der pharmazeutischen, chemischen und optischen Industrie beweist, wie erfolgreich das in deutschen Universitäten und Labors erworbene Wissen jenseits des Ozeans in Praxis umgesetzt werden konnte. Eine ganze Generation eingewanderter Chemiker und Feinmechaniker half den Vereinigten Staaten, Deutschland seine führende Rolle auf diesen Gebieten erfolgreich streitig zu machen.

Ottmar Mergenthaler, born in 1854 in Hachtel in the Tauber Valley, was only 44 years old when he died in 1899, in his adopted city of Baltimore.

Ottmar Mergenthaler, geboren 1854 in Hachtel im Taubertal, gestorben 1899, mit erst 44 Jahren, in seiner Wahlheimat Baltimore.

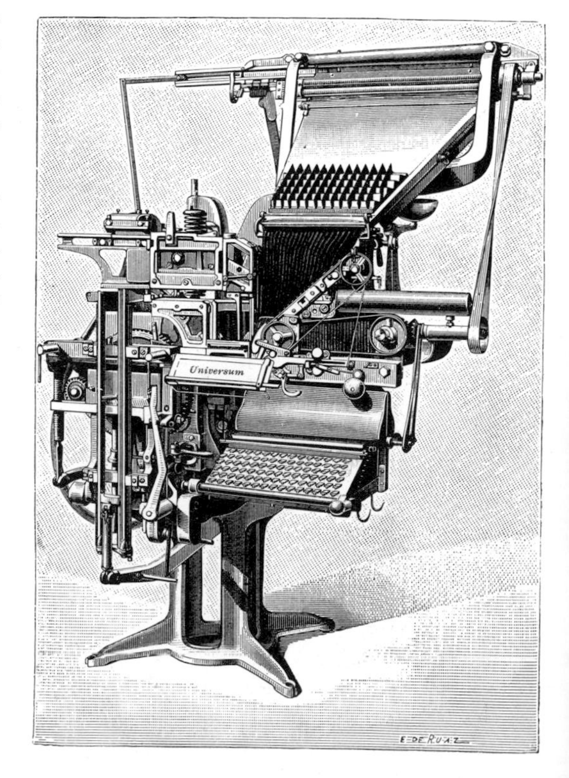

An early model of the "Linotype" typesetting machine which Mergenthaler developed, earning him the cognomen "the second Gutenberg". Its introduction in the last decade of the nineteenth century fundamentally revolutionized the printing industry, just as electronically controlled phototypography has done today.

Ein frühes Modell der »Linotype«-Zeilensetz- und -gießmaschine, deren Entwicklung Mergenthaler den Beinamen eines »zweiten Gutenberg« eintrug. Ihre Einführung in den 90er Jahren des 19. Jahrhunderts revolutionierte das Druckwesen ähnlich grundlegend, wie es heute durch den elektronisch gesteuerten Lichtsatz geschieht.

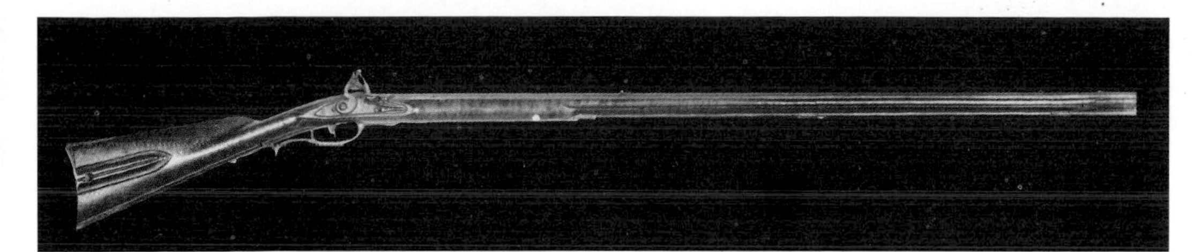

The "Kentucky Rifle", a venerable adjunct of the frontier myth.

Die »Kentucky Rifle«, eine Reliquie des »Frontier«-Mythos

The "Conestoga Wagon", a familiar object in American Westerns, can be traced back to prototypes from the southwestern region of Germany. The Pennsylvania Dutch family Studebaker produced about 750,000 of these covered wagons before turning its attention to the manufacture of automobiles.

Der »Conestoga Wagon«, noch heute aus Wildwestfilmen vertraut, geht auf Vorbilder aus dem südwestdeutschen Raum zurück. Die pennsylvaniendeutsche Familie Studebaker stellte etwa 750 000 solcher Planwagen her, ehe sie sich dem Automobilbau zuwandte.

The young immigrant and his lifework: an idealized portrayal of nineteen-year-old Johann Bausch from Wurttemberg upon his arrival in New York in 1849; in the background, the Bausch & Lomb Optical Company which he, together with his friend Heinrich Lomb, also a German immigrant, built up in Rochester.

Der junge Einwanderer und sein Lebenswerk: Idealporträt des 19jährigen Württembergers Johann Bausch bei seiner Ankunft in New York 1849; im Hintergrund die optischen Werke von Bausch und Lomb, die er gemeinsam mit seinem ebenfalls aus Deutschland stammenden Freund Heinrich Lomb in Rochester aufbauen sollte.

Albert Fink (1829–97), a "Forty-Eighter" who fled to America, erected this truss-frame bridge over the Monongahela River at Fairmount, West Virginia, in 1853. With a span of 290 feet and a length of over 880 feet, it was the longest bridge of its kind.

Albert Fink (1829–97), ein nach Amerika geflüchteter »Achtundvierziger«, errichtete 1853 diese eiserne Fachwerkbrücke über den Monongahela bei Fairmount, West Virginia. Mit einer Spannweite von 90 Metern und einer Länge von 270 Metern war sie die größte ihrer Art.

Cast-iron stove plate produced in the iron works of Heinrich Wilhelm Stiegel, who was born in Cologne in 1729 and emigrated to Pennsylvania in 1750. He was also a successful glass manufacturer and, because of his sumptuous life style, was nicknamed "Baron".

Gußeiserne Ofenplatte aus der Eisenhütte des 1729 in Köln geborenen und 1750 nach Pennsylvanien ausgewanderten Heinrich Wilhelm Stiegel, der auch als Glasfabrikant erfolgreich war und wegen seines großzügigen Lebensstils den Spitznamen »Baron« erhielt.

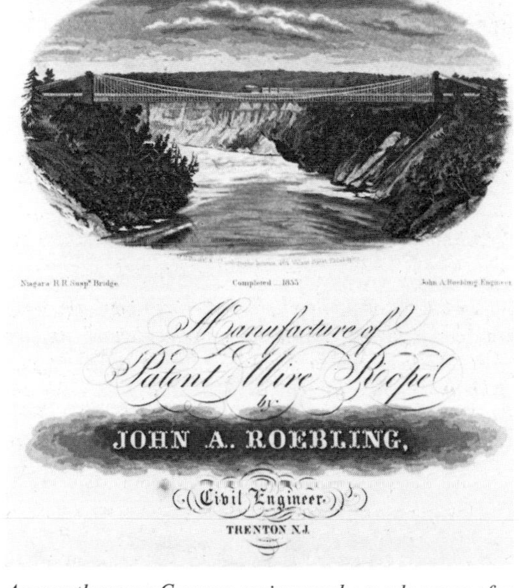

Among the many German engineers who made a name for themselves in American bridge construction, the most famous of all was John Augustus Roebling (1806–69), the pioneer of suspension bridge construction. The cover of a pamphlet advertising his wire-rope factory depicts the railroad suspension bridge over the Niagara River, completed in 1855.

Unter den vielen deutschen Ingenieuren, die gerade im amerikanischen Brückenbau hervorgetreten sind, war John Augustus Roebling (1806–69), der Pionier des Hängebrückenbaus, der berühmteste. Das Deckblatt einer Werbebroschüre seiner Drahtseilfabrik zeigt die 1855 vollendete Eisenbahn-Hängebrücke über den Niagara.

From this apothecary shop in Baltimore, in which Karl Dohme, who emigrated from Obernkirchen near Hanover in 1852, worked as an apprentice, emerged the pharmaceutical company of Sharp & Dohme.

Aus dieser Apotheke in Baltimore, in die der 1852 aus Obernkirchen bei Hannover ausgewanderte Karl Dohme als Lehrling eintrat, ging der Pharmaziekonzern Sharp and Dohme hervor.

The main building of the University of Göttingen as it looked in 1837. Not only had Benjamin Franklin been admitted to the Göttingen Academy of Science way back in 1766, but in the early 19th century a colony of American students formed here, making Göttingen an intellectual center of German-American fellowship.

Das Hauptgebäude der Universität Göttingen im Bauzustand von 1837. Nachdem bereits 1766 Benjamin Franklin in die Göttinger Akademie aufgenommen worden war, bildete sich hier im frühen 19. Jahrhundert eine amerikanische Studentenkolonie, die Göttingen zu einem geistigen Zentrum der deutsch-amerikanischen Begegnung machte.

George Ticknor (1791–1871) was born in Boston and studied in Göttingen from 1815 to 1817, during which time he once visited the aging Goethe. Ticknor later taught Romance languages at Harvard, where he sought to introduce the German system of nonrequisite, academic elective courses.

George Ticknor (1791–1871), in Boston geboren, studierte von 1815–17 in Göttingen, besuchte Johann Wolfgang von Goethe und wirkte später als Romanist in Harvard, wo er das deutsche System freier akademischer Wahlfächer einzuführen versuchte.

THESES,

QVAS,

ANNVENTE SVMMO NVMINE,

EX AVCTORITATE

ORDINIS PHILOSOPHORVM AMPLISSIMI

IN

ACADEMIA GEORGIA AVGVSTA

PRO

GRADV DOCTORIS

RITE CONSEQVENDO

DIE SEPTEMBRIS IX. cIↄIↄcccxx

LOCO HORAQVE SOLITA PVBLICE DEFENDET

GEORGIVS BANCROFT

MASSACHVSETTENSI - VIGONIENSIS,

REIPVBLICAE AMERICAE SEPTENTRIONALIS FOEDERATAE CIVIS,

IN ACADEMIA NEO - CANTABRIGIENSI ARTIVM BACCALAVREVS.

GOTTINGAE,

TYPIS J. C. BAIER, TYPOGR. ACAD.

After completing his studies in Göttingen in 1820 and returning to the U.S., the American historian George Bancroft (1800–91) was one of the co-founders of the famous Round Hill School in Northampton, Massachusetts, on the campus of which the immigrant Carl Beck, pupil of Jahn, established the first German-style athletic field in America, patterned after the Hasenheide near Berlin (illustration on page 92).

1820 promovierte in Göttingen der amerikanische Historiker George Bancroft (1800–91), der nach seiner Rückkehr 1823 die berühmte Round-Hill-Reformschule in Northampton, Massachusetts, mitbegründete. Dort richtete der Jahn-Schüler und Emigrant Carl Beck den ersten amerikanischen Turnplatz nach dem Modell der »Hasenheide« (vgl. S. 92) ein.

Practically unknown to those outside of his special field, the botanist Wilhelm N. Suksdorf (1850–1932) from Dransau in Holstein was the first to take a comprehensive inventory of the flora of the State of Washington; he also discovered numerous varieties of moss and mushrooms.

Außerhalb seines Fachbereichs fast unbekannt geblieben ist der Botaniker Wilhelm N. Suksdorf (1850–1932) aus Dransau in Holstein, der die erste umfangreiche Bestandsaufnahme der Flora des Bundesstaates Washington erarbeitete und zahlreiche Moos- und Piltzarten entdeckte.

Thomas Jefferson (1743–1826), author of the Declaration of Independence, third president of the U.S.A. and founder of the University of Virginia. He appointed the philologist Georg Blättermann of Göttingen to a professorship at the Virginia institution.

Thomas Jefferson (1743–1826), Autor der amerikanischen Unabhängigkeitserklärung, dritter Präsident der USA und Gründer der Universität von Virginia, an die er den Göttinger Sprachwissenschaftler Georg Blättermann berief.

Abraham Jacobi (1830–1919), the founder of pediatrics in the United States, surrounded by his grandchildren.

Abraham Jacobi (1830–1919), der Begründer der Pädiatrie in den Vereinigten Staaten, mit seinen Enkelkindern.

Abraham Jacobi's birthplace in Hartum, Westphalia (photo taken about 1900)

Abraham Jacobis Geburtshaus in Hartum in Westfalen (Foto um 1900)

Friedrich Valentin Melsheimer (1751–1814) came to America as an army chaplain for the Brunswick troops who fought on the British side during the Revolutionary War. He soon sought discharge from service, settled down in Pennsylvania to work as a Lutheran minister, and made a name for himself as an entomologist. The title page of a diary in which he recounted his experiences during the trip from Wolfenbüttel to Quebec, published in 1776, is reproduced here.

Friedrich Valentin Melsheimer (1751–1814) kam als Feldprediger der Braunschweigischen Truppen, die im Unabhängigkeitskrieg auf der Seite Englands kämpften, nach Amerika, wo er schon bald seinen Dienst quittierte, sich als lutherischer Geistlicher in Pennsylvanien niederließ und sich einen Namen als Insektenforscher machte.

A similarly significant contribution was made by German-trained and German-born physicians, in the second half of the 19th century. Numerous medical specialists and practitioners who came as refugees after 1933 followed in the footsteps of such men as Dr. Abraham Jacobi, the pioneer in pediatrics in America, who had arrived as a refugee after the aborted Revolution of 1848 and later became president of the American Medical Association.
Academic pursuits, of course, were not the objective of the mass of German immigrants, but some of their descendants acceded to chairs in American institutions of higher learning often after only one generation in the country. The colonial German clergy, almost all German-born, were among the best educated people in early America. Three of their number were appointed to the board of trustees of The College of Philadelphia as early as 1779. Some made significant contributions to America's budding science: Gotthilf Muhlenberg as a botanist, Valentine Melsheimer as an entomologist and Ferdinand Steinmeyer in a wide range of natural sciences. John Peter Miller, a graduate of Heidelberg and successor of Conrad Beissel as the head of the famed Ephrata Cloister of the German Seventh Day Baptists, was elected to the American Philosophical Society on the basis of his erudite writings and translations. Dr. Christopher Kunze taught ancient languages at Columbia College. Called by Thomas Jefferson from Göttingen in 1825 to the new University of Virginia, Dr. George Blättermann introduced the comparative study of languages.

Tagebuch
von der Reise
der Braunschweigischen
Auxiliär Truppen
von
Wolfenbüttel nach Quebec
entworfen
von
F. V. Melsheimer
Feldprediger bei dem Hochfürstl. Braunschweigischen
Dragoner Regiment.
Erste Fortsetzung.
Frankfurt und Leipzig,
1776.

Einen ähnlich bedeutenden Beitrag leisteten in Deutschland geborene und ausgebildete Mediziner in der zweiten Hälfte des 19. Jahrhunderts. Zahlreiche Fach- und Allgemeinärzte, die nach 1933 als politische Flüchtlinge in die USA kamen, traten dort in die Fußstapfen bedeutender Vorgänger wie Dr. Abraham Jacobis, des Pioniers der Kinderheilkunde in Amerika, der selbst als Flüchtling der gescheiterten Revolution von 1848 eingewandert und später Präsident der amerikanischen Ärztevereinigung geworden war.
Akademische Ehren zu erwerben war natürlich nicht das Ziel der großen Masse der deutschen Einwanderer, obwohl etliche ihrer Nachfahren, oft schon nach einer Generation, auf Lehrstühle höherer amerikanischer Bildungsinstitute gelangten. Die deutschamerikanischen Kleriker der Kolonialzeit, fast alle noch in Europa geboren, gehörten zu den gebildetsten Männern im frühen Amerika. Bereits 1779 wurden drei von ihnen ins Kuratorium des College von Philadelphia berufen. Einige leisteten bedeutende Beiträge zur knospenden Wissenschaft der Neuen Welt: Gotthilf Muhlenberg als Botaniker, Valentin Melsheimer als Entomologe und Ferdinand Steinmeyer auf einer Vielzahl von naturwissenschaftlichen Gebieten. Johann Peter Müller, später Miller, Absolvent der Universität Heidelberg und Nachfolger Conrad Beissels als Leiter des Klosters Ephrata der deutschen Siebentagbaptisten, wurde für seine gelehrten Schriften und Übersetzungen in die American Philosophical Society aufgenommen. Dr. Christopher Kunze lehrte als Altphilologe am Columbia College. Dr. George Blättermann, von ihrem Gründer Thomas Jefferson 1825 an die junge Universität von Virginia berufen, führte die vergleichende Sprachwissenschaft in Amerika ein.
Unter den Einwanderern, die, in verschiedenen Epochen der deutschen Geschichte, als Füchtlinge vor religiöser, politischer und rassischer Verfolgung nach Amerika kamen, war der Anteil an Intellektuellen und akademisch Gebildeten von jeher sehr hoch. Johann Kelpius und Henry Bernhard Koester, die ihre englischen Kirchenbrüder in den 90er Jahren des 17. Jahrhunderts mit der Gedankenwelt der deutschen Mystik bekanntmachten, stehen am Anfang dieser Liste. In den 20er und 30er Jahren des 19. Jahrhunderts trieben die „Demagogenverfolgungen" unter Metternich die erste Welle politischer Flüchtlinge in die USA. Unter diesen waren es besonders Karl Follen und Carl Beck, die ihre amerikanische Umgebung an der Universität Harvard, wo man sie aufgenommen hatte, beeinflußten. Der 1827 eingetroffene Franz Lieber schenke den Amerikanern ihre Nationalenzyklopädie, die vierzehnbändige *Encyclopedia Americana*, und wurde später Präsidentschaftsberater und einer der führenden Politikwissenschaftler. Frederick Rauch, ehedem an der Universität Gießen, führte die zeitgenössische deutsche Philosophie an den pennsylvanischen Colleges ein, an denen er lehrte. Rauch war auch der früheste Parteigänger Hegels in der Neuen Welt und wurde als solcher zum Vorläufer späterer deutschamerikanischer Hegelianer, unter denen vor allem H.C. Brokmeyer in St. Louis und Bernhard Stallo in Cincinnati zu erwähnen sind.

Among those immigrants who came as refugees from religious, political or racial persecution in various periods of German history, intellectuals and academically-trained leaders were numerous. Their list begins with Johann Kelpius and Henry Bernhard Koester, who acquainted their English fellow churchmen with the complex of German mystical thought in the 1690s. The repression of liberal ideas by police terror brought the first wave of political refugees in the 1820s and 30s. Notably Charles Follen and Carl Beck influenced the American environment into which they were received at Harvard University. Francis Lieber who came in 1827 gave Americans their native encyclopedia, the 14-volume *Encyclopedia Americana.* Lieber became a leading political scientist and presidential advisor. Frederick Rauch introduced contemporary German philosophy to the Pennsylvania colleges where he taught, having fled from Giessen University. Rauch was the earliest proponent of Hegel in the New World. As such he became the forerunner of later German-American Hegelians, notably H.C. Brokmeyer in St. Louis and John Bernhard Stallo in Cincinnati.

The largest group of university-trained men during the 19th century came with the Forty-Eighters. Their ranks included clergymen and freethinkers, painters, musicians, actors, professors and engineers, contractors, army officers, lawyers, journalists and the only active woman fighter, Mathilde Franziska Anneke, who bravely continued her fight for woman suffrage among the burdened immigrant women in America. Many of these exiles became leaders within the German-American community but a few also achieved national recognition in their new country. To their fellow Germans in America, who were referred to as an "army without generals", the Forty-Eighters came as "generals without an army" and for decades to come provided leadership in many fields.

Die größte Gruppe akademisch gebildeter Flüchtlinge im 19. Jahrhundert kam mit den „Achtundvierzigern". Zu ihnen gehörten Geistliche und Freidenker, Maler, Musiker, Schauspieler, Professoren und Ingenieure, Unternehmer, Offiziere, Rechtsanwälte, Journalisten und die einzige Frau, die aktiv für die deutsche Revolution gekämpft hatte, Mathilde Franziska Anneke. Sie setzte ihren einsamen Kampf für das Frauenwahlrecht unter ihren als Immigrantinnen in einem fremden Land schon doppelt belasteten deutschamerikanischen Geschlechtsgenossinnen fort. Auch viele andere der Exilanten gelangten in den deutschen Kreisen ihrer neuen Heimat zu Einfluß; einige wenige fanden sogar landesweite Anerkennung. Zu den deutschstämmigen Amerikanern, die man scherzhaft oft als „Armee ohne Generäle" bezeichnet hatte, gesellten sich nun die Achtundvierziger als „Generäle ohne Armee": sie sollten über Jahrzehnte hinweg auf vielen Gebieten Führungspositionen übernehmen.

Von den unzähligen deutschamerikanischen Universitätsprofessoren können hier nur wenige erwähnt werden. Franz Boas begründete die akademische Disziplin, die heute als Kulturanthropologie bekannt ist. Seine Forschungen und Deutungen hatten einen weitreichenden Einfluß auf unsere heutige Einstellung zu fremden Kulturen. Für Boas war eine Kultur ein Stadium in der individuellen und gesellschaftlichen Entwicklung der Menschheit, das nur an seinen eigenen Wertmaßstäben gemessen und beurteilt werden durfte. Seine Studien über die Ureinwohner Nordamerikas legten den Grundstein für unser modernes Verständnis der Indianer. Boas lehrte an der Columbia University und war Kurator des American Museum of Natural History. Hugo Münsterberg richtete an der Harvard University das erste psychologische Labor in Amerika ein. Während Münsterbergs Pionierarbeiten über die physiologischen Aspekte der Gehirntätigkeit und die Nutzanwendungen der Psy-

Franz (Francis) Lieber, who was born in 1800 in Berlin, fled to the United States in 1827 to escape repressive measures aimed at "demagogues". In America he edited the "Encyclopedia Americana" and, with his "Manual of Political Ethics" (1838/39), became the founder of American political science.

Franz (Francis) Lieber, 1800 in Berlin geboren, floh 1827 vor den »Demagogenverfolgungen« in die Vereinigten Staaten, wo er die »Encyclopedia Americana« herausgab und mit seinem »Manual of Political Ethics« (1838/39) zum Begründer der amerikanischen Politikwissenschaft wurde.

Karl (Charles) Follen, who was born in 1796 in Romrod, joined various politically radical student associations, founded a "Verein burschenschaftlicher Unbedingter" ("Society of Student Absolutists") to which Karl Ludwig Sand (the assassin of Kotzebue, cf. p. 38) also belonged. In 1824 he fled Germany and came to America, where he later taught at Harvard and also became a Unitarian preacher. His career was cut short by his death in 1840 when the ship he was on sank in Long Island Sound.

Karl (Charles) Follen, 1796 in Romrod geboren, schloß sich den radikalen Burschenschaften an, gründete einen »Verein burschenschaftlicher Unbedingter«, dem auch Karl Ludwig Sand (der Mörder Kotzebues, vgl. S. 38) angehörte, und mußte 1824 emigrieren. In den USA wirkte er als Professor in Harvard und als unitarischer Prediger, bis er 1840 bei einem Schiffsunglück den Tod fand.

Franz Boas, born in 1858 in Minden, emigrated in 1887 and died in 1942 in New York City. His research on the Kwakiutl Indians in the northwestern region of the United States enabled him to refute the pseudo-scientific arguments, widespread at the time, which were giving support to racist ideology.

Franz Boas, 1858 in Minden geboren, 1887 ausgewandert, gestorben 1942 in New York. Durch seine Forschungen an den Kwakiutl-Indianern des amerikanischen Nordwestens gelang es ihm, die zu seiner Zeit weit verbreiteten pseudo-wissenschaftlichen Begründungen des Rassismus zu widerlegen.

Henry Brokmeyer, the guiding light of the St. Louis school of philosophy. After an erratic life as a steel worker, huntsman, soldier, lawyer and, finally, hermit, Brokmeyer died in 1906 without his major work, a translation of Hegel's "Logic", having been published. "Just leave it in the attic for the vermin" were his last words concerning the manuscript.

Henry C. Brokmeyer, der führende Kopf der »St. Louis-Hegelianer«; nach einem unsteten Leben als Stahlkocher, Jäger, Soldat, Rechtsanwalt und endlich Einsiedler starb er 1906, ohne sein Hauptwerk, eine Übersetzung von Hegels »Logik«, veröffentlicht zu haben. »Überlaßt es doch dem Ungeziefer auf dem Speicher«, waren seine letzten Worte über das Manuskript.

The first dissertation in German philology in America, presented at Columbia College in 1886, and its author, Hugo Julius Walther (1863–96), the son of an immigrant "Forty-Eighter".

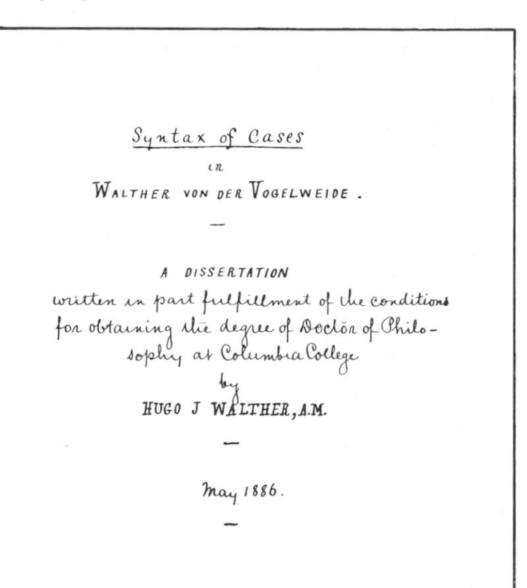

Syntax of Cases
in
Walther von der Vogelweide.

A Dissertation
written in part fulfillment of the conditions for obtaining the degree of Doctor of Philosophy at Columbia College
by
Hugo J Walther, A.M.

May 1886.

Die erste germanistische Dissertation in den USA, eingereicht am Columbia College im Jahre 1886, und ihr Autor Hugo Julius Walther (1863–96), der Sohn eines eingewanderten »Achtundvierzigers«.

A German archeologist of importance who became an American by chance: Heinrich Schliemann (1822–90), who later located and excavated Troy, happened to be on a business trip in California when it was granted statehood in 1850. He took advantage of the opportunity to become an American citizen, which he remained till his dying day, although he never again set foot on American soil (Portrait by Sidney Hodges)

Ein bedeutender deutscher Archäologe, der durch Zufall Amerikaner wurde. Heinrich Schliemann (1822–90), der spätere Ausgräber Trojas, befand sich 1850 auf einer Handelsreise in Kalifornien, als dieser Staat in die Union aufgenommen wurde. Er nutzte die Gelegenheit, amerikanischer Bürger zu werden, und blieb es bis zu seinem Tod, ohne später noch einmal in die USA zurückzukehren. (Porträt von Sidney Hodges)

Mathilde Franziska Anneke (1817–84) was already the editor of a feminist "Frauenzeitung" ("Women's Newspaper") in Germany before she took part in the insurrection of 1848/49 in Baden, serving as a combat orderly for her husband, Fritz Anneke. Together they emigrated to Milwaukee in 1849 where she founded the "Neue Frauenzeitung" ("New Women's Newspaper") and established a high school for girls. She remained a lifelong fighter for women's suffrage.

Mathilde Franziska Anneke (1817–1884), bereits in Deutschland Herausgeberin einer feministischen »Frauenzeitung«, am badischen Aufstand von 1848/49 als Gefechtsordonnanz ihres Mannes, Fritz Anneke, beteiligt, 1849 mit ihm nach Milwaukee emigriert, dort Gründerin der »Neuen Frauenzeitung« und einer Töchterschule sowie lebenslange Kämpferin für das Frauenwahlrecht (Porträt um 1840)

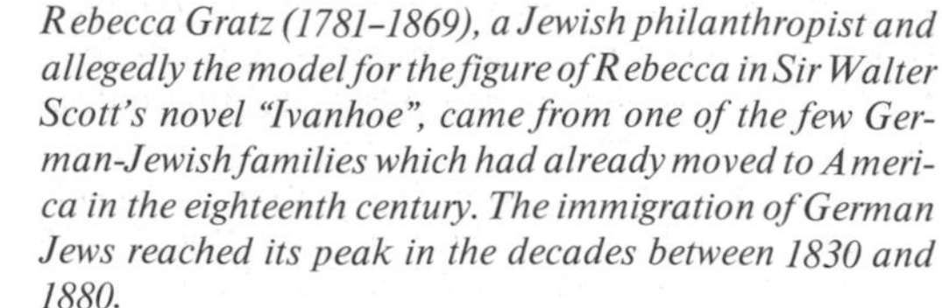

Rebecca Gratz (1781–1869), a Jewish philanthropist and allegedly the model for the figure of Rebecca in Sir Walter Scott's novel "Ivanhoe", came from one of the few German-Jewish families which had already moved to America in the eighteenth century. The immigration of German Jews reached its peak in the decades between 1830 and 1880.

Rebecca Gratz (1781–1869), jüdische Philanthropin und angebliches Vorbild für die Figur der Rebecca in Walter Scotts Roman »Ivanhoe«, entstammte einer der wenigen deutsch-jüdischen Familien, die bereits im 18. Jahrhundert nach Amerika übersiedelt waren. Ihren Höhepunkt erreichte die Einwanderung deutscher Juden in den Jahrzehnten von 1830 bis 1880.

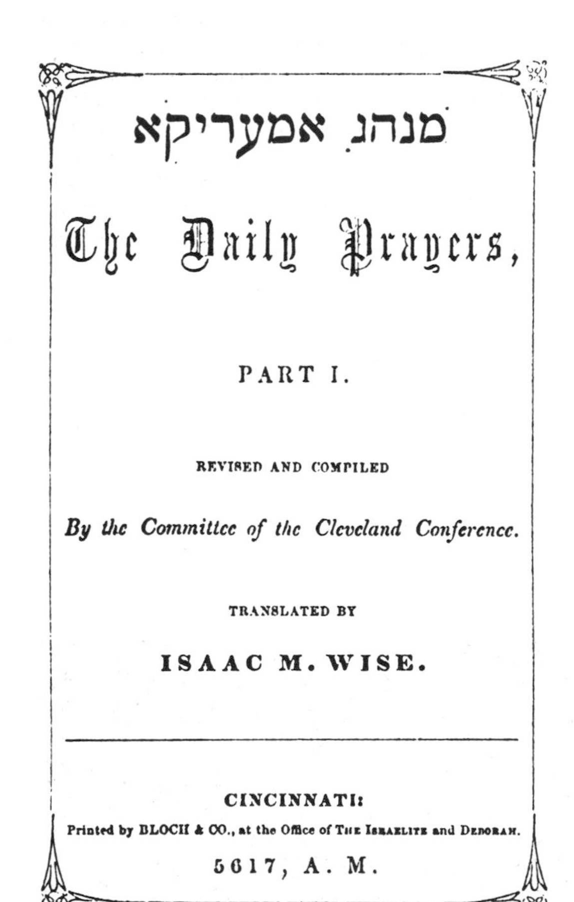

מנהג אמעריקא

The Daily Prayers,

PART I.

REVISED AND COMPILED

By the Committee of the Cleveland Conference.

TRANSLATED BY

ISAAC M. WISE.

CINCINNATI:

Printed by BLOCH & CO., at the Office of THE ISRAELITE and DEBORAH.

5617, A. M.

"Minhag America", a book of reformed rules for prayer, edited for the first time by Rabbi Wise in 1855 and containing simplified rituals as well as English and German translations of the Hebrew texts.

»Minhag America«, die von Rabbi Wise erstmals 1855 herausgegebene reformierte Gebetsordnung mit vereinfachtem Ritual sowie englischen und deutschen Übersetzungen der hebräischen Texte.

Rabbi Isaac Mayer Wise, born Isaak Weis in 1819 in Steingrub, Bohemia, emigrated in 1846 and made the unification of American Jewry his life's mission. After much discussion and debate, which lasted for decades, concerning the course Judaism in the United States should take, he was able to draw attention to his liberal program of religious reform through the publication of an English and a German-language journal ("American Israelite" and "Die Deborah"). As a result, in 1873 the Union of American Hebrew Congregations was founded and two years later this organization established its own theological seminary, the Hebrew Union College. Wise became president of the institution and retained this position until his death in 1900.

Rabbi Isaac Mayer Wise, als Isaak Weis 1819 in Steingrub in Böhmen geboren, emigrierte 1846 und machte die Einigung des amerikanischen Judentums zu seiner Lebensaufgabe. Nach jahrzehntelangen Auseinandersetzungen, bei denen er seinem liberalen Reformkurs mit einer englischen und einer deutschsprachigen Zeitschrift (»American Israelite« und »Die Deborah«) Gehör verschaffte, kam es 1873 zur Gründung der Union of American Hebrew Congregations und zwei Jahre später zur Einrichtung eines eigenen theologischen Seminars, des Hebrew Union College, dessen Präsident Wise bis zu seinem Tod im Jahre 1900 blieb.

Reinhold Niebuhr (1892–1971) attempted to reconcile Protestant theology with the findings of anthropology and the demands of social reality. An adherent of Paul Tillich, Niebuhr went on to develop a Christian philosophy of history.

Reinhold Niebuhr (1892–1971) versuchte, die evangelische Theologie mit den Erkenntnissen der Anthropologie und den Erfordernissen der sozialen Wirklichkeit zu versöhnen. Im Anschluß an Paul Tillich entwickelte er eine christliche Philosophie der Geschichte.

Karl Augustus Menninger, pioneer advocate of humanistic psychiatry, founded the "Menninger Clinic" (Topeka, Kansas) together with his father Charles in 1920. In 1941, Karl and his brother William established the "Menninger Foundation" for fundamental psychiatric research.

Karl Augustus Menninger, Vorkämpfer einer menschenwürdigen Psychiatrie, gründete 1920 zusammen mit seinem Vater Charles die »Menninger-Klinik« in Topeka, Kansas, und 1941 mit seinem Bruder William die »Menninger Foundation« zur psychiatrischen Grundlagenforschung.

The title page of Hugo Münsterberg's book on "The Americans" which first appeared in 1904.

Titelseite von Hugo Münsterbergs erstmals 1904 erschienenem Buch über »Die Amerikaner«

From the legions of German-American college professors only a few can be mentioned here. Franz Boas founded the discipline known today as cultural anthropology. His research and his interpretations have had a far-reaching impact on present-day attitudes towards other cultures. For him culture was a stage in human and communal development that could be measured and judged only by its own standards. His studies of the indigenous populations of North America laid the groundwork for the post-frontier understanding of the Native American. Boas taught at Columbia University and was curator of the American Museum of Natural History. Hugo Münsterberg set up the first psychological laboratory in America at Harvard University. While his pioneer work regarding the physiological aspects of the working of the mind and the application of psychology in industry are commonplace today, Münsterberg is best remembered for his German book, *Die Amerikaner,* in which he presented to his former countrymen a concise review of America's moral, cultural and political achievements. In the field of psychiatry the share of German immigrants and their descendants has been conspicuous. In 1925 a Kansas country doctor, Charles F. Menninger, and his sons, Karl A. and William C. Menninger, founded a clinic for the emotionally disturbed, whose renown has spread far beyond the United States. The Menningers employed specialists of various disciplines and treated patients in a home-like atmosphere. Born into a German-American pastor's family in Missouri, Reinhold Niebuhr moved from an obscure pastorate in Detroit to New York's Union Theological Seminary where his teachings and writings on theology earned him worldwide attention. Niebuhr's insistence on a strict Christian theology compatible with the secular demands of his times profoundly influenced modern religious thought. Carl Joachim Friedrich travelled to America as a student in 1922 and stayed, later to become a leading teacher of government science. As a professor at Harvard University, Friedrich shaped a generation of young Americans who later played important roles in government and public opinion. Boas, Münsterberg, the Menningers, Niebuhr and Friedrich are only a few examples of the thousands of German-American college teachers who preceded the waves of academic leaders who joined American faculties between 1933 and 1940.

chologie in Industrie und Wirtschaft heute Allgemeingut sind, bleibt sein Name mit seinem (auf deutsch geschriebenen) Buch über *Die Amerikaner* verbunden, in dem er seinen ehemaligen Landsleuten einen prägnanten Überblick über die sittlichen, kulturellen und politischen Errungenschaften Amerikas gab. Auf dem Gebiet der Psychiatrie ist der Beitrag deutscher Einwanderer und ihrer Nachfahren von jeher unübersehbar gewesen. Charles F. Menninger, ein Landarzt aus Kansas, gründete 1925 mit seinen Söhnen Karl und William eine Klinik für emotional gestörte Patienten, die bald weit über die Grenzen der USA hinaus berühmt wurde. Zu Menningers Konzept gehörte die interdisziplinäre Zusammenarbeit verschiedener Spezialisten und die Behandlung der Kranken in einer Atmosphäre, wie sie sie von zu Hause gewohnt waren. Reinhold Niebuhr, Abkömmling einer deutschamerikanischen Pastorenfamilie aus Missouri, begann seine Laufbahn mit einer kleinen Pfarrstelle in Detroit und krönte sie am Union Theological Seminary von New York, wo ihm seine theologischen Lehren und Schriften weltweite Aufmerksamkeit eintrugen. Niebuhrs Beharren auf einer streng christlichen Theologie, die gleichwohl mit den weltlichen Anforderungen seiner Zeit vereinbar sein sollte, hat das moderne religiöse Denken tiefgreifend beeinflußt. Carl Joachim Friedrich reiste 1922 als Student nach Amerika, entschloß sich zu bleiben, und wurde zu einem der führenden Lehrer in den Verwaltungswissenschaften. Als Professor an der Harvard University bildete Friedrich eine Generation junger Amerikaner heran, die später wichtige Rollen in Regierung und Öffentlichkeit spielen sollten. Boas, Münsterberg, die Menningers, Niebuhr und Friedrich sind nur einige Beispiele für die Tausende von deutschamerikanischen Universitätslehrern, die der Welle emigrierter Professoren vorausgingen, die zwischen 1933 und 1940 auf die Lehrstühle amerikanischer Colleges gelangten.

Hugo Münsterberg, born in 1863 in Danzig, surrounded by his assistants in his laboratory for experimental psychology in Freiburg. From here the pioneer of applied psychology and founder of "psychotechnics" was appointed to a position at Harvard through arrangements made by William James. Later he became director of the philosophy department there and, in 1916, he died in his lecture hall.

Hugo Münsterberg, 1863 in Danzig geboren, im Kreise seiner Mitarbeiter in seinem experimentalpsychologischen Labor in Freiburg. Von hier wurde der Pionier der angewandten Psychologie und Begründer der »Psychotechnik« durch die Vermittlung William James' nach Harvard berufen, wo er später die philosophische Fakultät leitete und 1916 in seinem Hörsaal starb.

One of the first strangleholds of the Nazi regime was directed against the freedom of expression at German universities. The number of well-known academic teachers and scientists among the refugees who came from Hitler's Germany was so large, that only a few internationally famous ones could hope for ready acceptance by American schools. Never before had so much talent and knowledge been transferred by men and women from one country to another. The first years in America were for many of them years of painful adjustment coupled with the learning of a new language, in order to be able to work in positions adequate to their training and competence. The Oberlaender Trust of the Carl Schurz Memorial Foundation, set up by a German-American textile manufacturer, was used up entirely in helping new refugees to get a foothold in their fields in America. A "University in Exile" was created at the New School for Social Research in New York to provide German scholars with teaching opportunities and research facilities. Columbia University was the home of the Institute of Social Research which had been founded in Frankfurt in the early 1920s and whose faculty came *en bloc* to New York in 1934. Many religious colleges of various denominations provided the first positions to uprooted professors from Germany. The rosters of Nobel prize laureates and the lists of distinguished personalities in academic life are full of the names of these men and women who came as exiles and became part of the elite of their new homeland. In 1944, only eleven years after the arrival of the first refugees, 106 of them had already become prominent enough in American science to be listed in the prestigious work *American Men of Science.*

Einer der ersten Würgegriffe des Naziregimes war gegen die Lehr- und Meinungsfreiheit an den deutschen Universitäten gerichtet. Die Zahl der prominenten akademischen Lehrer und Wissenschaftler unter den Flüchtlingen aus Hitlerdeutschland war so groß, daß nur die schmale Spitzengruppe der international bekanntesten auf eine baldige Aufnahme an amerikanischen Hochschulen hoffen konnte. Nie zuvor war eine ähnliche Konzentration an Wissen und Begabung von einem Land in ein anderes transferiert worden. Für viele der Flüchtlinge bedeuteten die ersten Jahre in Amerika einen schmerzlichen Anpassungsprozeß, der noch durch die Notwendigkeit erschwert wurde, erst die Sprache ihres Gastlandes zu erlernen, ehe sie wieder ihren Fähigkeiten und ihrer Ausbildung entsprechende Aufgaben übernehmen konnten. Der Oberlaender-Trust der Carl Schurz Memorial Foundation, eine Stiftung eines deutschamerikanischen Textilindustriellen, stellte sein gesamtes Stiftungsvermögen zur Verfügung, um neuankommenden Flüchtlingen Arbeitsmöglichkeiten auf ihren Fachgebieten zu verschaffen. An der New School for Social Research in New York wurde eine „Universität im Exil" gegründet, an der deutsche Wissenschaftler neue Lehr- und Forschungsaufträge erhielten. Die Columbia-Universität wurde zur neuen Heimat des Instituts für Sozialforschung, das in den frühen 20er Jahren in Frankfurt gegründet worden war und dessen Lehrkörper 1934 *en bloc* nach New York emigrierte. Viele der entwurzelten Akademiker aus Deutschland fanden auch an konfessionellen Colleges eine erste Heimstatt. Die Ehrentafeln der Nobelpreisträger und die Gelehrtenlexika sind voll von den Namen dieser Männer und Frauen, die als Exilanten kamen und Teil der geistigen Elite ihres Zufluchtslandes wurden. 1944, nur elf Jahre nach Beginn der Vertreibung, waren 106 der Flüchtlinge in der amerikanischen Wissenschaft bereits prominent genug, um in einem so angesehenen Nachschlagewerk wie den *American Men of Science* aufgeführt zu werden.

Gustav Oberlaender, self-made man, industrialist and philanthropist, born in Düren in the Rhineland in 1867, died in Reading, Pennsylvania, on November 30, 1936.

Gustav Oberlaender, Selfmademan, Industrieller und Philanthrop, geboren in Düren im Rheinland 1867, gestorben in Reading, Pennsylvanien, am 30. November 1936.

The main building of New York City's Columbia University, founded in 1754. In 1934, the school's president, Nicholas M. Butler, took in the "Frankfurter Institut für Sozialforschung" which previously had been turned away by the New School for Social Research. After World War II, Max Horkheimer (1895–1973), director of the institute, returned to Germany, as did Theodor Adorno (1903–69). Other prominent members and colleagues, such as Erich Fromm (1900–80), Herbert Marcuse (1898–1979), Franz Neumann, Karl A. Wittfogel and Leo Lowenthal, remained in the United States.

Das Hauptgebäude der 1754 gegründeten New Yorker Columbia University, deren Präsident, Nicholas M. Butler, 1934 das vorher von der New School for Social Research abgewiesene Frankfurter »Institut für Sozialforschung« aufnahm. Der Leiter des Instituts, Max Horkheimer (1895–1973), kehrte nach dem Krieg, ebenso wie Theodor W. Adorno (1903–69), nach Deutschland zurück. Andere prominente Mitglieder und Mitarbeiter, wie Erich Fromm (1900–80), Herbert Marcuse (1898–1979), Franz Neumann, Karl A. Wittfogel und Leo Lowenthal, blieben in den Vereinigten Staaten.

Prominent Emigrés to the United States:

In die USA emigrierten:

1933

Josef Albers (Maler/painter), Richard Bernheimer (Kunsthistoriker/art historian), Arnold Brecht (Politologe/political scientist), Gerhard Colm (Nationalökonom/political economist), Helene Deutsch (Psychoanalitikerin/psychoanalyst), Albert Einstein (Physiker/physicist), Hanns Eisler (Komponist/composer), Erik H. Erikson (Psychologe/psychologist), James Franck (Physiker/physicist), George Grosz (Maler/painter), Werner Hegemann (Architekt/architect), Hermann Kantorowicz (Politologe/political scientist), Otto Klemperer (Dirigent/conductor), Carl Landauer (Nationalökonom/political economist), Paul F. Lazarsfeld (Soziologe/sociologist), Emil Lederer (Nationalökonom/political economist), Kurt Lewin (Psychologe/psychologist), Otto Nathan (Nationalökonom/political economist), Johann von Neumann (Mathematiker/mathematician), Eugen Rosenstock-Huessy (Philosoph/philosopher), Albert Salomon (Soziologe/sociologist), Hans Simons (Jurist/jurist), Hans Speier (Soziologe/sociologist), Otto Stern (Physiker/physicist), Gustav Stolper (Nationalökonom/political economist), Paul Tillich (Theologe/theologian), Alfred Vagts (Historiker/historian), Heinz Werner (Psychologe/psychologist), Hermann Weyl (Mathematiker/mathematician), Billy Wilder (Filmregisseur/film director)

1934

Margarete Bieber (Archäologin/archaeologist), Felix Bloch (Physiker/physicist), Erich Fromm (Psychologe/psychologist), Albrecht Goetze (Assyrologe/assyriologist), Hajo Holborn (Historiker/historian), Max Horkheimer (Soziologe/sociologist), Guido Kisch (Rechtshistoriker/historian of jurisprudence), Erich Korngold (Komponist/composer), Leo Lowenthal (Soziologe/sociologist), Herbert Marcuse (Philosoph/philosopher), Fritz Morstein Marx (Politologe/political scientist), Sigmund Neumann (Politologe/political scientist), Erwin Panofsky (Kunsthistoriker/art historian), Curt Riess (Schriftsteller/author), Kurt Riezler (Geschichtsphilosoph/historian), Kurt Rosenfeld (sozialist. Politiker/socialist politician), Gerhard Seger (SPD-Politiker/SPD-politician), Ernst Toch (Komponist/composer), Robert Ulich (Pädagoge/educator), Max Wertheimer (Psychologe/psychologist), Karl August Wittfogel (Politologe/political scientist)

1935

Hans A. Bethe (Physiker/physicist), Rudolf Carnap (Philosoph/philosopher), Alfred Eisenstaedt (Photograph/photographer), Hermann Frankel (Philologe/philologist), Walter Friedlaender (Kunsthistoriker/art historian), Frieda Fromm-Reichmann (Psychoanalytikerin/psychoanalyst), Stefan Heym (Schriftsteller/author), Rudolf Katz (SPD-Politiker/SPD-politician), Richard Krautheimer (Kunsthistoriker/art historian), Heinrich Kronstein (Jurist/professor of law), Fritz Lang (Filmregisseur/film director), Lotte Lenya (Schauspielerin/ actress), Wolfgang Pauli (Physiker/physicist), Otto Rank (Psychologe/psychologist), Hans Rosenberg (Historiker/historian), Tony Sender (SPD-Politikerin/SPD-politician), Edward Teller (Atomphysiker/atomic physicist), Kurt Weill (Komponist/composer)

1936

Willi Apel (Musikwissenschaftler/musicologist), Arnold Bergstraesser (Historiker/historian), Konrad Bloch (Biochemiker/biochemist), Max Brauer (SPD-Politiker/SPD-politician), Heinz Fraenkel-Conrat (Biochemiker/biochemist), Felix Gilbert (Historiker/historian), Richard Goldschmidt (Zoologe/zoologist), Werner Jaeger (Philologe/philologist), Hubertus Prinz zu Löwenstein (Zentrumspolitiker/politician), Erika und Klaus Mann (Schriftsteller/authors), Arnold Schönberg (Komponist/composer), Leo Spitzer (Philologe/philologist), Ernst Toller (Schriftsteller/author), Karl Vietor (Literaturwissenschaftler/literary scholar)

1937

Heinrich Brüning (ehem. Reichskanzler/former chancellor), Max Delbrück (Biophysiker/biophysicist), Peter F. Drucker (Nationalökonom/political economist), Bruno Frank (Schriftsteller/author), Walter Gropius (Architekt/architect), Waldemar Gurian (Politologe/political scientist), Wolfgang Hallgarten (Historiker/historian), Carl G. Hempel (Philosoph/philosopher), Ernst Krenek (Komponist/composer), Erich Leinsdorf (Dirigent/conductor), Hans J. Morgenthau (Politologe/political scientist), Kurt Pinthus (Literaturwissenschaftler/literary scholar), Curt Sachs (Musikwissenschaftler/musicologist), Wilhelm Sollmann (SPD-Politiker/SPD-politician), Walter Sulzbach (Nationalökonom/political economist), Leo Szilard (Atomphysiker/atomic physicist)

1938

Theodor W. Adorno (Soziologe/sociologist), Hans Baron (Historiker/historian), Reinhard Bendix (Soziologe/sociologist), Ernst Bloch (Philosoph/philosopher), Hermann Broch (Schriftsteller/author), Ernst Caspari (Genetiker/geneticist), Karl Deutsch (Politologe/political scientist), Herbert Dieckmann (Literaturhistoriker/literary historian), Ernst Fraenkel (Politologe/political scientist), Manfred George (Journalist/editor), Alexander Gerschenkorn (Wirtschaftshistoriker/economic historian), Oskar Maria Graf (Schriftsteller/author), Erich von Kahler (Philosoph/philosopher), Robert Kempner (Jurist/jurist), Fritz Kortner (Schauspieler/actor), Thomas Mann (Schriftsteller/author), Ludwig Mies van der Rohe (Architekt/architect), Franz Oppenheimer (Nationalökonom/political economist), Frederick Praeger (Verleger/book publisher), Theodor Reik (Psychiater/psychiatrist), Max Reinhardt (Regisseur/theatrical producer), Arthur Rosenberg (Historiker/historian), William Steinberg (Dirigent/conductor), Leo Strauss (Philosoph/philosopher), Eric Vögelin (Philosoph/philosopher), Hans Wallenberg (Redakteur/editor), Max M. Warburg (Bankier/banker), Joseph Wechsberg (Schriftsteller/author), Franz Carl Weiskopf (Schriftsteller/author), Stefan Zweig (Schriftsteller/author)

1939

Bruno Bettelheim (Psychologe/psychologist), Herbert Bloch (Historiker/historian), Moritz Julius Bonn (Politologe/political scientist), Adolf Busch (Geiger/violinist), Joseph Buttinger (sozialist. Politiker/socialist politician), Alfred Einstein (Musikwissenschaftler/musicologist), Julius Epstein (Journalist/journalist), Ossip K. Flechtheim (Politologe/political scientist), Karl B. Frank (sozialist. Politiker/socialist politician), Curt Goetz (Dramatiker/playwright), Kurt R. Grossmann (Organisator der Flüchtlingshilfe/organizer of refugee aid programs), Albert C. Grzesinski (SPD-Politiker/SPD-politician), Paul Hertz (SPD-Politiker/SPD-politician), Wieland Herzfelde (Schriftsteller/author), Ernst Kantorowicz (Historiker/historian), Adolf Katzenellenbogen (Kunsthistoriker/art historian), Karl Löwith (Philosoph/philosopher), Ludwig Marcuse (Schriftsteller/author), Erwin Piscator (Regisseur/director), Wilhelm Reich (Psychologe/psychologist), Artur Schnabel (Pianist/pianist), Robert Siodmak (Filmregisseur/film director), Samuel P. Spiegel (Filmregisseur/film director), Fritz Sternberg (Nationalökonom/political economist), Veit Valentin (Historiker/historian), Berthold Viertel (Schriftsteller/author), Carl Zuckmayer (Dramatiker/ playwright)

1940

Rudolf Arnheim (Kunstpsychologe/psychologist of art), Siegfried Bernfeld (Psychologe/psychologist), Charlotte und Karl Bühler (Psychologen/psychologists), Richard Graf Coudenhove-Calergi (Paneuropa-Politiker/politician), Alfred Döblin (Schriftsteller/author), Lion Feuchtwanger (Schriftsteller/author), Ruth Fischer (ehem. kommunist. Politikerin/former communist politician), Friedrich Wilhelm Foerster (Pädagoge/educator), Konrad Heiden (Historiker/historian), Paul Hindemith (Komponist/composer), Hans Jacob (Journalist/editor), Ernst Jaeckh (Publizist/publicist), Fritz Kahn (Populärautor/author), Hans Kelsen (Jurist/professor of law), Hermann Kesten (Schriftsteller/author), Egon Erwin Kisch (Journalist/journalist), Adolf Löwe (Nationalökonom/political economist), Otto Loewi (Pharmakologe/pharmacologist), Emil Ludwig (Schriftsteller/author), Heinrich Mann (Schriftsteller/author), Alma Mahler-Werfel (Schriftstellerin/author), Otto Meyerhof (Biochemiker/biochemist), Ludwig von Mieses (Nationalökonom/political economist), Ferenc Molnár (Dramatiker/playwright), Norbert Mühlen (Journalist/journalist), Alfred Neumann (Schriftsteller/author), Max Nußbaum (Rabbiner/rabbi), Karl Otto Paetel (Publizist/publicist), Stefan T. Possony (Politologe/political scientist), Erich Maria Remarque (Schriftsteller/author), Alexander Roda-Roda (Schriftsteller/author), Hans Rothfels (Historiker/historian), Leopold Schwarzschild (Journalist/editor), Friedrich Stampfer (SPD-Politiker/SPD-politician), Fritz von Unruh (Schriftsteller/author), Bruno Walter (Dirigent/conductor), Herbert Weichmann (SPD-Politiker/SPD-politician), Franz Werfel (Schriftsteller/author)

1941

Erwin Ackerknecht (Medizinhistoriker/historian of medicine), Hannah Arendt (Philosophin/philosopher), Bertolt Brecht (Schriftsteller/author), Ernst Cassirer (Philosoph/philosopher)), Julius Deutsch (Politiker/politician), Max Ernst (Maler/painter), Heinz Hartmann (Psychoanalytiker/psychoanalyst), Joachim Joesten (Journalist/journalist), Siegfried Kracauer (Filmwissenschaftler/film historian), Alfred Kantorowicz (Journalist/journalist), Leo Lania (Publizist/publicist), Fritz Lipmann (Biochemiker/biochemist), Hans J. Meyer (Bankier/banker), Hermann Rauschning (konservat. Politiker/politician), Franz Schoenberner (Redakteur/editor), Konrad Wachsmann (Architekt/architect), Kurt Wolff (Verleger/publisher)

In American education, German influence was also felt on other levels. Since the early days of 18th-century immigration, German churches had maintained parochial schools; initially classes were always in German, but as acculturation progressed, bilingual and finally only English instruction prevailed. In 1750, the Mennonite schoolmaster, Christopher Dock, published his *Schulordnung* in Pennsylvania; it was the first American pedagogical work. The Herrnhuters, or Moravian Brethren, maintained well-known academies for boys and girls in Pennsylvania and North Carolina which attracted many outsiders, including children of non-German stock. Later waves of immigrants intensified the concern for education. As the name suggests, the kindergarten concept was introduced by Germans who had become familiar with Froebel's system of pre-school education. The first American kindergartens were operated by Caroline Frankenberg in Columbus, Ohio, and by Margarethe Meyer-Schurz in Watertown, Wisconsin. At the beginning, the movement spread only in German settlements but its success here and in Europe led to its introduction into the American educational system. For a time, cities with large German-speaking populations permitted bilingual public schools in which German-American teachers developed successful methods to teach immigrant children. The *Turner* societies, transplanted from Germany in the 1830s, also left a permanent mark on American schools at large. A government survey of 1898 showed that the school boards in Chicago, Cincinnati, Cleveland, Denver, Indianapolis, Kansas City, Milwaukee, St. Louis, St. Paul and San Francisco had "adopted German free and light gymnastics, and the directors of physical education are graduates of the Normal School of the North American *Turnerbund*."

Im amerikanischen Erziehungswesen hatten sich deutsche Einflüsse schon früher auch auf anderen Ebenen bemerkbar gemacht. Seit Beginn des 18. Jahrhunderts hatten deutsche Kirchen in den Haupteinwanderungsgebieten Pfarrschulen unterhalten, in denen anfangs nur auf deutsch, mit fortschreitender kultureller Anpassung jedoch zweisprachig und schließlich in englischer Sprache unterrichtet wurde. Im Jahr 1750 veröffentlichte der mennonitische Schulmeister Christopher Dock mit seiner deutschsprachigen *Schulordnung* die erste pädagogische Schrift in Amerika. Die Herrnhuter Brüdergemeine unterhielt in Pennsylvanien und Nord-Carolina bekannte Internatsschulen für Jungen und Mädchen, die zahlreiche Außenstehende, darunter auch Kinder nichtdeutscher Abstammung, anzogen. Spätere Einwanderungswellen verstärkten das Interesse an Erziehungsfragen. Wie schon der ins Amerikanische übernommene Name zeigt, kam der auf Friedrich Fröbels Konzept der Vorschulerziehung beruhende „Kindergarten" mit deutschen Einwanderern ins Land. Die ersten amerikanischen Kindergärten wurden von Caroline Frankenberg in Columbus, Ohio, und von Margarethe Meyer-Schurz in Watertown, Wisconsin, geführt. Nahm die Bewegung zunächst in deutschen Siedlungsgebieten ihren Anfang, so führte der Erfolg der Kindergärten hier und in Europa schließlich zu ihrer Einführung in das offizielle amerikanische Erziehungswesen. Städte mit einem großen deutschsprachigen Bevölkerungsanteil gestatteten vorübergehend auch die Einrichtung zweisprachiger öffentlicher Schulen, in denen deutschamerikanische Lehrer erfolgreiche Methoden zur Unterrichtung und Eingliederung der Einwandererkinder entwickelten. Die Turnvereine, erstmals in den 30er Jahren des 19. Jahr-

Christopher Dock, author of the German-language "School Regulations", published in 1750 in Germantown by the publishing house of Christopher Saur. Dock, who from 1714 to 1771 was employed as a teacher, also introduced the blackboard to America.

Christopher Dock, der Verfasser der deutschsprachigen »Schulordnung«, die 1750 im Verlag Christopher Saurs in Germantown erschien. Dock, der von 1714 bis 1771 als Pädagoge wirkte, führte auch die Wandtafel in Amerika ein.

Caroline Louisa Frankenberg, who was born in Eddigehausen near Göttingen, worked for six years together with Friedrich Fröbel, who originated the concept of the kindergarten, at his "General German Educational Institution" in Keilhau. After emigrating in 1858, Frankenberg set up the second American kindergarten in Columbus, Ohio.

Caroline Louisa Frankenberg, in Eddigehausen bei Göttingen geboren, arbeitete sechs Jahre lang mit Friedrich Fröbel, dem Vater der Kindergartenidee, in dessen »Allgemeiner deutscher Erziehungsanstalt« in Keilhau zusammen. Nach ihrer Emigration gründete sie 1858 in Columbus, Ohio, den zweiten amerikanischen Kindergarten.

Emma Marwedel, who introduced Fröbel's kindergarten system on the American West Coast.
Emma Marwedel, die das Kindergartensystem nach Fröbel an der amerikanischen Westküste einführte.

Poster commemorating the hundredth anniversary of the city of Watertown in 1936. Above left, the first American kindergarten: predecessor of five hundred which existed in 1882, a number which had increased to five thousand by 1901.

Gedenkblatt zum hundertjährigen Bestehen der Stadt Watertown, 1936. Links oben der erste amerikanische Kindergarten, aus dem 1882 bereits fünfhundert und im Jahre 1901 fünftausend geworden waren.

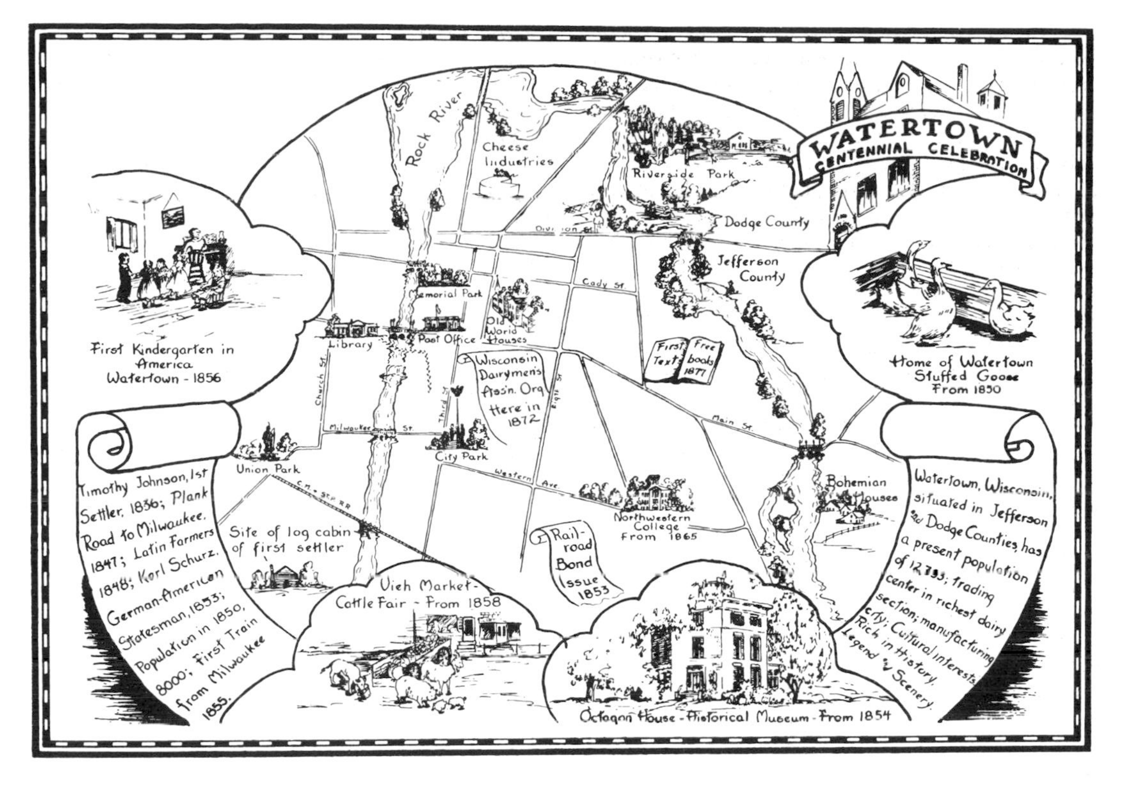

Margarethe Meyer-Schurz (1833–76) came from a family of Jewish merchants in Hamburg and became the wife of the emigrant "Forty-Eighter" Carl Schurz. In the fall of 1856 she opened the first American kindergarten in Watertown, Wisconsin, and introduced Elizabeth Peabody, who later founded the American Fröbel Institute (1867), to the concepts of the German reform educator.

Margarethe Meyer-Schurz (1833–76), einer jüdischen Hamburger Kaufmannsfamilie entstammende Ehefrau des emigrierten »Achtundvierzigers« Carl Schurz, eröffnete im Herbst 1856 in Watertown, Wisconsin, den ersten Kindergarten in den USA und machte Elizabeth Peabody, die spätere Gründerin des Amerikanischen Fröbel-Instituts (1867), mit den Konzepten des deutschen Reformpädagogen bekannt.

A model of Watertown's historic kindergarten which was opened at a time when the "autodidactic institutions", established in accordance with Fröbel's ideas, were outlawed in Prussia, where they originated, because of their allegedly "destructive tendencies in the areas of religion and politics".

Modell des historischen Kindergartens von Watertown, der hier zu einem Zeitpunkt eröffnet wurde, als die »autodidaktischen Anstalten« nach Fröbel in ihrem Herkunftsland Preußen wegen »destructiver Tendenzen auf dem Gebiet der Religion und Politik« verboten waren...

For more than two centuries German-language newspapers were the source of news and comfort for succeeding waves of newcomers. Their variety reflected the diversity of the immigrants. From Christopher Saur's *Pensylvanischer Geschicht-Schreiber* of 1739, which was read from New York to Georgia, to Manfred George's *Aufbau*, the outstanding weekly of the refugees from Nazi Germany with an international audience, the life and the concerns of immigrants are mirrored in the pages of hundreds of newspapers and periodicals published in the German language. In 1876 there were seventy-four German dailies with a total circulation of about 300,000; 374 weeklies with more than one million subscribers, plus numerous monthlies and annual almanacs. By 1894 the total number of German-language papers exceeded 800, but declining immigration reduced their number every year until the first World War dealt the death-blow to all but a few which managed to meet the government requirement of submitting translation of all German-language articles to the censors prior to publication. Although in 1920 some 275 German titles appeared again in the directories, most of them were house organs for fraternal and church organizations. Now there are hardly more than forty newspapers and periodicals on the list serving diverse interests. Among the papers which survived all vicissitudes are the New York *Staats-Zeitung und Herold* and the *Washington Journal,* now the oldest newspaper in the District of Columbia. German-American involvement in the press was not limited to German-language publications. Several of the colonial printers also published papers in English and descendants of German immigrants like Ochs (*New York Times*), Ridder and Nieman have their place in American newspaper history. Despite a large market of book imports from Europe, there has been a flourishing German book publishing business in America ever since Saur printed the first complete German Bible in 1743. In Philadelphia, Cincinnati, New York and a dozen other cities, a great variety of original and reprint titles appeared during the 19th century, among them Alexander Schem's *German-American Conversation Lexicon,* the only full-fledged foreign-language encyclopedia ever published in the United States, and editions of the collected works of German classic authors. Publishers like Ernst Steiger of New York issued many works by German-American authors whose audience rarely extended beyond the confines of their own linguistic community. The free atmosphere of the New World permitted time and again the publication of writings in German which were banned or censored in the homeland, a fact that also applied to many German-American newspapers. Some of Saur's outspoken comments on German princelings and their bigotry were not any more welcome in the old country than the liberal voices freely uttered in America in the times of Metternich and Bismarck. After the Nazi curtain had fallen over Germany, publishers in New York and California published many an exiled author in the original German, albeit in small editions. German-Americans, notably some from the midst of the emigrés from Nazi Germany, became well-known American publishers such as Frederick Praeger, Kurt and Helen Wolff, Curt Enoch and Walter Johnson. In the printing industry German immigrants repeatedly transferred the latest technical development to their new homeland. Almost all the early lithographers, among them two Forty-Eighters, Julius Bien and Louis Prang, were German-born.

Über zwei Jahrhunderte lang waren die deutschsprachigen Zeitungen für immer neue Wellen von Einwanderern Informationsquelle und Eingewöhnungshilfe zugleich. In ihrer Vielzahl spiegelte sich die Verschiedenartigkeit der Einwanderer wider. Von Christopher Saurs erstmals 1739 erschienenem *Pensylvanischem Geschicht-Schreiber*, der von New York bis Georgia gelesen wurde, bis zu Manfred Georges *Aufbau*, der herausragenden, international beachteten Wochenschrift der Flüchtlinge aus Hitlerdeutschland, berichten die Seiten von Hunderten von deutschsprachigen Zeitungen und Zeitschriften vom Leben und den Problemen der Einwanderer. Im Jahr 1876 existierten allein 74 deutsche Tageszeitungen mit einer Gesamtauflage von etwa 300 000 Exemplaren, dazu 374 Wochenblätter mit über einer Million Abonnenten und zahlreiche monatlich oder seltener erscheinende Periodika. 1894 erreichte die Gesamtzahl deutschsprachiger Zeitungen und Zeitschriften mit über 800 Titeln ihren Höhepunkt. In den folgenden Jahren setzte, parallel zur Entwicklung der Einwanderungszahlen, ein allmählicher Rückgang ein, bis schließlich im Ersten Weltkrieg die Zensurauflage, sämtliche Artikel vor der Veröffentlichung in englischer Übersetzung vorzulegen, für die meisten deutschen Blätter das endgültige Aus bedeutete. Zwar geben die Presseverzeichnisse bereits für 1920 wieder ca. 275 deutsche Titel an, doch handelte es sich dabei in der Mehrzahl um Hauszeitschriften kirchlicher oder bruderschaftlicher Vereinigungen. Heute weist die Liste kaum noch mehr als 40 Zeitungen und Zeitschriften auf, die einen breitgestreuten Leserkreis bedienen. Zu den Blättern, die alle Wechselfälle überdauert haben, gehören die New Yorker *Staats-Zeitung und Herold* und das *Washington Journal*, inzwischen die älteste noch erscheinende Zeitung im District of Columbia. Deutschamerikanisches Engagement im Pressewesen hat sich freilich nicht auf solche deutschsprachigen Publikationen beschränkt. Schon in der Kolonialzeit publizierten mehrere der deutschen Drucker auch englische Zeitungen, während Nachfahren späterer deutscher Einwanderer wie Ochs (*New York Times*), Ridder und Nieman heute ihren festen Platz in der amerikanischen Pressegeschichte innehaben.

Trotz umfangreicher Buchimporte aus Europa hat in Amerika seit 1743, als Saur seine erste deutsche Bibel druckte, immer auch ein florierender deutschsprachiger Verlagsbuchhandel bestanden. In Philadelphia, Cincinnati, New York und einem Dutzend anderer Städte erschienen im 19. Jahrhundert eine Vielzahl von erstveröffentlichten oder nachgedruckten Titeln, darunter Alexander Schems *Deutsch-Amerikanisches Conversationslexikon* – die einzige großangelegte Enzyklopädie, die in den USA je in einer fremden Sprache gedruckt wurde – und mehrere Gesamtausgaben deutscher Klassiker. Verleger wie Ernst Steiger in New York brachten Werke deutschamerikanischer Autoren heraus, deren Leserkreis sich jedoch kaum über die Grenzen der eigenen Sprachgemeinschaft hinaus erstreckte. Immer wieder konnten in der freien Atmosphäre der Neuen Welt auch Schriften publiziert werden, die in Deutschland der Zensur zum Opfer gefallen waren – eine Möglichkeit, von der auch die deutschamerikanischen Zeitungen Gebrauch machten. Saurs unverblümte Kommentare über deutsche Duodezfürsten und ihre Bigotterie waren im alten Heimatland ebensowenig willkommen wie zu Metternichs und Bismarcks Zeiten die liberalen Stimmen, die sich aus Amerika zu Wort meldeten. Nachdem der Vorhang der Naziherrschaft über Deutschland nieder-

New Yorker Staats-Zeitung und Herold

The "New Yorker Staats-Zeitung und Herold" first appeared on Christmas Eve, 1834. Its publishers, the Ridder family of German origin, now reign over an entire media empire in the U.S. Midwest, including newspapers, radio and television stations.

Erstmals am 24. Dezember 1834 erschien die »New Yorker Staats-Zeitung und Herold«, deren deutschstämmige Verlegerfamilie Ridder heute über ein Zeitungen, Rundfunkstationen und Fernsehsender umfassendes Medienimperium im Mittelwesten der USA gebietet.

AUFBAU
AMERICA'S LEADING GERMAN LANGUAGE NEWSPAPER
FOUNDED IN 1934
Vol. XLVIII, No. 37 New York, N.Y. Friday, September 10, 1982

The "Aufbau", originally founded in 1934 as the house organ of the New York "German-Jewish Club", is presently published by Hans Steinitz. Under the editorship of Manfred George, who fled Berlin in April of 1939, it acquired the widest circulation of any similar publication and became the leading voice of German opponents to Hitler in the U.S.A. Included among the members of its advisory board were Albert Einstein and Thomas Mann.

Der heute von Hans Steinitz geleitete »Aufbau«, 1934 als Vereinsblatt des New Yorker »Deutsch-jüdischen Clubs« gegründet, wurde unter der Redaktion des aus Berlin geflohenen ehemaligen Ullstein-Journalisten Manfred George (ab April 1939) zum führenden und auflagenstärksten Organ der deutschen Hitlergegner in den USA, zu dessen Beratergremium Albert Einstein und Thomas Mann gehörten.

Washington Journal

The German-language "Washington Journal" has the longest tradition of any newspaper in the U.S. capital.

Die traditionsreichste Zeitung der amerikanischen Bundeshauptstadt: das deutschsprachige »Washington Journal«

Eine Zeitung für Deutschamerikaner
AMERIKA WOCHE
AUSGABE FÜR CALIFORNIA
(415) 589-7881
Kommunisten in Christo: Die Hutterischen Brüder

One of the few new publications of today's German-American press, the "Amerika-Woche", which has been appearing regularly with several regional editions since 1973.

Eine der wenigen Neugründungen in der deutschamerikanischen Presse der letzten Jahre: die »Amerika-Woche«, die seit 1973 in verschiedenen Regionalausgaben erscheint.

Kurt Wolff, publisher of the works of Kafka and Heinrich Mann, left Germany in 1933, came to New York in 1941 and one year later, together with his wife Helen, founded "Pantheon Books", whose postwar publications included the first translations of Günter Grass's novels. The year 1961 marked the inception of the "Helen and Kurt Wolff Books" series at Harcourt-Brace and World, now managed by Helen Wolff since her husband's death in 1963. (Portrait by Felice Casorati, 1925)

Kurt Wolff, Verleger Franz Kafkas und Heinrich Manns, verließ 1933 Deutschland, kam 1941 nach New York und gründete dort im folgenden Jahr mit seiner Frau Helen die »Pantheon Books«, bei denen nach dem Krieg u. a. die ersten Übersetzungen der Romane von Günter Grass erschienen. 1961 folgte die Reihe der »Helen and Kurt Wolff Books« bei Harcourt-Brace and World, die seit Kurt Wolffs Tod 1963 von Helen Wolff fortgeführt wird. (Porträt von Felice Casorati, 1925)

Neujahrs-Glückwunsch der Träger des Berliner Journal

1888.

Wandkalender für 1888.

New Year's greetings for the year 1888, presented by the delivery boys of the local newspaper of Berlin, – the town of Berlin, Ontario, in Canada. At the time of World War I, the town was renamed "Kitchener" to sound more true-blue English. In the U.S., where many German place-names likewise disappeared in 1917/18, fifteen "Berlins" still exist today.

Neujahrsglückwünsche für 1888, entboten von den Austrägern der Lokalzeitung von Berlin – in Ontario, Kanada. Das kanadische Berlin wurde im Ersten Weltkrieg auf den urenglischen Namen »Kitchener« umgetauft; in den USA, wo 1917/18 ebenfalls viele deutsche Ortsnamen verschwanden, existieren heute noch fünfzehn Berlins.

1776. Dienstag, den 9 July. Henrich Millers 813 Stück.

Pennsylvanischer Staatsbote.

Diese Zeitung kommt alle Wochen zweymal heraus, näml. Dienstags und Freytags, für Sechs Schillinge des Jahrs.

N.B. All ADVERTISEMENTS to be inserted in this Paper, or printed singly by HENRY MILLER, Publisher hereof, are by him translated gratis.

Im Congreß, den 4ten July, 1776.

Eine Erklärung

durch die Repräsentanten der

Vereinigten Staaten von America,

im General-Congreß versammlet.

In the eighteenth century there already appeared a total of 38 different German-language newspapers in Pennsylvania and the other colonies. Next to Christopher Saur, the most prominent German printer was Heinrich Miller, whose "Pennsylvanischer Staatsbote" published the German translation of the Declaration of Independence on July 9, 1776.

Bereits im 18. Jahrhundert erschienen insgesamt 38 verschiedene deutschsprachige Zeitungen in Pennsylvanien und den anderen Kolonien. Neben Christopher Saur war der bedeutendste deutsche Drucker Heinrich Miller, dessen »Pennsylvanischer Staatsbote« am 9. Juli 1776 die deutsche Übersetzung der amerikanischen Unabhängigkeitserklärung veröffentlichte.

The photo of this U.S. newspaper stand was taken in 1922, only four years after the end of the First World War, during which publication of well-nigh all German-language papers was suspended.

1922, nur vier Jahre nach dem Ende des Ersten Weltkriegs, in dem die meisten deutschsprachigen Zeitungen der USA ihr Erscheinen einstellen mußten, entstand die Aufnahme dieses Zeitungsstandes.

Westliche Blätter
von
Otto Rappius
Sonntags-Ausgabe des Louisviller Anzeigers.
Jahrgang 1. No. 10. Louisville, den 10. Juli 1859.

When the "Louisviller Anzeiger" first appeared in 1859, there were about 13,000 Germans living in Louisville, Kentucky. At that time the total number of German-language newspapers and periodicals amounted to 250.

Als der »Louisviller Anzeiger« 1859 erstmals erschien, lebten in Louisville, Kentucky, etwa 13 000 deutsche Einwanderer; die Gesamtzahl deutschsprachiger Zeitungen und Zeitschriften in den USA betrug zu diesem Zeitpunkt 250.

A music rehearsal of the Moravians in Bethlehem. The minister and musician Jakob van Vleck, who received this miniature for his birthday in 1795, is seen at the keyboard accompanying a vocal quintet.

Musikstunde bei den Herrnhutern in Bethlehem: Vom Cembalo aus begleitet der Geistliche und Musiker Jakob van Vleck, der diese Miniatur im Jahre 1795 als Geburtstagsgeschenk erhielt, ein Gesangsquintett.

Due to the efforts of such immigrants as the orchestra conductor Leopold Damrosch, or the theater director Heinrich Conried (who, in 1903, brought to the Met the controversial premiere of "Parsifal"), Richard Wagner gained acceptance in America and today he even has a "second Bayreuth" in the state of Washington. The "Pacific Northwest Wagner Festival", held in the Seattle Opera, was initiated by Glynn Ross in 1975 and it offers the only opportunity in the world to hear the complete "Ring of the Nibelung" in parallel productions in two languages. Pictured here is the final scene from Wagner's "Rhinegold", directed by Lincoln Clark.

Richard Wagner, in Amerika durchgesetzt von Einwanderern wie dem Dirigenten Leopold Damrosch oder dem Intendanten Heinrich Conried (der 1903 die umstrittene »Parsifal«-Erstaufführung an die Met brachte), hat heute im Bundesstaat Washington sein »zweites Bayreuth«: das 1975 von Glynn Ross initiierte »Pacific Northwest Wagner Festival« der Seattle Opera, das als einziges der Welt komplette »Ring«-Aufführungen in zwei Sprachen anbietet. Abgebildet ist die Schlußszene aus »Rheingold« in der Regie von Lincoln Clark.

Deutsche

Musik-Zeitung

für die

Vereinigten Staaten,

redigirt von

P. M. Wolsieffer,

unter Mitwirkung tüchtiger Musiker aus der alten und neuen Welt.

Philadelphia:

Herausgegeben von Ph. Rohr, No. 512 Powell-Straße,

1856 und 1857.

Philipp Matthias Wolsieffer, who was born in the Rhenish Palatinate in 1808 and emigrated to Philadelphia in 1835, founded there and in Baltimore the first German-American men's choirs and edited the "German Music-Journal for the United States", a facsimile of which appears above.

Philipp Matthias Wolsieffer, 1808 in der Rheinpfalz geboren und 1835 nach Philadelphia ausgewandert, gründete dort und in Baltimore die ersten deutschamerikanischen Männerchöre und gab die oben faksimilierte »Deutsche Musik-Zeitung für die Vereinigten Staaten« heraus.

An odd piece of German-American music history was furnished by the Beethovens, who, on September 15, 1871, disembarked at New York. This newspaper clipping carries an account of an evening piano recital given in Toronto in 1872 by one "Madame von Beethoven", who, in actuality, was the German pianist, Maria Nitsche, wife of Ludwig Johann van Beethoven, a grandnephew of the famous composer. By leaving the country, both had sought to avoid impending apprehension by German authorities on charges of fraud and deceit. In America they honky-tonked their way from town to town, giving piano concerts and leaving behind unpaid bills until finally Maria returned to Europe and Ludwig recast himself in the role of one "Louis von Hofen", who succeeded in rising to the position of manager of the South Pacific Railway before his trail disappears around 1890.

Ein Kuriosum in der deutsch-amerikanischen Musikgeschichte lieferten die Beethovens, die am 15. September 1871 in New York an Land gingen. Bei »Madame von Beethoven«, von deren Klavierabend in Toronto 1872 der Zeitungsausschnitt berichtet, handelte es sich um die deutsche Pianistin Maria Nitsche, die mit Ludwig Johann van Beethoven, einem Großneffen des Komponisten, verheiratet war. Beide hatten sich durch die Auswanderung einer drohenden Verhaftung wegen Hochstapelei und Betrugs entzogen. In Amerika tingelten sie klavierspielend und unbezahlte Rechnungen hinterlassend von Stadt zu Stadt, bis Maria schließlich nach Europa zurückkehrte und Ludwig sich in einen »Louis von Hofen« verwandelte, der es noch zum Manager der South Pacific Railway brachte, ehe sich seine Lebensspuren um 1890 verlieren.

Conductor Theodore Thomas (1835–1905) was known as "America's Musical Missionary". Thomas, who immigrated to America as a lad of ten, was an advocate of a decentralized musical life in the U.S., with an accent on municipal orchestras similar to those in Germany.

Der Dirigent Theodore Thomas (1835–1905), der im Alter von zehn Jahren in die USA kam, setzte sich für ein dezentralisiertes Musikleben mit städtischen Orchestern nach deutschem Muster ein und erwarb sich so den Spitznamen »Amerikas Musikmissionar«.

The Leader,

TORONTO, TUESDAY, OCT. 29, 1872

LOCAL NEWS

MADAM VON BEETHOVEN.—We noticed in our impressions of Saturday and Monday that the above talented lady intended delivering a *piano-forte* recital at the Agricultural Hall. A very large assemblage attended to hear the performance, the crowd being so considerable that numbers had to stand. It became apparent from the moment that Madam Beethoven commenced the superb *sonata* 26 of her great uncle, that in delicacy of touch she can hardly be surpassed, and as the piece progressed through the *scherzo* and solemn *Funeral March*, it was clear she possessed feeling and execution in an equal degree. There has probably seldom been any *piano-forte* player in Toronto who would alone sit down to render the programme set before Mad. von Beethoven's company. From end to end it contained nothing but the most difficult of classical music, yet it is hard to mention one piece as being superior in its delivery to another. The programme comprised *The Sonata op. 26*, " Beethoven " ; *Andante and Rondo Capriccioso*, " Mendelssohn" ; *Meditation*, " Iaell" ; *Tannhæuser*, " Liszt" ; *Grand Sonata Pathetique*, " Beethoven " ; *Turkish March* (from Beethoven's, " The Ruins of Athens,") " Rubinstein " ; *Adelaide*, " Beethoven " ; *Egmont Overture*, " Beethoven." The *piano-forte* upon which the recital was given was unfortunately not equal to the occasion.

Juden gegen Wagner

Der Jude Otto Klemperer führte als „Generalmusikdirektor" der Kroll-Oper in Berlin die Generalattacken gegen Richard Wagner. Seine Inszenierung des „Fliegenden Holländer" wurde zu einem der größten Theaterskandale der Systemzeit. Als er am „Platz der Republik" abgewirtschaftet hatte, setzte er noch in der Staatsoper „Unter den Linden" sein zersetzendes Treiben mit einer ebenso berüchtigten „Tannhäuser"-Inszenierung fort. Klemperer ist nach der Machtübernahme in die Vereinigten Staaten emigriert. Dort läßt er sich als „Märtyrer" und „Opfer der deutschen Barbarei" feiern.

A historical document of the defamation of Jewish and progressive artists in the "Third Reich": A page taken from the Nazi inflammatory pamphlet "Degenerate Music" (1939), in which numerous composers and interpreters who had fled to the U.S. were portrayed with contempt. Otto Klemperer (1885–1973) headed the Los Angeles Philharmonic Orchestra from 1933 to 1940. After the war he returned to Europe and, in 1970, he made his final home in Israel. Here Klemperer is being assailed by the Nazis as one of those "Jews against Wagner", citing his emigration to America, where he had allegedly allowed himself to be celebrated as a "martyr" and a "victim of German barbarity".

Ein Dokument der Diffamierung jüdischer und progressiver Künstler im »Dritten Reich«: Seite aus der Nazi-Hetzbroschüre »Entartete Musik« (1939), in der zahlreiche in die USA geflüchtete Komponisten und Interpreten verächtlich gemacht wurden. Otto Klemperer (1885–1973) leitete von 1933 bis 1940 das Los Angeles Philharmonic Orchestra. Nach dem Krieg kehrte er nach Europa zurück und fand seine endgültige Heimat 1970 in Israel.

"Bix" Beiderbecke (1903–31), musician of German origin and pioneer of "white" jazz, here at far right, with his band, "The Wolverines", around 1923.

»Bix« Beiderbecke (1903–31), deutschstämmiger Pionier des »weißen« Jazz, hier ganz rechts mit seiner Band »The Wolverines« um 1923

Early German-American contributions in music were of a religious nature. The Kelpius group of mystics practiced choral and instrumental music and appeared in public as early as 1700. The Ephrata Cloister near Lancaster, Pennsylvania, produced not only numerous hymns (many of them composed by Conrad Beissel) – its nuns and monks also created illuminated music books of rare artistry. Beissel's music later fascinated Arnold Schönberg, and its wondrous tunes found their literary reflection in Thomas Mann's *Doctor Faustus*. In the towns founded by Moravian Brethren, orchestral music was part of the way of life. The *Collegium Musicum* orchestra at Bethlehem, Pennsylvania, was organized in 1744. Several of Mozart's and Haydn's symphonies and quartets had their premieres in Bethlehem just a few years after their composition.

While church-oriented musical activities were also cherished by most of the 19th century immigrants, and their descendants carried the hymns of the German Reformation over into their English hymnbooks, worldly choral singing was spread in the United States by German *Gesangvereine* which existed all over the country. Thousands of glee clubs and choruses today may trace their descent from German singing societies of which the Philadelphia *Männerchor* of 1834 was the first. At regular intervals they would meet for regional and national competition; the *Sängerfest* still being held regularly today, was the reward for endless hours of choral practice.

The share of Germans in the emergence of symphony orchestras need hardly be stressed. Many musical institutions were founded by them even in New England and the South, where German immigrants were not so numerous. George Henschel and William Gericke were the first conductors of the Boston Symphony Orchestra. In 1865, the New York Philharmonic Society counted 70 Germans among its 81 orchestra members. Leopold Damrosch, and his two sons, Frank and Walter, held prominent positions in American musical life for decades. Through extensive, regularly scheduled orchestra tours they brought music to towns from coast to coast. Theodore Thomas laid the foundations for the Chicago Symphony. This tradition was carried on by the American-born generations. Arthur Fiedler, whose German father had played in the Boston Symphony, will long be remembered for the "Pop Concerts" which carried classical tunes into the hearts of people who would not necessarily have entered a symphony hall for the more staid fare.

During the Nazi era Germany's loss became America's gain in musical life. For contemporaries most of the names need no introduction – Bruno Walter, Otto Klemperer, Kurt Herbert Adler, Fritz Reiner and Erich Leinsdorf as conductors, Adolf Busch and Artur Schnabel of concert hall fame and composers and teachers Paul Hindemith and Arnold Schönberg who were already established when they came to America's shores.

If this list were to be extended to the opera, operetta and musical it would be endless but Lotte Lehmann, one of the greatest sopranos of international opera, and Kurt Weill, who switched from the revolutionary music of his days in Weimar Germany to the American musical, must be named. Finally Leon Bismarck Beiderbecke, of Prussian parentage, took up his trumpet and plunged into America's most original form of music, Black jazz. Bix Beiderbecke proved that music knows no ethnic limits.

gegangen war, fand manch ein exilierter Autor in New York und Kalifornien Verleger, die seine Bücher in der Originalsprache veröffentlichten, wenn auch nur in kleinen Auflagen. Einige deutschstämmige Amerikaner, vor allem aus dem Kreis der Hitlerflüchtlinge, wurden selbst zu prominenten Verlegern, so Frederick Praeger, Kurt und Helen Wolff, Curt Enoch und Walter Johnson. Im Druckgewerbe führten deutsche Einwanderer mehrfach die jüngsten technischen Errungenschaften in ihrem neuen Heimatland ein. Fast sämtliche der frühen amerikanischen Lithographen, unter ihnen die Achtundvierziger Julius Bien und Louis Prang, waren in Deutschland geboren.

Die frühen Beiträge der Einwanderer zur amerikanischen Musik waren religiöser Natur. Die Mystiker um Johann Kelpius pflegten Chor- und Instumentalmusik und traten bereits um 1700 öffentlich auf. Im Kloster Ephrata bei Lancaster in Pennsylvanien entstanden nicht nur Hunderte von Kirchenliedern (viele von Conrad Beissel komponiert), sondern auch illuminierte Notenbücher von seltener Kunstfertigkeit. Beissels wundersame Melodien faszinierten später Arnold Schönberg und fanden ihren literarischen Niederschlag in Thomas Manns *Doktor Faustus*. In den von Herrnhutern gegründeten Städten gehörte orchestrale Musik zum alltäglichen Leben. In Bethlehem, Pennsylvanien, wurde schon 1744 die Orchestervereinigung des *Collegium Musicum* gegründet. Mehrere Symphonien und Streichquartette von Mozart und Haydn hatten dort nur wenige Jahre nach ihrer Veröffentlichung schon amerikanische Premiere. Während die Kirchenmusik auch von den Einwanderern des 19. Jahrhunderts weitergeleitet wurde und Kirchenlieder der deutschen Reformation schließlich in englische Gesangsbücher gelangten, wurde der weltliche Chorgesang in den Vereinigten Staaten durch die überall im Land entstehenden deutschen Gesangsvereine verbreitet. Tausende der heutigen *glee clubs* und Laienchöre können ihre Geschichte auf deutsche Gesangvereine des 19. Jahrhunderts zurückführen, unter welchen der philadelphische Männerchor von 1834 der erste war. Die Sänger und Sängerinnen trafen sich in regelmäßigen Abständen zu regionalen und nationalen Wettbewerben, den Sängerfesten, wie sie noch heute als Lohn für lange Probenstunden abgehalten werden.

Der Anteil der Deutschen an der Entstehung der amerikanischen Symphonieorchester braucht kaum betont zu werden. Selbst im Süden und in Neuengland, wo die deutschen Einwanderer weniger vertreten waren, haben sie zahlreiche musikalische Institutionen begründet. George Henschel und William Gericke waren die ersten Dirigenten des Bostoner Symphonieorchesters. Die New Yorker philharmonische Gesellschaft zählte 1865 unter ihren 81 Orchestermitgliedern 70 Deutsche. Leopold Damrosch und seine beiden Söhne, Frank und Walter, gehörten jahrzehntelang zu den tonangebenden Persönlichkeiten des amerikanischen Musiklebens. Durch umfangreiche, regelmäßig wiederholte Orchestertourneen machten sie die klassische Musik Europas von Küste zu Küste bekannt. Theodore Thomas gründete das Chicago Symphony Orchestra. Auch die schon in Amerika geborenen Generationen setzten diese große Tradition fort. Arthur Fiedler, dessen deutscher Vater schon im Bostoner Symphonieorchester gespielt hatte, bleibt für seine „Boston Pops"-Promenadenkonzerte unvergessen, mit denen er klassische Melodien in die Herzen von Menschen trug, die kaum in den Konzertsaal gefunden hätten, um sich ernstere Kost anzuhören.

Over the years, German-American literature has proved to be as diverse as the character of German immigration itself. Most authors who wrote in German were German-born. Their public was almost exclusively German-American. With the increasing disuse of the German language, the memory of the many poets and prose writers has faded. In perusing their works, an occasional line stands out that should not have suffered such neglect. This is true of the epigrams of the Forty-Eighter, Carl Heinrich Schnauffer who in the following epigram expressed the essence of freedom:

The precious diamond known as Freedom
Shatters not as common glass
On falling from the people's hand,
As oft as that may come to pass.

A vast amount of dialect literature stems from American-born writers. They have used the Pennsylvania-German language as their medium, a viable language derived from the Southwest German dialects of colonial immigrants which is still spoken today and understood by thousands in the original settlement area.
On quite another plane, and fully detached from the immigrant world into which their parents or grandparents came, we find that some of the best known names in the history of American letters belong to writers of German stock: Theodore Dreiser, Theodore Roethke, H.L. Mencken, Louis Untermeyer, Henry Miller, Peter Viereck, Sylvia Plath and Kurt Vonnegut, Jr. It was the latter who responded to the queries of a German-American research project that he felt "culturally" nothing but "purely American", and added that he qualifies as a German-American if the criteria of the American Kennel Club are applied!

One of the most prolific among the many forgotten German-speaking authors in America was Karl Knortz, who immigrated in 1864. Moved by Longfellow's epic poem, "Hiawatha", which he himself rendered into German, Knortz studied the Indian languages, edited a volume of legends and fables and, also in his own poetry, sided with native Americans ("Westward the Empire takes its way – follow it, voracious vultures!").

Während der Herrschaft der Nationalsozialisten wurden Deutschlands Verluste Amerikas musikalischer Gewinn. Die meisten der großen Namen bedürfen für den Zeitgenossen keiner weiteren Erklärung: Bruno Walter, Otto Klemperer, Kurt Herbert Adler, Fritz Reiner und Erich Leinsdorf unter den Dirigenten, Adolf Busch und Artur Schnabel als berühmte Instumentalisten, Paul Hindemith und Arnold Schönberg als Komponisten und Lehrer, die bereits anerkannt waren, als sie nach Amerika kamen.
Würde man diese Aufzählung auf Oper, Operette und Musical ausdehen, so wäre sie schier endlos. Trotzdem seien Lotte Lehmann, eine der größten Sopranistinnen der internationalen Operbühne, und Kurt Weill genannt, der mit politisch engagierter Musik im Berlin der Weimarer Jahre begann und später am Broadway Erfolge feierte. Und schließlich muß auch Leon Bismarck Beiderbecke erwähnt werden, Sohn preußischer Eltern, der zur Trompete griff und sich in Amerikas ursprünglichste Musikform stürzte, den schwarzen Jazz. Bix Beiderbecke bewies, daß Musik keine ethnischen Grenzen kennt.
Die deutschamerikanische Literatur hat sich im Lauf der Jahre als so vielfältig erwiesen wie die deutsche Einwanderung selbst. Die meisten der Autoren, die in Amerika in deutscher Sprache publizierten, waren noch in Deutschland geboren, Ihre Leserschaft bestand fast ausschließlich aus Deutschamerikanern. Als die deutsche Sprache zunehmend außer Gebrauch kam, begann auch die Erinnerung an diese vielen Dichter und Prosaschriftsteller zu verblassen. Läßt man ihre Werke heute Revue passieren, stößt man immer wieder auf Zeilen, die dieses Schicksal nicht verdient haben. Dies gilt für die Epigramme des Achtundvierzigers Carl Heinrich Schnauffer, der für das Wesen der Freiheit das folgende Bild fand:

Die Freiheit ist ein Diamant,
Der nie wie Glas zerschellt,
Wie oft er auch der zagen Hand
Des armen Volks entfällt.

Bei der mundartlichen Literatur stammt der überwiegende Teil von Autoren, die bereits in Amerika geboren sind. Ihr Medium war das Pennsylvaniendeutsche, das sich als unabhängige, lebendige Sprache aus den südwestdeutschen Dialekten der Einwanderer der Kolonialzeit entwickelt hat und in deren ursprünglichen Siedlungsgebieten noch heute von Tausenden gesprochen und verstanden wird.
Auf einer anderen Ebene, schon völlig abgelöst von der Welt der Einwanderer, der noch ihre Eltern und Großeltern angehört hatten, finden wir unter den bekanntesten Namen der amerikanischen Literatur etliche, die deutsche Abstammung verraten: Theodore Dreiser, Theodore Roethke, H.L. Mencken, Louis Untermeyer, Henry Miller, Peter Viereck, Sylvia Plath und Kurt Vonnegut jr. Es war der letztere, der auf die Frage eines deutsch-amerikanischen Forschungsprojekts zur Antwort gab, daß er sich „kulturell als reiner Amerikaner" fühle und als Deutschamerikaner nur, wenn man die Kriterien des Hundezuchtverbandes anlegen wolle.

Einer der fruchtbarsten unter den vielen in Vergessenheit geratenen deutschsprachigen Autoren Amerikas war Karl Knortz, der 1864 einwanderte. Angeregt von Longfellows Epos »Hiawatha«, das er selbst ins Deutsche übertrug, studierte er die Indianersprachen, gab indianische Märchen und Sagen heraus und ergriff auch in seinen eigenen Gedichten die Partei der amerikanischen Ureinwohner (»Westwärts zieht der Stern des Reiches – folget ihm, gefräß'ge Geier!«).

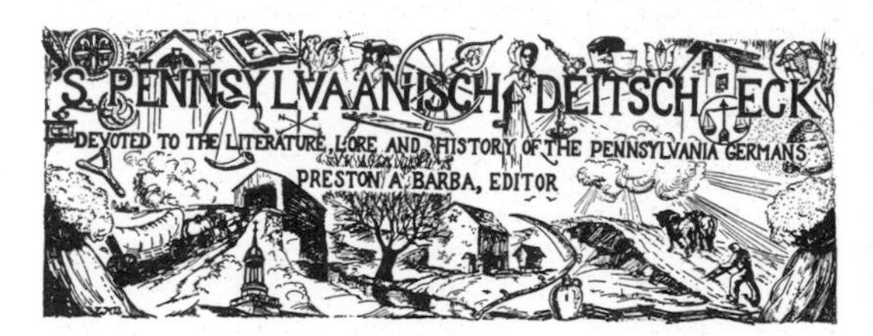

These two facsimiles are indicative of the whole range of German immigration and German-American literature. Above, the heading of a regularly appearing column in Pennsylvania Dutch dialect which even today is still spoken by half a million people in the U.S. Below, the title page of a book by the thwarted but indefatigable revolutionary and fugitive "Forty-Eighter" Karl Heinzen (1809–80), published by an association with the unambiguous name "Society for the Propagation of Radical Principles".

Die ganze Spannweite der deutschen Einwanderung und der deutschamerikanischen Literatur markieren diese beiden Faksimiles: oben der Kopf einer regelmäßig erscheinenden Dialektkolumne in Pennsylvaniendeutsch, das noch heute von einer halben Million Menschen in den USA gesprochen wird; unten ein Titel des verhinderten, aber unermüdlichen Revolutionärs und geflohenen »Achtundvierzigers« Karl Heinzen (1809–80), veröffentlicht von einer Gesellschaft mit dem schlichten Namen »Verein zur Verbreitung radikaler Prinzipien«.

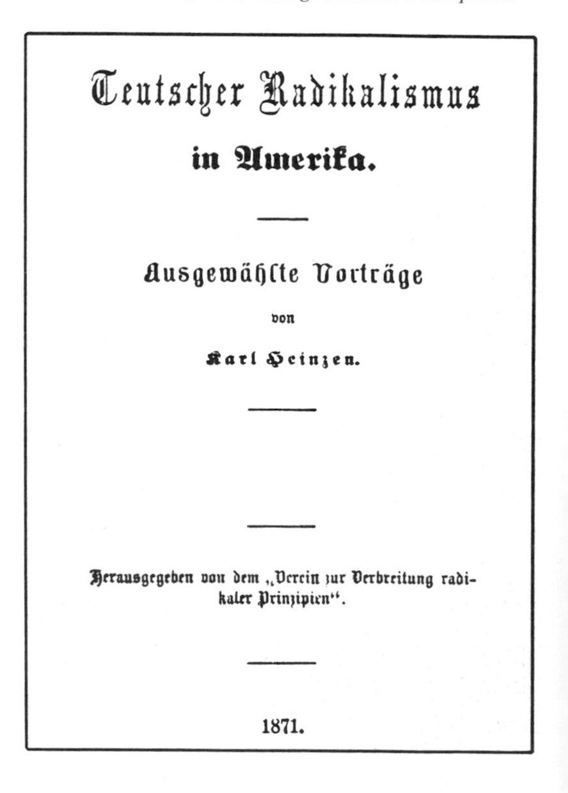

Teutscher Radikalismus
in Amerika.

Ausgewählte Vorträge
von
Karl Heinzen.

Herausgegeben von dem „Verein zur Verbreitung radikaler Prinzipien".

1871.

Kurt Vonnegut, Jr., born in 1922, survived the bombing of Dresden on the 13th and 14th of February, 1945 as a prisoner of war in the municipal slaughterhouse number 5. His novel "Slaughterhouse-Five or The Children's Crusade" was a literary attempt at overcoming this experience and in 1969 it made him famous.

Kurt Vonnegut jr., geboren 1922, überlebte als Kriegsgefangener im städtischen Schlachthof Nr. 5 die Bombardierung Dresdens am 13./14. Februar 1945. Sein Roman »Schlachthof 5 oder Der Kinderkreuzzug«, ein literarischer Bewältigungsversuch dieses Erlebnisses, machte ihn 1969 berühmt.

Henry Miller (1891–1980), the son of a tailor of German extraction, grew up in German surroundings in New York City. With the publication of his anarchic novels, "Tropic of Cancer" (1934) and "Tropic of Capricorn" (1939), which, because of their frank depiction of sexuality, were for years banned in the U.S.A., Miller emerged as one of the great liberators of 20th-century literature.

Henry Miller (1891–1980), als Sohn eines deutschstämmigen Schneiders in New York in deutscher Umgebung aufgewachsen, wurde mit seinen anarchischen und wegen ihrer sexuellen Freizügigkeit in den USA lange verbotenen Romanen »Wendekreis des Krebses« (1934) und »Wendekreis des Steinbocks« (1939) zu einem der großen Befreier in der Literatur des 20. Jahrhunderts.

The poet Sylvia Plath, who was born in Boston in 1932, committed suicide in London in 1963. Much of her poetry deals with her aggressive, self-tormenting struggle with her German origin.

Die Lyrikerin Sylvia Plath, 1932 in Boston geboren, beging 1963 in London Selbstmord; viele ihrer Gedichte behandeln ihre aggressive, selbstquälerische Auseinandersetzung mit ihrer deutschen Herkunft.

Theodore Dreiser (1871–1945), whose novels "Sister Carrie" (1900) and "An American Tragedy" (1925) brought to a close the naturalist period in American literary history, was born in Terre Haute, Indiana, the twelfth of thirteen children of an impoverished family of weavers who had emigrated to the United States in 1844.

Theodore Dreiser (1871–1945), als zwölftes von dreizehn Kindern einer 1844 ausgewanderten, verarmten Weberfamilie in Terre Haute, Indiana, geboren, wurde mit seinen Romanen »Schwester Carrie« (1900) und »Eine amerikanische Tragödie« (1925) zum Vollender des literarischen Naturalismus in Amerika.

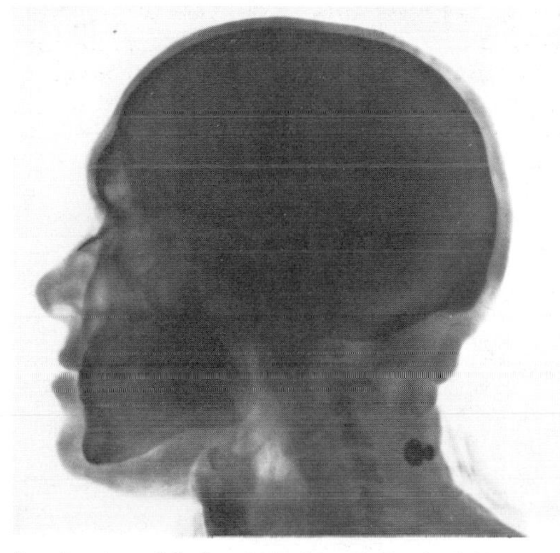

Interior view of the head which made Friedrich Nietzsche famous in America and helped Theodore Dreiser gain acceptance: an X-ray of H. L. Mencken (1880–1956) who, with his "American Mercury", became an institution of criticism in the United States.

Innenansicht des Kopfes, der Friedrich Nietzsche in Amerika bekannt machte und Theodore Dreiser durchzusetzen half: ein Röntgenbild von H. L. Mencken (1880–1956), der mit seinem »American Mercury« zu einer ähnlichen kritischen Institution wurde wie im deutschen Sprachraum Karl Kraus mit seiner »Fackel«.

Peter Lorre (1904–64) in Fritz Lang's classic film "M." (1931) which was made while they both were still in Germany. In his American career, Lorre appeared in such films as John Huston's "The Maltese Falcon" (1941), Michael Curtiz' "Casablanca" (1943) and Frank Capra's "Arsenic and Old Lace" (1944).

Peter Lorre (1904–64) in Fritz Langs noch in Deutschland gedrehtem Klassiker »M – eine Stadt sucht einen Mörder« (1931). In seiner amerikanischen Karriere trat Lorre u. a. in John Hustons »Die Spur des Falken« (1941), in Michael Curtiz' »Casablanca« (1943) und in Frank Capras »Arsen und Spitzenhäubchen« (1944) auf.

Max Reinhardt Workshop

PRESENTS

SHAKESPEARE'S
WOMEN, CLOWNS AND SONGS

Scenes from
TRAGEDIES AND COMEDIES

Directed by
MAX REINHARDT

Musical Interludes and Songs by
ERICH WOLFGANG KORNGOLD

MUSICAL DIRECTION: E. W. KORNGOLD, PIANO

Violin: GRISHA GOLUBOFF

SARI SCOTT, Assistant to MAX REINHARDT

AT THE
MAX REINHARDT THEATRE
6040 WILSHIRE BLVD. • • WILSHIRE AT FAIRFAX

•

WEDNESDAY, JULY 2nd . . . THURSDAY, JULY 3rd

CURTAIN 8:15

A program announcing a performance of the "Max Reinhardt Workshop", which the Austrian pioneer of modern theater-directing founded in Los Angeles immediately after his emigration in 1938.

Programmankündigung des »Max Reinhardt Workshop«, den der österreichische Pionier des modernen Regietheaters sofort nach seiner Emigration 1938 in Hollywood gründete.

Erich von Stroheim (1885–1957) came to America in 1906, was assistant director under the great D. W. Griffith and made the stereotype of the brutal Prussian officer his acting trademark. More significant, though less known, are his own films which, due to Stroheim's unwillingness to compromise on artistic matters of opinion, could not gain acceptance in Hollywood ("Blind Husbands" (1918), "Greed" (1923), "The Wedding March" (1928)).

Erich von Stroheim (1885–1957) kam 1906 nach Amerika, war Regieassistent bei dem großen D. W. Griffith und machte das Klischeebild des brutalen preußischen Offiziers zu seinem schauspielerischen Markenzeichen. Bedeutender, aber weniger bekannt sind seine eigenen Filme, die sich wegen ihrer künstlerischen Kompromißlosigkeit in Hollywood nicht durchsetzen konnten (u.a. »Blinde Ehemänner« (1918), »Gier nach Geld« (1923), »Der Hochzeitsmarsch« (1928)).

F. W. Murnau (1888–1931), born Friedrich Wilhelm Plumpe in Bielefeld, was welcomed in Hollywood with open arms. With the films he made there, "Sunrise" (1927), "Our Daily Bread" (1929) and "Tabu" (together with Robert Flaherty, 1929), he was nevertheless not able to continue the success of his classic works of German expressionism, "Nosferatu" (1922) and "Faust" (1926).

F. W. Murnau (1888–1931), als Friedrich Wilhelm Plumpe in Bielefeld geboren, wurde 1927 in Hollywood mit offenen Armen empfangen, konnte jedoch mit seinen dort gedrehten Filmen »Sunrise« (1927), »Our Daily Bread« (1929) und »Tabu« (zusammen mit Robert Flaherty, 1929) nicht mehr an die Erfolge seiner expressionistischen Klassiker »Nosferatu« (1922) und »Faust« (1926) anknüpfen.

Fritz Lang (1890–1976), who, like Otto Preminger and Billy Wilder, was born in Vienna, already had a European film career with such masterpieces as "Dr. Mabuse" (1922) and "Metropolis" (1926) to his credit when, in 1936, with "Fury", he began to conquer Hollywood.

Fritz Lang (1890–1976), wie Otto Preminger und Billy Wilder in Wien geboren, hatte bereits eine europäische Filmkarriere und Meisterwerke wie »Dr. Mabuse« (1922) und »Metropolis« (1926) hinter sich, als er 1936 mit »Fury« begann, sich die Hollywood-Genres zu erobern.

In the performing and creative arts as in American writing, the part played by Americans of German descent rarely has any specific relationship to their ethnic origins. They are to be found among the directors and producers of the early days, from Carl Laemmle and F.W. Murnau down to Eric Pommer, Ernst Lubitsch, William Dieterle, Billy Wilder and Max Reinhardt. Acting in movies and on stage involves the spoken language, which proved a handicap to some who had to be content with being typecast in roles where a German accent was desired; however, Marlene Dietrich and Peter Lorre transcended these limits successfully.
Before leaving the performing arts, we must step back into history in order to mention the fact that for some sixty years, from the 1850s to World War I, there was a lively, if not always financially thriving German stage in many American cities. The Irving Place Theatre in New York, under the management of Heinrich Conried from 1892 to 1907, was known among American theatre specialists for its innovations which were mostly transferred and adapted from contemporary stages in Europe. Cincinnati, Philadelphia, Chicago, Milwaukee, St. Paul and San Francisco were among the places where German theatres achieved professional status. Except for the four German theatres in New York City, most German-American stages were not receptive to modern works from Germany. They relied on a time-tested repertoire of classical and popular plays.

Ähnlich wie in der Literatur, hat die Rolle, die die Amerikaner deutscher Herkunft in den bildenden und in den darstellenden Künsten spielten, kaum eine spezifische Beziehung zu ihrem ethnischen Ursprung. Im Film finden sich deutsche Namen bei Regisseuren und Produzenten von der Frühzeit an, von Carl Laemmle und F.W. Murnau bis zu Eric Pommer, Ernst Lubitsch, William Dieterle, Billy Wilder und Max Reinhardt. Für Schauspieler erwies sich, im Film wie auf der Bühne, oft das gesprochene Wort als Hindernis, wenn sie sich nicht mit Rollen zufriedengeben wollten, in denen deutscher Akzent erwünscht war. Marlene Dietrich und Peter Lorre haben freilich bewiesen, daß auch diese Hürde erfolgreich zu überwinden war.
Wir dürfen die darstellenden Künste nicht verlassen, ohne noch einen Blick auf die deutschsprachigen Bühnen geworfen zu haben, die etwa sechzig Jahre lang, von der Mitte des 19. Jahrhunderts bis zum Ersten Weltkrieg, in vielen amerikanischen Städten lebendiges, wenn auch nicht immer finanziell erfolgreiches, Theater boten. Das Irving Place Theater in New York, von 1892 bis 1907 von Heinrich Conried geleitet, war unter amerikanischen Theaterspezialisten für seine Neuerungen bekannt, die größtenteils von zeitgenössischen europäischen Bühnen übernommen und adaptiert worden waren. Cincinnati, Philadelphia, Chicago, Milwaukee, St. Paul und San Francisco waren andere Städte, in denen deutschsprachige Theater professionellen Status erreichten. Abgesehen von den vier deutschen Theatern New Yorks, waren die deutschamerikanischen Bühnen für zeitgenössische, moderne Stücke aus der alten Heimat nicht sonderlich aufgeschlossen. Sie verließen sich auf ein bewährtes Repertoire an klassischen und populären Stücken.

"After the Performance – Dancing Party" appears on the bottom of this playbill announcing a German-American production of "Faust" in the year 1879.

»Nach der Vorstellung: Tanzkränzchen« – Theaterzettel für eine deutschamerikanische »Faust«-Aufführung im Jahre 1879

The show must go on – on the stage and in the audience. Scene from the "New Yorker Stadt-Theater", around 1860 the most prominent German language theater in the city.

Theater auf der Bühne und im Zuschauerraum: ein Blick ins »Deutsche Stadttheater« von New York, um 1860 die führende deutschsprachige Bühne der Stadt

The closest thing to a collective German-American contribution to American art was created by innumerable, mostly anonymous rural folk who were not aware that they were producing an art form. Pennsylvania German folk art, which only achieved its fullest recognition during the 20th century, had its origins among the German population of colonial times. From New York into North Carolina but mostly concentrated in eastern Pennsylvania, folk art was produced in many forms. Using Rhenish folk motifs, German craftsmen turned useful implements of everyday life into beautiful works of art. Furniture and tools were decorated with star-like flowers, tulips, sunwheels, hearts and colorful birds. The same symbols were worked into ornate *fraktur* writing, such as the Pennsylvania-Dutch birth certificates. This rural folk art became a firm component of a common American heritage to which present-day designers still resort for inspiration.

The individual artist of German birth or background was present in every generation. Painters and sculptors needed a more settled environment than the frontier society could provide. Hence we find the first, working as portraitists for the tidewater gentry and the seaport merchants. The earliest known artist was Justus Engelhardt Kuehn who painted portraits in Maryland from 1708 until 1717. Best remembered among the many 19th century painters, despite changing fashions and appreciation in art, are two disciples of the Düsseldorf school, Emanuel Leutze and Albert Bierstadt. Leutze's fame rests largely on the patriotic feelings evoked by his "Washington Crossing the Delaware" (1851), while Bierstadt's western landscapes have never lost their strong appeal.

Einem kollektiven deutschamerikanischen Beitrag zur amerikanischen Kunst kommt wohl am nächsten, was jene zahllosen, meist unbekannten Männer und Frauen aus der bäuerlichen Landbevölkerung geschaffen haben, die dabei selbst nicht ahnten, daß sie eine Kunstform begründeten. Die pennsylvaniendeutsche Volkskunst, die ihre größte Anerkennung erst im 20. Jahrhundert fand, geht auf die frühen Einwanderer der Kolonialzeit zurück. Von New York bis nach Nord-Carolina, vor allem aber im östlichen Pennsylvanien, entstanden naive Kunstwerke in vielerlei Gestalt. Deutsche Handwerker verschönten die nützlichen Dinge des Alltags mit rheinischen Volksmotiven. Möbel, Werkzeuge und Geräte wurden mit Sternblumen, Tulpen, Sonnenrädern, Herzen und farbenfrohen Vögeln verziert. Die gleichen Ornamente fanden auch in Fraktur-Kalligraphien wie den pennsylvaniendeutschen Geburtsurkunden Verwendung. Heute gehört diese bäuerliche Volkskunst zum gemeinsamen kulturellen Erbe der Amerikaner und ist für die Designer unserer Tage zu einer gern genutzten Inspirationsquelle geworden.

Individuelle Künstler deutscher Geburt oder Herkunft gab es in jeder Epoche der Einwanderungsgeschichte. Maler und Bildhauer brauchten eine ruhigere gesellschaftliche Umgebung, als sie die *frontier*, die Westgrenze, bieten konnte. So finden wir die ersten als Porträtisten des Blut- und Geldadels in den Hafenstädten. Der erste namentlich bekannte deutschstämmige Künstler war Justus Engelhardt Kuehn, der zwischen 1708 und 1717 in Maryland porträtierte. Unter den zahlreichen Malern des 19. Jahrhunderts sind zwei Mitglieder der Düsseldorfer Schule, Emanuel Leutze und Albert Bierstadt, trotz wechselnder künstlerischer Moden und Vorlieben die bekanntesten geblieben. Leutzes Ruhm beruht vor allem auf den patriotischen Gefühlsaufwallungen, die sein Historienbild von „Washingtons Übergang über den Delaware" (1851) hervorzurufen verstand, während Bierstadts monumentale Wildwestlandschaften ihre starke Wirkung nie verloren haben.

"Fractur" calligraphy, decorated with ornaments and motifs typical of Pennsylvania Dutch folk art.

Fraktur-Kalligraphie, dekoriert mit typischen Ornamenten und Motiven der pennsylvaniendeutschen Volkskunst

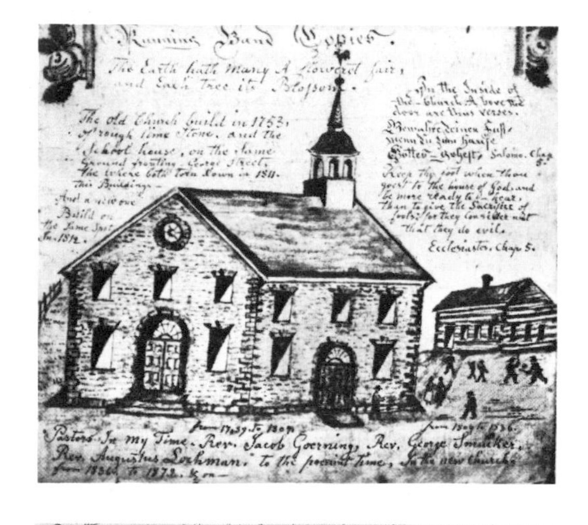

Around the turn of the eighteenth century, the German-American schoolmaster, Lewis Miller of York, Lancaster County, Pennsylvania, kept a diary consisting of both words and pictures. Today, this record of his is not only an invaluable source of cultural history but also an as yet undiscovered forerunner of the comic strip.

Ein Tagebuch in Worten und Bildern führte um die Wende vom 18. zum 19. Jahrhundert der deutschstämmige Schulmeister Lewis Miller in York, Lancaster County, Pennsylvanien: heute ist es eine unschätzbare kulturhistorische Quelle – und ein noch unentdeckter Vorfahr des Comic Strip.

Justus Engelhardt Kuehn, about whom it is only known that he immigrated before 1708 and until at least 1718 worked as a painter in Annapolis, Maryland, created this "Portrait of Eleanor Darnall", one of the early American oil paintings.

Justus Engelhardt Kuehn, von dem nur bekannt ist, daß er vor 1708 einwanderte und bis mindestens 1718 in Annapolis, Maryland, malte, schuf dieses »Porträt von Eleanor Darnall« – eines der frühen amerikanischen Ölgemälde.

"Sacramento Railroad Station" painted in 1875 by Carl William Hahn (1829–87). Hahn had studied together with the German-Americans Emanuel Leutze, Albert Bierstadt and Charles Wimar at the art academy in Dusseldorf and, in 1871, he too had emigrated.

»Bahnstation in Sacramento«, 1875 gemalt von Carl William Hahn (1829–87), der an der Düsseldorfer Kunstakademie im Kreise der Deutschamerikaner Emanuel Leutze, Albert Bierstadt und Charles Wimar studiert hatte und 1871 selbst ausgewandert war.

"A Sunday Morning in the Mines", the best known painting by Carl Christian Nahl (1819–78) from Kassel in Hessia. In 1848, he emigrated to America and, lured by the gold rush, made his way to California. When the dream of getting rich quick failed to materialize, he, together with his brother, opened up a studio in San Francisco.

»Sonntagmorgen auf den Goldfeldern«, das bekannteste Bild von Carl Christian Nahl (1819–78) aus Kassel, der 1848 auswanderte und vom »Goldrausch« nach Kalifornien gelockt wurde. Als sich der Traum vom schnellen Reichtum nicht erfüllte, eröffnete er zusammen mit seinem Bruder ein Atelier in San Francisco.

In 1850, Theodor Kaufmann, born in Uelzen, Lower Saxony, in 1814, published a series of etchings (including "The Enthronement of the Goddess of Reason" shown here) along with an accompanying speculative text under the title "The Development of the Idea of God". In the same year he emigrated to America, where he later took part in the Civil War as a private in the Union Army. He subsequently became well-known as a painter of Civil War themes.

»Die Inthronisation der Göttin der Vernunft«, aus einem Zyklus von Radierungen, die der 1814 in Uelzen geborene Theodor Kaufmann 1850 – im Jahr seiner Auswanderung – zusammen mit einem spekulativen Begleittext unter dem Titel »Die Entstehung der Gottesidee« veröffentlichte. In Amerika wurde Kaufmann als Maler des Bürgerkrieges bekannt, an dem er auf Seiten der Union als einfacher Soldat teilnahm.

"View of San Francisco" by Max Beckmann (1884–1950), a prominent representative of German Expressionism, who moved to the United States in 1947.

»Blick auf San Francisco« von Max Beckmann (1884–1950), dem führenden Repräsentanten des deutschen Expressionismus, der 1947 in die USA übersiedelte.

Street scene in New York, portrayed by George Grosz (1893–1959). In 1933 Grosz was expelled from Germany as a "degenerate artist", and subsequent to his emigration to America received U. S. citizenship in 1937.

Straßenszene in New York, gezeichnet von George Grosz (1893–1959), der 1933 als »entarteter Künstler« aus Deutschland vertrieben wurde und 1937 die amerikanische Staatsbürgerschaft erhielt.

The first folk sculptors were the stonecutters who lived in the early German settlements. Many of their surviving works have in recent years been given "historic landmark" status. It is in keeping with the American pioneer spirit that one of the first native American sculptors, William H. Rinehart, son of a German farm family in Maryland, began his career as a quarry worker. After studying in Baltimore and Rome, Rinehart created a myriad of works in the classical style. In many cities across the United States, statues and other monuments attest to the large number of Germans who helped adorn the parks and buildings of the rapidly growing cities, among them Albert Jaeger, Elisabeth Ney, Karl Bitter, Hans Schuler and F.W. Sievers.

Die ersten Bildhauer waren die Steinmetze in den frühen deutschen Siedlungen. Viele ihrer Werke, die bis heute überlebt haben, wurden in den vergangenen Jahren in den Rang von historischen Denkmälern erhoben. Es entspricht dem amerikanischen Pioniergeist, daß einer der ersten in Amerika geborenen Bildhauer, William H. Rinehart, der Sohn einer deutschen Bauernfamilie aus Maryland, seine Laufbahn als Arbeiter in einem Steinbruch begann. Nach Studienjahren in Baltimore und Rom wurde Rinehart zum Schöpfer zahlloser Arbeiten in klassizistischem Stil. Überall in den Vereinigten Staaten zeugen Statuen und andere Momumente vom Wirken weiterer deutschstämmiger Künstler, die die Grünanlagen und Bauwerke der rapide wachsenden Städte verschönten; genannt seien Albert Jaeger, Elisabeth Ney, Karl Bitter, Hans Schuler und F.W. Sievers.

Karl Bitter, who was born in Vienna and emigrated in 1889, created this equestrian statue of Franz Sigel (1824–1902), "Forty-Eighter" and major general of the Union Army in the Civil War.

Karl Bitter, in Wien geboren und 1889 ausgewandert, schuf dieses Reiterstandbild des »Achtundvierzigers« und Generalmajors der Unionsarmee im Bürgerkrieg, Franz Sigel (1824–1902)

A monument commemorating German immigrants in Texas, created in 1938 by Hugo Leo Villa.

Ein Denkmal für die deutschen Einwanderer in Texas, 1938 errichtet von Hugo Leo Villa

Due to a growing historical and self consciousness in German-Americans of the late 19th century, a consciousness which owed much to the bicentennial "Pioneer Jubilee" of 1883, immigration became a theme for representative monuments stylistically typical of the times. Shown here: "The Immigrants", a group of figures from Albert Jaeger's "German-American National Monument" in Germantown.

Das wachsende Geschichts- und Selbstbewußtsein der Deutschamerikaner des späten 19. Jahrhunderts, das einen wesentlichen Impuls aus dem zweihundertjährigen »Pionier-Jubiläum« von 1883 erhielt, ließ die Einwanderung zum Themenvorwurf für repräsentative Denkmäler im Stil der Zeit werden. Abgebildet: »Die Einwanderer«, eine Figurengruppe aus Albert Jaegers »deutsch-amerikanischem Nationaldenkmal« in Germantown.

"Molly Pitcher" (actually Maria Ludwig-Hayes), a folk heroine from the American Revolution, here immortalized by J. Otto Schweizer (1890–1965), an American sculptor of German-Swiss descent. This relief is from his Molly Pitcher Monument in Carlisle, Pa.

»Molly Pitcher«, eigentlich Maria Ludwig-Hayes, eine Volksheldin des amerikanischen Unabhängigkeitskrieges, verewigt dieses Relief aus einem Molly-Pitcher-Denkmal des amerikanischen Bildhauers deutsch-schweizerischer Abstammung J. Otto Schweizer (1890–1965)

Self-portrait of the sculptress Elisabeth Ney, born in Münster in 1833. While in Europe, Bismarck, Garibaldi and the Bavarian "dream king" Ludwig II sat for her. In 1870, at the high point of her brilliant career, she emigrated to Texas, where she died in 1907.

Selbstporträt der 1833 in Münster geborenen Bildhauerin Elisabeth Ney, der in Europa Bismarck, Garibaldi und der bayerische Märchenkönig Ludwig II. Modell saßen, ehe sie 1870 – auf dem Höhepunkt ihrer glänzenden Karriere – nach Texas auswanderte, wo sie 1907 starb.

From a tiny Bavarian village via the emigration port of Bremen to New York: the typical route of a 19th-century emigrant was taken in 1971 by a 20th-century piece of sculpture, the "Spherical Caryatid N. Y.", created by the German sculptor Fritz Koenig (also illustrated on back cover). Commissioned in 1968 by the New York Port Authority upon recommendation of Minuri Yamasaki, the architect of the World Trade Center, it today has a prominent place amidst the fountains adorning the World Trade Center Plaza – on that very island of stone which Peter Minnewit bought from the Algonquin Indians in 1626, and hardly a third of a mile away from the spot where millions of European immigrants first set foot on the soil of their "New World" as they emerged from the Castle Garden reception center. The sculpture, as ambiguous and abstract a work of art as it may be with its convoluted figure at the base either supporting, lifting, or being crushed by the massive globe, either being menaced by it or sheltered, as by a protective cranium, by this very evocative aspect may elicit thoughts of the immigrants, their motivations, hopes, fears and destiny...

The illustrations (top to bottom) show: the life-size plaster model of the 25-foot-high work, which was used for the casting in bronze in Munich; the completed bronze sculpture in front of the work-shed specially erected for the project in Koenig's Lower Bavarian village of Ganslberg, near Landshut; the "Spherical Caryatid N. Y." at its final destination, in front of the towers of the World Trade Center.

Aus einem kleinen Dorf in Bayern über den Auswanderungshafen Bremen nach New York: diesen typischen Weg eines Emigranten des 19. Jahrhunderts nahm 1971 die »Kugelkaryatide N. Y.« des deutschen Bildhauers Fritz Koenig, die auch auf dem hinteren Umschlag dieses Buches abgebildet ist. 1968 von der New Yorker Hafenbehörde auf Anregung des Architekten des World Trade Centers, Minuri Yamasaki, in Auftrag gegeben, steht die Skulptur heute im Zentrum der Brunnenanlage auf der Plaza des World Trade Center – auf eben jenem Felsen, den Peter Minnewit 1626 den Algonkin-Indianern abkaufte, und nur fünfhundert Meter entfernt von der Stelle, an der Millionen von europäischen Einwanderern beim Verlassen des Empfangszentrums von Castle Garden erstmals den Boden ihrer »Neuen Welt« betraten. Auch von den Schicksalen, Auswanderungsmotiven, Hoffnungen und Ängsten dieser Menschen vermag das vieldeutige, abstrakte Kunstwerk – eine tragende Figur, von der Kugelmasse niedergedruckt oder sie hebend, von ihr bedroht oder wie von einem Schädeldach beschützt – zu berichten.

Die Abbildungen zeigen (von oben nach unten): das 7,60 Meter hohe Gipsmodell der Plastik im Maßstab 1:1, nach dem in München der Bronzeguß vorgenommen wurde; die fertige Skulptur vor der Werkhalle in Koenigs Wohnort Ganslberg bei Landshut in Niederbayern, die eigens für dieses Projekt errichtet worden war; die »Kugelkaryatide N. Y.« an ihrem endgültigen Aufstellungsort vor den Türmen des World Trade Center.

Bethlehem, Pennsylvania, was founded in 1741 by missionaries of the Herrnhuter Brethren under Count Nikolaus von Zinzendorf, who sought to convert the Indians. Today a center of the American steel industry, the settlement and its typical structures around 1800 are shown here in an engraving by G. G. Lange.

Bethlehem, Pennsylvanien, heute ein Zentrum der amerikanischen Stahlindustrie, wurde 1741 von Indianermissionaren der Herrnhuter Brüdergemeine unter Nikolaus Graf von Zinzendorf gegründet. Der Stich von G. G. Lange zeigt die Siedlung und ihre typischen Bauten um 1800.

Thomas Ustick Walter, whose grandfather came to America when only seven years old, began work on the expansion of the Capitol in Washington in 1851, a project which was to take fourteen years. The illustration above shows the building around this time, still with its wooden dome and without the wings which were to be annexed by Walter. At left, ten years later, President Lincoln en route to be sworn in as the nineteenth president of the United States. The iron dome, already under construction in the illustration, is still a Washington landmark today.

Thomas Ustick Walter, dessen Großvater als Siebenjähriger nach Amerika gekommen war, begann 1851 mit dem Ausbau des Kapitols in Washington, der vierzehn Jahre in Anspruch nehmen sollte. Die Abbildung oben zeigt das Gebäude etwa zu diesem Zeitpunkt, noch mit der ursprünglichen Holzkuppel und ohne die von Walter hinzugefügten Erweiterungsflügel. Links, zehn Jahre später, rollt Präsident Lincoln auf dem Weg zu seiner Vereidigung als 19. Präsident der Vereinigten Staaten bereits auf die im Bau befindliche Eisenkuppel zu, die noch heute das Wahrzeichen Washingtons darstellt.

The "Times" Building at the corner of Broadway and 42nd Street in New York, designed by the architect and head of a construction firm, Otto M. Eidlitz.

Das »Times«-Gebäude, Ecke Broadway und 42. Straße in New York, entworfen von dem Architekten und Bauunternehmer Otto M. Eidlitz

American architecture also developed from the work of colonial craftsmen. The vernacular architecture of certain German settlements, notably Salem in North Carolina and Bethlehem in Pennsylvania, but also the often perfect simplicity of early houses and barns, are fully appreciated by a posterity that has come to cherish both style and harmony with the natural environment. In urban architecture, German-Americans were the creators of many well-known public buildings. John Adam Horlbeck built the magnificent customs house, the Exchange, in Charleston, South Carolina in 1767–71. The great iron dome of the United States Capitol in Washington was designed by Thomas Ustick Walter. John Smithmeyer and Paul J. Pelz, the latter a son of a Forty-Eighter, drew the plans for the original Library of Congress building. Some of New York's most prestigious hotels were the work of Henry J. Hardenbergh. The Times Building, a Manhattan landmark, was designed by Otto Eidlitz.

Auch die amerikanische Architektur erwuchs aus der Arbeit von Handwerkern der Kolonialzeit. Die volkstümliche Architektur bestimmter deutscher Siedlungen, vor allem Salems in Nord-Carolina und Bethlehems in Pennsylvanien, aber auch die oft ästhetisch perfekte Einfachheit der frühen Häuser und Scheunen finden den Beifall einer Nachwelt, die Stil und Harmonie mit der natürlichen Umgebung zu schätzen gelernt hat. In der städtischen Architektur schufen Deutschamerikaner zahlreiche bekannte öffentliche Gebäude. John Adam Horlbeck baute in den Jahren von 1767 bis 71 das imposante Zollamt von Charleston, Süd-Carolina. Die große Eisenkuppel des Kapitols in Washington wurde von Thomas Ustick Walter entworfen. John Smithmeyer und Paul J. Pelz, letzterer der Sohn eines Achtundvierzigers, zeichnete die Pläne für das ursprüngliche Gebäude der Kongreßbibliothek. Einige von New Yorks angesehensten Hotels sind Bauten von Henry J. Hardenbergh. Das Times Building, ein Wahrzeichen Manhattans, wurde von Otto Eidlitz entworfen.

This log cabin, built near New Ulm, Minnesota, by the immigrant Wilhelm Pfaender in 1856, represents simple, but aesthetically satisfying pioneer architecture. The L-shaped ground plan probably came about through later supplementary construction.

Einfache, aber in der Proportionierung durchaus anspruchsvolle Pionierarchitektur repräsentiert dieses Blockhaus mit L-förmigem (wahrscheinlich durch einen Anbau entstandenem) Grundriß, das der Einwanderer Wilhelm Pfaender 1856 bei New Ulm in Minnesota errichtete.

John L. Smithmeyer and Paul J. Pelz, who was born in Silesia in 1841, built the Library of Congress in Italian Renaissance style (in the photo with a modern annex in the background). The ornamentation and embellishment, designed by Pelz, were realized by Albert Weinert, a sculptor of German descent.

Im italienischen Renaissancestil errichteten John L. Smithmeyer und der 1841 in Schlesien geborene Paul J. Pelz das Gebäude der Kongreßbibliothek in Washington (auf dem Foto mit einem modernen Erweiterungsbau im Hintergrund). Die Ornamente und Ausschmückungen, von Pelz entworfen, wurden von dem deutschstämmigen Bildhauer Albert Weinert ausgeführt.

Once again this account must return to the refugees who came from Nazi Germany. Their impact on the creative arts can hardly be overestimated. One group might be singled out to stand here for all who not only brought their ideas and their experience from Europe but who readily adjusted their measures and scale to fit the spirit of the country that let them work freely. The *Bauhaus* of Weimar, a cooperative fraternity of artists and craftsmen concerned with the external structure and internal furnishings of contemporary buildings, was forcibly dissolved by the Nazi authorities. One after another, the whole faculty of the *Bauhaus* migrated to America, Walter Gropius, Ludwig Mies van der Rohe, Josef Albers, Herbert Bayer and Lyonel Feininger. Feininger was the grandson of a Forty-Eighter; although New York born, he spent half a century in Germany where he had joined the *Bauhaus* at its inception in 1919. Gropius, the founder of the *Bauhaus,* became director of the School of Architecture at Harvard, and van der Rohe became director of the School of Architecture at the Illinois Institute of Technology. Josef Albers, who taught at Yale after years of teaching at Black Mountain College in North Carolina, became one of the best known American painters of this century through his work with color modulation. Herbert Bayer's posters profoundly influenced American advertising. The works of these few men permeated and revolutionized design in buildings and homes all over the American continent.

Und wieder muß dieser Bericht auf die Flüchtlinge aus dem Deutschland Adolf Hitlers zurückkommen, deren Einfluß auf die schöpferischen Künste in den USA kaum überschätzt werden kann. Es sei gestattet, hier eine Gruppe stellvertretend für all jene zu behandeln, die nicht nur Ideen und Erfahrungen aus Europa mitbrachten, sondern auch bereitwillig auf die veränderten Maßstäbe und neuen Herausforderungen eingingen, die das Land, das ihnen freie Arbeitsmöglichkeiten gab, für sie bereithielt. Das in Weimar gegründete „Bauhaus", ein Zusammenschluß von Künstlern und Handwerkern, die an der Reform von Architektur und Innenausstattung zu einem gemeinsamen Gesamtkunstwerk arbeiteten, wurde von den Nationalsozialisten 1933 zwangsweise aufgelöst. Nach und nach übersiedelte sein gesamter Lehrkörper in die USA: Walter Gropius, Ludwig Mies van der Rohe, Josef Albers, Herbert Bayer und Lyonel Feininger. Letzterer war als Enkel eines Achtundvierzigers in New York geboren worden, hatte aber ein halbes Jahrhundert in Deutschland verbracht, wo er dem Bauhaus bereits bei der Gründung 1919 beigetreten war. Gropius, der Initiator des Bauhauses, wurde in Amerika Direktor der Schule für Architektur an der Harvard Universität; Mies van der Rohe übernahm die Leitung der Architekturschule des Illinois Institute of Technology. Albers, der jahrelang am Black Mountain College in Nord-Carolina und später an der Yale-Universität lehrte, wurde durch seine Arbeit mit Farbmodulationen zu einem der bekanntesten Maler Amerikas. Herbert Bayers Plakate waren von nachhaltigem Einfluß auf die amerikanische Werbegrafik. Die Arbeit dieser wenigen Männer durchdrang und revolutionierte Architektur und Produktdesign auf dem gesamten amerikanischen Kontinent.

"The Cathedral of Socialism": Lyonel Feininger's woodcut on the title page of the "Bauhaus Manifesto", published in 1919, illustrates the tradition and utopian aims of the Bauhaus.

»Die Kathedrale des Sozialismus«: Lyonel Feiningers Titelholzschnitt für das »Bauhaus-Manifest« von 1919 symbolisiert Tradition und Utopie des Bauhauses.

The Masters of the Bauhaus, who, in the tradition of the medieval lodges of the builders of Gothic cathedrals, strove to unite artists and craftsmen: (from left) Josef Albers, Scheper, Muche, Moholy-Nagy (founder of the "New Bauhaus" in Chicago, 1937), Bayer, Schmidt, Gropius, Breuer; the painters Kandinsky, Klee and Feininger; Gunda Stölzl and Oscar Schlemmer.

Die Meister des Bauhauses, das in der Tradition der mittelalterlichen Dombauhütten die Trennung zwischen Kunst und Handwerk aufheben wollte: (von links) Josef Albers, Scheper, Muche, Moholy-Nagy (1937 Gründer des »New Bauhaus« in Chicago), Bayer, Schmidt, Gropius, Breuer; die Maler Kandinsky, Klee und Feininger; Gunda Stölzl und Oscar Schlemmer.

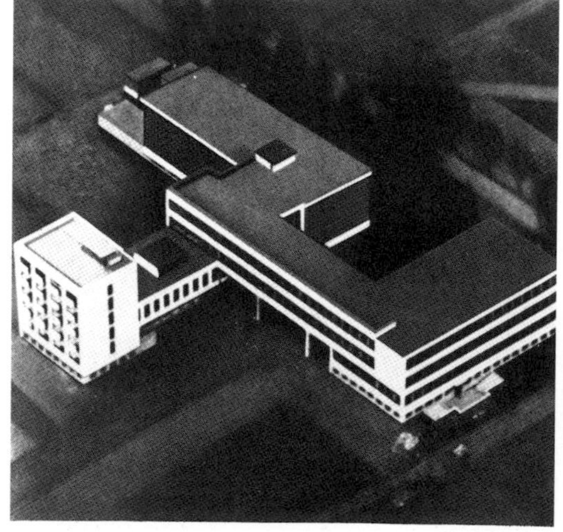

Aerial photo of the Bauhaus building in Dessau, designed by Walter Gropius (1883–1969). The Academy of Design, founded in Weimar in 1919, moved to Dessau in 1925.

Luftaufnahme des von Walter Gropius (1883–1969) entworfenen Bauhausgebäudes in Dessau, wohin die 1919 in Weimar gegründete Hochschule für Gestaltung 1925 übersiedelte.

"Form follows function". This classical maxim of modern architecture was equally true of early immigrant agricultural utility buildings: "barn raising" among the Amish in Pennsylvania, a community undertaking.

Daß die Form der Funktion zu folgen habe – eine klassische Maxime der modernen Architektur – galt für die landwirtschaftlichen Zweckbauten der frühen Einwanderer von jeher: »barn raising«, ein gemeinschaftlicher Scheunenneubau durch Nachbarschaftshilfe, bei den Amischen in Pennsylvanien.

The PanAm Building in New York, designed in 1952 by Walter Gropius.

Das Pan-Am-Gebäude in New York, 1952 erbaut von Walter Gropius

Josef Albers (1888–1976), once head of the Bauhaus's stained-glass workshop, painted compositions of squares which inspired and paved the way for the op-art movement of the 60s.

Josef Albers (1888–1976), im Bauhaus Leiter der Werkstatt für Glasmalerei, wurde mit seinen Quadratbildern Anreger und Vorläufer der Op-art der 60er Jahre.

Ludwig Mies van der Rohe's preceptive high-rise apartment houses on Lake Shore Drive (1951). Chicago was also the original site of modern skeleton construction, introduced toward the end of the 19th century by Louis H. Sullivan and the immigrant Dankmar Adler (1844–1900).

Die Wohnhochhäuser am Lake Shore Drive (1951), Ludwig Mies van der Rohes stilbildender Bau in Chicago, wo die moderne Stahlskelettbauweise gegen Ende des 19. Jahrhunderts von Louis H. Sullivan und dem Einwanderer Dankmar Adler (1844–1900) eingeführt wurde.

"Protected Blue", from the "Hommage to the Square" series, 1957. In his influential book, "Interaction of Color" (1967), Albers formulated a theory with respect to his geometric compositions based on the interaction of paints applied in pure form.

»Geschütztes Blau« aus der Serie »Huldigung an das Quadrat«, 1957. Eine Theorie seiner auf der Wechselwirkung von rein aufgetragenen Farben beruhenden geometrischen Kompositionen hat Albers in dem einflußreichen Buch »Interaction of Color« (1967) niedergelegt.

German immigration by Decade:
Deutsche Einwanderung nach Jahrzehnten:

Decade Jahrzehnt	Total Immigration	German Immigration	German as Percentage of Total Immigration
1820–29	128,502	5,753	4.5
1830–39	538,381	124,726	23.2
1840–49	1,427,337	385,434	27.0
1850–59	2,814,554	976,072	34.7
1860–69	2,081,261	723,734	34.8
1870–79	2,742,137	751,769	27.4
1880–89	5,248,568	1,445,181	27.5
1890–99	3,694,294	579,072	15.7
1900–09	8,202,388	328,722	4.0
1910–19	6,347,380	174,227	2.7
1920–29	4,295,510	386,634	9.0
1930–39	699,375	119,107	17.0
1940–49	856,608	117,506	14.0
1950–59	2,499,268	576,905	23.1
1960–69	3,213,749	209,616	6.5
1970	373,326	10,632	2.8
Total/Summe	45,162,638	6,917,090	15.3
	Gesamt- einwanderung	deutsche Einwanderung	Prozentanteil der Deutschen an der Gesamteinwanderung

U.S. Bureau of the Census

Geographical Distribution of German-born Americans:
Geographische Verteilung der deutschbürtigen US-Bevölkerung:

Region	Percentage of German-born 1850	1880	1920	1960	Gebiet
New England States	1.2	1.8	3.0	3.9	Neuenglandstaaten
Middle Atlantic States	36.0	30.0	30.1	38.5	Mittlere Ostküstenstaaten
East North-Central States	39.1	39.8	35.1	25.3	Nordöstliche Zentralstaaten
West North-Central States	9.0	16.6	17.4	7.1	Nordwestliche Zentralstaaten
South Atlantic States	6.6	3.6	2.4	5.8	Südliche Ostküstenstaaten
East South-Central States	3.0	2.0	1.0	0.9	Südöstliche Zentralstaaten
West South-Central States	4.6	2.9	2.8	2.2	Südwestliche Zentralstaaten
Mountain States	–	0.8	2.0	2.9	Rocky-Mountain-Staaten
Pacific States	0.6	2.5	6.1	13.2	Westküstenstaaten
	Prozentsatz der Deutschbürtigen				

U.S. Bureau of the Census

Having turned his back on the homeland: portrait of the emigrant Detmar Basse (1761–1836), who founded the settlements of Bassenheim and Zelianopel in Pennsylvania. Much more about him – for instance, what he looked like from the front – is not known....

Er kehrte seiner Heimat den Rücken: Porträt des Emigranten Detmar Basse (1761–1836), der in Pennsylvanien die Siedlungen Bassenheim und Zelianopel gründete. Mehr – etwa, wie er von vorne aussah – wissen wir über ihn nicht...

Numbers of German-born in Selected Cities, 1850 – 1950:
Deutschbürtiger Einwohneranteil ausgewählter Städte, 1850 – 1950:

City/Stadt	1850	1860	1870	1880	1890	1900	1910	1920	1930	1940	1950
New York	56,141	119,984	151,203	163,482	210,723	324,224	278,137	194,155	237,588	224,749	185,467
Chicago	5,035	22,230	52,316	75,205	161,039	203,733	182,289	112,288	111,366	83,424	56,635
Philadelphia	23,020	43,643	50,746	55,769	74,974	73,047	61,480	39,766	37,923	27,286	19,736
Milwaukee	7,271	15,981	22,509	31,483	54,776	68,969	64,816	39,771	40,787	28,085	18,259
Los Angeles	–	–	–	–	2,707	4,032	9,684	10,563	18,094	17,528	17,302
Detroit	2,838	7,220	12,647	17,292	35,481	42,730	44,675	30,238	32,716	23,785	17,046
San Francisco	–	6,346	13,602	19,928	26,422	35,303	24,137	18,514	18,608	14,977	12,394
Cleveland	–	9,078	15,855	23,170	39,893	44,225	41,408	26,476	22,532	15,427	9,629
Saint Louis	22,571	50,510	50,040	54,901	66,000	59,973	47,766	30,089	22,315	14,120	8,112
Buffalo, N.Y.	–	18,233	22,249	25,543	42,660	49,812	43,815	20,898	18,816	12,483	7,775
Baltimore	19,274	32,613	35,276	34,051	40,709	33,941	26,024	17,461	13,568	9,744	6,943
Cincinnati	33,374	43,931	49,446	46,157	49,415	38,308	28,426	17,833	13,944	8,856	6,013
Pittsburgh	–	6,049	8,703	15,957	25,363	36,838	29,438	16,028	14,409	9,805	5,898
Rochester, N.Y.	–	6,451	7,730	11,004	17,330	15,685	14,624	10,735	10,287	7,302	5,012
Newark, N.J.	3,822	10,595	15,873	17,628	26,520	25,251	22,177	14,041	12,508	7,813	4,977
Jersey City, N.J.	–	1,605	7,151	10,151	16,086	17,838	16,131	11,113	9,631	6,206	3,681
Boston	1,777	3,202	5,606	7,396	10,362	10,739	8,701	5,915	5,381	3,851	3,289
Columbus, Ohio	–	–	3,982	4,416	6,882	6,296	5,722	4,098	3,582	2,422	–
Louisville, Ky.	7,357	13,374	14,380	13,463	14,094	12,383	8,471	4,748	3,219	1,953	–
Albany, N.Y.	2,875	3,877	5,168	6,648	7,605	5,963	4,620	3,068	2,513	1,687	–
New Orleans	11,425	19,752	15,224	13,944	11,338	8,743	6,122	3,418	2,159	1,403	–

U.S. Bureau of the Census

Monument commemorating Oscar Straus, of German descent, Theodore Roosevelt's secretary of commerce and labor, and later associated with Woodrow Wilson at the time of the founding of the League of Nations. The allegorical figures, placed in front of the Department of Commerce in Washington in 1947, represent Freedom of Belief and the Voice of Reason.

Denkmal für Oscar Straus, den deutschstämmigen Arbeits- und Handelsminister im Kabinett von Theodore Roosevelt und späteren Mitarbeiter Woodrow Wilsons zur Gründungszeit des Völkerbundes. Die allegorischen Figuren, 1947 vor dem Handelsministerium in Washington aufgestellt, symbolisieren die Freiheit des Glaubens und die Stimme der Vernunft.

Since the arrival of the *Concord,* Germans in America have at no time lived in a vacuum. As a group, where they were numerous enough to organize their own institutions, or as individuals scattered among fellow-Americans of other origins, they shared, willingly or not, in the unfolding events of their chosen homeland. In turn, they exerted directly and often indirectly an influence on their neighbors. It was in this setting of give-and-take that Germans found themselves confronted with the same political and social problems as the population at large. Their response could never be unanimous, given the great diversity in their own ranks. What almost all had in common was the appreciation of the freedom America had offered to them. This common premise was shared by the conservative, the pious sectarian and the free-thinking revolutionary labor agitator.

Despite their considerable numbers, or maybe just because of them, most German-Americans throughout their history did not indulge in ethnic politics. There were a few exceptions, usually doomed from the beginning. From 1750 onwards German names appeared on the rosters of local officialdom, some in provincial assemblies, and after the Revolution, in state and federal legislatures. They became governors and members of cabinets. In the armed forces, they rose to generalship. Not one among the prominent men of German birth and descent considered himself as a representative of his ethnic group although his fellow Germans had frequently decided the vote in his favor. This was as true of Frederick Augustus Muhlenberg, Speaker of the First Congress of the United States, Carl Schurz, senator from Missouri and secretary of the interior, or Robert Ferdinand Wagner, senator from New York, as it was true of the numerous Germans in state and local governments.

Seit der Ankunft der *Concord* haben die Deutschen in Amerika zu keinem Zeitpunkt in einem gesellschaftlichen Vakuum gelebt. Als Gruppe, wo sie zahlreich genug waren, ihre eigenen Institutionen zu gründen, oder als einzelne, wenn sie verstreut unter Amerikanern anderer Herkunft lebten, haben sie stets, ob willentlich oder nicht, an der historischen Entwicklung ihrer gewählten Heimat teilgenommen. Es war in diesem Klima des Gebens und Nehmens, daß sich die Deutschen mit den gleichen politischen und sozialen Problemen konfrontiert sahen wie die übrige Bevölkerung. Ihre Reaktionen konnten so wenig einheitlich sein, wie es ihre gesellschaftliche Zusammensetzung war. Ihnen allen gemeinsam war jedoch die Wertschätzung der Freiheit, die Amerika ihnen bot. In diese gemeinsame Grundvoraussetzung teilten sich fromme Sektierer, politisch Konservative und freidenkende, revolutionäre Arbeiterführer gleichermaßen.

Trotz ihrer Zahlenstärke – oder vielleicht gerade deswegen – hat die große Mehrheit der Deutschamerikaner in keiner Phase ihrer Geschichte ein politisches Selbstbewußtsein als ethnische Gruppe entwickelt. Die wenigen Versuche, die in dieser Richtung unternommen wurden, waren meist von Anbeginn zum Scheitern verurteilt. Seit 1750 erschienen deutsche Namen auf den Listen lokaler Amtsträger, in Provinzversammlungen und nach der Revolution in Staats- und Bundesregierungen. Deutschamerikaner wurden Gouverneure und Kabinettsminister. Bei den Streitkräften stiegen sie in Generalsränge auf. Doch keiner dieser Prominenten von deutscher Geburt oder Herkunft betrachtete sich als Repräsentant seiner ethnischen Gruppe – auch wenn er etwa deutschamerikanischen Stimmen seine Wahl verdankte. Dies galt für Frederick Augustus Muhlenberg, den Sprecher des ersten Kongresses der Vereinigten Staaten wie für Carl Schurz, den Senator für Missouri und Innenminister, oder für Robert Ferdinand Wagner, den Senator für den Staat New York, und es galt nicht minder für die vielen Deutschen in bundesstaatlichen und lokalen Regierungsämtern.

The government of the short-lived Confederate States of America also had a secretary of German descent: Christoph Gustav Memminger, born in Wurttemberg in 1803, was treasurer of South Carolina and subsequent to secession in 1861 secretary of the treasury under Jefferson Davis.

Auch die Regierung der kurzlebigen Konföderierten Staaten von Amerika wies einen deutschstämmigen Minister auf: Christoph Gustav Memminger, 1803 in Württemberg geboren, zunächst Schatzmeister des Bundesstaates Süd-Carolina und nach der Sezession von 1861 Finanzminister unter Jefferson Davis.

In all wars German-Americans stood ready to defend the freedom of their country alongside all other Americans. Once, in the Civil War, roused by the men who had seen the defeat of liberty in Germany, they did far more than their share. Almost 200,000 German-born men served in the Union Army to end slavery and preserve the unity of their United States. Twice, they responded to the call to arms against the country of their forefathers or even their birth – some with a heavy heart, but respond they did.
Such sweeping statements are justified because the number of traitors and villains among German-Americans has been minute throughout this long history. Into what could have become a world of crass materialism – and it was the material side that attracted so many immigrants besides the prospect of freedom – many German immigrants brought with them across the Atlantic a faith and an idealism which has never been extinguished. Today, when tourists are shown the restored sites of what seemed once to contemporaries like unworldly utopias, at Ephrata, Bethlehem, Winston-Salem, Economy or New Harmony, they are awed by the idealism and faith that emanated from these communities. It was idealism in response to materialism that demanded the sacrifices of German workmen on the Haymarket in Chicago. The idealism of so many German-American movements has in no small way helped to maintain the precarious balance, without which unbridled materialism could easily have triumphed in the utter freedom of the continent. At first sight it seems like the bitter irony of history that twice men of German descent led the American armies to victory over the land of their ancestors. Neither Friedrich Pfoerschin nor Nikolaus Eisenhauer would have dreamed that their descendants, General John J. Pershing in 1918 and General Dwight D. Eisenhower in 1945, would step again on German soil as conquerors. But then the Washingtons who left England for Virginia did not imagine that a full-blooded Englishman like George Washington would accept the British surrender at Yorktown. Despite the vagaries of history, it has remained true for Americans what Thomas Jefferson wrote from the Rhineland two hundred years ago: "The neighborhood of this place is that which has been to us a second mother country."

In allen Kriegen haben Deutschamerikaner, Seite an Seite mit ihren Landsleuten anderer Herkunft, für die Verteidigung der Freiheit ihres Landes gekämpft. Einmal, im Bürgerkrieg, aufgerufen von den Männern, die die Unterdrückung der Freiheit in Deutschland miterlebt hatten, leisteten sie weit mehr, als ihr Teil gewesen wäre. Fast 200000 in Deutschland geborene Männer kämpften in der Unionsarmee für die Abschaffung der Sklaverei und die Bewahrung der Einheit ihrer Vereinigten Staaten. Zweimal folgten sie dem Ruf zu den Waffen, die Amerika gegen das Land ihrer Vorfahren oder selbst ihrer Geburt erhob – manche mit schwerem Herzen, doch sie folgten dem Ruf.
Was hier verallgemeinernd klingen mag, ist doch gerechtfertigt, da die Anzahl der Verräter und Schurken unter den Deutschamerikanern im Verlauf ihrer langen Geschichte von jeher klein war. In eine Neue Welt, die eine Welt des krassesten Materialismus hätte werden können – denn es war die materielle Seite, die neben Freiheitshoffnungen so viele Einwanderer anzog –, brachten zahlreiche deutsche Immigranten eine Gläubigkeit und einen Idealismus, die bis heute nicht erloschen sind. Wenn die Touristen unserer Tage in Ephrata und Bethlehem in Winston-Salem, Economy oder New Harmony die restaurierten Stätten besichtigen, die früheren Zeitgenossen als überirdische Utopias erschienen waren, so spüren sie etwas von der idealen Gesinnung und der Glaubenszuversicht, die von diesen Siedlungen ausstrahlte. Es war Idealismus, als Antwort auf den Materialismus, der den deutschen Arbeitern auf dem Haymarket in Chicago ihre Opfer abforderte. Der Idealismus so vieler deutschamerikanischer Bewegungen hat keinen geringen Beitrag dazu geleistet, jenes prekäre Gleichgewicht aufrechtzuerhalten, ohne welches der ungezügelte Materialismus im freien Klima dieses Kontinents sehr leicht die Oberhand gewonnen hätte.
Auf den ersten Blick kommt es einem wie eine bittere Ironie der Geschichte vor, daß es zweimal Männer deutscher Abstammung waren, die amerikanische Truppen gegen das Land ihrer Vorväter führten. Weder Friedrich Pfoerschin noch Nikolaus Eisenhauer hätten es sich träumen lassen, daß ihre Nachkommen, John J. Pershing im Jahre 1918 und General Dwight D. Eisenhower 1945, den Boden Deutschlands an der Spitze siegreicher Truppen wiederbetreten würden. Aber auch die Washingtons, die England mit dem Ziel Virginia verließen, hätten sich kaum vorstellen können, daß ein so reinblütiger Engländer wie George Washington die Kapitulation der Briten bei Yorktown entgegennehmen würde. Trotz solcher Launen der Geschichte ist für die Amerikaner wahr geblieben, was Thomas Jefferson vor zweihundert Jahren aus dem Rheinland nach Hause schrieb: „Die Nachbarschaft dieses Ortes nämlich ist uns ein zweites Mutterland gewesen".

John J. Pershing (1860–1948), descendant of Friedrich Pfoerschin who emigrated from Alsace in 1749. Commander-in-Chief of the American expeditionary forces in Europe in 1917/18, Pershing was the only other American besides George Washington to be awarded the rank of "General of the Armies"; the photo shows him on his arrival in France, June 13, 1917.

John J. Pershing (1860–1948), Nachfahre des 1749 ausgewanderten Elsässers Friedrich Pfoerschin, Oberbefehlshaber der amerikanischen Expeditionsstreitkräfte in Europa 1917/18 und neben George Washington der einzige Amerikaner, dem der Rang eines »General of the Armies« verliehen wurde; das Foto zeigt ihn bei seiner Ankunft in Frankreich am 13. Juni 1917.

Ephrata Cloister buildings in the 1934 painting by the American artist and photographer Charles Sheeler (1883–1965).

Klostergebäude in Ephrata, 1934 gemalt von dem amerikanischen Maler und Fotografen Charles Sheeler (1883–1965)

Dwight D. Eisenhower (1890–1969), Supreme Commander of the Allied Forces in Europe in 1944/45 and 34th president of the United States (from 1953–1961). A descendant of one Hans Nikolaus Eisenhauer from the Odenwald on his father's side, Eisenhower's mother stemmed from a Mennonite family which emigrated in order to avoid military service in Europe.

Dwight D. Eisenhower (1890–1969), oberster Befehlshaber der alliierten Streitkräfte in Europa 1944/45 und 34. Präsident der USA von 1953 bis 61, stammte väterlicherseits von Hans Nikolaus Eisenhauer aus dem Odenwald und mütterlicherseits von einer Mennonitenfamilie ab, die ausgewandert war, um in Europa keinen Kriegsdienst leisten zu müssen....

Biographical Sketches
Portraits of 47 German-Americans

Biographische Skizzen
47 deutschamerikanische Lebensläufe

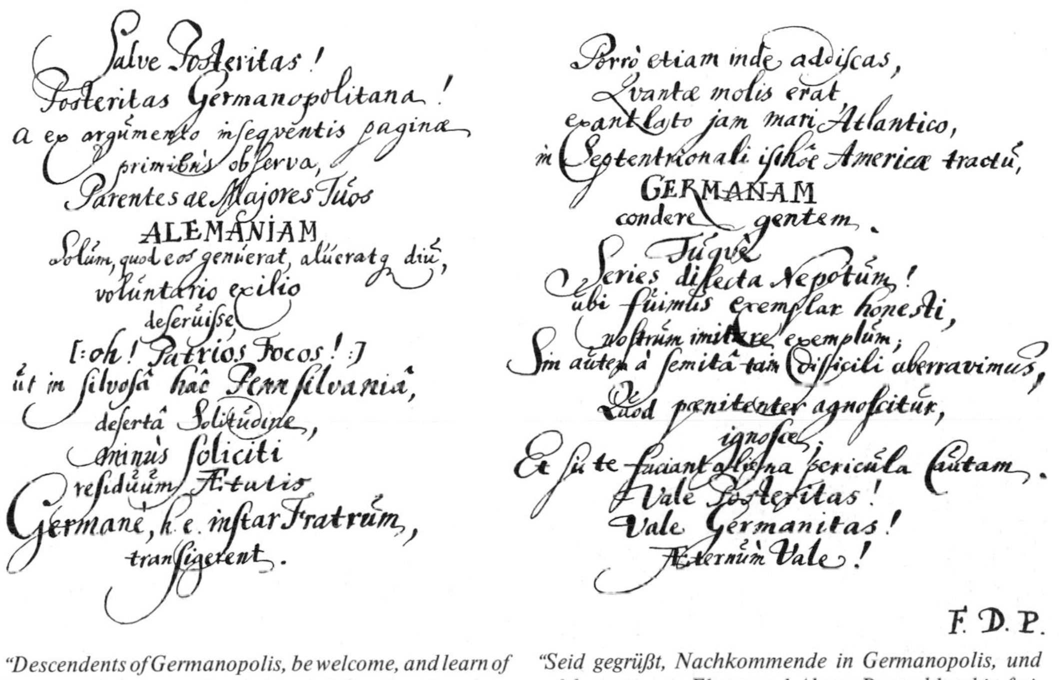

Salve Posteritas!
Posteritas Germanopolitana!
ex argumento insequentis paginae
primitus observa,
Parentes ac Majores Tuos
ALEMANIAM
Solum, quod eos genuerat, aluerat q diu,
voluntario exilio
deseruisse
[: oh! Patrios Focos! :]
ut in silvosa hac Pennsilvania,
deserta Solitudine,
minus soliciti
residuum Aetatis
Germane, h.e. instar Fratrum,
transigerent.

Porro etiam inde addiscas,
Quantae molis erat
exantlato jam mari Atlantico,
in Septentrionali isthoc Americae tractu,
GERMANAM
condere gentem.
Tuque
Series dilecta Nepotum!
ubi fuimus exemplar honesti,
nostrum imitare exemplum;
Sin autem a semita tam difficili aberravimus,
Quod poenitenter agnoscitur,
ignosce,
Et sic te faciant aliena pericula cautam.
Vale Posteritas!
Vale Germanitas!
Aeternum Vale!

F. D. P.

"Descendents of Germanopolis, be welcome, and learn of how your fathers and forefathers left Germany in voluntary exile..." – Francis Daniel Pastorius' greeting to posterity, the Latin dedication set down at the beginning of his Germantown "Land Register" – "Where we have been a model of righteousness, follow our example; where we have strayed from the difficult path, forgive us..."

"Seid gegrüßt, Nachkommende in Germanopolis, und erfahrt, wie eure Eltern und Ahnen Deutschland in freiwilliger Verbannung verlassen...« – Franz Daniel Pastorius' Gruß an die Nachwelt, als lateinisches Widmungsgedicht dem »Grund- und Lager-Buch« seines Germantown vorangestellt: »Wo wir ein Muster des Rechten waren, ahmt unser Beispiel nach, wo wir vom schwierigen Pfad abgewichen, vergebt uns...«

The Founder of Germantown

Francis Daniel Pastorius

Der Gründer Germantowns

In retrospect, Francis (Franz) Daniel Pastorius (1651–1719) seems to be a prophetic figure, a man with a clear vision of the kind of country which the United States later became. In his advocacy of separation of church and state, of religious and ethnic multiplicity, of the abolishment of slavery, he seems to have been ahead of his times. Yet his ideas of a just society were actually based on age-old utopian concepts; his thought and actions were in line with his outstanding humanistic education and a product of his times, the Age of Reason, and not the later era of the Enlightenment. The American and French Revolutions were developments Pastorius surely never dreamed of.

When he undertook the voyage to the "uncouth land and howling wilderness" which Pennsylvania was in those days, he brought five servants with him, and didn't forget to take his wig, with a good supply of powder for it. His first reaction to the city of Philadelphia, consisting then of nothing but a few blockhouses, was typical for a European gentleman: "...the rest was woods and underbrush, in which I got lost several times; I needn't describe the impression this made upon me, who had recently seen London, Paris Amsterdam and Ghent." When he organized a governing body for the new settlement of Germantown, there was no thought of having the officials elected by the townspeople. He was indeed a man of his times.

But he was an extraordinary man. He was born in Sommerhausen in Franconia and grew up in the imperial city of Windsheim, where his father became burgomaster. He studied law, theology and philosophy at the universities of Altdorf, Strasbourg, Basel and Jena, became doctor of laws at the age of twenty-five, and began the practice of law back home at Windsheim, but moved to Frankfurt three years later. In 1680 he became the tutor and travelling companion of a young nobleman; the next two and a half years took him through Germany, the Netherlands, England, France and Switzerland.

In der Rückschau mutet Francis (Franz) Daniel Pastorius, der von 1651 bis 1719 lebte, wie eine prophetische Persönlichkeit an, die eine klare Vorstellung von den Grundzügen jenes Staates hatte, der einmal in Gestalt der USA entstehen sollte. In seinem Eintreten für die Trennung von Kirche und Staat, für religiöse wie ethnische Toleranz und die Abschaffung der Sklaverei war er seiner Zeit weit voraus. Seine Vorstellung von einer gerechten Gesellschaft gründete jedoch auf altüberkommenen utopischen Konzepten. Sein Denken und Handeln entsprach seiner außergewöhnlichen humanistischen Bildung und war ganz dem Geist des Zeitalters der Vernunft verhaftet, nicht dem der späteren Epoche der Aufklärung. Die Amerikanische und die Französische Revolution waren historische Entwicklungen, von denen Pastorius mit Sicherheit niemals träumte.

Als er die Seereise ins »fremde Land, die wüste Wildnis«, was treffend den damaligen Zustand Pennsylvaniens umschreibt, antrat, nahm er fünf Diener mit und vergaß auch seine Perücke nicht nebst ausreichendem Pudervorrat für das gute Stück. Seine erste Reaktion beim Anblick der Stadt Philadelphia, die damals nur aus einigen Blockhäusern bestand, war typisch für den kultivierten Europäer: »das Übrige war Wald und Gestrüpp, worin ich mich mehrere Male verlor. Was für einen Eindruck solch eine Stadt auf mich machte, der ich eben London, Paris, Amsterdam und Gent besucht hatte, brauche ich nicht zu beschreiben«. Als er für die neu gegründete Siedlung Germantown eine kommunale Verwaltung organisierte, verschwendete er keinen Gedanken daran, deren Amtsträger durch die Einwohnerschaft wählen zu lassen. Bei aller Vortrefflichkeit war er durchaus ein Mann seiner Zeit.

Er wurde im fränkischen Sommerhausen geboren und wuchs in der Reichsstadt Windsheim auf, wo sein Vater Bürgermeister wurde. An den Universitäten von Altdorf, Straßburg, Basel und Jena studierte er die Rechte, Theologie und Philosophie, war bereits im Alter von 25 Jahren Doktor der Jurisprudenz und nahm seine Tätigkeit als Anwalt zu Hause in Windsheim auf, zog aber drei Jahre später nach Frankfurt um. 1680 wurde er Privatlehrer und Reisebegleiter eines jungen Adligen. Die nächsten zweieinhalb Jahre führten ihn quer durch Deutschland, die Niederlande, England, Frankreich und die Schweiz.

Sommerhausen, on the lower Main across from Winterhausen (near Würzburg), Pastorius' place of birth, has kept its historical townscape intact. Shown here, one of the original town gates, where the "Sommerhausener Torturmtheater", the smallest theater in Germany, is found today.

Pastorius' Geburtsort Sommerhausen, am unteren Main gegenüber von Winterhausen und nahe Würzburg gelegen, hat sein historisches Stadtbild unverändert bewahrt. Abgebildet: eines der Stadttore, in dem sich heute das »Sommerhausener Torturmtheater«, die kleinste Bühne Deutschlands, befindet.

The University of Altdorf, near Nuremburg, where the famous Thirty-Years'-War-General Wallenstein had already studied when Pastorius enrolled on July 31, 1668. It was also here that the latter submitted his "Inaugural-Disputation" in 1676. (Engraving from 1723)

Die Universität Altdorf bei Nürnberg, an der schon Wallenstein studiert hatte, als sich Pastorius am 31. Juli 1668 immatrikulierte. 1676 reichte er hier auch seine »Inaugural-Disputation« ein. (Stich aus dem Jahr 1723)

Jena in Thüringen, where, in addition to Strasbourg and Basel, Pastorius studied. Shown here in a contemporary engraving.

Jena in Thüringen, neben Straßburg und Basel ein weiterer Studienort von Pastorius, auf einem zeitgenössischen Stich

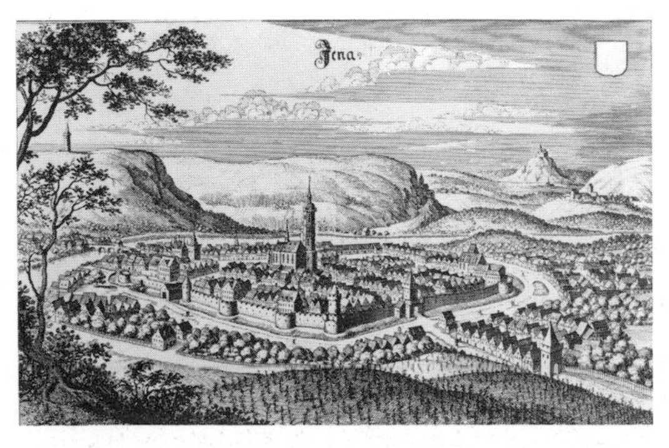

Idealized bust of Francis Daniel Pastorius by J. Otto Schweizer. Contemporary portrayals of the founder of Germantown were not handed down.

Idealisierende Büste des Franz Daniel Pastorius von J. Otto Schweizer; authentische Porträts des Gründers von Germantown sind nicht überliefert.

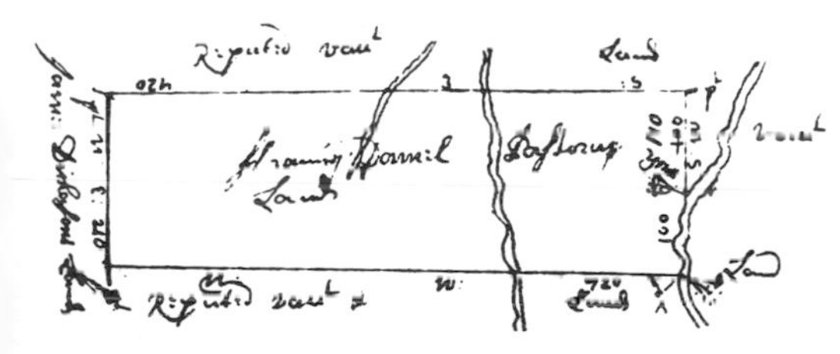

Lay-out plan of Pastorius' property, 1714.

Lageplan des Pastoriusschen Grundstücks aus dem Jahr 1714

Upon his return to Frankfurt, he was asked to become agent for a Pietist group's land purchase and settlement in the New World as a part of the Quaker William Penn's "holy experiment" to provide a haven for persecuted sectarians. During his travels, Pastorius had seen and developed a spiritual aversion to European social vanities, qualid poverty, inhumane civil law, and the fact that every populace was obliged to adhere to the religion of its local ruler. It is understandable that – although he was raised as a Lutheran – his sympathies were with the Pietists, the Mennonites and the Quakers, sects which commonly endorsed a quiet, kindly, pacifist Christian life, tolerant of the religious practices of others. The members of these sects were subject to persecution and abuse in Europe; most of their founders and leaders had been executed. Pastorius sailed to Pennsylvania on their behalf, arriving on board the *America* on 20 August 1683.

The original land purchasers, the Frankfurt Pietists, had changed their mind about emigrating, but other settlers were on their way, with whom Pastorius was to found Germantown, or "Germanopolis", as he also called it: thirteen Mennonite and Quaker families from Krefeld in the Rhineland, which Pastorius had visited to promote the great adventure before departing from Europe.

In the weeks while awaiting their arrival, Pastorius purchased a little house in Philadelphia to live in while his men were building him a new dwelling on a nearby lot that Penn had assigned to him. He had the area for the future Germantown – two hours north of Philadelphia – surveyed and subdivided into fourteen plots, for which the Krefeld men later drew lots for their home sites. Pastorius often dined with Penn and took rides through the virgin woods with him; conversing mainly in French, they had long discussions on matters of religion, philosophy and society. At Penn's home, Pastorius first met several Indian chieftains.

The Krefeld settlers arrived on the *Concord* (aptly termed the "German Mayflower") on 6 October 1683. The task immediately facing them was to construct adequate dwellings in which to survive the first winter. Clearing the forest proved extremely laborious, as they were mostly weavers by trade, making Pastorius wish they had brought along a few sturdy Tyrolean lumberjacks. But the autumn was mild and long and work was completed before an equally long and severe winter set in. Not until they were firmly established and prospering two years later did Pastorius build his own permanent home and join them in Germantown, at a time when they were reinforced by new arrivals from Kriegsheim. The original settlers had quickly begun to raise flax, and textiles became one of their main industries. The emblem which Pastorius designed for the town was a three-leaf clover representing "the vine, flax and weaving".

One of the earlier views of Germantown.

Eine der frühesten Ansichten von Germantown

Als er nach Frankfurt zurückkehrte, bat ihn eine Gruppe von Pietisten, Vermittler zu sein für den Landerwerb und die Gründung einer Siedlung in der Neuen Welt, die Teil von William Penns »Heiligem Experiment«, einer Zufluchtsstätte für verfolgte Quäker und andere Glaubensgenossen, sein sollte. Auf seinen Reisen hatte Pastorius den europäischen Standesdünkel, Elend und Armut, ein inhumanes Zivilrecht und die religiöse Unterdrückung derer, die den Glauben ihres Landesherrn annehmen mußten, kennen- und verabscheuen gelernt. So nimmt es nicht Wunder, daß – obwohl er lutherisch erzogen war – seine Sympathien den Pietisten, Mennoniten und Quäkern galten: Sekten, die alle eine friedfertige und menschenfreundliche christliche Lebensführung gemein hatten und die Religionsausübung anderer tolerierten. Mitglieder dieser Sekten wurden in Europa verfolgt und mißhandelt; die meisten ihrer Stifter und Führer waren auf dem Richtplatz gestorben. Um den Bedrängten zu helfen, reiste Pastorius nach Pennsylvanien, wo er am 20. August 1683 an Bord der *America* ankam.

Die ursprünglichen Landkäufer, die Frankfurter Pietisten, hatten sich inzwischen eines anderen besonnen und ihren Auswanderungsplan aufgegeben. Doch waren neue Siedler an ihre Stelle getreten, mit denen Pastorius Germantown oder »Germanopolis«, wie er es auch nannte, gründen wollte. Es waren dreizehn Mennoniten- und Quäkerfamilien aus Krefeld im Rheinland, das Pastorius besucht hatte, um das große Wagnis voranzutreiben, bevor er Europa verließ.

In den Wochen bis zu ihrer Ankunft kaufte Pastorius ein kleines Haus, während seine Bediensteten eine Unterkunft auf einem nahegelegenen Grundstück errichteten, das Penn ihm zugesprochen hatte. Das Gebiet für das künftige Germantown – es lag zwei Fußstunden nördlich von Philadelphia – ließ er vermessen und in vierzehn Parzellen einteilen, die die Krefelder später durch Losentscheid untereinander verteilten. Oft aß Pastorius mit Penn zu Mittag, und sie unternahmen gemeinsame Ausritte in die noch unberührten Wälder; in ihren hauptsächlich französisch geführten Gesprächen ging es um Religion, Philosophie und Fragen der Gesellschaft. Penns Wohnhaus war auch der Ort, wo Pastorius zum erstenmal Indianerhäuptlinge traf.

Die Krefelder Siedler trafen am 6. Oktober 1683 an Bord der zu Recht als »deutsche Mayflower« bezeichneten *Concord* ein. Ihre erste Aufgabe war es, sich Unterkünfte für den bevorstehenden ersten Winter zu schaffen. Da die meisten von ihnen Weber waren, taten sie sich bei den Rodungsarbeiten sehr schwer, so daß Pastorius wünschte, er hätte einige stämmige Tiroler Holzfäller mitgebracht. Doch der Herbst war mild und lang und die Arbeiten waren beendet, bevor der ebenso lange wie harte Winter einbrach. Erst als die Gründungsphase nach zwei Jahren überstanden war und sich das Leben in Germantown normalisierte, baute sich Pastorius dort ein eigenes Haus und schloß sich der Gemeinde an. Zur selben Zeit wurde die Einwohnerschaft bereits durch erste Neuankömmlinge aus Kriegsheim vergrößert. Die ersten Siedler hatten bald mit dem Anbau von Flachs begonnen, und die Leinweberei wurde ihr wichtigster Wirtschaftszweig. Das von Pastorius entworfene Ortssiegel war ein Kleeblatt, das *vinum, linum et textrinum* (»Wein, Lein und den Webeschrein«) symbolisierte.

1690 zählte Germantown bereits an die 175 Seelen, und der Niederlassung war urkundlich der Status einer unabhängigen Gemeinde zuerkannt. Man weiß zwar sicher, daß Pastorius selbst den Quäkern beitrat, doch ist bei seiner Erwähnung der 1686 gebauten Kirche

By 1690 the population was around 175 and the settlement had been chartered as an independent borough. It is established that Pastorius became a Quaker himself, but no denomination was mentioned when Pastorius wrote about the first Germantown chapel, built in 1686. Although Germantown was originally intended to be a permanent Germanic colony within an English colony, by 1727 people of Swedish, French and English stock were also living within its confines. Not foreseeing a revolution against English sovereignty and the formation of an independent nation, Germantown continued to cling to its basically German heritage well into the 18th century, for there was no reason to adopt English ways, despite occasional pressure from certain citizens of Philadelphia, including Benjamin Franklin. The devout townspeople were bound by a common effort to attain salvation by leading a proper Christian life, but they were neither tinged by the fanatic asceticism or doomsday mysticism of neighboring sects, nor by the puritanism of the New Englanders. They established schools, cultivated art and music, set up the first paper mill to operate in British America, printed books and a newspaper, and their textile and tanning industries prospered. They cultivated their own produce, trading surplus grain and cattle to the Barbados for rum, syrup, sugar and salt. They maintained friendly relations with the Indians, with whom they traded their own goods for furs, which they exported to England for manufactured products.

Germantowns von keiner Konfession die Rede. Obwohl Germantown ursprünglich als rein deutsche Siedlung innerhalb einer englischen Kolonie vorgesehen war, lebten dort im Jahr 1727 Schweden, Franzosen und Engländer. Nicht ahnend, daß eine Revolution gegen die englische Oberherrschaft und die Gründung einer unabhängigen Nation bevorstanden, hielten die Bürger von Germantown bis tief ins 18. Jahrhundert an ihrem deutschen Erbe fest und sahen, trotz gelegentlichen Drucks von Seiten der Bürger Philadelphias und nicht zuletzt Benjamin Franklins, keine zwingende Veranlassung, englische Lebensart anzunehmen. Ihr gemeinsames Bemühen, ihr Heil in einer christlichen Lebensführung zu finden, verband die Einwohner, doch frönten sie dabei weder einer asketischen Enthaltsamkeit noch der Endzeit-Mystik benachbarter Sekten oder dem Puritanismus der Neuengländer. Sie richteten Schulen ein, brachten Kunst und Musik zur Entfaltung, bauten die erste Papiermühle der Kolonien, druckten Bücher und bald eine Zeitung, und ihre Webereien und Gerbereien florierten. Sie entwickelten eine eigenständige Landwirtschaft und handelten ihre Überschüsse an Getreide und Vieh in Barbados gegen Rum, Sirup, Salz und Zucker ein. Mit den Indianern kamen sie gut aus und tauschten bei ihnen eigene Waren gegen Pelze, für die sie aus England Manufakturwaren bezogen.

Pastorius war der erste Bürgermeister von Germantown; außerdem wirkte er als Schulmeister, Schriftstel-

A

New Primmer

OR

Methodical Directions

To attain the

True Spelling, Reading & Writing of

ENGLISH.

Whereunto are added, some things Necessary & Useful both for the Youth of this Province, and likewise for those, who from forreign Countries and Nations come to settle amongst us.

By F. D. P.

All Blessings Come Down Even From God; His Infinite Kindness Love & Mercy, Now, of Old & Perpetually, Quickeneth Refresheth and Strengtheneth True Upright Willing Xtians & Young Zealots.

Examples prevail above Precepts.

Printed by William Bradford in New-York, and Sold by the Author in Pennsilvania.

"A New Primer" by "F.D.P.": the first grammar to appear in Pennsylvania

»Eine Neue Fibel, oder Methodische Anweisungen zum Erlernen des rechten Buchstabierens, Lesens und Schreibens des Englischen. Nebst beigefügtem Nötigem und Nützlichem für die Jugend dieser Provinz wie auch für jene, die aus fremden Ländern und Völkern kommen, um unter uns zu siedeln«: das früheste Lehrbuch Pennsylvaniens, verfaßt von »F.D.P.«

Pastorius' reports from Pennsylvania, printed and widely distributed in Germany, played a decisive role in influencing religiously motivated emigration to America. Reproduced here are title pages from his two earliest publications, "Reliable Information from America concerning the Country of Pennsylvania by a German who has Traveled There" (as early as 1684), and "Brief Geographical Description of the Lately Discovered American Country of Pennsylvania" (1692). These were followed by his "Detailed Description of the Lately Discovered Province of Pennsylvania" in 1700.

(1)

Sichere Nachricht auß America, wegen der Landschafft Pennsylvania / von einem dorthin gereißten Teutschen/

de dato Philadelphia, den 7. Martii 1684.

Einer schuldigen Obliegenheit so wol als auch meinem Abschiedlichen Versprechen ein Genügen zu leisten/sol ich etwas umbständlicher advisiren, wie und was ich hiesiger Landen gefunden und angemercket habe/ und weilen mir nicht unwissend / daß durch ungleiche Relation ihrer viel hinter das Licht geführet würden / versichere ich zum voraus/ daß ich mit ohnpartheyischer Feder ohne verfälschlichen Zusatz / beedes die Ungemächlichkeiten der Reiß und den Mangel hiesiger Provintz / als den von andern fast gar zu sehr gelobten Uberfluß desselben getreulich anführen wolle: Dann ich verlange an meinem wenigen Orte mehr nicht / als zu wandeln in den Fußstapffen deß jenigen / welcher ist der Weg / und zu folgen seinen heilsamen Lehren / weil Er die Warheit ist / auff daß ich unauffhörlich mit Ihm dem ewigen Leben vereinigt bleibe.

I. Ich will also den Anfang machen von der Seefart/ welche sicherlich so wol wegen der zu befürchten habender Schiffbrüche/ gefährlich/ als auch wegen der schlechten und harten Schiffskost/ sehr beschwerlich ist/ daß ich auß eigener Erfahrung nun ziemlich verstehe/ was David im 107. Psalm sagt / daß man auff dem Meer nicht nur die Wunderwerck deß HErrn / sondern auch den Geist deß Ungewitters verspühren und warnehmen könne. Dann meine Anheroreiß belangend/ bin ich mit 4. Knechten / 2. Mägden/ 2. Kindern und 1. Jungen/ den 10. Jun. von Deal abgesegelt/ hatten den gantzen Weg über meistens widrigen/ und nicht 12. Stund aneinander favorablen Wind/ viel Sturm- und Donnerwetter/ auch zerbrach der vorderste Mast zu zweyen malen/ so daß wir erst binnen 10. Wochen allhier arrivirt; jedoch sat cito, si sat bene. Massen es selten geschiehet/ daß einige viel zeitlicher anhero kommen. Die Crefelder/ welche den 6. Octobr. allhier angelangt/ waren ebenfals 10. Wochen auff der See/ und das Schiff das mit dem unsern von Deal außgefahren/ war 14. Tag länger unterwegs / auch starben einige Menschen darauff. Gedachte Crefelder haben auch zwischen Roterdam und Engelland eine erwachsene Tochter verloren/ welcher Verlust jedoch zwischen Engelland und Pennsilvanien mit der Geburt zweyer Kinder ersetzt worden. Auff unserm Schiff hingegen ist niemand Todes verfahren / auch niemand gebohren/ꝛc. Fast alle Passagiers waren etliche Tag lang Seekranck/ ich aber nicht über 4. Stund / herentgegen war ich andern Accidentien unterworffen/ da mir nemlich die zwey außgehauene Löben über unserer Schiffglock schier den Rucken eingeschlagen / und ich den 9. Jul. bey nächtlichen Sturm so ungestümm auff die lincke Seiten gefallen / daß ich einige Tag über deß Betts hüten muste. Diese beede Fäll erinnerten mich nachdrücklich deß ersten auff alle ihre posterität durchdringenden Falls unserer Urältern / welchen sie im Paradeiß / auch vieler der jenigen / die ich in diesem Jammerthal meines exilii begangen. Per varios casus, &c. allein gepreisst sey die Vatterhand göttlicher Barmhertzigkeit / welche uns so dickmals wieder auffrichtet/ und zurück hält/ damit wir nicht gäntzlich verfallen / in den Abgrund deß Argen. Görg Wertmüller fiel gleichmäßig über auß hart/ Thomas Gasper/ schlug am Leib sehr auß / die Englische Magd hatte das Rothlauff/ und Isaac Dilbreck/ der sonst dem äusserlichen Ansehen nach der stärckste/ lag am längsten darnieder. Hatte ich also einen kleinen Schiff-Hospital / wiewol ich allein von den Teutschen meine Lägerstätt unter den Englischen genommen/ꝛc. Daß ein Bootsgesell unsinnig/ und unser Schiff durch widerholtes auffschlagen eines Wallfisches zum Zittern bewegt worden/ hab ich in meinem

)o(letztern

FRANCISCI DANIELIS PASTORII

Sommerhusano-Franci.

Kurtze Geographische Beschreibung der letztmahls erfundenen Americanischen Landschafft

PENSYLVANIA,

Mit angehenckten einigen notablen Begebenheiten und Bericht-Schreiben an dessen Hrn. Vattern/ Patrioten und gute Freunde.

Vorrede.

ES ist denen Meinigen insgesamt zur Gnüge bekandt/ auf was Weise ich/ von meinen Kindesbeinen an/ auf dem Wege dieser Zeitlichkeit meinen Lebens-Lauff/ gegen die frohe Ewigkeit zu/ eingerichtet/ und in allem meinem Thun dahin getrachtet habe/ wie ich den allein guten Willen GOttes erkennen / seine hohe Allmacht fürchten / und seine unergründliche Güte lieben lernen möchte. Und obwohlen ich / nebst andern gemeinen Wissenschafften der freyen Künste/ das Studium Juris feliciter absolviret / die Italiänisch- und Frantzösische Sprachen ex fundamento begriffen / auch den so genannten grossen Tour durch die Landschafften gethan / so habe ich jedoch an allen Orten und Enden meinen grössesten Fleiß und Bemühung an anders nichts gewendet/ als eigentlich zu erfahren/ wo

A   doch

Pastorius' Berichte aus Pennsylvanien, die in Deutschland gedruckt wurden und weite Verbreitung fanden, waren von entscheidendem Einfluß auf die religiös motivierte frühe Amerikaauswanderung. Reproduziert sind die Titelseiten der beiden frühesten Publikationen, »Sichere Nachricht auß America« (bereits 1684) und »Kurtze Geographische Beschreibung« (1692), denen 1700 noch eine »Umständige Geographische Beschreibung Der zu allerletzt erfundenen Provintz Pensylvaniae« folgte.

Pastorius was the first mayor of Germantown; he also served as schoolmaster, scribe and judge. There was no major crime in the community, but an ordinance had to be passed to forbid the further sale of wine to the Indians. Pastorius was one of the most learned men in the colonies; he read and wrote seven languages, and found the time to write books on various subjects including poetry in Latin, German and English. At the age of 37 he married a woman who had emigrated from Mühlheim on the Ruhr, and their two sons were born in Germantown. When he died, sometime between late December 1719 and early January 1720, it was still a long time before the township he had founded became a battle site of the Revolutionary War, and longer still until it became the integral part of Philadelphia which it is today; yet he had every reason to believe that he had helped create something which would endure.

ler und Richter. Die Gemeinschaft hatte zwar keine groben Vergehen zu beklagen, doch mußte eine Verordnung erlassen werden, die den Weinverkauf an Indianer untersagte. Pastorius war einer der gelehrtesten Männer in den Kolonien; er konnte in sieben Sprachen lesen und schreiben und fand noch Zeit, mehrere Bücher zu verfassen und auf lateinisch, deutsch und englisch zu dichten. Im Alter von 37 Jahren heiratete er eine aus Mühlheim an der Ruhr emigrierte Frau, die in Germantown zwei Söhnen das Leben schenkte. Als er starb, irgendwann zwischen Ende Dezember 1719 und Anfang 1720, sollte es noch lange dauern, bis die von ihm gegründete Gemeinde zum Schauplatz einer Schlacht im Revolutionskrieg wurde und noch länger, bis sie der Vorort Philadelphias wurde, der sie noch heute ist. Dennoch durfte Pastorius gewiß sein, etwas mitgestaltet zu haben, das die Zeiten überdauern würde.

"Here is liberty of Conscience, wch is right & reasonable; here ought to be lickewise liberty of ye body, except of evildoers, wch is an other case. But to bring men hither, or to robb and sell them against their will, we stand against. In Europe there are many oppressed for Conscience sacke; and here there are those oppressed w[ch] are of a black Colour...": Facsimile (page 2) of the first documented protest against slavery in America, written and for the most part probably formulated by Francis Daniel Pastorius in April, 1688. After having been submitted to the Quaker monthly assembly, it was referred to the quarterly, and then to the annual assembly, where it was tentatively filed as being not ready for judgement. Pennsylvania did not enact a law against the importation of slaves until 1711, a law which was in turn nullified by the London government...

»Hier herrscht Freiheit des Gewissens, was recht und vernünftig ist; in gleicher Weise sollte hier Freiheit des Körpers herrschen, außer für Übeltäter, was ein anderer Fall ist. Aber dagegen, daß man Menschen gegen ihren Willen hierher bringt, sie raubt oder verkauft, erheben wir Einsprache. In Europa müssen viele Unterdrückung leiden, des Gewissens halber; und hier werden jene unterdrückt, die von schwarzer Farbe sind...«: Faksimile (Blatt 2) des ersten dokumentierten Protests gegen die Sklaverei in Amerika, niedergeschrieben und wahrscheinlich in wesentlichen Teilen formuliert von Franz Daniel Pastorius im April 1688. Die monatliche Quäkerversammlung, an die der Antrag gerichtet war, verwies ihn an die vierteljährliche und diese an die Jahresversammlung weiter, wo er als vorläufig nicht entscheidungsreif zu den Akten gelegt wurde. Erst 1711 erließ Pennsylvanien ein Gesetz gegen die Einfuhr von Sklaven, das jedoch von der Londoner Regierung annulliert wurde...

Though not exactly known, one can approximate the date of Pastorius' death as having occured sometime between December 26, 1719 – the date on his will – and the reading of the latter on January 13, 1720. Reproduced here, the inventory of his effects which was recorded on January 21: in addition to two cows and two horses, he left books in English, French, Greek, Latin, "High Dutch" and "Low Dutch", as well as fourteen dictionaries.

Pastorius' nicht überliefertes Todesdatum wird von seinem Testament vom 26. Dezember 1719 und von der Testamentseröffnung am 13. Januar 1720 eingegrenzt. Am 21. Januar wurde das hier abgebildete Inventar seines Nachlasses erstellt. Aufgeführt sind, neben zwei Kühen und zwei Pferden, Bücher in englischer, französischer, griechischer, lateinischer, »hochdeutscher« und »niederdeutscher« Sprache, sowie 14 Wörterbücher.

"A Book, which Treasures up all Learning in a Sum": index to Pastorius' "Alphabetical Beehive", where he amassed – in seven languages – everything he wanted to pass on to his sons with respect to factual knowledge and worldly wisdom. This monumental manuscript could actually be considered a precursor of the large encyclopedias which appeared during the enlightenment in Europe.

»Ein Buch, das allen Wissensschatz zusammenfaßt«: Indexseite aus Pastorius' »Alphabetischem Bienenstock«, in dem er in sieben Sprachen alles zusammentrug, was er seinen Söhnen an Faktenwissen und Lebensweisheit weitergeben wollte. Tatsächlich könnte man dieses monumentale Manuskript als Vorform der großen Enzyklopädien der europäischen Aufklärung bezeichnen.

Mennonite and Papermaker

William Rittenhouse

Mennonit und Papiermacher

William Rittenhouse, born near Mühlheim on the Ruhr in 1644 as either Wilhelm Rettinghaus or Ruttinghausen, was one of the outstanding personalities among the early citizens of Germantown. His motives for emigrating were surely not dissimilar to those of his contemporaries. The county of Broich where he lived as a practicing Mennonite and learned the craft of paper making was governed by an autocratic princeling who was known for the saying: "The dogs and soldiers should be set loose upon the sectarians". In the 70s, together with two brothers, Rittenhouse traveled to Arnhem in Holland, putting the intolerance out of reach. In 1688 he emigrated via New York to Pennsylvania to become a member of the Germantown community where his beliefs were shared.

Contemporary reports ascribe proficiency, business sense and strong religious commitment to the early German settlers. All of these attributes held for Rittenhouse, but not that with which Pastorius reprimanded his fellow citizens - a lack of public spirit. Rittenhouse donated the land for the first Mennonite church in the colonies and, as the first elected minister, served his community until his death in 1708. The extent of his service is reflected in the fact that he was offered the episcopate in 1703, an honor which he however did not accept.

In an evironment where affluence was honored as the just reward for hard work, Rittenhouse's reputation grew in proportion to his success as a paper maker. By 1690 he had set up the first paper mill in America, and this remained without competition for two decades, servicing areas as far away as New York. Managing to buy out his three partners within fifteen years, Rittenhouse made the mill into a family concern.

Rittenhouse the pioneer gained a considerable reputation, but lasting fame was reserved for his great-grandson: David Rittenhouse, who in later life became the first director of the young United States' mint, made a name for himself in the colonies as an astronomer, inventor, mathematician, and builder of an "orrery", an early planetarium. Even Thomas Jefferson considered him one of the greats of his time: "He has not indeed made a world, but he has intimately approached nearer its maker than any man who has lived."

William Rittenhouse, als Wilhelm Rettinghaus oder Ruttinghausen 1644 bei Mühlheim an der Ruhr geboren, war eine der herausragenden Persönlichkeiten unter den frühen Bürgern Germantowns. Die Motive seiner Auswanderung unterschieden sich freilich nicht von denen der Zeitgenossen: In der Grafschaft Broich, in der er als praktizierender Mennonit und Papiermüller gelebt hatte, regierte ein selbstherrlicher Duodezfürst, von dem der Ausspruch überliefert ist, man solle »die Hunde auf die Sektierer hetzen und die Soldaten auf sie loslassen«. Zusammen mit zwei Brüdern entzog sich Rittenhouse solcher Unduldsamkeit, ging in den 70er Jahren nach Arnheim in Holland und wanderte 1688 über New York nach Pennsylvanien aus, um sich den Glaubensgenossen in Germantown anzuschließen.

Zeitgenössische Berichte bescheinigen den frühen deutschen Siedlern Tüchtigkeit, Geschäftssinn und ein starkes religiöses Engagement. Auf Rittenhouse trafen diese Attribute zu, nicht aber der Vorwurf, den Pastorius seinen Mitbürgern pauschal machte - den des mangelnden Gemeinsinns: Rittenhouse stiftete das Land für die erste Mennonitenkirche in den Kolonien und betreute seine Gemeinde als erster gewählter Geistlicher bis zu seinem Tod im Jahr 1707. Das Ausmaß seiner Verdienste wird daran deutlich, daß ihm 1703 das Bischofsamt angetragen wurde, eine Ehre, die er jedoch nicht für sich in Anspruch nahm.

In einer Umgebung, die den Wohlstand als verdienten Lohn für harte Arbeit honorierte, wuchs sein Ansehen mit seinem Erfolg als Papiermacher. Schon 1690 errichtete Rittenhouse die erste Papiermühle auf amerikanischem Boden, die für zwei Jahrzehnte ohne Konkurrenz blieb und bis nach New York lieferte. Seine drei Teilhaber konnte er innerhalb von 15 Jahren abfinden und die Mühle zum Familienbetrieb machen.

Hatte es der Pionier Rittenhouse zu Ansehen gebracht, so war es seinem Urenkel vorbehalten, Berühmtheit zu erlangen: David Rittenhouse, im Alter noch erster Direktor der Münze der jungen USA, machte sich in den Kolonien als Astronom, Erfinder, Mathematiker und Erbauer des »orrery« - eines frühen Planetariums - einen Namen. Selbst Thomas Jefferson galt er als einer der Großen seiner Zeit: »Er hat zwar keine Welt geschaffen - aber aus ihrer innersten Kenntnis ist er ihrem Schöpfer nähergekommen als je ein Mensch zuvor.«

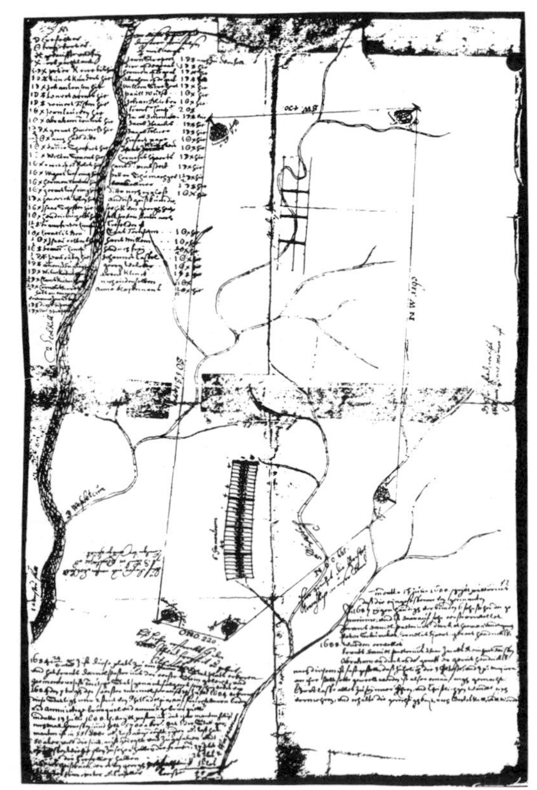

The "Germantonship in Pennsilvania, situated 6 English miles from Philadelphia" - so reads the caption on the earliest map of Germantown, drawn in 1688, the same year that William Rittenhouse immigrated.

"Situation der Germantonship in Pennsilvania, 6 Englische Meil von Philadelphia gelegen": die früheste Karte von Germantown, gezeichnet 1688, im Jahr der Einwanderung von William Rittenhouse.

William Rittenhouse's great-grandson David (1732-96), inventor, astronomer, and first director of the U.S. mint.

David Rittenhouse (1732-1796), Urenkel von William, Erfinder, Astronom und Direktor der staatlichen Münze der USA.

The Germantown house in which David Rittenhouse was born, built on the site where his great-grandfather William's papermill stood until 1707.

Das Geburtshaus von David Rittenhouse in Germantown. Bis 1707 stand hier die Papiermühle seines Urgroßvaters William.

From Baker's Apprentice to Prophet

Johann Conrad Beissel

Vom Bäckerlehrling zum Propheten

Contemporary silhouette, presumably a portrait of Conrad Beissel.
Zeitgenössischer Scherenschnitt, angeblich ein Porträt Conrad Beissels

Johann Conrad Beissel was born in Eberbach in the Palatinate of the Rhine in April of 1690, two months after the death of his father, a baker known throughout the town for his addiction to drink. Beissel's mother died when he was eight; shortly thereafter he became a baker's apprentice. The spiritual climate of Pietism with its visionary, subjective and personal practice of faith through individual devoutness must have left its mark on Beissel at an early age. In 1715 he was animated by a crucial experience of awakening, about which historical sources only cryptically inform us that it "involved renunciation of carnal love to womenfolk." Beissel sought contact with pietist circles, encountered the religious intolerance of secular authorities and, like many other sect members prevented from practicing their beliefs, emigrated in 1720 to Pennsylvania. Even there, where a sect culture unrivaled by its contemporaries in variety and color had developed in the first few decades of the Quaker colony, the new arrival was conspicuous for his rigorous asceticism and was quickly regarded as a commanding, charismatic personality. Although the trained baker had first sought a hermit's life, Beissel – despite a certain reluctance – felt himself chosen to found a new sect, the Seventh Day Baptists, so called because of its strict obervation of the sabbath and its belief in adult baptism. In 1732, his followers settled on Cocalico Creek. Within three years, the community had evolved into the Ephrata cloister, which would rapidly become a unique cultural center in Pennsylvania. While the community lived according to a rigorously ascetic regime entailing celibacy, restricted nourishment, and curtailment of sleep with nightly devotions, there was an eruptive burgeoning of creativity among the sisters and brethren, and particularly in Beissel himself. A cloister was built (today a museum) in an unprecedentedly austere architectural style inspired by mystical and theosophical notions. In 1748, eight years after setting up their own press, the cloister produced the most voluminous publication of American colonial times, the 1,514-page *Martyrs' Mirror.* The art of medieval miniaturist painting was resurrected and Beissel published diverse volumes with hundreds of hymns, whose dark symbolism, prophetic tenor and overblown sultry style could be considered – from a psychoanalytical viewpoint – the sublimated product of repressed desires. The most astonishing development at Ephrata, however, was in its music. Totally self-taught, Beissel invented his own vocal style and method of composition, with schematic part-harmonies freely following the rhythm of the hymn text – devices to which one could almost impute a naive anticipation of 20th-century techniques, while on the other hand, Beissel's hymns were purportedly the first musical works ever composed in America. Thomas Mann paid ironic but admiring tribute to Beissel's individualism in chapter 8 of his *Doctor Faustus.* The extent to which Ephrata's accomplishments were attributable to Beissel's inspiration was seen in the cloister's decline, which began under his successor, the likewise highly gifted Peter Miller, and ended with disbandment in 1814. Beissel died on 6 July 1768, "A former hermit who became a leader," as his tombstone says, "his spiritual age was 52, but his physical age was 77 years and 4 months."

Güldene
Aepffel
In
Silbern Schalen
Oder:
Schöne und nützliche
Worte und Warheiten
Zur Gottseligkeit.
Enthalten
In Sieben Haupt-Theilen/
die in diesem Buch zusamen gestellet sind;
Mit sonderbarem Fleiß von denen in der vorigen
Edition häufig eingeschlichenen
Druckfehlern gereiniget.
Nebst angehängten Vorreden/
und einem zweyfachen Register.

EFRATA, Im Jahr des Heils, 1745.
Verlegt durch etliche Mitglider der Mennonisten-gemeinde.

"Golden Apples in Silver Chalices": an early publication of the Ephrata Cloister press, established in 1745; following Benjamin Franklin's and Christopher Saur's, the third printing shop in Pennsylvania.

Ein früher Druck der 1745 eingerichteten Klosterpresse von Ephrata, die – nach Benjamin Franklin und Christopher Saur – die dritte Druckerei in Pennsylvanien war.

Sohn eines Bäckers und stadtbekannten Säufers, der zwei Monate vor der Geburt des Kindes starb, wurde Johann Conrad Beissel im April 1690 im kurpfälzischen Eberbach geboren. Mit acht Jahren war er Vollwaise, nur wenig später trat er in eine Bäckerlehre ein. Das geistige Klima des Pietismus mit seiner schwärmerisch-subjektiven, die individuelle Glaubenserfahrung suchenden Frömmigkeit muß ihn früh geprägt haben. 1715 widerfuhr ihm sein Erweckungserlebnis, von dem die Quellen nur kryptisch mitteilen, daß es »eine Abkehr von der natürlichen Liebe zum Weibe in sich schloß«. Beissel suchte Anschluß an pietistische Kreise, erlebte die religiöse Intoleranz der weltlichen Macht und entschloß sich, wie viele andere in ihrer Glaubensübung behinderte Sektierer, im Jahr 1720 zur Auswanderung nach Pennsylvanien. Selbst dort, wo sich in den wenigen Jahrzehnten seit der Gründung der Quäkerkolonie ein Sektenwesen entwickelt hatte, das an Buntheit und Vielfalt in der jüngeren Geschichte ohne Vergleich sein dürfte, stach der Neuankömmling durch seinen asketischen Rigorismus hervor und wurde bald als charismatische Führergestalt empfunden. Halb wider Willen, denn er hatte zunächst ein Leben als Einsiedler gesucht, sah sich der gelernte Bäcker zur Gründung einer neuen Sekte berufen: der nach Sabbatfeier und Erwachsenentaufe sogenannten »Siebentagbaptisten«. 1732 ließ er sich mit seinen Gefolgsleuten am Cocalico nieder; drei Jahre später hatte sich aus der Siedlungsgemeinschaft das Kloster Ephrata entwickelt, das bald zu einem einzigartigen kulturellen Zentrum in Pennsylvanien werden sollte. Unter asketischen Lebensbedingungen – sexuelle Enthaltsamkeit, reduzierte Ernährung, Schlafentzug durch nachtliche Andachten – begannen die Schwestern und Brüder, vor allem aber Beissel selbst, eine eruptive Kreativität zu entfalten. Es entstand eine vorbildlos-karge, von mystisch-theosophischen Vorstellungen inspirierte Klosterarchitektur (heute als Museum zugänglich). Eine Klosterpresse wurde gegründet, die mit dem 1500seitigen *Märtyrerspiegel* die umfangreichste Publikation der amerikanischen Kolonialzeit hervorbrachte. Die Buchmalerei blühte und Beissel selbst ließ mehrere Bände mit Hunderten von Hymnen erscheinen, die dunkle Symbolik und prophetischen Inhalt mit einem schwülstig-schwülen Stil verbinden, in dem eine psychoanalytische Betrachtungsweise die Wiederkehr des asketisch Verdrängten konstatieren würde. Die erstaunlichste Entwicklung nahm Ephrata jedoch in der Musik. Als völliger Autodidakt begann Beissel, einen neuen Gesangsstil und ein eigenes Kompositionsverfahren zu ersinnen, das die Harmonik schematisch behandelte, in seiner freien, dem zu komponierenden Text folgenden Rhytmik jedoch wie ein naiver Vorgriff auf das 20. Jahrhundert anmutet. Thomas Mann hat diesem Aspekt des Beisselschen Individualismus – wahrscheinlich den ersten in Amerika entstandenen Kompositionen überhaupt – im achten Kapitel seines *Doktor Faustus* ebenso ironisch wie bewundernd Tribut gezollt. Wie sehr die Blüte Ephratas von der Inspiration durch Beissel abhing, zeigt der Niedergang des Klosters, der bereits unter Beissels ebenfalls hochbegabtem Nachfolger Peter Miller einsetzte und 1814 zur Auflösung führte. Beissel selbst starb am 6. Juli 1768, »ein Einsamer nachmals aber geworden ein Anführer«, wie es auf seinem Grabstein heißt, »seines geistlichen Alters 52 Jahr, aber des natürlichen 77 Jahr 4 Monat«.

First to Print the Bible in the Colonies

Christopher Saur

Erster Bibeldrucker in den Kolonien

The driving force behind the influential German-language press in prerevolutionary America was the printer, publisher and journalist Christopher Saur (or Sower), who emigrated from Germany in 1724 as Johann Christoph Sauer, a 29-year-old tailor, and did not begin the amazing career which made him famous for another twelve years.

Saur was born on 2 February 1693 in the town of Ladenburg in the Palatinate, where his father was a deacon. Recent research has found his name on the 1713 roster of residents of the Wittgenstein village of Schwarzenau, where the 18-year-old is listed as "tailor". Only later did he spend a few years in the town of Laasphe (formerly thought to have been his birthplace), but then returned to Schwarzenau, where he bought a simple dwelling. He was a member of one of the stringently persecuted 18th-century Protestant sects, the "Inspirationalists", who believed that certain persons' lives were directly acted upon by the Holy Spirit, qualifying them to receive divine revelation and to pass it on to others. Persecution of the sect's adherents must have provided the impulse for Saur to emigrate to the more tolerant climate of Pennsylvania, where for a time he was associated with Conrad Beissel's Ephrata Community of Seventh-Day Baptists. Although Saur's sojourn at Ephrata was an unhappy one for him, he still maintained good relations with the community after he left it to open a printshop in nearby Germantown in 1738.

His initial publication, *An Earnest Exhortation to Young and Old,* was followed by a "High-German American Calendar" and almanac containing advice on health and care for the sick, along with historical, geographical and botanical information. The 1739 almanac was followed by a new edition annually until 1777. Saur's first large volume was a 792-page hymn book compiled by the Ephratra Brethren and bearing the exotic title, *The Zionite Hill of Incense or Mount of Myrrh.* On 20 August 1739, the first issue of Saur's *Hoch-Deutsch Pensylvanischer Geschicht-Schreiber* appeared. It was to become not only the first successful German newspaper in Pennsylvania, but the leader in its field for more than twenty years. In 1732, Benjamin Franklin had brought out a German-language edition of his *Pennsylvania Gazette,* but it did not survive more than two issues; the Germantown readers were aware of Franklin's contemptuous attitude toward Germans, and besides that, they were unaccustomed to reading Latin-style type. Saur's journal, printed with Gothic lettering, was such an immediate success that a new issue was able to appear monthly instead of quarterly, as originally planned. Starting in 1748 it came out every two weeks, and in 1751 enjoyed a circulation of four thousand, distributed throughout all of eastern Pennsylvania.

Saur's major claim to fame is the monumental task he planned and executed only four years after opening his shop: the publication of the first Bible in a European language to be printed in America. When his first edition (1743) of Luther's German translation of the Old and New Testaments was sold out two more followed in 1763 and 1776, printed by his son Christopher, Jr., who was born in Laasphe in 1721 before the family had left Germany. The elder Saur himself died in Germantown on 25 September 1758.

Treibende Kraft der einflußreichen deutschsprachigen Presse des vorrevolutionären Amerika war der Drukker, Verleger und Journalist Christopher Saur (auch Sower), der 1724 als Johann Christoph Sauer aus Deutschland emigrierte. Der 29-jährige Schneider sollte erst zwölf Jahre später seine erstaunliche Karriere beginnen.

Saur wurde am 2. Februar 1695 im pfälzischen Ladenburg geboren, wo sein Vater als Diakon wirkte. Jüngste Nachforschungen haben seinen Namen im Einwohnerverzeichnis von 1713 des Ortes Schwarzenau, Kreis Wittgenstein, entdeckt, in dem er als »Schneider« geführt ist. Erst später verbrachte er einige Jahre in Laasphe, das vordem als sein Geburtsort angenommen wurde, um wieder nach Schwarzenau zurückzukehren, wo er eine einfache Behausung erwarb. Er war Mitglied einer der vielen streng verfolgten, protestantischen Sekten des 18. Jahrhunderts, der »Inspirierten«, deren Glaube es war, daß Auserwählte mit dem Heiligen Geist in Verbindung stünden, was sie dazu qualifizierte, göttliche Eingebungen zu empfangen und diese an andere Personen weiterzugeben. Die Anfeindung solcher Sonderbündelei gab Saur sicherlich den Anstoß zur Auswanderung in das tolerantere Klima von Pennsylvanien, wo er sich eine Zeitlang Conrad Beissels Gemeinde der Siebentagbaptisten zu Ephrata anschloß. Trotz wenig erfreulicher Erfahrungen während seiner Ephrata-Episode bewahrte er zu dieser Gemeinschaft noch ein freundschaftliches Verhältnis, als er sie bereits verlassen hatte, um 1738 eine Druckerei im nahegelegenen Germantown zu eröffnen.

Seiner ersten Veröffentlichung, der *Ernstlichen Ermahnung an Junge und Alte,* folgte *der Hoch-Deutsch Americanische Calender,* ein Almanach, in dem sich Ratschläge für Gesundheit und Krankenpflege mit historischen, geographischen oder botanischen Informationen mischten. Dieser Almanach konnte von 1739 bis 1777 jedes Jahr neu aufgelegt werden. Saurs erster umfangreicher Druck war das 792seitige, von den Ephrata-Brüdern zusammengestellte Gesangbuch, mit dem charakteristischen Titel *Zionitischer Weyrauchs-Hügel oder Myrrhen-Berg.* Am 20. August 1739 erschien zum erstenmal der *Hoch-Deutsch Pensylvanische Geschicht-Schreiber,* der nicht nur die erste erfolgreiche deutsche Zeitung in Pennsylvanien werden, sondern zugleich für die nächsten zwanzig Jahre in seiner Art unübertroffen bleiben sollte. Bereits 1732 hatte Benjamin Franklin eine deutschsprachige Ausgabe seiner *Pennsylvania Gazette* herausgebracht, die aber ein zweimaliges Erscheinen nicht überdauerte; die Leserschaft von Germantown war sich Franklins Deutschfeindlichkeit nur allzu bewußt und überdies nicht gewohnt, Antiquaschriften zu lesen. Saurs Zeitung, in deutscher Fraktur Schrift gedruckt, traf derart ins Schwarze, daß er sie monatlich statt wie ursprünglich geplant vierteljährlich erscheinen lassen konnte. Ab 1748 konnte sie sogar vierzehntägig erscheinen und erreichte 1751 eine Auflage von 4000 Exemplaren, die im gesamten östlichen Pennsylvanien Verbreitung fanden.

Saurs Nachruhm gründet vor allem auf einem monumentalen Werk, das er schon vier Jahre nach der Eröffnung seiner Druckerei plante und durchführte: der Publikation der ersten in einer europäischen Sprache auf amerikanischem Boden gedruckten Bibel. Der Erstauflage dieser Lutherbibel von 1743 folgten zwei weitere in den Jahren 1763 und 1776, die Saurs Sohn Christopher jr. druckte, der 1721 in Laasphe geboren worden war, kurz bevor die Familie Deutschland verließ. Saur sr. starb in Germantown am 25. September 1758.

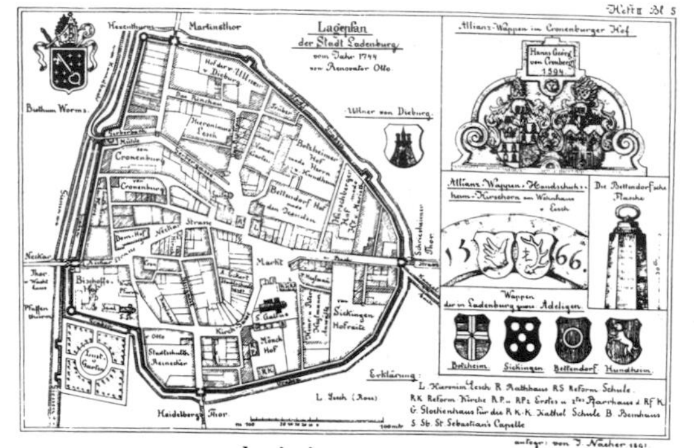

Historical map (1744) of Ladenburg, near Mannheim on the Neckar, where Christopher Saur was born.

Historischer Plan (1744) von Christopher Saurs Geburtsstadt Ladenburg, in der Nähe von Mannheim am Neckar gelegen

A map of Philadelphia and environs printed in Germany in the middle of the 18th century. At top in the middle is Germantown, the long, drawn-out ribbon village.

Philadelphia und Umgebung auf einer Mitte des 18. Jahrhunderts in Deutschland gedruckten Karte. Ganz oben in Kartenmitte ist das langgezogene Straßendorf Germantown zu erkennen.

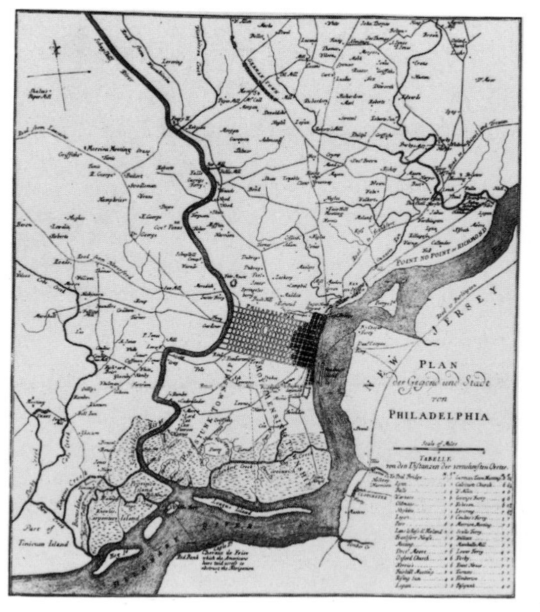

Contemporary woodcut of an early 18th-century printing press. Saur, who – as one source has it – "learned thirty crafts without an instructor", built his press and all his printing tools by himself.

Zeitgenössischer Holzschnitt einer Druckerpresse des frühen 18. Jahrhunderts. Saur, von dem eine Quelle berichtet, daß er »30 Handwerke ohne Lehrmeister erlernet« habe, baute sich seine Presse und alle sonstigen Druckwerkzeuge selbst.

BIBLIA,
Das ist:
Die
Heilige Schrift
Altes und Neues
Testaments,
Nach der Deutschen Uebersetzung
D. Martin Luthers,
Mit jedes Capitels kurtzen Summarien, auch
beygefügten vielen und richtigen Parallelen;
Nebst einem Anhang
Des dritten und vierten Buchs Esrä und des
dritten Buchs der Maccabäer.
Germantown:
Gedruckt bey Christoph Saur, 1743.

Title page of the first edition of the famous "Germantown Bible". Coming after the "Mamusse wunneetupnanatamwe up-biblum", an Indian bible printed in Cambridge, Massachusetts, in 1680 by missionaries, the Germantown Bible was the first bible to be printed in America in a European language.

Titelseite der Erstausgabe der berühmten »Germantown-Bibel«: nach der 1680 in Cambridge, Massachusetts, gedruckten »Mamusse wunneetupnanatamwe up-biblum«, einer Indianerbibel für Missionszwecke, war sie die erste in Amerika in einer europäischen Sprache erschienene Bibel.

Saur's "Pennsylvania Reporter, or: A Collection of Important Information from the Natural and Ecclesiastical Domains", printed in fractur type, which was formerly customary in Germany. As this type was not available in the colonies, Saur had to import it from the Egenolff-Luther type foundry in Frankfurt on the Main.

Saurs »Pensylvanischer Geschicht-Schreiber«, gedruckt in der damals im deutschen Sprachraum üblichen Frakturschrift. Da solche Typen in den Kolonien nicht verfügbar waren, mußte Saur sie aus der Egenolff-Lutherschen Schriftgießerei in Frankfurt am Main beziehen.

Der
Hoch-Deutsch
Pensylvanische
Geschicht-Schreiber,
Oder:
Sammlung
Wichtiger Nachrichten, aus dem Natur- und Kirchen-Reich.
Erstes Stück August 20/ 1739.

Geneigter Leser

UNter andern Abgöttern, denen die grobe und subtille Welt der sogenanten Christen dienet, ist nicht der Geringste der Vorwitz. Curiosität und Begierde gerne offt was neues zu Schauen, zu Hören und zu Wissen, auch zu Sagen. Diesem Athenienfischen Geist nun ein Opffer zu bringen mit Ausgebung dieser Sammlung/ ist man gantz nicht willens, nochweniger, sich selbst damit auszubreiten, oder Ruhm und Nutzen zu suchen, sondern weil man ehmahlen versprochen, die nützlichste und wichtigste Geschichte u. Begebenheiten bekant zumachen, und auch, weil denckwürdige Geschichte, wann sie den Menschen zu Ohren und Gesichte kommen, offters tieffern Eindruck und Nachdencken erregen, als Dinge die da täglich vorkommen; so wolle man dann hiermit einen Anfang machen, mit solchen Zeichen dieser Zeit so in diesem und andern Weltheilen kürtzlich und zuverläsig geschehen, in Hoffnung es werde nicht ohne einigen Nutzen, wenigst der Aufweckung und des Auffschauens bey einigen, die es lesen schaffen. Auch möchten wohl künfftig einige Anmerckungen und der Zeit dienliche Fragen ernstlichen Gemüthern zum Nachsinnen, oder auch wohl einige aufrichtige Antwort darauf zu geben, in dergleichen Sammlung herausgegeben werden. Der Leser lebe wohl/ und brauch es wie er soll.

Vor wenig Jahren hörte man, daß der Persianer und der Türcke grossen Krieg hatten; kaum hatte der Persianer mit dem Türcken Friede, so hatte er mit dem groß Mogel wie gegenwärtig Krieg; und der Römische Kayser hatte kaum Stillstand mit dem König von Franckreich, so ging er samt Moscau gegen die Türcken. Anfangs victorisirten die Moscowiter an den Türcken; bald wendete sich das Blatt um, und siegten die Türcken, jedoch stehen sie noch beyderseits miteinander zu Felde. Also auch der Kayser mit dem Türcken

wal

Christopher Saur's home and printshop in Germantown. It is assumed that somewhere on the grounds of the property, today the corner of Queen Lane and Germantown Road, Saur's as yet undiscovered grave is to be found.

Christopher Saurs Wohnhaus und Druckerei in Germantown. Auf dem zugehörigen Grundstück – heute die Ecke Germantown Road/Queen Lane – wird auch Saurs bis jetzt unentdecktes Grab vermutet.

The first of Benjamin Franklin's short-lived German edition of his "Pennsylvania Gazette", printed in Roman type.

Die erste Nummer von Benjamin Franklins kurzlebiger deutscher Ausgabe seiner »Pennsylvania Gazette«, gedruckt in moderner Antiqua-Schrift.

Der
Hoch-Deutsch
Americanische
Calender
Auf das Jahr
Nach der Gnaden-reichen Geburt unsers HERRN und
Heylandes Jesu Christi
1739.
(Welches ein gemein Jahr von 365 Tagen ist.)
In sich haltende: Die Wochen Tage; Den Tag des Monaths; Tage welche bemerckt werden; Des Monds Auf- und Untergang; Des Monds Zeichen und Grad; Voll und neu Licht; erst und letzt Viertel; Aspecten der Planeten samt der Witterung; Der 7 Sternen Aufgang, Sud-Platz und Untergang; Der Sonnen Auf- und Untergang; Nebst einer dazu gehörigen Vorede, Erklärung der Zeichen, Aderlaß-Täfflein, Anzeigung der Finsternüsse, Courten, Fären, Haupt-Straffen &c. &c. &c.
Eingerichtet vor die Sonnen Höhe von Pennsylvanien; jedoch an denen angrentzenden Landen ohne mercklichen Unterschied zugebrauchen.
Zum ersten mahl herauß gegeben
Germanton
Gedruckt und zu finden bey Christoph Saur; wie auch zu haben bey Johann Wister in Philadelphia.

One of Saur's earliest publications, the "High-German American Calendar" for 1739, which contained, among other things, "aspects of the planets as well as the weather; the ascent, southern meridian and descent of the seven stars; bloodletting table; eclipse dates, courts, ferries, main roads &c. &c. &c."

Einer der frühesten Saur-Drucke: der »Hoch-Deutsch Americanische Calender« auf das Jahr 1739, »in sich haltend«, unter anderem, »Aspecten der Planeten samt der Witterung; Der 7 Sternen Aufgang, Sud-Platz und Untergang; Aderlaß-Täfflein, Anzeigung der Finsternusse, Courten, Fären, Haupt-Strassen &c. &c. &c.«

(No. I.) … auf der

Philadelphische Zeitung.

SAMBSTAG, den 6 Mey. 1732,

An alle teutsche Einwohner der Provintz Pennsylvanien.

NACHDEM ich von verschiedenen teutschen Einwohnern dieses Landes bin ersuchet worden, eine teutsche Zeitung ausgehen zu lassen, und ihnen darinnen das vornehmste und merckwürdigste neues, so hier und in Europa vorfallen möchte, zu communiciren; doch aber hierzu viele mühe, grosse correspondentz und auch Unkosten erfordert werden: Als habe mich entschlossen, denen teutschen zu lieb, gegenwärtiges Specimen davon heraus zu geben, und ihnen dabey die Conditiones welche nothwendig zu der continuation derselben erfordert werden, bekent zu machen.

Erstlich, müsten zum wenigsten, um die unkosten die darauf lauffen, gut zu machen, 300 stücks können gedruckt und debitiret werden, und müste in jeder Township dazu ein mann ausgemachet werden, welcher mir wissen liesse, wie viel Zeitungen jedes mahl an ihn müsten gesandt werden, und der sie dan weiters einen jeglichen zustellen und die bezahlung davor einfordern müste.

Vor jede Zeitung muss jährlich 10 Shillinge erleget, und davon alle quartal 2 sh. 6 d. bezahlet werden.

Dagegen verspreche ich auf meiner seite, durch gute Correspondentz die ich in Holland und England habe allezeit das merkwürdigste und neueste so in Europa und auch hier passiret, alle woche einmahl, nemlich Sonnabends in gegenwärtiger form einer Zeitung, nebst denen schiffen so hier abgehen und ankommen, und auch das steigen oder fallen des Preisses der Güter, und was sonst zu wissen dienlich, bekandt zu machen.

Advertissemente oder Bekant machungen, welche man an mich schicken möchte, sollen das erste mahl vor 3 shill. 3 mahl aber vor 5 shil. hinein gesetzet werden.

Und weil ich nützlich erachte die gantze beschreibung der aufrichtung dieser provintz, mit allen derselben privilegien, rechten und gesetzen, bey ermangelung genugsamer Neuigkeiten, darinnen bekandt zu machen; solte nicht undienlich seyn, dass ein jeder, zumahl wer kinder hat, diese Zeitungen wohl bewahre, und am ende des jahres an einander heffte; zumahl da solche dann gleichsam als eine Chronica dienen können, die vorigen Geschichte daraus zu ersehen, und die folgende desto besser zu verstehen.

Auch wird anbey zu bedencken gegeben, ob es nicht rahtsam wäre, in jeder grossen Township einen reitenden Boten zu bestellen, welcher alle woche einmahl nach der stadt reiten und was ein jeder da zu bestellen hat, mit nehmen könne.

So bald nun die obgemeldte anzahl der Unterschreiber vorhanden, welche so bald als möglich ersuche in Philadelphia

The "Patron Saint" of Freedom of the Press

John Peter Zenger

Der »Schutzheilige« der Pressefreiheit

Among the three thousand Palatine emigrants who, in the course of the mass exodus of 1709, had been conveyed to New York with the support of England's Queen Anne, was a 13-year-old boy, in whose name an initial and precedent-setting victory for freedom of the press was to be achieved: Johann (henceforth, John) Peter Zenger.

The passengers had been brutally crowded together on board ship, and almost a fourth of them – including John's father – had not survived the crossing. So as not to become a burden upon the authorities, John was apprenticed – probably against the wishes of his mother – to the printer William Bradford, in whose shop he learned the trade, fulfilling his eight-year contract. Little is known about his journeyman years, except that they led him to Maryland and finally back to New York, where in 1725 he entered into a partnership with his former instructor, who in the meantime had founded the *New York Weekly Gazette*. Soon Zenger went into business for himself, largely publishing moral treatises, pamphlets and books until in the year 1733 opponents of the hated governor Cosby urged him to start an oppositional newspaper to counterbalance Bradford's *Gazette*, which was loyal to the colonial government. The new paper, which was really the first politically independent newspaper in America, was named the *New-York Weekly Journal*.

Ever since the takeover by the British, the colony of New York had had to suffer under a succession of corrupt governors and now William Cosby seemed to want to outdo all of his predecessors. Immediately after his arrival, he had laid claim to half of the salaries and other earnings of the provisional governor Rip van Dam and through manipulation of the courts and the dismissal of a judge from office, he prevented van Dam from legally offering any resistance. This was only the beginning of a whole series of infringements and breaches of the law.

The first issue of Zenger's *Journal* appeared on November 5, 1733, and in the months that followed, numerous articles were written denouncing the shady goings-on within the colonial government. Soon satirical verses, apparently also from Zenger's printshop, began circulating throughout the city and Cosby felt threatened.

In November 1734, just two weeks after the mayor and the town council had refused to participate in the burning of several issues of the *Journal*, Zenger was arrested on charges of having published various inflammatory pieces of slander. The disproportionately large sum of bail and the exclusion of two defense attorneys from the proceedings and from the bar made it obvious what kind of a trial it would be. While Zenger, with the help of his wife, continued to run the *Journal* from his jail cell, the general public in the colonies began to get interested in the case. And when finally even the famous Andrew Hamilton of Philadelphia expressed his willingness to take on Zenger's defense, the situation no longer appeared hopeless.

With an eloquent plea for the defense, which above all concentrated on the distinction between uncovering abuses and actual libel, the aged Hamilton convinced the jury, and in August 1735 he obtained a verdict of not guilty for his client. In addition, Hamilton's exposition managed to cripple the defamation clause, which had for so long blocked the path to freedom of the press.

In recognition of his services, John Peter Zenger was named official printer of the city of New York in 1737. He died on July 28, 1746, and five years later, the *Journal*, which his wife and his son had kept operating, was discontinued.

Unbeachtet unter den dreitausend Pfälzern, die im Zuge der Massenauswanderung von 1709 mit Unterstützung von Queen Anne nach New York transportiert worden waren, ging dort im Jahre 1710 ein Dreizehnjähriger an Land, in dessen Namen der erste und maßstabsetzende Sieg der Pressefreiheit in Nordamerika errungen werden sollte: Johann (von nun an: John) Peter Zenger. Sein Vater hatte, wie fast ein Viertel der grausam zusammengepferchten Passagiere, die Seereise nicht überlebt. Um den Behörden nicht als Halbwaise zur Last zu fallen, wurde John, wahrscheinlich gegen den Willen der Mutter, dem Drucker William Bradford zur Lehre übergeben, die er vertragsgemäß nach acht Jahren abschloß. Seine Wanderjahre, kaum dokumentiert, führten ihn nach Maryland und schließlich wieder nach New York zurück, wo er 1725 eine kurze Partnerschaft mit seinem einstigen Meister einging, der mittlerweile die *New York Weekly Gazette* gegründet hatte. Zenger machte sich bald selbständig, publizierte vorwiegend erbauliche Traktate, Pamphlete und Bücher, bis ihn im Jahre 1733 die Gegner des verhaßten Gouverneurs Cosby dazu bewogen, eine oppositionelle Zeitung zu starten, die ein Gegengewicht zu Bradfords regierungstreuer *Gazette* bilden sollte. Das neue Blatt, die wohl erste unabhängige politische Zeitung Amerikas, nannte sich *New-York Weekly Journal*.

Die Kolonie New York hatte seit der Eroberung durch die Engländer unter einer Reihe korrupter Gouverneure zu leiden gehabt. William Cosby schien dieser Tradition die Krone aufsetzen zu wollen: Sofort nach seiner Ankunft hatte er Anspruch auf die Hälfte der Gehälter und sonstigen Einkünfte des Interimgouverneurs Rip van Dam erhoben und diesen durch Manipulationen des Gerichts und Amtsentsetzung eines Richters daran gehindert, sich auf dem Rechtsweg zu wehren. Und dies war nur der Anfang einer ganzen Reihe von Übergriffen und Rechtsbrüchen.

Am 5. November 1733 erschien die erste Ausgabe von Zengers *Journal*, das in den folgenden Monaten die Machenschaften der herrschenden Clique anprangern sollte. Bald begannen auch Spottgedichte – anscheinend ebenfalls aus der Werkstatt Zengers – in der Stadt zu zirkulieren. Cosby fühlte sich bedroht.

Im November 1734, nur zwei Wochen, nachdem sich Bürgermeister und Magistrat der Stadt geweigert hatten, an der Verbrennung einiger *Journal*-Ausgaben teilzunehmen, wurde Zenger mit der Begründung verhaftet, er hätte mehrere aufrührerische Verleumdungen gedruckt. Die unangemessene Höhe der Kaution und der Ausschluß zweier Verteidiger aus dem Verfahren und aus der Anwaltschaft machten deutlich, welcher Art der Prozeß sein würde. Während Zenger das *Journal* mit Hilfe seiner Frau aus der Untersuchungshaft heraus weiterführte, begann sich die Öffentlichkeit der Kolonien für den Fall zu engagieren. Als sich schließlich gar der berühmte Andrew Hamilton aus Philadelphia bereiterklärte, die Verteidigung zu übernehmen, schien die Lage nicht mehr aussichtslos.

Mit einem beredten Plädoyer, das sich vor allem auf eine Differenzierung zwischen Offenlegung von Mißständen und tatsächlicher Verleumdung konzentrierte, überzeugte der greise Hamilton die Geschworenen und erreichte im August 1735 den Freispruch Zengers. Mehr noch: Hamiltons Auslegung entwertete die Diffamierungsklausel, die so lange den Weg zur Pressefreiheit versperrt hatte.

John Peter Zenger wurde 1737 in Anerkennung seiner Verdienste zum offiziellen Drucker der Stadt New York ernannt. Er starb am 28. Juli 1746; fünf Jahre später wurde das von seiner Frau und seinem Sohn fortgeführte *Journal* eingestellt.

Numb. II.

THE

New-York Weekly JOURNAL

Containing the freshest Advices, Foreign, and Domestick.

MUNDAY November 12, 1733.

Mr. *Zenger*.

INcert the following in your next, and you'll oblige your Friend,

CATO.

Mira temporum felicitas ubi sentiri quæ velis, & quæ sentias dicere licit.

Tacit.

THE Liberty of the Press is a Subject of the greatest Importance, and in which every Individual is as much concern'd as he is in any other Part of Liberty: therefore it will not be improper to communicate to the Publick the Sentiments of a late excellent Writer upon this Point. such is the Elegance and Perspicuity of his Writings, such the inimitable Force of his Reasoning, that it will be difficult to say any Thing new that he has not said, or not to say that much worse which he has said.

There are two Sorts of Monarchies, an absolute and a limited one. In the first, the Liberty of the Press can never be maintained, it is inconsistent with it; for what absolute Monarch would suffer any Subject to animadvert on his Actions, when it is in his Power to declare the Crime, and to nominate the Punishment? This would make it very dangerous to exercise such a Liberty. Besides the Object against which those Pens must be directed, is their Sovereign, the sole supream Magistrate; for there being no Law in those Monarchies, but the Will of the Prince, it makes it necessary for his Ministers to consult his Pleasure, before any Thing can be undertaken: He is therefore properly chargeable with the Grievances of his Subjects, and what the Minister there acts being in Obedience to the Prince, he ought not to incur the Hatred of the People; for it would be hard to impute that to him for a Crime, which is the Fruit of his Allegiance, and for refusing which he might incur the Penalties of Treason. Besides, in an absolute Monarchy, the Will of the Prince being the Law, a Liberty of the Press to complain of Grievances would be complaining against the Law, and the Constitution, to which they have submitted, or have been obliged to submit; and therefore, in one Sense, may be said to deserve Punishment, So that under an absolute Monarchy, I say, such a Liberty is inconsistent with the Constitution, having no proper Subject in Politics, on which it might be exercis'd, and if exercis'd would incur a certain Penalty.

But in a limited Monarchy, as *England* is, our Laws are known, fixed, and established. They are the streight Rule and sure Guide to direct the King, the Ministers, and other his Subjects: And therefore an Offence against the Laws is such an Offence against the Constitution as ought to receive a proper adequate Punishment; the severa Constil

The second issue of Zenger's "Journal", the main author of which was James Alexander. Each number of the newspaper opened with an anonymous letter to Zenger – de facto an editorial. Zenger never appeared as an author himself, but had to accept responsibility for the unsigned contributions of his political friends.

Nummer zwei von Zengers »Journal«, dessen Hauptautor James Alexander war. Jede Nummer der Zeitung wurde mit einem anonymen, an Zenger gerichteten Brief – de facto einem Leitartikel – eröffnet. Zenger selbst trat nicht als Autor in Erscheinung, mußte aber für die ungezeichneten Beiträge seiner politischen Freunde die Verantwortung übernehmen.

Lawyer James Alexander, founder of the American Philosophical Society and owner of the largest legal library in the colonies, supported Rip van Dam against Cosby and, together with his colleague Smith, initiated Zenger's "Journal".

Rechtsanwalt James Alexander, Gründer der American Philosophical Society und Besitzer der größten juristischen Bibliothek in den Kolonien, unterstützte Rip van Dam gegen Cosby und initiierte gemeinsam mit seinem Kollegen Smith das Zengersche »Journal«.

William Cosby issued a proclamation offering a twenty-pound reward for the arrest of the author of two "scandalous" poems directed against the colonial government.

William Cosby setzt eine Belohnung von 20 Pfund für die Ergreifung des Autors zweier Spottgedichte auf die Kolonialregierung aus.

By his Excellency

William Cosby, Captain General and Governour in Chief of the Provinces of *New-York*, *New-Jersey*, and Territories thereon depending in America, Vice-Admiral of the same, and Colonel in His Majesty's Army.

A PROCLAMATION.

WHereas Ill-minded and Disaffected Persons have lately dispersed in the City of *New-York*, and divers other Places, several Scandalous and Seditious Libels, but more particularly two Printed Scandalous Songs or Ballads, highly defaming the Administration of His Majesty's Government in this Province, tending greatly to inflame the Minds of His Majesty's good Subjects, and to disturb the Publick Peace. *And Whereas* the Grand Jury for the City and County of New-York did lately, by their Address to me, complain of these Pernicious Practices, and request me to issue a Proclamation for the Discovery of the Offenders, that they might, by Law, receive a Punishment adequate to their Guilt and Crime. *I Have* therefore thought fit, by and with the Advice of his Majesty's Council, to issue this Proclamation, hereby Promising *Twenty Pounds* as a Reward, to such Person or Persons who shall discover the Author or Authors of the two Scandalous Songs or Ballads aforesaid, to be paid to the Person or Persons discovering the same, as soon as such Author or Authors shall be Convicted of having been the Author or Authors thereof.

GIVEN under My Hand and Seal at Fort-George in New-York this Sixth Day of November, *in the Eighth year of the Reign of Our Sovereign Lord* GEORGE *the Second, by the Grace of* GOD *of* Great-Britain, France *and* Ireland, KING, *Defender of the Faith, &c. and in the year of Our* LORD, 1734.

By his Excellency's Command,
Fred. Morris, *D. Cl. Conc.*

W. COSBY.

GOD Save the KING

As attorney general of Philadelphia, speaker of Pennsylvania's assembly and judge of the admiralty, Andrew Hamilton became the most famous legal scholar in the colonies. Despite old age, when James Alexander called upon him for help, he made the trip to New York and won Zenger's acquittal.

Andrew Hamilton wurde als Generalstaatsanwalt von Philadelphia, Sprecher der Bürgerversammlung von Pennsylvanien und Richter der Admiralität zum bekanntesten Juristen der Kolonien. Von James Alexander zu Hilfe gerufen, nahm er trotz hohen Alters die Reise nach New York auf sich und erreichte den Freispruch Zengers.

Mr. James Alexander & Mr. William Smith.

I John Peter Zenger do hereby Authorize and Desire you or either of you to be my Attorney or Attorneys in all Actions & Suits whatsoever that are or Shall be brought against me in any Courts within this Province of New York Witness my hand this 18th Nov. 1734

Jno Peter Zenger

At a Supream Court of Judicature held for the province of New York at the City Hall of the City of New York on Wednesday the 16th Day of April 1735

Present The hon.ble James De Lancey Esq.re Chief Justice
The hon.ble Fred.k Philipse Esq.r Second Justice

James Alexander Esq.r and William Smith attorneys of this Court having presumed (notwithstanding they were forewarned by the Court of their displeasure if they should do it) to sign and having actually signed and put into Court Exceptions in the name of John Peter Zenger thereby denying the Legality of the Judges their Commissions tho' in the usual form, and the being of this Supream Court It is therefore Ordered that for the said Contempt the said James Alexander and William Smith be excluded from any farther practice in this Court and that their names be struck out of the Role of attorneys of this Court

p Cur James Lyne Cl Cur

Facsimile of the court decree disbarring Alexander and Smith, issued in April, 1735.

Faksimile des Gerichtsbeschlusses, durch den Alexander und Smith im April 1735 aus dem Verfahren und aus der Anwaltschaft ausgeschlossen wurden.

On November 17, 1734, the day after his arrest, John Peter Zenger entrusted the lawyers Alexander and Smith with his defense.

Einen Tag nach seiner Verhaftung am 17. November 1734 beauftragt John Peter Zenger die Anwälte Alexander und Smith mit seiner Verteidigung.

Andrew Hamilton, having succeeded in bringing the jury to a verdict contrary to the recommendation of the presiding judge – a persuasive tour de force no one had thought possible –, is carried out of the court room in triumph: the end of the Zenger trial in August, 1735, as conceived by a 19th-century illustrator.

Andrew Hamilton, dem das von niemandem erwartete Kunststück gelungen war, die Geschworenen zu einem Spruch gegen die Rechtsauslegung des vorsitzenden Richters zu veranlassen, wird im Triumph aus dem Gerichtssaal getragen: das Ende des Zenger-Prozesses im August 1735, frei nachempfunden von einem Illustrator des 19. Jahrhunderts.

Luther's Champion in America

Henry Melchior Mühlenberg

Luthers Mann in Amerika

The man generally acknowledged as being the organizer of Lutheranism in America, Henry Melchior Mühlenberg, was born on September 6, 1711, in Einbeck, Hanover. He was the seventh of nine children, the son of Nicolaus Melchior Mühlenberg, a master-shoemaker, deacon and town councilor, and his wife, Anna Maria, daughter of a retired army officer. From an early age he came under the influence of his family's religion, the Augsburg Confession of the Lutheran Church, to which Henry adhered throughout his life. He began his education in a good local school which emphasized classical studies. But when the death of his father in 1723 left the family in difficult circumstances, he had to interrupt his schooling for three years to work for an elder brother. In this period he learned to play the organ and later completed his preliminary education in classical schools at Einbeck and Zellerfeld.

In 1735, Mühlenberg began studying theology at the University of Göttingen and during this time he opened up a school for the teaching of poor children. Upon completion of his studies in 1738, he was appointed teacher at the famous orphanage in Halle where he met G.A. Francke. A year later he was ordained in Leipzig and accepted a position as co-pastor and inspector of an orphanage at Grosshennersdorf in Upper Lusatia. In 1741, while visiting in Halle, Francke presented him with a call to the United Congregations (Philadelphia, New Providence, New Hanover) in Pennsylvania. Mühlenberg took six weeks to consider the proposal and then accepted. After spending some time in London, he sailed to America, arriving at Charleston, South Carolina, in the fall of 1742, and three weeks later, on November 25, 1742, he reached Philadelphia.

His arrival was a rather dismal one since no one knew of his coming. He found the Philadelphia congregation divided into two factions and the other congregations, located in distant rural areas, received him with some degree of distrust and skepticism. Nevertheless, he immediately set out to win their support and confidence, making it his task not just to serve three isolated congregations but to establish one Church. This he undertook with great diligence, perseverance and knowledge which, in addition to his intellectual capabilities and his classical training, commanded respect and admiration wherever he went. Especially his mastery of languages was astounding: he preached not only in his native German but also in English; in Dutch as well as in Latin.

Henry (Heinrich) Melchior Mühlenberg, der als Begründer der Lutherischen Kirche Amerikas gelten darf, wurde am 6. September 1711 in Einbeck bei Hannover geboren. Er war das siebte von neun Kindern, Sohn des Nicolaus Melchior Mühlenberg, eines Schuhmachermeisters, Diakons und Stadtrats, und seiner Frau Anna Maria, Tochter eines Offiziers im Ruhestand. Schon in jungen Jahren beeinflußte ihn die Religion seiner Familie, die Augsburger Konfession der lutherischen Kirche, der er sein ganzes Leben weihen sollte. Seine Ausbildung begann in einer Gemeindeschule, die besonderen Wert auf die humanistischen Fächer legte. Als der Tod des Vaters im Jahr 1723 die Familie in Bedrängnis brachte, mußte er drei Jahre lang die Schule unterbrechen und für einen älteren Bruder arbeiten. In dieser Zeit lernte er Orgel spielen. Später schloß er seine vorbereitende Ausbildung an altsprachlichen Schulen in Einbeck und Zellerfeld ab.

1735 nahm Mühlenberg an der Universität Göttingen das Studium der Theologie auf und eröffnete eine Schule für die Armen. Nach Beendigung seines Studiums wurde er im Jahre 1738 als Lehrer am berühmten, von August Hermann Francke gegründeten Waisenhaus von Halle eingestellt, wo er Franckes Sohn Gotthilf August kennenlernte. Im Jahr darauf empfing Mühlenberg in Leipzig die Priesterweihe und nahm eine Stelle als Nebenpastor und Inspektor eines Waisenhauses in Großhennersdorf in der Oberlausitz an. Als er 1741 in Halle weilte, überreichte ihm Francke ein Berufungsschreiben der Vereinten Kongregationen (Philadelphia, New Providence, New Hanover) von Pennsylvanien. Nach sechswöchiger Bedenkzeit nahm Mühlenberg das Angebot an. Mit einem Zwischenaufenthalt in London reiste er nach Amerika und kam im Herbst 1742 in Charleston, South Carolina, an. Drei Wochen später, am 25. November 1742, erreichte er Philadelphia.

Die Ankunft war enttäuschend, da er unangekündigt kam und ihn niemand erwartete. Er fand die Philadelphische Kongregation in zwei Lager gespalten und wurde von den übrigen, weiter entfernten Gemeinden im Landesinneren mit einem gewissen Mißtrauen empfangen. Dennoch bemühte er sich sofort um Unterstützung und Vertrauen, wobei er sich die Aufgabe stellte, nicht nur Seelsorger dreier Gemeinden zu sein, sondern diese zu einer geschlossenen Bekenntnisgemeinschaft zusammenzuführen. Er verfolgte dieses Ziel mit Sorgfalt, Ausdauer und Umsicht, was ihm im Verein mit seinen intellektuellen Fähigkeiten und seiner humanistischen Bildung überall Respekt und Bewunderung eintrug. Vor allem überraschte seine Fremdsprachenkenntnis, die ihn befähigte, nicht nur auf deutsch, sondern auch in englischer, niederländischer und lateinischer Sprache zu predigen.

Bald wurde Mühlenberg zum Pastor der Vereinten Kongregationen ernannt, die zum Herzstück des deutschen Luthertums in den Kolonien werden sollten. Um

Henry Melchior Mühlenberg (1711–1787)

The stone church in the "Trappe" which Mühlenberg built and, at its consecration on 6 October 1745, named the "Augustus Church" in honor of August Hermann Francke, the founder of the orphanages at Halle. Mühlenberg was buried in this church's cemetery on 10 October 1787.

Die steinerne Kirche in »Trappe«, die Mühlenberg errichtete und bei ihrer Weihe am 6. Oktober 1745 zu Ehren des Gründers der Halleschen Waisenhäuser, August Hermann Francke, auf den Namen »Augustuskirche« taufte. Hier wurde Mühlenberg am 10. Oktober 1787 auch begraben.

Upon arrival in America, Henry Melchior Mühlenberg preached in a barn in New Providence, then still populated by Germans, and called – in their dialect – the "Trappe".

Henry Melchior Mühlenberg predigt nach seiner Ankunft in Amerika in einer Scheune in New Providence, das damals noch – im Dialekt seiner deutschen Bewohner – »die Trappe« hieß.

Mühlenberg was soon made pastor of the United Congregations which became the nucleus of German Lutheranism throughout the colonies. In response to the need for greater organization among the newly formed congregations, the Evangelical Lutheran Ministerium of Pennsylvania was established in 1748. This was also the result of the many trips Mühlenberg had made to Lutheran enclaves scattered from the Hudson River to the Potomac. Once dubbed "The Saddle-Bag Preacher", he continued ministering to remote groups of Lutherans until the outbreak of the Revolutionary War. During that period he returned to his rural retreat in New Providence, where he resided with his wife Anna Maria (née Weiser). They had married in 1745 and she had borne him eleven children, the most famous of whom was John Peter Muhlenberg, the "Fighting Pastor". The last years of his life were spent in gradual retirement but he did manage to complete work on a hymnal which was published in 1786. On October 7, 1787, the patriarch of the Lutheran Church in America died at his home in New Providence, Pennsylvania.

die Weiterentwicklung der jungen Gemeinden zu gewährleisten, gründete man 1748 das Evangelisch-Lutherische Ministerium von Pennsylvanien, dessen Zustandekommen nicht zuletzt Ergebnis der vielen Vermittlungsreisen war, die Mühlenberg zu den lutherischen Gemeinden vom Hudson River bis an den Potomac unternommen hatte. Einmal mit dem Spitznamen »Satteltaschenprediger« betitelt, versah er bis zum Ausbruch des Revolutionskrieges sein geistliches Amt und suchte weiterhin auch die entlegensten lutherischen Kongregationen auf. Während der Kriegsjahre lebte er mit seiner Frau Anna Maria, einer geborenen Weiser, auf einem Landsitz in New Providence. Aus der 1745 geschlossenen Ehe gingen elf Kinder hervor, von denen John Peter Muhlenberg, »der kämpfende Pastor«, am bekanntesten wurde. In den letzten Jahren seines Lebens setzte sich Henry Melchior mehr und mehr zur Ruhe und widmete sich nur noch der Fertigstellung eines Hymnars, das 1786 erschien. Am 7. Oktober 1787 starb der Patriarch der Lutherischen Kirche Amerikas in seinem Haus in New Providence in Pennsylvanien.

John Peter Gabriel Muhlenberg (1746–1807), the oldest of Henry's six sons, became known as the "Fighting Pastor" during the Revolution, leading a regiment of German volunteers while bearing the rank of a brigadier general. The relief by Otto Schweizer portrays his famous sermon in January, 1776, in Woodstock, Virginia. With the following words he threw off his robe to reveal the uniform of his volunteer regiment: "There is a time for all things. There is a time to preach and a time to fight; and now is the time to fight!" Three hundred community members spontaneously enlisted.

John Peter Gabriel Muhlenberg (1746–1807), der älteste von Henrys sechs Söhnen, wurde im Unabhängigkeitskrieg als »Fighting Pastor« und Führer eines deutschen Freiwilligenregiments im Rang eines Brigadegenerals bekannt. Das Relief von Otto Schweizer zeigt seine berühmte Predigt in Woodstock, Virginia, im Januar 1776, wo er mit den Worten: »Ein jegliches hat seine Zeit; predigen hat seine Zeit; und kämpfen hat seine Zeit. Und die Zeit zum Kampf ist gekommen!« seinen Talar ablegte, unter dem er bereits die Uniform seines Freiwilligenregiments trug: dreihundert Gemeindemitglieder schlossen sich spontan der Revolutionsarmee an.

Frederick Augustus Conrad Muhlenberg, another of Henry's sons, earned the epithet of an "American Linnaeus" for his botanical work. From 1789–91 he was also speaker of the First Congress of the United States. His brother, John Peter Gabriel, became vice-governor of Pennsylvania after the war.

Frederick Augustus Conrad Muhlenberg, ein weiterer Sohn Henrys, erwarb sich als Botaniker den Beinamen eines »amerikanischen Linné« und war von 1789–91 der Sprecher des ersten Kongresses der Vereinigten Staaten. Sein Bruder John Peter Gabriel wurde nach dem Krieg Vizegouverneur von Pennsylvanien.

The Mühlenberg Monument, created for the Mt. Airy Theological Seminary in Germantown by the sculptor J. Otto Schweizer. The latter was born in Zurich and emigrated to America in 1894.

Das Mühlenberg-Denkmal des in Zürich geborenen und 1894 ausgewanderten Bildhauers J. Otto Schweizer, geschaffen für das Mt. Airy Theological Seminary in Germantown

"Ike's" Ancestor from the Odenwald

Hans Nikolaus Eisenhauer

»Ikes« Ahn aus dem Odenwald

Hans Nikolaus Eisenhauer, who emigrated to America around the middle of the eighteenth century, can, with all due respect, not be considered one of the great German-born Americans. He did not achieve wealth or fame or make any substantial contribution to his newfound home; nor was he an ingenious inventor or a freedom-seeking artist. Nonetheless he deserves some attention, for he was the ancestor of Dwight David Eisenhower, World War II general and 34th president of the United States. Due to the difficulty of recovering records from the time Eisenhauer lived, not a great deal is known about him. We do however know that he was born about 1691 in Eiterbach in Southern Odenwald, a part of the former Electorate of the Palatinate in what is now the State of Hessen. In an excellent piece of genealogical research, the name (which is German for "ironcutter") has been traced in the region north of the Neckar river all the way back to 1450. Hans Nikolaus was the youngest of seven children born to the bondsman Hans Peter Eyssenhauer and his second wife Ann Catharina. As the youngest son, there was apparently no opportunity for him to work on his father's farm and so he left it, earning his living most likely as a weaver or lumberman. Around 1712 he married his first wife (whose name is unknown) and had two sons, Johannes and Hans Peter. His second wife, Anna Margaretha Strubel, whom he wedded around 1725, gave birth to three children, Johannes, Martin and Maria Magdalena. In 1741, at the age of 50, Eisenhauer sailed with his family on the ship *Europe* from Rotterdam to America, landing on November 17 at the mouth of the Delaware River. Three days later, together with his three oldest sons, he took his oath of allegiance at Philadelphia. This family moved on and settled in Lebanon County, Pennsylvania, where Eisenhauer was granted a tract of land in an area still populated by Indians. It has been recorded that they were roaming about the neighborhood and even set fire to Eisenhauer's house. The date of Eisenhauer's death has not been ascertained, but we know that he was still alive in 1760 when he attested his signature to the will of his son Martin.

Hans Nikolaus Eisenhauer, der Mitte des achtzehnten Jahrhunderts nach Nordamerika auswanderte, zählt, bei allem Respekt, nicht zu den großen in Deutschland geborenen Amerikanern. Er wurde weder reich noch berühmt und trug nicht mehr als Millionen andere zum Werden der Nation bei. Ebensowenig war er ein genialer Erfinder oder ein die amerikanische Freizügigkeit suchender Künstler. Dennoch verdient er unser Interesse, denn er war der Ahnherr von Dwight David Eisenhower, dem General im Zweiten Weltkrieg und 34. Präsidenten der Vereinigten Staaten.
Bisher gelang es kaum, Genaueres über Eisenhauers Leben in Erfahrung zu bringen. Er soll um 1691 in Eiterbach im südlichen Odenwald geboren worden sein, einem Landesteil, der damals dem pfälzischen Kurfürstentum angehörte und heute im Bundesland Hessen liegt. Einer umfangreichen genealogischen Studie ist es gelungen, den Namen »Eisenhauer« bis ins Jahr 1450 zurückzuverfolgen, wo er im Gebiet nördlich des Neckar beheimatet war. Hans Nikolaus war das jüngste von sieben Kindern des Knechts Hans Peter Eyssenhauer und dessen zweiter Frau Anna Katharina. Als ›Benjamin‹ der Familie hatte er kaum Aussicht, auf dem kleinen Hof seines Vaters ein Auskommen zu finden, und so ging er fort und verdiente seinen Lebensunterhalt als Weber und Holzfäller. Um das Jahr 1712 heiratete er seine erste Frau, deren Name bis heute nicht bekannt ist, und hatte mit ihr die beiden Söhne Johannes und Hans Peter. Seine zweite Frau Anna Margaretha Strubel, die er um 1725 heiratete, schenkte ihm drei Kinder, Johannes, Martin und Maria Magdalena.
1741, Eisenhauer war mittlerweile fünfzig Jahre alt, schiffte er sich mit seiner Familie in Rotterdam auf der *Europa* ein und kam am 17. November in Nordamerika an der Mündung des Delaware an. Drei Tage später leistete er zusammen mit seinen Söhnen in Philadelphia den Treueid. Die Eisenhauer-Familie zog nach Lebanon County in Pennsylvanien, wo ihr ein Landstrich zugesprochen worden war, der allerdings von Indianern bewohnt wurde. Es soll zu Kämpfen gekommen sein und einmal stand das Haus der Eisenhauers sogar in Flammen. Das Todesdatum von Hans Nikolaus Eisenhauer ist so unbekannt wie sein übriges Leben, aber noch im Jahr 1760 setzte er seine Unterschrift unter das Testament, in dem er seinen Besitz dem Sohn Martin vermachte.

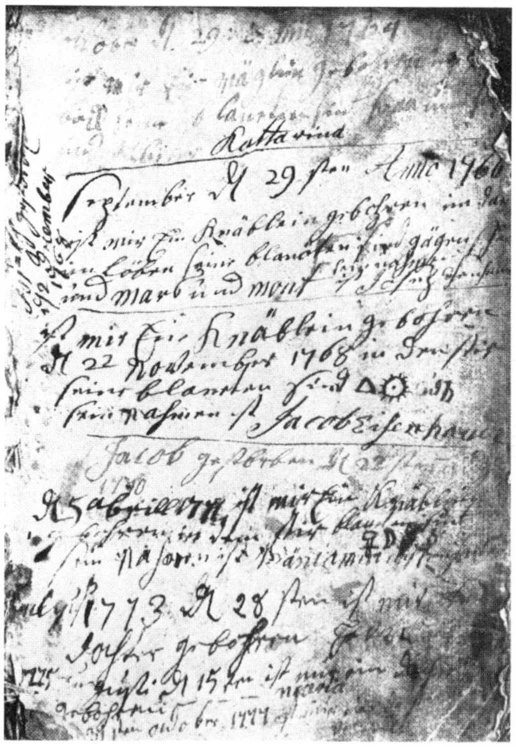

First of the Eisenhower generation born in America, 1760 and 1768: entered in the family bible brought with him from Europe, the children of John Eisenhauer, himself the child of Hans Nikolaus' second marriage.

Geburtseintragungen der ersten in Amerika geborenen Eisenhower-Generation, 1760 und 1768 von Johannes Eisenhauer, dem Sohn aus zweiter Ehe, in seiner aus Europa mitgebrachten Familienbibel vorgenommen.

View of the city of Lindenfels in the western Odenwald from around 1634; the old fortress tower on the outer right is still known today as the "Eisenhauer Tower".

Ansicht der Stadt Lindenfels im westlichen Odenwald um 1634; der Festungsturm rechts außen ist noch heute unter dem Namen »Eisenhauer-Turm« bekannt.

Water-driven forge-hammer in the Odenwald, from a wood engraving dated 1495. Even at that time the name "Eisenhauer" (Ysenhawer, Eisenhawer, Ysenhäuer, Eyssenhauer), designating a profession associated with iron mining, is on the records in Hans Nikolaus Eisenhauer's area of origin.

Eisenhammer im Odenwald auf einem Holzschnitt aus dem Jahr 1495; bereits damals ist der Name »Eisenhauer« (Ysenhawer, Eisenhawer, Ysenhäuer, Eyssenhauer), ein Berufsname aus dem Erzbergbau, im Herkunftsgebiet Hans Nikolaus Eisenhauers beurkundet.

Hero of the Revolutionary War

Johann de Kalb

Held des Unabhängigkeitskrieges

Johann Georg Kalb, born on June 29th, 1721, in Hüttendorf near Erlangen, was the second son of a peasant couple, Leonhard and Margarethe Kalb. He left his parents' farm at the age of 16. Six years later he reappeared in a German regiment of the French army as "Lieutenant de Kalb", having conferred upon himself a fictitious nobleman's title to advance his career (in those days only noblemen could become officers). In his new surroundings, Kalb made a mark for himself by his intelligence, bravery, cultivated manners and fluent French. His military instructor was Maurice of Saxony, with whom he took part in the War of Austrian Succession. When France entered the Seven Years' War, de Kalb was promoted to first lieutenant. After the war he retired from the French military, having served for 21 years and acquired a considerable fortune. He purchased the palace of Milon la Chapelle near Paris (with its associated baronetcy) and, in 1764, married Anna Elizabeth van Robais, the daughter of a linen manufacturer. At this point Baron de Kalb might have led the leisurely existence of a landed nobleman, but the 47-year-old ex-soldier longed for further glories. His opportunity came in 1768 when the French government sent him on a secret mission to North America with the task of sensing the mood of the English colonies. When the War of Independence broke out in 1776 de Kalb immediately offered his services. In the following year he again journeyed to America, this time in the company of the young Marquis de Lafayette, whose mentor he was. Here, after some delay caused by the American Congress, he entered the Continental Army with the rank of general. He took part in the Battle of Germantown and accompanied Washington to his dismal winter quarters at Valley Forge. In 1779 de Kalb was sent to South Carolina to support the local troops. He was joined at Deep River by General Gates who, against de Kalb's advice, immediately set out to Camden. Here they encountered the British "Lobsterbacks" under Lord Cornwallis. While Gates quickly withdrew from the battle with the main wing, de Kalb stood his ground with the Maryland and Delaware regiments, suffering defeat. His horse shot out from under him, he continued to fight sword in hand until he fell to the ground, bleeding from eleven wounds. Three days later, on August 18th, 1780, he died of his wounds in Camden.

Johann Georg Kalb kam am 29. Juni 1721 in Hüttendorf bei Erlangen als zweitgeborener Sohn der Bauersleute Leonhard und Margarethe Kalb zur Welt. Mit sechzehn verließ er den elterlichen Hof und tauchte schon sechs Jahre später als »Leutnant de Kalb« in einem deutschen Regiment der Französischen Armee auf. Den Adelstitel hatte er sich, des besseren Fortkommens wegen, selbst zugelegt: Verständlich, denn damals durften nur Adelige Offizier werden. Kalb behauptete sich in seiner neuen Umgebung durch Klugheit, Tapferkeit, gute Manieren und fließendes Französisch. Sein militärischer Lehrmeister war Moritz von Sachsen, mit dem er am Österreichischen Erbfolgekrieg teilnahm. Als Frankreich in den Siebenjährigen Krieg eintrat, rückte de Kalb zum Oberstleutnant auf. Nach Ende des Krieges und nach 21 Dienstjahren zog sich de Kalb aus dem französischen Militär zurück. Wohlhabend geworden, kaufte er das Schloß Milon la Chapelle bei Paris (nebst dazugehörigem Baronat) und heiratete 1764 die Tuchfabrikantentochter Anna Elizabeth van Robais. Baron de Kalb hätte nun das müßige Leben eines Landedelmannes führen können, doch den 47jährigen dürstete es nach weiterem Ruhm. Die Gelegenheit bot sich, als er 1768 in geheimer Mission der französischen Regierung nach Nordamerika geschickt wurde: Er sollte die Stimmung in den englischen Kolonien erkunden. Als 1776 der amerikanische Unabhängigkeitskrieg begann, bot de Kalb sogleich seine Dienste an. Zusammen mit dem jungen Marquis de Lafayette, dessen Mentor er war, reiste er 1777 erneut nach Amerika, wo er, nach einigen Verzögerungen durch den amerikanischen Kongreß, der Kontinentalarmee als General beitreten konnte. Er nahm an der Schlacht von Germantown teil und zog mit Washington ins triste Winterlager von Valley Forge. 1779 wurde de Kalb zur Unterstützung der dortigen Truppen nach Süd-Carolina entsandt. In Deep River schloß sich ihm General Gates an, der, entgegen Kalbs Rat, sofort nach Camden weitermaschierte. Hier stießen sie auf die britischen »Rotröcke« unter Lord Cornwallis. Während sich Gates mit dem Hauptflügel bald aus der Schlacht absetzte, hielt de Kalb mit den Regimentern »Maryland« und »Delaware« bis zur bitteren Niederlage stand. Nachdem ihm das Pferd unter dem Leib weggeschossen worden war, kämpfte er mit dem Schwert in der Hand weiter, bis er, aus elf Wunden blutend, zu Boden stürzte. Drei Tage später, am 18. August 1780, erlag er seinen Verletzungen in Camden.

Johann de Kalb (1721–1780)

Germans and Americans of German descent joined in Hüttendorf in 1960 to commemorate the 180th anniversary of Kalb's death. In the photo, American historian Ralph C. Wood addresses the audience.

Deutsche und Amerikaner deutscher Abstammung versammelten sich 1960 in Hüttendorf, um des 180. Todestages von de Kalb zu gedenken. Das Foto zeigt den amerikanischen Historiker Ralph C. Wood bei einer Ansprache.

Entry of Johann Leonhard Kalb's birth in the parish register of Hüttendorf near Erlangen.

Geburtseintrag des Johann Leonhard Kalb im Kirchenbuch von Hüttendorf bei Erlangen

Drillmaster and Democrat

Friedrich Wilhelm von Steuben

Drillmeister und Demokrat

He entered American history by a roundabout path. Friedrich Wilhelm Ludolf Gerhard Augustin von Steuben was born on September 17th, 1730, in Magdeburg. Like his father before him, he became a Prussian officer. For a while he was on the general staff of Frederick the Great, but as a result of drastic budget reductions in the aftermath of the Seven Years' War he was discharged with the rank of captain after 17 years of service. An altercation with the king's adjutant general was another deciding factor.
Impoverished and seeking a new field of activity, he established contacts with influential persons in Paris who arranged his dispatch to America. The American envoy Benjamin Franklin, the French Minister of War St. Germain, and the well-known playwright Beaumarchais jointly recommended von Steuben to the American Congress and to George Washington, Commander-in-Chief of the rebel forces, for service in the Continental Army. As the rank of captain would never have sufficed to obtain Steuben a position equal to his military capabilities and potential, he was presented to the Americans as a former lieutenant general of Frederick the Great.
On February 22, 1778, Steuben reached Washington's winter quarters at Valley Forge. Here he found the troops demoralized, ridden with hunger and increasing desertions. At Washington's suggestion, von Steuben was appointed inspector general of the troops of the United States, with the rank of a major general and the task of disciplining, training and provisioning the troops. Drawing on guidelines which he worked out during the winter months, von Steuben devised a uniform code of drill for the American army, entitled *Regulations for the Order and Discipline of the Troops of the United States* and known, because of its blue binding, simply as the "Blue Book". It contained all the important training regulations for officers and enlisted men.
Yet von Steuben proved his mettle not merely as a drill master but also as a military leader. Less well known but no less noteworthy are the memoranda he composed, among them a concept for a national defense system drawn up at Washington's request. Equally significant was his plan for the erection of a military academy, which became a reality under the Jefferson administration in 1802 with the founding of West Point.
The United States of North America became von Steuben's new home, and this formerly monarchist officer was transmuted into a confirmed advocate of the principles of democracy. This change was documented on many occasions, among them in a letter written to a friend in Germany: "What a fortunate, progressive land this is! No kings, no high clergy, no parasitic landlords or idle gentry! ... I am gladly prepared to die for a country which honors me in this way with its confidence and trust."
After being discharged from active service, von Steuben was to spend only a few happy years on his estate, a gift from the State of New York. On November 28th, 1794, he died near Remsen in Oneida County, New York.

Sein Weg in die amerikanische Geschichte war verschlungen. Der am 17.9.1730 in Magdeburg geborene Friedrich Wilhelm Ludolf Gerhard Augustin von Steuben wurde wie sein Vater preußischer Offizier. Obwohl eine Zeitlang im Generalstab Friedrich des Großen, mußte er nach 17jähriger Dienstzeit am Ende des Siebenjährigen Krieges infolge drastischer Sparmaßnahmen im Range eines Hauptmanns aus der friderizianischen Armee ausscheiden. Hierzu trug auch bei, daß er sich mit dem Generaladjutanten überworfen hatte.
Der Verbindung zu einflußreichen Personen in Paris verdankte der verarmte, um ein neues Betätigungsfeld bemühte von Steuben seine Entsendung nach Amerika. Der amerikanische Gesandte in Paris, Benjamin Franklin, der französische Kriegsminister St. Germain und der bekannte Dichter Beaumarchais waren übereingekommen, dem amerikanischen Kongreß und George Washington, dem Oberbefehlshaber der Revolutionstruppen, die Übernahme von Steubens in die »Kontinentalarmee« zu empfehlen. Da aber von Steuben als Hauptmann trotz seiner militärischen Fähigkeiten niemals eine ihm angemessene Wirkungsmöglichkeit erhalten hätte, wurde er den Amerikanern als ehemaliger Generalleutnant Friedrichs des Großen vorgestellt.
Als von Steuben am 23. Februar 1778 in Washingtons Winterquartier in Valley Forge eintraf, fand er eine hungernde und demoralisierte Truppe vor, in der sich die Desertionen häuften. Auf Vorschlag Washingtons ernannte der Kongreß von Steuben zum Generalinspekteur der Truppen der Vereinigten Staaten im Range eines Generalmajors, der für die militärische Disziplin, die Ausbildung und die Versorgung der Truppe verantwortlich war.
Auf der Grundlage der von ihm in den Wintermonaten erarbeiten Richtlinien schuf von Steuben ein einheitliches Exerzierreglement für die amerikanische Armee, die *Regulations for the Order and Discipline of the Troops of the United States,* wegen des blauen Einbandes allgemein *Blue Book* genannt. Es enthielt alle wichtigen Ausbildungsvorschriften für Soldaten und Offiziere.
Aber nicht nur als Exerziermeister hat sich von Steuben bewährt, sondern auch als Truppenführer. Weniger bekannt, aber darum nicht weniger bedeutend, sind seine Denkschriften - darunter eine im Auftrag Washingtons verfaßte Konzeption eines nationalen Verteidigungssystems. Von gleichfalls großer Bedeutung war sein Plan zur Errichtung einer Militärakademie, der 1802, unter der Regierung Jefferson, mit der Gründung der berühmten Akademie West Point verwirklicht wurde.
Daß ihm die Vereinigten Staaten von Nordamerika zur Heimat wurden und sich in ihm, dem einst monarchistischen Offizier, ein Wandel vollzog, der ihn zu einem überzeugten Verfechter demokratischer Prinzipien machte, geht neben vielen sonstigen Belegen aus einem Brief an einen Freund in Deutschland hervor: »Was ist das für ein fortschrittlich-glückliches Land ohne Könige, ohne hohen Klerus, ohne blutsaugende Pächter, ohne faule Großgrundbesitzer ... Gerne bin ich bereit, für eine Nation zu sterben, die mich so mit ihrem Vertrauen ehrte«.
Nach seinem Ausscheiden aus dem aktiven Dienst waren von Steuben nur wenige Jahre des privaten Glücks auf seinem Landsitz, einem Geschenk des Staates New York, beschieden. Er verstarb am 28. November 1794 bei Remsen in Oneida County im Staate New York.

Friedrich Wilhelm von Steuben (1730–1794)

George Washington and von Steuben inspecting the squalid conditions at Valley Forge

George Washington und von Steuben inspizieren die entmutigenden Zustände im Winterlager von Valley Forge.

Wrapped in his officer's coat, Friedrich Wilhelm von Steuben was buried in a simple grave. This monument in the "Sacred Grove", close to the villages of Steuben and Remsen in Oneida County, New York, was not erected until 1804.

Friedrich Wilhelm von Steuben wurde nach seinem Tod, in seinen Offiziersmantel gehüllt, in einem einfachen Grab beigesetzt. Erst 1804 erhielt er dieses Grabmonument im »Heiligen Hain« nahe den Ortschaften Steuben und Remsen in Oneida County im Staat New York.

Title page of the famous "Blue Book" which first appeared in 1779

Titelseite des erstmals 1779 erschienen »Blauen Buches«

REGULATIONS
FOR THE
ORDER AND DISCIPLINE
OF THE
TROOPS OF THE UNITED STATES.
BY BARON DE STUBEN,
TO WHICH ARE PREFIXED THE
LAWS AND REGULATIONS
FOR
GOVERNING AND DISCIPLINING
THE MILITIA OF THE UNITED STATES.
AND THE
LAWS FOR FORMING AND REGULATING
THE
MILITIA OF THE STATE OF NEW HAMPSHIRE.

PUBLISHED BY ORDER OF THE HON. GENERAL-COURT OF THE STATE OF NEW-HAMPSHIRE.

PORTSMOUTH:
PRINTED BY J. MELCHER, PRINTER TO THE STATE OF

Sketch of the Steuben Monument in Washington, for which Congress invited entries in 1903. Seven years later, in 1910, German-American sculptor Albert Jaeger unveiled his creation.

Skizze des 1903 vom amerikanischen Kongreß ausgeschriebenen und 1910 enthüllten Steuben-Denkmals in Washington, das der deutschamerikanische Bildhauer Albert Jaeger schuf.

"Steuben Receives the Surrender Overture of Cornwallis," by Conrad Linke. Artist's conception of the conclusion of the battle of Yorktown, at which Steuben commanded the front-line troops and was the first to be apprised that the British were prepared to negotiate.

»Steuben erhält das Kapitulationsangebot von Cornwallis«: Historienbild von Conrad Linke mit einer freien Darstellung des Endes der Schlacht von Yorktown, in der von Steuben die vordersten Linien kommandierte und als erster von der Verhandlungsbereitschaft der Briten erfuhr.

The Steuben Parade has been a yearly event in New York since 1958 and is presently indicative of the role that Steuben has played in facilitating identification among Americans of German descent since the late 19th century. Marching in the photo of the 1979 parade (from left): chairman of the parade committee, William H. Handeler; Minister President of Baden-Wurttemberg and guest of honor, Lothar Späth; and Edward J. Koch, mayor of New York.

Die Rolle, die von Steuben seit dem späten 19. Jahrhundert als Integrationsfigur für die Amerikaner deutscher Abstammung spielt, wird heute vor allem in der New Yorker Steubenparade deutlich, die seit 1958 alljährlich abgehalten wird. Das Foto aus dem Jahr 1979 zeigt als Mitmarschierer (von links) den Vorsitzenden des Paradekomitees, William H. Handeler, den Baden-Württembergischen Ministerpräsidenten Lothar Späth als Ehrengast und Edward J. Koch, den Oberbürgermeister von New York.

Emblems for the South

Nicola Marschall

Embleme für den Süden

Of the many Germans who came to America in the middle of the 19th century, one, whose name has all but been forgotten, has left an indelible mark on American history. For it was Nicola Marschall, a German painter, who gave to America the two symbols which would forever come to be associated with that belligerent attempt to rend the nation asunder: the first flag of the Confederate States of America, the "Stars and Bars", and the gray uniforms of the South.
Marschall was born in 1829 in St. Wendel, the son of a tobacco factory owner, Emanuel Marschall. Rather than take up the familiy business as was the custom, the young Nicola followed his artistic leanings and dedicated himself to portrait painting which he studied at the art academy in Düsseldorf. The turbulent 1840s not only brought political upheaval to Germany but also economic impoverishment to much of the middle class which, together with the competition introduced by a technological innovation, the Daguerrotype (the forerunner of photography), led to Marschall's decision to try his luck in the New World. With his father's blessings and an official exemption from military service, at the age of eighteen Marschall sailed to New Orleans.
Settling in Marion, Alabama, he found employment as a teacher of painting, music and the French and German languages at the women's seminary and remained there until 1857, when he returned to Prussia for two years to study art and to travel.
Returning again to Marion, Marschall enjoyed much success painting portraits of wealthy planters and prominent Southerners. When the war broke out, one of the South's loyal daughters, Mrs. Napoleon Lockett, engaged Marschall to design a flag and a uniform for the Confederacy. Prussian uniforms he had seen on his travels in Italy served as a model for his design. Record has also been made of Marschall's having served briefly in the Alabama Militia. In 1873 Marschall moved with his family to Louisville, Kentucky, where he set up a studio to paint portraits, many of which were of Northern military and civilian leaders of the Civil War period. He died in his Louisville home on 24 February 1917, at the age of 88.

Von den zahllosen Deutschen, die Mitte des 19. Jahrhunderts in die Vereinigten Staaten auswanderten, hat einer, dessen Name fast vergessen ist, der amerikanischen Geschichte ein bleibendes Zeichen aufgeprägt: Es war Nicola Marschall, ein deutscher Maler, der Amerika die Symbole schenkte, die für immer an die Sezession und ihren blutigen Krieg erinnern werden – die erste Fahne des Konföderierten Staaten von Amerika, die *Stars and Bars,* und die grauen Uniformen der Südstaatler.
Marschall, der Sohn des Tabakwarenfabrikanten Emanuel Marschall, wurde 1829 in St. Wendel geboren. Statt im Familienunternehmen mitzuarbeiten, wie es damals üblich war, folgte der junge Nicola seinen künstlerischen Neigungen und studierte an der Düsseldorfer Kunstakademie Porträtmalerei. Die turbulenten vierziger Jahre brachten nicht nur politische Umwälzungen, sondern auch den wirtschaftlichen Niedergang für viele mittelständische Betriebe. Diese Konstellation und die aufkommenden Konkurrenz der Daguerrotypie, der Wegbereiterin der Fotografie, ließen in Marschall den Entschluß reifen, sein Glück in der Neuen Welt zu versuchen. Mit des Vaters Segen und der amtlichen Befreiung vom Militärdienst reiste er im Alter von 18 Jahren nach New Orleans.
Er ließ sich in Marion in Alabama nieder und fand eine Anstellung als Lehrer für Malerei, Musik, Französisch und Deutsch an einer Töchterschule. Dort blieb er bis 1857. Für zwei Jahre kehrte er dann nach Preußen zurück, unternahm Reisen und setzte das Malereistudium fort.
Nach Marion zurückgekehrt, hatte Marschall großen Erfolg als Porträtist vermögender Pflanzer und prominenter Südstaatler. Als der Krieg ausbrach, engagierte ihn die loyale Südstaatlerin Mrs. Napoleon Lockett als Entwerfer für die Fahne und die Uniform der Konföderierten Truppen. Preußische Uniformen, die Marschall auf einer Italienreise gesehen hatte, dienten ihm dabei als Vorbild. Aktenkundig ist auch sein kurzfristiger Dienst in der Bürgermiliz von Alabama.
1873 zog Marschall mit seiner Familie nach Louisville, Kentucky, wo er ein Atelier eröffnete und viele Offiziere und Prominente der Bürgerkriegsära porträtierte. Dort starb er in seinem Haus am 24. Februar 1917 im Alter von achtundachtzig Jahren.

Nicola Marschall (1829–1917)

Abraham Lincoln, leader of the northern states, posthumously painted by Nicola Marschall, designer of the Confederate flag

Abraham Lincoln, der Führer der Nordstaaten, postum porträtiert von Nicola Marschall, dem Schöpfer der Südstaatenflagge.

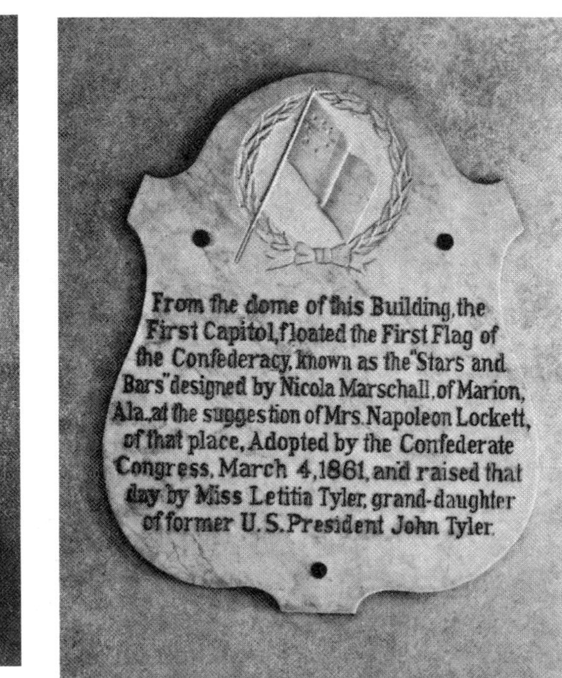

Marble commemorative plaque in the first capitol of the Confederate States of America in Montgomery, Alabama

Marmorne Gedenktafel im ersten Kapitol der Konföderierten Staaten von Amerika in Montgomery, Alabama

Painter of the Wild West

Albert Bierstadt

Der Maler des Wilden Westens

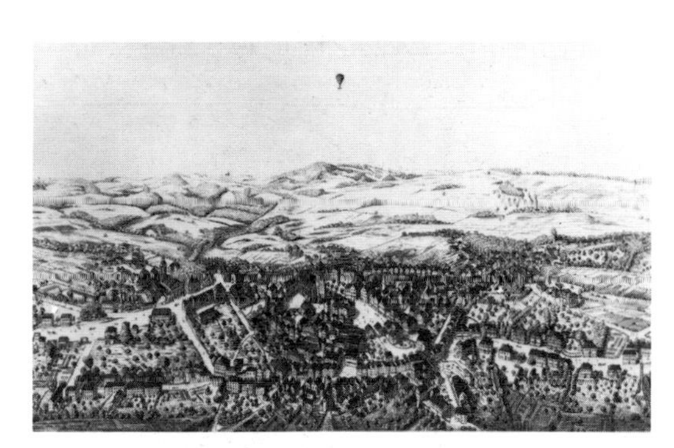

View of Solingen from around the middle of the 19th century, not far from Düsseldorf, where Bierstadt was later to study

Solingen, nicht weit von Bierstadts späterem Studienort Düsseldorf gelegen, auf einer Ansicht um die Mitte des 19. Jahrhunderts.

"Last of the Buffalo," one of Bierstadt's later works: at the time of this painting the title had almost become reality.

»Die letzten Büffel«, ein Spätwerk Bierstadts, gemalt zu einer Zeit, da sein Titel fast Realität geworden war

Albert Bierstadt, who was born in Solingen in 1830 and at the age of two moved with his family to America, returned to Germany in 1853 to study at Düsseldorf under C. F. Lessing, Andreas Achenbach, and the German-American Emanuel Leutze, who was 14 years his senior. A profound change was taking place in European landscape painting at that time: idealized landscapes, often serving as backgrounds for romanticized figures out of myths or stories, were beginning to give way to painting from nature, realistically capturing the outdoor moods. It was particularly Andreas Achenbach who exercised a lasting influence on Bierstadt, who managed to combine what he learned in Germany with the American feeling for space exemplified by the famous Hudson River School, and come up with his own unmistakable personal style.

In 1859, back in America, Bierstadt took part in General Frederick Lander's surveying expedition on the Oregon Trail. There he came into contact with what was to become the central subject of his art: the frontier landscapes and above all, the Rocky Mountains, whose dramatic presence seemed to reflect the spirit of the epoch, the great westward migration. During this trip and three later ones, Bierstadt made hundreds of drawings and oil sketches for use back in his studios in Irvington on the Hudson and New York as models for his large-scale paintings, which successfully combined a realistic perception of nature with a romantic spirit and sure-fire theatrical effects. In the course of the 1860s he became one of the most sought-after and highest paid American painters. But in the 1890s, as the French Impressionists came into vogue, Bierstadt sank into oblivion. When he died in 1902, time seemed to have passed his work by. However, only half a century later, historical distance permitted a new impartiality and Bierstadt's importance as a landscape artist was rediscovered and acknowledged. Even outside the museums he was posthumously honored by having Mt. Bierstadt and Lake Bierstadt on the Bierstadt Trail named after him.

Als der am 7. Januar 1830 in Solingen geborene und bereits im Alter von zwei Jahren ausgewanderte Albert Bierstadt 1853 nach Düsseldorf zurückkehrte, um dort unter C.F. Lessing und Andreas Achenbach und bei dem vierzehn Jahre älteren Deutschamerikaner Emanuel Leutze zu studieren, vollzog sich in der europäischen Landschaftsmalerei ein tiefgreifender Wandel: die Ideallandschaften, oft vollgestellt mit romantisierenden Historienstaffagen, begannen dem Malen nach der Natur und der realistischen Stimmungserfassung zu weichen. Vor allem Andreas Achenbach wurde so für Bierstadt zu einem prägenden Einfluß, den er mit dem amerikanischen Raumverständnis der berühmten Hudson River School zu einem unverwechselbaren Personalstil zu verschmelzen verstand.

1859, in die USA heimgekehrt, nahm Bierstadt an General Frederick Landers Landvermessungsexpedition auf dem Oregon Trail teil und fand dort sein großes Thema: die Landschaften der *frontier*, vor allem der Rocky Mountains, in deren Dramatik sich der Geist der Epoche, der großen Westwärtsbewegung, selbst widerzuspiegeln schien. Bierstadt nahm, was sich seinem Auge auf dieser und drei späteren Reisen bot, in Hunderten von Ölskizzen und Zeichnungen auf, aus denen er in seinen Ateliers in Irvington am Hudson und in New York großformatige Gemälde komponierte, die realistische Naturdarstellung mit virtuosen Lichteffekten zu einer höchst erfolgsträchtigen Mischung verbanden. Im Lauf der 60er Jahre wurde Bierstadt zu einem der begehrtesten und höchstbezahlten amerikanischen Maler – um freilich ab 1890, als die Impressionisten in Mode zu kommen begannen, desto gründlicher in Vergessenheit zu geraten.

Als Bierstadt am 19. Februar 1902 in New York starb, war die Zeit über sein Werk hinweggegangen. Erst ein Halbjahrhundert später, als die historische Distanz neue Unbefangenheit erlaubte, wurde seine Bedeutung als Landschaftsmaler wiederentdeckt – und auch außerhalb der Museen erinnern heute noch der postum benannte Mt. Bierstadt und der Bierstadt-See, erreichbar über den Bierstadt Trail, an diesen deutschstämmigen Meister der amerikanischen Landschaft.

Dean of Classical Music

Leopold Damrosch

Wegbereiter der klassischen Musik

With their exceptional combination of musical talents, indefatigable drive and organizational prowess, Dr. Leopold Damrosch and his sons Frank and Walter were vitally instrumental in raising the quality of concert and opera performances in America to European professional standards, and making good music accessible to wider audiences.
Leopold Damrosch was born on 22 October 1832 in Posen. In accordance with the wish of his parents, he studied medicine, receiving his M.D. in 1854 from the Berlin University. But then he promptly turned his attention from the staff of Aesculapius to the musical staff. Within a year he was conducting at minor theaters, making appearances as solo violinist, and was hired by Franz Liszt, then conductor at the Weimar Court Opera, as leading violinist of its Grand Ducal Orchestra. Following several years in Weimar, during which time he met and married the young singer Helene von Heimburg, he was appointed conductor of the orchestra at Breslau in 1858. For the next thirteen years, apart from directing the Philharmonic Society and conducting at Breslau's municipal theater, he undertook tours with von Bülow and Tausig, appeared as soloist in Leipzig and Hamburg, founded a choral society in Breslau, and participated in chamber music evenings there. Both of his sons were born in Breslau; Frank (named after Franz Liszt) on 22 June 1859, and Walter on 30 January 1862. Among the regular guests at the Damrosch home, whom the boys met as children, were Wagner, Liszt, Joachim, Anton Rubinstein and Clara Schumann.
The outbreak of the Franco-Prussian War in 1870 so distressed Dr. Damrosch that he eagerly accepted an invitation to become conductor of the New York Arion Society in 1871. He took an instant liking to America and enthusiastically bid his family to join him in New York, where he founded the Oratorio Society in 1873 and the Symphony Society in 1878. In 1880 Columbia College added the honorary degree of Doctor of Music to his M.D. In 1881 he organized a mammoth music festival with a chorus of 1200 and orchestra of 300 musicians, and in addition to his other activities found time to compose a symphony, a violin concerto and seven cantatas. When the initial season of Italian opera at the Metropolitan (1883) proved a failure, Damrosch took over the directorship, sailed to Europe to hire singers for a season of German opera, and saved the institution. His productions firmly established Wagner's works in the Met's repertoire; yet he gave equal attention to non-German composers from Berlioz and Tschaikovsky to Verdi.
Overtaxed by the strain of the 1884/85 season, Leopold Damrosch succumbed to pneumonia on 15 February 1885. His duties at the Met were taken over by his 23-year-old son Walter, who had returned from musical studies in Europe, and who later became famous as symphonic conductor, composer of operas, and popularizer of music on the radio. But it was a not even 30-year-old Walter Damrosch who persuaded Andrew Carnegie to build the great concert hall named after him. Walter Damrosch remained active in music until his death on 22 December 1950, a month before his 89th birthday. His older brother Frank, who made a name for himself as choral conductor, founder of musical organizations, educator and author, died on 21 October 1937.

Ebenso reich an musikalischem wie an organisatorischem Talent und mit der nötigen Zähigkeit zur Durchsetzung ihrer Pläne begabt, haben Dr. Leopold Damrosch und seine Söhne Frank und Walter entscheidend dazu beigetragen, daß Oper und Konzert in den USA den professionellen Standard Europas erreichten und gute Musik einem breiten Publikum zugänglich wurde.
Leopold Damrosch wurde am 22. Oktober 1832 in Posen geboren. Dem Elternwunsch entsprechend, studierte er Medizin und promovierte 1854 an der Universität Berlin. Schon bald jedoch wandte er seine Aufmerksamkeit vom Merkurstab ab und dem Dirigentenstab zu. Schon nach einem Jahr dirigierte er an kleineren Theatern, trat als Geigenvirtuose auf und wurde von Franz Liszt, damals Hofkapellmeister an der Weimarer Oper, als erster Konzertmeister an das großherzogliche Orchester engagiert. Nach mehrjährigem Aufenthalt in Weimar, wo er auch seine Frau Helene von Heimburg kennenlernte und heiratete, wurde Damrosch 1858 zum Kapellmeister in Breslau ernannt. Neben seiner Dirigententätigkeit im Orchesterverein und am Stadttheater unternahm er in den folgenden dreizehn Jahren Konzertreisen mit von Bülow und Tausig, trat als Solist in Hamburg und Leipzig auf und gründete einen Gesangverein in Breslau, wo er sich auch an Kammerkonzerten beteiligte. Seine Söhne wurden beide in Breslau geboren – Frank (benannt nach Franz Liszt) am 22. Juni 1859 und Walter am 30. Januar 1862. Regelmäßige Gäste im Hause Damrosch, denen die Kinder dort begegneten, waren Wagner und Liszt, der Geiger Joachim, Anton Rubinstein und Clara Schumann.
Der Ausbruch des deutsch-französischen Krieges 1870 traf Damrosch so schwer, daß er 1871 ohne Zögern der Einladung folgte, Dirigent des New Yorker Arion-Vereins zu werden. Er faßte eine spontane Zuneigung zu Amerika und bat seine Familie in begeisterten Briefen, ihm nach New York zu folgen, wo er 1873 die Oratorien-Gesellschaft und 1878 die Symphonische Gesellschaft gründete. 1880 fügte das Columbia College seinem Dr. med. den Ehrendoktor für Musik hinzu. 1881 organisierte Damrosch ein Mammutkonzert mit 1200 Sängern und 300 Instrumentalisten. Daneben fand er Zeit, eine Symphonie, ein Violinkonzert und sieben Kantaten zu komponieren. Als sich 1883 die Eröffnungssaison der Metropolitan Opera mit einem italienischen Programm als Mißerfolg entpuppte, übernahm Damrosch die Leitung, reiste nach Europa, engagierte Sängerinnen und Sänger für eine Saison mit deutschen Opern und konnte so den Ruin des Hauses abwenden. Seine Aufführungen machten die Werke Wagners zum festen Bestandteil des Met-Repertoires, doch widmete er nichtdeutschen Komponisten, von Berlioz und Tschaikowsky bis zu Verdi, die gleiche Aufmerksamkeit.
Von den Anstrengungen der Saison 1884/85 erschöpft, erlag Leopold Damrosch am 15. Februar 1885 einer Lungenentzündung. Die Verpflichtungen an der Met übernahm sein 23jähriger Sohn Walter, der von seinem Musikstudium in Europa zurückgekehrt war und später als Konzertdirigent, Opernkomponist und Pionier der Musikübertragungen im Rundfunk hervortreten sollte. Walter Damrosch war noch nicht 30, als er Andrew Carnegie zur Stiftung des nach ihm benannten Konzertsaals überredete, und er nahm bis zu seinem Tod am 22. Dezember 1950, nur einen Monat vor seinem 89. Geburtstag, aktiv am Musikleben teil. Sein älterer Bruder Frank, der sich als Chorleiter, Gründer von Musikvereinen, Pädagoge und Buchautor einen Namen machte, starb am 21. Oktober 1937.

Leopold Damrosch (1832–1885)

An open-air mass choir in New York in the 90s, directed by Frank Damrosch from a mezzanine window

Ein Freiluft-Massenchor im New York der 90er Jahre, aus einem Fenster im Hochparterre dirigiert von Frank Damrosch

Power, Wealth and Integrity

Henry Villard

Macht, Reichtum und Integrität

Henry Villard (1835–1900)

The classically American success story of Henry Villard, journalist, railroad tycoon and philanthropist, began in Germany, where he was born as Heinrich Hilgard in Speyer (Rhenish Palatinate) on 10 April 1835. He grew up in the town of Zweibrücken, where as a youth, his republican sentiments put him at odds with both his father and the regime, and he decided, as so many of the 48ers, to depart for America. At the age of eighteen, with no money, no connections and no knowledge of English, he arrived in New York. In 1854, under his new name, Henry Villard, he moved to the German-settled areas of Illinois and, with the aid of a cousin, Villard began his first career as a journalist, writing for German-language newspapers. He became a supporter of abolitionism, covered the great historical events of the era, such as the Lincoln-Douglas debates and the Civil War, became friends with Lincoln and within a decade worked himself up to the position of Eastern correspondent for the *Chicago Tribune*. In 1866 he married Fanny Garrison, daughter of William Lloyd Garrison, and, after a trip to Paris, the couple settled down in Boston where Villard became secretary of the American Social Science Association.

Villard's second career as railroad entrepreneur began in 1873 on a trip to Germany, where he met with German railroad investors who were concerned about their American holdings in the Oregon & California Railroad. As their agent, he returned to investigate the operation of that company, reorganize it and eventually become its president. He achieved his first important financial success by helping the Kansas Pacific Railway out of difficulties through a merger with the Union Pacific. And in 1881, with a total sum of 20 million dollars contributed by friends in a "blind pool", he was able to gain control of the Northern Pacific Railroad and dominate the transportation industry in the entire Pacific Northwest. Villard nevertheless remained active in other fields. He realized a dream of his by acquiring control of the New York *Evening Post*. In 1890, Villard bought out Thomas Alva Edison's companies, to which he had already provided financial backing, and combined them into the Edison General Electric Company, which three years later evolved into the General Electric Company. And before his death at Dobbs Ferry, New York, on 12 November 1900, he left an architectural monument to New York City – the Italian-style apartment house between Madison and Park Avenue, formerly the Villard Mansion and now known as the Helmsley Palace.

Die prototypische amerikanische Erfolgsgeschichte Henry Villards, des Journalisten, Eisenbahnmagnaten und Philanthropen, begann in Speyer, Rheinland-Pfalz, wo er am 10. April 1835 als Heinrich Hilgard geboren wurde. Er wuchs in Zweibrücken auf. Seine Begeisterung für republikanisches Gedankengut stellte den jungen Villard gegen Vater und Obrigkeit, und, wie so viele »Achtundvierziger«, verließ er die Heimat. Als Achtzehnjähriger kam er in New York an, ohne Geld, Verbindungen oder Englischkenntnisse zu besitzen. 1854 zog er unter seinem neuen Namen Henry Villard in das von Deutschen besiedelte Gebiet von Illinois und startete, von einem Vetter unterstützt, seine erste Karriere als Journalist mit Beiträgen für deutschsprachige Zeitungen. Er setzte sich für die Abschaffung der Sklaverei ein, kommentierte die großen Ereignisse seiner Zeit, wie die Debatte zwischen Lincoln und Douglas und den Bürgerkrieg, wurde ein persönlicher Freund Lincolns und arbeitete sich zum Oststaatenkorrespondenten der *Chicago Tribune* hoch. 1866 heiratete er Fanny Garrison, die Tochter des Abolitionisten William Lloyd Garrison. Nach einer Parisreise ließ sich das Paar in Boston nieder, wo Villard Geschäftsführer der Amerikanischen Gesellschaft für Sozialwissenschaften wurde.

Die zweite Erfolgslaufbahn schlug er 1873 als Agent einer Eisenbahngesellschaft bei einem Deutschlandbesuch ein, wo er mit Aktionären zusammentraf, die sich um ihre Oregon & California Railroad-Aktien sorgten. Daraufhin strengte er entsprechende Untersuchungen an, erwirkte Verbesserungen und wurde schließlich Präsident des Unternehmens. Sein erster finanzieller Geniestreich war die Fusionierung der Kansas Pacific Railway, die in erheblichen Schwierigkeiten war, mit der Union Pacific. Nachdem befreundete Unternehmer ohne Kenntnis des Verwendungszwecks zwanzig Millionen Dollar in einen Fond gezahlt hatten, erwarb er die Aktienmehrheit der Northern Pacific Railroad und beherrschte damit das gesamte Transportnetz des Nordwestens. Auch als Eisenbahn-Tycoon blieb Villard noch auf anderen Gebieten aktiv. Er erfüllte sich einen alten Traum, als er die New Yorker *Evening Post* unter seine Kontrolle brachte, und im Jahre 1890 übernahm er die Gesellschaften des Erfinders Thomas Alva Edison, den er schon vorher finanziell unterstützt hatte: Aus Edison Betrieben wurde die »Edison General Electric Company«, aus der drei Jahre später die heutige General Electric Company hervorging. Und auch ein architektonisches Monument hinterließ Henry Villard bei seinem Tod am 12. November 1900 in Dobbs Ferry im Staat New York: die Villa im italienischen Stil, die heute Teil des Helmsley Palace Hotels in New York ist, war ursprünglich sein Wohnhaus.

Maiden run of the Northern Pacific's "Gold Spike Special" in September 1883 along the stretch built by Villard (from St. Paul, Minnesota, to Portland, Oregon).

Eröffnungsfahrt des »Gold Spike Special«-Sonderzugs der Northern Pacific auf der von Villard gebauten Strecke von St. Paul in Minnesota nach Portland, Oregon, im September 1883

Villard's villa in New York, today dwarfed by a skyscraper and part of a hotel.

Villards New Yorker Villa, heute von einem Wolkenkratzer überragt und Teil eines Hotels

The Father of Modern Political Cartooning

Thomas Nast

Der Begründer der modernen politischen Karikatur

Thomas Nast, the son of a Bavarian army bandsman, was born in 1840 in Landau, in the Rhenish Palatinate. At the age of six he came to America with his family. Before he learned English he was able to express himself with simple drawings on his slate. His artistic talent enabled him to enter an art school at an early age, but he had to leave at fifteen in order to support his family. Upon his first interview he was immediately hired as illustrator for *Leslie's Weekly* at four dollars per week. He began his career with a cartoon attacking civic corruption. In 1860, at the age of 20, he covered a heavyweight championship in London for the *New York Illustrated News*. From there he joined the forces of Garibaldi in Italy as war correspondent. With the outbreak of the American Civil War, he returned to the United States, where he married his fiancée Sarah Edwards, a well-educated young lady who contributed in no small measure to her husband's success. In the spring of 1862 Nast joined the staff of *Harper's Weekly* as Civil War correspondent, visiting the battlefields in the South and the Border States and sending back on-the-scene sketches. At the end of the war, Nast had become a nationally known figure as political cartoonist. From now on he took up nearly every national issue of political and social significance. Nast was a champion of the underprivileged and a protagonist of equal rights for all citizens – not only for the newly freed Negro slaves, but for other minority groups as well, such as the American Indians. He also took sides with the Chinese after their immigration had been restricted. He criticized the administration, which pretended to serve "the public good", lampooned bigotry in the Catholic Church, dealt with economic and monetary issues and made Victoria Woodhull and her theories of "Free Love" the receptacle for his stinging irony. Between 1861 and 1884, Thomas Nast and *Harper's Weekly* were considered bulwarks of Republicanism and Nast's greatest influence was obviously in politics. He was even called the "president maker", since every presidential candidate whom he supported was elected. Nast popularized several political symbols: the Democratic donkey, the Republican elephant, the Tammany tiger. He also gave us our present-day conception of Uncle Sam, John Bull and Columbia. The figure Nast drew, which was based on *Pelznikel*, the St. Nicholas of his German ancestors, is the famous Santa Claus, now known to everybody in the country.

After the death of Nast's friend and supporter Fletcher Harper, a younger generation of editors changed the policy of the magazine. It became less liberal and Nast's career declined. Not willing to tolerate any censorship, Nast thought that after more than twenty-five years of work, it was time to travel, to rest, and to devote more of his hours to his family. He put together a collection of Christmas drawings, which were published in 1890 under the title, *Thomas Nast's Christmas Drawings for the Human Race*.

When one of his cherished plans, publishing his own magazine, failed, he fell into debt. Therefore he accepted an appointment as Consul General to Ecuador, offered to him by one of his old admirers, Theodore Roosevelt. But the tropical heat and the unsanitary living conditions in Ecuador were too much for the sixty-two-year-old artist. On December 7, 1902, he succumbed to an epidemic of yellow fever – not without having paid back his debts and leaving some money for his family.

Thomas Nast wurde am 26. September 1840 als Sohn eines bayerischen Militärmusikers in Landau in der Pfalz geboren. Als Sechsjähriger wanderte er mit seiner Familie nach Amerika aus. Noch nicht des Englischen mächtig, konnte sich der Knabe mit Zeichnungen auf seiner Schiefertafel verständlich machen. Schon früh durfte er eine Kunstschule besuchen, mußte sie jedoch mit 15 wieder verlassen, um zum Familienunterhalt beizutragen. Nach der ersten Vorsprache bei *Leslie's Weekly* wurde er für vier Dollar die Woche als Illustrator engagiert. Nasts Laufbahn begann mit einer Karikatur über die Korruption in der Stadtverwaltung. Der Zwanzigjährige berichtete aus London für die *New York Illustrated News* über einen Schwergewichtsboxkampf und schloß sich in Italien Garibaldis Truppen als Bildberichterstatter an. Bei Ausbruch des amerikanischen Bürgerkrieges kehrte er in die Vereinigten Staaten zurück und heiratete seine Verlobte Sarah Edwards – eine gebildete, junge Dame, die nicht wenig zu seinem Erfolg beitrug. Im Auftrag von *Harper's Weekly* suchte Nast während des Krieges die Schlachtfelder des Südens auf und schickte von dort so eindrucksvolle Skizzen nach Hause, daß er am Ende des Krieges im ganzen Land bekannt war. Von nun an gab es kaum ein Problem von politischer oder sozialer Brisanz, das Nast nicht als Karikaturist aufgriff. Sein Eintreten für die Gleichberechtigung aller Bürger galt nicht nur den gerade befreiten schwarzen Sklaven, sondern auch anderen Minoritäten wie z. B. den Indianern und den Chinesen. Mit spitzem Zeichenstift attackierte er die Stadtverwaltung, die vorgab dem »Gemeinwohl« zu dienen, enthüllte die Bigotterie der katholischen Kirche und nahm Wirtschafts- und Währungsprobleme ebenso aufs Korn wie die Verfechterin der »Freien Liebe«, Victoria Woodhull.

Zwischen 1861 und 1884 galten Thomas Nast und *Harper's Weekly* als Bollwerk der Republikaner und zweifellos war Nasts Einfluß im politischen Bereich am größten. Man nannte ihn sogar den »Präsidentenmacher«, da jeder von ihm unterstützte Kandidat gewählt wurde. Nast machte mehrere politische Symbolfiguren populär: den Esel für die Demokraten, den Elefanten für die Republikaner und den Tiger für die korrupten Tammany-Demokraten. Auch unserer gegenwärtigen Vorstellung von Uncle Sam, John Bull und der Columbia verlieh er Gestalt. Und den berühmten Santa Claus hat Nast nach dem Vorbild des »Pelznikel«, des Sankt Nikolaus seiner deutschen Vorfahren, gestaltet.

Der Tod seines Gönners Fletcher Harper brachte eine jüngere Redakteursgeneration ans Ruder. Die Politik des Blattes war nicht mehr so liberal und Nast nicht mehr so erfolgreich. Da er keine Zensur von oben dulden wollte, zog er sich nach mehr als 25jähriger Tätigkeit zurück. Seine letzte Arbeit für *Harper's* war die Zusammenstellung seiner gesammelten Weihnachtszeichnungen, die 1890 unter dem Titel *Thomas Nast's Christmas Drawings for the Human Race* veröffentlicht wurde.

Durch das Scheitern eines seiner Lieblingspläne – der Herausgabe einer eigenen Karikaturzeitschrift – geriet Nast in Schulden. Als ihm daraufhin sein alter Bewunderer Theodore Roosevelt den Posten eines Generalkonsuls in Ecuador anbot, nahm er diesen Vorschlag an. Doch das tropische Klima und die unhygienischen Lebensbedingungen waren zuviel für den 62jährigen Künstler. Am 7. Dezember 1902 starb er am Gelbfieber – nicht ohne vorher seine Schulden beglichen und seiner Familie etwas Geld hinterlassen zu haben.

Thomas Nast (1840–1902)

The artist with the pointed pencil: Nast's self-caricature with the self-ironic headline "Reform is necessary".

Der Künstler mit dem spitzen Stift: Selbstkarikatur Nasts vor der beziehungsreichen Schlagzeile »Reform tut not«

Nasts bissige Karikatur von Victoria Woodhull, der »schrecklichen Sirene«, die auch die erste englische Übersetzung des kommunistischen Manifests druckte und sich im Jahre 1872 als erste Frau um die amerikanische Präsidentschaft bewarb.

Nast's malicious cartoon of Victoria Woodhull, "the terrible siren", who was also the printer of the first English translation of the Communist Manifesto, and, in 1872, the first woman to run for the presidency.

The Nast Medallion, since 1978 first prize in a biannual caricature contest for German and American artists sponsored by Landau, Nast's city of origin. In addition to the medallion, the winner is also entitled to his weight in Palatinate wine.

Die Nast-Medaille, seit 1978 der Hauptpreis eines von Nasts Heimatstadt Landau in zweijährigem Turnus ausgeschriebenen Karikaturenwettbewerbs für deutsche und amerikanische Zeichner. Zusätzlich zum Gewinn der Medaille wird der Sieger in pfälzischem Wein aufgewogen.

Nast at the time of the Civil War, in a portrait by the famous photographer, Mathew Brady. Nast's drawings were so committed to the Union cause that they prompted President Lincoln to remark: "Thomas Nast has been our best recruiting sergeant."

Nast zur Zeit des amerikanischen Bürgerkriegs, porträtiert von dem berühmten Fotografen Mathew Brady. Nasts zeichnerisches Engagement für die Union veranlaßte Präsident Lincoln zu dem Ausspruch: »Thomas Nast war unser bester Truppenwerber.«

Nast derived his "Santa Claus" from "Pelznikel", the St. Nicholas of Palatinate folklore, and for thirty years it appeared on the title page of every Christmas edition of "Harper's Weekly".

Vom »Pelznikel«, der Nikolausgestalt der pfälzischen Folklore, leitete Nast seinen »Santa Claus« ab, den er dreißig Jahre lang auf der Titelseite jeder Weihnachtsnummer von »Harper's Weekly« auftreten ließ.

In the Federal Republic of Germany, where Nast was practically unknown, the past several years have surprisingly seen a veritable Nast boom. The photo shows its leading initiator and curator of the Nast Museum in Landau, Hermann Glessgen, at the opening of a Nast exhibition in Bonn. Also present are the American ambassador and the Minister President of the Rhenish Palatinate, Bernhard Vogel.

In der Bundesrepublik Deutschland, wo Nast so gut wie unbekannt war, zeichnet sich in den letzten Jahren ein überraschender Nast-Boom ab. Das Foto zeigt dessen Hauptinitiator, den Kurator des Landauer Nast-Museums, Hermann Glessgen, bei der Eröffnung einer Nast-Ausstellung in Bonn in Gegenwart des amerikanischen Botschafters und des Ministerpräsidenten von Rheinland-Pfalz, Bernhard Vogel.

John Peter Altgeld

John Peter Altgeld, the first Democratic governor of Illinois after the Civil War, was the son of an illiterate and indigent German immigrant who had come to the U.S. shortly after the birth of his son on December 30, 1847. Growing up near Mansfield, Ohio, Altgeld received little formal education. Nevertheless, after serving 100 days as a private in the Union Army (1864/65), he worked as a school teacher in Missouri. He subsequently began to study and practice law there and, in 1874, was elected district attorney of Andrew County, Missouri.
Moving to Chicago in 1875, Altgeld soon became an active Democrat. He was judge of the Superior Court of Cook County from 1886 to 1891 and was its chief justice when he retired. At that time, his influence among Illinois Democrats was such that he was nominated for governor in 1892; his ensuing election to a four-year term in that office came as part of the wave of Democratic success - chiefly due to farm and labor voters - after 1890.
A little treatise on crime (1884) had been early evidence of Altgeld's belief that the poor and unfortunate had less than a fair chance in American life. Accordingly, now as governor, he embarked on a program of reform which included the improvement of prison conditions, education, and working conditions in factories.
During his term as governor, Altgeld was discussed and condemned with whole-hearted bitterness in the daily press, especially in 1893, when he pardoned the three surviving anarchists convicted of alleged conspiracy in the Haymarket Riot of 1886. This action and his protest to President Cleveland regarding the use of federal troops in the Pullman strike (1894) aroused considerable opposition among conservative elements, and Altgeld was not re-elected in 1896.
Altgeld was a champion of free silver and an active supporter of William J. Bryan for the presidency in 1896 and 1900. He died suddenly in 1902, shortly after he had lost the large fortune which he had accumulated through speculation in Chicago real estate.

John Peter Altgeld, erster Gouverneur der Demokraten in Illinois nach dem Bürgerkrieg, war der Sohn eines unbemittelten deutschen Immigranten, der kurz nach der Geburt seines Sohnes am 30. Dezember 1847 in die USA auswanderte. Ohne eigene Schulbildung in der Nähe von Mansfield, Ohio, aufgewachsen, begann Altgeld in Missouri zunächst als Lehrer zu arbeiten, nachdem er in der Schlußphase des Bürgerkriegs noch 100 Tage als Soldat der Unionsarmee gedient hatte. Ein Studium der Jurisprudenz und die Eröffnung einer Anwaltskanzlei schlossen sich an. 1874 wurde Altgeld zum Staatsanwalt gewählt. Ein Jahr später übersiedelte er nach Chicago und wurde in der demokratischen Partei aktiv. Als er sich 1891 nach fünfjähriger Tätigkeit als höchster Richter aus dem Obersten Gerichtshof von Chicago zurückzog, war sein Einfluß bereits so groß geworden, daß er im folgenden Jahr als Kandidat für die Gouverneurswahl aufgestellt wurde. Sein Wahlsieg spiegelte nicht zuletzt den Rückhalt wider, den die Demokraten seit 1890 vor allem bei den Farmern und Arbeitern gefunden hatten.
Schon früh - 1884 - hatte Altgeld in einer kurzen Denkschrift über die Kriminalität seine Überzeugung vertreten, daß dem Besitzlosen in den USA keine faire Chance bliebe. Als Gouverneur setzte er sich nun für ein Reformprogramm ein, das in erster Linie auf Verbesserungen im Strafvollzug, im Erziehungswesen und bei den Arbeitsbedingungen in den Fabriken abzielte.
Während seiner Amtszeit wurde Altgeld immer wieder Ziel erbitterter Angriffe der Presse, besonders als er 1893 die drei noch lebenden Anarchisten begnadigte, die wegen angeblicher konspirativer Tätigkeit bei den Haymarket-Unruhen von 1886 verurteilt worden waren. Dies und sein Protest gegen die von Präsident Cleveland angeordnete Entsendung von Bundestruppen zur Niederschlagung des Pullman-Streiks (1894) setzten Altgeld der Kritik vieler Konservativer aus.
Nach seiner Wahlniederlage 1896 engagierte sich Altgeld stark in der Silber-Frage und in den beiden Wahlzügen William J. Bryans zum Präsidenten. Nach dem Verlust seines Vermögens, das er als Immobilienspekulant erworben hatte, starb er unerwartet am 12. März 1902.

John Peter Altgeld (1847-1902)

Execution of anarchists in the wake of the Haymarket Bombing of 4 May 1886. Three who received jail sentences despite lack of conclusive evidence against them, were pardoned by Altgeld in June 1893.

Hinrichtung von Anarchisten nach dem Haymarket-Attentat vom 4. Mai 1886. Drei weitere Verurteilte, gegen die ebenfalls ein Gesinnungsurteil ohne schlüssigen Beweis ihrer Schuld gefällt worden war, begnadigte Altgeld im Juni 1893.

Having already become a controversial figure because of the pardons, Altgeld became the definitive bogeyman of the conservative press after the 1894 Pullman strike. W.A. Rogers' caricature in "Harper's Weekly" of July 21, 1894, shows him at right, the leader of a horde of anarchists.

Schon durch die Begnadigungen umstritten, wurde Altgeld nach dem Pullman-Streik von 1894 endgültig zum Buhmann der konservativen Presse. Die Karikatur von W. A. Rogers aus »Harper's Weekly« vom 21. Juli 1894 zeigt ihn ganz rechts als Anführer der Anarchistenhorde.

First to Record Sound on Discs

Emile Berliner

Der Vater der »Schellacks«

Emile Berliner with his most famous invention.
Emile Berliner mit seiner bekanntesten Erfindung

Street in Hannover's old town where Emile Berliner was born in 1851.
Straße in der Altstadt von Hannover, wo Emil Berliner 1851 geboren wurde.

Many of the objects which we have come to take for granted in our modern world owe their very existence to ingenious figures of the past. So it is with the common phonograph record which, if it hadn't been for the German-born inventor, Emile Berliner, might still be a wax cylinder.
Berliner was born in Hanover on May 20, 1851, the fourth of eleven children of a Jewish merchant, Samuel Berliner, and his wife, Sarah. He attended the Samson School in Wolfenbüttel for four years and, upon graduating in 1865, began working, first in a print-shop and later as a clerk in a dry goods store. When a friend of the family, Nathan Gotthelf, a prosperous Washington merchant, came to visit, bringing with him descriptions of America as a land of unlimited opportunities, Berliner resolved to leave his drab existence and, in April 1870, shortly before the outbreak of the Franco-Prussian War, he sailed to America.
After three years in Washington as a clerk in Gotthelf's store, he went to New York where he worked at a number of odd jobs, including bottlewasher in the laboratory of Dr. Fahlberg, the discoverer of saccharin. He was so fascinated by this experience of science that he began reading books on physics and electricity. Upon returning to Washington in 1876, he continued to study and experiment at home, where he set up a small electrical laboratory. He became particularly interested in Bell's telephone. His first invention was a much improved transmitter (microphone), patented in 1877, as a result of which he was invited to join the Bell Telephone Company. Then he turned his attention to Edison's "talking machine". Convinced that sound could be recorded without distortions, he developed the first "gramophone" to record horizontally on a flat disc-record which he designed, instead of vertically on a cylinder. Soon thereafter he founded the Berliner Gramophone Company in Philadelphia.
After the turn of the century Berliner continued to do work in the field of acoustics. But a greater part of his time was dedicated towards humanitarian projects such as the reduction of the infant mortality rate (his son Henry having nearly died) and the movement to introduce pasteurization in the U.S. On August 3, 1929, Berliner died in Washington D.C.

Vieles, was wir in unserer modernen Welt als selbstverständlich hinnehmen, verdanken wir dem Erfindungsgeist genialer Persönlichkeiten der Vergangenheit. So verhält es sich auch mit der allseits bekannten Schallplatte, die ohne den in Deutschland geborenen Erfinder Emil (anglisiert Emile) Berliner vielleicht immer noch die Gestalt eines Wachszylinders hätte.
Berliner wurde am 20. Mai 1851 in Hannover als viertes von elf Kindern des jüdischen Kaufmanns Samuel Berliner und dessen Frau Sarah geboren. Er besuchte vier Jahre lang die Samson-Schule zu Wolfenbüttel und verdingte sich nach dem Abschluß 1865 zunächst in einer Druckerei, später als Gehilfe in einem Textilgeschäft. Als Nathan Gotthelf, ein Freund der Familie und wohlhabender Kaufmann, aus Washington zu Besuch kam und von Amerika als dem Land der unbegrenzten Möglichkeiten schwärmte, entschloß sich Berliner zur Probe aufs Exempel und reiste im April 1870, kurz vor Ausbruch des deutsch-französischen Krieges, nach Amerika.
Nach dreijähriger Hilfsarbeit in Gotthelfs Geschäft in Washington ging er nach New York, wo er sich mit Gelegenheitsarbeiten durchschlug und unter anderem als Flaschenspüler im Labor von Dr. Fahlberg, dem Erfinder des Saccharin, arbeitete. Dieser erste Kontakt mit der Wissenschaft beeindruckte Berliner so nachhaltig, daß er sich in Bücher über Physik und Elektrizität zu vertiefen begann. 1876 kehrte er nach Washington zurück und setzte seine Studien und Experimente zuhause fort, wo er ein kleines Labor eingerichtet hatte.
Vornehmlich interessierte ihn Bells Telefon. Als erstes erfand er dazu ein 1877 patentiertes neuartiges Mikrophon, das ihm das Angebot eintrug, der Bell Telephone Company beizutreten. Danach widmete sich Berliner Bells »Sprechapparat«. Überzeugt, daß Klänge verzerrungsfrei wiedergegeben werden können, entwickelte er das erste »Grammophon« zum horizontalen Abspielen einer selbsterfundenen Schallplatte, mit der er den vertikalen Zylinder ersetzte. Wenig später gründete er in Philadelphia die Berliner Gramophone Company.
Nach der Jahrhundertwende setzte Berliner seine Arbeit auf dem Gebiet der Akustik fort. Einen Großteil seiner Zeit widmete er jedoch humanitären Zwecken, wie der Minderung der Kindersterblichkeitsrate – sein Sohn Henry hätte fast dieses Schicksal geteilt – und der Bewegung zur Einführung der Pasteurisierung in den Vereinigten Staaten. Am 3. August 1929 starb Berliner in Washington, D.C.

The original Gramophone: a model from 1889. Production of records in quantities did not begin until the end of the following decade.
Das Ur-Grammophon: ein Modell aus dem Jahr 1889. Die serienmäßige Schallplattenherstellung begann erst gegen Ende des folgenden Jahrzehnts.

A New Method of Language Teaching

Maximilian Berlitz

Erneuerer der Sprachpädagogik

Maximilian Delphinius Berlitz, the founder of the Berlitz Schools, was born in 1852 in Wurttemberg. Although his exact birthplace has never been ascertained, it is known that he came from a family of teachers and mathematicians in the Black Forest.
In 1872, Berlitz came to Rhode Island where he worked for a while as a private language teacher in Westerly before accepting a permanent position as a teacher of French and German at the Warner Polytechnical College in Providence. Although the institute wasn't doing very well, in 1878 Berlitz purchased it from its owner, becoming not only the director but also the only teacher. Not long afterwards, he hired a young Frenchman, Nicholas Joly, to assist him. Joly arrived in Providence to find his new employer sick and feverish due to overwork. Moreover, Berlitz discovered, much to his dismay, that his new instructor spoke no English. Nevertheless, he directed Joly to take over the French classes - he was to teach them by pointing to objects, naming them and explaining verbs using only French.
After his recuperation six weeks later, Berlitz was amazed to find that, contrary to his expectation, his pupils had made more progress in the same period of time than they had under traditional methods of language instruction. He was quick to realize that this was the seed of a new kind of teaching method, which he immediately began employing in his school. The success Berlitz achieved with his new method encouraged him to open up a second language school in Boston in 1880. Soon other schools followed in New York and Washington, D. C. Eventually he established schools all over America and even exported them abroad. Between 1880 and 1900 he not only taught but managed to set his ideas down in writing, developing them into a systematic method which he then presented at the World's Fair in Paris in 1900.
After the turn of the century, Berlitz traveled extensively and received many honors and distinctions from countries all over the world. However, he remained an active language instructor until his death on April 6, 1921, in New York City.

Maximilian Delphinius Berlitz, Gründer der Berlitz-Schulen, wurde 1852 in Württemberg geboren. Zwar ist sein Geburtsort unbekannt, doch weiß man zumindest, daß er einer Familie von Lehrern und Mathematikern aus dem Schwarzwald entstammte.
1872 kam Berlitz in Rhode Island an, wo er eine Zeitlang in Westerly privaten Sprachunterricht gab, bevor er eine feste Anstellung als Lehrer für Französisch und Deutsch am Warner Polytechnical College in Providence erhielt. Bedauerlicherweise war es um das Institut nicht gerade gut bestellt, und 1878 kaufte es Berlitz dem Besitzer ab, was ihn nicht nur zum Direktor, sondern auch zum einzigen Lehrer der Schule machte. Wenig später holte er den jungen Franzosen Nicholas Joly als Assistenten zu sich. Joly kam nach Providence und fand seinen Arbeitgeber infolge von Überarbeitung krank und fiebernd vor. Zu allem Überfluß mußte Berlitz auch noch feststellen, daß sein neuer Dozent kein Wort Englisch sprach. Dennoch überantwortete er Joly den Französischunterricht, den dieser meisterte, indem er auf Gegenstände deutete, sie auf Französisch benannte und sogar Zeitwörter nur in seiner Muttersprache erklärte. Als Berlitz sechs Wochen später vom Krankenbett aufstand, stellte er verwundert fest, daß die Schüler entgegen seinen Befürchtungen weiter fortgeschritten waren, als es die traditionelle Lehrmethode erlaubt hätte. Es wurde ihm schnell klar, daß er den Schlüssel zu einer neuartigen Lehrmethode in Händen hielt, mit der er in seiner Schule sofort zu experimentieren begann. Durch den mit der neuen Methode erzielten Erfolg ermutigt, eröffnete er 1880 eine zweite Sprachenschule in Boston, der bald weitere in New York und Washington und schließlich auch im übrigen Amerika und im Ausland folgten. Zwischen 1880 und 1900 fand er neben seiner Lehrtätigkeit noch Zeit, sein pädagogisches Programm schriftlich niederzulegen und zu einer systematischen Methode weiterzuentwikkeln, die er auf der Pariser Weltausstellung im Jahre 1900 präsentierte.
Nach der Jahrhundertwende unternahm Berlitz ausgedehnte Reisen, und es wurden ihm aus aller Welt viele Auszeichnungen und Ehrentitel zuteil. Trotzdem arbeitete er weiterhin aktiv als Sprachlehrer, bis er am 6. April 1921 in New York starb.

Maximilian Berlitz (1852–1921)

One of the first foreign establishments: the Berlitz School on Oxford Street, London; in the photo from 1904 the festive adornment is in honor of Edward VII's coronation.

Eine der ersten Auslandsgründungen: die Berlitz School in der Oxford Street in London, auf dem Foto aus dem Jahre 1904 festlich geschmückt zu Ehren der Krönung Eduards VII.

Instruction of small groups at the Berlitz School in Milwaukee, 1900. Above right, the sign informs visitors that they should pay in advance.

Kleingruppenunterricht in der Berlitz-Schule in Milwaukee im Jahre 1900. Auf dem Schild rechts oben ist zu lesen, daß Vorkasse erbeten wird.

The Berlitz School – Milwaukee – 1900

The "Wizard of Schenectady"

Charles Proteus Steinmetz

Der »Zauberer von Schenectady«

Inventors among themselves: Thomas Alva Edison (ca. 1,000 patents, left) visiting Charles Proteus Steinmetz (ca. 200 patents) in his laboratory.

Erfinder unter sich: Thomas Alva Edison (ca. 1000 Patente, links) zu Besuch im Labor von Charles Proteus Steinmetz (ca. 200 Patente).

Charles Proteus Steinmetz, nicknamed toward the end of his career the "Wizard of Schenectady", was born Karl August Rudolf Steinmetz on April 9, 1865, in Breslau (now Wroclaw, Poland). The only child of a lithographer, Karl Heinrich, and his first wife Caroline, the boy Steinmetz exhibited an amazing aptitude in school, especially in the subjects of mathematics and physics but also in the classics, and he graduated from secondary school with honors. In 1882 he began his studies at the University of Breslau and, within a few years, was excelling in such complex fields of science as theoretical physics and electrical engineering. But in spite of his diligence, Steinmetz still found time to participate in the social life of the university which included becoming involved in student politics. In 1884 he joined a student socialist group and later worked as editor of the party newspaper, *The People's Voice*.

Four years later, just before receiving his doctoral degree, he was forced to flee the country because of an inflammatory editorial he had written. He first settled in Zurich where he lived for a year and then, in 1889, he sailed by steerage to the United States, arriving in New York in early summer.

With a letter of introduction from the German editor of an electrical journal, Steinmetz soon found a job as a draftsman for Rudolf Eickemeyer of Eickemeyer and Osterheld Manufacturing Company. But before long he established a laboratory of his own where he conducted much of his scientific research. There he developed the law of hysteresis which dealt with power loss in electrical devices and, while still in his twenties, he worked out a practical method for calculating alternating current circuits. When the company was bought by General Electric, Steinmetz was part of the deal and eventually became consulting engineer in Schenectady, the company's headquarters.

A conspicuous figure due to a physical deformity, Steinmetz was the author of many books, held two professorships and gave numerous lectures throughout the country while, as a Socialist Party member, he remained active in local American politics. He died in Schenectady on October 26, 1923.

Charles Proteus Steinmetz, auf dem Höhepunkt seiner Karriere unter dem Beinamen »Zauberer von Schenectady« bekannt, wurde als Karl August Rudolf Steinmetz am 9. April 1865 in Breslau, dem heutigen Wroclaw in Polen, geboren. Er war einziges Kind des Lithographen Karl Heinrich Steinmetz und dessen erster Frau Caroline, fiel früh durch hervorragende Leistungen in Mathematik und Physik, aber auch in den humanistischen Fächern auf und schloß das Gymnasium mit Auszeichnung ab. 1882 begann er in Breslau Elektrotechnik und theoretische Physik zu studieren. Trotz seines Lerneifers fand Steinmetz genügend Zeit, sich am studentischen Leben zu beteiligen, was auch politische Betätigung mit einschloß. Er trat einer sozialistischen Studentenvereinigung bei und wurde Herausgeber ihrer Zeitung *Stimme des Volkes*. Nach vier Jahren, kurz vor seiner Promotion, mußte er wegen eines aufrührerischen Leitartikels außer Landes fliehen. 1889 entschloß er sich, nach einjährigem Aufenthalt in Zürich, zur Überfahrt in die Vereinigten Staaten und kam im Frühsommer in New York an. Dem Empfehlungsschreiben des Herausgebers einer deutschen Fachzeitschrift für Elektrotechnik verdankte er die sofortige Anstellung als Konstrukteur bei der Eickemeyer and Osterfeld Manufacturing Company. Es dauerte nicht lange, bis Steinmetz über ein eigenes Laboratorium verfügte, in dem er den größten Teil der Forschungsarbeiten im Alleingang leistete. Dort löste er das Problem der Hystereseverluste in Elektromotoren und entwickelte, noch keine dreißig Jahre alt, eine einfache Methode zur Berechnung von Wechselstromkreisen. Als General Electric den Betrieb aufkaufte, war es vor allem Steinmetz, den man durch diesen Kauf erwerben wollte. Schließlich arbeitete er als technischer Berater in Schenectady, dem Hauptsitz des Konzerns.

Durch seine verwachsene Gestalt auch äußerlich eine markante Persönlichkeit, verfaßte Steinmetz zahlreiche Bücher, bekam zweimal die Professorenwürde verliehen und hielt als weiterhin aktives Mitglied der Sozialistischen Partei landesweit viele Vorträge. Er starb am 26. Oktober 1923 in Schenectady.

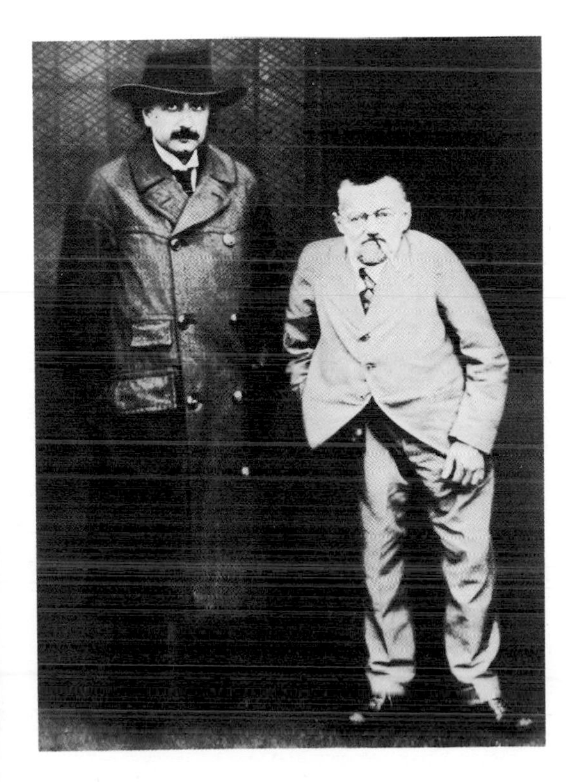

When Charles Proteus Steinmetz (seen here together with physics colleague Albert Einstein in 1921) immigrated in 1889, he nearly was rejected by the authorities because of his deformity (cf. par. 6 of the passenger agreement, reproduced on p. 44).

Charles Proteus Steinmetz, der bei seiner Einwanderung 1889 von den Behörden wegen seiner verwachsenen Gestalt fast zurückgewiesen worden wäre (vgl. § 6 des »Schiffs-Accords« auf S. 44), mit dem Physikerkollegen Albert Einstein im Jahre 1921.

The "Wizard of Schenectady" in his laboratory, where he worked for up to 18 hours a day – and where he had snakes and alligators as pets.

Der »Zauberer von Schenectady« in seinem Labor, in dem er bis zu 18 Stunden täglich arbeitete – und sich Schlangen und Alligatoren als Haustiere hielt.

The First German "Film Emigrant"

Carl Laemmle

Der erste deutsche »Film-Emigrant«

Carl Laemmle, one of Hollywood's founding fathers, was born on January 17, 1867, the tenth of 13 children of a Jewish building superintendent in Laupheim near Ulm. In 1884, at the apex of German emigration to America, the 17-year-old Laemmle resolved to seek his fortune "over there". Like many Jewish immigrants, he started in the textile trade, and rose through the ranks to branch manager of a firm in Oshkosh, Wisconsin. He quit in 1905 to "go into business" for himself, although what he chose was in those days not considered business but rather vaudeville. His first nickelodeon, the Whitefront Theater in Chicago, opened in 1906 and was a smashing success. Within a few years, Laemmle owned not only a chain of cinemas but also his own distributorship, and he also began to produce his own films in 1909. He founded the Independent Motion Picture Company (IMP), which would soon challenge another company started in January the same year, the Motion Picture Patents Company (MPPC), a syndicate of seven leading film and equipment producers led by Thomas Alva Edison. It was a tough battle but David conquered Goliath: The MPPC was ordered to break up for violating anti-trust legislation while Laemmle's IMP became Universal Studios in 1912 in Los Angeles. Three years later, Laemmle opened Universal City in the San Fernando Valley, the largest movie lot of its time. His years as a movie tycoon had begun. He produced among other things the first films of a headstrong Erich von Stroheim, made Rudolph Valentino the romantic idol of the Roaring Twenties and discovered Irving Thalberg, later a producer at MGM. But his avocation was philanthropy, with special interest for projects in his homeland, Germany, to which he was able to dedicate full time after passing the reins of business to his son, Carl Laemmle Jr., in 1929. A financial crisis in Universal in 1936 forced him to resign as president. Three years later, on 24 September 1939, he died in Hollywood.

Carl Laemmle, einer der Gründerväter Hollywoods, wurde am 17. Januar 1867 als zehntes von 13 Kindern eines jüdischen Hausverwalters in Laupheim bei Ulm geboren. 1884, auf dem Höhepunkt der deutschen Amerikaauswanderung, entschloß sich auch der siebzehnjährige Laemmle, sein Glück »drüben« zu versuchen. So wie zahlreiche jüdische Einwanderer faßte er in der Textilbranche Fuß und brachte es, über viele Zwischenstationen, bis zur Filialleitung eines Kaufhauses in Oshkosh, Wisconsin. Dort kündigte er 1905, um sich selbständig zu machen. Er entschied sich für eine Branche, die damals noch nicht Industrie, sondern Jahrmarktsvergnügen war: das Kino. Sein erstes »Nickelodeon«, das 1906 in Chicago eröffnete Whitefront Theater, entpuppte sich als solcher Erfolg, daß Laemmle innerhalb weniger Jahre eine Kinokette und einen eigenen Verleih sein eigen nannte und schon 1909 damit begann, seine Filme auch selbst zu produzieren. Er gründete die »Independent Motion Picture Company« (IMP), mit der er gegen das Kartell der im Januar desselben Jahres gegründeten »Motion Picture Patents Company« antrat, einer Monopolgesellschaft, zu der sich die sieben führenden Film- und Geräteproduzenten unter der Führung Thomas Alva Edisons zusammengeschlossen hatten. Der Konkurrenzkampf wurde mit harten Bandagen ausgefochten, und David blieb über Goliath siegreich: Die MPPC mußte schließlich wegen Verstößen gegen das Anti-Trust-Gesetz aufgelöst werden, während aus Laemmles IMP 1912 die Universal Studios in Los Angeles hervorgingen. Drei Jahre später eröffnete Laemmle im San Fernando Valley die »Universal City«, das größte Studiogelände der Zeit. Seine Jahre als Movie Tycoon begannen. Er produzierte, unter anderem, die ersten Filme des schwierigen Erich von Stroheim, machte Rudolph Valentino zum romantischen Idol der Goldenen Zwanziger und entdeckte Irving Thalberg, den späteren MGM-Produzenten. Nebenbei widmete er sich philanthropischen Projekten, vor allem in seiner alten Heimat Deutschland, die er zu seiner Hauptaufgabe machte, nachdem er 1929 die Produktionsleitung an seinen Sohn Carl Laemmle jr. abgetreten hatte. 1936 zwang ihn eine Finanzkrise der Universal, von seinem Präsidentenposten zurückzutreten. Drei Jahre später, am 24. September 1939, starb Carl Laemmle in Hollywood.

Carl Laemmle (front right) with Sergei Eisenstein (center) and his colleagues in Hollywood

Carl Laemmle (vorne rechts) mit Sergei Eisenstein (Mitte) und dessen Mitarbeitern in Hollywood

Prussian spiked helmets in Hollywood: the film version of Erich Maria Remarque's anti-war novel, "All Quiet on the Western Front", produced by Laemmle's son, Carl Laemmle, Jr., was one of Universal Studio's most famous films. It was directed by Lewis Milestone in 1930.

Preußische Pickelhauben in Hollywood – in einem der berühmtesten Filme der Universal, der von Laemmles Sohn Carl Laemmle jr. 1930 produzierten Verfilmung des Antikriegsromans »Im Westen nichts Neues« von Erich Maria Remarque. Regie führte Lewis Milestone.

Advertisement for Laemmle's film distributing agency, bluntly promoted as the "Biggest and Best Film Renter in the World"; from the era of the antitrust struggles.

Werbeanzeige des Laemmleschen Filmverleihs, kurz und bündig als »größter und bester Filmverleih der Welt« bezeichnet, aus der Anti-Trust-Kampfzeit.

Banker and Philanthropist

Paul Moritz Warburg

Bankmann und Philanthrop

Paul Moritz Warburg, banker and architect of the Federal Reserve System, was born on August 10, 1868, in Hamburg, the third son of Moritz and Charlotte Warburg. His father was head of the family-run banking house of M.M. Warburg & Co., founded in 1798 by Paul's great-grandfather.
Warburg was raised in the tradition of conservative Judaism mitigated by the more worldly atmosphere associated with his family's affluence. After graduating from secondary school, he was apprenticed to banking houses in London and Paris and subsequently made an extended journey around the world before becoming a partner in the family firm in 1895. In that same year, while serving as best man at his brother Felix's wedding to Frieda Schiff in New York, he met her mother's considerably younger sister, Nina Loeb, and a year later they were married. When Nina's brother-in-law and Frieda's father, Jacob Schiff, made him an employee in his firm, Kuhn, Loeb & Co., Warburg decided, though not without some degree of reluctancy, to make his American sojourn permanent.
His contribution to reforming the American banking system began when in 1907 he issued a pamphlet advocating centralization of the banking structure in the United States. Warburg's efforts in getting his proposals realized ran the gamut from delivering public speeches to private audiences with bankers, merchants and other influential leaders. Finally he won over Nelson Aldrich, head of the National Monetary Commission in Taft's administration and helped draw up a proposal, known as the Federal Reserve Bill, which became law in December 1913. In the summer of 1914 Warburg was appointed by President Wilson to be a member and the vice-chairman of the Federal Reserve Board, a position he held for four years. After the war he concentrated his energies on the formation of the International Acceptance Bank which was to stimulate post-war international trade. However, he received his greatest disappointment with American finance when the stock market failed in 1929, a disaster he had warned against as early as the mid-20s. A quiet man but one of great moral courage, Warburg retired to his house at White Plains where on January 24, 1932, he died.

Paul Moritz Warburg, Bankier und Vater des Federal Reserve System (Zentralbanksystem der USA), wurde am 10. August 1868 in Hamburg als dritter Sohn von Moritz und Charlotte Warburg geboren. Sein Vater leitete das familieneigene Bankhaus M. M. Warburg & Co., das 1798 von Pauls Urgroßvater gegründet worden war.
Warburg wurde in der Tradition des konservativen Judentums erzogen, dem allerdings eine weltoffene, vom Wohlstand der Familie geprägte Lebensart die Waage hielt. Nachdem er die höhere Schule absolviert hatte, ging er bei Bankhäusern in London und Paris in die Lehre. Anschließend unternahm er eine ausgedehnte Weltreise und trat 1895 als Partner in das Familienunternehmen ein. Als er im selben Jahr an der Hochzeit seines Bruders Felix mit Frieda Schiff in New York als Trauzeuge teilnahm, lernte er Nina Loeb, die erheblich jüngere Schwester der Mutter von Frieda Schiff, kennen und heiratete sie ein Jahr später. Als Ninas Schwager, also Friedas Vater Jakob Schiff, ihn in seinem Unternehmen Kuhn, Loeb & Co anstellte, entschloß sich Warburg nach einigem Zaudern, in Amerika zu bleiben.
Sein Beitrag zur Reform des amerikanischen Bankwesens begann 1907 mit einem Rundschreiben, in dem er für die Zentralisierung des Bankensystems in den Vereinigten Staaten plädierte. Warburgs Anstrengungen zur Verwirklichung seiner Vorschläge schlossen auch Reden vor einer ausgesuchten Zuhörerschaft von Bankiers, Großkaufleuten und einflußreichen Führungskräften ein. Schließlich überzeugte er Nelson Aldrich, Chef der National Monetary Commission in Tafts Regierung, und half bei der Erstellung eines Gesetzentwurfs, der, als Federal Reserve Bill bekannt, im Dezember 1913 in Kraft trat. Im Sommer des Jahres 1914 ernannte Präsident Wilson Warburg zum Mitglied und Vizepräsidenten des Federal Reserve Board, ein Amt, das er vier Jahre lang betreute. Nach dem Krieg bemühte er sich vor allem um die Gründung der International Acceptance Bank, die den internationalen Handel beleben sollte. Eine große Enttäuschung über das amerikanische Finanzwesen blieb ihm dennoch nicht erspart, als es 1929 zum Börsenkrach kam – ein Desaster, vor dem er schon Mitte der zwanziger Jahre gewarnt hatte. Warburg, ein zurückhaltender, doch in hohem Maße mit unverbrüchlicher Lauterkeit ausgestatteter Mann, zog sich auf sein Haus in White Plains zurück, wo er am 24. Januar 1932 starb.

View of the stock exchange in Hamburg, around the time the bank of M. M. Warburg & Co. was founded in 1798.

Zeitgenössische Ansicht der Börse in Hamburg, wo das Bankhaus von M. M. Warburg & Co. 1798 gegründet wurde.

Paul Moritz Warburg (middle) in 1931, receiving an honorary doctorate from Occidental College in Los Angeles. (Left, the president of the college, R. D. Bird, right, J. P. Young, Professor of Economy.)

Paul Moritz Warburg (Mitte) erhält 1931 die Ehrendoktorwürde des Occidental College von Los Angeles. (Links der Präsident des College, R. D. Bird, rechts J. P. Young, Professor an der Wirtschaftsfakultät)

Manhattan with the Brooklyn Bridge and (foreground left) Castle Garden at the time of Paul M. Warburg's arrival in New York (photo from the German magazine "Illustrirte Welt")

Manhattan mit der Brooklyn-Bridge und (links vorne) Castle Garden zur Zeit der Ankunft Paul M. Warburgs in New York (Abbildung aus der deutschen Zeitschrift »Illustrirte Welt«)

Plane Flight into Oblivion

Gustave Whitehead

Am Ruhm vorbeigeflogen

Gustave Whitehead, the great unknown in the history of aviation, was born on New Year's Day in 1874 in the Frankonian town of Leutershausen as Gustav Albin Weisskopf. As a child, he is supposed not only to have studied birds in flight, but to have built a glider when he was thirteen - with which he crashed from the roof in an attempted night flight. He unexpectedly lost both parents in the same year, and, on his own, decided to seek work as a shipboy. Years later he returned shortly to Germany where he began a correspondence with Otto Lilienthal, who, since 1891, had been conducting the first successful flights with gliders. In 1895 Whitehead finally emigrated to Boston, where an aeronautical society already existed.
Well received due to his contact to the famous Lilienthal, Whitehead was able to build two flying machines in Boston: one glider and one "Boston Flyer", an ornithopter which was to be propelled by man power. The attempted flight, however, again ended in a crash landing. Depressed, Whitehead left the city and, living from hand to mouth from part-time work, spent the next several years in New York, Buffalo and Pittsburgh. In Pittsburgh Whitehead constructed his first motorized aircraft, driven by a steam-engine. In May 1899, one experiment ended against the outside wall of a house - whether before or after take-off can not be confirmed with certainty. Whitehead in any case abandoned steam propulsion and began work on a special, lighter motor which ran on oxyacetylene. With this new motor and yet another new craft - Nr. 21 in a consecutive series - Whitehead, early on the morning of August 14, 1901, in the vicinity of Fairfield, Connecticut, is supposed to have made the first motorized flight in aeronautic history: 90 seconds long, 850 meters in distance and more than two years prior to the Wright Brothers' similarly short spurts. With the exception of three reports in local newspapers, the pioneer flight went without public notice, as was also the case with ensuing trial flights in 1902, one of which allegedly covered over 12 kilometers. Amazing as this seems, it was also the case with the Wright Brothers' experiments in 1903, which also attracted but slight attention. Whitehead, moreover, was not prone to publicizing his achievements as were his successors. We can conceive of him as a genial home-mechanic, the fate of his small motor factory which he opened in Bridgeport, Connecticut testifying to his worldly innocence: he built without calculation, often investing more in a motor than he had counted on, and ultimately forfeited his shop and construction plans. When he died of heart failure on October 10, 1927 - he had already given up his flying experiments fifteen years earlier - he left his family, in addition to the house he had built himself, all of eight dollars. His final resting place was in an anonymous pauper's grave.
There is no existent photographic documentation of Whitehead's early flights. But accounts by witnesses and other indications collated in past years render them plausible - with the exception perhaps of the twelve-kilometer flight in 1902. Irrespective of the acknowledgement of historical priority, in 1964 John Dempsey, governor of Connecticut, officially proclaimed Gustave Whitehead to be the "Father of Aviation in Connecticut".

Gustave Whitehead, der große Unbekannte der Luftfahrtgeschichte, wurde am Neujahrstag 1874 in der mittelfränkischen Kleinstadt Leutershausen als Gustav Albin Weißkopf geboren. Bereits in jungen Jahren soll er den Vogelflug studiert und mit dreizehn einen Gleiter gebaut haben, mit dem er bei einem nächtlichen Flugversuch vom Hausdach stürzte. Im selben Jahr verlor er überraschend beide Eltern, war auf sich selbst gestellt und beschloß, als Schiffsjunge anzuheuern. Nach mehreren Jahren kehrte er zu einem kurzen Aufenthalt nach Deutschland zurück, knüpfte einen Briefwechsel mit Otto Lilienthal an, der seit 1891 die ersten erfolgreichen Gleitflüge durchgeführt hatte, und wanderte schließlich 1895 nach Boston aus, wo zu diesem Zeitpunkt bereits eine »Aeronautische Gesellschaft« existierte.
Durch seinen Kontakt mit dem berühmten Lilienthal bestens eingeführt, konnte Whitehead in Boston zwei Fluggeräte bauen: einen Gleiter und ein "The Boston Flyer" benanntes Schlagflügelflugzeug, das durch Menschenkraft angetrieben werden sollte. Der Flugversuch endete abermals mit einer Bruchlandung. Deprimiert verließ Whitehead die Stadt und schlug sich in den folgenden Jahren in New York, Buffalo und Pittsburgh mit verschiedenen Gelegenheitsarbeiten durch.
In Pittsburgh konstruierte Whitehead sein erstes Motorflugzeug, das durch eine Dampfmaschine angetrieben wurde. Ein Flugexperiment im Mai 1899 endete an einer Hauswand - ob vor oder nach dem Abheben läßt sich nicht mit letzter Sicherheit entscheiden. Whitehead jedenfalls gab den Dampfantrieb auf und begann mit der Konstruktion eines eigenen Flugmotors, der mit Azetylengas arbeitete und ein günstigeres Leistungsgewicht erreichte. Mit diesem Motor und einem neuen Flugzeug - das, bei fortlaufender Numerierung, bereits die Nr. 21 trug - soll ihm am frühen Morgen des 14. August 1901 bei Fairfield, Connecticut, der erste Motorflug der Luftfahrtgeschichte gelungen sein: anderthalb Minuten lang, 850 Meter weit und mehr als zwei Jahre vor den ähnlich kurzen ersten Luftsprüngen der Brüder Wright.
Abgesehen von drei Berichten in lokalen Zeitungen fand der Pionierflug - dem 1902 weitere Flüge, angeblich über Strecken bis zu 12 Kilometern, folgten - kaum öffentliche Resonanz. Das mag verwundern, findet jedoch gerade bei den Brüdern Wright eine Parallele, deren Experimente im Jahre 1903 zunächst ebenfalls wenig Aufsehen erregten. Und anders als seine Nachfolger war Whitehead nicht der Mann, seine Errungenschaften selbst publik zu machen. Man wird ihn sich als genialischen Bastler vorstellen dürfen, von dessen Weltfremdheit das Schicksal der kleinen Motorenfabrik Zeugnis ablegt, die er in Bridgeport in Connecticut eröffnete: er konstruierte ohne Kalkulation, steckte oft mehr in einen Motor hinein, als er dafür berechnete, und verlor schließlich Werkstatt und Konstruktionsunterlagen durch Pfändung. Als er am 10. Oktober 1927 an einem Herzleiden starb - die Flugexperimente hatte er bereits fünfzehn Jahre zuvor aufgegeben -, hinterließ er seiner Familie neben dem selbsterbauten Haus ganze acht Dollar und fand seine letzte Ruhestätte in einem anonymen Armengrab.
Foto- oder Filmdokumente von Whiteheads frühen Flügen existieren nicht. Zeugenaussagen und Indizien, die in den letzten Jahren zusammengetragen wurden, machen sie jedoch plausibel - vielleicht mit Ausnahme des Zwölf-Kilometer-Fluges von 1902. Unabhängig von der Anerkennung seiner historischen Priorität wurde Gustave Whitehead 1964 vom Gouverneur des Staates Connecticut, John Dempsey, zum »Vater der Luftfahrt in Connecticut« proklamiert.

Gustave Whitehead with his flying machine Nr. 21 and with one of his unconventional motors. The wire bristles around the cylinders are intended to be a cooling device.

Gustave Whitehead mit seiner Flugmaschine Nr. 21 und mit einer seiner unkonventionellen Motorentwicklungen. Die Drahtborsten rund um die Zylinder sollen der Luftkühlung dienen.

A "Conservative Revolutionary" in L. A.

Arnold Schönberg

Der »konservative Revolutionär« in L. A.

Schoenberg with his children and wife Gertrud in Los Angeles

Schönberg mit seiner Frau Gertrud und den Kindern in Los Angeles

Arnold Schoenberg grew up in the fin-de-siècle Vienna of Sigmund Freud, Gustav Mahler und Arthur Schnitzler. In an effort to free music of overripe post-romantic decadence, he developed a bold new method of composition, completely discarding the thousand-year-old principle of European music being organized around a modal or tonal center – and became perhaps the most heatedly discussed, though rarely performed, major 20th-century composer.

The son of a Jewish merchant, Schoenberg was born in Vienna on 13 September 1874. He was basically self-taught in music, except for a brief period as pupil of his future brother-in-law, the composer Alexander von Zemlinsky. His early works, culminating with the dramatic *Gurre-Lieder* for soloists, chorus and large orchestra (written between 1900 and 1911), were stylistically in the mainstream of post-Wagnerian romanticism. In 1909 he was already experimenting with non-tonal music, and in *Pierrot Lunaire* (1912) he had not only abandoned traditional harmony but also reduced the massive body of performers to a single vocalist and five instrumentalists. Yet not until the 1920s, during his stay in Berlin as professor at the Prussian Academy of Fine Arts, did Schoenberg systemize his technique of composition based on a "12-tone row". Works composed during this period include the *Variations for Orchestra* op. 31 and the opera *Moses and Aaron.*

In 1933 Schoenberg voluntarily resigned his Berlin post, anticipating an inevitable dismissal because of his Jewish origins. Having previously converted to Lutheranism, he now returned to his Jewish faith and took up a life in exile, settling in Los Angeles and eventually adopting American citizenship (1941). For years he was professor of music at the University of Southern California and then at the University of California, which now jointly administer the Schoenberg archives, and where his outstanding abilities as a teacher attracted a large and influential circle of devoted students. Despite an occasional return to conservative elements in his music, it was still mainly ignored by the public and vilified by the press.

The horrors of World War II led him to write two powerful indictments of authoritarianism, a setting of Byron's *Ode to Napoleon* (1942) and the cantata *A Survivor from Warsaw* (1947). When he died in Los Angeles on 13 July 1951, his reputation with the public was still as controversial as his commanding position in music history was assured.

Arnold Schönberg wuchs in der Fin-de-siècle-Atmosphäre des Wiens von Arthur Schnitzler, Sigmund Freud und Gustav Mahler auf. Er versuchte, die Musik vom Ballast spätromantischer Dekadenz zu befreien und wurde zum Erfinder einer wegweisenden Kompositionsmethode, die mit der tausendjährigen Vorherrschaft der Tonalität in der europäischen Musikgeschichte brach – und damit zum wohl umstrittensten, wenngleich selten gespielten, unter den großen Komponisten des 20. Jahrhunderts.

Als Sohn eines jüdischen Kaufmanns wurde Schönberg am 13. September 1874 in Wien geboren. Musikalisch war er Autodidakt, abgesehen von einem kurzen Studium des Kontrapunkts bei Alexander von Zemlinsky, seinem zukünftigen Schwager. Die frühen Arbeiten Schönbergs – kulminierend in den hochdramatischen *Gurre-Liedern* für Soli, Chor und großes Orchester (1900–11) – stehen in der unmittelbaren Nachfolge der Wagnerschen Spätromantik. 1909 experimentierte Schönberg bereits mit atonaler Musik; in *Pierrot lunaire* (1912) hatte er sich nicht nur von der traditionellen Harmonik gelöst, sondern auch das massive Orchesteraufgebot auf eine Sprech- und fünf Instrumentalstimmen reduziert. In den zwanziger Jahren schließlich, während seiner Lehrtätigkeit an der Preußischen Akademie der Künste in Berlin, vollzog Schönberg den entscheidenden Schritt von der Atonalität zur Reihentechnik seiner »Komposition mit zwölf nur aufeinander bezogenen Tönen«. In diese Schaffensphase fallen seine *Variationen für Orchester* op. 31 und die Oper *Moses und Aron.*

1933 gab Schönberg, einer Entlassung wegen seiner jüdischen Abkunft zuvorkommend, die Stellung in Berlin auf und wählte das Exil. Früher zum Luthera-nertum konvertiert, kehrte er demonstrativ zum mosaischen Glauben zurück und ließ sich in Los Angeles nieder, wo er 1941 die amerikanische Staatsbürgerschaft erwarb. Als Lehrer an der University of Southern California und später an der University of California – die heute gemeinsam das Schönberg-Archiv verwalten – zog seine geniale pädagogische Begabung eine große und später einflußreiche Schar von engagierten Schülern an. Obgleich Schönbergs Kompositionen aus jener Zeit gelegentlich auf traditionelle Techniken zurückgreifen und seine Ästhetik – unabhängig von den avancierten Mitteln des Komponierens – von jeher konservativ war, blieb sein Werk beim amerikanischen Publikum unbeachtet und wurde von der Kritik verunglimpft.

Erschüttert von den Greueln des Zweiten Weltkriegs, komponierte Schönberg in Amerika zwei leidenschaftliche Anklagen gegen jeglichen Totalitarismus: eine Vertonung von Byrons *Ode to Napoleon* (1942) und die auf einem authentischen Brief aus dem Warschauer Getto beruhende Kantate *A Survivor from Warsaw* (1947). Als er am 13. Juli 1951 in Los Angeles starb, war sein Ansehen beim Publikum noch ebenso kontrovers, wie seine überragende Position in der Musikgeschichte gewiß.

Arnold Schoenberg's death-mask, taken in Los Angeles by Alma Mahler-Werfel on the morning of July 14, 1951.

Arnold Schönbergs Totenmaske, am Morgen des 14. Juli 1951 in Los Angeles abgenommen von Alma Mahler-Werfel

Uprooted in Chicago

Emerenz Meier

Entwurzelt in Chicago

Schiefweg, in a sequestered corner of the world near Waldkirchen in the lower Bavarian Forest, is where Emerenz Meier, the daughter of a peasant innkeeper, was born on 3 October 1874. The place where she died in her New World, only 54 years later, could not have provided a greater contrast to her verdant birthplace: the American metropolis of Chicago, to which she emigrated with her family in 1906.

The motive behind the Meier family's resettling was no different from that which had already resulted in waves of emigration from the sparsely settled, climatically ill-favored Bavarian/Bohemian border region around 1850, and again in the years 1868 and 1876: economic distress, conjoined with the tempting conception – still current in Germany – of America as the "land of unlimited possibilities", a phrase originally coined in 1902 by one Ludwig Goldberger.

For Emerenz, who probably only accompanied her family to the United States out of a sense of loyalty to her parents, brothers and sisters, emigration presented dimmer prospects. In Germany, where she had already established the foundation for a career as a writer, her woodland tales had earned her artistic recognition, if as yet little financial reward. But her inspiration was integrally bound to the stimulus of her bucolic environment, from which her deracination put an abrupt end to her literary production. She remained the sensitive observer who experienced the travails of immigrant life more intensively and smartingly than others, and was able to describe them vividly in her letters to her girl friend Auguste back in Waldkirchen.

At first, things seemed to be taking a good turn: "My father," begins one of Emerenz's letters, "a 70-year-old hoary peasant, ... immediately found work, and is not only able to support himself and mother well, but also to start saving..." However the very first biographical fact we learn about Emerenz in the New World tells a different story: she married the first man she met in Chicago, one who came from the same area of the Bavarian Forest as she herself; mutual homesickness must have been their sole common bond, for the strange new environment plus alcohol soon contributed to their marriage breaking up. Then came the First World War, giving rise to anti-German sentiment: "The indignities we had to endure here, the intolerance and abuse, were simply despicable. Posters were to be seen on every street corner showing brave Yankees slaughtering the hated "Huns" like pigs. And (we) Germans had to pay the piper..." The failure to become integrated led to a growing embitterment and even resentment. "This big American city is something awful, ugly and morose," says one of her letters; yet on the other hand the desolate conditions in postwar Germany kept her from returning there. Instead, like so many other immigrants, Emerenz tried to persuade those who had remained behind to join her, for which plenty of enticing arguments could still be found: "Delicacies which one couldn't even dream of back home, can be indulged in daily here, even if one's income is small." But no one took to her pitch, and Emerenz became increasingly isolated. She sought consolation in something not unseemly for a Bavarian innkeeper's daughter – but in the days of strict nationwide Prohibition, she even had to brew her own beer at home.

Prohibition was still in effect when Emerenz Meier died on 28 February 1928, following a long sickness, disillusioned and forgotten in her detested Chicago. Alienated from both her old and new homelands, she had forsaken her Catholic religion in America: her body was cremated.

In einem abgeschiedenen Winkel des Weltgeschehens, in Schiefweg bei Waldkirchen im unteren Bayerischen Wald, wurde am 3. Oktober 1874 die Gastwirts- und Bauerntochter Emerenz Meier geboren. Sie starb, nur 54 Jahre später, in einer Neuen Welt, wie sie verschiedener von ihrer grünen Heimat nicht sein konnte – der amerikanischen Metropolis Chicago, in die sie mit ihrer Familie 1906 ausgewandert war.

Das Auswanderungsmotiv der Familie Meier war dasselbe, das im dünnbesiedelten, klimatisch benachteiligten bayerisch-böhmischen Grenzgebiet schon um 1850 und in den Jahren 1868 und 1876 zu Auswanderungswellen geführt hatte: wirtschaftliche Not, die das aktuelle Schlagwort vom »Land der unbegrenzten Möglichkeiten« – es war 1902 von einem gewissen Ludwig Goldberger geprägt worden – nur umso verführerischer leuchten ließ.

Für Emerenz mußte die Auswanderung freilich eine zusätzliche Dimension haben: Sie hatte in Deutschland den Grundstein zu einer Schriftstellerkarriere gelegt und sich mit Erzählungen aus dem Waldlermilieu zwar wenig Geld, aber künstlerische Anerkennung verdient. Daß sie ihre Eltern und Geschwister, wohl aus Familiensolidarität, in die USA begleitete, setzte ihrer Schriftstellerei, die ganz auf die Anregungen der bäuerlichen Heimat angewiesen war, ein abruptes Ende. Übrig blieb die sensible Beobachterin, die die Probleme des Einwandererlebens schmerzlicher und intensiver als andere erlebte und in ihren Briefen an die Freundin Auguste in Waldkirchen darzustellen wußte.

Zunächst schienen sich die Erwartungen zu erfüllen: »Mein Vater«, so Emerenz in einem Brief, »ein 70jähriger Bauerngreis, (...) hat gleich zu verdienen angefangen, und nicht bloß sich und Mutter reichlich ernährt, sondern noch erspart dazu...« Doch schon das erste biographische Detail, das wir über Emerenz in der Neuen Welt erfahren, spricht eine andere Sprache: der Mann, den sie in Chicago als ersten kennenlernte und heiratete, stammte aus derselben Ecke des Bayerischen Waldes wie sie selbst. Heimweh scheint die beiden zusammengeführt zu haben, und in der fremden Umgebung ging die Ehe dann auch am Alkohol zugrunde. Es folgten die Jahre des Weltkriegs und der Deutschenfeindlichkeit: »Was wir hier erleiden mußten an Schmähungen, Unterdrückungen und Verfolgungen, das ist einfach erbärmlich. An allen Straßenecken waren Plakate zu sehen, darauf tapfere Yankees die verhaßten ›Hunnen‹ abschlachteten wie Säue. Und die Deutschen mußten dies ansehen und blechen...« Das Scheitern der Eingliederung ließ Verbitterung, ja Ressentiment wachsen. »Diese amerikanische Großstadt ist etwas Fürchterliches, Häßliches, Freudloses«, heißt es in einem Brief, doch umgekehrt verboten die desolaten Zustände im Deutschland der Nachkriegszeit die Rückkehr. Stattdessen versuchte Emerenz, wie so viele Einwanderer, die Daheimgebliebenen zum Nachkommen zu bewegen, wofür sich immer noch genügend Anreize fanden: »Genüsse, von denen einem draußen niemals träumt, kann man hier für wenige Kröten sich täglich gestatten, mag auch das Einkommen klein sein.« Doch die Köder verfingen nicht, und Emerenz vereinsamte zusehends. Sie suchte Zuflucht bei dem, was ihr als bayerischer Wirtstochter das Nächstliegende schien – aber selbst das Bier mußte sie sich zu Hause selber brauen, galt doch im ganzen Land die strenge Prohibition...

Sie war noch nicht aufgehoben, als Emerenz Meier am 28. Februar 1928, nach langem Kränkeln, enttäuscht und vergessen in ihrem ungeliebten Chicago starb. Ihrer alten Heimat ebenso entfremdet wie der neuen, hatte sie in Amerika auch den katholischen Glauben abgelegt: ihre Leiche wurde verbrannt.

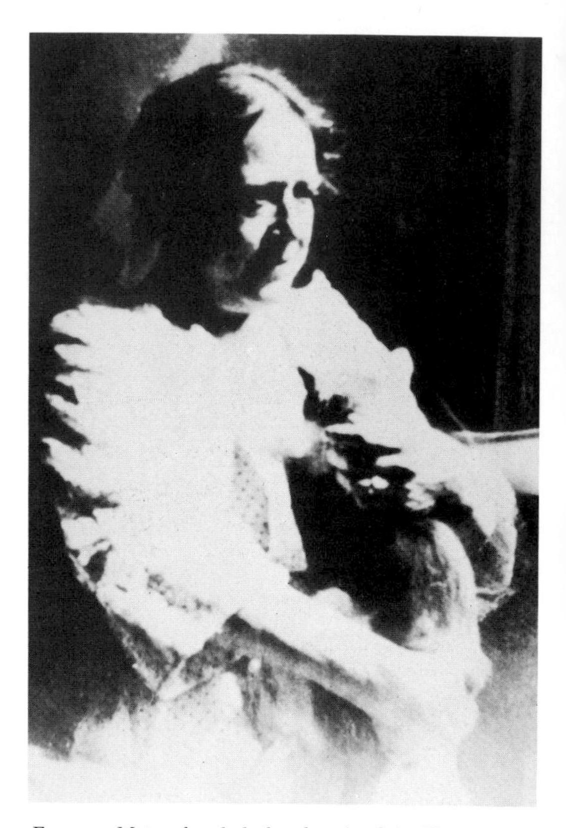

Emerenz Meier shortly before her death in Chicago
Emerenz Meier kurz vor ihrem Tod in Chicago

A sign of early popularity: a postcard of the young writer Emerenz Meier and the house where she was born in Waldkirchen, around 1900.

Ein Zeichen früher Popularität: die junge Schriftstellerin Emerenz Meier und ihr Geburtshaus auf einer Ansichtskarte ihrer Heimatgemeinde Waldkirchen, um 1900

Music as an Ethical Force

Bruno Walter

Musik als geistige Kraft

Portrait of young Bruno Schlesinger, who changed his name to "Bruno Walter" in 1911 in honor of his favorite Wagner characters, Walter von Stolzing and Walther von der Vogelweide.

Jugendbildnis von Bruno Schlesinger, der seinen Namen 1911 nach seinen bevorzugten Wagner-Charakteren Walter von Stolzing und Walther von der Vogelweide in »Bruno Walter« ändern ließ.

The constants in Bruno Walter's life were (besides the masters from Mozart to Mahler) the honors bestowed upon him wherever his career took him, the esteem in which he was held for his integrity as man and musician, and his belief in "the immense moral force of music....with its uplifting influence on the human soul." The variables in his life were the many cities of his early career as a rapidly up-and-coming pianist and conductor, and the countries of his later career after fleeing Nazi Germany.

He was born as Bruno Schlesinger on 15 September 1876 in a poor and crowded district of Berlin, where his father made a modest living as a bookkeeper. In his autobiography, *Theme and Variations* (1947), Walter writes that in his family, members of the liberal Reform Jewish Community, "peace, kindness, and decency prevailed." The first music he heard was played and sung by his mother, who had been a conservatory student. The extraordinarily gifted Bruno began his studies at the same conservatory, and at the age of 17 already had his first job conducting at the Cologne Opera. By the time he was 25 he had gained experience at the opera houses of Hamburg, Breslau, Pressburg, Riga and Berlin. In 1901 he was invited by Gustav Mahler to assist at the Vienna Opera, where he remained for 11 years, until he was called to Munich to succeed Felix Mottl as *Königlich Bayerischer Generalmusikdirektor.* During his two decades at Vienna and Munich, two of the most important music centers of Europe, his fame as "the singer among conductors" spread worldwide. In the early 20s Walter made guest appearances in America and England; in 1925 he became musical director of the Berlin Municipal Opera, and 1929–33, of the Leipzig Gewandhaus Orchestra.

With the accession to power of the National Socialists, Walter returned to Austria, where he succeeded Felix Weingartner at the Vienna State Opera, and conducted at the Salzburg Festival, which he had earlier helped found and develop. When the Germans occupied Austria, Walter resigned his posts and went to France, where, having previously been named "Commander of the Legion of Honor", the government immediately made him a French citizen. However, since he was in America as guest conductor of the NBC Symphony and the Los Angeles Philharmonic when war broke out, he again resettled and became an American citizen, spending the final two decades of his life as one of the most honored, popular, and sought-after conductors throughout the United States. He died in Beverly Hills, California, on 17 February 1962.

Die Konstanten in Bruno Walters Leben waren (neben den großen Meistern von Mozart bis Mahler) die Ehrungen, die ihm überall zuteil wurden, wohin ihn seine Laufbahn führte; die Hochachtung, die man ihm für seine menschliche und musikalische Integrität entgegenbrachte; und sein Glaube an die »gewaltige moralische Kraft der Musik... mit ihrer erhebenden Wirkung auf die menschliche Seele«. Die Variablen waren die vielen Städte seiner frühen Karriere als kometenhaft aufsteigender Pianist und Dirigent – und in seiner späteren Laufbahn die verschiedenen Länder, in die es ihn nach seiner Flucht vor den Nationalsozialisten verschlug.

Als Bruno Schlesinger wurde er am 15. September 1876 in einem ärmlichen und dicht bevölkerten Viertel von Berlin geboren, wo sein Vater als Buchhalter einen bescheidenen Lebensunterhalt verdiente. In seiner Autobiographie *Thema und Variationen* (1947) schreibt Walter, daß in seiner Familie, die einer liberalen jüdischen Reformgemeinde angehörte, »Friede, Güte und Anstand herrschten«. Die erste Musik, die er hörte, wurde ihm von seiner Mutter vorgespielt und -gesungen, die an demselben Konservatorium studiert hatte, an dem auch der hochbegabte Junge seine Ausbildung begann. Schon mit 17 gab er sein Dirigentendebüt am Kölner Stadttheater, und mit 25 hatte er bereits in Hamburg, Breslau, Preßburg, Riga und Berlin Opernerfahrung gesammelt. 1901 holte ihn Gustav Mahler als Assistenten an die Wiener Oper, wo er elf Jahre blieb, bis er als Königlich Bayerischer Generalmusikdirektor und Nachfolger von Felix Mottl nach München berufen wurde.

Während seiner beiden Jahrzehnte in Wien und München – zwei der wichtigsten europäischen Musikzentren – verbreitete sich Walters Ruhm als »der Sänger unter den Dirigenten« auf der ganzen Welt. In den frühen 20er Jahren gab er Gastspiele in Amerika und England, war ab 1925 Generalmusikdirektor der Städtischen Oper Berlin und von 1929–33 Gewandhauskapellmeister in Leipzig.

Als die Nationalsozialisten an die Macht kamen, kehrte Walter nach Österreich zurück, wo er Felix Weingartner an der Wiener Staatsoper ablöste und bei den Salzburger Festspielen dirigierte, an deren Gründung und Aufbau er ebenfalls mitgewirkt hatte. Nach dem »Anschluß« Österreichs 1938 legte Walter seine Ämter nieder und ging nach Frankreich, wo er, schon früher zum »Kommandeur der Ehrenlegion« ernannt, sofort die französische Staatsbürgerschaft erhielt. Als ihn der Kriegsausbruch 1939 als Gast des NBC-Symphonieorchesters und der Los Angeles Philharmonic in den USA überraschte, verlegte er seinen Wohnsitz erneut und wurde amerikanischer Staatsbürger. Die beiden letzten Lebensjahrzehnte verbrachte er als einer der geachtetsten, beliebtesten und umworbensten Dirigenten in den Vereinigten Staaten. Er starb am 17. Februar 1962 in Beverly Hills, Kalifornien.

Bruno Walter in Prague in 1908 with Gustav Mahler (left). After Mahler's death, Walter conducted the world premieres of Mahler's 9th Symphony and "Lied von der Erde".

Bruno Walter 1908 in Prag mit Gustav Mahler (links), von dem er die 9. Symphonie und das »Lied von der Erde« zur postumen Uraufführung brachte.

Bruno Walter conducting the New York Philharmonic Orchestra

Bruno Walter am Pult der New Yorker Philharmoniker

The Physicist as a Moral Authority

Albert Einstein

Der Physiker als moralische Instanz

Einstein was born on March 14, 1879, in Ulm, "a German", as he explicitly noted in a short autobiography. His impressionable youthful years were spent in Munich, where his father and uncle manufactured electrical equipment.

As a 12-year-old student at Munich's Luitpold Gymnasium, Einstein experienced his first major conflict. His reading books on popular science led him to draw the conclusion that the authoritarian doctrines he was being taught in school in religion class as the "ultimate truth" could not possibly be correct. "The result", he reported, "was a fanatical freethinking, combined with the impression that young people were being deliberately misled by the state." Experiences of this sort gave rise to his distrust of authority in any form. At an early age he began to form his own ideas about everything – about the laws governing nature and those governing human society.

His genius developed almost clandestinely. His professors at the Swiss Federal Technical Institute in Zurich (known then as the Polytechnic) took little note of him as was also the case with his colleagues later on at the patent office in Bern, where – in retrospect, an irony of history – he was employed as "technical expert, third class".

Einstein was made to suffer much iniquity in Germany. But German scholars can claim one thing to their credit. They were the first to recognize the significance of Einstein's theories and to help in their breakthrough. For instance, what Max Planck found fascinating about the special theory of relativity of 1905 was that while it overthrew the absolute nature of space and time as postulated by Newton and Kant, it yet confirmed the speed of light and Planck's own universal constant as absolute quantities. Also in 1905, Einstein came out with the no less revolutionary hypothesis of light quanta. Fifteen years later, his explanation of the photoelectric effect won him a Nobel Prize.

Einstein wurde am 14. März 1879 in Ulm geboren, »als Deutscher«, wie er in einer kurzen Autobiographie ausdrücklich vermerkte. Die entscheidenden Jugendeindrücke hat er in München empfangen, wo sein Vater und sein Onkel eine Fabrikation elektrotechnischer Artikel betrieben.

Als Schüler des Münchner Luitpoldgymnasiums erlebte Einstein mit zwölf Jahren seinen ersten großen Konflikt. Durch die Lektüre populärwissenschaftlicher Bücher kam er zu dem Schluß, daß das im Religionsunterricht autoritär als Wahrheit Verkündete unmöglich richtig sein konnte. »Die Folge war«, berichtete er, »eine geradezu fanatische Freigeisterei, verbunden mit dem Eindruck, daß die Jugend vom Staate mit Vorbedacht belogen wird.« Aus solchen Erlebnissen wuchs sein Mißtrauen gegen jede Art von Autorität. Frühzeitig hat er sich über alles seine eigenen Gedanken gemacht: über die Gesetze der Natur und über die Gesetze des menschlichen Zusammenlebens.

Das Genie entwickelte sich im Verborgenen. An der Eidgenössischen Technischen Hochschule in Zürich (damals noch Polytechnikum genannt) fiel er seinen Professoren ebensowenig auf wie später seinen Kollegen am Patentamt in Bern, wo er, Ironie der Geschichte, als »Experte dritter Klasse« angestellt war.

In Deutschland ist Einstein viel Übles geschehen. Eines aber dürfen sich deutsche Gelehrte zur Ehre anrechnen: Sie haben als erste die Bedeutung der Einsteinschen Theorien erkannt und ihnen zum Durchbruch verholfen. So faszinierte Max Planck an der Speziellen Relativitätstheorie von 1905, daß Raum und Zeit ihren von Newton und Kant postulierten absoluten Charakter verlieren, gleichzeitig aber die Lichtgeschwindigkeit und die von Planck selbst entdeckte Naturkonstante (das später sogenannte Wirkungsquantum) als absolute Größen bestätigt werden. Gleichfalls 1905 trat Einstein auch mit seiner nicht

A.

Nr. 224.

Ulm am 15. März 1879.

Vor dem unterzeichneten Standesbeamten erschien heute, der Persönlichkeit nach bekannt, der Kaufmann Hermann Einstein, wohnhaft zu Ulm Bahnhofstraße B Nr. 135 israelitischer Religion, und zeigte an, daß von der Pauline Einstein geb. Koch seiner Ehefrau israelitischer Religion, wohnhaft bei ihm zu Ulm in seiner Wohnung am vierzehnten März des Jahres tausend acht hundert siebenzig und neun Vormittags um elf ein halb Uhr ein Kind männlichen Geschlechts geboren worden sei, welches den Vornamen Albert erhalten habe.

Vorgelesen, genehmigt und unterschrieben
Hermann Einstein

Der Standesbeamte.
Hartmann

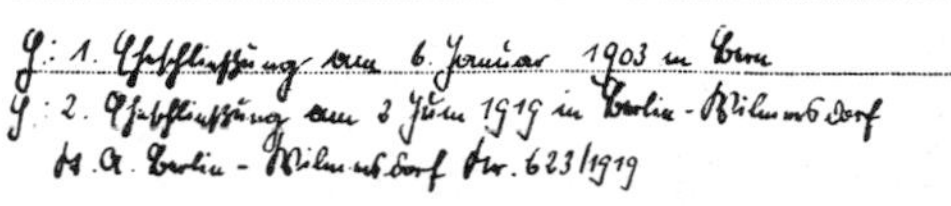
g: 1. Eheschließung am 6. Januar 1903 in Bern
g: 2. Eheschließung am 2. Juni 1919 in Berlin-Wilmersdorf
H.A. Berlin-Wilmersdorf Nr. 623/1919

Albert Einstein's birth certificate from the city of Ulm's municipal archives. At the bottom there are entries on his marriages: in 1903 in Berne he wed his fellow student Mileva Maritsch, who bore him two sons, and in 1919 in Berlin his cousin Elsa became his second wife.

Albert Einsteins Geburtsurkunde aus den Akten des Ulmer Standesamtes. Ganz unten sind Einsteins Eheschließungen vermerkt: 1903 in Bern mit seiner ehemaligen Kommilitonin Mileva Maritsch, mit der er zwei Söhne hatte, und 1919 in Berlin mit seiner Cousine Elsa.

Albert Einstein around 1905 – when he was employed at the Patent Office in Berne as "technical expert, third class", and spending his spare time working out the special theory of relativity and the hypothesis of light quanta which later earned him a Nobel Prize.

Albert Einstein um 1905 – als er am »Eidgenössischen Schutzamt für geistiges Eigentum« in Bern als »Experte dritter Klasse« angestellt war und in seiner Freizeit die spezielle Relativitätstheorie und die Lichtquantenhypothese (die ihm später den Nobelpreis brachte) ausarbeitete.

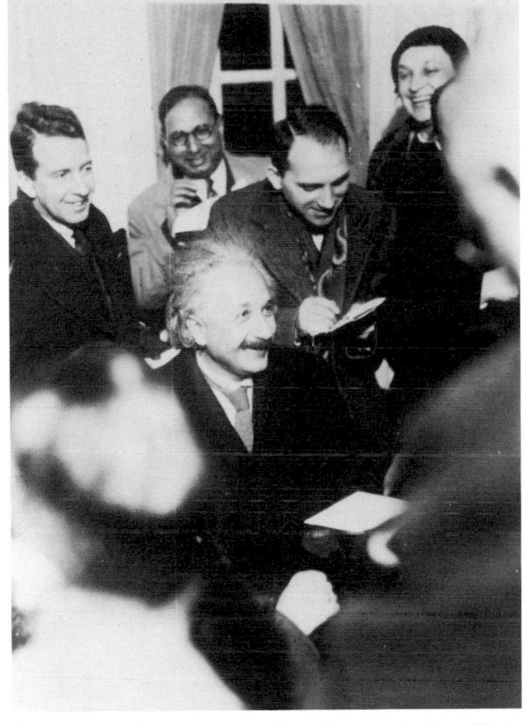

Beleaguered by reporters: Albert Einstein in New York, 1930. His spontaneous and witty retorts made him a welcome quarry for journalists wherever he went.

Von Reportern umlagert: Albert Einstein 1930 in New York. Seine spontanen und witzigen Antworten machten ihn überall zu einem gesuchten Opfer der Journalisten.

The cover of a 1930 Berlin weekly radio guide showing Einstein as the honored main speaker at the opening of the German radio and phonograph trade fair in Berlin

Berlin, den 29. August 1930

Funk-Post

Wochenschrift mit den Programmen aller Sender

31. August - 6. September

Heft 35

Einstein spricht

Der große Gelehrte bei der Eröffnung der Deutschen Funkausstellung und Phonoschau Berlin 1930

Phot. Keystone

Einstein als prominenter Redner bei der Eröffnung der Berliner Funkausstellung, 1930

Einstein's profound humanitarianism led to his being respected as a venerable sage more than any other scientist of his time. He is seen here together with the Indian philosopher, poet and Nobel prizewinner Rabindranath Tagore (1861–1941).

Einstein, der dank seiner Menschlichkeit wie kein anderer Wissenschaftler seiner Zeit das Ansehen eines Weisen genoß, mit dem indischen Philosophen, Dichter und Nobelpreisträger Rabindranath Tagore (1861–1941)

Einstein came to Los Angeles with Charlie Chaplin in 1931 to attend the premiere of Chaplin's film "City Lights"; they were given an enthusiastic ovation by the crowd, which led Chaplin to comment, "They all applaud you because nobody can understand you; they all applaud me because everyone can understand me."

Einstein mit Charlie Chaplin, 1931 in Los Angeles bei der Premiere des Chaplin-Films »City Lights«; beide wurden von der Menge begeistert begrüßt, was Chaplin zu dem Kommentar veranlaßte: »Ihnen applaudieren die Leute, weil Sie keiner versteht, und mir, weil mich jeder versteht.«

Albert Einstein received an honorary doctorate from Harvard University on 20 June 1935. The picture shows Einstein with Professor James B. Conant who subsequently served as President of Harvard and High Commissioner of Germany (from 1953 to 1955).

Albert Einstein bei der Verleihung der Ehrendoktorwürde der Harvard Universität am 20. Juni 1935. Neben ihm James B. Conant, später Präsident von Harvard und von 1953 bis 1955 Hoher Kommissar der USA in Deutschland.

With Einstein, a new epoch in human thought had begun. At first, only physicists took notice. The public followed in a few years. After World War I, two British solar eclipse expeditions produced preliminary proof of his general theory of relativity, which had been published in 1916, when Einstein was at work in Berlin as a member of the highly prestigious Prussian Academy of Science.

Great political upheavals followed the collapse of the German empire. Anti-Semites claimed that Jews were responsible for all of society's ills. Since Einstein was Jewish, so their simplistic argument went, his theory of relativity must have been a sinister concoction brewed up to poison sound scientific thought.

But what was really happening was symptomatic of a true scientific revolution. Einstein's general theory of relativity made radically new statements about the structure of the macrocosmic universe. His quantum theory furthermore changed the prevailing concept of the microcosmic atom. In the history of science, there certainly had been other revolutions. But that of the 20s was singularly typified by the heatedness of the debate and the political resentment that accompanied it.

In 1933, Einstein emigrated to the United States. The departure of the "Pope of Physics" to the New World had symbolic significance. Germany's world leadership in the field of physics had ended and was passed on to the United States.

minder revolutionären Lichtquantenhypothese hervor. 15 Jahre später trug ihm die Erklärung des Photoeffektes den Nobelpreis ein. Mit Einstein begann eine neue Epoche im Denken des Menschen. Zuerst wurden die Physiker aufmerksam, ein paar Jahre später auch die Öffentlichkeit. Nach dem Ende des Ersten Weltkrieges erbrachten zwei britische Sonnenfinsternisexpeditionen einen (allerdings nur vorläufigen) Beweis seiner Allgemeinen Relativitätstheorie. Einstein hatte die Theorie 1916 veröffentlicht, als er schon in Berlin wirkte und Mitglied der hochangesehenen Preußischen Akademie der Wissenschaften war.

Nach dem Zusammenbruch des Kaiserreichs tobten heftige politische Auseinandersetzungen im Lande. Antisemiten machten für alles Übel die Juden verantwortlich, und da Einstein Jude war, mußte nach ihrer simplen Schlußweise auch die von ihm hervorgebrachte Relativitätstheorie ein Machwerk sein, geeignet, die bisher so gesunde Wissenschaft zu vergiften.

Was sich da abspielte, waren die Begleitumstände einer wissenschaftlichen Revolution. Die Allgemeine Relativitätstheorie machte neue und ganz ungewohnte Aussagen über die Struktur des Makrokosmos, des Weltganzen, und parallel dazu veränderte die Quantentheorie die bisherigen Auffassungen über den Mikrokosmos Atom. In der Geschichte der Wissenschaft hatte es schon früher Revolutionen gegeben; einmalig

Einstein and his stepdaughter Margot become United States citizens in Trenton, New Jersey, on 1 October 1940, by swearing the oath to support the American Constitution.

Zusammen mit seiner Stieftochter Margot legt Einstein am 1. Oktober 1940 in Trenton, New Jersey, den Eid auf die Verfassung ab und wird Bürger der USA.

Einstein's famous letter to President Roosevelt which initiated the development of the atomic bomb. He composed the letter in conjunction with fellow physicist Leo Szilard (1898–1964).

Einsteins berühmter Brief an Präsident Roosevelt, der den Anstoß zur Entwicklung der amerikanischen Atombombe gab; Einstein verfaßte den Brief gemeinsam mit seinem Physiker-Kollegen Leo Szilard (1898–1964).

Albert Einstein
Old Grove Rd.
Nassau Point
Peconic, Long Island

August 2nd, 1939

F.D. Roosevelt,
President of the United States,
White House
Washington, D.C.

Sir:

Some recent work by E.Fermi and L. Szilard, which has been communicated to me in manuscript, leads me to expect that the element uranium may be turned into a new and important source of energy in the immediate future. Certain aspects of the situation which has arisen seem to call for watchfulness and, if necessary, quick action on the part of the Administration. I believe therefore that it is my duty to bring to your attention the following facts and recommendations:

In the course of the last four months it has been made probable - through the work of Joliot in France as well as Fermi and Szilard in America - that it may become possible to set up a nuclear chain reaction in a large mass of uranium,by which vast amounts of power and large quantities of new radium-like elements would be generated. Now it appears almost certain that this could be achieved in the immediate future.

This new phenomenon would also lead to the construction of bombs, and it is conceivable - though much less certain - that extremely powerful bombs of a new type may thus be constructed. A single bomb of this type, carried by boat and exploded in a port, might very well destroy the whole port together with some of the surrounding territory. However, such bombs might very well prove to be too heavy for transportation by air.

-2-

The United States has only very poor ores of uranium in moderate quantities. There is some good ore in Canada and the former Czechoslovakia, while the most important source of uranium is Belgian Congo.

In view of this situation you may think it desirable to have some permanent contact maintained between the Administration and the group of physicists working on chain reactions in America. One possible way of achieving this might be for you to entrust with this task a person who has your confidence and who could perhaps serve in an inofficial capacity. His task might comprise the following:

a) to approach Government Departments, keep them informed of the further development, and put forward recommendations for Government action, giving particular attention to the problem of securing a supply of uranium ore for the United States;

b) to speed up the experimental work,which is at present being carried on within the limits of the budgets of University laboratories, by providing funds, if such funds be required, through his contacts with private persons who are willing to make contributions for this cause, and perhaps also by obtaining the co-operation of industrial laboratories which have the necessary equipment.

I understand that Germany has actually stopped the sale of uranium from the Czechoslovakian mines which she has taken over. That she should have taken such early action might perhaps be understood on the ground that the son of the German Under-Secretary of State, von Weizsäcker, is attached to the Kaiser-Wilhelm-Institut in Berlin where some of the American work on uranium is now being repeated.

Yours very truly,
A. Einstein
(Albert Einstein)

Lecture at the Institute for Advanced Study in Princeton, where Einstein pursued his activities from 1933 until his death on 18 April 1955.

Vorlesung im Institute for Advanced Study in Princeton, wo Einstein von 1933 bis zu seinem Tod am 18. April 1955 wirkte.

No later than 1907 and long before his fellow physicists, Einstein had recognized that in principle, it must be possible to produce energy through nuclear reaction. In 1938, Einstein finally saw its technical feasibility proven, when Otto Hahn and Fritz Strassmann discovered how to split the atom.

On the eve of World War II, in his famous letter of 2 August 1939, Einstein pointed out to the American president the dangers then threatening the world. Einstein saw more clearly than many others what Hitler might come up with in the offing. Thus it was that Einstein, the dedicated pacifist, acting out of dread of the National Socialists' hybris, gave the impetus for developing the atomic bomb.

und typisch für die zwanziger Jahre war aber die Schärfe, mit der die Auseinandersetzung geführt wurde, und das politische Ressentiment.

1933 emigrierte Einstein in die Vereinigten Staaten. Der Umzug des »Papstes der Physik« in die Neue Welt wurde als Symbol verstanden: Die Führung, die Deutschland in der Physik innegehabt hatte, war beendet und ging auf die Vereinigten Staaten über. Lange vor allen anderen Physikern, spätestens im Jahre 1907, hatte Einstein erkannt, daß es prinzipiell möglich sein müsse, aus Atomkern-Umwandlungen Energie zu gewinnen. Nach der Entdeckung der Kernspaltung durch Otto Hahn und Fritz Straßmann Ende 1938 verstand Einstein sofort, daß nunmehr die Zeit der technischen Realisierung gekommen war.

In seinem berühmten Brief vom 2. August 1939 machte Einstein – am Vorabend des Zweiten Weltkrieges – den amerikanischen Präsidenten auf die Gefahren aufmerksam, die der Welt drohten. Besser als viele andere hatte Einstein begriffen, was von Hitler zu erwarten war. So kam es, daß Einstein, der überzeugte Pazifist, aus Furcht vor der Machthybris der Nationalsozialisten den Anstoß gab zur Entwicklung der Atombombe.

In honor of its famous native son, the city of Ulm christened the new building of its adult education center "Einstein House". The photo shows the ceremony at the laying of the cornerstone in January 1967.

Zur Erinnerung an ihren größten Sohn taufte Einsteins Heimatstadt Ulm den Neubau ihrer Volkshochschule auf den Namen »Einstein-Haus«. Das Foto zeigt die Feier der Grundsteinlegung im Januar 1967.

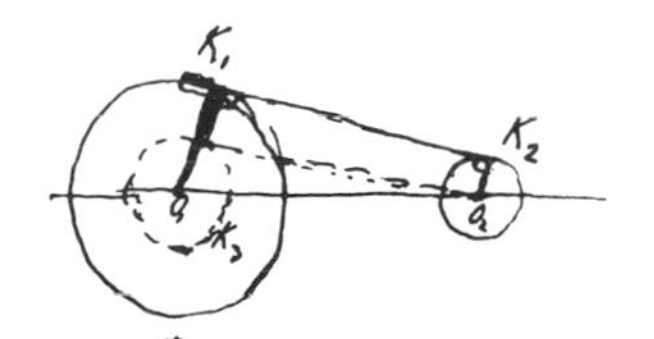

The radius of K_3 is the difference $r_3 = r_1 - r_2$.
The tangent $O_2 \rightarrow K_3$ is || to the tangent on K_1 and K_2 and can be easily constructed. This gives the solution.
A. E.

Einstein's reply to an American schoolgirl who wrote to him asking for help on her homework.

Einsteins Antwort für ein amerikanisches Schulmädchen, das ihn um Hilfe bei den Hausaufgaben gebeten hatte.

Jewish children who found refuge in the U.S. as "Displaced Persons" paid Einstein a visit at his home in Princetown on 14 March 1949 to congratulate him on his 70th birthday. Deeply moved by the cruel fate which befell European Jewry, Einstein evinced a patent solidarity with his fellow Jews.

Jüdische Kinder, als »Displaced Persons« in die USA gekommen, besuchen Einstein zu seinem 70. Geburtstag am 14. März 1949 in seinem Haus in Princeton. Begründet durch die Härte des jüdischen Schicksals wurde für Einstein das Gefühl der Solidarität mit jüdischen Menschen die stärkste innere Bindung.

Champion of the Underdog

Robert F. Wagner

Anwalt der Unterdrückten

"Champion of the Underdog" – this term is often used to describe Senator Robert Wagner, born in Nastätten, Germany, on June 8, 1877. Wagner moved with his family from Germany to New York when he was eight years old. He grew up in a slum area in Upper Manhattan, but, financially aided by his brother, managed to work his way through City College (1898) and Law School (1900). It was not Wagner's academic credentials which helped launch his political career, however, but Tammany Hall – a political machine not necessarily noted for propriety. Although Tammany leaders at first regarded Wagner with suspicion, they soon came to recognize his loyalty and intelligence. With Tammany support he was elected to the New York State Assembly in 1904 and served in the state legislature up to 1918. During this time Wagner showed that his support for reform was not simply a matter of expediency. As a member of the New York Factory Investigating Commission he sponsored more than sixty bills to ensure humane working conditions and a minimum wage. His experiences in the Committee were also crucial for his further career. For both as justice of the New York Supreme Court (1918–26) and as a member of the U.S. Senate (1926–49) Wagner deeply committed himself to innovating labor law.

In the late 1920s, notably before the Depression, Wagner worked tirelessly – though in vain – to obtain passage of legislation to control unemployment. Only in 1932, when the Great Depression was at its height, did Congress pass the Relief and Construction Act, the first legislation that gabe the federal government the responsibility for preserving a satisfactory employment level.

Wagner later helped draft and pass through the Senate several other important bills that committed government agencies to aiding the nation's economy. Among the most important were the National Industrial Recovery Act, designed to improve labor standards and to prevent unfair competition, and the National Labor Relations Act, the "Magna Charta" of American unionism. Due to this act, Wagner is still today referred to as the "legislative pilot of the New Deal". He died on May 4, 1953.

»Anwalt der Unterdrückten« – dieser Titel gebührt Senator Robert Wagner, der am 8. Juni 1877 in Nastätten im Taunus geboren wurde. Mit seiner Familie emigrierte Wagner als Achtjähriger nach New York, wo er in einem Slumviertel in Upper Manhattan aufwuchs. Dank finanzieller Hilfe seines Bruders gelang ihm 1898 der erfolgreiche Abschluß des City College und 1900 der eines Jurastudiums. Zum Eintritt ins politische Leben verhalfen ihm allerdings nicht seine akademischen Leistungen, sondern Tammany Hall – eine politische Organisation, die nicht unbedingt für ihre lauteren Methoden berühmt wurde. Den anfänglichen Argwohn der Tammany-Führung zerstreute Wagner bald durch Intelligenz und Loyalität. Mit Tammanys Unterstützung gelang ihm 1904 der Sprung ins Abgeordnetenhaus des Staates New York, wo er bis 1918 Delegierter blieb. In dieser Zeit wurde deutlich, daß Wagners Reformbestrebungen nicht von politischem Kalkül bestimmt waren. Als Mitglied des Untersuchungsausschusses für Fabrikwesen brachte er mehr als 60 Anträge zur Humanisierung der Arbeit und zur Fixierung eines Mindestlohnes ein. Diese Erfahrungen waren entscheidend für seinen weiteren politischen Werdegang: Sowohl als Richter des Obersten Gerichtshofs von New York (1918–1926) als auch als Senator (1926–49) widmete sich Wagner vor allem der Verbesserung der Arbeitsgesetzgebung. Bereits vor der Depression setzte er sich unermüdlich für eine gesetzliche Regelung der Arbeitslosenfrage ein. Doch erst 1932, auf dem Tiefpunkt der Wirtschaftskrise, verabschiedete der Kongreß den *Relief and Construction Act,* der der Bundesregierung erstmals die Verantwortung für die Eindämmung der Arbeitslosigkeit übertrug. Auch später wirkte Wagner bei der Gestaltung weiterer wichtiger Gesetze zur staatlichen Einflußnahme auf die Wirtschaft mit. Zu den bedeutendsten gehörten dabei der *National Industrial Recovery Act,* der auf die Verbesserung der Arbeitsverhältnisse und Wahrung des Wettbewerbs abzielte, sowie der *National Labor Relations Act,* die Magna Charta des amerikanischen Gewerkschaftswesens. Sie brachten ihm den Ruf des »Vaters der New-Deal-Gesetzgebung« ein. Robert F. Wagner starb fünfundsiebzigjährig, am 4. Mai 1953.

Robert Ferdinand Wagner (1877–1953)

Robert F. Wagner, left, next to President Franklin D. Roosevelt, at the signing of the Social Security Act of 1935, which he co-initiated

Robert F. Wagner, links neben Präsident Franklin D. Roosevelt, bei der Unterzeichnung des von ihm mitinitiierten »Social Security Act« von 1935

The old city hall in Wagner's place of birth, Nastätten – the scene of a German tragicomedy: it was here, in the 20s, that Robert Ferdinand Wagner was elected his home town's first honorary citizen, and it was here, in the 30s, that his honorary citizenship was revoked. Between these two events Wagner had held a speech that won worldwide respect, a speech against Nastätten's second honorary citizen – Adolf Hitler. Wagner's photo was absent from the Nastätten city hall until the arrival of American troops in April, 1945, when it suddenly reappeared...

Das alte Rathaus von Wagners Geburtsort Nastätten – der Schauplatz einer deutschen Tragikomödie: Hier wurde Robert Ferdinand Wagner in den 20er Jahren zum ersten Ehrenbürger seiner Heimatstadt gewählt, und hier wurde ihm diese Ehrenbürgerschaft in den 30er Jahren wieder aberkannt. Denn inzwischen hatte Wagner eine weltweit beachtete Rede gegen den zweiten Ehrenbürger von Nastätten gehalten – Adolf Hitler. Erst beim Einmarsch amerikanischer Truppen im April 1945 hing plötzlich wieder ein Wagner-Foto in Nastättens Rathaus...

Reinvigorating Christian Thought

Paul Tillich

Erneuerer christlichen Denkens

Paul Tillich (1886–1965)

An eminent 20th-century theologian and philosopher who illuminated and bound together the realms of religion and culture, Paul Tillich is considered a central figure in the intellectual life of his time both in his native Germany and later in his adopted homeland, the United States. Tillich, the son of a Lutheran minister, was born in the village of Starzeddel, Prussia, on 20 August 1886. After conclusion of his theological studies at various German universities (1911) and his ordination (1912), Tillich served as a military chaplain during World War I. The war was a shattering experience to him, not only for its carnage and destruction, but it made him lose his belief in 19th-century humanism and led him to question the adequacy of the traditional concept of God in modern times. He devoted the rest of his life to redefining this concept and directing man to "the God beyond God".

After the war Tillich taught at the universities of Berlin, Marburg (where he met Heidegger), Dresden, Leipzig and Frankfurt. He also became an active leader in the Religious Socialist movement and wrote extensively, publishing over 100 essays, articles and reviews in the period up to 1933. The first non-Jewish professor to be dismissed from a teaching post for criticizing the intimidating actions of Hitler's "Brown Shirts," Tillich went to the U.S. in 1933. Without knowledge of the English language, he joined the faculty of the Union Theological Seminary in New York. As chairman of the Council for a Democratic Germany, he continued to pursue his political interests. In the post-war years he taught at Columbia University, Harvard (1955–62) and the University of Chicago (1962–65). His public lectures and books reached large audiences. *Systematic Theology,* Tillich's major statement of the meaning of Christian faith, together with *The Courage to Be* and *Dynamics of Faith* revealed the comprehensiveness of his thought and made him the most influential theologian of his time in North America. Tillich died in Chicago on 22 October 1965.

Der Versuch, die Inhalte von Religion und Kultur in ihren Wechselwirkungen zu verstehen, machte Paul Tillich zu einem der herausragenden Theologen und Philosophen des 20. Jahrhunderts und zu einem der wichtigsten zeitgenössischen Intellektuellen sowohl in seinem Geburtsland Deutschland wie in seiner späteren Wahlheimat Amerika. Tillich wurde als Sohn eines protestantischen Pfarrers am 20. August 1886 im preußischen Starzeddel geboren. Nach Beendigung seines Theologiestudiums an mehreren deutschen Universitäten (1911) und seiner Ordination (1912) diente Tillich als Militärpfarrer. Die erschütternden Erfahrungen in den Blutbädern des Ersten Weltkieges nahmen ihm den Glauben an einen Humanismus, wie ihn das 19. Jahrhundert gelehrt hatte, und weckten seine Zweifel an der Gültigkeit des traditionellen Gottesbegriffs. Den Rest seines Lebens widmete Tillich der Neubestimmung des Konzepts und der Lehre vom »wahren Gottwesen«.

Nach dem Krieg lehrte Tillich in Berlin, Marburg (wo er u.a. Heidegger traf), Dresden, Leipzig und Frankfurt. Darüber hinaus engagierte er sich im Bund religiöser Sozialisten und veröffentlichte bis 1933 über 100 Aufsätze, Artikel und Rezensionen. Wegen seiner Kritik am Hitlerregime wurde er 1933 als erster nichtjüdischer Professor seines Ordinariats entbunden; noch im gleichen Jahr ging er in die USA, wo er, obwohl des Englischen nicht mächtig, einen Lehrauftrag am Union Theological Seminary in New York erhielt. Als Vorsitzender des »Council for a Democratic Germany« setzte er sein politisches Engagement fort. In den Nachkriegsjahren lehrte Tillich an der Columbia University, in Harvard (1955–62) und an der University of Chicago (1962–65). Seine Vorlesungen und Bücher fanden große Beachtung. Vor allem die *Systematische Theologie,* sein Hauptwerk über die Inhalte christlichen Glaubens, sowie die Schriften *Der Mut zum Sein* und *Wesen und Wandel des Glaubens* verdeutlichen jene Vielseitigkeit im Denken, die ihn zum einflußreichsten zeitgenössischen Theologen in Amerika machte. Tillich starb in Chicago am 22. Oktober 1965.

A monument in Paul Tillich Park in New Harmony. The town was founded by George Rapp, a German immigrant from Wurttemberg. Later, the early British socialist, Robert Owen, took over this utopian socialist settlement in Indiana. Paul Tillich himself prescribed that his ashes be scattered at this site.

Gedenkstein im Paul-Tillich-Park in New Harmony, der von dem Württemberger Georg Rapp gegründeten und später von dem englischen Frühsozialisten Robert Owen übernommenen sozialutopischen Siedlung in Indiana. Paul Tillich selbst bestimmte, daß seine Asche an diesem Ort verstreut werden sollte.

Paul Tillich (left) together with the publisher of "Time", Henry Luce, in May, 1963. Tillich was the main speaker at the celebration commemorating the magazine's fortieth anniversary.

Paul Tillich (links) mit »Time«-Verleger Henry Luce im Mai 1963; Tillich war Hauptredner bei einer Feier zum 40jährigen Bestehen des Nachrichtenmagazins.

From the Bauhaus to the Capital of Modern Architecture

Ludwig Mies van der Rohe

Vom Bauhaus in die Hauptstadt der modernen Architektur

Ludwig Mies van der Rohe, one of the most significant architects in the first half of the twentieth century, was born in Aachen on March 27, 1886, as the son of a stonemason, Mies. He later added his mother's Dutch maiden name to his own, and began his career in his father's workshop and amidst the noise and dirt of construction sites. After completing elementary school, he attended the building trade school in Aachen and, starting at the age of fifteen, spent two years as an architect's apprentice. In 1905 he moved to Berlin where he continued his training as a pupil of Bruno Paul, the famous furniture designer. Three years later, he joined the office of Peter Behrens, the most innovative architect in Germany at that time. Behrens' work, emphasizing the relationship between architecture and industry as well as the romantic neoclassicism of the Berlin architect, painter and set designer, Karl Friedrich Schinkel (1781–1841), was to have an important impact on Mies until the war. A year in Holland was followed by his return to Berlin in 1913, where he opened his own atelier.

The First World War marked a change in Mies' style which, in the 20s, was strongly influenced by German expressionism, Dutch *stijl* and Russian constructivism. Among his most notable buildings in this period are the Weissenhof housing project in Stuttgart (1927) and the German pavilion at the international exhibition in Barcelona (1929), both of which showed Mies' fascination for modern designs and his novel use of concrete-steel and glass. In 1930 he was made director of the famous *Bauhaus* until it was dissolved in 1933 under pressure from the Nazis. As artistic freedom in Germany continued to erode, Mies took advantage of a business trip to the United States in 1937 to remain there. A year later he was made head of the School of Architecture at Chicago's Armour Institute (later the Illinois Institute of Technology), and in 1944 he became an American citizen.

As a result of his redesigning the I.I.T. campus, Mies' fame spread rapidly in America, and Chicago soon became a mecca for students of architecture from all over the world. With towering skyscrapers such as the Lake Shore Drive apartments in Chicago and the Seagram Building in New York, he left his mark on America's urban skyline for years to come. On August 17, 1969, at the age of 83, Mies van der Rohe died in Chicago.

Ludwig Mies van der Rohe, einer der bedeutendsten Architekten der ersten Hälfte des 20. Jahrhunderts, wurde am 27. März 1886 in Aachen als Sohn des Steinmetzen Mies geboren und fügte dem Familiennamen später den holländischen Mädchennamen seiner Mutter an. Seine Laufbahn begann in der Werkstatt des Vaters und auf Baustellen inmitten von Lärm und Schutt. Nach der Volksschule besuchte Mies eine Baugewerbeschule in Aachen und ging im Alter von fünfzehn Jahren bei einem Architekten in die Lehre. 1905 setzte er seine Ausbildung in Berlin als Schüler des berühmten Möbeldesigners Bruno Paul fort. Drei Jahre später wurde er Mitarbeiter im Planungsbüro von Peter Behrens, dem damals schöpferischsten Architekten Deutschlands. Behrens Arbeit, die einerseits die Beziehung zwischen Architektur und Industrie betonte, gleichzeitig aber den romantischen Neoklassizismus des Berliner Architekten, Malers und Bühnenbildners Karl Friedrich Schinkel (1781–1841) wieder aufnahm, sollte bis Kriegsbeginn starken Einfluß auf Mies ausüben. Einem einjährigen Hollandaufenthalt folgte 1913 die Rückkehr nach Berlin, wo er ein eigenes Atelier eröffnete.

Mies van der Rohes Stil erfuhr durch den Ersten Weltkrieg einen Wandel und orientierte sich in den zwanziger Jahren am heimischen Expressionismus, dem holländischen *Stijl* und dem russischen Konstruktivismus. Zu den bemerkenswertesten in dieser Zeit entstandenen Bauwerken zählt die 1927 errichtete Weißenhofsiedlung in Stuttgart und der deutsche Pavillion auf der Weltausstellung in Barcelona 1929, die beide Mies' Vorliebe für modernes Design und seine neuartige Verwendung von Stahlbeton und Glas verdeutlichten. Dem berühmten *Bauhaus* stand er ab 1930 als Direktor vor, bis es unter nationalsozialistischem Druck 1933 aufgelöst werden mußte. Als die künstlerische Freiheit in Deutschland zunehmend erstickt wurde, nutzte Mies 1937 eine Geschäftsreise in die Vereinigten Staaten, um sich dort niederzulassen. Ein Jahr darauf folgte er einem Ruf nach Chicago an die Architektenschule des Armour Instituts, dem späteren Illinois Institute of Technology, 1944 wurde er amerikanischer Staatsbürger.

Die Neugestaltung des IIT – Hochschulgeländes machte seinen Namen auf dem gesamten Kontinent bekannt und trug dazu bei, daß Chicago bald zum Mekka für Architekturstudenten aus aller Welt wurde. Mit Wolkenkratzern wie den Wohnhochhäusern am Lake Shore Drive in Chicago und dem Seagram Building in New York setzte er auf Jahre hinaus Akzente im amerikanischen Städtebau. Mies van der Rohe starb am 17. August 1969 im Alter von 83 Jahren in Chicago.

The angular cityscape of Aachen, where Mies van der Rohe was born in 1886. Today, architectural development seems to have returned from Mies van der Rohe's expansive style to smaller structures such as these.

Das winkelige Stadtbild Aachens, wo Mies van der Rohe 1886 geboren wurde. Heute scheint die Entwicklung der Architektur von Mies van der Rohes Großflächigkeit zu solchen Kleinstrukturen zurückzukehren.

The School of Architecture at the Illinois Institute of Technology: Mies van der Rohe continued his work in one of his most famous buildings.

Die Schule für Architektur auf dem Campus des Illinois Institute of Technology: Mies van der Rohes Wirkungsstätte und einer seiner bekanntesten Bauten.

The Seagram Building in New York, built 1954 to 1958, designed by Mies van der Rohe and Philip Johnson.

Das Seagram Building in New York, von 1954 bis 1958 erbaut von Mies van der Rohe und Philip Johnson

Prima Donna in Vienna and New York

Lotte Lehmann

Primadonna in Wien und New York

Lotte Lehmann in New York as the Marschallin in a Metropolitan Opera production of Richard Strauss' "Rosenkavalier".

Lotte Lehmann als Marschallin im »Rosenkavalier« von Richard Strauss in einer Aufführung der Metropolitan Opera, New York

Until the appearance on the scene of soprano Lotte Lehmann, the singing of the classic German repertoire was largely the province of abundantly proportioned ladies with often strident voices. Lehmann's career brought in an era of subtlety and sincerity in the interpretation of the vocal music of Beethoven, Wagner and Strauss.

Born in Perleberg near Berlin on February 27, 1888, she studied singing in the capital with Mathilde Mallinger, the first Eva in *Die Meistersinger,* making her own inauspicious operatic début in the alto role of the third boy in Mozart's *Zauberflöte* in Hamburg in 1909. Her first performance in Vienna, as Agathe in Weber's *Freischütz* in 1914, so impressed the management of the theatre that Vienna soon became her artistic home. She became a permanent member of the company in 1916.

Of regal bearing and voice, Lehmann is probably best remembered for her interpretations of noble tragic heroines. The first artist to sing all three leading soprano parts in Strauss's *Rosenkavalier,* she soon made the Marschallin her trade mark, the composer's declared favorite. Strauss later wrote three of his best-known roles for her, the dyer's wife in *Die Frau ohne Schatten,* the title role in *Arabella,* and the composer in *Ariadne* auf Naxos.

A woman of great principle, Lehmann renounced her German citizenship when the Nazis came to power, and then left her adopted country of Austria when that nation was annexed. In 1938, she settled in the United States, soon to become a citizen of that country.

An accomplished author and poet herself, Lehmann brought her keen intelligence and understanding especially into play in her interpretations of the concert repertoire, and counted such eminent musicians as Bruno Walter among her recital accompanists. Her performing career ended in 1951 on the stage of New York's Town Hall where she announced her retirement with characteristic humility and then proceeded to burst into tears shortly before completing her final encore, Schubert's "An die Musik".

But the end of her performing career was by no means the last the public would hear of Lotte Lehmann. Moving to Santa Barbara, California, she became head of the vocal music department of the Music Academy of the West, and numbered prominent artists such as Grace Bumbry among her pupils. She amplified these activities by writing books, recording German poetry, appearing on radio and television and directing opera, including a production of *Der Rosenkavalier* at the Metropolitan in 1961.

After receiving most of the honors the musical world of two continents can bestow, and witnessing the naming of a street in Salzburg and a concert hall in California for her, Lotte Lehmann died on August 26, 1976, aged eighty-eight.

Bevor Lotte Lehmann die Arena der Sopranistinnen betrat, beherrschten Damen mit oft üppigen Ausmaßen und nicht selten schrillem Diskant die Szene der deutschen Klassik. Lotte Lehmanns Karriere leitete eine Ära der Feinfühligkeit und Klarheit in der Interpretation der Vokalmusik von Beethoven, Wagner und Strauss ein.

In Perleberg nahe Berlin am 27. Februar 1888 geboren, studierte sie in Berlin Gesang bei Mathilde Mallinger, der ersten Eva aus Wagners *Meistersingern* und gab ihr wenig glücklich verlaufenes Operndebut in der Altrolle des dritten Knaben in Mozarts *Zauberflöte* 1909 in Hamburg. Ihr erster Auftritt in Wien im Jahr 1914 – sie sang die Agathe in Webers *Freischütz* – beeindruckte die Intendanz dermaßen, daß sie Wien bald zu ihrer künstlerischen Heimat machen konnte. 1916 wurde sie ein festes Mitglied des Ensembles.

Dank ihrer königlichen Stimme und Ausstrahlung bleibt Lotte Lehmann hauptsächlich als Interpretin nobler und tragikumwitterter Opernheroinen in Erinnerung. Sie sang als erste alle drei großen Sopranrollen im *Rosenkavalier* von Richard Strauss und machte die Marschallin, die erklärte Lieblingsfigur des Komponisten, zu ihrer Glanzrolle.

Als Frau mit klaren moralischen Grundsätzen legte Lotte Lehmann nach der nationalsozialistischen Machtergreifung die deutsche Staatsangehörigkeit ab und verließ, als Österreich annektiert wurde, auch ihre Wahlheimat. 1938 ließ sie sich in den Vereinigten Staaten nieder und wurde kurz darauf Staatsbürgerin dieses Landes.

Selbst eine versierte Autorin und auch mit eigenen Gedichten hervorgetreten, brachte Lotte Lehmann ihre künstlerische Intelligenz und Sensibilität vor allem im Liedgesang zur Geltung, bei dem sie so prominente Musiker wie Bruno Walter zu ihren Begleitern zählen konnte. Sie beschloß ihre sängerische Laufbahn mit einem Konzert in der Carnegie Hall in New York, wo sie mit charakteristischer Bescheidenheit ihren Abschied bekanntgab, jedoch in Tränen ausbrach, ehe sie ihre letzte Zugabe, Schuberts »An die Musik«, beendet hatte.

Lotte Lehmanns Rückzug vom Podium war jedoch noch keineswegs ihr Rückzug aus der Öffentlichkeit. Im kalifornischen Santa Barbara wurde sie Leiterin der Gesangsklasse an der Music Academy of the West und hatte unter ihren Schülern so berühmte Künstler wie Grace Bumbry. Darüber hinaus schrieb sie mehrere Bücher, las deutsche Lyrik für Schallplattenaufnahmen, arbeitete für Radio- und Fernsehproduktionen und führte mehrfach Opernregie, darunter bei einer Produktion des *Rosenkavaliers* an der Metropolitan Opera im Jahre 1961.

Nachdem sie fast alle Ehrungen erhalten hatte, die die Musikwelt zweier Kontinente zu vergeben hat, und miterleben konnte, daß eine Straße in Salzburg und ein Konzertsaal in Kalifornien nach ihr benannt wurden, starb Lotte Lehmann im Alter von 88 Jahren am 26. August 1976.

Lieder recital with Bruno Walter

Ein Liederabend mit Bruno Walter

Lotte Lehmann's first concert with Arturo Toscanini in New York, 1934; in the same year, still before moving permanently to the United States, she made her Met debut in Richard Wagner's "Valkyrie".

Lotte Lehmanns erstes Konzert mit Arturo Toscanini in New York, 1934; im selben Jahr, noch vor der endgültigen Übersiedlung in die USA, debütierte sie an der Met als Sieglinde in Richard Wagner »Walküre«

Eminent Authority on Art History

Erwin Panofsky

Klassiker der Kunstgeschichtsschreibung

Erwin Panofsky, generally referred to as one of the founders and main representatives of the iconological approach to art history, was born in Hanover, Germany, on March 30, 1892. Educated at the Berlin, Munich, and Freiburg Universities, he received his Ph. D. in 1914 with a work on Dürer's art theory. The following years he continued working on theoretical problems of art at the reputable Warburg Library in Hamburg, where he met Aby Warburg and other well-known "art intellectuals". In close cooperation with this circle of scholars, Panofsky – appointed professor at the Hamburg University in 1926 – began to develop the "iconological" approach, in which art, in addition to its mere visual meaning, is always charged with the attitude toward life of the civilization that produced it. Two works, *Hercules at the Crossroads* (1930) and *Studies in Iconology* (1939), an elaborate "manifesto" of the new approach, established him as the most prominent figure of this school of art history.
Hitler's seizure of power in 1933 forced Panofsky to emigrate to the United States, where he had been visiting professor at New York University between 1931–33. In 1935, he became professor of art history at the Institute for Advanced Study in Princeton, New Jersey. Panofsky published numerous books and articles, many of which were devoted to the study of iconographic, stylistic, and theoretical aspects of medieval and Renaissance art. In *Early Netherlandish Painting* (1953) he combined iconographic interpretation with analysis of style, while his *Renaissance and Renascences in Western Art* (1960) was a historical synthesis of all schools and epochs of western European art. His major work, *Meaning in the Visual Arts* (1955), is a collection of essays dealing with the subjects and ideas represented throughout the history of art, examining them as manifestations of cultural traditions. Central to all these writings was the profoundly humanistic view that form and content in a work of art are indissoluble.
Panofsky died on March 15, 1968, in Princeton. He is still today considered one of the most important art historians of our time.

Erwin Panofsky, Mitbegründer und Hauptvertreter der Ikonologie in der Kunstgeschichte, wurde am 30. März 1892 in Hannover geboren. Nach seinem Studium in Berlin, München und Freiburg promovierte er 1914 mit einer Arbeit über die Kunsttheorie Dürers, eine Thematik, die auch in den folgenden Jahren im Mittelpunkt seiner Arbeit stand. Zunächst am renommierten Warburg Institut und ab 1926 als Professor an der Universität Hamburg tätig, traf er bekannte Kunstsachverständige wie Aby Warburg, die ihm wichtige Impulse zur Entwicklung seines ikonologischen Ansatzes gaben. Kern dieses Ansatzes ist die Forderung, daß ein Kunstwerk nicht nur nach seiner bildlichen Bedeutung befragt, sondern immer auch in seinem kulturellen Kontext betrachtet werden sollte. Panofskys Bücher *Hercules am Scheidewege* (1930) und *Studies in Iconology* (1939), das grundlegende Werk zur Theorie und Praxis der Ikonologie, machten ihn zum »Vater« dieser neuen kunsthistorischen Disziplin.
Nach Hitlers Machtergreifung 1933 emigrierte Panofsky in die USA, die er zuvor als Gastprofessor an der New York University (1931–33) kennengelernt hatte. 1935 wurde er als Professor für Kunstgeschichte an das Institute of Advanced Study in Princeton, N.J., berufen. Hier schrieb Panofsky zahlreiche Bücher und Artikel, v. a. zu ikonographischen, stilistischen und theoretischen Aspekten der Kunst des Mittelalters und der Renaissance. In seinem Werk über *Frühe niederländische Malerei* (1953) verband er ikonographische Interpretation mit Stilanalyse, während er in *Renaissance and Renascences in Western Art* (1960) zu einer kunsthistorischen Synthese der westeuropäischen Kunst aller Schulen und Epochen ausholte. Sein Hauptwerk, die Aufsatzsammlung *Sinn und Deutung in der bildenden Kunst* (1955) ist der Formulierung von Gegenstand und Idee der Kunstgeschichte und ihrem Verständnis als einem Ausdruck kultureller Traditionen gewidmet. Im Mittelpunkt all dieser Bücher stand dabei stets ein stark humanistisch geprägtes Verständnis der Kunst als Einheit von Form und Gehalt.
Panofsky starb am 15. März 1968 in Princeton. Noch heute gilt er als einer wichtigsten zeitgenössischen Kunsthistoriker.

Erwin Panofsky (1892–1968)

Fuld Hall, the old main building of the Institute for Advanced Study at Princeton which was founded in 1930 and where Panofsky taught from 1935 to 1962. This school of research for the scholarly elite (which was not a part of Princeton University) also became the new academic home of Albert Einstein.

Fuld Hall, das alte Hauptgebäude des 1930 gegründeten Institute for Advanced Study in Princeton, an dem Panofsky von 1935 bis 1962 wirkte. Auch Albert Einstein fand an dieser (nicht zur Universität Princeton gehörenden) Elite-Forschungsstätte eine neue wissenschaftliche Heimat.

As an art historian, Aby Warburg (1866–1929), Paul Moritz Warburg's brother, greatly influenced Panofsky's generation. (Photo from around 1925)

Aby Warburg (1866–1929), ein Bruder von Paul Moritz Warburg, übte als Kunsthistoriker großen Einfluß auf die Generation Panofskys aus. (Foto um 1925)

A Bavarian Writer in New York

Oskar Maria Graf

Ein Heimatschriftsteller in New York

The Bavarian writer Oskar Maria Graf, whose round, ruddy-colored countenance and large figure reflected his southern German homeland, was born on July 22, 1894, in the little resort town of Berg on Lake Starnberg. He was the ninth child of a baker and a woman of peasant stock and, like his older brothers, he had to learn the baking business. Nevertheless, he managed to do a lot of surreptitious reading while delivering warm rolls on his morning rounds.

At sixteen he ran away to nearby Munich, determined to become a writer. While earning a living at various menial tasks, he spent his spare time writing stories and book reviews and became initiated into his "university", the bohemian culture of prewar Munich. During World War I he served on the Russian front but his refusal to fire upon the enemy and other acts of insubordination got him a short prison term and a brief spell in an insane asylum. Back in Munich in 1918, he witnessed the attempted revolution under Kurt Eisner and the eventual overthrow of the *Räterepublik*. His description of those events in *Prisoners All* (published in 1927) first brought him international recognition as an author. In 1933 he voluntarily went into exile in Austria in reply to Hitler's seizure of power and, when the Nazis decided to spare Graf's works in their crackdown on German writers, he protested: "Burn me!" he angrily demanded in a Viennese newspaper, whereupon his books were added to the flames at the Munich University. One of the first to be stripped of his citizenship, he fled to Czechoslovakia in 1934 and four years later emigrated to America.

Graf spent the rest of his life in his adopted country although, due to his anti-militaristic convictions, he was never issued a passport and hardly learned a word of English. He maintained ties with the old homeland only by keeping to touch with other German expatriates in New York whose experiences in America he portrayed in *Taking Refuge in Mediocrity* (1959). But disgusted by the renewal of provincial narrow-mindedness in postwar Germany, Graf never again returned there to live. Ironically however, after his death in 1967, his remains were given a final resting place in a cemetery in Bogenhausen, an elegant section of Munich.

Oskar Maria Graf, before having published a single line, had the epithet "Bavarian Writer" printed on his calling card. And throughout his life he tried – even in his habilement, complete with Lederhose – to hide behind this mask...

»Heimatschriftsteller« ließ Oskar Maria Graf auf seine Visitenkarte drucken, ehe er sonst eine Zeile veröffentlicht hatte – und auch in seiner äußeren Erscheinung versuchte er zeitlebens, sich hinter dieser Maske zu verstecken...

House where Graf was born in Berg on Lake Starnberg

Grafs Geburtshaus in Berg am Starnberger See

Der bayerische Schriftsteller Oskar Maria Graf, dessen breites, gerötetes Gesicht und grobschlächtige Figur beredtes Zeugnis seiner oberbayerischen Herkunft waren, wurde am 22. Juli 1894 in Berg am Starnberger See geboren. Neuntes Kind eines Bäckers und einer Frau bäuerlicher Herkunft mußte er, wie seine älteren Brüder, schon früh in der elterlichen Bäckerei mitanpacken. Freie Augenblicke kannte er nur beim allmorgendlichen Semmelaustragen – und die nutzte er schon als Kind zum Lesen.

Mit sechzehn lief er von Zuhause weg, um im nahegelegenen München Schriftsteller zu werden. Während er mit verschiedensten Hilfsarbeiten seinen Lebensunterhalt verdiente, schrieb er in der Freizeit Erzählungen und Buchrezensionen und wurde in die Kreise der Münchner Vorkriegsbohème eingeführt, die er »seine Universität« nannte. Im Ersten Weltkrieg diente er an der russischen Front, weigerte sich jedoch, auf den Feind zu schießen, was ihm, zusammen mit anderen Widersetzlichkeiten, eine Haftstrafe und einen kurzen Aufenthalt in einer psychiatrischen Anstalt eintrug. 1918, wieder in München, erlebte er die Novemberrevolution unter Kurt Eisner und die Niederschlagung der Räterepublik. Seine Beschreibung dieser Ereignisse in *Wir sind Gefangene* (1927) brachte ihm die erste internationale Anerkennung als Autor. 1933 ging er als Reaktion auf Hitlers Machtergreifung nach Österreich ins Exil. Als die Nazis bei ihrem Rundumschlag gegen die deutsche Literatur einen Großteil seiner Werke ausklammerten, protestierte er mit einem wütenden Brief in einer Wiener Zeitung: »Verbrennt mich!«, worauf auch seine Bücher den Scheiterhaufen vor der Münchner Universität hinzugefügt wurden. Als einer der ersten, denen die Staatsbürgerschaft aberkannt wurde, floh er 1934 in die Tschechoslowakei und emigrierte vier Jahre später nach Amerika.

Graf verbrachte den Rest seines Lebens in der Wahlheimat, obwohl er sich als konsequenter Pazifist weigerte, den Verfassungseid (in dem die Bereitschaft zum Waffendienst für die USA gefordert wird) abzulegen und daher nie einen amerikanischen Paß erhielt. Auch um die englische Sprache bemühte er sich kaum. Eine gewisse Verbindung zur Heimat hielt er durch Kontakte zu anderen in Amerika lebenden Deutschen aufrecht, deren Erfahrungen er in *Die Flucht ins Mittelmäßige* (1959) beschrieb. Er selbst kehrte zu Lebzeiten nicht mehr nach Deutschland, dessen Restauration in der Nachkriegszeit er als provinziell empfand, zurück: Erst nach seinem Tod im Jahre 1967 wurden seine sterblichen Überreste nach München überführt, wo sie auf dem Künstlerfriedhof in Bogenhausen ihre letzte Ruhestätte fanden.

Invitation from Oskar Maria Graf and his cronies to an Artists' Grand Costume Ball.

Oskar Maria Grafs New Yorker Stammtisch lädt zu einem Künstlerball ein.

Philosopher of the "New Left"

Herbert Marcuse

Der Philosoph der »Neuen Linken«

Born of a well-to-do Jewish family in Berlin on July 19, 1898, Herbert Marcuse was trained as a professional philosopher at the Universities of Berlin and Freiburg. In 1933 he became a member of the Institute for Social Research in Frankfurt and remained actively committed to its projects until 1942. When the Nazi takeover resulted in the Institute's transplantation (first to Geneva and then to New York City), its members included Max Horkheimer, Theodor Adorno, Erich Fromm, Leo Lowenthal and (after 1936) Franz Neumann. The climate of the Institute was decidedly Marxist, though not dogmatically so. It was there that Marcuse, the Institute's resident expert on philosophy and political theory, became interested in the ideological origins of fascism. Having emigrated to the U.S. with the Institute, Marcuse subsequently worked at the Office of Strategic Services, the Office of Intelligence Research and the State Department from 1942 until 1950. This period was a sort of moratorium, providing him with the opportunity to reassess his thought. He became convinced that Marxism could only play a role in the post-fascist era if it underwent certain modifications. After considering French existentialism, Marcuse rejected Sartre's concept of freedom as political quietism and turned to Freud. *Eros and Civilization* (1954) was the culmination of this reflection. Here Marcuse united Marx and Freud, claiming that the latter was revolutionary and thoroughly sociological. From the 1950s until his death Marcuse taught at various universities including Columbia, Harvard, Brandeis and California at San Diego. With the publication of *One-Dimensional Man* in 1964, he became almost a cult figure among engaged student groups. His essay "Repressive Tolerance" (1965) maintained that the apparent freedom to dissent in America was a way of disarming radical opposition, and that this "tolerance" was in fact a form of intolerance. But the popularity of Marcuse's own dissent was short-lived, and the revolution he believed in failed to crest, relegating him to the relics of the 60s. Marcuse died from a stroke on July 29, 1979 in Starnberg, Bavaria, while a guest of the Max Planck Society.

Herbert Marcuse, am 19. Juli 1898 als Sohn einer gutsituierten jüdischen Familie in Berlin geboren, studierte Philosophie in Berlin und Freiburg. Von 1933 bis 1942 war er Mitarbeiter des Instituts für Sozialforschung. Hitlers Machtübernahme erzwang die Verlegung des Instituts von Frankfurt nach Genf, dann nach New York. Weitere Institutsmitglieder waren Max Horkheimer, Theodor W. Adorno, Erich Fromm, Leo Lowenthal und, nach 1936, Franz Neumann. Das Institut orientierte sich deutlich am Marxismus, jedoch ohne ihn ideologisch zu propagieren, und bot so für Philosophen und Politikwissenschaftler die idealen Bedingungen zur theoretischen Aufarbeitung der Ursprünge des Faschismus. Von 1942 bis 1950 stand Marcuse im Dienst des Office of Strategic Services, dem späteren CIA, des Office of Intelligence Research und des Außenministeriums. Während dieser Zeit akademischer Abstinenz erhielt Marcuse Impulse, die auf seine späteren Werke wesentlichen Einfluß haben sollten. Zunächst wurde ihm klar, daß die Marxismus-Diskussion nach der Ära des Faschismus nicht mehr unter den überkommenen Prämissen fortzusetzen war. Ebenso intensiv setzte er sich mit dem französischen Existentialismus auseinander; Marcuse verwarf Sartres Freiheitsbegriff als apolitisch und wandte sich Sigmund Freud zu. 1957 erschien *Eros und Kultur*, 1965 unter dem Titel *Triebstruktur und Gesellschaft* neu aufgelegt, das seinen philosophischen Brückenschlag zwischen Marx und Freud vollendete, wobei Marcuse gerade letzteren als besonders revolutionären und soziologisch relevanten Denker herausstellte. Ab 1950 lehrte Marcuse an den Universitäten Columbia, Harvard und Brandeis und an der University of California in San Diego. Mit dem Erscheinen des Buches *Der eindimensionale Mensch* im Jahr 1967 wurde Marcuse zu einer Vaterfigur der Neuen Linken. In seinem Essay »Repressive Tolerance« von 1965 entlarvte er die vielgepriesene amerikanische Freizügigkeit als getarntes Verschleißinstrument oppositioneller Kräfte. Doch auch die von Marcuse angeführte Protestwelle ebbte ab, und die erhoffte revolutionäre Springflut verlief in den siebziger Jahren im Sande. Am 29. Juli 1979 erlag Herbert Marcuse während eines Aufenthalts am Max-Planck-Institut in Starnberg, Bayern, den Folgen eines Schlaganfalls.

Herbert Marcuse (1898–1979)

The campus of Columbia University, where Marcuse first continued his work in America. It was here that the Institute for Social Research, after having emigrated from Frankfurt, was offered generous opportunities to further its investigations.

Marcuses erste amerikanische Wirkungsstätte: der Campus der Columbia-Universität, an der das Frankfurter Institut für Sozialforschung nach der Emigration großzügige neue Arbeitsmöglichkeiten erhielt.

Herbert Marcuse in the great lecture hall of the Free University, Berlin, during student unrest in May 1968. To the disappointment of many in the audience, Marcuse refused to voice any opinion on "revolutionary practice", withdrawing instead to theoretical ground.

Herbert Marcuse während der Studentenunruhen im Mai 1968 im Auditorium Maximum der Freien Universität Berlin; zur Enttäuschung eines Großteils seiner Zuhörer verweigerte Marcuse jede Stellungnahme zur »revolutionären Praxis« und zog sich auf seine theoretische Position zurück.

From Berlin to Broadway

Kurt Weill

Vom Kurfürstendamm zum Broadway

While the music of Kurt Weill is just as popular today, over thirty years after his death, as it was during his lifetime, Weill's musical language and intentions are often still the object of rank misconception. Both his early move from the field of symphonic and chamber music to work for the musical theater on social-critical themes, as well as his later move to the sphere of the Broadway musical, have been criticized as a kind of demeaning self-betrayal. Yet it can be demonstrated that he used his extraordinary versatility as a means of remaining true to his inner self; his capacity to adapt to new and changing environments served his disrelish for conformity.

The fifty years of Kurt Weill's life exactly spanned the first half of our century, a time whose ills, turbulence and hopes are reflected in his compositions. The son of a cantor, Weill was born in Dessau on 2 March 1900, and began to study music at fourteen. His First Symphony and Violin Concerto were among the results of his studies in Berlin (1918-23) as a pupil of Humperdinck and Busoni. Successful collaborations with Bert Brecht which made him famous *(The Three Penny Opera,* 1928; *Mahagonny, 1930; The Seven Deadly Sins of the Petty Bourgeois,* 1933) were followed by his Second Symphony (world premiere by Bruno Walter and the Concertgebouw Orchestra in Amsterdam, 1934). He and his wife Lotte Lenya (for whom he wrote many of his leading roles) had fled to Paris from Nazi Germany in 1933, and in 1935 they emigrated to New York, where Weill spent the last fifteen years of his life writing mainly for the Broadway stage.

In America, as in Berlin, Weill managed to work together with the finest writers of his time. He created *Knickerbocker Holiday* (1938) together with Maxwell Anderson; *Lady in the Dark* (1941) with Moss Hart and Ira Gershwin; *One Touch of Venus* (1943) with S. J. Perelman and Ogden Nash; *Street Scene* (1947) with Elmer Rice and Langston Hughes; *Love Life* (1948) with Alan Jay Lerner; and *Lost in the Stars* (1949) with Maxwell Anderson, based on the novel *Cry, the Beloved Country* by Alan Paton.

When Kurt Weill died in New York on 3 April 1950, he was acknowledged as one of the leading American theater composers.

Obwohl die Musik von Kurt Weill heute, dreißig Jahre nach seinem Tod, ebenso populär ist wie zu seinen Lebzeiten, werden Weills Musiksprache und Absichten noch häufig mißverstanden. Seine frühe Abkehr von Symphonik und Kammermusik und die Hinwendung zum sozialkritischen Musiktheater sowie der spätere Schritt in den Umkreis des Broadway-Musicals wurden als chamäleonhafter Opportunismus kritisiert. Ohne weiteres ließe sich aber zeigen, daß Weill seine außerordentliche Vielseitigkeit als Mittel benutzte, um die Treue zu sich selbst wahren zu können; seine Gabe, sich neuen und wechselhaften Verhältnissen anzupassen, ergänzte sich mit seinem Widerwillen gegen jeden Konformismus.

Die fünfzig Jahre seines Lebens umspannen genau die erste Hälfte unseres Jahrhunderts, eine Zeit, deren Mißstände, Verwerfungen und Sehnsüchte sich in seinen Kompositionen widerspiegeln. Weill wurde als Sohn eines Kantors am 2. März 1900 in Dessau geboren und begann im Alter von 14 Jahren, Musik zu studieren. Seine erste Symphonie und das Violinkonzert waren Ergebnisse seiner Berliner Studienzeit (1918 bis 1923) unter Humperdinck und Busoni. Der erfolgreichen Zusammenarbeit mit Bert Brecht, die ihn berühmt machte *(Die Dreigroschenoper,* 1928; *Aufstieg und Fall der Stadt Mahagonny,* 1930; *Die sieben Todsünden der Kleinbürger,* 1933), folgte seine zweite Symphonie, die unter Bruno Walter 1934 in Amsterdam vom Concertgebouw-Orchester uraufgeführt wurde. Weill war mit seiner Frau Lotte Lenya, für die er viele Hauptrollen schrieb, 1933 aus Hitlers Deutschland nach Paris geflohen und emigrierte mit ihr 1935 nach New York, wo er in den verbleibenden fünfzehn Lebensjahren hauptsächlich für den Broadway schrieb.

In Amerika wie in Berlin konnte Weill mit den besten Librettisten seiner Zeit arbeiten. So schuf er 1938 mit Maxwell Anderson *Knickerbocker Holiday,* 1941 mit Moss Hart und Ira Gershwin *Lady in the Dark,* 1943 mit S. J. Perelman und Ogden Nash *One Touch of Venus,* 1947 mit Elmer Rice und Langston Hughes *Street Scene,* 1948 mit Alan Jay Lerner *Love Life* und 1949 mit Maxwell Anderson *Lost in the Stars* nach dem Roman *Denn sie sollen getröstet werden* von Alan Paton.

Als Kurt Weill am 3. April 1950 in New York starb, war er allgemein als einer der großen amerikanischen Theaterkomponisten anerkannt.

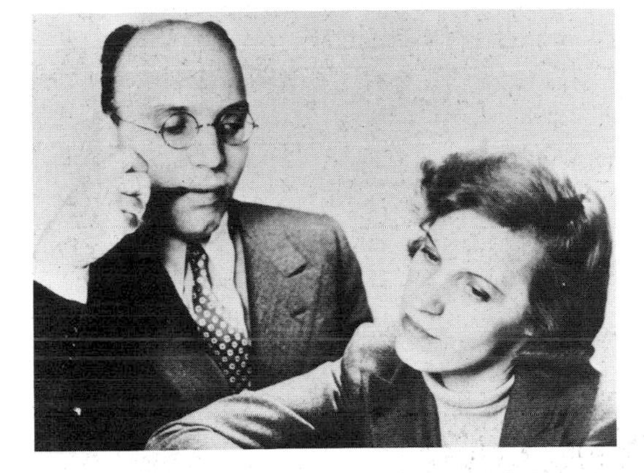

Kurt Weill with his wife and congenial interpreter, the actress and singer Lotte Lenya, shortly after their arrival in New York in 1935

Kurt Weill mit seiner Frau und kongenialen Interpretin, der Sängerin und Schauspielerin Lotte Lenya, kurz nach der Ankunft in New York im Jahre 1935

Der "Schöpfer" der
Dreigroschenoper
KURT WEILL, PERSÖNLICH
und seine Handschrift mit dem Selbstbekenntnis aus der „Dreigroschenoper":
„ . . . nur wer im Wohlstand lebt, lebt angenehm."

Weill and one of his famous melodies from the "Three Penny Opera", quoted in the inflammatory pamphlet "Degenerate Music" with the purpose of denouncing them

Weill und eine seiner berühmten Melodien aus der »Dreigroschenoper«, in denunziatorischer Absicht zitiert in der nationalsozialistischen Hetzschrift »Entartete Musik«

Kurt Weill with Maxwell Anderson (2nd from left) on an aircraft spotting-tower in 1942, looking out for German planes

Kurt Weill mit Maxwell Anderson (2. v. l.), 1942 auf einem Luftbeobachtungsturm nach deutschen Flugzeugen ausspähend

The “Blue Angel” Hits Hollywood

Marlene Dietrich

Mit dem »Blauen Engel« nach Hollywood

Maria Magdalena (“Marlene”) Dietrich took the vamp character created by Theda Bara, Nita Naldi and Pola Negri, among others, into the talking pictures and gave these “fallen women” of another era motivation, dimension and intelligent understanding. Born on December 27, 1901, in Berlin, the daughter of an officer, she originally aspired to being a concert violinist, but a wrist injury put an end to that ambition, whereupon she decided on a theatrical career. During the heady ferment which was Berlin in the 1920s, Dietrich performed in theatres and night clubs, married, bore a daughter (actress Maria Riva), and established a career as one of Germany’s leading motion picture actresses. She was almost 30 when her international breakthrough came in a production that represented one of the last masterworks of the golden age of German films, *The Blue Angel,* directed by Viennese-born American director, Joseph von Sternberg, who had emigrated to the United States as a child, returning to Europe for this film version of Heinrich Mann’s novel, *Professor Unrat.* The success of this film in 1930 brought her to America, where she starred in one motion picture after another, including von Sternberg’s *Morocco, Catherine the Great* and *Shanghai Express.* Moving on from naughty showgirl parts, she soon became the embodiment of the slightly soiled woman of the world, such as *Mata Hari,* possessed nevertheless with fundamental human decency.

Marlene Dietrich became a United States citizen in 1939, after turning down offers to return to Hitler’s Germany. From 1943 to 1946 she entertained American troops in Europe and made broadcasts to German soldiers for the Office of Strategic Services. These activities won her a Medal of Freedom, the highest civilian award granted by the U.S. government.

Following the war, Dietrich continued both her motion picture and her night club career, appearing to enthusiastic crowds in London, Paris and Moscow. She was less enthusiastically received during a 1960 tour of Germany, where many people still considered her activities in World War II treasonous. At the age of 77 she appeared in the cameo role of the bordello madam in David Hemmings’ motion picture *Just a Gigolo,* a film inspired by the milieu in which her career began, Berlin in the 1920s.

Maria Magdalena (»Marlene«) Dietrich führte den Typ des »Vamp«, der, unter anderem, von Theda Bara, Nita Naldi und Pola Negri geprägt worden war, in den Tonfilm ein und gab diesen »gefallenen Frauen« aus einer anderen Zeit Hintergrund, Tiefe und intelligentes Verständnis. Als Tochter eines Offiziers wurde sie am 27. Dezember 1901 in Berlin geboren und wollte eigentlich Konzertviolinistin werden, doch eine Handgelenksverletzung setzte diesem Vorhaben ein Ende, und so schlug sie die Theaterlaufbahn ein. Marlene Dietrich trat in Theatern und Nachtlokalen im turbulenten Berlin der zwanziger Jahre auf. Dort heiratete sie auch, bekam eine Tochter (die spätere Schauspielerin Maria Riva) und begründete ihre Karriere als eine der führenden Filmschauspielerinnen Deutschlands. Sie war noch nicht dreißig, als ihr der internationale Durchbruch mit einer Produktion gelang, die zu den letzten Meisterwerken aus der Glanzzeit des deutschen Films zählt: *Der Blaue Engel,* unter der Regie des in Wien geborenen Amerikaners Joseph von Sternberg, der als Kind in die Vereinigten Staaten ausgewandert war und für diese Filmversion des Romans *Professor Unrat* von Heinrich Mann nach Europa zurückkehrte. Die Woge dieses Filmerfolgs trug die Dietrich 1930 nach Amerika, wo sie eine Hauptrolle nach der anderen bekam, unter anderen in Sternbergs Filmen *Marokko, Katharina die Große* und *Shanghai-Express.* Sie hörte auf, das freche Tingeltangelmädchen zu spielen und wurde bald die Verkörperung der nicht ganz unbefleckten Dame von Welt à la *Mata Hari* – aber mit einem grundanständigen Kern.

Schon vor ihrer Einbürgerung 1939 hatte Marlene Dietrich alle Angebote abgelehnt, ins Deutschland Hitlers zurückzukehren. Von 1943 bis 1946 trat sie in Europa vor amerikanischen Soldaten auf und wandte sich im Auftrag des Office of Strategic Services (des späteren CIA) über den Rundfunk an die deutschen Soldaten. Diese Verdienste wurden durch die Verleihung der Medal of Freedom gewürdigt, der höchsten Auszeichnung, die die amerikanische Regierung für Zivilisten zu vergeben hat. Nach dem Krieg setzte die Dietrich ihre Film- und Nachtklubkarriere fort und trat in London, Paris und Moskau vor begeisterten Zuschauern auf. Weniger überschwenglich war ihr Empfang während einer Deutschlandtournee im Jahr 1960, da viele Deutsche ihre Aktivitäten während des Zweiten Weltkrieges immer noch als Verrat ansahen.

Im Alter von 77 Jahren spielte Marlene Dietrich in einer brillianten Einlage die Besitzerin eines anrüchigen Etablissements in David Hemmings Film *Schöner Gigolo, armer Gigolo,* der die Atmosphäre jenes Ambiente atmet, in dem ihre Karriere begann – das Berlin der zwanziger Jahre.

31. Juli 1930
Nummer 31
39. Jahrgang

Berliner
Illustrirte Zeitung

Preis des Heftes 20 Pfennig

Verlag Ullstein Berlin SW 68

Ein Schönheitstypus unsrer Zeit.
Neueste in Hollywood gemachte Aufnahme der Bühnen- und Filmschauspielerin Marlene Dietrich.

Fot. Irving Chidnoff

“A standard of beauty in our age. The latest photo, made in Hollywood, of the stage and screen actress Marlene Dietrich,” runs the caption under this picture on the cover of the “Berliner Illustrirte Zeitung”.

»Ein Schönheitstypus unserer Zeit. Neueste, in Hollywood gemachte Aufnahme der Bühnen- und Filmschauspielerin Marlene Dietrich«, lautet die Unterschrift dieses Titelfotos der »Berliner Illustrirten Zeitung«.

Marlene as Lola-Lola in the “Blue Angel”. The script for this filming of Heinrich Mann’s novel “Professor Unrat oder Das Ende eines Tyrannen” (1905) was written by Carl Zuckmayer, who emigrated to the U.S. in 1939. Heinrich Mann followed him to America a year later.

Marlene als Lola-Lola im »Blauen Engel«. Das Drehbuch zu dieser Verfilmung des Romans »Professor Unrat oder Das Ende eines Tyrannen« (1905) von Heinrich Mann schrieb Carl Zuckmayer, der 1939 in die USA emigrierte. Heinrich Mann folgte ein Jahr später.

It’s off to Hollywood. Marlene bidding farewell at the Lehrte train station in Berlin on April 1, 1930.

Auf dem Weg nach Hollywood: Marlenes Abschied auf dem Lehrter Bahnhof in Berlin am 1. April 1930

Unmasking Totalitarianism

Hannah Arendt

Entlarverin des Totalitarismus

Hannah Arendt (1906–1975)

The political theorist and controversial author Hannah Arendt was born on October 10, 1906, in Hannover but grew up in Königsberg (Kaliningrad). When she was seven, her father died and she was raised by her mother, a progressive woman, a social democrat and a non-religious Jew. Arendt demonstrated an amazing precocity in school and in 1924 she entered the University of Marburg as a student of philosophy, theology and Greek. During her first and only year there she formed a close relationship with the philosopher Martin Heidegger, who awakened in her a passionate love for philosophical thinking. After one semester under Edmund Husserl at Freiburg, she received her doctorate Heidelberg under Heidegger's friend, Karl Jaspers. In 1929 she married her first husband, Günther Anders (later to become a prominent author in his own right), and they moved to Berlin, where Arendt began writing *Rahel Varnhagen: The Life of a Jewess* (published in 1957). She was arrested by the Gestapo in 1933 for collecting material on German anti-Semitism and, after her release, she eventually made her way to Paris, where she worked for various Jewish relief organizations. In 1940 she married Heinrich Blücher, and a year later the couple, together with Arendt's mother, fled to the United States. Arendt spent the war years in New York, contributing articles to various German-Jewish and American publications. Later she did research for the Conference on Jewish Relations and was employed as a senior editor at Schocken Books. However, with the publication of her essays in 1951 under the title *The Origins of Totalitarianism,* Arendt was immediately recognized as an important post-war thinker. A more general philosophical work, *The Human Condition,* appeared in 1958, and a year later she was invited to become a full professor at Princeton. Her later works include *On Revolution* (1963) and her controversial *Eichmann in Jerusalem: A Report on the Banality of Evil* (1964). In addition, she held professorships with the University of Chicago's Committee on Social Thought and at the New School for Social Research. On December 12, 1975, while working on her last book, *The Life of the Mind* (published in 1979), she died in New York.

Hannah Arendt, Politologin und leidenschaftlich diskutierte Autorin, wurde am 10. Oktober 1906 in Hannover geboren, wuchs aber in Königsberg, dem heutigen Kaliningrad, auf. Ihr Vater starb als sie sieben Jahre alt war. Sie wurde von der Mutter, einer fortschrittlichen Sozialdemokratin und nicht praktizierenden Jüdin, aufgezogen. Schon in der Schule fielen ihre erstaunlichen geistigen Fähigkeiten auf, und 1924 schrieb sie sich an der Universität von Marburg für die Fächer Philosophie, Theologie und Griechisch ein. Während ihres ersten und zugleich letzten Jahres an dieser Universität schloß sie sich eng an den Philosophen Martin Heidegger an, der in ihr die Leidenschaft zum philosophischen Denken geweckt hatte. Nach einem Semester bei Edmund Husserl in Freiburg promovierte sie in Heidelberg bei Heideggers Freund Karl Jaspers. Mit ihrem ersten Ehemann, Günther Anders, der später selbst ein bekannter Autor wurde, zog Hannah Arendt nach Berlin, wo sie an dem Buch *Rahel Varnhagen. Lebensgeschichte einer deutschen Jüdin aus der Romantik* (deutsch 1959) zu schreiben begann. 1933 wurde sie von der Gestapo verhaftet, weil sie belastendes Material über den deutschen Antisemitismus sammelte. Nach ihrer Freilassung ging sie nach Paris, wo sie für verschiedene jüdische Wohlfahrtsorganisationen tätig wurde. 1940 heiratete sie Heinrich Blücher und floh im folgenden Jahr mit ihm und ihrer Mutter in die Vereinigten Staaten. Hannah Arendt verbrachte die Kriegsjahre in New York und schrieb Beiträge für deutsch-jüdische und amerikanische Publikationen. Später übernahm sie Forschungsarbeiten für die Conference on Jewish Relations und wurde Cheflektorin des Schocken Verlags. Seit dem Erscheinen ihres Essaybandes *Elemente und Ursprünge totalitärer Herrschaft* (deutsch 1955) zählte man Hannah Arendt zu den bedeutenden Theoretikern der Nachkriegszeit. 1958 erschien die philosophische Abhandlung *The Human Condition,* deutsch 1960 unter dem Titel *Vita activa oder Vom tätigen Leben,* und ein Jahr später wurde ihr von der Princeton University eine ordentliche Professur angeboten. Zu ihren späteren Werken gehören *Über die Revolution* (deutsch 1965) und ihr umstrittenes *Eichmann in Jerusalem. Bericht von der Banalität des Bösen* (deutsch 1964). Zugleich war sie Dozentin im Committee on Social Thought der University of Chicago und an der New Yorker School for Social Research. Hannah Arendt starb am 12. November 1975 in New York während der Arbeit an ihrem Buch *Vom Leben des Geistes*, das 1979 erschien.

Two extreme poles of the lot of the Jews and the work of Hannah Arendt: Rahel Varnhagen von Ense (1771–1833), a celebrated German Jewess of the Romantic period and the heroine of Arendt's most popular book, and Adolf Eichmann, one of those responsible for the murder of six million Jews and Hannah Arendt's chief witness in support of the concept of the "banality of evil", a term which she herself coined. (Photo taken at the trial in Jerusalem in 1961.)

Zwei extreme Pole des jüdischen Schicksals und des Arendtschen Werkes: Rahel Varnhagen von Ense (1771–1833), umschwärmte deutsche Jüdin der Romantik und Heldin von Hannah Arendts populärstem Buch; und Adolf Eichmann, Mitverantwortlicher des sechsmillionenfachen Judenmords und Hannah Arendts Kronzeuge für den von ihr geprägten Begriff von der »Banalität des Bösen« (Foto aus dem Prozeß in Jerusalem 1961)

Wernher von Braun

Ein Leben für die Raumfahrt

When Wernher von Braun, who was born in the East Prussian town of Wirsitz on March 23, 1912, joined the small band of rocket enthusiasts grouped around Rudolf Nebel which had founded the "Rocket Air Field" in Berlin, he was eighteen years old, and at that time, except for knowledge of the basic principles, there existed hardly anything in the way of liqui rocketry. That from these basic principles a functioning technology developed which not only carried the first men to the moon but also enabled "weapons of retaliation" to descend upon London, is Wernher von Braun's greatest achievement in life and at the same time his personal tragedy.

It remains without a doubt that from the beginning von Braun was concerned only with the peaceful use of rocket technology. As a young boy, his enthusiasm for the remote possibility of space travel was first aroused by Hermann Oberth's visionary book, *Rockets to Planetary Space* (1923). Thus, the experimental beginnings on the "Rocket Air Field" in the year 1930 were purely a result of private initiative and were correspondingly poorly financed. But soon the aroused interest of the military leadership during the Weimar regime, an interest which rapidly grew during the "Third Reich", opened up employment prospects for the barely twenty-year-old von Braun and to dismiss them would have meant giving up the realization of his great dream – the force of temptation which is difficult to reprimand.

Considered apart from its military aspect, the development of the "Aggregate 4" (later renamed by Goebbels "weapon of retaliation" (V-2), forerunner of all modern rockets, can be thought of as one of the boldest chapters in the history of technology. Starting almost from scratch, in the few years between 1937 and 1944 von Braun and his team in Peenemünde progressed by leaps and bounds in all phases, creating the foundation upon which all future rocketry developments were based – including the lunar mission's Saturn V launch vehicle.

After von Braun had the honor of temporarily being taken into custody by Himmler's SS-men shortly before the end of the war on grounds of alleged disinterest in the military employment of the A-4, and after the collapse of Germany, he and his most important coworkers turned themselves in to the American troops. They were taken to Fort Bliss near the White Sands testing area where, for a daily wage of six dollars, they continued their development program – again for military purposes –, first using captured A-4 rockets, and soon, new types.

In 1950, Braun was named director of the U.S. Army Ballistic Missile Agency at Huntsville, Alabama; in 1955 he became a naturalized citizen, and his shining hour came as a result of the "Sputnik shock" of 4 October 1957. Within four months, Braun succeeded in responding to the Soviet challenge with the launching of the first U.S. satellite, Explorer I. The space race which now commenced between the two superpowers finally led to the creation of a civilian agency, the National Aeronautics and Space Administration (NASA), founded in 1959 and provided with sufficient means to realize Wernher von Braun's long-standing dream: rocket flight to the moon.

Von Braun's base in Huntsville was put under NASA supervision and renamed the George C. Marshall Space Flight Center in honor of the statesman who initiated the Marshall Plan. It was here that von Braun

Als Wernher von Braun, am 23. März 1912 im ostpreußischen Wirsitz geboren, mit achtzehn Jahren zu der kleinen Gruppe von Enthusiasten rund um Rudolf Nebel stieß, die den »Raketenflugplatz Berlin« gegründet hatte, existierte vom Flüssigkeitsraketenantrieb außer der Kenntnis des Grundprinzips praktisch nichts. Daß aus diesem Grundprinzip eine funktionierende Technologie entwickelt wurde, die Menschen zum Mond trug und »Vergeltungswaffen« auf London niedergehen ließ, ist Wernher von Brauns Lebensleistung und persönliche Tragik.

Daß es ihm selbst von Anbeginn nur um die friedliche Nutzung der Raketentechnik ging, unterliegt keinem Zweifel. Es war Hermann Oberths visionäres Buch *Die Rakete zu den Planetenräumen* (1923), das den jungen von Braun für die ferne Möglichkeit der Raumfahrt begeisterte, und die praktischen Anfänge auf dem »Raketenflugplatz« im Jahre 1930 waren eine rein private und entsprechend unterfinanzierte Initiative. Erst das bald erwachende Interesse der Militärs der Weimarer Republik, das sich im »Dritten Reich« rapide verstärkte, eröffnete dem kaum Zwanzigjährigen Arbeitsmöglichkeiten, die auszuschlagen einen völligen Verzicht auf die Verwirklichung seines großen Traums bedeutet hätte: eine Dynamik der Verführung, über die schwer zu rechten ist.

Versucht man, vom militärischen Aspekt abzusehen, so darf die Entwicklung des »Aggregats 4« – der später von Goebbels in »Vergeltungswaffe 2« umgetauften Ahnin aller modernen Raketen – als eines der heroischen Kapitel der Technikgeschichte gelten. Unter größten Entwicklungssprüngen auf nahezu allen Gebieten schufen von Braun und sein Team in Peenemünde in den wenigen Jahren von 1937 bis 1944 praktisch aus dem Nichts heraus die Grundlagen, auf denen alle späteren Raketenentwicklungen bis hin zur Saturn V der Mondmissionen aufbauten.

Nachdem ihm kurz vor Kriegsende noch die Ehre widerfahren war, von Himmlers SS unter dem Vorwurf des Desinteresses an der militärischen Anwendung des A 4 vorübergehend festgenommen zu werden, stellte sich von Braun nach dem Zusammenbruch mit seinen wichtigsten Mitarbeitern den amerikanischen Truppen. Für eine Tagesgage von 6 Dollar wurden sie nach Fort Bliss in der Nähe des Testgeländes von White Sands gebracht, wo sie ihre Arbeit mit erbeuteten A-4-Raketen und bald auch neuen, abermals militärischen, Entwicklungen fortsetzten.

1950 zum Direktor des Raketenforschungszentrums der amerikanischen Armee in Huntsville, Alabama, ernannt und 1955 naturalisiert, schlug von Brauns große Stunde mit dem »Sputnik-Schock« vom 4. Oktober 1957. Innerhalb von vier Monaten gelang es ihm, die sowjetische Herausforderung mit dem Start des ersten amerikanischen Satelliten Explorer I zu beantworten. Das nun einsetzende Weltraum-Wettrennen der beiden Supermächte führte mit der Gründung der NASA im Jahre 1959 endlich zur Schaffung einer zivilen Behörde, die mit den nötigen Mitteln zur Verwirklichung von Wernher von Brauns ältestem Plan ausgestattet war: des Flugs zum Mond.

Von Brauns Dienststelle in Huntsville wurde der NASA unterstellt und (nach dem Initiator des Marshallplans) in George C. Marshall Space Flight Center umbenannt. Hier entwickelten von Braun und seine Mitarbeiter die gigantische Saturn-V-Trägerrakete, mit deren Hilfe sich der Menschheitstraum der Mondlandung am 20. Juli 1969 erfüllte.

The early beginnings in Reinickendorf, a section of Berlin, in 1930. Wernher von Braun together with Rudolf Nebel (1894–1978, left), and a letterhead of the "Rocket Air Field", an amateur society which was initially financed from donations. Soon, however, it caught the attention of the German military authorities who saw in these rockets a new kind of weapon not included in the Treaty of Versailles.

Die Anfänge in Berlin-Reinickendorf, 1930: Wernher von Braun mit Rudolf Nebel (1894–1978, links) und ein Briefkopf des »Raketenflugplatzes«, der sich als Liebhaberverein zunächst aus Spenden finanzierte, bald aber die Aufmerksamkeit der deutschen Reichswehr auf sich zog, die in den Raketen eine neuartige, nicht in den Versailler Verträgen erfaßte Waffe witterte.

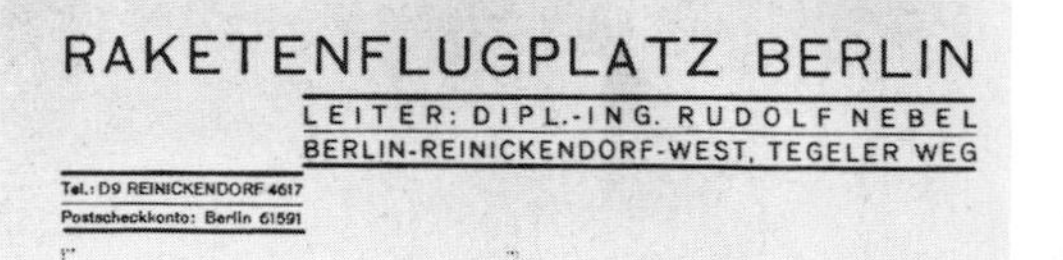

RAKETENFLUGPLATZ BERLIN
LEITER: DIPL.-ING. RUDOLF NEBEL
BERLIN-REINICKENDORF-WEST, TEGELER WEG
Tel.: D9 REINICKENDORF 4617
Postscheckkonto: Berlin 61591

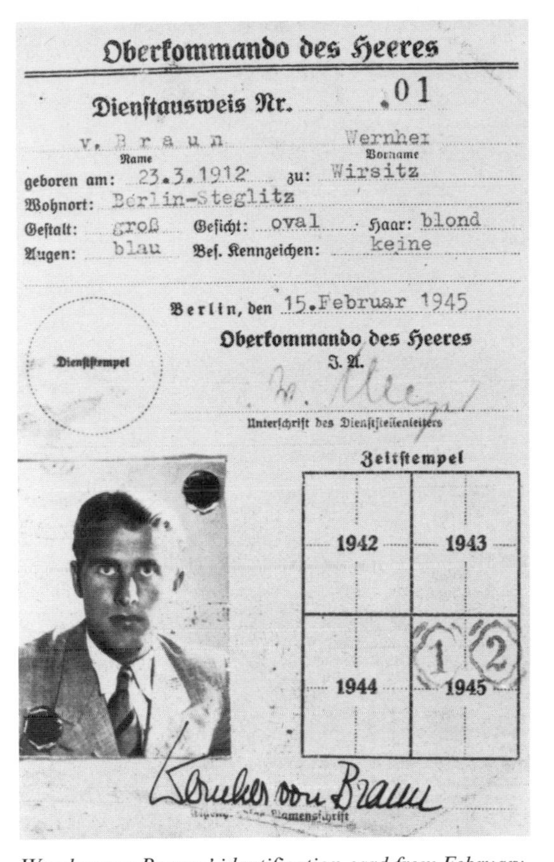
Oberkommando des Heeres

Dienstausweis Nr. 01

v. Braun — Wernher
Name — Vorname

geboren am: 23.3.1912 zu: Wirsitz

Wohnort: Berlin-Steglitz

Gestalt: groß Gesicht: oval Haar: blond

Augen: blau Bes. Kennzeichen: keine

Berlin, den 15.Februar 1945

Oberkommando des Heeres

I. A.

Dienststempel

Unterschrift des Dienststellenleiters

Zeitstempel

1942	1943
1944	1945

Wernher von Braun

Namensschrift

Wernher von Brauns' identification card from February, 1945. Although von Braun was himself a civilian, as technical director of the "Army Experimental Station" in Peenemünde he was subject to the authority of the High Command of the German Army. His military superior, General Walter Dornberger, emigrated to America in 1947 and later became the vice president of the Bell Aircraft Corporation.

Wernher von Brauns Dienstausweis vom Februar 1945; obwohl selbst Zivilist, unterstand von Braun als technischer Direktor der »Heeresversuchsanstalt Peenemünde« dem Oberkommando des Heeres. Sein militärischer Vorgesetzter, General Walter Dornberger, wanderte 1947 in die USA aus und wurde später Vizepräsident der Bell Aircraft Corporation.

and his staff developed the gigantic and mighty Saturn V launch vehicle, by means of which that ancient dream of mankind, travel to the moon, was achieved on 20 July 1969.

After the Apollo spacecraft program came to a close, following nine flights and six successful lunar landings, Wernher von Braun, who had become assistant director of NASA in 1970, returned to private industry. He succumbed to a very terrestrial disease, cancer, on 16 June 1977.

The date, July 16, 1969. Apollo 11, mounted atop a Saturn V rocket, starts on its historic journey to the moon. (The picture here is a photo montage. In actuality, the distance between the starting ramp and the spectators was a little over three miles.)

16. Juli 1969: an der Spitze einer Saturn-V-Rakete startet Apollo 11 zum Mond. (Bei der Aufnahme handelt es sich um eine Fotomontage; tatsächlich betrug der Sicherheitsabstand zwischen Startrampe und Zuschauern volle fünf Kilometer.)

A view inside the control center during take off. Kurt Debus, also formerly from Peenemünde and long-time director of the Space Center at Cape Canaveral, together with Hans Gruene, Wernher von Braun and Eberhard Rees (from left to right).

Im Kontrollzentrum während eines Starts: die ehemaligen »Peenemünder« Kurt Debus – langjähriger Direktor des Startkomplexes von Cape Canaveral –, Hans Gruene, Wernher von Braun und Eberhard Rees (von links)

Nachdem das Apollo-Programm nach neun Mondflügen und sechs erfolgreichen Landungen ausgelaufen war, zog sich Wernher von Braun, der 1970 stellvertretender Direktor der NASA geworden war, in die Privatwirtschaft zurück. Er starb am 16. Juni 1977, sehr irdisch an Krebs.

A captured A-4 rocket with a scientific payload (contained in the elongated tip) on the U.S. testing grounds in White Sands, New Mexico.

Eine A-4-Beuterakete mit wissenschaftlicher Nutzlast (in der verlängerten Spitze) auf dem amerikanischen Versuchsgelände von White Sands in Neu-Mexiko.

Wernher von Braun experiencing simulated weightlessness on board an airplane flying part of a parabolic course where centrifugal force and gravity cancel out one another. The space pioneer didn't personally ever get to experience the true weightlessness of outer space.

Wernher von Braun in simulierter Schwerelosigkeit: an Bord eines Flugzeugs, das ein Teilstück einer Parabelbahn fliegt, auf der sich Fliehkraft und Erdanziehung aufheben. Die wirkliche Schwerelosigkeit des Weltraums lernte der Raumfahrtpionier selbst nicht mehr kennen.

From the Lectern to the Conference Tables of the World

Henry Kissinger

Vom Katheder an die Konferenztische der Welt

The most prominent American of German descent living today is decidedly Henry Alfred Kissinger. Many of his political concepts and opinions, which he first formulated as a political scientist, were realized in his influential capacity as politician and secretary of state under Presidents Nixon and Ford. Kissinger was born in Franconian Fürth on May 27, 1923, where his father was a secondary school teacher. In 1938 his family, being Jewish, was forced to emigrate to the United States. Kissinger completed high school in New York in 1941 and received American citizenship two years later. In 1947 he completed his military service at the age of 24, on duty with the U.S. military government in Bensheim an der Bergstrasse. Kissinger subsequently studied at the esteemed Harvard University, completing his Ph.D. in political science in 1954. He then collaborated on various research projects in New York which dealt with foreign affairs, nuclear strategy, and diplomacy, before returning to Harvard as a professor.
When Nelson Rockefeller ran for the Republican nomination for the presidency in 1968, he recruited Kissinger as a staff specialist for foreign affairs. The concepts which he developed in this capacity apparently impressed Nixon, who ultimately won the nomination. Shortly after the latter's presidential election, Kissinger was asked to serve as special advisor on national security questions. As "Assistant to the President for National Security Affairs" from 1969 on, and then from 1973 to 1977 as secretary of state, Kissinger played the key role in forming and instrumenting a foreign policy which was characterized by repeated, hectic "shuttle diplomacy", not infrequent secretiveness (even vis-à-vis closely allied parties), surprise tactics and the conviction that diplomatic initiative also brings results.
Among the most important accomplishments of his restless activity were the opening of diplomatic relations with China, a truce for Vietnam (for which he and the North Vietnamese Le Duc Tho received the Nobel Peace Prize), détente with the Soviet Union, and his strenuous mediatory endeavors in the Middle East after the Yom Kippur War in 1973.
Kissinger is the perfect example of a political theoretician who, having become an active politician with increasing desire to exercise influence, attempted to realize his concept of an international order based on mutual understanding. His political style of behind-the-scenes international diplomacy, his dramatic propensity and his strong belief in power and success did not remain uncontested, forming the basis for characterizations such as "Hercules Henry" or "Lion Tamer of the International Spirit".
Accustomed to success, this lead actor in an eventful era of American foreign policy vehemently defended his policies in two volumes of recently published memoirs. Kissinger views "Watergate" as the self-destruction of a president through internal politics, of the same president who had won unexpected esteem and respect as an international politician. Kissinger thinks and feels as an American, as a representative of a world power with legitimate claim to a leading role within its political alliances, and he has seemingly relegated Europe, his former homeland, to a historical position of secondary significance. That this epitome of American self-assurance should be embodied in an immigrant is only seemingly a whim of historical irony – one need but look at comparable biographies within the long history of immigration.

Der prominenteste amerikanische Zeitgenosse deutschen Ursprungs ist zweifellos Henry Alfred Kissinger, der seine politischen Gedanken und Vorstellungen zunächst als Wissenschaftler formulierte und vieles davon später als einflußreicher Politiker und Außenminister unter den Präsidenten Nixon und Ford verwirklichte. Am 27. Mai 1923 im fränkischen Fürth als Sohn eines Studienrats geboren, mußten seine jüdischen Eltern mit ihm 1938 nach Amerika emigrieren, wo er 1941 in New York die Oberschule abschloß und 1943 die amerikanische Staatsbürgerschaft erhielt. Seine Militärdienstzeit beendete er mit 24 Jahren in der US-Militärregierung in Bensheim an der Bergstraße. Danach studierte Kissinger an der angesehenen Harvard-Universität, an der er 1954 im Fach Politische Wissenschaften promovierte, arbeitete dann in New York an verschiedenen Forschungsvorhaben über Außenpolitik, Nuklearstrategie und Diplomatie und kehrte 1959 als Professor nach Harvard zurück.
Als sich Nelson Rockefeller 1968 um die Präsidentschaftskanditur der Republikanischen Partei bemühte, holte er Kissinger als außenpolitischen Sachverständigen in seinen Stab. Die Ideen, die Kissinger dort entwickelte, blieben offenbar auch auf den schließlich siegreichen Gegenkandidaten Nixon nicht ohne Eindruck, der Kissinger kurz nach seiner Wahl zum Präsidenten aufforderte, sein Sonderberater für Fragen der nationalen Sicherheit zu werden. Als »Assistant to the President for National Security Affairs« ab 1969 und dann als Außenminister von 1973 bis 1977 war Kissinger Hauptarchitekt und Schlüsselfigur bei der Realisierung einer Außenpolitik, die durch oft hektische Reisediplomatie (Flugzeug-Blitzreisen), häufige Geheimhaltung (auch gegenüber engen Verbündeten), Überraschungstaktiken und die Überzeugung geprägt war, daß diplomatische Initiative auch Resultate bringt.
Die wichtigsten Ergebnisse seiner rastlosen Aktivitäten waren die Eröffnung von diplomatischen Beziehungen zu China, ein Friedensabkommen für Vietnam (für das er zusammen mit dem Nordvietnamesen Le Duc Tho den Friedensnobelpreis erhielt), die Entspannungspolitik mit der Sowjetunion, und Vermittlungsbemühungen nach dem Jom-Kippur-Krieg 1973 durch eine diplomatische Parforce-Tour im Nahen Osten.
Kissinger ist das Musterbeispiel eines politischen Denkers, der später als handelnder Politiker mit wachsender Lust an der Ausübung von Macht sein Konzept einer neuen internationalen Ordnung, die auf Verständigung beruhen sollte, zu verwirklichen suchte. Sein politischer Stil einer Weltdiplomatie hinter den Kulissen, sein Hang zum Dramatischen, und sein starker Glaube an Macht und Erfolg waren durchaus nicht unumstritten und bildeten die Grundlage von Charakterisierungen wie »Henry Herkules« oder »Großdompteur des Weltgeistes«.
Der erfolgsgewohnte Hauptakteur einer bewegten Zeit amerikanischer Außenpolitik hat in seinen jüngst erschienen zweibändigen Memoiren in einem wortgewaltigen Plädoyer seine Politik verteidigt. In »Watergate« sieht er die innenpolitische Selbstzerstörung eines Präsidenten, der als Weltpolitiker Ansehen und Respekt in einem unerwarteten Ausmaß gewonnen hatte. Kissinger denkt und fühlt als Amerikaner, als Repräsentant einer Weltmacht, mit legitimem Führungsanspruch innerhalb ihrer politischen Allianzen, dem seine alte Heimat Europa historisch ins zweite Glied zurückgetreten scheint. Das sich ein solches amerikanisches Selbstbewußtsein in der Person eines Einwanderers verkörpert, ist – betrachtet man vergleichbare Lebensläufe innerhalb der langen Einwanderungsgeschichte – durchaus nur scheinbar von historischer Ironie.

Prewar aerial photograph of Fürth, the town where Henry Kissinger was born, and from which he fled with his family in 1938, only a few days prior to the anti-Semitic spree of violence known as the "Crystal Night".

Vorkriegs-Luftaufnahme von Henry Kissingers Heimatstadt Fürth, die er 1938, wenige Tage vor den antisemitischen Ausschreitungen der »Reichskristallnacht«, mit seiner Familie verließ.

Henry Kissinger's birthplace in Fürth: the house at 23 Mathilden St. (photo taken in 1981)

Henry Kissingers Geburtshaus in der Mathildenstraße 23 in Fürth (Ansicht aus dem Jahr 1981)

The eleven-year-old Henry Kissinger with his brother Walter (right) in Fürth (1934)

Der elfjährige Henry Kissinger mit seinem Bruder Walter (rechts) 1934 in Fürth

A sensational secret mission carried out by Henry Kissinger was the starting point for the normalization of diplomatic relations between the U.S. and the People's Republic of China. The photo shows him and his delegation in Peking to prepare the way for the American presidential visit of February 1972.

Mit einer spektakulären Geheimreise leitete Henry Kissinger die politische Normalisierung zwischen den USA und der Volksrepublik China ein. Das Foto zeigt ihn in Peking mit seiner Verhandlungsdelegation zur Vorbereitung des amerikanischen Präsidentenbesuchs vom Februar 1972.

Kissinger and Le Duc Tho in Paris on 23 January 1973, after the initialing of the Vietnam agreement, which provided the basis for the pullout of American troops from Vietnam; in October of the same year the two statesmen shared the Nobel Peace Prize.

Kissinger und Le Duc Tho am 23. Januar 1973 in Paris nach der Paraphierung des Vietnam-Abkommens, das die Voraussetzungen für den Rückzug der amerikanischen Truppen aus Vietnam schuf; beide erhielten dafür im Oktober desselben Jahres den Friedensnobelpreis.

Kissinger and President Nixon within the Kremlin walls. The picture was taken during the first state visit of an American president to the capital of the Soviet Union in May 1972.

Kissinger mit Präsident Nixon in den Mauern des Kreml. Die Aufnahme entstand während des ersten Staatsbesuchs eines amerikanischen Präsidenten in der Hauptstadt der Sowjetunion im Mai 1972.

When Henry Kissinger was awarded the Golden Medal of the City of Fürth by his native town in 1975, he referred to his visit as "symbolic of the exceptional renewal of the friendship between the American and German people". In the photo of the celebration, the following personalities can be identified: second from left the German Foreign Minister Genscher; next to him, Mrs. Nancy Kissinger; the former Bavarian Minister President Goppel; Henry Kissinger; the Lord Mayor of Fürth, Scherzer; Mrs. Barbara Genscher; Henry Kissinger's parents, Louis and Paula, and his brother Walter.

Ein »Symbol für die außerordentliche Erneuerung der Freundschaft zwischen dem amerikanischen und dem deutschen Volk« nannte Henry Kissinger 1975 seinen Besuch in seiner Heimatstadt, die ihn mit ihrer Goldenen Bürgermedaille ausgezeichnet hatte. Das Foto des Festaktes zeigt, beginnend mit dem zweiten von links, den deutschen Außenminister Genscher, Mrs. Nancy Kissinger, den damaligen bayerischen Ministerpräsidenten Goppel, Henry Kissinger, den Oberbürgermeister der Stadt Fürth, Scherzer, Frau Barbara Genscher, Henry Kissingers Eltern Louis und Paula und seinen Bruder Walter.

Appendix Anhang

Chronology

1683 Encouraged by the American Quaker William Penn (1644–1718), Franz Daniel Pastorius (1651–c. 1720) organizes the immigration of 13 Mennonite families from Krefeld. On October 6, they sail into Philadelphia harbor on the Delaware River on the vessel "Concord", and subsequently establish Germantown.

1688 Pastorius writes the first manifesto condemning the institution of slavery.

1689 The community of Germantown is incorporated with Pastorius as the first mayor.

1691 Jacob Leisler (born 1635), governor in New York from 1689 to 1691, is falsely accused of treason and executed.

1694 Johann Kelpius (1673–1708) leads a group of German mystics to America and forms a brotherhood on Wissahickon Creek near Philadelphia.

1701 The first Germantown Fair, which later becomes a center for trade in crafted goods in colonial Pennsylvania.

1702 Pastorius establishes the first German-American school in Germantown; in Germany, Daniel Falckner (1666–1741) publishes his *Curieuse Nachricht von Pennsylvania,* stimulating migration of German sectarians.

1708 Joshua Kocherthal (1669–1719) brings 61 Protestant emigrants from the Rhenish Palatinate to America; thousands more from the region follow in 1709.

1710 A first group of German and Swiss immigrants settles in North Carolina.

1714 Christopher von Graffenried (1691–1744) brings ore miners from Siegen, Westphalia, to Virginia to work Governor Spotswood's iron mines.

1719 Peter Becker brings the first German Baptist "Dunkers" to Germantown; the founder of the sect, Alexander Mack (1679–1735), comes to America with another group ten years later.

1727 The German population of Pennsylvania already numbers around twenty thousand.

1730 Conrad Beissel (1696–1768), a Seventh Day Dunker from the Palatinate, has Benjamin Franklin print the first collection of Pennsylvania-German sacred songs.

1732 Benjamin Franklin publishes the first German language newspaper in America, the *Philadelphische Zeitung.* Beissel founds the Ephrata Cloisters near Lancaster.

1733 Members of the Schwenkfelder sect from Silesia settle in Montgomery County, Pennsylvania.

1735 The Herrnhuters or Moravians found their first settlement under the leadership of August Gottlieb Spangenberg (1704–1792).

Johann Peter Zenger (1697–1746), publisher of the *New York Weekly Journal,* is acquitted of the charge of libel: a first victory for freedom of the press.

1738 The eminent printer Christopher Saur (1693–1758) opens a printshop in Germantown.

1739 Caspar Wistar (1696–1752) builds a glass factory near Allowaystown, New Jersey.
Saur begins publication of the newspaper *Pennsylvanische Geschicht-Schreiber.*

1741 Hans Nicholas Eisenhauer, ancestor of President Dwight D. Eisenhower, emigrates from the Palatinate.

1742 Nikolaus Ludwig, Count of Zinzendorf and Pottendorf (1700–1760), founds the Moravian settlement of Bethlehem, Pennsylvania.

1743 Saur prints a German-language Bible, the first complete Bible ever to be published in America.

1744 The Moravian brotherhood found their *Collegium Musicum* orchestra in Bethlehem.

1746 The Moravians found their first school for girls.

1748 George Washington first encounters German immigrants in the Shenandoah Valley. Ephrata monks complete their monumental 1514-page German edition of the *Martyrs' Mirror,* the largest book produced in the colonies.

1750 The schoolmaster Christopher Dock (died 1771) publishes his *Schulordnung,* the first American pedagogical work.

1759 Michael Hillegas (1729–1804) opens America's first music store in Philadelphia.

1762 Henry Miller begins publication of his newspaper *Staatsbote.* In 1776 it was the first paper in America to print the news of the Declaration of Independence.

1767 David Rittenhouse (1732–1796) of Germantown constructs the first planetarium; it can demonstrate astronomical phenomena over a period of five thousand years.

1774 Goethe's *Werther* enjoys popularity in America.

1778 Friedrich Wilhelm von Steuben (1730–1794) takes over the training of the Continental Army.

1779 As Inspector General, von Steuben completes the "Blue Book" of troop regulations for the Revolutionary Army.

1783 John Jacob Astor of Walldorf in Baden arrives in New York after studying commerce and the English language in London.

1785 The Treaty of Amity and Commerce is concluded between the young Union and Prussia.

1792 David Rittenhouse is appointed director of the newly established United States Mint.

1804 George Rapp (1770–1847), founder of a communal religious sect, establishes the settlement of Harmony in Pennsylvania.

1819 The first steamship crosses the ocean from America to Europe in 26 days, ushering in a new era of transatlantic travel.

1825 Charles Follen (1796–1840) introduces German language courses at Harvard, where he receives a professorship in 1830. Karl Beck (1798–1886) is co-founder of the first American gymnastics center fitted out with Jahn's equipment.

1827 Francis Lieber (1800–1872) comes to Boston to direct the Tremont *Turner Gymnasium* and begins editing his monumental 14-volume *Encyclopedia Americana* based on the Brockhaus *Conservations-Lexikon.*

1835 Frederick A. Rauch (1806–1841): *Psychology, A View of the Human Soul.*
Foundation of the Giessen Society, aiming at establishing a "new Germany" in the United States.
The male chorus "Männerchor von Philadelphia" is the first German-American "Gesangsverein" (choral society).
The Rappites sell New Harmony, Indiana, to the English socialist Robert Owen and trek back to Pennsylvania.

1838 Wilhelm Weitling (1808–1871): *Humanity as it is and as it Should be.*

1841 Publication of *Das Kajütenbuch (The Cabin Book)* by Karl Anton Postl (1793–1864) under his pseudonym Charles Sealsfield.

1844 Under the patronage of the "Mainzer Adelsverein", Prince Carl von Solms-Braunfels (1812–1875) brings the first German settlers to Texas; in the following year he founds the town of New Braunfels.

1848 Establishment of the first German-style gymnastics club in Cincinnati, Ohio; other American cities follow suit in the succeeding years.

The Forty-Eighter Friedrich Hecker (1811–1881) is greeted by a crowd of 20,000 German-Americans upon his arrival in New York.

Zeittafel

1683 Auf Anregung des amerikanischen Quäkers William Penn (1644–1718) organisiert Franz Daniel Pastorius (1651–1719 oder 1720) die Auswanderung der Krefelder Mennoniten. Sie treffen am 6. Oktober auf der »Concord« in Philadelphia ein und gründen Germantown.

1688 Pastorius verfaßt erste Resolution gegen Sklaverei.

1689 Germantown wird kommunale Körperschaft mit Pastorius als erstem Bürgermeister.

1690 Pastorius' Abhandlung *Vier Kleine und Doch Ungemeine und Sehr Nützliche Tractätlein* erscheint in Germantown, Pennsylvanien.

1691 Jacob Leisler (1635–1691), von 1689 bis 1691 Gouverneur von New York, wird aus politischen Gründen hingerichtet.

1694 Mit Johann Kelpius (1673–1708), einem Schüler Jacob Böhmes, hält das Rosenkreuzertum in Amerika Einzug.

1701 Erster Jahrmarkt in Germantown, der zu einer Art Handelsmesse des kolonialen Pennsylvanien wurde.

1702 Pastorius gründet die erste deutsch-amerikanische Schule in Germantown. Die *Curieuse Nachricht von Pennsylvania* von Daniel Falckner (1661–1741) veranlaßt viele Deutsche zur Auswanderung.

1708 Josua Kocherthal (1669–1719) bringt 61 protestantische Emigranten aus der Pfalz nach Amerika. Tausende von Pfälzern folgen im Jahr darauf.

1710 Die ersten deutschen und schweizerischen Einwanderer kommen in North Carolina an.

1714 Grubenarbeiter aus Siegen in Nordrhein-Westfalen folgen Christopher von Graffenried (1691–1744) nach Amerika und arbeiten dort in den Zechen von Gouverneur Spotswood.

1719 Peter Becker bringt die ersten Tunker nach Germantown. Der Gründer der Sekte, Alexander Mack (1679–1735), kommt 1729 mit einer weiteren Gruppe in Amerika an.

1727 In Pennsylvanien leben bereits ungefähr 20 000 Deutsche.

1730 Das erste Buch mit pennsylvanien-deutschen Liedern *Göttliche Liebes und Lobes Gethöne* von Benjamin Franklin für den Pfälzer Conrad Beissel (1696–1768) gedruckt.

1732 Die erste fremdsprachige Zeitung in Amerika ist die *Philadelphische Zeitung* von Benjamin Franklin.
Beissel trennt sich von den Tunkern und gründet Ephrata.

1733 Die Schwenckfelder aus Schlesien lassen sich in Montgomery County, Pennsylvanien, nieder.

1735 Unter der Führung von August Gottlieb Spangenberg (1704–1792) gründen die Herrnhuter die erste Moraviersiedlung.
Johann Peter Zenger (1697–1746), Leiter des *New York Weekly Journal,* wird von der Anklage übler Nachrede freigesprochen: ein erster Sieg für die Freiheit der Presse.

1738 Christoph Sauer (1693–1758) eröffnet in Germantown eine Druckerei.

1739 Caspar Wistar (1696–1752) baut Glasmanufaktur bei Allowaystown, New Jersey.

Der *Hoch-Deutsch Pennsylvanische Geschichtschreiber* von Sauer erscheint.

1741 Hans Nicholas Eisenhauer verläßt die Pfalz. Von ihm stammt Dwight D. Eisenhower ab, Präsident der Vereinigten Staaten von 1953 bis 1961.

1742 Nikolaus Ludwig Graf von Zinzendorf (1700–1760) gründet die Herrnhuter Niederlassung Bethlehem

1743 Sauer druckt die erste deutsche Bibel in Amerika.

1744 Die Moravier gründen das »Collegium Musicum« zur Aufführung von Kammermusik. Erste Organisation dieser Art in Amerika.

1746 Die Moravier gründen in Bethlehem die erste Mädchenschule.

1748 George Washington begegnet im Shenandoah-Tal zum erstenmal deutschen Einwanderern.
Ephrata-Mönche drucken das umfangreichste Buch der Kolonien: *Martyrs' Mirror* mit 1514 Seiten.

1750 Christopher Dock (gestorben 1771) veröffentlicht die *Schulordnung,* das erste schulpädagogische Werk in Amerika.

1759 Am 3. Dezember eröffnet Michael Hillegas (1729–1804) die erste Musikalienhandlung Amerikas in Philadelphia.

1762 Henry Miller aus Waldeck gründet die Zeitung *Staatsbote.* Sie bringt am 5. Juli 1776 die erste Nachricht von der Unabhängigkeitserklärung.

1767 David Rittenhouse (1732–1796) aus Germantown baut das erste »Planetarium«. Es zeigt die Sonnenerscheinungen über einen Zeitraum von 5000 Jahren.

1774 Goethes *Werther* wird in Amerika zum Bestseller.

1778 Friedrich Wilhelm von Steuben (1730–1794) aus Magdeburg trifft am 23. Februar in Valley Forge ein und übernimmt die Ausbildung der Kontinental-Armee.

1779 Steuben verfaßt das »Blue Book«, das als offizielles Reglement der amerikanischen Armee anerkannt wird.

1783 Johann Jacob Astor (1763–1848) kommt in New York an und wird zum Prototyp des erfolgreichen Einwanderers.

1785 Abschluß des Freundschafts- und Handelsvertrages zwischen der jungen Union und Preußen.

1792 David Rittenhouse wird erster Präsident der amerikanischen Münze in Philadelphia.

1804 Georg Rapp (1757–1847) und die Anhänger seiner Sekte gründen Harmony.

1819 In 26 Tagen fährt zum erstenmal ein Dampfschiff von den USA nach Europa. Eine neue Epoche der Transatlantik-Schiffahrt beginnt.

1825 Charles Follen (1796–1840) führt in Harvard das Fach Deutsch ein. 1830 erhält er die Professur.
Karl Beck (1798–1866) gründet das erste Turnergymnasium.

1827 Franz Lieber (1800–1872) wird Direktor des Tremont Turnergymnasiums in Boston und beginnt mit der Arbeit an der 14bändigen *Encyclopaedia Americana,* die auf dem Brockhaus-Konversationslexikon basiert.

1835 Frederick A. Rauch (1806–1841), *Psychology, A View of the Human Soul.*
Gründung der Gießen-Gesellschaft, die sich zum Ziel setzt, ein neues Deutschland in den USA zu verwirklichen.
Der »Männerchor von Philadelphia« konstituiert sich als erster deutsch-amerikanischer Gesangsverein.

1838 Wilhelm Weitling (1808–1871): *Die Menschheit wie sie ist und wie sie sein sollte.*

1841 *Das Kajütenbuch* von Charles Sealsfield (1793–1864), eigentlich Karl Anton Postl, aus Mähren erscheint.

1844 Auf Betreiben des Mainzer Adelsvereins bringt Prinz Carl von Solms-Braunfels (1812–1875) die ersten Deutschen nach Texas, wo er am 21. März 1845 New Braunfels gründet.

1848 In Cincinnati, Ohio, wird der erste amerikanische Turnverein nach deutschem Vorbild gegründet. In Jahresabständen folgen Boston, Philadelphia und Louisville.

20 000 Deutsch-Amerikaner begrüßen den 48er Friedrich Hecker (1811–1881) bei seiner Ankunft in New York.

1849 Massenauswanderung politischer Flüchtlinge nach den USA: die sogenannten 48er. Erstes Sängerfest in den Vereinigten Staaten.

1849 Mass emigration of political refugees, the so-called Forty-Eighters, to the United States. The first "Sängerfest" in the United States.

1850 Wilhelm Weitling (1808–1871) organizes a labor movement, the *Allgemeiner Arbeiterbund,* in New York.

1852 Carl Schurz (1829–1906) arrives in America.

1853 Heinrich Steinweg (1797–1881) founds the firm Steinway & Sons in New York.

1855 Castle Garden is opened as a processing center for immigrants in New York.

1861 Carl Schurz is United States envoy to Spain, where he tries to gain sympathy for the Union cause. German-Americans fight on both sides in the Civil War.

1867 Completion of the suspension bridge over the Ohio at Cincinnati, designed by Johann August Roebling (1806–1869).

1873 The violinist, conductor, composer, and M. D. Dr. Leopold Damrosch (1832–1885) from Posen founds the New York Oratorio Society.

1877 Carl Schurz (1829–1906) becomes Secretary of the Interior under President Rutherford B. Hayes (1822–1893) and holds this office until 1881. He pushes through the civil service reform and attempts to revise the prevailing policy towards the Indians.

1878 Leopold Damrosch founds the New York Symphony Society.

1883 Construction of the Brooklyn Bridge, designed by Roebling, is completed by his son Washington Augustus (1836–1927).

1884 Ottmar Mergenthaler (1854–1899) invents the Linotype in America. The *New York Tribune* is the first newspaper to use it, in 1886.

1887 Emil Berliner (1851–1929) invents the first sound recording on disc.

1892 On January 1, Ellis Island is opened as the new United States Immigration Center; in the 62 years till it was closed on November 12, 1954, approximately twenty million immigrants passed through its portals.

1903 Manager of the Metropolitan Opera House Heinrich Conried (1855–1909), born in Silesia, presents the first production of Wagner's *Parsifal* outside of Bayreuth.

1907 Conried invites Gustav Mahler (1860–1911) to conduct at the "Met". From 1909 to 1911 Mahler is musical director of the New York Philharmonic at what was then the largest salary ever paid a conductor ($ 30,000 per annum).

1914 "German-American Alliance": Mass meeting for the purpose of a resolution against American participation in the war.

1917 April 6: the United States declares war against the Central Powers.

1918 November 11: signing of the armistice. Carl Laemmle (1867–1939) produces the silent film *Blind Husbands,* directed by Erich von Stroheim (1885–1957). *The Devil's Passkey* followed in 1919, and *Foolish Wives* in 1921.

1919 June 8: the Versailles Peace Treaty.

1927 *Der Steppenwolf* by Hermann Hesse (1877–1962). Almost 40 years later, this novel experiences a renaissance through the American hippie movement.
Guest appearance in New York of Berlin's "Deutsches Theater" with its director, Max Reinhardt (1873–1943).

1928 Köhl, Hünefeld and Fitzmaurice are the first to fly over the Atlantic from east to west.

1933 Start of the emigration of German artists and intellectuals to the United States; among them, Paul Tillich (1886–1965), Billy Wilder (born 1906), Georg Grosz (1893–1959), and Albert Einstein (1879–1955), who joins the Institute for Advanced Studies at Princeton.

1935 The Labor Relations Act introduced by Senator Robert F. Wagner is signed into law by President Roosevelt (1882–1945).

1936 *Fury,* the first film directed in the United States by Fritz Lang (1890–1976), is a box-office success.

1937 The Bauhaus, prohibited in National Socialistic Germany, is carried on in Chicago as the "New Bauhaus" under the guidance of Laszlo Moholy-Nagy (1895–1946).

1941 December 11: Hitler declares war on the United States.

1944 The play *Jacobowsky and the Colonel* by Franz Werfel (1890–1945) receives its world premiere in New York.

1945 May 8: unconditional surrender of Germany to the Allies. On May 3, the team of German rocket scientists from Peenemünde and their director, Wernher von Braun (1912–1977) are interned by the Americans in Reutte, Austria, and later flown to the United States.

1947 Bertolt Brecht (1898–1956) presents a revised version of his play *The Life of Galilei* in Los Angeles, with Charles Laughton (1899–1962) in the leading role.

1951 *The Origins of Totalitarianism* by Hannah Arendt (1906–1975) is published.

1952 Following the signing of the German-American Culture Agreement, the Fulbright program includes exchange grants for professors, instructors, and students.

1953 The Nobel Prizes for Medicine and Physiology go to Dr. Hans A. Krebs, who emigrated in 1933, and Dr. Fritz Lippmann, who emigrated in 1941.

1968 Between 1949 and 1968 around 1800 scientists and 5000 technicians leave the Federal Republic of Germany for the United States.

1969 The American astronaut Neil Armstrong, member of the crew of Apollo XI, is the first man to set foot on the moon. Wernher von Braun's participation in the American space program was an important factor in its success.

1983 Tercentenary celebration of German immigration to the United States.

1850 Wilhelm Weitling (1808–1871) organisiert in New York den »Allgemeinen Arbeiterbund«.

1852 Carl Schurz (1829–1906) kommt in Amerika an.

1853 Heinrich Steinweg (1797–1881) gründet in New York die Firma »Steinway & Sons«.

1855 Castle Garden wird als Durchgangslager für Immigranten in New York eröffnet.

1861 Ernennung von Schurz zum Gesandten der Vereinigten Staaten in Spanien, wo er um Sympathien für die Union wirbt.

1867 Die von Johann August Roebling (1806–1869) geplante Hängebrücke über den Ohio bei Cincinnati wird vollendet.

1873 Der Geigenvirtuose, Dirigent und Komponist Leopold Damrosch (1832–1885) aus Posen gründet die New Yorker Oratorien-Gesellschaft.

1877 Carl Schurz wird während der Regierungszeit von Präsident Rutherford B. Hayes (1822–1893) bis 1881 amerikanischer Innenminister. Er führt eine Reform des öffentlichen Dienstes durch und beginnt eine Neuordnung der Indianerpolitik.

1878 Leopold Damrosch gründet die »New York Symphony Society«.

1883 Die von Roebling entworfene Brooklyn Bridge wird unter der Leitung seines Sohnes Washington Augustus (1836–1927) fertiggestellt.

1884 Ottmar Mergenthaler (1854–1899) entwickelt eine Schriftsetzmaschine im Zeilengußverfahren. Diese »Linotype« wird bei der »New York Tribune« erstmals 1886 zur Herstellung einer Zeitung verwendet.

1887 Emil Berliner (1851–1929) entwickelt das Schallplatten-Grammophon.

1892 Ellis Island wird am 1. Januar neue Einwanderungsstelle für Immigranten. Nach 62 Jahren wird sie am 12. November 1954 geschlossen. In diesem Zeitraum passierten ungefähr 20 Millionen Einwanderer die Insel.

1903 Der in Schlesien geborene Heinrich Conried (1855–1909) produziert, als Intendant der Metropolitan Opera, die erste Aufführung von Wagners Parsifal fern von Bayreuth.

1907 Conried holt Gustav Mahler (1860–1911) als Gastdirigent an die »Met«. Von 1909 bis 1911 ist Mahler Dirigent der New Yorker Philharmoniker und erhält dafür das bis dahin höchste Dirigentenjahresgehalt von 30 000 Dollar.

1914 »German-American-Alliance«: Massentreffen zur Resolution gegen die Teilnahme Amerikas am Krieg.

1917 6. April: Die USA treten in den Krieg gegen Deutschland ein.

1918 11. November: Waffenstillstand.
Carl Laemmle (1867–1939) produziert Erich von Stroheims (1885–1957) Film *Blind Husbands,* 1919 *The Devil's Passkey* und 1921 *Foolish Wives.*

1919 28. Juni: Friedensvertrag von Versailles.

1927 Hermann Hesse (1877–1962): *Der Steppenwolf;* dieser Roman erlebt fast vierzig Jahre später seine ›Renaissance‹ in der amerikanischen Hippie-Bewegung.
Max Reinhardt (1873–1943) gastiert mit seinem »Deutschen Theater« in New York.

1928 Köhl, Hünefeld und Fitzmaurice überfliegen am 12./13. April als erste den Atlantik in Ost-West-Richtung.

1933 Beginn der Emigration deutscher Künstler und Intellektueller in die Vereinigten Staaten, unter ihnen Prominente wie Paul Tillich (1886–1965), Billy Wilder (geboren 1906) und Georg Grosz (1893–1959). Albert Einstein (1879–1955) emigriert und wird Mitarbeiter des »Institute for Advanced Studies« in Princeton.

1935 Die von Senator Robert F. Wagner (1877–1953) verfaßte »Labor Relations Act« wird von Präsident Roosevelt (1882–1945) unterzeichnet.

1936 Fritz Langs (1890–1976) erster in den USA vollendeter Film *Fury* wird zu einem großen Erfolg.

1937 Das im nationalsozialistischen Deutschland verbotene Bauhaus wird in Chicago unter Leitung von Laszlo Moholy-Nagy (1895–1946) als »New Bauhaus« weitergeführt.

1941 11. Dezember: Hitler erklärt den USA den Krieg.

1944 Franz Werfels (1890–1945) *Jakobowski und der Oberst* wird in New York uraufgeführt.

1945 Am 3. Mai wird das Team der Raketenforscher aus Peenemünde mit ihrem Chef Wernher von Braun (1912–1977) in Reutte, Österreich, von Amerikanern interniert und später in die USA ausgeflogen.
8. Mai: Bedingungslose Kapitulation Deutschlands vor den Alliierten.

1947 Bert Brecht (1898–1956) inszeniert in Los Angeles eine Neufassung von *Leben des Galilei* mit Charles Laughton (1899–1962) in der Hauptrolle.

1951 *The Origins of Totalitarianism* von Hannah Arendt (1906–1975) erscheint.

1952 Im Rahmen des deutsch-amerikanischen Kulturabkommens wird auch die Bundesrepublik in das Fulbright-Programm einbezogen. Es fördert den Austausch von Professoren, Lehrern und Studenten.

1953 Die Nobelpreise für Medizin und Physiologie gehen an Dr. Hans A. Krebs, 1933 emigriert, und Dr. Fritz Lippmann, der 1941 emigrierte.

1968 Zwischen 1949 und 1968 gingen etwa 1800 Naturwissenschaftler und 5000 Techniker aus der Bundesrepublik in die USA.

1969 Am 21. Juli betreten drei Amerikaner erstmals den Mond. Maßgeblichen Anteil an dem Apollo 11-Unternehmen hatte Wernher von Braun.

1983 Dreihundertjahrfeier der deutschen Auswanderung nach Amerika.

Index Register

Figures in italics refer to pictures and captions. The list of prominent emigrés from 1933 to 1941 on page 87 is not included.

Kursive Ziffern verweisen auf Bilder und Bildlegenden. Die Liste der prominenten Emigranten aus den Jahren 1933 bis 1941 auf Seite 87 wurde nicht aufgenommen.

Bibliography Bibliographie

Abbott, Edith, *Historical Aspects of the Immigration Problem,* Chicago, 1926
Adler, Jacob, *Claus Spreckels. The Sugar King of Hawaii,* Honolulu, 1967
Arndt, Karl J. R. and May Olson, *German-American Newspapers and Periodicals 1732–1955,* Heidelberg, 1961
--, *The German-Language Press of the Americas 1732–1968,* Pullach, 1973
Arndt, Karl J. R., *George Rapp's Harmony Society 1785–1847,* Philadelphia, 1965

Bachmann, Calvin G., *The Old Order Amish of Lancaster County,* Norristown, Pa., 1961
Billigmeier, Robert Henry, *Americans From Germany: A Study in Cultural Diversity,* Belmont, Calif., 1974
Bittinger, Lucy, *The Germans in Colonial Times,* New York, 1906 (Reprint: 1968)
Bodnar, John E., ed., *The Ethnic Experience in Pennsylvania,* Lewisburg, 1973
Bowers, David F., ed., *Foreign Influences on American Life,* London, 1967
Boyers, Robert, ed., *The Legacy of the German Refugee Intellectuals,* New York, 1972

Cazden, Robert E., *German Exile Literature in America, 1933–1950,* Chicago, 1970
Child, Clifton J., *The German-Americans in Politics 1914–1917,* Madison, Wisc., 1939
Conzen, Kathleen Neils, *Immigrant Milwaukee 1836–1860: Accomodation and Community in a Frontier City,* Cambridge, Mass., 1976
Cronau, Rudolf, *Drei Jahrhunderte deutschen Lebens in Amerika,* Berlin, 1909
Cunz, Dieter, *The Maryland Germans,* Princeton, 1948

Davis-Dubois, Rachel, and Emma Schweppe, *The Germans in American Life,* New York, 1936
Diamond, Sander A., *The Nazi-Movement in the United States 1924–1941,* Ithaca, 1974
Dräcker, Edmund F. (für Friedemann), *Die Positiv-negativ-Wirkung privater Bindungen in den deutsch-amerikanischen Beziehungen unter besonderer Berücksichtigung der Eheerfahrungen des Verf. mit Kate Barbara Silverwork-Smith, geschiedene Gräfin Itzenplitz-Kippenburg,* Boston und Gräfelfing, 1923
Dujmovits, Walter, *Die Amerikawanderung der Burgenländer, Stegersbach, 1975*

Easum, Chester V., *The Americanization of Carl Schurz,* Chicago, 1929
--, *Carl Schurz. Vom deutschen Einwanderer zum amerikanischen Staatsmann,* Weimar, 1937
Eisenberg, Azriel and Hannah Grad Goodman, *Eyewitnesses to American Jewish History. Part II: The German Immigration, 1800–1875,* New York, 1977
Ernst, Robert, *Immigrant Life in New York City 1825–1863,* New York, 1979
Esslinger, Dean R., *Immigrants and the City,* Port Washington, N.Y., 1975

Faust, Albert B., *The German Element in the United States,* Boston 1909 (Reprint: New York, 1969)
--, *Das Deutschtum in den Vereinigten Staaten,* Leipzig, 1912
Fermi, Laura, *Illustrious Immigrants: The Intellectual Migration from Europe 1930–1941,* Chicago, 1968
Friesen, Gerhard K., and Walter Schatzbert, eds., *The German Contribution to the Building of the Americas. Studies in Honor of Karl J.R. Arndt,* Hanover, N.H., 1977
Froeschle, Hartmut, ed., *German-Canadian Yearbook/ Deutschkanadisches Jahrbuch,* Toronto, 1975 ff.

Gelberg, Birgit, *Auswanderung nach Übersee,* Hamburg, 1973
Gerlach, Russel, *Immigrants in the Ozarks,* Columbia, Mo., 1976
Gilbert, Glenn, ed., *The German Language in America. A Symposium,* Austin, 1971
Glanz, Rudolf, *Jews in Relation to the Cultural Milieu of the Germans in America Up to the 1880s,* New York, 1947
Glazer, Nathan, and Daniel P. Moynihan, *Beyond the Melting Pot,* New York, 1963 (2nd ed. Cambridge, Mass., 1970)
Gleason, Philip, *The Conservative Reformers: German-American Catholics and the Social Order,* Notre Dame, Ind., 1968
Gordon, Milton M., *Assimilation in American Life,* New York, 1964
Graeff, A.D., *The Pennsylvania Germans,* Princeton, N.J., 1943

Hagedorn, Herman, *The Hyphenated Family,* New York, 1960
Hagen, Victor von, *Der Ruf der Neuen Welt,* München, 1970
Handlin, Oscar, *Immigration as a Factor in American History,* New York, 1959
--, *The Uprooted,* Boston, 1951 (2nd ed. 1973)
Hartmann, Edward G., *The Movement to Americanize the Immigrant,* New York, 1948
Hawgood, John A., *The Tragedy of German-America,* New York, 1940
Higham, John, *Strangers in the Land: Patterns of American Nativism 1860–1925,* New Brunswick, 1955
--, *Send These to Me: Jews and Other Immigrants in Urban America,* New York, 1975
Hirshler, Eric E., *Jews from Germany in the United States,* New York, 1955
Holland, Ruth, *The German Immigrants in America,* New York, 1969
Hostetler, John A., *Amish Society,* Baltimore 1968
--, *Hutterite Society,* Baltimore, 1974
Huebener, Theodore, *The Germans in America,* Philadelphia 1962

Iverson, Noel, *Germania, U.S.A. Social Change in New Ulm, Minnesota,* Minneapolis, 1966
Jordan, Terry G., *German Seed in Texas Soil: Immigrant Farmers in 19th-Century Texas,* Austin, 1966

Kapp, Friedrich, *Aus und über Amerika: Thatsachen und Erlebnisse,* Berlin, 1876
Kellner, George Helmuth, *The German Element on the Urban Frontier: St. Louis 1830–1860,* Ann Arbor, 1975
Kennedy, John F., *A Nation of Immigrants,* New York, 1964
Kloss, Heinz, *Atlas of 19th and Early 20th Century German-American Settlements,* Marburg, 1974

Learned, Marion D., *The Life of Francis Daniel Pastorius,* Philadelphia, 1908
Learsi, Rufus, *The Jews in America,* Cleveland, 1954
Luebke, Frederick C., *Bonds of Loyalty: German-Americans and World War I,* DeKalb, Ill., 1974
Lüönd, Karl, *Schweizer in Amerika. Karrieren und Mißerfolge in der Neuen Welt,* Olten, 1979

Marzio, Peter C., ed., *A Nation of Nations,* New York, 1976
Mittelberger, Gottlieb, *Journey to Pennsylvania* (1750), Philadelphia, 1898
Moltmann, Günter, ed., *Aufbruch nach Amerika. Friedrich List und die Auswanderung aus Baden und Württemberg 1816/17,* Tübingen, 1979
--, ed., *Deutsche Amerikaauswanderung im 19. Jahrhundert. Sozialgeschichtliche Beiträge,* Stuttgart, 1976
Morrison, Joan, et. al., *American Mosaic: The Immigrant Experience in the Words of Those Who Lived It,* New York, 1980
Myers, Gustavus, *History of the Great American Fortunes,* New York, 1907

Novotny, Ann, *Strangers at the Door: Ellis Island, Castle Garden and the Great Migration to America,* Riverside, 1971

O'Connor, Richard, *The German-Americans. An Informal History,* Boston, 1968
--, *Die Deutsch-Amerikaner. So wurden es 33 Millionen,* Hamburg, 1970
O'Dwyer, William J. and Stella Randolph, *History by Contract. The Beginning of Motorized Aviation: August 14, 1901, Gustave Whitehead, Fairfield, Conn.,* Leutershausen, 1978
Olson, Audrey Louise, *St. Louis Germans 1850–1920: The Nature of an Immigrant Community and its Relation to the Assimilation Process,* Ann Arbor, 1971
Pennypacker, S. W., *The Settlement of Germantown, Pennsylvania, and the Beginning of German Immigration to North America,* Lancaster, Pa., 1899 (Reprint: New York, 1969)
Pershing, E.J., *The Pershing Family in America,* Philadelphia, 1926
Piltz, Thomas, ed., *1776–1976. Zweihundert Jahre deutsch-amerikanische Beziehungen / Two Hundred Years of German-American Relations,* München, 1975
--, *Die Deutschen und die Amerikaner / The Americans and the Germans,* München 1978
Pitkin, Thomas M., *Keepers of the Gate: A History of Ellis Island,* New York, 1975

Radkau, Joachim, *Die deutsche Emigration in den USA. Ihr Einfluß auf die amerikanische Europapolitik 1933–1945,* Düsseldorf 1971
Ravenswaay, Charles Van, *The Arts and Architecture of German Settlements in Missouri,* Columbia, Mo., 1977
Rippley, LaVern J., *The German-Americans,* Boston, 1976
Rogge, John O., *The Official German Report: Nazi Penetration 1924–1942,* New York, 1962
Rutherfurd, Livingston, *John Peter Zenger. His Press, His Trial,* New York 1904 (Reprint: New York, 1968)

Sallet, Richard, *The Russian-German Settlements in the United States,* Fargo, 1974
Schappes, Morris, *Documentary History of the Jews in the United States,* New York, 1950
Schelbert, Leo, *Swiss in North America,* Philadelphia, 1974
--, *Swiss Migration to America. The Swiss Mennonites,* New York, 1980
Schnücker, George, *Die Ostfriesen in Amerika,* Cleveland, 1917
Schrader, Frederick F., *The Germans in the Making of America,* New York, 1924
Schurz, Carl, *Reminiscences, Vols. 1 and 2,* New York, 1917
--, Reminiscences, Vol. 3, New York, 1909
--, *Lebenserinnerungen, Band 1 und 2,* Berlin, 1920 u. 23
--, *Lebenserinnerungen, Band 3,* Berlin, 1912
Seidensticker, Oswald, und Max Heinrici, *Geschichte der Deutschen Gesellschaft von Pennsylvanien 1764–1917,* Philadelphia, 1917
--, *Die erste deutsche Einwanderung in Amerika und die Gründung von Germantown 1683. Festschrift zum deutsch-amerikanischen Pionier-Jubiläum am 6. Oktober 1883,* Philadelphia, 1883
Skaggs, William H., *German Conspiracies in America,* London, 1915
Skal, G. V., *History of German Immigration in the United States,* New York, 1908
Smith, C. Henry, *The Coming of the Russian Mennonites,* Berne, Ind., 1927
Spaulding, Wilder, *The Quiet Invaders: The Story of the Austrian Impact upon America,* Vienna, 1968
Stephenson, George M., *A History of American Immigration,* Boston, 1926

Thernstrom, Stephan, ed., *Harvard Encyclopedia of American Ethnic Groups,* Cambridge, Mass., 1980
Tolzmann, Don Heinrich, *German-Americana: A Bibliography,* Metuchen, N.J., 1975
--, ed., *German-American Literature,* Metuchen, N.J., 1977

Ueberhorst, Horst, *Turner unterm Sternenbanner,* München, 1978
--, *Friedrich Wilhelm von Steuben,* München, 1981

Vagts, Alfred, *Deutsch-amerikanische Rückwanderung,* Heidelberg, 1960

Wersich, Rüdiger, ed., *Carl Schurz. Revolutionär und Staatsmann / Revolutionary and Statesman,* München, 1979
Wilk, Gerard, *Americans from Germany,* New York, 1976
Wittke, Carl, *The German-Language Press in America,* Louisville, Ky., 1957
--, *We Who Built America,* New York, 1946 (2nd ed. Cleveland, 1964)
--, *Refugees of Revolution: The German Forty-Eighters in America,* Philadelphia, 1952
Walker, Mack, *Germany and the Emigration 1816–1885,* Cambridge, Mass., 1964
Wood, Ralph, ed., *The Pennsylvania Germans,* Princeton, 1942
Wust, Klaus, *The Virginia Germans,* Charlottesville, 1969

Zucker, A.E., ed., *The Forty-Eighters,* New York, 1950

Addresses

In the U.S.:

Embassy of the Federal Republic of Germany,
4645 Reservoir Road, N.W., Washington, D.C. 20007-1998
Consulate General of the Federal Republic of Germany,
1000 Peachtree Center Cain Tower, 229 Peachtree St. N.E., Atlanta, Georgia 30043-3201

Consulate General of the Federal Republic of Germany in Atlanta,
Branch Office Miami, 100 N. Biscayne Blvd., Miami, Florida 33132
Consulate General of the Federal Republic of Germany,
535 Boylston Street, Boston, Mass. 02116
Consulate General of the Federal Republic of Germany,
104 South Michigan Ave., Chicago, Ill. 60603
Consulate General of the Federal Republic of Germany,
2200 Book Building, Washington Blvd., Detroit, Mich. 48226
Consulate General of the Federal Republic of Germany,
1900 Yorktown, Suite 405, Houston, Texas 77056
Consulate General of the Federal Republic of Germany, Houston,
Branch Office New Orleans, 2834 International Trade Mart, 2 Canal Street, New Orleans, LA. 70130
Consulate General of the Federal Republic of Germany,
6435 Wilshire Blvd., Los Angeles, Calif. 90048
Consulate General of the Federal Republic of Germany,
460 Park Avenue, New York, N.Y. 10022
Consulate General of the Federal Republic of Germany,
601 California Street, San Francisco, CA. 94108–2870
Consulate General of the Federal Republic of Germany,
1617 IBM Building, 1200 Fifth Avenue, Seattle, Wash. 98101
American Association of Teachers of German (AATG), 523 Bldg., Suite 201, Rte, 38, Cherry Hill, N.J. 08034
American Association of University Women
2401 Virginia Ave. N.W., Washington D.C. 20037
American Council for Nationalities Service
20 West 40th Street, New York, N.Y. 10018
American Council on Education
One Dupont Circle, Washington D.C. 20036
American Council on Germany, Inc.
680 Fifth Avenue, New York, N.Y. 10019
American Field Service (Schüleraustausch)
313 43rd Street, New York, N.Y. 10017
American Friends Service Committee
(Social Welfare) (AFSC),
1501 Cherry Street, Philadelphia, PA. 19102

Americans for Democratic Action
1424 16th St., N.W., Washington D.C. 20036
American Home Economics Association
2010 Massachusetts Ave. N.W., Washington D.C., 20036
American Youth Abroad
84 University Station, Minneapolis, Minn. 55401
American Youth Hostels, National Campus
Delaplane, VA 22025
Association for Academic Travel Abroad
280 Madison Ave., New York, N.Y. 10016
Association for World Travel Exchange
38 West 88th Street, New York, N.Y. 10024
AFS International/Intercultural Programs
(International Exchange AFSIIP)
213 East 43rd Street, New York, N.Y. 10017
Boy Scouts of America (BSA)
P.O. Box 61030, Dallas/FA Worth Airport, TX 75261
Camp Fire Girls
1750 Broadway, New York, N.Y. 10019
Camp Fire, Inc. (York)
4601 Madison Avenue, Kansas City, Mo 64112
Carnegie Corporation of New York
437 Madison Ave., New York, N.Y. 10022
Carnegie Endowment for International Peace
11 Dupont Circle, N.W., Washington, D.C. 20036
Central Bureau of the Catholic Central Union of America
3835 Westminster Place, St. Louis, Mo. 63108
The Cleveland International Program for Youth Leaders and Social Workers (CIP)
2123 East 9th Street, Cleveland, Ohio 44101
Concordia Historical Institute
801 De Mun Avenue, St. Louis, Mo. 63105
Council for International Exchange of Scholars (CIES)
11 Dupont Circle, N.W. Washington, D.C. 20036
Council on Foreign Relations, Inc.
The Harold Pratt House, 58 East 68th Street, New York, N.Y. 10021
Council of Mennonite Colleges (CMC)
Eastern Mennonite College, Harrisburg, VA 22801
Department of Health Education and Welfare, Office of Education, Division of International Education
330 Independence Avenue, S.W., Washington, D.C. 20418
Eisenhower Exchange Fellowship, Inc.
256 South Sixteenth Street, Philadelphia, Pa. 19102
Experiment in International Living (International Exchange)
U.S. Headquarters, Brattleboro, VT 05301
Farmers' Educational and Cooperative Union of America
P.O. Box 39251, Denver, CO 80251
Federation of German Citizens of German Descent
460 Chapman Street, Irvington, N.J. 07111
Ford Foundation
320 East 43rd Street, New York, NY 10017
Foreign Policy Association
250 Lexington Avenue, New York, N.Y. 10016

German Academic Exchange Service (DAAD)
535 Fifth Avenue, Apt. 1107, New York, N.Y. 10017
German American Chamber of Commerce, Inc.
666 Fifth Avenue, New York, N.Y. 10019
German-American National Congress (DANK)
999 Elmhurst Rd. Suite 33, Mt. Prospect, IL 60056
German Information Center
410 Park Avenue, New York, N.Y. 10022
German National Tourist Office
630 Fifth Avenue, New York, N.Y. 10011
104 South Michigan Avenue, Suite 306, Chicago, Ill. 60603
323 Geary St., San Francisco, Calif., 94102
German Society of the City of New York
Deutsche Gesellschaft der Stadt New York
150 Fifth Ave., New York, N.Y. 10011
German Society of Pennsylvania
Deutsche Gesellschaft von Pennsylvanien
611 Spring Garden St., Philadelphia, Pa. 19123
Girl Scouts of the US, International Division
830 Third Ave., New York, N.Y. 10022
Goethe-Institut
German Cultural Center, 400 Colony Square
Street Level, Atlanta, Georgia 30361
Goethe-Institut
German Cultural Center for New England,
170 Beacon Street, Boston, Mass. 02116
Goethe-Institut
German Cultural Center
401 North Michigan Avenue, Chicago, Ill. 60611
Goethe-Institut
German Cultural Institute
1014 Fifth Avenue, New York, N.Y. 10028
Goethe-Institut
German Cultural Center
3400 Montrose Blvd., Suite 808, Houston, Tex. 77006
Goethe-Institut
530 Bush Street, San Francisco, Ca. 94108
Goshen College, Goshen, Ind. 44526
Governmental Affairs Institute
(Betreuung von ausländischen Besuchern)
1776 Massachusetts Avenue, N.W., Washington, D.C. 20036
Guggenheim Foundation
120 Broadway, New York, N.Y. 10005
Heifer Project, Inc.
(Hilfsorganisation für Landwirte)
825 W. Third Street, Little Rock, AR 72203
Institute of International Education
809 United Nations Plaza, New York, N.Y. 10017
International Association for the Exchange of Students of Technical Experience (IAESTE)
American City Bldg., Suite 217, Columbia, Md. 21044
International Christian Youth Exchange
74 Trinity Place, New York, N.Y. 10006
International Friendship League (Correspondence)
22 Batterymarch Street, Boston, MA 02109
International Road Educational Foundation
1023 Bldg., Washington, D.C. 20013
Johnson Foundation, Inc.
P.O. Box 547, Racine, Wisconsin 53401
W.K. Kellog Foundation
400 Morth Avenue, Battle Creek, Michigan 49016
Lalor Foundation
4400 Lancaster Pike, Wilmington, Delaware 19899
League of Friendship
(Vermittlung von Briefwechsel)
P.O. Box 509, Mount Vernon, Ohio 43050
Letters Abroad Inc.
209 East 56th St., New York, N.Y. 10022
Liberal Religious Youth
25 Beacon Street, Boston, Mass. 02108
Lions Club International (Service Club)
300-22nd Street, Oak Brook, IL 60570
Lisle Fellowship (International Exchange)
1623 Belmont Street, N.W., Washington, DC 20009
Lutheran World Federation,
USA National Committee
315 Park Avenue South, Suite 1910, New York, N.Y. 10010

Marquette University, Institute of German Affairs
Milwaukee, Wis.
Max Kade Foundation
100 Church Street, Rm. 10604, New York, N.Y. 10007
Mennonite Central Committee
(Mennonitischer Hauptausschuß)
21 South Twelfth St., Akron., Pa. 17501
Modern Language Association of America
62 Fifth Ave., New York, N.Y. 10011
National Academy of Sciences - National Research Council
2101 Constitution Avenue, N.W., Washington, D.C. 20418
National Association of Educational Broadcasters
1346 Connecticut Ave., Washington, D.C. 20036
National Association of Travel Organizations
1100 Connecticut Ave. N.W., Washington, D.C. 20036
National Council of the Churches of Christ in the USA, Department of Church World Service
475 Riverside Drive, New York, N.Y. 10027
National Education Association of the US
1201 16th St., N.W., Washington D.C. 20036
National Federation of Business and Professional Women's Clubs, Inc.
2012 Massachusetts Avenue, N.W., Washington, D.C. 20036
National 4-H Club Foundation
7100 Connecticut Avenue, Washington, D.C. 20015
National League of Cities
1301 Pennsylvania Avenue, N.W., Washington, D.C. 20004
Overseas Education Fund (Citizenship)
2101 L. Street, N.W., Suite 916, Washington, DC 20037
Overseas Education Fund of the League of Women Voters
1730 M.St., N.W., Washington, D.C. 20036
Pennsylvania German Society
Box 97, Breinigsville, PA 18301
People-to-People International
2440 Pershing Rd., G-30 Kansas City, MO 64108
Rockefeller Foundation
1133 Avenue of the Americas, New York, NY 10036
Rotary International
1600 Ridge Ave., Evanston, Ill. 60201
Salzburg Seminar in American Studies, American Office
17 Dunster St., Cambridge, Mass. 02138
Society for the History of the Germans in Maryland
231 St. Paul Place, Baltimore, Md. 21202
Steuben Society of America
6705 Fresh Pond Rd., Ridgewood, N.Y. 11385
Student Letter Exchange
Waseca, Minn. 56093
Unitarian Universalist Service Committee
78 Beacon St., Boston, Mass. 02108
United States International Communication Agency
Washington, D.C. 20547
United States National Association (USNSA)
International Commission
2115 S St. N.W., Washington, D.C. 20008
World Pen Pals
1690 Como Avenue, St. Paul, MN 55108
World University Service
c/o Lehman College, Bedford Park Blvd., Bronx, N.Y. 10468
Young Men's Christian Associations of the US (YMCA)
101 N. Wacker St., Chicago, IL 60606
Young Women's Christian Association of the US (YWCA) Foreign Division
600 Lexington Ave., New York, N.Y. 10022
Youth of all Nations
16 Saint Luke's Place, New York, N.Y. 10014

Adressen

IN GERMANY:

Botschaft der Vereinigten Staaten von Amerika
Mehlemer Aue, D-5300 Bonn-Bad Godesberg
Generalkonsulat der Vereinigten Staaten von Amerika
Clayallee 170, D-1000 Berlin 33
Generalkonsulat der Vereinigten Staaten von Amerika
Präsident-Kennedy-Platz 1, D-2800 Bremen
Generalkonsulat der Vereinigten Staaten von Amerika
Cecilienallee 5, D-4000 Düsseldorf
Generalkonsulat der Vereinigten Staaten von Amerika
Siesmayerstraße 21, D-6000 Frankfurt
Generalkonsulat der Vereinigten Staaten von Amerika
Alsterufer 27, D-2000 Hamburg 36
Generalkonsulat der Vereinigten Staaten von Amerika
Königinstraße 2, D-8000 München 22
Generalkonsulat der Vereinigten Staaten von Amerika
Urbanstraße 7, D-7000 Stuttgart
A.I.E.S.E.C. - Association Internationale des Etudiants en Sciences Economiques et Commerciales
Internationale Vereinigung der Studenten der Wirtschaftswissenschaften
Deutsches Komitee der AIESEC e.V.
Habsburgerring 24-26, D-5000 Köln 1
Alexander-von-Humboldt-Stiftung
Jean-Paul-Straße 12, D-5300 Bonn 2
American Chamber of Commerce in Germany
Roßmarkt 12, D-6000 Frankfurt
American Field Service (Schüleraustausch)
St.-Benedict-Straße 22, D-2000 Hamburg 13
Amerika-Gesellschaft e.V.
Tesdorpfstraße 1 (Amerika-Haus),
D-2000 Hamburg 13
Arbeitsgemeinschaft Westdeutscher Partnergemeinden Amerikanischer Städte
c/o Institut für Auslandsbeziehungen
Charlottenplatz 17, D-7000 Stuttgart 1
Arbeitsgemeinschaft für Internationalen Kulturaustausch
c/o Friedrich-Ebert-Stiftung
Adenauerallee 149, D-5300 Bonn
Arbeitskreis Internationaler Gemeinschaftsdienste in Deutschland (AIG)
Auf der Körnerwiese 5, D-6000 Frankfurt 1
(Durchführung internationaler Arbeitslager)
Atlantik-Brücke e.V.
Sanderskoppel 15, D-2000 Hamburg 64
Auslandsstelle des Deutschen Bundesstudentenringes
Lennéstraße 1, D-5300 Bonn
Auswärtiges Amt, Abt. 6 (Kulturabteilung)
Adenauerallee 101, D-5300 Bonn
Benjamin-Franklin-Stiftung
Württembergische Straße 6-10, D-1000 Berlin 31
Carl-Duisberg-Gesellschaft für Nachwuchsförderung e.V.
Hohenstaufenring 30-32, D-5000 Köln 1
Carl-Schurz-Gesellschaft e.V.
Tivoli-Hochhaus, Bahnhofsplatz 29, D-2800 Bremen
Christopher Columbus Youth Council
Evezastraße 7, D-5050 Porz-Zündorf
Columbus-Gesellschaft e.V. München
Deutsch-Amerikanische Gesellschaft
Karolinenplatz 3, D-8000 München
Deutsche Atlantische Gesellschaft e.V.
Thomas-Mann-Straße 62, D-5300 Bonn 1
Deutsche Forschungsgemeinschaft
Kennedyallee 40, D-5300 Bonn-Bad Godesberg
Deutsche Gesellschaft für Amerika-Studien
c/o Anglistisches Seminar der Universität Mannheim
Schloß, D-6800 Mannheim
Deutsche Gesellschaft für Auswärtige Politik e.V.
Adenauerallee 137, D-5300 Bonn
Deutsche Gesellschaft für internationalen Jugendaustausch
Lennéstraße 1, D-5300 Bonn
Deutsche Welle
Raderberggürtel 50, D-5000 Köln 1
Deutscher Akademischer Austauschdienst (DAAD)
Kennedyallee 50, D-5300 Bonn 2
Deutscher Bauernverband e.V.
(Praktikantenaustausch)
Godesberger Allee 142-148, D-5300 Bonn 2
Deutscher Fremdenverkehrsverband
Beethovenstraße 61, D-6000 Frankfurt 1
Deutscher Gewerkschaftsbund, Abteilung Ausland
Hans-Böckler-Straße 39, D-4000 Düsseldorf
Deutsches Institut für Internationale Pädagogische Forschung
Schloßstraße 29, D-6000 Frankfurt
Deutsches Jugendherbergswerk
Bülowstraße 26, D-4930 Detmold

Deutschlandfunk
Raderberggürtel 40, D-5000 Köln 51
Das Experiment e.V.
Vereinigung für praktisches Zusammenleben der Völker (Deutsche Sektion des „Experiment in International Living")
Schopenhauerstraße 3, D-4990 Lübbecke
Federation of German-American Clubs
Verband der Deutsch-Amerikanischen Clubs e.V.
Ferdinand-Keller-Straße 29, D-7500 Karlsruhe 21
Foundation Luftbrückendank (Stipendien)
Martin-Luther-Straße 105, D-1000 Berlin 62
Freie Universität Berlin
John-F.-Kennedy-Institut für Amerikastudien
Lansstraße 7–9, D-1000 Berlin 33
Fremdenverkehrsamt der Vereinigten Staaten von Amerika
United States Travel Service
Roßmarkt 10, D-1000 Frankfurt 1
Friedrich-Ebert-Stiftung e.V.
Kölner Straße 149, D-5300 Bonn-Bad Godesberg
Fulbright Kommission
Kommission für den Studenten- und Dozentenaustausch zwischen der Bundesrepublik und den Vereinigten Staaten
Theaterplatz IA, Postfach 200208, D-5300 Bonn-Bad Godesberg

Gesellschaft für Auslandskunde e.V.
Theatinerstraße 32/III, D-8000 München 2
Gesellschaft zur Pflege des Schwesterstadtverhältnisses
Hagerstown/USA – Wesel/Deutschland e.V.
Hohe Straße, D-4320 Wesel
Goethe-Institut zur Pflege deutscher Sprache und Kultur im Ausland e.V. (Zentralverwaltung/Central Office)
Lenbachplatz 3, D-8000 München 2
Heimatstelle Pfalz
(Erforschung der Auswanderung aus der Pfalz, Mundartforschung)
Museumsplatz 1, D-6750 Kaiserslautern
Institut für Auslandsbeziehungen
Charlottenplatz 17, D-7000 Stuttgart 1
Internationale Jugendgemeinschaftsdienste e.V.
(Durchführung von internationalen Arbeitslagern)
Kaiserstraße 43, D-5300 Bonn
Internationaler Arbeitskreis Sonnenberg
Gesellschaft zur Förderung internationaler Zusammenarbeit
Bankplatz 8, D-3300 Braunschweig
Internationaler Christlicher Schüleraustausch der Arbeitsgemeinschaft der Evangelischen Jugend Deutschlands
Kiefernstraße 45, D-5600 Wuppertal-Barmen
Inter Nationes e.V.
Kennedyallee 91–103, D-5300 Bonn 2

Junior Year in München und Freiburg
Leopoldstraße 23, D-8000 München 40
Friedrichstraße 1, D-7800 Freiburg

Kirchliches Außenamt der Evangelischen Kirche in Deutschland
Bockenheimer Landstraße 109, D-6000 Frankfurt
Kultusminister-Konferenz
Dokumentations- und Auskunftsdienst
Nassestraße 11/II, D-5300 Bonn
Lions International, Sekretariat des Gesamt District 111
Rheinstraße 4, D-6200 Wiesbaden
Lutherischer Weltdienst · Deutscher Hauptausschuß
(Austauschprogramm für kirchliche Mitarbeiter)
Stafflenbergstraße 78, D-7000 Stuttgart
Mennonite Voluntary Service
Mennonitischer Freiwilliger Hilfsdienst
(Durchführung von Arbeitslagern)
Bruchstraße 13, D-6750 Kaiserslautern
Pädagogischer Austauschdienst (PAD)
Nassestraße 8, D-5300 Bonn
Presse- und Informationsamt der Bundesregierung
Welckerstraße 11, D-5300 Bonn
Rationalisierungs-Kuratorium der Deutschen Wirtschaft (RKW) e.V.
Gutleutstraße 163, D-6000 Frankfurt
Schiller College
Schloß, D-7121 Kleiningersheim
„Stanford in Germany"
Stiftstraße 30, D-7056 Beutelsbach
Steuben-Schurz-Gesellschaft in Düsseldorf e.V.
Gesellschaft zur Pflege der deutsch-amerikanischen Beziehungen
Benrather Straße 19, D-4000 Düsseldorf
Steuben-Schurz-Gesellschaft e.V. Berlin
Kurfürstendamm 188, D-1000 Berlin 15

Steuben-Schurz-Gesellschaft e.V.
Gesellschaft zur internationalen Zusammenarbeit
Backhausstraße 18, D-6000 Frankfurt
Studienstiftung des deutschen Volkes
Mirbachstraße 7, D-5300 Bonn 2
United States Information Service
(USIS/Germany)
c/o Amerikanische Botschaft
Mehlemer Aue, D-5300 Bonn-Bad Godesberg
Universität Frankfurt, Amerika-Institut
Kettenhofweg 130, D-6000 Frankfurt
Universität Köln, Anglo-Amerikanische Abteilung des Historischen Seminars
Albertus-Magnus-Platz, D-5000 Köln 41
Universität Mainz,
Lehrstuhl für Amerikanistik und Neueste Anglistik
Jakob-Welder-Weg 18, D-6500 Mainz
Universität München, Amerika-Institut
Schellingstraße 3, D-8000 München 22

Universität Marburg, Institut für Englische und Amerikanische Philologie
Krummbongen 28 D, D-3550 Marburg
Universität Tübingen, Seminar für Englische Philologie, Abt. für Amerikanistik
Wilhelmstraße 50, D-7400 Tübingen
Verband Deutscher Studentenschaften (VDS)
Auslandsreferat
Georgstraße 25–27, D-5300 Bonn
Verein der Ausländischen Presse in Deutschland e.V.
Heußallee 2, D-5300 Bonn
World University Service, Deutsches Komitee e.V.
Lessingstraße 32, D-5300 Bonn
Zentralkomitee der Deutschen Katholiken, Außenamt
Hochkreuzallee 246, D-5320 Bad Godesberg
Zentralstelle für Arbeitsvermittlung
Feuerbachstraße 42, D-6000 Frankfurt

Amerika-Häuser und ähnliche Einrichtungen

Amerika-Haus Berlin
Hardenbergstraße 22–24, D-1000 Berlin
Deutsch-Amerikanische Gesellschaft,
John-F.-Kennedy-Haus
Kasinostraße 3, D-6100 Darmstadt
Deutsch-Amerikanische Bücherei,

Internationales Bildungswerk
„Die Brücke" e.V.
Alleestraße 49–51, D-4000 Düsseldorf

Deutsch-Amerikanisches Institut
Sophienstraße 12, D-6900 Heidelberg
Carl-Schurz-Haus
Kaiser-Joseph-Straße 266, D-7800 Freiburg
Amerika-Haus Hamburg
Testorpfsstraße 1, D-2000 Hamburg 13
Amerika-Haus Hannover
Prinzenstraße 9, D-3000 Hannover
Deutsch-Amerikanische Gesellschaft
John-F.-Kennedy-Haus
Kasinostraße 3, D-6100 Darmstadt
Amerika-Haus München
Karolinenplatz 3, D-8000 München
Deutsch-Amerikanisches Institut
Gleißbühlstraße 13, D-8500 Nürnberg
Deutsch-Amerikanisches Institut
Haidplatz 8, D-8400 Regensburg
Amerika-Haus Saarbrücken
Berliner Promenade 16, D-6600 Saarbrücken
Amerika-Haus Stuttgart
Friedrichstraße 23a, D-7000 Stuttgart
Deutsch-Amerikanische Bücherei
Weberbach 25, D-5500 Trier
Deutsch-Amerikanisches Institut
Karlstraße 3, D-7400 Tübingen

Sources of Illustrations   Bildnachweis

Harry N. Abrams Inc., New York (1); Amerika-Haus, München (1); Amerika-Institut der Universität München (23); American Jewish Archives (2); American Jewish Historical Society (1); Amerika-Woche (1); Antiquariat Gaetjens, Hamburg (1); Karl J. R. Arndt, Worcester, Mass. (4); Art Museum of the City of Sacramento (1); Aufbau, New York (1); Bauhaus Archiv, Berlin-West (4); Bausch and Lomb, Rochester (1); Bayerische Hypotheken- und Wechsel-Bank, München (1); Bayerische Staatsbibliothek, München (27); Bettmann Archive Inc., New York (3); Lutz Bormann, München (1); Bruckmann Verlag, München (1); Bundesbildstelle, Bonn (5); Burson-Marsteller GmbH, Frankfurt (8); Collection of Edgar William and Bernice Chrysler Garbisch (1); Columbia University, New York (1); E. B. Crocker Gallery, Sacramento, Calif. (1); Cunard Line, London (1); Deutsche Bundespost, Bonn (1); Deutsche Presse Agentur, Frankfurt (2); Deutsches Museum, München (6); Deutschkanadisches Jahrbuch, Toronto (1); Henry Francis Du Pont Winterthur Museum, Wilmington/Delaware (3); Enoch Pratt Free Library, Baltimore (3); Evangelisches Verlagswerk, Stuttgart (1); Foto Lossen, Heidelberg (1); Friedl-Brehm-Verlag, Feldafing (2); Gemeinde Berg (2); German Society of Pennsylvania, Philadelphia (3); Hermann Glessgen, Landau (7); Goethe Institute, Boston (2); Graphische Sammlung, München (2); Dr. A. Hahn, Heidelberg (1); Edith Handeler, New York (1); Hapag-Lloyd, Hamburg (6); Helmsley Palace Hotel, New York (1); Hessisches Hauptstaatsarchiv, Wiesbaden (5); Hessisches Landesmuseum, Darmstadt (1); Historisches Museum am Hohen Ufer, Hannover (1); Hochschule für Fernsehen und Film, München (9); Hotel Drei Mohren, Augsburg (1); Fritz Koenig, Ganslberg (6); Kommunalarchiv Minden (2); Kommunalverwaltung Wiernsheim (1); Kunsthalle Bremen (1); Kurpfälzisches Museum Heidelberg (1); Landesbildstelle Berlin (7); Walter Leisler-Kiep, Hamburg (1); Hans-Günther Loher, Ruhstorf (3); Library of Congress, Washington D. C. (15); Lufthansa AG, Köln (1); Majer Verlag, Leutershausen (2); Angelika Marsch, Hamburg (1); Maryland Historical Society, Baltimore (2); Mergenthaler-Museum, Hachtel (2); Museum für Hamburgische Geschichte, Hamburg (1); Museum of Fine Arts, Boston (2); Museum of Fine Arts, Springfield (1); National Aeronautics and Space Administration, Washington D. C. (4); National Archives, Washington D. C. (4); National Carl Schurz Association, Philadelphia (19); New York City Library (1); New Yorker Staats-Zeitung und Herold (1); New York Historical Society (2); New York Public Library (6); New York State Historical Association (1); Niederländische Botschaft, Bonn (1); Niedersächsische Staats- und Universitätsbibliothek Göttingen (7); Northern Pacific Railroad (2); Thomas Ostwald, Braunschweig (1); Pennsylvania Historical Society, Philadelphia (7); Josephine Pfaender, New Ulm (1); Philadelphia Museum of Art (1); Thomas Piltz, München (4); Piper Verlag, München (1); Polygram GmbH, Hannover (2); Pommerscher Zentralverband e. V., Hamburg (2); Abby Aldrich Rockefeller Folk Art Collection, Colonial Williamsburg, Virginia (1); Rose and Son, Princeton (1); Rowohlt Verlag, Reinbek bei Hamburg (1); Michael Ruetz, Hamburg (2); Rosalie Scheibe, Fredericksburg, Texas (1); Schiffahrtsmuseum Bremerhaven (6); Seattle Opera, Seattle, Washington (1); Smithsonian Institution, Washington D. C. (4); Stadtarchiv Aachen (1); Stadtarchiv Aschaffenburg (1); Stadtarchiv Basel (1); Stadtarchiv Erlangen (2); Stadtarchiv Frankfurt (6); Stadtarchiv Gießen (1); Stadtarchiv Groß-Gerau (1); Stadtarchiv Heidelberg (5); Stadtarchiv Krefeld (4); Stadtarchiv Ladenburg (1); Stadtarchiv Ulm (2); Stadtarchiv Walldorf (3); Stadtarchiv Worms (3); Stadtbibliothek Frankfurt (3); Stadtbibliothek München (11); Stadtbibliothek Zürich (1); Stadtverwaltung Eichtersheim (2); Stadtverwaltung Fürth (3); Stadtverwaltung Nastätten (1); Stadtverwaltung Solingen (1); Steinway and Sons, Hamburg (4); Stiftung Preußischer Kulturbesitz, Berlin-West (5); Suhrkamp Verlag, Frankfurt (1); Time-Life, New York (1); Horst Ueberhorst, Bochum (5); United Feature Syndicate, Inc. (1); United Press International, Frankfurt (1); United States Information Service, Bonn (20); Universitätsarchiv Göttingen (2); Universitätsbibliothek München (7); Washington Journal, Washington D. C. (1); E. T. Wherry (1); Klaus Wust, New York (1); Zentralinstitut für Kunstgeschichte, München (1); all others/alle übrigen: Verlagsarchiv